SECOND EDITION

Approaches to
Psychology

SECOND EDITION

Approaches to *Psychology*

WILLIAM E. GLASSMAN

Open University Press
Buckingham · Philadelphia

Open University Press
Celtic Court
22 Ballmoor
Buckingham
MK18 1XW

and

1900 Frost Road, Suite 101
Bristol, PA 19007, USA

First edition published 1979
Reprinted 1984, 1986, 1988, 1989, 1991

First published in this second edition 1995

A catalogue record of this book is available from the British Library

ISBN 0 335 19259 9 (pb)

Library of Congress Cataloging-in-Publication Data
Glassman, William E., 1947–
    Approaches to psychology / William E. Glassman. — 2nd ed.
      p.   cm.
    Includes bibliographical references and index.
    ISBN 0–335–19259–9 (pbk.)
    1. Psychology. I. Title.
    BF121.G56   1995   95–1904
    150—dc20   CIP

Typeset by Graphicraft Typesetters Limited, Hong Kong
Printed in Great Britain by Redwood Books, Trowbridge, Wilts.

Never did any science originate,
but by a poetic perception.
Ralph Waldo Emerson

Dedication

To my father, for teaching me
that vision is more than simply eyesight,
and wisdom is more than simply knowledge.
W.E.G.

Contents

3 The Behaviourist Approach

4 The Cognitive Approach

5 The Psychodynamic Approach

6   The Humanistic Approach

7 Perspectives on Development

8 Perspectives on Social Behaviour

List of Figures

Preface to the Second Edition

At the university where I teach, and most others, introductory psychology is one of the most popular courses. This reflects the interest which most people have in understanding human behaviour – both their own, and that of others. While an introductory course should acknowledge this interest, it must also be an introduction to psychology as a discipline. In meeting these goals, the choice of a textbook is often crucial.

There are many possibilities in selecting course materials for introductory psychology. My own experience as a student involved a course which had no text, but rather a set of readings which included several short books and a number of articles. While this gave the impression of encountering psychologists 'in their own words', it represented a very heavy burden of reading, and little coherence. Indeed, it was long after the introductory course that I began to really grasp the outlines of the discipline, and what made it distinct from other fields of study. Hence, the course failed one of the important requirements for an introductory course – to provide a coherent understanding of the nature of psychology.

While using a textbook might seem to present a simple solution, there are literally dozens of introductory texts in print, and most seem to follow a formula which is less than satisfactory. Over more than twenty years, I have encountered many texts, and used several. From my experiences as a teacher, and the feedback from several thousand students, I have come to recognize certain factors which seem important in a textbook.

Most textbooks today tend to be rather large volumes which provide an impressive amount of factual knowledge. Unfortunately, as teaching tools, these texts tend to have several limitations. First, they are both too large and too expensive. No student can really hope to assimilate all the detail which is provided, and often they find the mass of information overwhelming. Second, most students come to psychology with an interest in *human* behaviour, yet find a large proportion of their text is devoted to research on other species. While such research clearly is part of psychology, it is often not handled in ways that help students to understand its relevance to understanding human behaviour. Third, by presenting a survey of various sub-areas such as 'learning', 'development' and 'personality', texts fail to provide a coherent framework for the discipline as a whole. In the end, it becomes as disjointed for students as my own text-less experience was.

Out of these concerns emerged the first edition of this book. At that time, a group of colleagues and I decided to create a text which would offer a relatively brief, coherent introduction to psychology which emphasized the understanding of human behaviour. The emphasis on human behaviour was the easiest goal to meet, since much of psychological research is focused on people; animal research is included only where it clearly relates to our understanding of human behaviour. The goal of brevity was met by making a conscious decision to be selective rather than encyclopaedic. In order to define criteria for such selection, it was necessary to choose some organizing principles – which in fact related to the third goal, coherence.

Historically, psychology has been based on several different conceptual frameworks, each with its own assumptions, methods and theories. It was decided to make the presentation of five such frameworks (or approaches, as they are called in this text) the central focus of the book. Further, underlying this was a concern with the process of *how* we arrive at knowledge of behaviour – not just that different approaches exist, but how and why they came to be. In doing so, it was recognized that the processes of perception can be used to explain both human behaviour and also the nature of the discipline of psychology. That organizing structure has proven remarkably popular with students and those instructors who have tried using it. In this edition, this theme is reinforced by addressing the role of perception and the nature of the scientific process in both the initial and final chapters. Overall, this book remains faithful to the basic concepts and goals of the earlier edition.

The changes in this edition involve three goals: to clarify and update the material of the first edition where necessary, to expand on the application and comparison of the approaches, and to provide more structural aids to readers. With regard to the first goal, this book represents a complete rewrite of the previous edition, and includes new material in every chapter. Although the previous edition had a remarkable life-span of almost fifteen years in print, any text eventually becomes dated in some respects. Readers will find discussion of new developments, and many new references for both research and further reading. The purpose of such changes has not been to be current for currency's sake, but to select that material which contributes to the original goals of the text. The new edition also amplifies on the approaches where the previous text seemed too narrow – for example, the psychoanalytic chapter has been revised to acknowledge other psychodynamic theories. In the interests of greater clarity and integration, the processes of perception and their relationship to the methods of science have been combined into the first chapter, whereas they were in separate chapters in the previous edition. Hence, the changes are meant to enhance the original conception, not to alter it.

The second change, expansion of discussions on the application and comparison of the five approaches, is also intended to make the book better balanced. In the previous edition, the three application areas – development, social behaviour and abnormal behaviour – were given much more limited attention; in retrospect, it seemed desirable to elaborate both the concepts and the content. Similarly, an Appendix on research methods and statistics has been added, although the text itself also discusses major aspects of these subjects. In the interests of both clarity and reader appeal, the number of illustrations has been approximately tripled. Overall, the book is modestly larger than the previous edition, but still provides a brief introduction to psychology – and one which provides a coherent understanding of the origins and nature of the discipline.

In terms of providing guidance to readers, several features have been added to this edition to make it more helpful. In addition to an extensive Glossary, important terms are also highlighted and defined in context where they first occur, with formal definitions being provided in the margin. Also, each chapter begins with an overall Outline to help readers grasp the structure of what lies ahead, and concludes with a point-form Summary and list of Key Terms and

Concepts. It is hoped that these features will aid students in the process of studying and reviewing, without distracting from the flow of the text itself.

A further addition is the use of discussion questions, which are dispersed throughout the book with the label 'For further consideration'. These questions are meant to encourage readers to apply the ideas within the text as a means of enhancing understanding. In general, they go beyond simple rote review, but are not intended to be completely open-ended. Some ask students to reflect on their own experiences, others may prove amenable to group discussions. While 'critical thinking' has become a much-abused buzz-word in the past few years, these questions are intended to provoke involvement and reflection.

A minor point of style is worth noting. In recent years, there has been an increased awareness of the problems of sexism in language. This is an important issue, but one which is not always easy to address in ordinary English usage. In particular, the use of 'he/she' seems an awkward construction. Since English lacks a gender-neutral pronoun for the third person singular, I have tried to avoid the need for its usage where possible. However, it is not always elegant or appropriate to use 'one', or plurals like 'individuals'. Consequently, I have adapted a usage which is not technically proper, but seems to be becoming more common, and may eventually become generally accepted: where 'he/she' or 'his/her' would seem to be called for, I have used 'they' and 'their'. It is hoped that readers will understand this usage, and not attribute it to grammatical failings of the author.

In writing this book, I have been only too clearly aware of my own limitations, and of my debts to others. The first edition of this book was a collaborative effort of six people, including myself. For various reasons, none of the others became involved in this edition, although all seem happy that it is proceeding. Much of the basic framework of this book was the result of extended discussions and interactions before and during the writing of the earlier edition. While it is impossible to say who provided what insight, there is clearly a large intellectual debt involved. I wish to thank those colleagues who contributed to the previous volume: Gordon R. Emslie, Paul H. Hirschorn, Judith Kelly Waalen, John Medcof and John Roth. In particular, by serving as editors as well as contributors to the earlier book, John Medcof and John Roth helped shape the final product, and encouraged and prodded the rest of us as needed. To all of them, I give my thanks.

A further debt must be accorded to those colleagues who read and criticized the draft versions of various portions of this book. Mary Easton, Isaac Engel, Brian Rabinowicz, Craig Ramsey, Isaac Smith and Dana Williams – all faculty at Ryerson Polytechnic University – provided thoughtful comments and valuable criticism; in particular, Brian Rabinowicz deserves thanks for his efforts in reading a large portion of the manuscript. I feel strongly that the book is better for their efforts. For any faults which remain, I must accept responsibility.

I also wish to thank my family, who sacrificed in many ways during the nearly two years that this project consumed. My older son, David, has grown from toddler to child during this project, and his interruptions have been a frequent relief when the task has grown heavy. My younger son, Daniel, who was born even as this book was being born, has reminded me of just how remarkable our existence is. My wife, Lies Weijs, has been invaluable, emotionally, intellectually and logistically. She has provided encouragement when I needed it, and bore the burdens of family demands when I could not fulfil them. Further, as a reader who has never taken psychology, she provided insightful and intelligent feedback from the viewpoint of a non-expert. Family life and career often seem at odds in our society; in this case, my family has my gratitude and love for all that they have given to this project, and to my life.

At Open University Press, I wish to thank Nick Evans, psychology editor, for being what a good editor should be: a source of encouragement, a valuable source of advice and a gentle critic when necessary. His suggestions have added greatly to this book in ways that readers should appreciate. In addition, I wish to thank Jacinta Evans, publisher, for her commitment to producing this book, and Joan Malherbe of the editorial staff for her efforts in seeing the manuscript through the complexities of publication.

William E. Glassman
Toronto, 1994

┃ Behaviour and Psychology

The Magic of Behaviour

When I was a child, my father sometimes took me to see magic shows. To a boy of 10, this was a wondrous and exciting event. The tricks performed were usually pretty standard – producing objects from hats or boxes, making things disappear, and so on. I knew even then that these feats were not supernatural, but based on some sort of deception or gimmickry – in a word, 'tricks'. Nonetheless, they held me spellbound, wondering how it was all accomplished.

I was reminded of this recently, while teaching a course in problem solving. One day after class, a student in his thirties told me of having recently seen a magic show. After describing some of the tricks, he had the inevitable question: 'How is it done?'

As children or adults, we are curious about the world, and when faced with the unexpected or unexplained, we are driven to increase our understanding. Magic shows represent a special kind of mystery, because what we *think* we see is somehow different from the underlying reality. Indeed, one of the most basic tools in a magician's repertoire is *misdirection* – getting the audience to focus on an irrelevant detail, while ignoring a crucial manoeuvre by the magician. By manipulating our attention and expectations, magicians draw us into a world which entertains us precisely because it is hard to understand.

Studying psychology in some ways is like viewing a magic show, in that the study of behaviour evokes the desire to understand, and often challenges our expectations. In trying to make sense of behaviour, psychologists encounter both the wondrous and the baffling. Consider the case of a horse called 'clever Hans'. Hans had been 'educated' by his owner for four years, and subsequently seemed capable of answering questions in history, geography, mathematics and more.

People came from near and far to see clever Hans, and most went away convinced that he really *was* educated. Ultimately, it was a psychologist named Oskar Pfungst who figured out the true explanation. (Of course, Hans really didn't understand history and so on; later in this chapter, we will discuss what was really happening.) Although an 'educated' horse is unusual, it is not really surprising that a psychologist was involved in understanding it. Understanding behaviour in all its forms is, after all, the primary goal of psychology.

Introduction

Throughout human history, people have sought ways to make sense of the world, and there have been many attempts to formalize the understanding of behaviour. Astrology, for example, arose out of the belief that human actions were influenced by the stars. Often, theories of behaviour have been stimulated by developments in other fields. For instance, in the eighteenth century, anatomists studying the brain proposed that there was a relationship between brain size and mental abilities. This led to the development of **phrenology**, which asserted that one could assess ability by examining the shape of the skull. While phrenology and astrology have been largely discredited, their goal of understanding and explaining the way people act seems similar to that of psychology. So what makes psychology different?

phrenology a now discredited eighteenth-century theory which asserted that one could assess ability by examining the shape of the skull

The simple answer is that psychology differs in the method it uses in the search for understanding. Unlike astrology, phrenology or even 'common sense', psychology utilizes a form of systematic observation and analysis that is often called 'the scientific method'. In fact, **psychology** is often defined as 'the scientific study of behaviour'. Definitions, of course, have limitations, and this one does too. For example, some psychologists would interpret 'behaviour' to mean both overt responses and conscious experience, while others would be more restrictive. Similarly, some psychologists include the behaviour of other species, while some are concerned only with human behaviour. Despite such variations in the focus of interests, the *methods* used in psychology are *scientific*. That is, the methods are primarily based on a tradition which originated with the natural sciences of physics, chemistry and biology.

psychology the scientific study of behaviour and experience

The Challenge of Psychology

All scientists emphasize certain common principles, like the importance of careful observation, minimizing sources of error and testing alternative explanations. At the same time, the methods of psychologists differ from those of physicists or chemists, because what they study is different: the actions (and interactions) of living creatures. This means that psychologists face challenges which are unique to their discipline.

One challenge is related to complexity. Physicists studying atomic particles typically deal with only a limited number of particles at once – a hundred particles interacting would be a very complex system. By contrast, a physiological psychologist studying the human brain is dealing with a structure composed of several *billion* interconnected cells – the most complex structure in the universe! Even for non-physiological researchers, there is tremendous diversity to consider – for example, studying language is complicated by the several thousand languages and dialects known, each with its own vocabulary and grammar. Given the richness of human behaviour, psychologists must contend with a vast range of possibilities, and a correspondingly large variety of data (observations). By comparison, the possible interactions between two chemical elements, or the dynamics of a moving object, are relatively simple.

A second challenge faced by psychologists is sometimes referred to as the problem of self-awareness (Hofstadter 1979). While physicists studying atoms are themselves composed of atoms, most researchers would say that this has no impact on the problems they study. By contrast, psychologists studying human behaviour are simultaneously *producing* human behaviour. At first glance, this may not seem like a problem – it might even be seen as a convenience. In fact, historically, a number of noted psychologists studied their own behaviour as part of their broader studies: Sigmund Freud, the founder of psychoanalysis, studied his own dreams as well as those of his patients (Freud 1900). William James, a pioneering American psychologist, favoured introspectionism – studying the contents of one's conscious awareness – over laboratory research. (In doing so, he popularized the phrases 'stream of consciousness' and 'armchair psychology' (James 1890).) Eventually, however, it was recognized that self-observation is prone to many sources of error, not the least of which is bias – researchers may falsely interpret their own behaviour as consistent with their theoretical ideas.

Observing the behaviour of others can also pose difficulties. While measurement can be demanding even in simple physical systems, psychological observation is complicated by the fact that one is dealing with independent, living organisms, not inanimate particles. In particular, observing human behaviour can lead to **reactivity**, the tendency for people to alter their behaviour when they are being observed. (As a simple case, consider how many people who sing to themselves, stop if they realize someone is listening.) In order to deal with reactivity, psychologists often resort to complicated research designs, sometimes including deliberate deception. (The methods used will be discussed in more detail later in this chapter.) In the end, observing human behaviour proves more difficult than observing simple physical systems.

reactivity the tendency for people to alter their behaviour when they are being observed

Another challenge arises in terms of identifying the causes of behaviour. Traditionally, science has taken as one of its goals the identification of causes, and psychology has tended to accept that this is important to what we mean by 'understanding'. However, the reality is that many different factors can influence behaviour in a given situation. Consider an example: the child welfare authorities are called in when someone is reported to have hit their child. It turns out the father was drinking, had just lost his job, and was himself abused as a child. Is the cause of his abusive behaviour the alcohol, the job loss, his early upbringing, a combination of these, or some factor not identified? In any situation, there are many factors which influence behaviour: some are internal, some are part of the immediate situation, some are part of past history. Each of these represents a type of cause, but developing a complete description of such causes in a given situation is a difficult (if not impossible) task.

Why Different Approaches?

It is not surprising, given the richness and complexity of behaviour, that psychologists have evolved different approaches to understanding behaviour. Ideally, we would have one simple set of principles which would explain every aspect of human experience. At present, no such theory has been developed which has met with broad acceptance. Instead, there are a range of approaches which differ in terms of their basic assumptions, their methods and their theoretical structures. In effect, each approach represents a distinct framework for the study of behaviour. While most psychology books emphasize the research findings in psychology, organized according to traditional topic areas like learning and perception, this book focuses instead on the major approaches which have influenced psychology. By understanding how these frameworks arose, and how they differ, one can better evaluate the significance of each approach, as well as make sense of the field as a whole.

The traditional model of science says that scientists formulate theories based on the information they have gathered from research. Hence, one might imagine that each approach arose as an attempt to improve on existing theories. This viewpoint, while a bit simplistic, is partially valid. In some cases, theorists *do* react against what they see as limitations or errors in the work of others. For example, Carl Jung split from his mentor, Sigmund Freud, partly because of disagreements about the meaning of sexuality. At the same time, other factors also come into play. Thomas Kuhn (1970), a specialist in the philosophy of science, has argued that the acceptance or rejection of particular frameworks or approaches (which he calls 'paradigms') depends on human preferences as well as the available evidence (see Chapter 10 for more on Kuhn's ideas). That is, the development and evaluation of a theory depends not simply on the available data, but also social and personal factors, including the life experience of the researcher. To understand this, we need to examine how we actually perceive the world.

Perception and Theorizing

Most individuals tend to assume that what we experience depends on what is 'out there' – that is, that our senses simply convey information about the physical stimuli which we encounter. This implies a direct record of the external world, similar to the way a video camera records a scene. However, the process of perceiving is actually much more complex. **Perception** is an *active* process involving selection, organization and interpretation, *not* a passive mirroring of the external world.

perception the process of selection, organization and interpretation of information about the world conveyed by the senses

Let us consider first the process of selection. At every moment, we encounter a tremendous variety of stimuli: sights, sounds, smells, etc. Unfortunately, the human brain has a limited capacity to deal with incoming information. (Imagine going to a television store, and trying to watch several channels on different televisions simultaneously – parts of one or more programmes are inevitably missed.) In order to cope with the sensory barrage, our perceptual system focuses on some aspects of the situation, while ignoring others. This process of

Fig. 1.1 Ambiguous figures Is this a rabbit or a duck? What we see can change, even when the stimulus stays the same.

A I3 C

Fig. 1.2 Ambiguous figures What do you see between the A and the C? Compare this with Fig. 1.3.

I2 I3 I4

Fig. 1.3 Ambiguous figures What do you see between the 12 and the 14? Compare this with Fig. 1.2; note how context alters our expectations, and thereby what we perceive.

selective attention the perceptual process of selectively focusing on particular stimulus elements

choosing stimuli is called **selective attention**. One example is the way we focus on one conversation, while filtering out other voices and sounds, at a crowded party. (The nature of attentional limits will be discussed further in Chapter 4.)

Perception, then, is partly determined by the external stimuli that we encounter, as filtered by selective attention (this stimulus-based process is sometimes called 'bottom-up' processing). At the same time, perceptual experience is also influenced by more complex internal factors, such as our prior experience and expectations. These factors (referred to as 'top-down' processing) influence both the way that we interpret selected stimuli, and also what we select. Consider two examples: in Fig. 1.1, what do you see? (Look *now*!) While the figure *could* be interpreted as either a duck or a rabbit, most native English speakers see the rabbit first, because they have learned to scan images in a left-to-right sequence. In this case, past experience influences the processing order. (Try making a copy of the image reversed, and show it to a friend to see what happens.) In Fig. 1.2, what are the letters? Now, compare this with Fig. 1.3. What are the elements in

Fig. 1.4 The Gestalt concept of closure What do you see in these two figures? Note that both are easily recognizable, even though both are based on incomplete outlines.

ambiguous figure any stimulus which can be perceived in more than one way

Gestalt theory a theory of behaviour pioneered in the early part of this century by Kohler, Wertheimer and others, which emphasized the active, creative nature of perception and learning (*Gestalt* is German, and means roughly 'organized whole')

closure in perception, the tendency to fill in incomplete patterns to produce a coherent whole

the centre – numbers, or the letter B? In this situation, the presence of other letters or numbers leads us to interpret the same stimulus elements differently.

So-called **ambiguous figures**, which can be interpreted in different ways, have long been of interest to psychologists studying perception. Such figures illustrate that what we perceive is not based simply on what is 'out there', but is also influenced by internal processes. On first encounter, it may seem that ambiguous figures have little to do with everyday experience – but they actually underscore the processes which are part of *all* perception. In trying to make sense of the world, we look for familiar patterns, and we interpret what we encounter based on our prior experiences. When faced with a situation where there is incomplete information, we fill in the gaps according to what seems probable. This view of perception as an active, creative process was pioneered in the early part of this century by **Gestalt theory** (the word *Gestalt* is German, and means roughly 'organized whole'). Gestalt psychologists argued that perceptual experience is the result of active synthesis, based on a number of basic principles. Among the most important of these was the concept of **closure**, which is the tendency to fill in incomplete patterns to produce a coherent whole (see Fig. 1.4).

The interpretations we make when perceiving are seldom random; instead, they reflect the way we have structured our previous knowledge and experience. From early infancy, we analyse and interpret our experience, seeking patterns to help us make sense of the world. Some of these patterns are fairly simple concepts, like 'food' or 'chair'. As we develop, we form more complex structures called **schemata**. Some schemata are scripts to guide our actions in particular situations. For example, a 'restaurant' script tells us that in a restaurant we order from a menu, are served by someone, and are expected to pay for what we order, among other things. Schemata can also be used to organize our knowledge of objects and people. For example, a schema for 'bedroom' would include knowledge of the various objects found in a bedroom, as well as their functions. Our attitudes towards people, such as stereotypes, can also be considered schemata. As the structure underlying our beliefs and expectations about the world, schemata have even been suggested as the basis of personality (Kelly 1955).

schema (pl. 'schemata') a mental framework which organizes knowledge, beliefs and expectations, and is used to guide behaviour

Whether simple or complex, schemata influence the way we perceive the world around us. Depending on one's schemata, the same situation may be interpreted differently. For example, an old chair at a flea market may be perceived as junk by one person, but another person, more knowledgeable about furniture, may recognize it as a Georgian antique. A Brazilian settler may see a rainforest as something to be cleared in order to create a farm, whereas an environmental activist may see the same forest as a priceless ecosystem. Schemata reflect our values, experiences and expectations about the world. In turn, they also influence how we see the world.

In many cases, it is impossible to label a particular interpretation as correct or incorrect. In the above examples, both points of view have meaning. At the same time, it should be obvious that the use of schemata also creates the risk of distortions in the way we see the world. Sometimes the distortions may be relatively benign, but in other cases the errors may be more serious – especially when our schemata involve faulty or inaccurate assumptions. Consider social stereotypes: It can be argued that stereotypes are formed initially around some 'kernel of truth', an observation of one or more individuals. The **stereotype** is created when this information is then generalized to apply to *all* members of a group, regardless of circumstances. The difficulty comes when circumstances change, but the stereotype doesn't, or when a stereotype is used as a substitute for gathering accurate information about a person. A friend once reported an experience that his six-year-old son had at school. The teacher had asked the children to 'draw a picture of your father relaxing'. When the teacher saw the boy drawing a picture of a man chopping wood, she said, 'No, I said draw him *relaxing*'. Bursting into tears, the six-year-old exclaimed (correctly), 'But my Daddy *does* chop wood to relax!' (By contrast, his father's 'work' involved sitting at a desk all day.) The teacher's stereotype, not the boy's drawing, was the problem. Stereotypes, as mental schemata, can lead us to prejudge others – and *all* schemata carry this risk of distorting reality.

stereotype an oversimplified and often inaccurate perception of an individual based on generalizing from schemata related to the individual's group membership

Even when we are not consciously aware of using schemata, they are part of our perceptual process. Our perceptions of friends and family members are based on many, many experiences. Over time, the schemata we form from these experiences can have more influence on our perceptions than the present reality. Consider the following examples: As parents, we tend to overlook the changes in our maturing children, and fail to recognize that they are no longer as dependent as they were as toddlers. As adults, we can be shocked to realize that our elderly parents now need to be cared for as if *we* were the parents. Friends may change both physically and emotionally, and we may fail to notice. In each case, the mental schema is inconsistent with the person before us. Yet we all tend to believe that family and friends are the people we know best, because we have such elaborate schemata to deal with them.

Ironically, the danger of distortion is greatest when we are most confident that we are correct – because we are less likely to look for information that might reveal our error. This tendency to seek out confirming information, and ignore potentially discrepant information, is sometimes called **confirmation bias**. A doctor with thirty years of experience is less likely to recognize when he has made a diagnostic error than a newly graduated intern precisely because greater experience instils greater confidence (Halpern 1989).

confirmation bias a form of cognitive error based on the tendency to seek out information which supports one's beliefs, and ignore contradictory information

This is not to say that schemata are undesirable – most of the time, they aid us in processing efficiently and accurately the vast amount of sensory information that we encounter. Rather, it is to emphasize that perception is an imperfect process, even as it is a crucial one in our dealings with the world. Coupled with selection and interpretation, organizational schemata enable us to make sense of the wealth of sensory information around us. On balance, the risk of errors is largely offset by the benefits gained from organizing our experiences. In addition, by *understanding* the perceptual process, we are more likely to avoid the kinds of errors we have discussed.

We began this discussion of perceptual processes in response to the question, 'Why different approaches?' By now it should be obvious that researchers depend on the same perceptual processes as other people, with the same limitations. Still, it may not be apparent as to how these perceptual limitations have led to divergent approaches within psychology. To understand this, recall what was said earlier about the challenges involved in studying behaviour. In particular, we noted that human behaviour is almost infinitely complex and variable. Faced with this complexity and variability, how is a researcher to proceed?

Since 'studying everything' seems impossible, some degree of selection is inevitable in research. Researchers make choices, focusing on one aspect or type of behaviour (e.g. physiological processes, or a problem like aggression), or sometimes one species (humans, primates, bees, etc.). The choices made may reflect the researcher's interests, theoretical assumptions, or other aspects of the individual's schemata. In other words, the process of deciding what to study, and how to study it, is influenced by the processes of perception which we have been discussing.

Thus, the process of doing research involves selection in the same sense that perception in general does. Faced with a range of choices, many individuals interested in behaviour decide to follow a research path already defined by others. In some cases, however, circumstances and schemata combine in a way that leads certain individuals to break new ground. In effect, they make choices of what to study, and the methods used, that come to define a new framework or approach to the study of behaviour. In the long run, the development of any approach involves the contributions of many people, but in the beginning there is usually a key figure, whose personal choices serve to define the nature of the approach.

Psychology as a discipline is characterized by not one, but several, different approaches. The major part of this book will be devoted to exploring five major ones: the biological, behaviourist, cognitive, psychodynamic and humanistic approaches. In each case, we will explore the origins of the approach, the individuals involved in its development, and the assumptions and methods which characterize it. Inevitably, you will find points of disagreement between the approaches, as well as apparent limitations of each. Faced with this situation, you may well wonder which approach is the 'real' psychology. While such an impulse is natural, it may not be the most productive way to view the situation.

It is frequently noted in introductory texts that psychology is a relatively young field, tracing its origins back only about 100 years or so. This is just as frequently followed by statements about how one cannot expect much coherence from a young field, as if apologizing for a toddler who doesn't eat tidily. This sentiment not only downplays the accomplishments of psychology, but is also likely erroneous, because it assumes that coherence is *necessary* to a mature field. (Modern physics, by comparison, still grapples with differing models of basic forces, without having a unified theory.)

This general issue deserves more detailed exploration, but the purpose here is to suggest that disagreement is not always a weakness. Physics, a much older discipline than psychology, has long recognized the concept of **complementarity** – different frameworks may be separately valid, without being reducible one into the other (Blackburn 1971). For example, light can be described as a wave or a particle, depending on the circumstances. Each representation has value, without implying that one is right and one is wrong in an absolute sense. In the same way, the differing approaches to behaviour which we will consider may also reflect complementarity. Seen this way, the basic concern becomes how *useful* an approach is, not which is completely correct.

complementarity a concept developed by physicists to deal with the existence of two models which are both useful, but not directly reconcilable

If the preceding example seems too abstract, consider the following story: A group of blind men were making a pilgrimage together in India, when they met a man leading an elephant. None of the blind men had ever encountered an elephant before, and they proceeded to touch it. One man, grasping the trunk, exclaimed, 'Oh! An elephant is like a snake!' Another, wrapping his arms around one of the elephant's legs, said, 'No! An elephant is like a tree, with rough bark!' A third, grasping the end of the elephant's tail, countered, 'You're both wrong! An elephant is hairy, like a camel!' They proceeded to argue vehemently, never realizing that they were each partly right, but that none was completely right. Their differences stemmed from emphasizing different observations, and making different interpretations of those observations. In a similar way, each approach to psychology may be a partial view of the whole subject. And, like the interpretations of the blind men, each approach may have something to offer in our attempt to understand behaviour, even if no one approach can answer all questions.

In considering the five approaches, the process of perception can help us understand how the origin of each approach is related to the schemata of the individuals who pioneered it. While personal experiences play an important role in forming an individual's schemata, people do not live (or work) in a vacuum; each of us is influenced by the ideas and attitudes of the society we live in. (Consider, for example, changes in social attitudes from the 'hippie' 1960s to the 'hungry' 1990s.) Consequently, it is desirable to consider also the intellectual and social context in which the approaches were developed. In so far as possible, these aspects will be discussed in the following chapters, but we should also look at the general context in which psychology as a discipline emerged.

For further consideration

In what ways do you think your own perceptions of the world may be influenced by your previous experiences? Have you ever misjudged someone on first encounter?

The Origins of Psychology

Psychology did not exist as a specific discipline until the end of the nineteenth century. Formally, its inception is usually traced to the creation of Wilhelm Wundt's laboratory of experimental psychology, established in Leipzig in 1879. While it is convenient to point to a specific date, psychology is not a baby with a specific 'birth date'; its genesis really involved a number of elements, from the creation of laboratories, to the formation of university psychology departments, to the growth of public recognition of the discipline. In this sense, its 'birth' really extends over roughly the last three decades of the nineteenth century.

In a broader sense, it can be argued that the origins of psychology go back even further. What has been called the first 'psychology experiment' was performed in ancient Egypt, in about 700 B.C. (Hunt 1993). The king of Egypt arranged for a child to be reared by a shepherd, who was ordered never to speak to the boy. The goal was to determine if language was innate. When the grown child was later presented to the king, supposedly the first sounds he made sounded like the Egyptian word for 'bread' – satisfying the king's desire to demonstrate the inherent superiority of Egyptian culture!

In general terms, psychology emerged out of two traditions: philosophy and natural science. Philosophers have always been concerned with understanding the meaning of human experience, and many basic concepts in psychology trace their origin back to philosophy. For example, John Locke was deliberating the role of learning in behaviour in his *Essay Concerning Human Understanding*, published in 1690. In addition, philosophy, like the humanities more generally, has posed questions about awareness, motivation and values that have also been of concern to psychologists. Along with philosophy's interest in human experience, psychology has been influenced by the study of the natural world. Physics and the other natural sciences have been important to psychology both conceptually and in terms of methods of study. In particular, the success of the physical sciences in using experiments to develop explanations based on causation led to psychology seeking to do the same. Later, as the biological sciences began to develop, they too became sources of influence in the development of psychology. An oft-cited example is the impact of Darwin's work on evolution, with its emphasis on the innate origins of behaviour.

Hence, both philosophy and science have been influential in shaping the nature of psychology. The continuity of these influences is indicated in a 1970 review of research on memory by Tulving and Madigan. Looking at the then current findings, they began by suggesting, only partly in jest, that there was very little that would have surprised Aristotle (perhaps the greatest of the early Greek philosopher-scientists)! To see more clearly how psychology developed from these sources, we will consider two of the great pioneers: Wilhelm Wundt and William James. Taken together, their contributions laid the foundation for most of modern psychology, while reflecting the impact of philosophy and natural science.

Wilhelm Wundt was born in Germany in 1832, and received a medical degree at the University of Heidelberg, graduating at the top of his class in 1855. Shortly after, he went to Berlin, to study for a short time under Johannes Müller, who had earlier established the first laboratory of experimental physiology. Wundt's contact with Müller, while brief, had a significant influence on him, inspiring him to give up medicine to pursue research in physiological processes. Wundt's training led him to study behaviour by examining elementary sensory processes. His background in medicine made it natural to emphasize physiological aspects of behaviour, though he also hoped that eventually psychology could analyse higher mental processes. By today's standards, his equipment and techniques were primitive, but the impact of his work was far-reaching. A prolific writer as well as researcher, he published almost 500 articles and books, totalling almost 60,000 printed pages.

Wilhelm Wundt

Wilhelm Wundt (1832–1920) was born in Baden, Germany, the son of a Lutheran pastor. He received a degree in medicine from the University of Heidelberg in 1855, graduating at the top of his class. Over time, his interests turned towards research in physiology, particularly sensory processes. This led him to an interest in psychology, and in 1879 he founded what is regarded as the first laboratory of experimental psychology, at the University of Leipzig. Wundt hoped that eventually the study of sensory processes would lead to an understanding of higher mental processes, and he wrote prolifically on all aspects of psychology, from physiological processes to social behaviour. As a teacher and researcher, he influenced many early psychologists, but the approach he took to the study of behaviour, called *structuralism*, has been supplanted by other approaches within psychology. Despite this, Wundt is often regarded as the founder of modern psychology.

At this time, psychology did not exist as a distinct discipline; as a result, Wundt's appointment at the University of Leipzig was as professor of 'scientific philosophy' (as opposed to classical philosophy). Thus, a man whose training was in medicine and physiology became a founder of psychology, while teaching as a philosopher! Out of this strange combination emerged the new discipline, and Wundt played a significant role, both through his own work and his impact on his students. While Wundt himself was designated a 'philosopher', he advocated the creation of a new field of experimental psychology. By the end of the century, psychology departments were created at several universities, and some of the founders of these programmes (e.g. E.B. Titchner and J.M. Cattell) studied under Wundt. As a result, Wundt's conception of an experimental psychology – physiologically oriented, emphasizing basic sensory processes – was an important influence in the early development of psychology.

Interestingly, one of the other early giants of psychology, William James, also began as a medical student. James, the elder brother of the novelist Henry James, was born in Boston, Massachusetts in 1842. Ten years younger than Wundt, he came from a wealthy family, and travelled extensively during his career, from the salons of Europe to the jungles of Brazil. His academic career was spent at Harvard University, first as a student, then as a professor. Unlike Wundt, his student days were undistinguished: he started in chemistry, switched to medicine, took a foray into biology, and eventually, after several interruptions, finished his medical degree when he was almost thirty. In 1872 he was asked to teach half of a course in physiology at Harvard; within three years the course had evolved into a study of 'The Relations between Physiology and Psychology'. Three years after that, he dropped the physiological component and began teaching a course which was explicitly psychological.

It was at this time that James was asked by publisher Henry Holt to prepare a textbook on psychology. He accepted, thinking it would be a straightforward task. After all, he was fluent in German and French as well as English, and knew most of the existing literature (including Wundt's work). In reality, writing the book turned into a mammoth enterprise, consuming almost twelve years, and

William James

William James (1842–1910) was one of the most influential and articulate of the early American psychologists. Indeed, his writing is so clear and engaging that it has been said that he wrote like a novelist. (Interestingly, his younger brother Henry is often regarded as the creator of the psychological novel.) The son of a wealthy Boston family, William James was an indifferent student, who tried several fields before finally receiving a medical degree from Harvard in 1869. He began his teaching career as in instructor in physiology at Harvard, but gradually incorporated more psychological content, so that by 1878 the course was purely psychological in focus. At this time, he was approached to write a psychology textbook; the task took more than a decade to complete, but his *Principles of Psychology* became one of the most influential texts in the history of the discipline, and is still in print. Over time, however, his interests shifted towards philosophy, and he finished his career in the philosophy department at Harvard. Within psychology, he is perhaps best known for coining the phrase 'the stream of consciousness'; the approach he founded, called *functionalism*, has remained influential, particularly among cognitive psychologists.

resulting in two massive volumes totalling approximately 1000 pages. James himself was ultimately dissatisfied with his efforts, telling Holt, '*1st*, that there is no such thing as a *science* of psychology, and *2nd*, that W.J. is an incapable' (quoted by Fancher 1979: 160). In fact, by the time of the publication of *Principles of Psychology* in 1890, James' interests had turned towards philosophy, and with the exception of *Varieties of Religious Experience* (1902), his significant later work was all philosophical, not psychological. Ultimately, his appointment at Harvard was in philosophy.

From this brief biography, and James' own comment, one might conclude that his efforts in psychology had little impact on the developing field. In fact, nothing could be further from the truth. Like his brother Henry, William James was a gifted writer, and his *Principles of Psychology* was both influential and widely read – it is probably the best-selling textbook in the history of psychology. (It is still in print.) More importantly, he was an incisive thinker, and his analysis of basic problems set the framework for later research in many areas, from emotion to consciousness. An indifferent experimentalist (although he *did* set up a laboratory for teaching purposes in 1875, the same year as Wundt), he favoured analysing how the mind functioned rather than observing its basic parts. Consequently, he expressed little interest in Wundt's approach, which he once compared to trying to understand a house by studying each of its bricks (James 1884). In turn, Wundt was less than impressed with James, saying of *Principles of Psychology*, 'It is literature, it is beautiful, but it is not psychology' (quoted by Fancher 1979: 128).

Wundt and James each played a major role in shaping the direction of psychology as a discipline. Contemporaries, each began as a medical student and ended as a professor of philosophy (at least in title, if not content). In this sense, they highlight the double heritage of psychology – the natural sciences and philosophy. At the same time, they differed significantly in their approach to the

functionalism an approach to the study of behaviour pioneered by William James, which emphasizes the analysis of the processes by which the mind works, as opposed to the study of the mind's contents advocated by structuralism

structuralism an approach to psychology pioneered by Wundt which attempted to analyse the contents of the mind, using the introspectionist method

study of behaviour and the mind. James' approach, with its emphasis on how the mind works, came to be known as **functionalism**, whereas Wundt's study of basic mental processes became known as **structuralism**. Wundt was a precise and prolific experimenter, while James cared little for the laboratory. Yet, taken together, they point towards two crucial aspects of modern psychology: the importance of making careful observations, and the importance of asking the proper questions. While neither man's views are accepted completely today, their efforts and insights provided much of the foundation for the new discipline. If psychology today seems to see farther than they did, it is partly because (as Isaac Newton once said of his own accomplishments) it is standing on the shoulders of giants.

Psychology, then, traces its origins to rather divergent roots. This diversity is still evident in the current form of the discipline, which extends in many directions. Today, there are individuals involved in psychology who look at everything from intracellular chemistry, to the causes of forgetting, to the nature of romantic love. In some cases, they may feel more comfortable talking with colleagues in other disciplines than with other types of psychologists. Some would see this as a failing, and it is *possible* that time will support that view. At present, though, one can view this diversity as simply a reflection of the complexity of both psychology's origins and its subject matter. One might draw an analogy to the medieval world view which saw man as the measure of all things, and placed humanity at the centre of the universe. Psychology is clearly not the measure of all things, but it is perhaps fitting that the study of human behaviour should have links extending into all the domains of human knowledge, from natural sciences to humanities.

Methods of Studying Behaviour

The Role of the Scientific Method in Psychology

Given the complexity and diversity of human behaviour, how does one go about studying it? While the five approaches differ in the methods they emphasize, all psychologists share a belief in the observational methods of science as the foundation of psychological research. We noted earlier that psychology is distinguished from pursuits like astrology or phrenology, or even commonsense wisdom like proverbs, by being a science. But what exactly does that mean?

First and foremost, psychology is **empirical** – that is, it is based on making observations. Precisely what observations researchers are interested in varies according to the approach, but there is a common emphasis on *objective* observation; normally, this means that observations can be verified by different observers. In this sense, psychology is a public endeavour, which cannot depend on secret knowledge or mystic inspiration. (More will be said about this in conjunction with introspectionism.)

empirical based on making observations, as in an *empirical* theory

The emphasis on empiricism is important, but what determines what is to be observed, and how? A friend of mine likes to 'people watch' by sitting in a sidewalk cafe; if I join him, does that make our observations scientific? To decide, one has to remember that the goal of psychology is to understand behaviour – and understanding requires more than a random cataloguing of observations. By itself, counting how many people go by a sidewalk cafe has no scientific value. At the very least, one must *classify* those observations in some way, which may lead to relating them to something else (perhaps the weather, or time of day, or some other factor). That is, science depends on organized observation, in the belief that classification of observations will ultimately lead to an explanation of those observations (Robinson 1985). Understanding and explanation require the formulation of general principles. At the highest level, a structured set of principles is called a **theory**. A theory provides a coherent structure for relating various observations, and often permits prediction of future observations. Traditionally, theories in science have explained observed events by identifying their causes; at the very least, a theory provides a way of generalizing across specific observations. Hence, observations and theories are complementary to each other.

theory a structured set of principles intended to explain a set of phenomena
induction a process of reasoning based on forming general principles from specific observations
deduction the process of drawing specific conclusions from a set of general principles
hypothesis a statement describing a proposed relationship between two types of variables; a conclusion derived from a theory which can be evaluated by making further observations

Essentially, observations and theory are connected by two basic cognitive processes: inductive and deductive reasoning. **Induction** involves forming general principles from specific observations. The story of Isaac Newton discovering gravity by being hit by a falling apple is doubtless folklore. What is *not* folklore is that Newton saw a connection between falling apples and orbiting planets – that is, gravity was a general principle that could be used to link these observations. **Deduction**, by contrast, involves drawing specific conclusions from a set of general principles. For example, Freud believed that aggression is an innate drive which can be expressed in destructive behaviour. From this, it follows that if someone commits murder, it is because of this innate drive. Most commonly in science, deduction is used to derive a **hypothesis**, a specific conclusion from a theory which can be evaluated by making further observations.

Which comes first, you may ask, inductively forming principles from observations, or deductively deriving hypotheses to be tested by observing? In reality, this is much like the old chestnut about whether the chicken or the egg comes first – there is no clear answer. In practice, researchers use both processes, in a more or less continuous interaction (see Fig. 1.5). Sometimes, past experience will lead to an interest in particular phenomena, and then observations will lead to a theoretical insight. Alternatively, thinking about a theory may lead to the discovery of a new implication, which then must be tested for accuracy by making appropriate observations. As we will see in the following chapters, both types of process have played important roles in the development of the five approaches. As supporters of the scientific method, all approaches share common concerns: to make careful, consistent observations, to avoid errors and to develop clear theories. Despite the general agreement on these principles, there is still room for a range of particular techniques when gathering information.

Introspectionism and Public Observation

introspectionism a method of gathering data in which the individual attempts to analyse the content of their conscious mind; associated with the structuralist approach

At first glance, it might seem that the best way to learn about behaviour is to carefully analyse your own behaviour. After all, whom do you know more intimately than yourself? This approach, called **introspectionism**, was in fact used in various forms by a number of early psychologists, including Wundt and

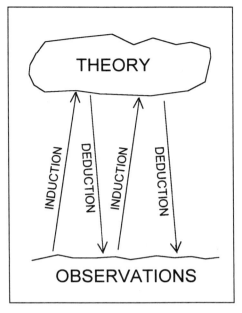

Fig. 1.5 The interaction of induction and deduction in research Research involves an interaction between generalizations derived from observations (induction) and the formulation of predictions about reality derived from theory (deduction). Most researchers use both, and trying to say which comes first is rather like the question about the chicken and the egg.

James. Despite its early popularity, introspectionism (literally, 'looking within') proved to be a questionable technique. Even when it involved carefully structured forms of self-analysis, as in Wundt's case, the method ultimately failed. In part, this was due to the limitations inherent in the perceptual process, as we have discussed. But a second weakness stems from its inherently private nature: Suppose two people, trained in Wundtian introspection, view two colour samples. One person says one is red and one is pink – that is, they differ in one sensory characteristic, defined by colour. The other says that they are both the same colour, but that they differ in saturation (purity of the colour), with the 'pink' one being a mixture of red and white. In essence, they disagree as to whether their experience of the stimuli reflects one quality or two. How can we resolve this dispute? One may be wrong, or each may be correct about their own experience, but since we have no way to determine, we are no closer to a general understanding of what is involved in perceiving a colour sample.

To avoid these dilemmas, psychology, like other forms of science, has come to emphasize public techniques of observation, which make it possible for observers to agree on what has occurred. Even so, this principle takes many forms, since researchers sometimes disagree as to what is 'public'. In general, any aspect of behaviour which can be observed consistently (that is, produces agreement among observers) is considered open for possible study. For example, an arm movement is a public observation. Many physiological responses can also be considered 'public', in that the technologies used for measuring them produce results which observers can agree on. When one refers to mental states, it becomes more ambiguous; some psychologists believe that reports of mental states are inherently unreliable, and cannot be considered public. Others argue that as long as the results of such reports are consistent, then it is possible to devise public measures of mental events. For example, studies of memory depend on what people are able to report remembering.

Some researchers also extend the requirement for public observation to the way terms are defined. So-called **operational definitions** must be based on observable events. For example, to define *love* as 'a feeling in the heart' is not acceptable as an operational definition, because it is not based on an observable event. However, defining it as 'giving a dozen roses to someone' is operational. The difficulty with such definitions, as this example suggests, is that sometimes an operational definition seems unrelated to the concept which it supposedly defines. Consequently, while all researchers accept the importance of being able to confirm observations, not all psychologists see value in operational definitions.

operational definition a term whose meaning is derived from the processes or observable events used to measure it

Measures of Behaviour, Research Settings and Research Methods

In doing research on behaviour, there are a number of ways of gathering information. As a result, a researcher must make choices in terms of how to measure behaviour, what sort of setting to use, and what type of research method to employ. In the remainder of this chapter, we will be looking at the various possibilities in some detail. However, before doing so, it is useful to describe briefly the kinds of options that exist.

Generally speaking, observation can be based on two different ways of measuring behaviour: self-report and direct observation. **Self-report** involves asking the person to indicate their behaviour or mental state in some way. Self-report procedures are used in many situations, but most commonly in interviews, surveys and psychological testing. For example, a survey might ask individuals how often they consume alcohol. Self-report has the attraction of seeming very direct, and in some cases it allows researchers to access information which is otherwise unobtainable. For example, in cognitive research, experimenters may ask people to think aloud while trying to solve a problem. The comments are transcribed as **think-aloud protocols**, which may reveal information about the participants' thought processes.

self-report a method of gathering data which involves asking an individual to describe their behaviour or mental state in some way, such as an interview, survey or psychological inventory
think-aloud protocol a transcript of the comments made when an individual is asked to describe their thoughts and behaviour while working on a task such as problem solving

The alternative to self-report procedures is for researchers to use **direct observation** of the behaviour of interest; in this case, the researcher observes behaviour in some way that does not depend on what the individual says. Direct observation by an independent person tends to be more neutral or objective than self-report, and is more easily verified by having multiple observers. Overall, observation is used most frequently in experiments, although observational methods take many forms, as we will see. The choice of whether to use self-report or direct observation as a method of measuring behaviour represents one of the basic decisions a researcher must make when beginning study of a particular problem. In addition, there are decisions about what type of setting to use, and the type of research method.

The choice of **research setting** concerns whether to observe behaviour in a *laboratory setting*, which involves having participants come to a special location (the laboratory), or in a *field setting*, which requires going to where the people are that the researcher wishes to observe. In a laboratory setting, it is possible to create particular conditions, in order to see how people behave in that situation. However, bringing individuals to a laboratory is also somewhat artificial,

research setting the context in which research is conducted, either a *laboratory setting* (which involves having participants come to a special location) or a *field setting* (which requires going to where the people are that the researcher wishes to study) since participants will be very aware of being observed. By contrast, a field setting is more natural, but necessarily more difficult to control. For example, a researcher may be interested in how children interact while playing. Bringing them into a laboratory would make it possible to control what toys are available and other factors, but may also lead to non-spontaneous behaviour. By contrast, going to a playground to observe such interactions would be more natural, but would allow no control over what was played, by whom, or for how long, thus making comparisons more difficult. Hence, each type of setting has advantages and disadvantages.

The choice of setting is often closely linked to the **research method** chosen. An **experiment** is a procedure whereby a researcher systematically varies one or more factors in order to see what effect the changes have on behaviour. For example, in order to examine the effects of alcohol on coordination, a researcher might vary systematically the amount of alcohol which different subjects consume in the experiment. Experiments are normally conducted in a laboratory setting, since this normally makes it easier to control the factors one wishes to vary systematically. **Non-experimental methods**, sometimes called descriptive/ correlational designs, do not involve direct control of any factor, in contrast to experiments. For example, testing individuals' coordination before and after they visit a bar would not provide any direct control over how much alcohol people drank. Consequently, such comparisons would not directly tell us anything about how *alcohol* affects coordination. Non-experimental methods include naturalistic observation, case studies and surveys, among others.

The three characteristics of research method, setting and measurement type can be used to describe virtually all of the techniques used in psychological research. As we consider some specific techniques, you should ask yourself where they fit in terms of these characteristics.

At this point, the description of research techniques may seem very abstract. Why, for example, would a researcher choose to use self-report in a particular situation? To understand how psychologists make such decisions, let us consider a real-world problem: why do people help or not in an emergency? In recent years, there have been all-too-frequent reports in the news media of situations where someone is in trouble, and onlookers don't get involved. In one well-known case, a young woman named Kitty Genovese was on her way home from her job as a waitress in a New York restaurant. It was late, and the street was virtually deserted as she neared the building where she lived. Unfortunately, before she reached it, a man attacked her, stabbing her. She screamed, and her assailant ran off. Before she could reach home or other shelter, he returned. This time, a man leaned from his apartment window to yell at him, and the attacker retreated once more. She tried to seek refuge in the lobby of an apartment building, only to be attacked again. Sadly, she died from the attack.

As shocking as this story is, most people were more shocked to learn that despite her screams, *no-one telephoned the police*, even though the whole sequence took nearly forty minutes. At first glance, it appears to be a case of utter callousness: someone must have heard; why wouldn't they call? The police and reporters combed the area to seek witnesses, and found thirty-eight people living close to the scene who acknowledged having been home at the time. (One man said the sound of his window air conditioner blocked outside noise – on a night when it was nearly freezing!) Obviously, none of these people telephoned the

research method a procedure for examining a problem and gathering observations; in broad terms, research methods are either experimental or non-experimental
experiment a procedure whereby a researcher systematically varies one or more factors (called independent variables) in order to see what effect the changes have on behaviour
non-experimental methods research methods which do not involve direct control of any factor, in contrast to experiments; sometimes called descriptive/ correlational designs

bystander apathy the failure of onlookers to intervene in an emergency; despite the label, the cause is often unrelated to apathy

For further consideration

interview a method of gathering data in which a researcher asks an individual questions; the format may be pre-planned and highly structured, or relatively free-flowing and unstructured

survey a technique for determining attitudes of many individuals by providing a pre-planned series of questions to which individuals respond

bias a source of error which results in a systematic distortion of results

police. How can we understand this? Is it really the result of callousness and apathy? The tragic death of Kitty Genovese, and other similar incidents, led to the coining of a new term, **bystander apathy**, used to describe situations in which people do not intervene in an emergency. For researchers, as for society in general, the challenge is to understand why such incidents happen; ideally, such understanding might lead to ways of increasing helping behaviour in the future. Faced with a problem like this, it is possible to proceed in many ways. Let us explore this situation further, seeing how psychologists might try to learn more about the underlying behaviour.

Based on what has been said so far, do you think that self-report or direct observation provides a more accurate means of determining how someone behaves or of how someone feels or thinks?

Interviews and Surveys as Self-report Procedures

The police and reporters used one possible method, interviews. In an **interview**, a researcher asks questions, which may be pre-planned and highly structured, or relatively free-flowing and unstructured. The responses from the person interviewed represent *self-report* data, since the person is describing their own behaviour. In the Genovese case, for example, a number of the people interviewed reported hearing the screams, or even watching the attack from their windows, and wondering why the police hadn't arrived. Rather than being apathetic, these people seemed very upset. When questioned as to why they hadn't telephoned the police, they typically stated that they *assumed* someone *else* had done so already. Of course, the reality was that no-one had. Assuming the self-reports were accurate (as opposed to being a rationalization for not having helped), the interviews showed that these people had failed to telephone because of a faulty assumption, *not* because they were apathetic. By suggesting an alternative to apathy as an explanation of the incident, the self-reports were very useful.

Another approach to the issue of bystander apathy would be to do a survey. A **survey** is a technique for determining the attitudes of a large number of people. Some surveys use predetermined questions and response options; this is commonly called a *fixed-alternative* survey. For example, a researcher might ask, 'Would you be willing to aid a stranger in distress?', and allow the answers, 'Yes', 'No' or 'I'm not sure'. For other questions, the researcher might give a rating scale, with several options, from very positive to very negative. The fixed-alternative technique has several advantages, including being easy to administer and easy to analyse. Its major limitation is that it allows little flexibility in answers, and thereby limits how much information can be obtained from respondents; in the worst case, the questions and response alternatives are seen as inappropriate by the person responding.

By contrast, *open-ended* surveys use skilled interviewers; they ask pre-arranged questions, but allow the respondent to give a spontaneous response. At first glance, this may seem more useful than a survey with fixed alternatives, but it has several drawbacks. First, it requires a skilled interviewer to get clear responses without coaching or leading the person answering (coaching could, of course, lead to **bias**, a systematic distortion of the results). Second, it takes considerable effort to analyse the sometimes lengthy responses, and it becomes difficult to summarize responses from a large group of people. Even if one is willing to face these obstacles, responses may not always be very meaningful. In one survey which asked people 'What do you think is the most pressing problem facing the world today?', the majority of responses simply restated the day's newspaper headlines! Without adequate time to reflect on the questions, there is the danger of such superficial responses; the more complex the issue, the greater this problem is likely to be. In such cases, a series of carefully developed, fixed-alternative questions may actually give more meaningful information about people's views than will open-ended questions.

Surveys, even when open-ended, are more structured than interviews, and are intended to provide information from a relatively large number of individuals. Today, surveys are used extensively by governments, political groupings, corporations, the news media and other groups. Sometimes it seems we are bombarded by surveys, many of which are less than insightful. (Does it surprise you, for example, that immediately after the Berlin Wall came down, most Germans were optimistic about the future of their country?)

Surveys and Sampling Procedures

Whether the issues are earthshaking or trivial, all surveys face a common problem: who to survey? At first glance, this may seem very straightforward – simply select a large number of people. Unfortunately, large numbers do not guarantee that a survey will provide meaningful results. To understand why, we need to consider two concepts: population and sample. A **population** is the group whose views one wishes to determine; a **sample** is the subgroup of the population which one actually studies. For example, if a political party wished to determine the attitudes of Canadian voters towards the prime minister, the population would be all Canadians eligible to vote. Since contacting some 15 million people would obviously be impossible, the researchers must use a smaller sample group; in a case like this, they would probably contact between 200 and 1000 people. In selecting a sample, the goal is to obtain a **representative sample** – that is, one which fairly represents the population of interest – and thereby reduce the likelihood of bias in the results. In the case of the election poll, suppose the researcher went to a large shopping centre in Toronto at lunchtime, and stopped every third person that went by. This procedure would not result in a representative sample, since not all Canadian voters are likely to be found at that site. While various techniques exist for selecting a sample, they all share the goal of seeking a balanced representation of the population of interest. (For more information about sampling, see the Appendix.)

As you might expect, sampling procedures in surveys (and in other forms of research) always have some potential for error. In order to deal with this, proper surveys always calculate the probable margin of error, and report this with the results. If you don't see such figures indicated, be cautious, especially when comparing numbers which are close in size. For example, an election survey reported the percentage of people who favoured each political party in an upcoming election (Toulin 1993). In this survey, the margin of error was ±2 per cent, meaning if a reported value was 12 per cent, the actual figure in the population was likely to be between 10 and 14 per cent. In this case, the margin

population in statistics, the group whose characteristics one wishes to determine, and from which a sample is chosen
sample in statistics, a subgroup drawn from a population; in research, the group which one actually studies
representative sample in statistics, a sample whose composition matches the population from which it is drawn

of error meant that the apparent difference between the party in third place (12 per cent) and the party in fifth place (8 per cent) was more apparent than real.

Obviously, the process of obtaining a sample for a survey is not a simple matter, and one must be cautious in looking at survey results, especially when the numbers are taken out of context. Nonetheless, when properly conducted, surveys provide an excellent tool for determining the views of a large group of people.

Limitations of Self-reports

Self-report procedures, like interviews and surveys, are an important method of measuring behaviour, but their use also poses some problems. One basic concern is with accuracy: is self-report an accurate reflection of behaviour? After all, individuals may not always be clear about their own behaviour, because of lapses of attention, memory distortions or other factors. This problem was highlighted by a classic study of racial discrimination, which examined attitudes of restaurant and hotel owners towards racial minorities (LaPiere 1934). (Because the study was done in the United States in the 1930s, human rights legislation was not a strong governing factor.) Travelling across the country with a young Chinese couple, LaPiere kept records of their experiences. Out of 251 establishments visited, only *one* refused to serve the couple (who typically went in first). Six months after their trip, a letter asking about policies was sent to the same establishments. The letter asked, 'Will you accept members of the Chinese race in your establishment?' Overall, 51 per cent replied to the letter, and of these 92 per cent said they would *not* serve Chinese people. In this case, the owners *said* they were more discriminatory than they actually *behaved*! More frequently, a person may actually lie to a researcher, in order to create a more favourable impression. For example, the man who said his air conditioner prevented him from hearing anything when Kitty Genovese was attacked was presumably lying, given the cold weather; in this case, the lie served to justify his failure to intervene. Because of such uncertainties, researchers using self-report procedures must always consider the possibility that what people report is not what they do (Wicker 1971).

Naturalistic Observation and Unobtrusive Measures

Since self-reports may be distorted in various ways, one might prefer to study behaviour through direct observation. One form of direct observation is **naturalistic observation**, which, as the name suggests, involves observing behaviour in a natural setting. Depending on the type of behaviour a researcher is interested in, this technique may be relatively simple, or quite difficult. In the case of bystander apathy, a major hurdle is the unpredictability of emergencies, which makes it nearly impossible for a researcher to be present as events unfold. When the behaviour of interest is more frequent and/or more predictable, naturalistic observation has the advantage of presenting behaviour in a real-world context. Observing in a natural setting avoids the potential artificiality of the laboratory, and for many behaviours, such as social interactions, this can be a great benefit.

At the same time, naturalistic observation has some limitations. One obvious concern, referred to earlier, is *reactivity*; when people know they are being

naturalistic observation a research method which is based on observing behaviour in a natural setting, without interfering or attempting to control conditions watched, they may act differently. In practice, this is often not a serious concern, since there are a number of ways to deal with this problem. One technique, made famous by the American television show, *Candid Camera*, is to use a hidden camera. In other cases, researchers will be able to use a one-way mirror, or other form of blind, to make their presence less noticeable. (The day-care centre at my university has a one-way mirror, allowing students in the early learning pro- gramme to observe the children at play.) Sometimes, simply staying in a situ- ation long enough to make one's presence familiar is sufficient to reduce reactivity. Alan King, a Canadian documentary film-maker, is noted for spending weeks or months with the people he wishes to film. He has commented, 'I carry the camera from day one, but there's no film in it for the first week or so. After that, they're so used to it, they forget about my presence'. (In one memorable film, *A Married Couple*, King ended up recording the break-up of a marriage: King 1971.)

Very close to King's approach is a variation of naturalistic observation called participant observation. In **participant observation**, the researcher becomes part of a group they wish to observe. One recent example is described in *Among the Thugs*, in which author Bill Buford joined a group of English rowdies to learn more about fan violence (Buford 1991). His involvement became so intense that he was injured during a post-game riot! Apart from personal risk, participant observation also poses a risk of biasing the results, since the researcher's inter- action with the group may alter what would otherwise occur.

In order to avoid the problem of reactivity, researchers will sometimes use **unobtrusive measures** as a means of recording behaviour. As the name implies, unobtrusive measures involve recording behaviour indirectly, rather than poss- ibly disrupting it by direct observation. Examples would include checking the frequency of borrowing of various library books as a means of determining which is most popular, or checking sales of travel insurance after an airline crash to measure changes in anxiety among travellers (Webb *et al.* 1972). Inventing unobtrusive ways to measure various behaviours can be a challenging creative exercise, but such measures can also be very difficult to interpret. In one in- stance, an archaeologist attempted to determine whether men or women lived longer in ancient Rome by counting the number of tombstones for each sex. The assumption was that, among married couples, the first to die would be more likely to receive a tombstone; thus, finding more tombstones for men meant women lived longer! Of course, this ignores a wide number of possible factors, from cultural norms about death to the impact of war on male mortality rates. Consequently, when using unobtrusive measures, there is always a need to make sure the characteristic observed is in fact measuring what one intends.

participant observation a non-experimental research method in which the researcher becomes part of a group he or she wishes to observe

unobtrusive measure an indirect measure of behaviour intended to avoid the reactivity which can occur with direct observation; such measures typically require making complex assumptions about the relationship of the measure to actual behaviour

For further consideration

case study a detailed description of a single individual, typically used to provide information on the person's history and to aid in interpreting the person's behaviour

Try to think up your own example of an unobtrusive measure. What do you want to measure? Do you see any ambiguities or other weaknesses with your example?

Case Studies

One of the most fascinating aspects of psychology for many readers is the use of case studies. A **case study** is a detailed description of a single individual.

Like a well-written biography, a good case study gives a sense of capturing the essence of a particular person's behaviour. While this sense of drama is certainly one of the attractions for readers of case studies, as a research tool the value of the case study method stems from the contextual detail it provides about the behaviour of an individual. Case studies basically arose out of medical practice, where developing a clear picture of a patient's background and current symptoms formed an important diagnostic tool. Many basic advances in psychological understanding have come from case studies, particularly in the area of brain function. For example, the discovery of the speech area in the brain came about through the study of a patient who lost the ability to speak after a head injury (see Chapter 2 for more detail). Case studies are found in other areas as well. For example, Sigmund Freud (whose training was in medicine) emphasized case studies as a basic tool of psychoanalysis.

An effective case study can aid in treatment, and can also deepen our insight into behaviour in general. However, like other methods, case studies have their limitations. One important concern is representativeness: a case study is essentially a sample of one and, consequently, a researcher must be careful in generalizing to a larger population. In many situations, the important aspects of a case may well be applicable to a broader group, for example when studying basic neurological functions. (One of my early psychology mentors, whose specialization was the visual system, used to comment, 'In physiology, a sample of one is sufficient'.) Unfortunately, one cannot always be certain whether a case is representative or not. In one well-known instance, Russian neurologist A.R. Luria reported on a man who had a remarkable memory, so remarkable that he essentially never forgot *anything* (Luria 1968). In fact, the man (referred to as S.) would write down things which he *wanted* to forget, in the hope that his mind would no longer be obliged to retain them! As Luria studied S., he discovered that he was also unusual in that his senses appeared 'cross-wired': sounds could create visual images, and had textures and colours as well. This sensory linkage, called *synaesthesia*, apparently was a factor in his unusual memory. Luria's account makes remarkable reading, but it is not clear how relevant the case is to our general understanding of either memory or sensory functioning. Such cases are extremely rare. Richard Cytowic, an American neurologist who has studied another individual with synaesthesia, estimates that fewer than ten people in a million show any real indications of the phenomenon (Cytowic 1993). Consequently, such cases seem rather unrepresentative. As disappointing as this is, it does point out one of the ways in which researchers evaluate representativeness – by looking for similar cases. If similar cases are found, this bolsters the representativeness of the behaviour.

A second limitation of most case studies is not so easily remedied. By their nature, clinical cases arise when people seek treatment; as a result, the doctor/ researcher is presented with a situation whose causes are not directly known. (One of the purposes of developing a clinical history, of course, is precisely to try to learn about what preceded the current situation.) This frequently limits the ability to draw conclusions about causation, particularly for behaviour. For example, a doctor examines a teenage boy who has been in trouble with both school officials and the police. The case history reveals that the boy's delivery at birth was difficult, and may have resulted in minor brain damage. The boy's mother died when he was seven, and his father, who has remarried, is emotionally remote and physically abusive. Which of these factors, if any, account for the boy's current problems? In this type of situation, it is difficult to draw clear conclusions. In particular, there is a risk of confusing factors which may be significant with those which may be coincidental. Even in situations where some type of pre- and post-treatment comparisons might be possible, ethical standards require that concerns for the patient's well-being transcend any research goals. Consequently, case studies can be helpful in suggesting further directions for research, but are generally a poor tool for understanding the *causes* of behaviour.

Correlational Research

Like surveys and naturalistic observation, most case studies represent non-experimental forms of research. Typically, the purpose of a case study is simply *descriptive*, to provide an accurate portrait of behaviour in a particular situation. While accurate descriptions of behaviour are an important starting point in research, description cannot conclusively tell us *why* behaviour occurs. Instead, a researcher may look for patterns which link different aspects of behaviour, such as age and willingness to help in an emergency. Any characteristic which can vary (like age) is called a **variable**; a pattern observed between two variables is called a **correlation**. Thus, if a person's willingness to help is related to their age, then this would represent a correlation. This correlational approach is commonly used in non-experimental studies, since finding patterns is one of the important ways of increasing our understanding of behaviour. Correlational methods are used to identify possible relationships between factors being studied (age and probability of helping, in the example above).

Correlations can enable researchers to make sense out of what might otherwise seem a jumble of data. For example, Fig. 1.6 shows performance on a term examination compared with term paper grades for students in a course I recently taught. In this situation, I wanted to see how performance on the exam compared with that on the papers, since the scores reflect different types of assessment. By using a measurement called a **correlation coefficient**, it is possible to show that there is a moderately strong relationship between the two variables – that is, students tended to get similar grades on the two evaluations. Without the aid of correlational techniques, it would be difficult to know if there is a pattern or not. Thus, a researcher looking for links between sets of observations can find correlations very helpful. (For a more detailed discussion of correlations and how they are measured, see the Appendix.)

The desire to find patterns in observational data is part of a larger goal, which is to understand how and why behaviour occurs. At the same time, this desire to find correlations as a way of making sense of what we observe is not restricted to researchers. Studies have shown that the search for patterns is a natural human trait. Most of the time, finding patterns in our environment is adaptive; for instance, a young child quickly learns that brightly glowing objects, like stove burners and lights, are usually hot. Unfortunately, sometimes we see patterns where none actually exists; when this happens, it is called an **illusory correlation** (Halpern 1989). B.F. Skinner, the behaviourist, has suggested that many forms of superstitious behaviour arise when people falsely perceive connections between their behaviour and a desired or feared outcome (Skinner

variable any measured characteristic which shows variation across cases or conditions
correlation a pattern or relationship observed between two variables

correlation coefficient a descriptive statistic measuring the degree of relationship between two variables. For positive correlations, it is a number which varies between 0.0 and +1.0, and for negative correlations between 0.0 and −1.0; in both cases, the closer the value is to 1, the stronger the relationship between the two variables

illusory correlation a cognitive error in which an individual perceives a relationship between variables where none actually exists

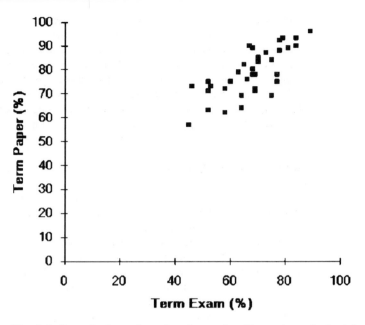

Fig. 1.6 Correlation of academic grades These data, obtained from an actual class, show that there is a positive correlation (+0.75) between performance on term exams and on term papers.

1948a). In essence, such superstitions arise out of illusory correlations. (My favourite example from everyday life is watching people wait for elevator doors to close: often they tap the edge of the door, push the 'close' button repeatedly, or engage in other odd actions – most of which do nothing to alter the programmed cycle of the elevator!) Hence, while seeking patterns can be useful, in everyday life we should be wary of our tendency to see patterns even where none exist.

While finding correlations can help us to make sense of the world, correlations are limited in what they can tell us. The most important limitation concerns explaining *why* an observed pattern occurs. Ideally, we would like to be able to say something like 'A causes B' when we observe a correlation between variables A and B. Unfortunately, a correlation does *not* prove causation. In the above example, rather than exam performance directly causing term paper performance (or vice versa), it is likely that there are underlying factors (e.g. ability and hard work) that affect both types of grades.

It can be very tempting to draw conclusions about cause and effect when we see a pattern in events, but this is also a very error-prone process. For example, most people know that different species of birds have distinctly different songs (e.g. robins *vs* sparrows *vs* finches) – that is, there is a correlation between song type and species. From this, one might conclude that each species sings its particular song *because* of its species (that is, that the song is genetically programmed). While this is consistent with everyday observations and plausible in terms of genetic theory, in fact it is wrong – birdsong requires *learning*, somewhat like human language does (Marler 1970). Or consider the following example:

a study done in Hamburg, Germany found that over a period of years, there was a correlation between the number of storks nesting in the city and the number of human babies born. That is, more storks were found nesting in those years in which more human babies were born. Obviously, folk tales about storks bringing babies are not true, despite this observed pattern! (The reason for this pattern *may* be a series of underlying links in terms of storks choosing chimneys as nesting sites, and the number of chimneys increasing as human population grows – *or*, it may be coincidence!)

In the end, finding a correlational pattern doesn't tell us *why* the pattern occurred; further research is required to find out its origin. Generally, one of three possible explanations applies: (1) one variable actually causes changes in the other; (2) there is some underlying link between the observed variables (as in the example of student grades); or (3) the observed pattern is really coincidental, and would not re-occur in a new set of similar observations. While one might gather further information by doing additional descriptive or correlational research, the best way to address questions of causation is by doing experiments.

Experiments

All of the methods we have discussed thus far, from interviews to naturalistic observation, share the same limitation – they cannot answer questions about the causes of behaviour. In large part, this stems from the complexity of behaviour, and the many possible influences on it. For example, let us consider again the case of clever Hans, the 'educated' horse. As was described earlier, Hans' owner spent several years trying to teach him maths, geography and other information, and seemed to have succeeded. Hans was able to answer questions correctly by tapping his foot to spell words, or shaking his head to answer yes or no. Finally, after Hans had become rather famous, a psychologist named Oskar Pfungst came to observe him (Pfungst 1911).

Mr von Osten, the horse's owner, had already invited a number of psychologists and animal trainers to observe Hans, and all had come away convinced that the horse's ability was real. Pfungst was sceptical, however, and asked that some simple experiments be performed. One experiment showed that Hans could still perform if his owner was absent (thus ruling out fraud by the owner). A second test involved comparing how Hans performed when blindfolded or not. The results led to the conclusion that Hans used some sort of visual cues to determine his responses, since his performance was poor when wearing blinders. Eventually, by varying the conditions, Pfungst was able to identify the mechanism by which Hans figured out answers: members of the audience who knew the answer would unconsciously make minor head and facial movements in anticipation of Hans' response (e.g. slightly tilting the head down when expecting him to tap). While the cues varied from person to person, the general conclusion was supported by a further experiment, in which no-one in the horse's view knew the answer; under these conditions, Hans could not answer correctly. Thus, rather than learning maths, history and geography, Hans had learned to read non-verbal cues in the onlookers, as a way of getting rewards of praise and carrots!

What is most striking in this story is how successful Hans was, and how long it took to discover the truth. Note that his owner was *not* engaged in deliberate fraud – he genuinely believed Hans was clever, and encouraged scientists and others to find an explanation. Only Pfungst was able to do so, by doing experiments. *Experiments*, unlike the most careful of descriptive and correlational methods, allow us to manipulate and control conditions in ways that make determining causation possible. In essence, these two factors – manipulation of a variable of interest, and control of factors that might confuse the situation – are what distinguish experimental methods from other forms of research. The experiments that Pfungst did all involved testing a single subject (Hans) under various conditions (e.g. with or without blinders). This is what is called a *within-subject design*, involving comparisons of the same individual under different conditions. As we will see, most experiments involve comparing different groups of individuals, a procedure called a *between-groups design*. Since Pfungst did his tests in Hans' ordinary environment, it represents an example of a **field experiment** (as compared to experiments done in a *laboratory setting*).

> **field experiment** an experiment done in a natural setting, usually without the explicit awareness of participants; as contrasted to experiments done in a laboratory setting

In any experiment, the researcher begins with a *hypothesis*, a statement describing a proposed relationship between two types of variables; the experiment is then designed as a way of testing the accuracy of this hypothesis. One type of variable, called an **independent variable**, is controlled by the researcher, in order to see what effect it has on behaviour. For example, Pfungst looked at the influence of blinders versus no blinders on Hans. The other type of variable, called a **dependent variable**, is a measure of the behaviour under study. In Pfungst's experiments, the dependent variable was always whether Hans answered correctly or not. In most experiments, there is a single independent and a single dependent variable, although as we will see, more complex designs are possible.

> **independent variable** a variable in an experiment which is systematically varied by the researcher, in order to see what effect it has on behaviour
>
> **dependent variable** in an experiment, the behaviour measured in order to evaluate the effects of the independent variable

In order to see how researchers use experiments to test hypotheses, let us return to the problem of bystander apathy. As you may recall, the results of interviews with nearby residents indicated that although no-one intervened, those who observed the attack on Kitty Genovese were hardly apathetic about the experience. Faced with the phenomenon that people seemed concerned but did not react, two social psychologists, Bibb Latané and John Darley, decided to explore the issue further (Latané and Darley 1969). As was noted previously, the interviews suggested that most people assumed *someone else* had already telephoned the police. Given that several apartment buildings overlooked the location, it seemed reasonable for someone to imagine that other people were also aware of the attack, and therefore that others would have telephoned already. This meant that people had acted according to what they thought others were doing. Latané and Darley recognized that emergencies represent an unfamiliar and sometimes ambiguous situation, and that in such circumstances people often guide their behaviour by what others do. Consequently, Latané and Darley decided to explore the effects of the presence of others on behaviour in an emergency. They did a series of experiments, of which we will discuss two.

The first experiment was done in a laboratory, and was dubbed 'A Lady in Distress'. Participants were recruited through ads asking for volunteers to take part in a consumer research study (Latané and Darley recognized that telling people the true purpose of the study might distort their responses). The **subjects** (the term refers to participants in research) either came alone or with a friend; if alone, they found either another volunteer, a confederate of the experimenters who was pretending to be a volunteer, or no-one. These variations represented

> **subject** in research, an individual who is the object of study or the participant in an experiment

the independent variable – being alone, with a friend, with a stranger, or with a stooge. Latané and Darley wanted to see what effect these variations had on the likelihood of someone intervening in a (staged) emergency; the measure of intervention became the dependent variable. In this experiment, the emergency involved an apparent injury to the woman conducting the consumer survey. When the subjects arrived, they were greeted by a woman wearing a white lab coat, who gave them a questionnaire, and then went into the next room. Through the partially opened door, the subjects could hear the sounds of someone climbing on a chair, and then a crash, followed by a scream and sounds of evident distress. If you were sitting in the waiting room, would you go to help? Would it matter to you if a friend or stranger was present? What do you think Latané and Darley found?

The primary measure of helping behaviour was whether the subjects did anything to intervene, ranging from going next door to simply calling out. (A second dependent variable was the time subjects waited before responding; while we will not discuss this variable in detail, it is worth noting that experiments can have more than one dependent variable.) The main result was that individuals alone were the most likely to help (70 per cent intervened). Groups consisting of two friends also showed a 70 per cent response rate, but since there were two people present, this is actually lower than would be expected if they acted independently. (Probability theory states that the likelihood that at least one would respond, given the 70 per cent figure for a single person, is 91 per cent.) When two strangers witnessed the emergency, only 40 per cent of the time did one or both react (again, this is significantly less than the 91 per cent expected if they acted independently). When a stooge was present who deliberately ignored the emergency, the rate of intervention by the subjects dropped to 7 per cent! Clearly, in this situation, the presence of another person reduced the rate of intervention.

Despite the relatively high level of response by individuals who were alone, Latané and Darley were concerned that the situation may have been too artificial. After all, the participants had come to a laboratory for a form of psychological research; maybe they were suspicious. While it would be difficult to conduct research on bystander apathy without some form of deception, Latané and Darley felt that the use of a laboratory design may have limited the usefulness of the research in terms of what is called external validity. **External validity** concerns the degree to which one can generalize the results beyond the specific situation. Obviously, if participants saw the situation as somehow artificial, the experiment would have low external validity.

external validity an assessment of the degree to which one can generalize research results beyond the specific situation

Faced with this concern, Latané and Darley decided to try a further experiment, which would be a field experiment. Like naturalistic observation, field experiments are done in a natural setting, without telling participants that their behaviour is being observed. Unlike naturalistic observation, field experiments involve the same elements of manipulation and control which are found in laboratory experiments. In this case, Latané and Darley decided to examine how people respond to a perceived theft in a store. Dubbed 'The Case of the Stolen Beer', the experiment involved repeatedly staging a 'theft' at a store selling beer in suburban New Jersey. (The store operator, of course, was a knowing participant, and the 'thieves' were actually confederates of the researchers.) As in the previous experiment, Latané and Darley were interested in the influence of another person's presence on response rates, but in this case they also added a second independent variable – that is, the number of robbers (one or two). As before, their hypothesis was that an individual would be more likely to intervene when alone than when others were present. The 'robbery' scenario was rehearsed to be consistent: while one or two customers (remember, the number of people present is an independent variable) were in the store, the robber (or robbers) would enter, ask the lone clerk for an item not on display, and while the clerk went to check the storeroom, the robbers would glance around, pick up a case of beer from a floor display, and walk out. When the clerk returned, he would ask the other customers if they'd seen what happened to the now-disappeared person(s). The customers, of course, did not know this was a staged event; from their point of view, the robbery was genuine. To measure rates of helping (the dependent variable), Latané and Darley defined helping as telling the clerk about the theft (they felt it was unreasonable to insist on actively attempting to prevent the theft!).

One of the challenges of doing field experiments is the need to preserve consistency of conditions, while at the same time not revealing to participants that an experiment is in progress (note that, as in the previous study, this involved an element of deception). In order to fulfil the conditions of Latané and Darley's experiment, it was necessary for the number of customers required (one or two) not to change during the staging of the robbery; thus, if a customer entered or left the store *during* the scenario, the staging was aborted. While a number of aborted trials were necessary, eventually the researchers obtained results from ninety-two trials, half involving one customer, and half involving two. Since the customers did not know the robbery was staged, a secondary concern was to prevent harm to the confederates who were acting as robbers. Fortunately, no-one attempted any heroic intervention that posed risk to those involved.

What would *you* do if you witnessed a theft like this? Would you attempt to stop the thieves, tell the clerk, or pretend you'd not noticed the theft? The results from The Stolen Beer experiment are shown in Fig. 1.7. Note that the data are presented in a two-dimensional table, because there are two independent variables: the number of customers (subjects) and the number of robbers (confederates). Look carefully at the results: note that overall people were more likely to respond when there were two robbers rather than one! Why do you think this was the case? (One possibility overlooked by Latané and Darley is that failure to actively intervene was *easier to justify* when there were two robbers because of the increased risks, so that customers were more willing to admit having seen the robbery in this circumstance.) Also, the pattern found in the previous study was supported: people are more likely to intervene when alone than when others are present.

The experiments by Latané and Darley thus support the hypothesis that the presence of others reduces helping behaviour in emergencies. This takes us a step further than the interview data or naturalistic observation, in suggesting that it is not apathy, but a social process of some sort, that inhibits helping behaviour. What exactly is the nature of that social process? Latané and Darley offered two possibilities: diffusion of responsibility and social influence. *Diffusion of responsibility*, which can occur in any group situation, including committees, is the tendency to feel less personal responsibility when others are also perceived as responsible. (This is consistent with the reports in the Kitty Genovese case,

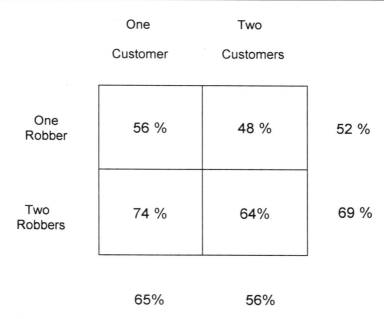

	One Customer	Two Customers	
One Robber	56 %	48 %	52 %
Two Robbers	74 %	64%	69 %
	65%	56%	

Fig. 1.7 Latané and Darley's field experiment This experiment actually used two independent variables: the number of customers present and the number of robbers involved. As the table shows, both variables had an influence, with people being most likely to report the theft when it was a single customer faced with two robbers (data from Latané and Darley 1969).

when people assumed someone else must have called the police. While no real group existed, people apparently *perceived* themselves as part of a social unit defined by the locale.) *Social influence*, which is more subtle, refers to the tendency to look to others for guidance, particularly when facing an unfamiliar situation. For example, if you were at a formal banquet, and were uncertain which fork to use for the salad, you might try to see what fork other people were using. (Since the people who saw the Genovese murder were isolated from each other, this is a less likely explanation of their behaviour.) Unfortunately, the experiments described above cannot determine which of these two explanations is more important. (Subsequent work has indicated that in fact *both* factors play a role in most emergency situations, as will be discussed in Chapter 8.) What the research *does* tell us is that 'bystander apathy' is a misnomer, since people who don't intervene behave that way for reasons very different from simple apathy.

For further consideration

Do you think that the experiments by Latané and Darley are plausible as a means of studying bystander apathy? Would naturalistic observation during real emergencies be better in your view? Why or why not?

Ethics in Psychological Research

As we have seen, the desire to understand behaviour has led to the development of a variety of methods based on scientific principles. Over time, the application of these methods has significantly increased our understanding of human behaviour. While it would be comforting to portray psychology as simply the neutral and impartial pursuit of understanding, it is also true that research can be intrusive, and possibly even harmful. To say this is not to portray psychologists as evil, like some lab-coated villain in a low-budget movie, but to acknowledge that no human activity is value-free. The concern for values applies to all scientific endeavour, but the focus on living beings (animals as well as people) in psychology makes concerns about ethics more immediate than in the natural sciences. In part to foster high standards, the psychological associations in every major country publish codes of ethics for their members. Despite this attempt at uniformity, ethical standards in research, like all social standards, are shifting thresholds, which seldom produce universal agreement.

The most basic ethical concern is the desire to avoid causing harm. While this seems very straightforward, in practice it can be more ambiguous. Consider the following example from recent medical research. In the late 1980s, it was discovered that the drug AZT had some possible benefit in the treatment of acquired immunodeficiency syndrome (AIDS). Since the drug was unapproved, doctors began a double-blind study to test its safety and effectiveness. However, because no other treatment existed for AIDS (a fatal disorder), trials were halted before the study was completed, in order to provide AZT to all participants. In this case, the concern was that it was unethical to withhold a promising drug from those in need (the placebo group). Unfortunately, cancellation of the study had the negative effect of slowing the process of evaluating AZT; consequently, it was not discovered until 1993 that AZT was not appropriate for those who were HIV-positive but not yet showing symptoms of AIDS. Should the researchers have continued the original study, even if it meant denying some individuals with AIDS full dosages of AZT? Or did the immediate need outweigh the concern for future knowledge? In circumstances like this, one sometimes finds conflicts between different ethical principles.

A case which directly involves psychological research relates to a famous study of obedience to authority (Milgram 1963). This study was concerned with how people respond to authority figures when instructed to do something they feel unwilling to do. (While often described as an 'experiment', Milgram's original study actually had no control group.) Subjects were recruited through a newspaper ad to participate in 'a study of learning and teaching methods'. When they arrived at the laboratory, a researcher in a white coat showed them an impressive-looking device which, it was explained, was used to punish wrong answers with a series of electric shocks. The volunteer was to be the 'teacher', while a 'learner' in the next room would receive the shocks. The teacher met the learner (actually a confederate of the experimenter) and watched while the electrodes were strapped to his wrists; the learner expressed some apprehension as to how the shocks might affect his heart condition. The researcher stated that, 'Although the shocks can be extremely painful, they cause no permanent tissue damage'. During the actual 'learning' session, the teacher and learner communicated from adjacent rooms, via an intercom. As the 'experiment' progressed, the researcher instructed the subject to increase the shock each time a wrong answer was given. (The shock apparatus had a series of switches in 15 volt increments, going from 15 to 450 volts – the latter was also labelled 'Danger XXX'.) Despite possible personal misgivings, protests from the learner and, finally, no sound at all from the learner, the subject acting as teacher was instructed by the researcher to go to the highest voltage level. It is hard, while sitting comfortably reading this account, to imagine how upsetting the participants found this situation. It may be even harder to understand why they continued, for in Milgram's original study, 65 per cent continued to the maximum shock level!

Milgram's study has subsequently become well-known, both for its results and the controversy over its methods. After participating in the study as described above, the subjects discussed the experience with the researcher (a process called *debriefing*). At this time, the subjects were told that the apparatus, as well as the entire situation, was simply a ruse; the 'learner' was never actually shocked, and his protests were carefully scripted acting. The *real* purpose of the study was to see how far people would go to obey an authority figure. The fact that most people went to the top of the scale, Milgram has argued, shows how important it is to understand the roots of obedience.

At the same time, many of Milgram's subjects found complying very upsetting, since they believed that the learner was actually suffering real shocks. For those who fully complied, this upset was perhaps compounded by the realization that, had the shocks been real, they might have killed someone. The debate then comes down to this: does the knowledge gained about obedience offset the emotional upset to the subjects? Milgram himself has gone to great lengths to justify the study, and has used follow-up studies of the original subjects to indicate that no enduring trauma ensued: after one year, 84 per cent were either glad or very glad to have taken part (Milgram 1964). However, this might be explained by the theory of cognitive dissonance, which says we tend to alter beliefs to fit with past actions (Festinger 1957); from this viewpoint, the subjects might have been trying to justify their compliant behaviour.

Critics have suggested Milgram was insensitive to the suffering of his subjects. For example, Baumrind (1964) criticized Milgram for statements like 'a mature and initially poised businessman . . . within 20 minutes . . . was reduced to a twitching, stuttering wreck'. Brandt (1982) has offered a meta-analysis of the situation, suggesting that subjects' willingness to inflict suffering in the name of research was paralleled by Milgram's own willingness in the same cause. From this viewpoint, Brandt argues, the experiment was unnecessary, since Milgram's own attitude would tell him how others would respond. It seems clear that Milgram was not deliberately malevolent, and did in fact take considerable care to debrief his subjects after their participation. At the same time, it seems probable that a less harmful technique could have been found to test the concept of obedience – although the results also would likely be perceived as less applicable to the real world. Ultimately, ethical standards *do* evolve, and it is probable Milgram's research might *not* be approved if it were to be proposed today (at my university, the rules of the ethical standards code state that the perceived benefits of research cannot be used to justify causing harm to research subjects). In the end, Milgram's study highlights the difficulties of achieving consensus on ethical matters.

Milgram's study also points out the ethical conflicts raised by another issue: the use of deception in research. Technically, *deception* occurs whenever participants are not fully informed about their participation in research – although this is a rather stringent, and possibly unrealistic, standard. As has been noted already, the phenomenon of reactivity makes it impossible to provide full disclosure in all research situations. In naturalistic observation, for example, the researcher cannot typically seek the consent of those being observed before doing research, since that could lead to altered behaviour. In social psychology in general, whether observing in the field or doing experiments in the laboratory, research requirements often make it necessary to withhold information or even to actively deceive participants. Obviously, deception (and with it, the lack of opportunity for informed consent) is open to abuse, and must be used with caution. Most ethical codes, such as that of the American Psychological Association (APA), allow deception to be used, with certain restrictions: that the research cannot be done otherwise, that subjects are not coerced to participate, that subjects will be fully debriefed after participating, and that there is a justifiable value to the outcome of the research (normally an increase in understanding of behaviour). While most researchers agree with this code, and argue that under these conditions no real harm occurs to participants, the issue is still contentious. Kelman has argued that the use of deception can undermine the relationship between researcher and participants, and suggests deception should only be used when there is no alternative way to do the research (Kelman 1967). Warwick (1975) goes even further, suggesting that the willingness to use deception contributes to undermining public perceptions of the trustworthiness of public institutions. Brandt (1982) has argued that essentially the APA code amounts to saying the end justifies the means – it's all right to deceive subjects if society gets something out of it.

The concern about the long-term effects of deception is illustrated by a follow-up to Milgram's study, which sought to demonstrate that the same effects could occur in the real world (Hofling *et al.* 1966). In this case, the researchers set up a field experiment, in which nurses at a hospital received a telephone call from an unfamiliar staff doctor, instructing them to administer what appeared to be a toxic dose of medication to a patient. The doctor explained that he was on his way to the ward and would sign the authorization at that time. Of course, the situation was designed to ensure no harm came to patients, and true to expectation, all but one of twenty-two nurses tried to administer the toxic dosage! This study demonstrated the external validity of Milgram's results, and is cited approvingly by Zimbardo (1992) for this reason. What is *ignored* by both the original researchers and Zimbardo is the question of how this experience affected the nurses subsequently: did it make them more distrustful, and if so, is that ultimately good or bad? The consequences of such deceptions seem to extend well beyond the confines of the experiment itself.

In the end, this is an issue upon which it is impossible to find universal agreement. Having served on ethical review boards, I know that good researchers recognize that they bear a moral responsibility for their work, although cases do arise where researchers are not sufficiently sensitive to possible ethical conflicts. Ethical boards exist, in fact, to ensure that the proponent of a study is not the only one to evaluate its suitability. In my own research on cognitive processes, deception is not an issue, and the greatest risk to subjects is the possibility of boredom. However, some types of researchers have no such luxury, and must often balance their desire to know against other kinds of values. At the very least, it is to the credit of the discipline that the debates about ethical issues are publicly argued. Psychology exists to enhance our understanding of ourselves, and as long as researchers remain sensitive to the ethical responsibility this entails, then psychology will represent *humane* behaviour as well as *human* behaviour.

For further consideration

Consider the experiment by Schachter and Singer described in Chapter 4 (p. 176), in which participants were misinformed about the effects of a drug injection. How would you feel about it? Do you think it is an ethical study? If yes, why? If no, why not?

Conclusion

In this chapter, we have looked at the history and basic characteristics of psychology as a discipline. In the process, two basic themes have emerged. The first is that the process of understanding behaviour is influenced by the perceptual processes which we use in interpreting everything which we experience. One aspect of this is the selective nature of perception. Given the complexity of behaviour, researchers inevitably must be selective in what they study, and this is reflected in the nature of the different approaches to psychology which this book considers. Perception is also important in that we actively interpret the world, and the interpretations we make are based on the schemata which we use to organize our thinking. Psychological theories are one example of the attempt to organize our understanding of the world. Hence, the existence of different approaches within psychology can be partly understood in terms of the processes of perception.

The second basic theme is that psychology faces particular challenges in the process of gathering information. Like the natural sciences, psychology is empirical, and emphasizes the importance of observations in developing an understanding of behaviour. However, physics or chemistry deal with inanimate matter, and the concepts can seem remote from personal experience. By contrast, psychology is concerned with the understanding of our own actions and experiences. Because people are self-aware, researchers must be careful that the process of observing does not alter the behaviour of interest. This concern underlies many of the research methods employed, from naturalistic observation to field experiments. In addition, because psychology deals with living creatures, ethical concerns exist which do not arise in the natural sciences. These two factors make psychology very different from the natural sciences.

At this stage, you may feel that the challenges are overwhelming, not only for psychologists as researchers, but also for you as a reader. If so, don't despair. This chapter has tried to outline some basic themes, but it cannot tell the whole story. Indeed, while much of the meaning lies in the themes, the excitement lies in the details – the specifics of how we act, and why. In the chapters ahead, you will encounter more of the specifics, and also develop a better understanding of the broader themes and issues. As you proceed, you will find that each chapter adds to your understanding of both behaviour and the way psychologists study it.

Each of us has wondered what we are, and why; psychologists have dedicated their lives to answering these questions. While no final answers can be offered, in the chapters ahead we will see that even partial answers can offer both excitement and insight.

Chapter Summary

♦ Psychology is defined as 'the scientific study of behaviour'. By *behaviour*, researchers variously mean observable responses, inner experience (thoughts, feelings, etc.), or both – the variations are one of the factors that distinguish the different approaches within psychology. It is *scientific*, in that it is based on the methods of systematic observation and analysis which are part of all science.

♦ The task of understanding behaviour can be related to *perception*. Rather than being a passive representation of sensory input, perception is an active process of *selecting* and *interpreting* the information provided by our senses. Faced with the complexity and diversity of behaviour, psychologists make choices in terms of what aspects to study, the research methods to be used, and other issues.

♦ These choices are reflected in the different *approaches* to the study of psychology, which differ in their basic assumptions about behaviour, as well as their methods and theories. In effect, each approach represents a distinct framework for the understanding of behaviour.

♦ Psychology developed from two different traditions, associated with philosophy and natural science. The influence of the natural sciences is seen in the work of Wilhelm Wundt, who founded the first major laboratory for psychology at Leipzig in 1879. The influence of philosophy is reflected in the ideas of William James, an American contemporary of Wundt's, who wrote a highly influential text on psychology.

♦ Five major approaches have been influential within psychology: the *biological*, *behaviourist*, *cognitive*, *psychodynamic* and *humanistic*.

♦ In psychology, there are many possible ways of collecting observations, which vary in terms of *measurement techniques* (*self-report* or *direct observation*), *setting* (in a *laboratory* or in the *field*) and *research method* (*experimental* or *non-experimental*).

♦ Non-experimental techniques include *interviews*, *surveys*, *case studies*, *naturalistic observation* and the use of *unobtrusive measures*. Non-experimental methods are *correlational* – that is, they assist us in finding patterns in behaviour, but do not directly identify the causes.

♦ Experimental methods always involve systematically varying one or more *independent variables* in order to see how the changes affect behaviour. This systematic manipulation, together with control of other factors in the situation, is intended to aid in understanding the *causes* of behaviour.

♦ One issue which is common to all psychological research is the importance of *ethics*. Two particular concerns are the possibilty of causing harm and the use of deception.

Key Terms and Concepts

case study
correlation
dependent variable
empirical
experiment
hypothesis
independent variable
interview
naturalistic observation

population
psychology
representative sample
sample
schemata
self-report
survey
theory
unobtrusive measure

Suggestions for Further Reading

Fancher's *Pioneers of Psychology* provides a highly readable historical overview of psychology, focusing on the major figures who helped shape the discipline.

Luria's *The Mind of a Mnemonist* is a short book which shows the value of case studies while providing a vivid account of a remarkable individual.

Pygmalion in the Classroom, by Robert Rosenthal and Lenore Jacobson, is a classic account which presents Rosenthal's ideas about experimenter bias in a very relevant setting.

The Varieties of Religious Experience is a remarkable work, William James' last on psychology. It offers both an excellent introduction to James' thinking, and a still relevant exploration of one of the most profound aspects of human experience.

Unobtrusive Measures: Non-reactive Research in the Social Sciences, by Webb *et al.*, is an interesting account of how to do research without intruding.

2 The Biological Approach

Looking for the Mind

One of the most profound, and yet easily overlooked, aspects of our behaviour is that we are able to ask questions about ourselves – that is, we are self-aware. This capacity to reflect on our own existence has long been a source of both wonder and perplexity. In the seventeenth century, the French philosopher René Descartes, trying to find a foundation for his philosophical system, arrived at his now famous conclusion, '*Cogito, ergo sum*' ('I think, therefore I am'). Conscious awareness, for Descartes, was the one element of experience that could be trusted as being real. Descartes's ideas have had a profound impact on the way we think about the nature of the mind, but one need not look to philosophy to recognize the complexity of our own awareness. The practice of medicine, for example, often poses strange puzzles.

Oliver Sacks, a neurologist who is also a gifted writer, has described a remarkable case that he encountered (Sacks 1985). 'Dr P.' was a music professor who was referred to Sacks because of a visual problem. He would confuse common objects, on one occasion mistaking his wife's head for his hat. Given a live rose to identify, he described it as 'a convoluted red form with a linear green attachment'. Shown photographs, he could identify only those with a distinguishing feature, such as Einstein's unruly hair. On the street, he some-

phantom limb a mysterious phenomenon in which individuals who have lost a limb will often continue to experience sensations which seem to come from the missing limb

mind the inner subjective experience of conscious awareness; the term has no direct reference to physical form

times patted a fire hydrant, thinking it was the head of a child. Indeed, he could only recognize people by voice, not by sight. Yet his eyes were fine – he could even spot a pin on the floor. In other respects, Dr P. seemed normal; in fact, his musical gifts (with the exception of no longer being able to read music) were considerable. The only evident symptom, apart from his problems with visually recognizing faces and complex shapes, was a slight abnormality of reflexes on the left side. Here was a bizarre puzzle: how could someone identify a pin, yet think that his wife's head was a hat? How is our awareness related to what our senses tell us?

If that seems puzzling, consider the phenomenon known as **phantom limb**. When individuals lose a limb, they will often continue to experience sensations which seem to come from the missing limb. Sometimes, the sensations are relatively benign – a feeling of cold, or an itching sensation (that sometimes can be relieved by scratching where the limb would be!) – but often the sensation is one of intense pain in the missing limb. Since the pain is experienced in a non-existent limb, conventional pain remedies are typically of no value. Sometimes, the afflictions are even stranger than simple pain. Sacks has reported one case of a man who experienced his missing finger as extending straight out – accompanied by the fear that if his hand came near his face, the phantom finger would poke him in the eye! He *knew* the finger didn't exist, but could not escape the sensation, or the accompanying fear. Despite great efforts to understand and treat the problem, the full explanation of phantom limb remains a mystery.

Both of these phenomena call into question the relationship between mind and body. Traditionally, **mind** is used to refer to our experience of awareness, or consciousness; it has no direct reference to physical form. The **body**, of course, refers to our physical being, and includes what many feel is the basis of mind – the brain. Are mind and body separate, and does their separateness account for cases like those above? Or are mind and body simply different aspects of an underlying unity? If they are a unity, then what accounts for the sometimes bizarre discrepancies between the two? William James, in his *Principles of Psychology*, stated that, 'The explanation of consciousness [i.e. mind] is the ultimate question for psychology'. Although James made the statement one hundred years ago, and much has been learned since, the answer to the question is still beyond our grasp. However, if we *do* find the answer, many believe it will come from research based on the biological approach.

Introduction

The biological approach to psychology, as its name implies, views man as a biological organism. What we do, and even what we think, is seen as having its basis in our physiological structure. The approach has developed out of interest in two major concerns: the relationship between mind and body, and the influence of heredity on behaviour. Each is a reflection of our biological nature, and the study of them often leads to overlaps, but the two aspects have separate histories.

As one might guess, biological researchers tend to view behaviour as being purely physical. As a doctor commented while discussing possible physical causes of schizophrenia, 'Of *course* it has to be physical. There isn't anything else up there'. By 'up there', he was referring to the brain. His assumption was that the brain determines behaviour. Although you may not find that very surprising, in earlier times it would have been seen as very radical. Even in the seventeenth century, most people believed the body was controlled by an intangible soul. Among those who believed in the soul was René Descartes. A keen observer, but also deeply religious, Descartes tried to reconcile the apparent physical nature of the body with the intangible nature of the soul. The human body, he felt, was constructed like that of an animal – both were basically *machines*. However, he also believed that people (unlike animals) had a soul, which interacted with the physical body through a small gland in the brain called the pineal gland. Since in French the same word (*l'âme*) can be used for both 'mind' and 'soul', Descartes's idea became interpreted as referring to the relation between the mind and body; his view that mind and body are distinct, but can interact, became known as **dualism**.

dualism the view, first attributed to Descartes, that mind and body are distinct; Descartes believed the two could interact via the pineal gland in the brain

The primary alternative to dualism is called *monism*, the belief that mind and body are a single entity. In most respects this is equivalent to **materialism**, which assumes all behaviour has a physiological basis. At one level, Descartes was actually a materialist, seeing the body's functioning in machine-like terms. However, his interactionist view (physical body interacting with intangible soul) was also a compromise. By viewing the body as a machine, dualism was a step forward, but it also created a split which has been the subject of much subsequent controversy. In any event, it was left to others to take the final step to materialism in its modern form.

materialism the assumption that all behaviour has a physiological basis

As often happens, the crucial insight came about almost by accident. In 1745 (about one hundred years after Descartes), a French priest-turned-physician named Julien de La Mettrie contracted a fever, and noticed that this physical condition affected his mental state as well as his physical state. Reflecting on this after his recovery, he wrote a book called *L'histoire naturelle de l'âme* (*The Natural History of the Soul*). In the book, he argued that the body is but a machine, *and* that the soul is no different than the mind. Further, he said the mind was part of the body. This assertion, which clearly went beyond Descartes's position, caused a tremendous outcry, but he held fast to his views. Ultimately, the opposition from religious and political authorities forced him to leave France for his personal safety.

By the time of the French Revolution (less than fifty years after La Mettrie), a physician named Cabanis was able to argue that guillotine victims were not conscious after beheading, because consciousness was the function of the brain, just as digestion was the function of the stomach. Still, no-one had shown a specific connection between physiological structures and behaviour. Then, in 1861, a doctor at the insane asylum at Bicêtre, Paul Broca, encountered a case in which a man lost the ability to speak coherently after a head injury. Later, Broca was able to demonstrate, by post-mortem autopsy, that the cause of the man's deficit lay in damage to a specific point in the brain. The proof of this **localization of function** (connecting a specific behaviour to a specific brain area) was the final step in the progression of ideas. The acceptance of this finding completed the gradual change in attitude, from seeing behaviour as

localization of function the assumption that specific functions are associated with specific areas of the brain governed by an intangible soul, to the modern view of behaviour as having a physiological basis. Of course, many others also contributed to the development of knowledge and ideas. The brief history given here is simply meant to indicate how the basic assumptions about mind and body arose.

The other main aspect of the biological approach, the role of heredity in behaviour, also had a gradual development (**heredity** refers to the biological transmission of characteristics from one generation to another). In the eighteenth century, people believed that each species of plant and animal had been independently created: as the Bible says, 'every living creature after his kind'. Still, there were indications that this might not be literally true. The great biologist Linnaeus had published a catalogue of over 4000 plant and animal species in 1735, and his orderly categories suggested connections among species. Then, in 1809, a French naturalist named Lamarck presented the first widely known theory of species development, or evolution. Lamarck believed that variations developed through inheritance of acquired characteristics. For instance, giraffes acquired long necks because each generation strained a little further to get food, slightly stretching their necks, and passed this difference on to their offspring. Today, Lamarckian theory is generally discredited, but it was a significant step forward in suggesting that characteristics have a hereditary basis.

heredity the biological transmission of characteristics from one generation to another

The real revolution in thought came with the work of Charles Darwin. Darwin's theory, published in *The Origin of Species* (1859), was that variations among individuals of a species would occur by chance, but could in turn be passed on. His doctrine of 'survival of the fittest' meant that only those variations which helped the individuals survive long enough to breed would be passed on. Darwin was not only advocating the inheritance of characteristics, but also an evolutionary link between humans and all other species. In 1872, he made this even clearer by writing *The Expression of the Emotions in Man and Animals*. (Actually, Darwin proposed the concept of inheritance, but specified no biological mechanism for its operation; it remained for the re-discovery of the work of an Austrian monk, Gregor Mendel, for a specific mechanism for heredity to be suggested.)

Like La Mettrie, Darwin came into conflict with religious doctrine, this time with the view that man was created 'in God's image'. In part, the controversy concerned how literally one should interpret the biblical concept. The controversy raged for many years, and is still not completely ended, but in time the evolutionary viewpoint expressed by Darwin became dominant. Despite not specifying precisely how heredity operated, Darwin's theory laid the basis for the study of hereditary influences on behaviour.

Today, these two concepts – materialism and heredity – are the foundation of the biological approach to psychology. The assumptions involved (that mind has a physiological basis, and that behaviour can be inherited) influence both the questions asked and the type of data collected. Compared with other approaches, the biological approach emphasizes 'getting inside the black box' – that is, looking at the internal structure of the organism. Broca showed that a specific defect in the brain could destroy speech in an otherwise normal person. Darwin showed that what we are is at least partly due to what our parents are. In this chapter, we will look at how these ideas have been applied to enhance our understanding of behaviour.

The Nature of the Physiological System

As previously noted, the biological approach emphasizes the physiological basis of behaviour. While the approach can be applied to any aspect of behaviour, the most challenging questions seem to be those relating to the interactions between mind and body. In everyday life, we encounter situations in which the body affects the mind (as when coffee makes you tense), and also situations in which the mind affects the body (as when executives get ulcers). What is the mechanism of such interactions? In this section, we will try to deal with this question in terms of what is currently known about the physiological basis of behaviour, and also consider some of the problems psychologists face in trying to develop answers.

Mind, Brain and the Central Nervous System

In trying to understand the interaction of mind and body, the first difficulty encountered is dealing with the terms involved. For instance, where is 'the mind'? Where is the 'self' that we experience? Terms, like these, while seemingly clear in everyday usage, are not so clear when one tries to relate them to physiological structures.

Most people would equate 'mind' with 'brain', and this is partially correct. But in more precise terms, the word 'mind' refers to a psychological concept, not a physiological one. The *mind* is usually regarded as the seat of consciousness or awareness, not as a physiological structure. Current knowledge indicates that the brain is, indeed, involved in our experience of consciousness, but no-one is currently certain just how, or whether consciousness involves only the brain. So in discussing interactions of the physical (brain) and mental (mind), one is restricted to saying that somehow the two are connected, or even fundamentally the same, but the specifics are not clear. (As noted earlier, in part, this is an *assumption* that researchers make. However, the alternative – that the mind is non-physical, perhaps a soul – would not only take us back before Descartes, but would also make scientific study irrelevant.) While no final answers can be given here, we will examine what is known about the structure of the physiological system and its influence on behaviour.

Neurons and the Nervous System

neuron a cell of the nervous system (also called a nerve cell)
synapse the junction between two neurons, represented by a small physical gap which is bridged by the flow of neurotransmitter chemicals from the terminals of the 'sending' neuron

The human body is a remarkably complex system, comprised of trillions of individual living cells of many specialized types. Certain cells in the stomach lining, for example, do nothing but produce digestive secretions. Other cells fight disease, transport oxygen or store energy. Coordinating the activity of the many body systems requires communication, and this is one of the key functions of the nervous system. The specialized cells of the nervous system, called nerve cells or **neurons**, are like wires in that they carry an electrochemical message from one point to another. Each time a neuron connects to another neuron, at a junction called a **synapse**, it is possible for a message to be switched to other areas. The brain, together with the nerve pathways of the spinal cord, forms the

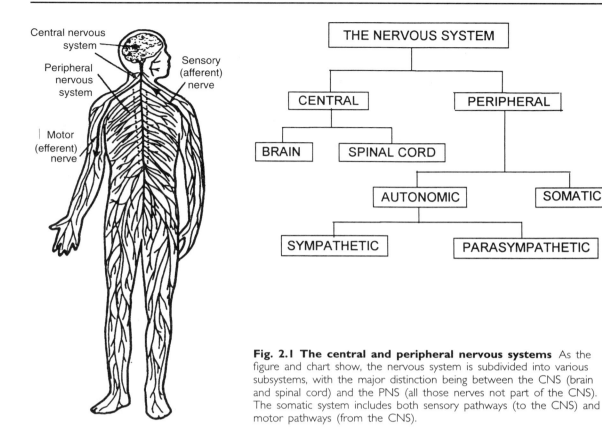

Central nervous system

Peripheral nervous system

Sensory (afferent) nerve

Motor (efferent) nerve

THE NERVOUS SYSTEM

CENTRAL

PERIPHERAL

BRAIN

SPINAL CORD

AUTONOMIC

SOMATIC

SYMPATHETIC

PARASYMPATHETIC

Fig. 2.1 The central and peripheral nervous systems As the figure and chart show, the nervous system is subdivided into various subsystems, with the major distinction being between the CNS (brain and spinal cord) and the PNS (all those nerves not part of the CNS). The somatic system includes both sensory pathways (to the CNS) and motor pathways (from the CNS).

central nervous system (CNS) the brain, together with the nerve pathways of the spinal cord

peripheral nervous system (PNS) those nerve pathways which lie outside the central nervous system, involving sensation, motor control and regulation of internal organs

sensory nerves neural pathways in the PNS which carry information from the sense receptors to the CNS

motor nerves those neurons which are responsible for initiating muscle activity

nerve impulse the electrical signal generated when a neuron is active, which normally passes from the dendrites, along the axon, to the terminals

central nervous system (or CNS). Those nerve pathways outside the central nervous system form the **peripheral nervous system** (or PNS). **Sensory nerves** in the PNS carry messages from the outside world to the CNS via the sense receptors, such as those located in the eyes and ears, while **motor nerves** are responsible for initiating muscle activity, under the direction of the CNS. Although the brain is responsible for integrating incoming information and directing muscle activity, the spinal cord is a vital relay station. For instance, the first connection (or synapse) between your big toe and the brain is where the pathway enters your spinal cord. For protection, the spinal cord passes within the bones (vertebrae) of the spinal column, like wires in a flexible casing. Despite this protection, a back injury can result in disruption of the spinal cord, which can cause loss of all feeling (sensory input) and movement (motor control) below the point of injury (see Fig. 2.1).

The basic unit of the nervous system is the neuron. In a sense, a neuron is like a wire through which an electrical signal passes. This signal, called a **nerve impulse**, stays essentially the same as it passes along the 'wire' or **axon**, and is also the same in every neuron (see Fig. 2.2). While all neurons show the same basic structure and serve the same basic purpose, they show many differences in their details. One of the most striking variations is in size – the central wire or axon may range from less than 1 mm (for neurons in the brain) to about 1 m

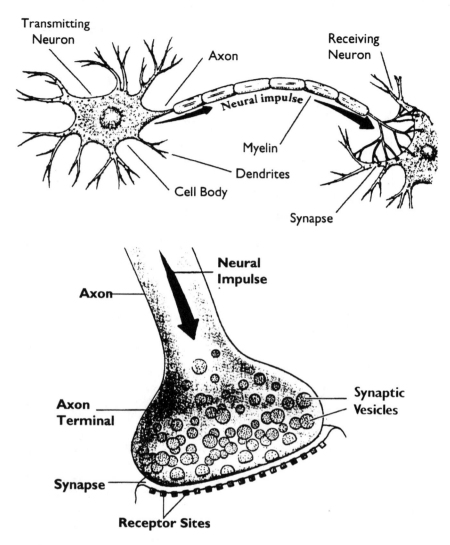

Fig. 2.2 Neurons and neural transmission The structure of a neuron is illustrated in the upper figure, with the various parts. A neural impulse ('signal') travels from the dendrites, along the axon, to the terminals, where it must cross a physical gap, the synapse. Transmission across the synapse is by means of neurotransmitters, chemicals released by the synaptic vesicles, which then flow across the gap, to lock into receptor sites on the receiving neuron (see lower figure).

axon the relatively elongated portion of a neuron between the cell body and the terminals which provides the signal pathway for a nerve impulse

(for peripheral neurons between the spinal cord and the toes)! Neurons also differ in terms of whether they are insulated or not; as with ordinary electrical wires, insulation improves efficiency by reducing signal losses. In neurons, the insulation consists of a fatty substance called **myelin** (the myelin is actually composed of another specialized type of cell called a Schwann cell, which wraps itself around the axon to provide an insulating sheath). Not all neurons in either the CNS or PNS are insulated ('myelinated'), although most of those in the brain of a healthy adult are. The process of forming myelin begins in the foetus, and the process is largely completed by about age three, though formation (and repair) continues throughout life. Across species, the degree of completion at birth is roughly paralleled by the degree of behavioural capacities; a newborn calf, for example, is both better myelinated and more capable at birth than a human infant. At the same time, destruction of the myelin sheath (in disorders like multiple sclerosis) can have disastrous effects of the nervous system and behaviour. Whether the neuron is insulated or not, the nerve impulse travels only within the axon of a single neuron. At the junction between neurons is a small physical gap, called a synapse. Communication across the synapse depends on chemicals called **neurotransmitters**. As we will see in the next section, neurons can also differ in terms of what neurotransmitter chemicals they use.

While the pathways of the peripheral nervous system are crucial in providing our links to the outer world for both sensation and movement, the central nervous system, with responsibility for integrating and controlling the whole system, is much more complex. As noted above, damage to the spinal cord can result in loss of feeling and paralysis; the brain itself is also vulnerable. (In the peripheral nervous system, severed nerves will often repair themselves; cases of a severed arm or leg being successfully reattached after an accident attest to this. Unfortunately, nerves in the central nervous system do not regenerate – hence damage to the spinal cord can result in permanent paraplegia.)

The Brain

Considered visually, the **brain** is not very impressive – a greyish lump weighing approximately three pounds, with an irregular surface of ridges and valleys. However, that superficial impression belies both its complexity and its capabilities. The brain consists of about one hundred billion neurons (no-one knows the exact number, since estimates are based on examining a small region, and extrapolating the number found to the whole structure). In turn, each neuron makes connections to possibly hundreds of other neurons, resulting in a network of some one million billion connections in the cortex (the outer layer of the brain) alone (Edelman 1992).

Like the nervous system as a whole, the brain can be subdivided into many areas. Early anatomists looked for physical divisions (like the fissures on the cortex, or the almond shape of the amygdala in the limbic system), and then tried to deduce the functions. As we will see, much has been achieved based on this assumption that specific functions are associated with specific areas, called *localization of function*. At the same time, the brain is a highly interconnected system, and it is worth keeping that in mind as we discuss what is known about the functions of different parts of the brain.

If you were to remove the top portion of a person's skull, you would see the pink, somewhat wrinkled outer layer of the brain, called the **cortex** (Greek for 'bark', as on a tree) (see Fig. 2.3). Its wrinkled ('convoluted') appearance results from the cortex being folded on itself. Since maximum surface area seems important (simpler organisms have both smaller and less convoluted brains), this crumpling effect allows a large sheet to be compressed into the relatively small confines of the skull. (Imagine crumpling a large sheet of paper into a small wad.)

myelin in a neuron, an insulating sheath around the axon, composed of the spirally wound membrane of Schwann cells, which serves to improve the efficiency of neural conduction

neurotransmitter a chemical released by the terminals of a neuron which plays a role in communication between neurons, across the synapse

brain the portion of the central nervous system which lies within the skull

cortex the pink, somewhat wrinkled outer layer of the brain which controls many of our higher functions like speech and perception; from the Greek for 'bark' (as on a tree)

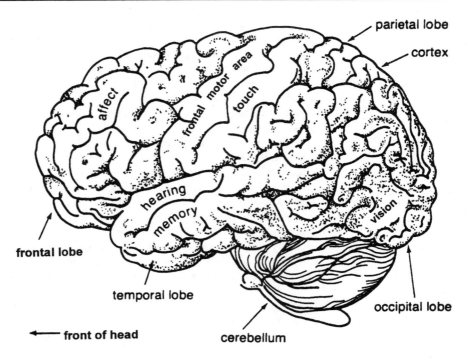

parietal lobe

cortex

frontal motor area

touch

affect

hearing

memory

vision

frontal lobe

temporal lobe

occipital lobe

◄─── **front of head**

cerebellum

Fig. 2.3 Exterior view of the cortex showing the left hemisphere and areas of primary functions.

frontal lobe the area of the cortex in front of the central fissure, and above the lateral fissure; it is involved in the interpretation of emotion and experience
frontal lobotomy an operation, popular in the 1940s and 1950s, which involved cutting off or removing portions of the frontal lobes, in an attempt to treat cases of manic depression or chronic pain; later shown to be largely ineffective as a therapeutic procedure
association areas areas of the cortex which have no primary function (such as receiving direct sensory data), but rather play a role in integrating activity from other brain areas
frontal motor area the area of the frontal lobes just before the central fissure which controls all voluntary movements of the muscles

The cortex is made up of two distinct hemispheres, left and right, each of which basically controls the opposite side of the body (e.g. muscle movements in your right hand are initiated by your left hemisphere). In turn, the hemispheres can be broken down into smaller regions called *lobes*, which are identified by the valleys or 'fissures' on the surface. Surprisingly, there is considerable variation across individuals in the precise shape and location of the convolutions; despite this, the ridges and valleys make reliable landmarks for distinguishing major regions of the cortex. The two major landmarks are the central fissure, which divides each hemisphere roughly in half front-to-back, and the lateral fissure, which runs along the side of each hemisphere. The **frontal lobe** is the area in front of the central fissure, and above the lateral fissure; it is associated with subtle colourings of emotional response and experience. For this reason, an operation called a **frontal lobotomy**, which involved cutting off or removing portions of the frontal lobes, was once used in an attempt to treat cases of manic depression or chronic pain. The procedure, popular in the 1940s and 1950s, ultimately was shown to be a poor treatment, and such frontal lobotomies have been largely abandoned (Goldstein 1950; Blakemore 1977). Much of the frontal lobes seem to have no primary function (such as receiving direct sensory data), but rather play a role in integrating activity from other brain areas; as a result, they are labelled **association areas**. By contrast, the area of the frontal lobes just before the central fissure is called the **frontal motor area**, because it controls all voluntary movements of the muscles. Interestingly, the body areas

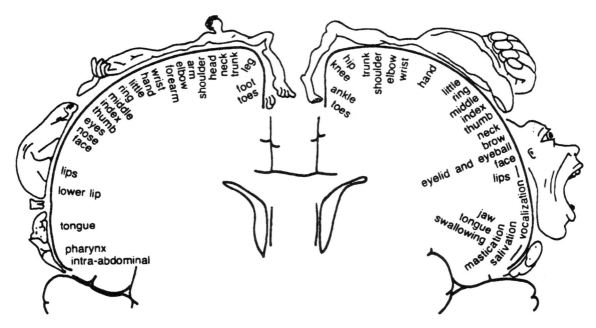

Fig. 2.4 Tactile and motor representation in the cortex Penfield's research using electrical stimulation of the cortex has helped clarify the localization of touch and motor control along the central fissure. (In the figure, the brain has been cut vertically along the fissure which divides the frontal motor area from the sensory region of the parietal lobe; cf. Fig. 2.3.) Note the relative size of the parts shows the relative degree of cortical representation (after Penfield and Rasmussen 1957).

parietal lobe the portion of the cortex just behind the central fissure and above the lateral fissure, whose primary function is the sense of touch

capable of very subtle motor control (e.g. hands, lips) show a greater representation in the frontal motor area than other body regions. In fact, researchers have created maps of the frontal motor area, detailing the body areas controlled. A similar mapping for the sense of touch exists for the portion of the **parietal lobe** just behind the central fissure (see Fig. 2.4).

We also have some understanding of other portions of the cortex. Hearing is located in the region below the lateral fissure, in the **temporal lobe**. Our memory for past experience also seems to be represented in the temporal lobe. The **occipital lobe**, at the rear of the cortex, is devoted solely to vision. Given the large area devoted to it, one might speculate that vision is either very complex, or very important, or both; the evidence suggests it is indeed both. The experience of seeing, like the other senses, is dependent on brain activity as well as sensory activity. In the extreme case, a person with damage to the occipital lobe would be functionally blind, despite having perfectly functioning eyes. Recognition of this connection between brain function and sensory experience is another reason why researchers feel comfortable identifying the mind with the brain.

temporal lobe the region of the cortex below the lateral fissure; its primary functions are hearing and memory
occipital lobe the rearmost portion of the cortex, which is devoted solely to vision

visual agnosia a general term for disorders which result in disruption of visual recognition

In the introduction to this chapter, we discussed the peculiar case of Dr P., who could see but often failed to recognize what he saw – particularly faces. His problem is an example of **visual agnosia**, which refers to problems with visual recognition. Clearly, the primary visual areas of the brain were intact, since he

Fig. 2.5 Internal view of the brain showing the relatively 'old' parts of the brain which are normally hidden by the cortex.

limbic system a series of subcortical structures which connect the cortex with other parts of the brain and which are important in many basic functions; among the main parts of the limbic system are the thalamus, hypothalamus, amygdala and hippocampus

hypothalamus one of the most important elements in the limbic system, the hypothalamus both regulates behaviours associated with hunger, thirst, sex and other basic drives, and also plays a role in regulating hormonal functions

hippocampus a structure within the limbic system which is important to memory function

cerebellum ('little brain' in Latin) two small hemispheres located beneath the cortical hemispheres, at the back of the head; the cerebellum plays an important role in directing movements and balance

brainstem the region at the top of the spinal cord, composed of three primary structures: the medulla, the pons and the midbrain

medulla a small swelling at the top of the spinal cord composed of the cell bodies

could recognize simple forms like a pin, and had no difficulty avoiding obstacles in his path. Instead, his problem involved *integrating* the sensory information into a coherent whole, and relating it to other information, such as his memories of people. Disorders like this can be very perplexing, and indeed, in describing this case, Sacks (1985) does not specify the precise physiological basis. However, it is very likely that it involves the role of the association areas for vision, which link visual sense data to functions in other parts of the brain. In particular, the pattern of problems (trouble in integrating complex patterns, along with abnormal motor reflexes on the left side of the body) suggests damage to the association areas of the right occipital lobe. Despite the apparent localization of many cortical functions, we must always remember that the brain functions as a whole.

As noted, the cortex is like a crumpled sheet of paper; at the same time, it surrounds the other sections of the brain, much as the bark of a tree covers the interior. Below the cortex are subcortical networks which connect the cortex with other parts of the brain, notably the limbic system and the brainstem (see Fig. 2.5). These regions are sometimes referred to as the 'primitive brain'. As the name implies, these structures control fundamental aspects of behaviour that we share with many lower organisms. The main parts of the **limbic system** are identified in Fig. 2.5; among these, the most important is the **hypothalamus**, which both regulates behaviours associated with hunger, thirst, sex, and other basic drives, and also plays a role in regulating hormonal functions. The **hippocampus** is important to memory function; in a well-known case, a man who suffered damage to the hippocampus lost the ability to recall subsequent experiences (Milner 1965). Other regions of the limbic system have been associated with the primitive emotions of fear and rage, and possible maternal behaviour.

Nestled beneath the large cortical hemispheres, at the back of the head, are two smaller hemispheres. These two hemispheres form the **cerebellum** (literally 'little brain' in Latin). The cerebellum plays an important role in directing movements and balance, particularly fine motor control activities like sewing or of neurons whose axons extend to the heart and other internal organs; its role is to regulate basic bodily processes

pons (Latin for 'bridge') a region in the brainstem below the medulla which provides connections between the cortex and cerebellum

reticular formation a diffuse network of nerve fibres which runs through the brainstem and limbic system, with connections both up to the cortex and down to the spinal cord; the reticular formation acts as a relay network controlling sensory inputs, and thereby plays a key role in regulating arousal level, alertness and sleep

For further consideration

playing the piano, and also complex movements like gymnastics. It does this by receiving information from both the sensory nervous system and the cortex, with much of this information passing through an adjacent centre, the brainstem.

The **brainstem** is the region at the top of the spinal cord, and is composed of three primary structures: the medulla, the pons and the midbrain. The **medulla**, a small swelling at the top of the spinal cord, has neurons whose axons extend to the heart and other internal organs; its role is thus to regulate basic bodily processes. Above it, the **pons** (Latin for 'bridge') provides connections between the cortex and cerebellum. A significant structure of the brainstem is the **reticular formation** (reticular means 'finely interwoven'), a diffuse network of nerve fibres which runs through the brainstem and limbic system, with connections both up to the cortex and down to the spinal cord. The reticular formation acts as a relay network, controlling sensory inputs; as such, it plays a key role in regulating our arousal level, controlling alertness and sleep.

Thus, the brain and nervous system are made up of a number of specific structures, which must function as an integrated system to regulate our behaviour. The description given here should not be taken as complete, but simply as an introduction to this incredible system. At the same time, this discussion has said little about *how* we know these things – for example, how do we know that motor functions are located in the frontal lobe?

Based on what we have discussed about the workings of the brain, consider the following science fiction scenario. A mad scientist kidnaps you, and renders you unconscious. Then he takes your brain, and places it in a bowl which provides nutrients, and is connected to a computer to provide 'sensations'. When you awake, would you be able to tell your brain was no longer in your body? If yes, why? If no, why not?

Studying the Brain

As with other approaches to psychology, our understanding of the brain has long been dependent on observation. At one time, researchers had to rely on clinical cases to study the workings of the brain. The use of clinical observation (*case studies*) has its drawbacks, particularly in terms of lack of control. For example, a person may receive a severe blow to the back of the head, and subsequently complain of numbness in one arm. Unfortunately, one cannot easily interpret the connection between the blow and the symptom, because the impact would have been transmitted throughout the skull. Thus, in this case, it does *not* mean that the occipital lobe (closest to the site of the blow) is involved in the sense of touch (the symptom). Occasionally, though, the clinical method can lead to important breakthroughs: Broca's discovery of the speech centre is one example. In this case, it was possible to study the patient in detail, since the problem existed for many years. In addition, after the patient's eventual death, an autopsy clearly showed a lesion (tissue injury) in the left frontal lobe, providing the basis for Broca's conclusion.

Today, researchers have available a variety of techniques for identifying the function of various brain structures. One method which has been very effective is *electrical stimulation* of nerve cells. In this technique, small clusters of cells are activated by inserting a fine wire into the desired area, and then applying a

Wilder Penfield

Wilder Penfield (1891–1976) was born in Spokane, Washington. He was educated at Princeton University, and subsequently attended Oxford University as a Rhodes Scholar. It was at Oxford that the direction of his career took shape, as he met the distinguished neurologist Sir Charles Sherrington. After returning to the United States to obtain a medical degree at Johns Hopkins University, he returned to Oxford to study with Sherrington for two more years. Eventually, he established a practice in neurosurgery, first in the United States, and then in Montreal, Canada. At Montreal, he became a professor at McGill University, and founded the Montreal Neurological Institute. This institute became one of the world's leading centres for neurology, and it was here that Penfield did his pioneering work on the mapping of cortical functions. In the course of doing surgery for epilepsy and other disorders, Penfield would identify the functions of various cortical regions by using electrical stimulation as the patient lay conscious on the operating table. This work has been widely hailed, and among other honours, Penfield became a member of the Royal Society. He died in Montreal at the age of eighty-five.

small electric current. Often this research must proceed by analogy, looking at effects in animals and then extrapolating the results to humans, but in some cases researchers have observed people directly. One example is the pioneering work of Wilder Penfield, a Montreal neurosurgeon. In treating epileptics suffering from severe seizures, Penfield would sometimes operate, in order to destroy cells in the area where the seizure originated. (In such cases, epileptic seizures are triggered by random bursts of activity in a focal region, which then spreads to other parts of the cortex.) In order to avoid damage to essential functions, Penfield would first stimulate various areas of the cortex, and observe the effects reported by the patient (who was conscious throughout the operation). From this, he would produce a 'map' of the cortex and its functions, making the surgery itself more accurate. In cases like this, both the search for knowledge and the alleviation of suffering can be served. (Electrical stimulation will be discussed in more detail later in the chapter.)

More recently, a variety of techniques have been developed to study brain activity without having to examine the brain directly. These **computerized imaging** techniques, which use computers to assist in the analysis of information, are enabling researchers to gain new insights about brain function. While the details of each technique differ, they are similar in that the computer is used to convert a series of two-dimensional images into a three-dimensional model of the brain which can be viewed on a television monitor. The earliest method, the *computerized axial tomography* (CAT) scan, uses a series of X-ray images to create a three-dimensional picture of the brain. The limitation of the CAT scan, however, is that, like any X-ray, it shows physical structures, but reveals nothing about the *activity* within the brain. Newer methods, notably *positron emission tomography* (PET) and *magnetic resonance*, have overcome that hurdle. In a PET scan, a short-lived radioactive substance is injected into the bloodstream

computerized imaging
techniques for studying brain function which use computers to convert information into a three-dimensional model of the brain which can be viewed on a television monitor

along with glucose; when it reaches the brain, the active areas absorb more of the glucose, and with it, the radioactive tracer. Sensitive detectors then pinpoint the location of the tracer, and thereby tell researchers which parts of the brain are most active. Magnetic resonance scans (variously identified as either 'nuclear magnetic resonance scans' or 'magnetic resonance imaging') do not require injection of a radioactive tracer; instead, they utilize the response of electric charges within cells to large magnetic fields (called resonance) to identify areas of activity. The new generation of scanning techniques enables researchers to examine aspects of brain function never before possible, without the need for invasive procedures like surgery. As such, scanning methods provide a new tool to assist in the treatment of a range of disorders. For example, PET scans have identified markedly reduced activity in the cortex of depressed patients compared with normal individuals, and reduced frontal lobe activity in individuals with schizophrenia. The drawbacks of these systems are two-fold: first, they are very expensive, and their use is unlikely to become routine for some time to come; second, at present, they are limited in their ability to pinpoint activity precisely – far less than electrical stimulation, for example. However, since PET scans and magnetic resonance are barely 10 years old, further improvements are likely to be seen in the years ahead.

In different ways, each of the above methods has contributed to our understanding of the brain. In many cases, the evidence seems to support the concept of localization of function. However, one must keep in mind that the brain is highly interconnected, and its activity is highly integrated (more of the brain is devoted to integration, via association areas, than to primary functions). Despite the existence of specialized functions, no one part can really be considered without the others. (An analogy might be an automobile: examining one part, such as the transmission, will not reveal the way the system as a whole functions.) As the example of Dr P. shows, it is through the working of the whole that psychological processes are best seen.

Chemistry and Behaviour

As discussed in the preceding section, the CNS plays an essential role in co-ordinating behaviour. Neurons transmit sensory messages and allow motor responses to occur nearly instantaneously; the process of touching a hot stove and quickly removing one's hand is a good example. (This represents an example of a so-called spinal reflex arc, the simplest form of neural circuit; it involves only a sensory neuron and a motor neuron, which connect via a synapse in the spinal cord.) Despite the impression we may have from such experiences, nerve conduction is not truly instantaneous: the fastest speed for nerve impulses is about 150 metres per second in large myelinated sensory nerves, slowing to a mere tenth of a metre per second (point-to-point) in the brainstem. Our **reaction time** to respond to a stimulus is a reflection of the limits of this communication system. For example, in driving a car, it takes about three-quarters of a second to begin lifting your foot off the gas, from the moment of seeing something you should stop for. At eighty kilometres an hour, you cover almost seventeen metres in that time – and that doesn't count the time for the brakes to physically stop the car!

reaction time the time required to make a response to a stimulus, as measured by the interval between the stimulus and the response

Neurotransmitters

Despite being less than instantaneous, the nervous system is very effective in fulfilling its role as the body's communication network. Messages continually criss-cross, enabling us to perceive and respond to both our internal and external environments. In this system, the primary signals are the nerve impulses, racing along the axons. While the axon of a neuron may be compared to a wire which relays an electrical signal, a nerve impulse only travels within the neuron which generated it. At the junction between two neurons is a physical gap, the *synapse*. In order to bridge this gap, communication between neurons depends on an exchange of chemicals. These chemicals, called *neurotransmitters*, are released by the terminals of one neuron, and flow across the synaptic gap to the receptors of the next neuron. The first such substance identified was *acetylcholine*, which activates muscle fibres, among other functions. *Adrenaline* is another neurotransmitter. Since acetylcholine was first identified in the 1930s, approximately one hundred chemicals have been found which are involved in neural transmission, most of them in the past fifteen years! Neurotransmitter substances can function in various ways. Some neurotransmitters trigger activation of the neuron, called *excitation*; this is a bit like stepping on the gas while driving a car. Others act to prevent the neuron from firing, called *inhibition*; by reducing neural activity, this is somewhat like stepping on the brakes while driving. Still other substances act to block the excitatory or inhibitory chemicals, or to clear them away after they have done their job. As we will see below, this system provides the basis for a wide range of effects.

While well-adapted to providing quick responses, neuronal control has its limitations. Neurons only communicate while they are active, and while changes in activity can take place over fractions of a second, a neuron cannot remain active indefinitely. Faced with constant stimulation, neurons begin to reduce their response, a phenomenon called **habituation**. This means that the nervous system is not well-suited to the regulation of slower-changing processes like metabolism, growth and reproduction. How, then, are such processes regulated?

habituation a reduction in neural response due to continual stimulation

Hormones

The answer lies not with nerve conduction and neurotransmitters, but with another class of chemicals produced by glandular cells. These cells 'communicate' by means of chemical secretions. The most significant glands, from this standpoint, are the **endocrine glands**. These are a number of glands which secrete chemicals called **hormones** directly into the bloodstream, where they are carried to all parts of the body (see Fig. 2.6). Given the time it takes for circulation through the body, the effects of these chemical messengers is not as swift as neural transmission – often it can be minutes, hours, weeks, or longer before the response occurs. Not surprisingly, though, the effects are typically much longer-lasting than those processes which are under direct neural control. In this sense, neural and hormonal processes are not competitive, but complementary.

At one time, the distinctions between neural and hormonal processes seemed both clear-cut and neat: the nervous system handled short-term functions with fast responses, and the endocrine system handled slower, long-term functions. Instead, research in recent years has shown that the boundaries are not quite so

endocrine glands ('ductless glands') glands which secrete chemicals called hormones directly into the bloodstream
hormone a chemical secreted by an endocrine gland; hormones are involved in many aspects of metabolism and long-term functioning of the body

Endocrine Glands
and their functions

Pineal—melatonin (circadian rhythm)

Pituitary—growth hormone
ACTH—stress
hormones for labour
and milk production

Thyroid—metabolism

Parathyroids—calcium levels

Pancreas—insulin

Adrenals—stress response
metabolism

Gonads—sex hormones

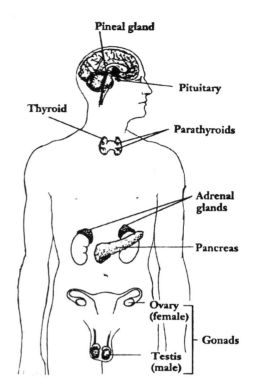

Fig. 2.6 The endocrine system and hormonal functions The major hormone-secreting glands are illustrated, along with the functions of some of the major hormones produced.

distinct. One reason for this new view is the realization that the two systems interact directly. The *pituitary gland*, for example, which is sometimes called 'the master gland' because of its role in regulating other endocrine glands, also has direct linkages to the hypothalamus, whereby it can influence the nervous system. The hypothalamus, in turn, releases small amounts of hormones, which affect the endocrine system. While such interactions actually make sense – links between the systems presumably let the body function more effectively overall – it makes separating their roles much harder. A couple of examples will indicate the concept. *Norepinephrine*, also called noradrenaline, is one example of such dual-purpose chemicals: it is one of the primary secretions of the adrenal glands, and also a neurotransmitter found in many parts of the nervous system (the neurons which use it as a neurotransmitter are called 'noradrenergic pathways'). *Vasopressin*, first identified as a hormone which influences blood pressure, is also used as a neurotransmitter by the hypothalamus, and has been shown to enhance memory and learning.

In addition, it has been discovered that some chemicals influence neural transmission, while retaining roles as hormones. Variously called **neuropeptides** or neurohormones, they have further influenced our ideas about how the body functions, even as we try to puzzle out their role (Cooper *et al.* 1991). As time

neuropeptide a chemical, comprised of a short chain of amino acids, which can function both as a neurotransmitter and as a hormone; also called a neurohormone passes, our understanding of the underlying chemical processes will doubtless increase. At present, the new-found complexity is exciting, even as it cautions us to never assume we have the final picture.

Interactions of Mind and Body in Behaviour

Both neural and chemical processes are important to our understanding of the relationship between the brain and behaviour. In this chapter, we cannot cover all that is known about these processes. Rather, the intent is to give a basic description of how these physiological processes fit into the biological approach as a means of understanding behaviour. At the beginning of this chapter, we noted that the biological approach assumes that the mind is ultimately a product of the brain, with a physical basis. This assumption is often referred to as *materialism*. At the same time, no-one can presently explain precisely *how* mind and brain are connected, despite the progress made in understanding more basic functions. A person may be a type of 'machine' in the materialist sense, but it is an exceedingly complex machine, as a study of the interactions between mind and body shows.

As already noted, it is impossible to identify the 'mind' with one particular brain structure, or portion of the body. In some sense, the entire body is the receptacle of the mind. Consciousness may depend on a normally functioning cortex, but other aspects of behaviour depend on other elements of the system. If we cannot identify the mind as a portion of the body, how is it possible to study interactions of the two? Precisely because they are separate conceptually and require different types of description, one can seek parallels. It is almost like trying to translate between two languages – words may not always be easy to match up, but in the end the ideas can be communicated. In this case, we are trying to translate between physiologically based 'body' and psychologically based 'mind'.

The Effects of Body on Mind

When we speak of effects of the body on the mind, we are referring to the effects of physically identifiable events (e.g. changes within the body) on psychological functioning and behaviour. Nearly all of the identifiable events can be described in terms of neural and/or chemical processes. Obviously, this can include a wide range of effects, both transitory (e.g. a cup of coffee as a drug) and enduring (e.g. spinal injury or alcohol-induced memory deficits). In this section, we will focus on some problems which have significance because of what they tell us about the bases of behaviour. These include drugs, the electrical nature of brain activity and specialization in the brain.

The Study of Drug Effects

Technically, a drug is any substance which has an effect on living cells. Since this could include virtually any substance, including water, we will take a more restricted meaning of the term 'drug'. *Drugs* are chemical substances which are foreign to the body, either totally or in the form introduced (for example, adrenaline is a hormone, but it may also be *injected* as a drug). It is worth noting that not all drugs have discernible effects on *behaviour*. For example, penicillin reduces infections, but does not affect how we act directly. Nor need drugs always be medically prescribed: a morning cup of coffee is an example of drug use (or abuse), as is the illegal use of cocaine. The study of psychoactive (mind-affecting) drugs is a concern in both psychology and medicine, and has given rise to a hybrid field called *psychopharmacology*.

The use of **psychoactive drugs** is probably as old as recorded history. Nearly every culture has used some type of fermented grain or vegetable to produce an alcoholic drink. For example, some South American tribes have long traditions of eating plants in order to produce hallucinations for religious rites. But it is only relatively recently that doctors have considered the use of drugs as a therapeutic tool, or that researchers have had effective methods to study drug effects.

Psychopharmacology today has become a complex field, but in the early days of drug research, research techniques were very pragmatic. Many psychoactive substances were first identified by studying plants which had already been used for folk remedies. For example, reserpine, one of the first tranquillizers, was originally isolated from Indian snakeroot; aspirin was isolated from willow bark. In other cases, researchers even experimented on themselves. Heinrich Kluver, a man noted for his contributions in other areas of physiological research, wrote a paper on his experience with mescaline, a hallucinogenic drug derived from a type of mushroom (Kluver 1966). Today, research techniques have become more formal and sophisticated.

The methods typically used today for research on psychoactive drugs are much like those for other types of drugs. Experimental animals are used to assess toxicity, strength and basis of effects. These assessments may involve intricate techniques and precision chemical analyses, such as injecting tiny amounts of the drug directly into specific regions of the brain, and then examining changes in neurotransmitter concentrations at nearby synapses. These methods often yield important information about the mechanism of drug actions, which is important to the preliminary screening of new drugs. Unfortunately, they do not provide sufficient information by themselves.

Ultimately, psychoactive drugs must still be assessed by use on human subjects. There are several reasons for this. First, even the use of closely related species like chimpanzees does not always produce the same results as with people. Second, even if the effects are the same, assessing them in animals can be difficult. By definition, the key aspect of psychoactive drugs is their effect on behaviour, which can include changes in alertness, responsiveness, mood, memory and even perceptions. Obviously, it is difficult to assess these effects in animals. This leads to the most fundamental problem: how to categorize the effects of drugs.

By their nature, drugs operate on the physical system, yet the behavioural changes are primarily mental (perception, memory, etc.). This leads back to the problem of linking mind and body. Consider some of the possible difficulties: (1) Some drugs will affect only certain clinical groups, and not other types of patients or normal individuals. (2) Some drugs affect sensory capacities in ways that are not directly expressed in behaviour. Consequently, even with verbal

psychoactive drug a chemical agent which has a discernible effect on mental state or behaviour reports from subjects, it can be difficult to determine what is happening. (3) It is convenient to categorize drugs, but the categories may not always fit well with the subtleties of drug effects. For example, the label 'anti-depressant' focuses on one aspect of mood; however, drugs operate by affecting all neurons which have appropriate receptors, and this may involve much more than mood functions. The result can be a temptation to focus on an intended effect while overlooking various side-effects. (For example, many drugs used to treat schizophrenia do so by affecting a neurotransmitter called *dopamine*. While such drugs can often reduce delusional thoughts and hallucinations, they can also affect motor responses, which also depend on dopamine.) In the end, it can be very difficult to match behavioural descriptions, which are partly based on culture, to drug effects, which depend on complex sets of neural pathways (Snyder 1980). These problems are not insurmountable, as the increasing sophistication of psychopharmacology shows, but they do present continual challenges to researchers.

In addition to understanding in what ways a drug alters behaviour, we need to understand how it operates in the body. In this regard, there has been tremendous progress in recent years. Almost all drugs operate by affecting communication between neurons. As was described earlier, communication across the synapse is dependent on neurotransmitters. These chemical messengers are released by the terminals at the end of the axon, and flow across the synaptic gap to the receptors on the next neuron (see Fig. 2.2). The relationship of the receptor and the neurotransmitter may be compared to a lock and a key – only a particular shape of neurotransmitter molecule will fit in a given receptor. (There are also variations on this basic theme. Sometimes, a molecule will seem to fit, but not influence the neuron; this is something like a key which fits a lock, but won't turn. By blocking the receptor site, such a chemical may prevent the proper neurotransmitter from reaching its target receptor. Alternatively, some chemicals attack neurotransmitters in the synapse, destroying them before they can reach the receptors.) While this lock-and-key metaphor applies to all neurotransmitters and psychoactive drugs, it was the basis for one of the great discoveries of modern psychopharmacology: endorphins.

The story begins with interest in opiates, a family of drugs which includes morphine, heroin and opium, all derived from the opium poppy. Although opiates have been used for hundreds of years (notably through the smoking of opium), the basis for their euphoric effects was unknown. As psychopharmacology developed, it became clear that drugs that affect behaviour must do so by affecting neural activity. This suggested that there might be a type of neural receptor which opiates activate. Based on this reasoning, a young researcher named Candace Pert began looking for opiate receptors in the brain. After several failures, she succeeded – there were indeed opiate receptors in the human brain. What's more, tests in other species found that *many* had such receptors – all the way down to the hagfish, which has existed essentially unchanged for 350 million years. This raised a new question: why should a 350 million-year-old fish have receptors for a chemical derived from a flower? The only reasonable answer seemed to be that there must be a similar chemical which occurs naturally in the brain! Given that the opiate receptor sites which Pert found were located in regions of the limbic system and brainstem that are associated with pain and emotion, it suggested that the body may produce its own natural painkillers. The race was on to find such chemicals, and within a year the search was successful.

endorphin (endogenous – 'naturally occurring' – morphine) a neuropeptide which plays a significant role in pain and mood states

The first discovery was dubbed *enkephalin* (Greek for 'in the head'); shortly after, C.H. Li found what have become known as **endorphins** (for *end*ogenous – 'naturally occurring' – m*orphine*) (Villet 1978).

It was quickly recognized that endorphins were not typical neurotransmitters, but were rather small molecules called peptides; their discovery prompted increased interest in such *neuropeptides* – chemicals which function as both hormones and neurotransmitters (see the section on 'Chemistry and Behaviour' above). The discovery of endorphins is like a detective story – finding clues, making deductions about what they mean, until the solution is found. It also provides a good model for how drugs are discovered and evaluated today – by examining the molecular shape, and matching it with receptor sites in the brain.

Types of Psychoactive Drugs

Advances in psychopharmacology have led to an increasing diversity of psychoactive drugs, and also to more widespread usage. At the same time, the frequency of their use has led to a change in social attitudes, so that drugs are more widely accepted, and in fact may be actively sought. (Studies suggest well over half of visits to doctors include writing a prescription; in part, because patients have come to see drugs as a panacea.) In addition to prescription drugs, there are a number of other drugs which have behavioural effects, but are often overlooked by consumers because of their non-prescription nature. Let us briefly examine some commonly encountered drugs and their effects.

Psychoactive drugs are commonly divided into various categories, according to the general nature of their effects on behaviour (although, as noted previously, such categories are often imprecise). One category often overlooked in daily experience is the stimulants. **Stimulants** act on both the CNS and the autonomic nervous system (a portion of the peripheral nervous system that controls such functions as heart rate and breathing, as well as general arousal level). These drugs tend to decrease fatigue, increase physical activity and alertness, diminish hunger, and produce a temporary elevation of mood. Both *caffeine* and *nicotine* are stimulants, although not as powerful as the prescription drugs known as *amphetamines*.

stimulant a drug which increases activation of the CNS and the autonomic nervous system; these drugs tend to decrease fatigue, increase physical activity and alertness, diminish hunger and produce a temporary elevation of mood

Because stimulants tend to diminish hunger, amphetamines are sometimes prescribed as 'diet pills'. Smokers often experience a related effect when they reduce their smoking: the reduced nicotine level leads to an increase in appetite. Amphetamines are also sometimes prescribed for treating hyperactive children, who show unusually high activity levels and an inability to concentrate; for reasons which are not clear, amphetamines seem to calm them down. Beyond these uses, stimulants have very few legitimate applications. They do not really reduce depression, nor are they a proper substitute for sleep when fatigued. Yet their use (and misuse) is widespread – sometimes users are even unaware, since stimulants like caffeine can be found in many common foods.

Caffeine is found not only in coffee, but also in tea, cola and even chocolate bars. Children exposed to average amounts of cola and candy may be accustomed to caffeine long before they ever taste coffee. Nicotine, found in cigarettes, is also a stimulant. Although caffeine and nicotine are treated casually in our culture, they nonetheless can cause adverse effects. Like other types of drugs, the body tends to adapt to their presence over long intervals. This can result in the phenomenon of *tolerance*, whereby one needs higher and higher doses to maintain the effect. In extreme cases, misuse of drugs can lead to *addiction*, which is determined by the occurrence of symptoms of physical *withdrawal*; when a person is addicted, stopping usage of the drug provokes vomiting, muscle and heart tremors, and seizures (note that addiction is *not* limited to stimulants – the pattern can arise with a variety of drugs). While withdrawal symptoms to caffeine and nicotine are usually relatively mild, amphetamine abuse can be more serious. Chronic high doses of amphetamines can lead to marked side-effects, including hallucinations, delusions and even a psychosis very similar to paranoid schizophrenia.

Curiously, individuals often confuse stimulants with **depressants**, which reduce CNS activity, and in large doses can cause coma and even death. People often regard alcohol as a stimulant, because in small doses it reduces inhibitions and increases talkativeness. In reality, these effects are due to differential sensitivity to the depressant effects by different parts of the brain. The 'higher' functions of the cortex are the first to be affected, which can lead to less self-consciousness and a reduction in learned inhibitions. In large enough quantities, alcohol (like other depressants) is a general anaesthetic, producing loss of consciousness. (Depressants also affect some of the same receptors as tranquillizer drugs, which accounts for the anti-anxiety effects of alcohol.) Over time, large doses of alcohol can also cause severe physiological effects, including memory deficits and liver damage.

depressant a drug which reduces CNS activity; in large doses, depressants can cause coma and even death

Abuse of alcohol may well be endemic in our culture: it has been estimated that 5 per cent of the population in both the United States and Canada have a serious drinking problem, and alcoholism is a problem in virtually all Western countries. In France it is involved in one of every ten chronic hospital cases. No-one is certain whether alcoholism is based on a physiological malfunction or is based on learned drinking patterns. There is evidence that it runs in families, but this may mean either that there is a genetic cause, or that the children learn patterns from their parents. In either case, most treatments show only limited rates of success. Alcohol may well be our largest drug problem.

The chronic, casual use of drugs can be a danger in many ways. As noted, prolonged use can lead to tolerance and addiction. In other cases, side-effects may be infrequent but severe. For example, Prozac, a widely used anti-depressant, can severely suppress appetite in some individuals; at one time, its manufacturer considered seeking certification for its use as a diet pill. Another potential problem can arise due to the interaction of a drug with other drugs or even certain foods. Barbiturates (a depressant sometimes used as a sedative), for example, tend to interact with alcohol (also a depressant) in a *synergistic* manner – that is, the effect of the two together is greater than for either alone. Some cheeses, such as Blue or Roquefort, can also be dangerous or even lethal if consumed while taking certain drugs. Not long ago, there was a public scare when it was discovered that some non-prescription hay fever remedies could interact with a common antibiotic, erythromycin, to produce potentially deadly heart irregularities.

Our knowledge of synergistic effects is limited at present, and undiscovered combinations may exist. Unfortunately, casual attitudes towards drugs may lead to underestimating possible risks. For the present, the best approach seems to be caution: never take a drug without reason, and then only under a doctor's supervision. Always tell a doctor about medicines being taken which may have been prescribed by another doctor. If you take a drug, watch for drowsiness or other side-effects that may impair your ability to deal with your surroundings.

Mood-altering drugs are not new, nor are the circumstances that lead people to seek relief from anxiety. However, our understanding of the mechanism of such drugs is growing. The methods of research are becoming more sophisticated, and with them our ability to use drugs as a therapeutic tool. While no amount of research can ever determine social attitudes, ideally such attitudes are based on knowledge. To this end, the next few years offer hope of great strides in our ability to understand the role of drugs in mind–body interactions.

For further consideration

If you use caffeine (found in coffee, tea, cola and chocolate) or nicotine (found in tobacco), you might consider whether you notice any stimulant effects the next time you ingest the drug. If you don't notice any effects, could this mean you have developed a *tolerance* for the drug?

Electrical Stimulation of the Brain

electrical stimulation of the brain (ESB) artificial stimulation of neurons by means of a current applied through an implanted electrode

While chemical processes are important, brain activity is also electrical. This aspect of the brain's functioning is emphasized by research on **electrical stimulation of the brain** (ESB). ESB refers to artificial stimulation of neurons by means of a current applied through an implanted electrode. By applying tiny electrical currents to brain tissue, one can force neurons to activate. Although the details are complex, the basic concept is quite simple.

It has long been known that the brain somehow involves electrical activity. In ancient Rome, Pliny the Elder recommended the shock of an electric fish, applied to the forehead, to ease the pain of childbirth. Without knowing the mechanism, Pliny recognized that the shock stunned the patient, reducing conscious awareness (including pain). The electrical nature of nerve activity was first recognized by Luigi Galvani, an Italian anatomist in 1791. Galvani observed that a frog's leg could be made to twitch at the touch of dissimilar metals. (Apparently he first noticed the effect when a butcher reached for some frogs' legs with metal tongs!) Galvani thought, wrongly, that the frog's leg generated the impulse, rather than being activated by the metal probe, which actually created a battery. While it was not long before the true nature of the process was recognized, the possible implications were ignored for nearly a century. It was only about seventy years ago that researchers began to study electrical activity in the brain in a systematic manner.

electroencephalograph (EEG – 'writing the electricity of the brain') a device for recording the electrical activity of the brain

In the 1920s, the first recordings of brain-wave activity (as the electrical signals are called) were made using the **electroencephalograph** (EEG – 'writing the electricity of the brain'). The EEG allowed researchers to *record* activity, but it was not until the 1950s that techniques permitted more direct intervention. In 1954, researchers at Yale University discovered that stimulation of certain regions of the limbic system and midbrain in animals seemed to produce pain (Delgado *et al.* 1954). This was not too surprising: since an electrical shock to the fingertip can be painful, why not in the brain? However, in the same year, James Olds, working independently, discovered that stimulation of certain areas of the limbic system could also produce *pleasure* (Olds and Milner 1954). Both groups were studying areas of the 'primitive brain' in animals, and the effects they discovered seemed to reflect primitive emotions and drives. At the same time, however, Wilder Penfield, a neurosurgeon at the Montreal Neurological Institute, was working with epileptic patients. As part of the surgical method of treatment, he discovered the effects of stimulation of the cortex in conscious individuals (see the section on 'Mind, Brain and the Central Nervous System' above).

These discoveries set the stage for more sophisticated approaches. In the early 1960s, a doctor working with hospitalized mental patients reported pleasurable/ painful effects from midbrain stimulation in conscious patients (Heath 1972). Other researchers found that ESB could be used to control particular behaviours. The possibilities were illustrated in headline-making form by Jose Delgado of Yale University when he went into an arena with a full-grown, electrode-implanted bull, and used ESB to stop the bull in mid-charge (Delgado 1969)!

Leaving such dramatic demonstrations aside, ESB poses some basic questions about the brain and mind. One of the most basic issues concerns the localization of functions. The materialist view argues that all functions of the mind are based on activity in the body. The simplest form of this view says that each aspect of behaviour is produced by a specific location in the brain – that is, that functions are localized. Broca offered support for this position when he pinpointed speech functions in the left cortical hemisphere. Similarly, Penfield's work using ESB indicated that specific regions of the cortex control particular movements, sensations and even memories (refer back to Fig. 2.4 for his findings). Thus, it would seem that ESB may allow us to identify – and ultimately control – all aspects of behaviour.

This line of thought can give rise to all sorts of scenarios, from people using ESB instead of drugs to control mood, to governments enforcing laws by means of computer-controlled systems implanted in each citizen's brain. These possibilities can seem frightening and Orwellian, and critics have been quick to raise questions. Typically, the questions focus on the moral aspect: who is to control the computers that control the ESB, and what sort of behaviours should be rewarded or punished? Ironically, the ethical dilemmas posed have already been raised by the work of Heath, who used hospitalized individuals to explore the effects of ESB. Since most patients had schizophrenia, it seems unlikely they were capable of giving informed consent. But before accepting this as a purely moral crisis, one should look more carefully at the scientific basis of the issue.

Problems *do* exist with ESB, and in some sense they are all connected with the issue of localization of function. If one accepts it in its simplest form, then there exists a specific centre responsible for any type of behaviour. At present, there is inadequate evidence to support this view. Lower animals show a great degree of physiological predetermination of their behaviour (often called 'instincts'). In humans, however, there appear to be relatively few such patterns, even for comparable behaviour. For example, while male stickleback fish show stereotyped courtship rituals, human males do so only to the extent that their culture dictates. If true localization of function does not exist, one must question whether complete control of every action would ever be possible. (Gerald Edelman, a Nobel laureate in physiology, has also noted that while the general patterns of brain structure are similar across individuals, the details of neural connections differ significantly. This implies that mapping of functions must still be done on a case-by-case basis, even if localization exists: Edelman 1992.)

While ESB has greatly aided our understanding of the brain, it does have limitations as a research tool. First, ESB is an artificial process. Inserting an electrode destroys a few hundred cells in the immediate vicinity, and the effects of the stimulation itself are not the same as normal neural activity. Typically, the current applied is either some form of alternating current, or a series of brief direct-current pulses. The effect in either case is to stimulate artificially all the neurons in the immediate area, perhaps a few thousand cells. These cells then fire *in synchrony*, which is hardly typical of normal neural function over such a region. Thus, current techniques of ESB do initiate brain activity, but they do *not* duplicate the normal workings of the brain. Given the approximately ten *billion* neurons in the cortex alone, it is unlikely that ESB will ever mimic the brain's patterns over any significant area.

Like drug research, ESB has been useful in increasing our understanding of the brain. In addition, clinical work like Penfield's has led to better, simpler methods of treating disorders like epilepsy. At the same time, it is inherently limited, in that it cannot tell us about how the brain functions as a whole. This means that larger-scale functions, like consciousness, are unlikely to be revealed by ESB. For that, we must look to other research methods.

The Split Brain and the Whole Mind

According to the materialist view, consciousness *must* have a physical basis, most probably in the brain. The problem for researchers has been to find a way of identifying it. Techniques like ESB have produced support for the principle of localization of function by demonstrating control of a remarkable range of behaviours, but they still leave the question hanging: where is the mind?

Normally, our experience of the world, our inner thoughts and feelings, seems unitary – that is, we have only a single consciousness. Yet the structure of the brain, especially the cortex, is basically two symmetrical halves. These halves, made up of the cortex and underlying structures, are called the **cerebral hemispheres**. Connecting the two hemispheres is a wide band of nerve fibres called the **corpus callosum**. Researchers have long known that each hemisphere is basically responsible for the opposite side of the body (e.g. your left hemisphere receives sensations from, and gives motor commands to, the right side of your body). Now, if consciousness is really associated with the cortex, then it implies that the unitary nature of our experience and awareness is based on the integration of the two hemispheres. This reasoning led pioneering psychologist Gustav Fechner to speculate, more than one hundred years ago, that if the two hemispheres would somehow be separated, we would have *two* separate consciousnesses. Fechner never thought that this could be tested, but time has proven differently.

Research in the 1950s by psychologist Roger Sperry, working with monkeys, suggested that cutting the fibres of the corpus callosum, thereby separating the two hemispheres, had no grave effects on behaviour – certainly less than procedures like frontal lobotomy. Still, this gave no indication of what might happen in humans. One obvious difference between primates and people is that monkeys do not speak, and Broca had shown that speech was found in only one hemisphere. Consequently, no-one was sure what would happen if the hemispheres were separated in a person.

The answer to the question came as a result of medical needs. In the 1960s,

cerebral hemispheres two half spheres, made up of the cortex and underlying structures, which comprise the major portion of the brain
corpus callosum a wide band of nerve fibres which connect the two hemispheres

Roger W. Sperry

Roger Walcott Sperry (1913–   ) is an American neurological researcher who pioneered much of our understanding of hemispheric specialization. His career began relatively slowly, receiving his doctorate in zoology at the University of Chicago at the age of twenty-eight. While there, he worked with the biophysicist Paul Weiss, studying how the connections between neurons and muscles are formed. This led to further work on the regeneration of neural connections between the retina and brain in amphibians. While doing this work, he met biologist Norma Dupree, with whom he collaborated; they married in 1949. In 1952, he moved to the California Institute of Technology, where he remains a professor emeritus of psychobiology. In 1953, one of his graduate students, Ronald Myers, invented the split-brain procedure, the study of which later led to Sperry's most important discoveries; ironically, Myers' initial role is seldom cited in this regard. They first studied the effects of severing the corpus callosum in cats and primates; however, it was Sperry's later work on epileptic patients, in collaboration with neurosurgeon Joseph Bogen, that eventually led to Sperry sharing the 1981 Nobel Prize in Physiology or Medicine. Sperry's contributions continue to be carried further by his students, including Jerre Levy and Michael Gazzaniga.

a Los Angeles surgeon name Joseph Bogen was trying to treat patients with a long history of epilepsy. While in many cases epileptics could be treated with anti-seizure drugs (and more progress has been made since then), these patients did not respond to drug treatment; consequently, they had major seizures on the average of twice a week. In epilepsy, the random neural activity of a seizure usually starts at a point in one hemisphere and spreads, creating sensory distortions and convulsions. In cases of *grand mal* attacks, the seizure activity spreads from one hemisphere to the other across the bridge provided by the corpus callosum. In such cases, the recurring seizures can disrupt normal life, and even present a life-threatening situation. When all other treatments failed, Bogen tried a new and radical approach. By cutting the fibres of the corpus callosum, he hoped to restrict the seizure activity to one hemisphere, and thus prevent grand mal attacks. While he knew of Sperry's work, and there had been occasional clinical reports of damage to the corpus callosum, no-one had ever purposely separated the hemispheres before. Bogen and his patients were venturing into new territory.

Medically, the treatment worked. Not only did it prevent further grand mal attacks, but (for reasons still unclear) it also reduced the frequency of more limited seizures. At the same time, it was desirable to know what negative effects, if any, the surgery had caused. Knowing of Sperry's research, Bogen asked him to collaborate on evaluating the patients. The results were a surprise to all concerned.

Initial observations suggested that the patients were remarkably normal. Everyday actions like walking and eating seemed to occur naturally. However, by a series of ingenious testing procedures, Sperry, Bogen and their associates discovered that, in fact, these individuals had an unusual mental syndrome. As Sperry reported, 'Instead of the normally unified single stream of consciousness, these patients behave in many ways as if they have two independent streams of conscious awareness, one in each hemisphere, each of which is cut off from and out of contact with the mental experience of the other' (Sperry 1968: 724). In other words, *two* minds, each functioning separately from the other. Fechner's prediction had been correct! (Ultimately, Sperry's research on the split brain led to his receiving the Nobel Prize in physiology in 1981.)

To assess the effects of the surgery, the researchers had to use techniques whereby information was presented to only one hemisphere. The simplest case involved touch: if the split-brain person were given an object in their *left* hand while blindfolded, the left hand could later pick it out again, by touch, from a selection of several objects. However, if the *right* hand attempted to pick out the article previously held by the left hand, it did no better than chance. In the case of vision, the situation is a bit more complicated, because each eye is connected to *both* hemispheres. The division of visual processing is such that the visual world of each eye is divided in two, so that objects on the *left* side of the visual world (or *visual field*) are seen by the *right* hemisphere, while objects on the *right* side are seen by the *left* hemisphere, regardless of which eye is used (see Fig. 2.7). Thus, if a person looks straight ahead and an image appears briefly to the left, only the right hemisphere receives the information. This led to an interesting discovery: because only the left hemisphere had language, a split-brain person presented with a word or picture on the left side (and thus conveyed to the right hemisphere) could not say what they had seen! Only the left hemisphere seemed able to talk, while the right was silent. (Note, of course, that these effects only apply when the corpus callosum has been cut; in a normal individual, there is continual exchange of information between the two hemispheres.)

As it turns out, the differences are not quite what they first seemed. The right hemisphere, while unable to speak, is not completely ignorant of language. If presented with a word or picture, it can *point* to a corresponding picture or word. Thus, seeing the word 'key', the left hand can correctly choose a key. At the same time, the right hemisphere has musical and spatial abilities which seem to be lacking in the left hemisphere. If given geometric figures to copy (such as a circle overlapping a square), the left hand (right hemisphere) does a better job of copying it than does the right hand (left hemisphere). This is particularly striking, since the patients Sperry tested were all right-handed, so in principle one might expect the right hand to be more skilled. For handwriting, the right hand *is* better; for drawing, it is not. (This raises a fascinating problem: since lettering is a type of artistic skill, why is it that the left hand, so superior for other drawing tasks, cannot reproduce letters and words? So far, this aspect of the split-brain phenomenon has not been fully explored.)

Despite the apparent handicap and dual-consciousness which they possess, split-brain individuals manage to cope very well. Even tasks requiring motor coordination of the two hemispheres, such as riding a bicycle, can be mastered. Over time, it even seems that indirect methods of communicating between the two sides develop. For example, in one experiment, Sperry flashed either a red or a green card to the left visual field (right hemisphere), and then asked the person to name (left hemisphere) the colour. As expected, the left hemisphere, not having seen the colour, did poorly. However, if allowed to reconsider, the person was always correct. What seemed to happen was that the right hemisphere, hearing the spoken response of the left hemisphere, would produce grimaces and

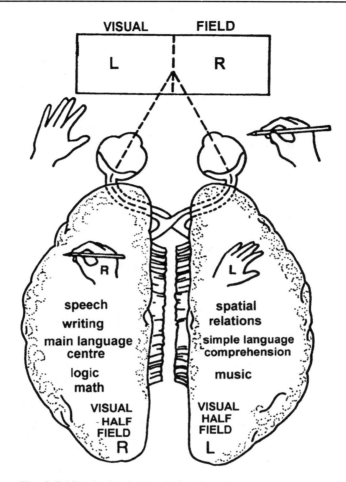

Fig. 2.7 Hemispheric specialization Roger Sperry's work with split-brain individuals (note the cut fibres of the corpus callosum between the hemispheres) has helped to identify differences in the functions of the two sides of the brain (after Sperry 1968).

other gestures if the answer was wrong. These cues let the left hemisphere know its error, which it then corrected!

Since Sperry's original research, a large number of studies have been done, even though the number of split-brain individuals is quite small (between 1962 and 1968, Bogen operated on a total of nine patients). Overall, the results have supported Sperry's original work, although it is now recognized that the differences between the hemispheres are not absolute (Trevarthen 1987). Still, the research does suggest several things: (1) If the corpus callosum is cut, the two hemispheres function independently. (2) Each hemisphere seems to possess consciousness, but without awareness of the other. (In one case, a patient, seeing her left hand make a response, exclaimed, 'I didn't do that!') (3) The two hemispheres seem to show different types of specialized abilities, with the left hemisphere possessing language, logic and maths skills, the right hemisphere spatial and musical skills.

The Split Brain and the Normal Brain

The striking nature of the split-brain findings makes it tempting to extend the conclusions to normal individuals. At the same time, it must be recognized that severing the corpus callosum is not a natural condition, and in the intact brain the two hemispheres communicate freely. Still, research seeking to test these findings in normal individuals does indicate that the two hemispheres tend to become specialized in ways similar to what has been observed in split-brain individuals. For example, clinical cases show that damage to the left hemisphere, whether by disease or trauma, can impair speech. (It should be noted that in a small percentage of people, primarily left-handers, the pattern of hemispheric specialization is modified or reversed.)

One issue that has arisen out of split-brain research is an increased interest in **cerebral dominance**, the tendency for one hemisphere to be superior for particular functions. In most individuals, one hand, foot, eye and ear are usually preferred for many actions; for instance, if standing, we begin walking with the dominant foot. Similarly, if using a camera or telescope, we usually focus with the dominant eye. Such preferences have been noted since ancient times, and the origin of cerebral dominance has caused much speculation among researchers. Evidence suggests that dominance, as seen in preferences for one side, is already developing at birth.

cerebral dominance the tendency for one hemisphere to be superior for particular functions

Handedness, which is the most visible indicator of dominance, has often been the focus of social prejudice. In many languages and cultures, being left-handed is viewed negatively. This can be seen in the way we use words: a 'left-handed compliment' is not really a compliment. To be 'right' is to be correct. A suspicious person is 'sinister' (Latin for left-handed), while a skilful person is 'dextrous' (Latin for right-handed). Similarly, a 'gauche' (French for left) remark is in bad taste. These usages reflect a form of cultural bias, and lead to questions about the origin of handedness, and dominance more generally.

Theories of the origin of handedness range from genetic factors to learning (speech being connected to right-hand gestures) to congenital brain damage (left-handedness being the result of such damage). At present, there is no conclusive evidence for any of these theories. While it is known that dominance is somehow related to hemispheric specialization (for example, stuttering in adults correlates highly with forcing right-hand use for a left-handed child), no-one is sure exactly what the connection is. Attempts to alter dominance *do* seem to have some impact on skills like language, but that does not prove that dominance is the source of specialization. In fact, the *pattern* of hemispheric specialization seems basically the same in both left- and right-dominant individuals (although left-handers are slightly more likely to show a reversed or mixed pattern of hemispheric specialization). In addition, there is no clear explanation as to why right-handedness (dominant left hemisphere) is the norm across races and cultures. Like many aspects of brain function, we still have many unanswered questions about handedness, dominance in general and hemispheric specialization. Even so, most researchers would agree that despite social prejudices, one should not interfere if a child shows a preference for being left-handed.

The research on the split brain and cerebral dominance brings us back to our initial questions: is localization of function correct, and does consciousness reside in the brain? The research on split-brain individuals seems to indicate that consciousness involves the cortex, for separating the cerebral hemispheres seems to split consciousness as well. However, since it involves such a large-scale division, it offers us very little information in terms of determining precisely *where* consciousness resides. After all, the hemispheres each involve cortex, underlying subcortical tissue, limbic system structures, and so on, down into the brainstem, spinal cord and beyond. To say that the two sides of the body can each have their own consciousness does not tell us what sort of structure *produces* consciousness. A materialist view which assumes localization of function would argue that we should be able to find some particular neural circuit that represents conscious awareness. At present, no study has found such a circuit; current attempts to do so tend to limit themselves to particular aspects of consciousness, such as visual awareness (Crick and Koch 1992). The resulting ambiguity has led different researchers to take different points of view. In a book written shortly before his death, Penfield noted the absence of any evidence for the localization of consciousness. Consequently, he concluded consciousness was not a function of the brain, and he essentially reverted to a form of dualism (Penfield 1975). Sperry, by contrast, simply rejects the idea that consciousness is localized, without abandoning materialism. He views consciousness as an *emergent property* of the brain (that is, a phenomenon which emerges from the system working as a whole), and suggests that no study of individual parts will enable us to pin it down (Sperry 1969). If Sperry is correct, the mind *is* connected to the body – but the terms may remain forever separate in our descriptions.

For further consideration

Are you left- or right-handed? Consider the types of skills that are associated with each hemisphere. Do you see any relationship between your own dominant hemisphere and your relative abilities? (Remember, the preferred hand is associated with the *opposite* hemisphere.)

The Effects of Mind on Body

'Mind over matter'. The phrase has been used to describe many things, from accomplishing a difficult task to claims of levitation. The most common meaning is to describe how physical reactions are seemingly altered by mental processes. The view that this is paradoxical or impossible can be traced to Descartes's dualistic conception of mind and body, in which the mind has no physical basis. In this sort of framework, it becomes difficult to imagine how mental states could affect specific body functions. By contrast, in a materialist framework, where mind and body are linked, it becomes easier to conceive of such interactions. 'Mind' and 'brain' may represent different levels of description, but materialism assumes that they have a common physical foundation.

This unified view can help us to understand what would be otherwise inexplicable phenomena. A common example is the reaction to painful stimuli; repeatedly, one finds that different people react differently to similar physical traumas. To one person a trip to the dentist may be terrifying, whereas to another it is no more painful than scratching an itch. In our culture, childbirth is usually regarded as an intensely painful experience, yet members of some other cultures experience it differently (Melzack 1973). Thus, response to painful stimuli seems to show considerable variation. Pain researcher Ronald Melzack believes that such variations across individuals are due to differing cognitive expectations and perceptions. Since cognitive processes (including perception and attitudes) are regarded as functions of the cortex, Melzack's theory says that the effects of expectations on pain response are mediated by cortical influences. Phantom limb phenomena, as mentioned in the Introduction, may also be the product of the way the person interprets sensory inputs, rather than an automatic response (Melzack 1992). If the way we think can affect the way we perceive our own body, then such cognitive effects on physical state truly represent what is meant by 'mind over matter', or the effect of mental states on physical functioning and behaviour. In this section, we will consider some of the research that is helping to improve our understanding of the processes involved.

Stress

Like pain, stress is a common human experience. We are all familiar with those moments: the boss wants to see you *now* about the last quarter's sales figures; or you're late for an appointment, so you gulp down lunch; or you go to bed, only to hear the neighbour's stereo blaring away. The pulse-pounding, gut-wrenching sensations that result from such moments are common in modern life. When we recognize the feelings, we may experience the desire to run away to a desert island. Unfortunately, even this may not solve the problem of stress.

According to Hans Selye, the doctor who pioneered stress research, **stress** is the non-specific response of the body to any demand on it (Selye 1978). Simply being alive is 'stressful'; in this sense, there is no escape from stress. But not all stress situations are alike, nor are all reactions harmful. To understand this, first consider what happens when one experiences stress.

Biologically, stress reactions are an emergency response intended to prepare one for 'fight or flight'. A significant link in the body's chain of reactions to stressful situations is the release of hormones by the adrenal glands. The **adrenal glands**, located just above the kidneys, are made up of two portions, the *cortex* or outer covering, and the *medulla* or inner core. When stimulated, the adrenal medulla secretes *epinephrine* (also called adrenaline) and *norepinephrine* (noradrenaline). Each of these hormones plays a role in stress reactions (as noted previously, the same chemicals also function as neurotransmitters).

The release of *epinephrine* into the bloodstream triggers effects in both the brain and the peripheral nervous system. In the brain, it increases activity (particularly in the reticular formation, which controls overall arousal). In turn, the reticular formation sends signals to the autonomic branch of the peripheral nervous system, which shuts off digestion, increases heart rate and raises blood pressure, among other reactions (see Fig. 2.8). Since among the organs affected by the autonomic nervous system are the adrenal glands, the sequence of responses is a so-called 'closed loop', which means that the stress reaction produced by epinephrine can be prolonged. Anyone who has been startled or has otherwise experienced sudden stress knows that the racing heart beat and other signs can linger beyond the moment of stress.

Norepinephrine also plays a role in stress reactions, but more indirectly. Travelling through the bloodstream, it goes to the brain, where it activates another gland, the **pituitary gland**, which in turn releases another hormone, adrenocorticotrophic

stress a term coined by Hans Selye to describe the non-specific response of the body to any demand on it
adrenal glands endocrine glands, located just above the kidneys, which play an important role in arousal and stress; the outer layer (the cortex) secretes corticosteroids, and the *medulla* (the inner core) secretes *epinephrine* (adrenaline) and *norepinephrine* (noradrenaline)

pituitary gland a small gland adjacent to the hypothalamus which regulates many endocrine functions, including growth, and also interacts with the nervous system via hypothalamic connections; in stress, it releases a hormone called ACTH, which triggers the release of steroids by the cortex of the adrenal glands; sometimes called 'the master gland' because of its many functions

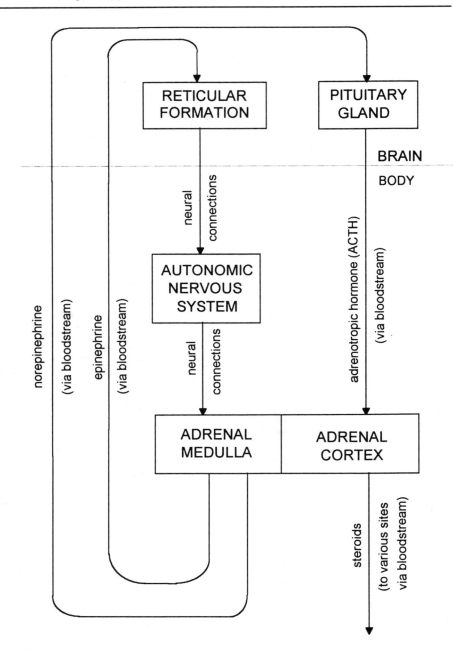

Fig. 2.8 A schematic diagram of the body's response to stress Stress reactions involve a series of effects involving an interaction of the nervous system and the hormonal system. Note that the response involving epinephrine is a 'closed loop', which tends to be self-maintaining in the absence of off-setting interventions by the parasympathetic division of the autonomic nervous system.

steroids hormones produced by the cortex of the adrenal glands which are involved in the regulation of water and sugar metabolism, immune system function, and other basic bodily processes; sometimes called 'corticosteroids'

hormone (ACTH). ACTH in turn reaches the adrenals, causing the adrenal cortex to produce hormones called steroids. (Note that the adrenal *medulla*, not the *cortex*, produces norepinephrine and epinephrine.)

Steroids (sometimes called 'corticosteroids') play a role in a diverse range of body processes. They are involved in the normal regulation of water and sugar metabolism, including the quick release of sugar for energy under stress. They also affect the immune system, including inflammatory response. Synthetic forms of the steroids (e.g. cortisone) are also used in medicine for treatment of allergic reactions, arthritis and shock. Steroids can also affect mood: one reaction to large doses of cortisone can be severe depression.

While this description may seem to emphasize the role of the adrenal glands, the changes associated with stress are actually a complex sequence involving many parts of the body, as noted above. This sequence, sometimes called the 'fight or flight' response, has its origins far back in the evolution of the brain (similar patterns are found in all mammals, for example). The adrenals play a major role (e.g. injections of adrenaline can initiate many of the effects), but stress is an integrated response of the body to whatever is perceived as an emergency situation.

This set of physiological reactions evolved as a means of coping with danger, but it presents two major problems for modern humans. First, the 'danger' may often be psychological rather than physical (e.g. pressure to meet a deadline), and hence no physical response is either required or appropriate. This means that one is left with a surge of activity-oriented chemical changes, and no outlet for the energy. Second, the stress response may carry beyond the moment of crisis; under conditions of chronic stress, there can be severe effects due to excess production of steroids and related changes. These effects include suppressing the body's immune system. Insomnia, asthma, herpes and rheumatoid arthritis are among the disorders which may be affected by stress responses (Selye 1976; Solomon 1990).

general adaptation syndrome a model of stages of stress identified by Hans Selye, ranging from acute stress (alarm), to outward coping (resistance) and, finally, to depletion of bodily resources (exhaustion)

Selye identified what he called the **general adaptation syndrome** of stress, involving three stages. The initial, acute stress response identified above is called *alarm*. If the stress continues, there is a second stage, *resistance*, in which the organism seems to be coping with the stress and *outward* signs of arousal disappear (internally, hormonal production, etc., continues). If the situation persists, the final stage, *exhaustion*, may be reached, in which the body's resources are depleted; in studies with experimental animals, this has resulted in sickness or death. Autopsies on these animals reveal enlarged adrenal glands, severe ulcers of the stomach, and shrinkage of the thymus gland and lymph nodes, which are involved in the body's immune system.

Interestingly, what first led Selye to the study of stress was an observation he made as a second-year medical student in 1926. As part of their clinical training, the students encountered patients suffering from a variety of disorders. Selye noted that 'they all looked sick'. His professors and fellow students laughed at his suggestion that disease, no matter what its nature, could produce certain consistent changes. Some ten years later, Selye returned to this question, and named the syndrome 'stress'. The term, borrowed from physics, was meant to refer to the effects of resisting an outside force (Selye 1978).

The effects of chronic stress have been indirectly confirmed by research by two psychiatrists. In the late 1940s, Dr Thomas Holmes became interested in the

A BAROMETER OF STRESS

Stressful experiences can have great impact on a person's ability to function. But what are stressful circumstances, and what types of experience typically cause the greatest stress? A long-term study by Rahe, referred to in the text, attempted to answer these questions by looking at the effects of various events on the probability of becoming ill. Generally, the effects were found to be additive—that is, people who went through more life changes were more likely to get sick. High stress levels seem to impair the body's ability to function.

A look at the table below will show you the estimated stress-value of various events. Rahe suggested that if your stress total went above 150 for any twelve-month period, you were in a high-risk group, and should heed the storm warnings of the stress barometer.

Rank	Life Event	Stress score
1	Death of spouse	100
2	Divorce	75
3	Marital separation	65
4	Jail term	63
5	Death of close family member	63
6	Personal injury or illness	53
7	Marriage	50
8	Fired from job	47
9	Marital reconciliation	45
10	Retirement	45
18	Change to different line of work	36
25	Outstanding personal achievement	28
27	Begin or end school	26
32	Change residence	20
40	Change in eating habits	13
41	Vacation	13
43	Minor violations of the law	11

Fig. 2.9 The Holmes–Rahe Life-Change Scale (adapted from Rahe 1972).

effects of major life-changes on the health of his patients. For this purpose, he examined the case histories of more than 5000 patients, and developed a 'stress barometer' of life changes (see Fig. 2.9). Later, Dr Richard Rahe used Holmes' work as the basis for a study of 2500 men in the US Navy. Using the stress scale as a predictor of illness over a twelve-month period, he found that those who underwent the highest number of life-changes suffered nearly twice as many ailments as those in the lowest category (Rahe 1972). While this research is correlational (as is much of the research on stress), the pattern has been supported in other studies (e.g. Brown and Harris 1989), and overall the results tend to suggest stress is a significant factor in determining health (the possible mechanisms for this will be discussed below; see the section on 'Medicine and the mind').

One may well ask if the negative consequences of stressful events are inevitable. Research suggests that, in fact, options exist. While stress can be created by life situations, one's perception of the situation and one's mode of responding can make an important difference. Psychologists David Glass and Jerome Singer have explored how our perceptions affect our response to stressful situations (Glass and Singer 1972). Their work, which concerns sources of urban stress, arose out of the observation that it is very hard to get agreement about what is a **stressor** (source of stress). For example, a person who has been thinking of making a career change may welcome an offer of early retirement, whereas a person content in their job may be very upset at a similar offer. Similarly, being pushed into cold water may sound stressful, yet every New Year's Day members of 'polar bear clubs' willingly jump into icy lakes or oceans. Thus, having control (or even feeling you have control) of the situation can reduce the effects of a stressor. This element of *perceived control* was also confirmed in a field experiment performed in a nursing home (Langer and Rodin 1976). Another factor influencing the impact of stressors is *predictability*. People who live near subways or railroad tracks often show no discomfort from the sounds, which tend to occur at fixed times. Visitors, however, may be greatly stressed by what they see as 'unpredictable' noise. Thus, the way we perceive the situation may be an important factor in reducing our susceptibility to stress.

stressor any factor which triggers a stress response in an individual

Hans Selye has suggested that the way one *reacts* to a stressor is also an important factor. He distinguishes between those responses intended to *resist* the situation (*catatoxic* reactions) and those intended to help one *adapt* to the situation (*syntoxic* reactions). If someone cuts in front of you on the highway, you may get angry and upset (an aggressive, catatoxic response), or you can laugh and dismiss the other driver's behaviour as foolish (an adaptive, syntoxic response). According to Selye, the syntoxic response is often the preferable one. However, sometimes people are caught in a double bind: when they are passive they wish they could be aggressive, and when they are aggressive they feel guilty. This self-conflict is itself stressful, and Selye concedes that we sometimes need catatoxic reactions of anger to act as a safety valve. Unfortunately, Selye offers very little in terms of defining which situations merit which response, causing critics to say his concept is either circular or meaningless. Certainly the criteria are imprecise, but as Glass and Singer have noted, stressors are very difficult to define; it may be that defining an 'appropriate' response is also imprecise. Given the variations in the way individuals respond, Selye's message seems to come down to recognizing when you are stressed, and developing a range of possible coping responses.

The individual's interpretation of the situation may in fact be the most important determinant of the effects of 'stressful' situations. As was discussed in Chapter 1, individuals perceive any situation in terms of their own cognitive schemata. Since materialists would argue that cognitive processes are embedded in the cortex, the link between perceptions and stress becomes potentially understandable as an interaction of the mind and body. Perhaps the best illustration of positive adaptation was offered by Selye's own behaviour. At the time of writing his last book, he would normally get up at dawn to cycle five miles to his office and then work until eight at night – and this from a sixty-eight-year-old man with two artificial hips!

For further consideration

What are the primary stressors in your life? Given the preceding discussion, can you envision steps you could take to reduce your level of stress?

Meditation and Altered States of Consciousness

Our reactions to stressful events clearly suggest that mental processes can affect our physical state – that is, the influence of mind over body. One of the issues raised by these processes concerns our definitions of reality. Usually, we think of reality as being objective; for example, the existence of an object like a chair is verifiable independently of a particular observer. However, when it comes to studying behaviour, we are forced to acknowledge that reality as we experience it is subjective, for the same external stimulus does not always result in the same response by a person. While the materialist view asserts that such variations must be due to internal physiological changes, the nature of these changes is often impossible to pinpoint (recall, for example, the different views on localization of consciousness). It is this aspect of the mind–body relation that has fascinated thinkers. At one time, questions about the relationship between mental states and perceived reality were left to mystics and philosophers, because psychologists lacked techniques to get at the problem. In recent years, however, researchers have been able to examine seriously the nature of mental states. Usually, this is referred to in terms of the study of altered states of consciousness.

Often, when people hear the term 'altered states of consciousness', it conjures up images of drugs and/or mysticism. However, this is too limited a view. Basically, an **altered state of consciousness** is any (subjective) state of awareness which differs from normal waking awareness. As such, the term could apply to psychosis, meditation and even sleep, as well as drug states and mysticism. Even fever can induce an altered state of consciousness, as Julien de la Mettrie realized over two hundred years ago. Because the issues (both technical and theoretical) raised by these states are basically the same, we will focus on only one, meditation.

altered state of consciousness any state of awareness which differs from normal waking awareness; examples could include meditation, sleep, drug states and psychosis

meditation a technique or practice that seeks to achieve mental and physical relaxation, a more passive, receptive awareness, and harmony of mind and nature

Until very recently, meditation was primarily practised in Eastern cultures. Now, for many reasons (including a concern with stress and the search for new medical therapies), Westerners have begun to explore various meditative disciplines. In a broad sense, **meditation** refers to a variety of techniques that seek to achieve mental and physical relaxation, a more passive, receptive awareness, and harmony of mind and nature. Often practitioners will use metaphors like 'existing in the here and now' or 'becoming part of the circle of being'. While intended as a way to communicate the nature of the experience, such statements can sound like claims for Dr John's Miracle Cure to those who have not experienced such states. For the researcher, it becomes a challenge to define meditation in a measurable way (i.e. forming an operational definition in terms of how meditation affects physical functioning).

The nature of meditation as a subjective experience is difficult to define, because in many respects it is non-verbal. Instead, practitioners tend to talk about the process or technique involved. Most forms involve focusing awareness on some stable source of stimulation for a given period of time. This may involve sitting and focusing on nothing, as in Za-Zen (sitting Zen), or chanting, as in transcendental meditation (TM), or focusing one's full concentration on a task, as in Do-Zen (moving Zen). It is claimed that such practices result in relaxation, greater awareness of one's surroundings and renewed energy. The difficulty with these claims has been finding a way to assess them.

Research on meditation has focused on two aspects: (1) seeking changes in brain activity that might define the mental state, and (2) seeking effects of meditation on other aspects of physiology. In terms of brain activity, the typical method has been to look at changes in brain-wave patterns by means of an EEG. It has long been known that brain waves change with level of alertness (e.g. actively thinking *vs* relaxation *vs* sleep), and the brain waves found during relaxation have been labelled the *alpha rhythm*. (This pattern is characterized by relatively uniform slow waves of about 8–12 Hz, compared to the larger, slower waves of sleep or the shorter, faster waves of a fully alert person.) Most studies of meditation, of whatever form, have found that advanced practitioners show increased alpha waves during meditation (e.g. Ornstein 1972).

Of particular interest are the results of a study of advanced Zen states by a Japanese researcher (Hirai 1978). One of the metaphors used in describing *satori*, or Zen enlightenment, is a sense of freshness to all events; each moment exists for itself. Studies of human physiological response to sudden noise usually indicate a startle response, measurable by EEG, which gradually fades if the sound occurs repeatedly. In a study done with three Zen masters, they did not show this fading of response (called *habituation*), but rather reacted to each repetition of the sound as if it truly were a fresh event. In this instance, the metaphorical description seems to be supported by the measurements of brain activity.

Another area of study has been to look for other types of changes in physical functioning. For example, studies of physiological effects associated with TM have reported a general reduction of sympathetic nervous system activity (Wallace and Benson 1972). Since the sympathetic nervous system responds to stress by increasing its activity, this study suggests meditation may help to counter the effects of stress. In fact, Benson believes there is an integrated response pattern mediated by the hypothalamus which is the opposite of the 'fight or flight' response; he calls it the 'relaxation response' (Benson 1976). Interestingly, meditation is also being tried as a means of reducing chronic pain and alleviating the distress of chronic disease. John Kabat-Zinn, a doctor at Johns Hopkins, has worked with patients who have exhausted other alternatives. Even when participants had no prior experience with meditation and were initially sceptical of its value, the majority found that four weeks of training produced significant improvement in their overall condition (Kabat-Zinn *et al.* 1985).

One interesting area of study has been changes in vital body functions like heart rate and breathing. For many years, it was assumed that such functions could not be deliberately altered or controlled. However, more recent research has led to modification of our theoretical understanding (see 'Autonomic Conditioning and Biofeedback' in Chapter 3). One of the first studies to examine this issue scientifically was done by psychologist Neal Miller. Using an airtight chamber and sophisticated monitoring equipment, he found that a yogi (a practitioner of yoga) was able to control heart rate, breathing and other metabolic processes to a degree previously assumed to be impossible. Zen masters and practitioners of TM have also shown changes in these measures. Such demonstrations indicate that meditation as a mental state can in fact have physical effects.

In recent years, as research has advanced, meditation has achieved more general recognition and acceptance. Clinics at a number of schools and hospitals have been seeking new ways to apply meditative techniques in medical treatment (e.g. Borysenko 1990). Limitations do exist, however, in terms of both our knowledge and the possible impact of meditation on bodily processes. As yet, there have been no studies of experienced practitioners which attempt to separate the effects of meditation from other factors such as diet and general lifestyle. In addition, we have very little understanding of individual differences in susceptibility (as found in Kabat-Zinn's work). With time and more research, we may increase our understanding of these issues.

Overall, the evidence on meditation supports the idea that states of awareness can be consciously altered, and that the effects of such changes can be measured physically. This has great significance in expanding our theoretical understanding of the interactions between mind and body. At the same time, the results point towards a whole new domain: if meditation can reduce the negative effects of stress, is it possible that bodily processes can be consciously influenced in other positive ways? The prospect of such possibilities has opened a whole new area of research, whose limits are not yet known.

Medicine and the Mind

At first glance, the notion that individuals can influence their health by their thoughts or feelings seems bizarre. After all, we have grown up accepting a model of health in which disease processes are due to pathological agents – either invading germs, or defective cell processes. Surely such events have nothing to do with laughter or loneliness!

In fact, research today seems to point to a very different conception of health and healing. Consider some of the clues offered in the research considered already. While neural and hormonal pathways appear distinct, the two systems are also highly interrelated. Processes like chronic stress affect both systems – and also affect the immune system. Meditation in some ways appears to be the opposite of stress, with beneficial effects on body processes. At the same time, these effects are fairly diffuse, and certainly don't adequately explain how mental states could affect the course of disease.

Still, the possibility of mental states affecting the course of medical treatment has a long, if unconventional, history. Every doctor can tell stories about patients who have recovered despite an unfavourable prognosis, or conversely, of patients who *should* have survived, but died. Traditionally, if they spoke of such cases at all, doctors referred to 'the will to live' or similar phrases. One such case has become well-known. In the 1970s, Norman Cousins, the long-time editor of *Saturday Review* magazine in the United States, was diagnosed with Hodgkin's disease, a form of cancer which attacks the immune system. His doctors were pessimistic about the outcome, but Cousins decided that giving up would only hasten his end. So while treatment (chemotherapy, etc.) was in progress, he embarked on a determined programme to bolster his spirits; perhaps the best-known aspect of his plan involved viewing classic comedy films in his hospital room. In the end, Cousins recovered. Although he was grateful to his doctors for their treatment, he was also convinced that, in the old phrase, laughter is truly the best medicine. As a result, he embarked on a quest to both document this belief, and to understand the processes involved (Cousins 1989).

placebo effect a phenomenon whereby inert substances labelled as drugs (such as a painkiller) produce effects similar to the real drug

psychoimmunology the study of mental states and their effect on health, as expressed through the functions of the immune system; sometimes referred to as psychoneuroimmunology

At the time of his recovery, Cousins' ideas were widely dismissed as delusional or, at best, a type of **placebo effect**, an effect which refers to the phenomenon of inert substances labelled as drugs (e.g. a painkiller) producing effects similar to the real drug (this in itself is something of a medical puzzle!). Then, as new discoveries were made about the functioning of the immune system, new theories and data began to emerge. Today, the study of mental states and their effect on health is referred to as **psychoimmunology** (or sometimes psychoneuro-immunology). Just as research led to recognition of the interrelations between the nervous system and the endocrine system, so too there is a new awareness of the relationship of both of these to the functioning of the immune system.

Psychoimmunology is a fast-developing field, and it is impossible to summarize all of the current research, but a few examples can help to clarify the direction in which the field is moving (for general reviews, see Cousins 1989; Ornstein and Swencionis 1990). A variety of life events have been identified as measurably suppressing the immune system, including the death of a loved one or marital conflict (Maier and Laudenslager 1985; Solomon 1990). As noted in discussing stress, it has long been known that high stress levels increase the likelihood of disease (recall Holmes and Rahe); the more recent research suggests that a wide range of social environmental factors may do so, and that the underlying linkage is suppression of immune functions. On the positive side, patients recovering from heart attacks progress faster if they have a pet for company (Cousins 1989). The question is, how do such circumstances get translated into immune responses?

While Hans Selye correctly noted that chronic stress resulted in deterioration of the immune system in experimental animals, he did not know the precise mechanism. Today, advances in biochemical techniques are helping to provide answers. One crucial clue seems to be the role of neuropeptides, particularly the 'natural opiates' called endorphins. As noted earlier, neuropeptides play a role in both the nervous system and as hormones. Endorphins serve as natural pain-killers in the brain, and receptors for them have been identified at a number of sites, particularly in the brainstem. Interestingly, recent studies have shown that a number of types of immune cells, collectively called *monocytes*, also have receptors for endorphins, and that the endorphins play a role in regulating the activity of the immune cells (Maier and Laudenslager 1985; Pert 1990). At a higher level, there is evidence of interactions between the hypothalamus (involved in the 'fight or flight' response, and probably meditation) and the immune system. While many details remain to be clarified, the notion of mental states affecting health is no longer a delusion or fantasy.

At the same time, one must be cautious about drawing conclusions based on the available research. While mental states may play a role in health, none of the researchers involved is suggesting abandoning conventional medical treatment. If anything, the implication seems to be that doctor–patient relationships are more important than ever to effective health care: a good 'bedside manner', for some years overlooked in the pressure to keep up with medical technology, becomes once more a powerful adjunct to medical treatment. A second concern was raised by Marcia Angell, editor of the *New England Journal of Medicine*: in the absence of compelling evidence, telling patients (particularly those with terminal illnesses) that their attitudes and behaviour produced their condition is adding an unjustified burden of guilt on those already afflicted (Angell 1985). Cancer, for example, may arise despite 'positive thinking', since other factors are clearly involved (including genetic factors and environmental hazards). Regardless of what future research on psychoimmunology reveals, the multifaceted nature of health is unlikely to change. What is likely to change, however, is the concept that individuals must be passive in the face of illness.

From the point of view of psychology, the research on psychoimmunology adds a further dimension to our understanding of the relationship between mind and body. In some ways, it brings us full circle from where we started this chapter. We have seen how processes in the body affect our mental state, and in turn how mental processes can affect the body. Obviously, many questions remain, but the basic assumption of the materialists – that 'mind' and 'body' are different ways of talking about the same thing – seems relatively secure. While we may never be able to do away with one or the other term, research on mind–body issues has led to exciting discoveries about the way we function. In the end, it is the advances in our understanding that justify the biological approach.

Still, there is one element of our biological nature that has not been discussed. The human brain is an incredibly complex structure, unparalleled (so far as we know) in the universe. The body, too, with its highly integrated systems, is a wondrous thing. How did it arise? How do nerve cells grow and develop into the specialized networks that make up the brain? What determines the variability found between individuals – not just in height or eye colour, but also in the brain (Edelman 1992)? To try to answer such questions, we must look at another aspect of the biological approach – the study of heredity.

For further consideration

Do you have a pet (e.g. a cat or dog)? In terms of the current research on psychoimmunology, discuss why recovery from heart attacks is enhanced by having a pet.

The Hereditary Basis of Behaviour

In the 1970s, a group of researchers announced that they had found a genetic pattern associated with criminal behaviour. They had discovered that certain men were born with an extra Y chromosome; individuals with the resulting XYY pattern, the researchers argued, tended to become criminals. This assertion led to great controversy, both among researchers and the general public. If someone could be identified at birth as a potential criminal, advocates argued, they could be closely watched, or even locked up before they could cause harm. Opponents questioned both the evidence and the moral principle of prejudging guilt. Soon, other researchers discovered that many XYY men existed who had no apparent history of criminal actions. Given this and other contrary evidence, the XYY-criminality theory was cast into doubt, and the controversy died (Gould

1981). Still, it is significant that, throughout the debate, no-one really questioned the underlying assumption that behaviour *could* be inherited.

The concept of inherited traits has become so widely known and accepted that it is difficult for us to recognize its impact on our thinking. Yet it is not much more than a hundred years since Charles Darwin suggested that variations could be passed on from one generation to another. 'Like father, like son', we say – but how *much* like, we barely realize. Even Darwin, although he believed in the phenomenon of inheritance, had no clue as to how heredity actually functioned.

Darwin's ideas about inheritance between generations were closely linked to another concept, **evolution**. He recognized that variations existed within a species, and believed that such traits could be transmitted from parents to offspring. In turn, he believed that the same process which produces variations within a species *also* produces the variations which are ultimately labelled as different species. Thus, all species are ultimately related through the mechanism of evolution. This concept of continuity between species was contentious in Darwin's day (and sometimes still is), but it has significantly influenced the way we view behaviour. For example, one can use comparisons of human behaviour and physiology to that of other species as a tool for improving our understanding (chimpanzees, for example, are genetically very similar to humans). This is not to say that chimpanzee studies, or those involving other species, are a substitute for research on humans. Rather, comparisons of similarities and differences can lead us to new questions. In a similar vein, work by palaeoanthropologists helps us to understand the ancestors of humanity. Ultimately, the goal of such studies is not to diminish the wonder of human existence, but to better understand and appreciate who and what we are.

These concepts – *heredity* and *evolution* – have been significant in improving our knowledge of human behaviour. As we shall discuss, the pace of research in genetics in particular has been accelerating tremendously in the past few years, and no account can be fully current. However, an understanding of the foundations and assumptions underlying current research can help us to better understand the significance of what George Beadle, a Nobel laureate in genetics, has called 'the language of life' (Beadle and Beadle 1966).

evolution a theory to account for the development of species diversity; while various theories have been proposed, Darwin's theory based on natural selection is the most broadly recognized

Basic Mechanisms of Heredity

The word 'genetics' was coined by the English biologist William Bateson. In an article published in 1902, he urged his fellow researchers to look at the causes of inherited resemblances and differences, to understand 'the essential process by which the likeness of the parent is transmitted to the offspring'. At first, Bateson drew little response. For many years, the study of genetics was considered a bit eccentric, being based on taking inventories, raising generations of fruit flies, keeping animal pedigrees, and talking about concepts like 'dominance', 'unit characters' and 'ratios'. At the same time, chemists were working on the chemical structures of enzymes and other organic chemicals. While it took many years before they realized it, both groups were working on the same problem. Ultimately, the result was the breaking of 'the code of life', embodied in the chemical structure of genes. The **gene** came to be recognized as the basic unit of heredity, made up of strings of 'building blocks' called amino acids.

gene the basic unit of heredity, made up of strings of 'building blocks' called amino acids; it is estimated that humans possess about 100,000 different genes, each regulating a different process

Altogether, it is estimated that humans possess about 100,000 different genes, each regulating a different process. At present, only about 1 per cent have been identified, but an international research effort called the Human Genome Project is seeking to map the entire structure within the next several years (Lee 1991). Today, genetics research often take place at the molecular level, but the beginnings were far less sophisticated.

What is perhaps most fascinating about the development of genetics is that the early population geneticists (like Bateson) came to a clear understanding of the basic properties of genetic inheritance *without* any knowledge of the underlying biochemistry. Consider the following: the structure of DNA, which holds the basic structure of chromosomes of which genes are a part, was deciphered by James Watson and Francis Crick in 1953. However, it took roughly another *twenty* years before anyone isolated a single gene! Clearly, the key to heredity is the gene; clearly, too, the basic concepts of inheritance can be largely understood without any direct reference to the biochemical processes involved. In fact, the basic patterns of inheritance were actually worked out over a hundred years before the first gene was directly identified.

In the 1860s, Gregor Mendel was living as a monk in an Austrian monastery. The son of a farmer, he became interested in problems of plant hybridization (the crossing of different strains to produce new varieties). Working with garden peas, he set up an experimental plot to see if he could determine some orderly principles underlying the results of hybridization. As it turns out, he was wrong on many details, but correct in the general outline. Mendel discovered that an inherited characteristic passed from parent to offspring. (Mendel, of course, did not know that it was a *chemical* process, but he knew there must be a mechanism.) In any individual, this code is made up of two genes, forming a pair. When reproduction takes place, the gene pair is split, so that one parent contributes only one gene to the offspring; the other member of the offspring's gene pair comes from the other parent. Thus, the offspring carries genetic information from both parents.

As time went on, it was discovered that the mechanism of splitting and recombining depends on the chromosomes. Composed of double strands of DNA and proteins, **chromosomes** are the large-scale structures of heredity, containing the genes. In humans, there are twenty-three pairs of chromosomes, each holding thousands of genes, like pearls on a necklace. Because each of the twenty-three pairs of chromosomes splits and recombines independently of the others during reproduction, there are 2^{23} possible chromosome combinations from each parent, meaning that genetic recombination provides for almost limitless variety. (With over 8.4 million combinations from a single set of parents, the likelihood of even two siblings having identical sets of chromosomes is very small.) The result is that genetic mechanisms provide a basis for variability, as well as similarity, from parent to offspring.

The genetic code which an individual carries in the DNA of their cells is called their **genotype**. Genes function in pairs, and the gene-pair members for particular characteristics (e.g. blood type, eye colour) come in several variants, called *alleles*. Each allele represents the chemical code for a single variation. For example, basic blood types in people are based on three alleles, representing A, B and O. Normally, for a characteristic based on a single gene (i.e. one pair, called **unigenic** or Mendelian **inheritance**), one allele, called the *dominant* allele,

chromosomes thread-like genetic structures composed of double strands of DNA and proteins, containing the genes; in humans, there are twenty-three pairs of chromosomes

genotype the genetic code which an individual carries in the DNA of their cells

unigenic inheritance genetic transmission which is dependent on the action of a single pair of genes; also called Mendelian inheritance, in recognition of Gregor Mendel's pioneering work

MENDELIAN (UNIGENIC) INHERITANCE APPLIED TO EYE COLOUR

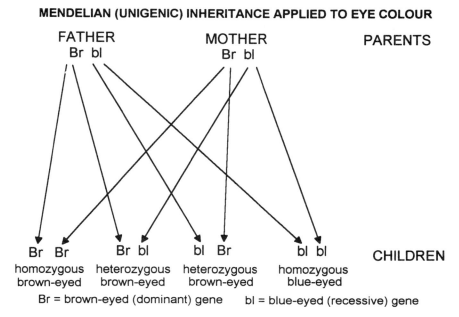

Fig. 2.10 **Unigenic inheritance** As discussed in the text, observed characteristics like eye colour depend on the individual's genetic make-up, inherited from the parents. If both parents are heterozygous brown-eyed, then the unigenic model says there is a 25 per cent chance of any child being homozygous blue-eyed, as the combinations suggest.

will be expressed (i.e. active) whenever it occurs in the gene pair. Other alleles will only be expressed (i.e. active, and therefore observable in the individual) if both members of the gene pair are the same. Because they are not as influential as the dominant form, these genes are called *recessive* alleles. For eye colour, brown is the dominant form, while blue is recessive (see Fig. 2.10). Thus, the observed form of the characteristic depends upon what pairing of dominant and/ or recessive alleles of the gene is present. (*Note*: this description is based on the classical model of unigenic inheritance; while it works very well for the vast majority of cases, research in recent years has indicated ways in which it over-simplifies, and hence occasionally leads to faulty predictions. For the purpose of understanding the basics of heredity, these subtleties are not critical.)

One must distinguish between the genotype, defined by the genes, and the *observed* characteristics of the individual, called the **phenotype**. One reason for this distinction has already been noted: a person may possess a recessive gene for blue eyes, but it will not be expressed if they also have a dominant gene for brown eyes. In terms of appearance, they would seem no different than a person with two brown genes. Hence, one cannot always determine the genotype simply by observing the phenotypic appearance.

More importantly, genes only determine a *potential* for a characteristic, which must then be realized through a long sequence of biochemical processes. Along the way, other factors, including environmental influences, may intervene. For example, an individual may be born with phenylketonuria (PKU), a metabolic

phenotype the observed characteristics of the individual, based on the combination of genetic expression and environmental influences disorder based on a recessive gene. If untreated, it can result in severe mental retardation. However, appropriate medical treatment and dietary restrictions can compensate if the disorder is detected early, and the individual need never suffer the effects. Depending on the particular characteristic, the amount of influence the environment has differs. The genetic code for most aspects of our physical structure is relatively rigid, for instance dictating the location of the eyes. For traits related to behaviour, such as intelligence, the reverse may be true – environment may play a decisive role. Consequently, one cannot easily generalize about genetic expression, except to note that the observed characteristics of an individual (the phenotype) is based on a combination of genotype and environmental influences. For psychologists, this is one of the most important aspects of heredity.

To summarize thus far, inheritance of characteristics is based on a chemical code carried by genes, which are themselves carried by the chromosomes. Genes function in pairs, and various forms (alleles) of the gene for a characteristic exist. The recombination of genes from parents to offspring provides a basis for genetic variability within families. Ultimately, though, the observed characteristics of an individual depend on the interaction of genetic and environmental factors. As we will discuss, determining the relative role of these factors in behaviour has been one of the major concerns of psychologists studying heredity.

One other issue needs to be considered in relation to genetic mechanisms – that is, the origin of new traits. Although recombination provides for considerable variation, it does not provide for the creation of any *new* traits. Thus, if heredity functioned only in the way described above, there would be no possibility of evolution. Darwin recognized this, even without knowing anything about the basis of hereditary mechanisms. Along with the normal sequence of biochemical processes, it is possible for new gene forms, called **mutations**, to occur. Mutations are very rare, happening perhaps once in a million times. However, when they do occur, by whatever random process, a new trait may appear. Again, Darwin was alert to the significance of such events, which he expressed in the law of natural selection: any new trait which offers an advantage in terms of survival will tend to be passed on (because the individual is more likely to survive to reproduce). Conversely, any trait which weakens the ability to survive will normally disappear (if the individual dies before reproducing). Today, this is often referred to as 'survival of the fittest'. Recently, the possibility of a second mechanism for genetic variation has been identified – that is, the transfer of genes between different species (Amábile-Cuevas and Chicurel 1993). Whether by mutation or other mechanism, the emergence of new traits due to genetic variation is the basis of *evolution*, the development of species diversity. From a psychological point of view, this is significant, because it indicates that the development of human characteristics has a long history. The structure of our brain is linked to the structure of the brains of other species. In the same way, hands are related to flippers and wings. Darwin recognized these connections, but also knew that his contemporaries would not be likely to accept it. So in his first book, *The Origin of Species*, he carefully avoided any mention of *human* evolution (Darwin 1859). Only in his later writings did he become more explicit.

Heredity, then, is an important key to understanding behaviour. To the extent that it provides the organizational code for the developing embryo, it underlies

mutation a change in the genetic material of a cell; while rare, mutations can result in new characteristics which may be transmitted to descendants of the original cell all that we have talked about in terms of physiological processes. Through evolution, humans have developed the characteristics and abilities that distinguish us from other species. The cortex of our brains, which in many respects seems more highly developed than in other species, has played an important part in those gains. At the same time, the environment, through the effects of experience, has a significant impact on our cortex. What we are depends on both our genotype and our environment. For psychologists, the major challenge is to understand precisely how these two factors interact.

Nature and Nurture in Behaviour

Of all the disputes in psychology, perhaps the most contentious has been that concerning the relative importance of heredity and experience. Long before Mendel formed his genetic theory, people had an intuitive belief that something like heredity existed. Plato, for example, talked about knowledge being inborn or 'native' to the person, rather than being acquired through experience. This led to the view of knowledge and behaviour called **nativism**, the belief that characteristics are innate (Weimer 1973).

However, not everyone has taken this viewpoint. Other thinkers have maintained that all newborn babies are basically alike, and only develop unique characteristics as a result of differing experiences. John Locke, an English philosopher, expressed this view in 1690, saying the mind at birth is like a blank paper, on which experience is gradually written (Locke 1690). This view, which emphasizes the importance of environmental influences, is often called **empiricism**.

The philosophical split between nativism and empiricism has led to arguments about the relative importance of heredity ('nature') and environmental factors ('nurture') in various aspects of human functioning. Advances in our knowledge of genetics have made it possible to identify specific genes related to a variety of disorders, such as Huntington's disease and Tay-Sachs disease (both disorders affect the nervous system). With behaviour, the situation is more complex, in part because behavioural traits are likely influenced by a variety of genes, rather than a single gene as in the cases above. Intelligence, for example, is a characteristic for which the relative contributions of nature and nurture are still being assessed. Similarly, the role of heredity in mental disorders like schizophrenia is still not well understood. With such complex aspects of behaviour, the techniques involved in 'mapping' genes may prove of limited help for some time to come. Consequently, the study of genetic influences on behaviour typically involves methods familiar to traditional population genetics – tracing observed traits among related individuals.

Ideally, one would like to have total control of both genetic and environmental factors, so that they could be studied experimentally. Although this is impossible both technically and ethically, one can often approximate the ideal by doing concordance studies. **Concordance** (literally, 'agreement') studies examine characteristics of individuals whose genetic relationship is known. In these studies, *identical twins* are the preferred subjects, because they come from the same fertilized egg, and therefore have the same genetic make-up. (*Fraternal twins*, by contrast, are conceived at the same time, but because they come from

nativism the philosophical view, held by Plato and others, that knowledge and behaviour are innate in origin

empiricism the philosophical position, first attributed to John Locke, that all knowledge is based on experience; hence, the basis of the view that behaviour is learned

concordance a technique for studying inheritance by examining characteristics of individuals whose genetic relationship is known separately fertilized eggs, they are genetically no more alike than any two siblings.) Because of the similar genetic make-up of identical twins, if a particular trait is controlled by the genes, then the twins should develop similarly, whether they are raised together or in different settings. Conversely, if environment plays the major role in a trait, then the degree of similarity between identical twins should depend on how they were raised: if raised in the same family, they should show some similarities, as do any siblings. If raised separately, however (e.g. in adoptive families), identical twins should be more like members of their adoptive families than like each other. Concordance studies also examine other genetic links, such as fraternal twins or other siblings, or parent–child comparisons. In each case, the goal is to measure behavioural similarities in accordance with what would be expected based on the degree of genetic similarity (for example, on average, any child shares 50 per cent of their genes with each parent).

Unfortunately, although the concept of concordance is fairly straightforward, the methodology is not as clear-cut as it may seem. Although identical twins are the preferred group, such twins are quite rare, and finding cases where they have been separated at an early age (due to parental death, family break-ups, etc.) are rarer still. In addition, the fact of separation may make it difficult to locate both twins at a later time. (In some cases of separation in infancy followed by adoption, the children are not informed that they have a twin.) When separated twins *are* located, the degree of separation can be hard to assess. In one case, a researcher described twins as 'separated' who had been separated in name only – one twin was raised by the parents and the other by a maiden aunt living only one hundred yards away (Shields 1962). Recently, by accessing adoption records, a group at the University of Minnesota has been able to identify a sizeable group of identical twins separated near birth (Bouchard *et al.* 1990). Determining early history is a crucial factor to the validity of concordance studies, because when twins actually have contact despite living under different roofs, it cannot be claimed that the environments are truly different. Even when twins are separated at birth and raised separately, they still share the same prenatal environment in the mother's womb. (In this regard, fraternal twins are likely to be more alike than other siblings, since they are conceived and born at the same time.) Consequently, it is a practical impossibility to find identical twins who have grown up in completely different environments.

At the other end of the scale from looking at individuals with identical genotypes is the idea of studying two individuals (regardless of genotype) who have grown up in identical environments. Unfortunately, this is equally tricky. Twins raised in the same family appear, superficially, to meet this criterion because both prenatal and postnatal circumstances are shared. However, even when two children grow up in the same family, there is no guarantee that they will have identical experiences, or be treated in exactly the same way. This becomes especially clear when one considers fraternal twins of different sexes. Regardless of their shared prenatal environment, they are likely to encounter increasingly different circumstances as time goes on, due to social factors.

In analysing the results of concordance studies, researchers employ a variety of statistical procedures, most of which are related to correlations. One common measure which has been used to try to estimate the relative importance of heredity versus environment for specific traits is the **heritability index**. The heritability index looks at the overall variability in a set of data (e.g. IQ scores for sets of

heritability index a measure of the influence of heredity within a group based on comparing the estimated genetic variability for the particular characteristic to the overall variability within the group twins), and then attempts to determine what proportion of the overall variance is due to genetic variability within the group observed. Mathematically, it can be expressed as a ratio:

$$H\ (\text{heritability}) = \frac{\text{genetic variability}}{\text{total variability}}$$

where total variability = (genetic variability + environmental variability).

It should be noted that this ratio is *only* meaningful when applied to a *group*; it is impossible to calculate a heritability index for a single individual. Thus, while one might conclude that within a particular group, 70 per cent of the observed variations in IQ are due to genetic differences, one *cannot* say the same for any single person in the group. In addition, the calculated result can only be properly applied to the group observed, since it depends on the actual values of genetic and environmental variability. It is interesting to note what happens to heritability ratios under hypothetical circumstances. If, for example, one could clone individuals (create a group of genetic duplicates), then heritability would be *zero*, since there would be no genetic variability. On the other hand, in an imaginary world where everyone was raised in an identical environment, all observed differences would be related to genetic differences, and so heritability would be 100 per cent. The paradox that this leads to is as follows: while those who believe in a democratic society would like to see everyone receive equal environmental circumstances, the consequences of such actions would be to *increase* differences due to hereditary factors! And creating a 'brave new world' of genetic duplicates would simply emphasize any *environmental* differences! Ironically, in each case, the results are likely to be exactly *opposite* to what advocates of the particular approach would desire (for a further discussion of current research results, see Chapter 7).

Despite the difficulties of conducting rigorous studies, concordance research has added to our knowledge of the role of nature and nurture in development. At one time, the tendency was to ask whether a characteristic was due to heredity *or* environment, implying that the answer must be one or the other. Today, we recognize that the picture is more complex, at least with regard to most forms of behaviour. Modern psychologists largely accept an interactionist view, which suggests that genetic and environmental influences are interwoven in determining the final shape of behaviour. In this sense, the answer to the question 'Is it nature or nurture?' is actually, 'Both'.

For further consideration

Suppose that scientists created a clone (genetic duplicate) of you. Would you expect it to be identical to you when grown? What does your response tell you about your own view of the nature–nurture issue?

Conclusion

The biological approach is oriented towards understanding the physiological and genetic basis of our behaviour. Within psychology, it is the only approach which tries to explain behaviour in terms of the workings of the physical system. By contrast, consider psychoanalysis (see Chapter 5). Although Freud was trained in neurology, and believed that ultimately the system was biologically based, psychoanalysis uses concepts which are purely psychological, not physiological. Behaviourism (see Chapter 3) is even more extreme, regarding the body as a black box, whose workings are neither known nor relevant to psychological theory. Hence, the biological approach is alone in emphasizing the physical system.

The biological approach, by its nature, focuses on the internal factors associated with physiology and genetics. As important as these processes are in understanding behaviour, they are not the only source of influences. Each individual's behaviour represents a unique combination of genetic factors (*heredity*) and life experiences (*environment*). While the biological approach acknowledges the role of environmental factors such as stressors, it does not place primary emphasis on these factors, or the impact they can have on behaviour. Rather, the study of environmental influences is the focus of other approaches, such as behaviourism.

Over two hundred years ago, Julien de La Mettrie made the assumption that the mind has its physical basis in the brain. In the time since, this concept of *materialism* has gained increasing acceptance. Today, as our understanding of physiological processes increases, it seems more and more evident that mind and body *are* fundamentally linked. This is not to suggest that all the questions, such as the nature of consciousness, have been fully answered; in part, 'mind' and 'brain' may represent different levels of description, and hence the issue may never be completely reconciled. Still, our knowledge is increasing, and perhaps most significantly, the insights are being applied – in medicine, in business and in everyday activities. The concept of stress has become widely known, as have methods for coping with it. The use of psychoactive drugs has radically altered the treatment of mental disorders, with the number of hospitalized patients in the United States being more than halved between 1955 and 1971. Advances in areas like psychoimmunology may have even greater impact in the future.

At the same time, problems remain. One of the greatest challenges concerns the complexity of the physiological system. There are approximately *ten billion* neurons in the cortex of the brain alone, which are interconnected in manifold ways. In addition, there are countless chemical interactions involving *neurotransmitters*, *hormones* and *neuropeptides*, plus environmental influences. This complexity makes achieving a complete understanding of the processes affecting behaviour a daunting goal. Even on a more limited scale, the ways in which factors interact make it difficult to make specific statements about one factor (e.g. stress as a cause of heart attacks) in the absence of knowledge about other factors (e.g. exercise and family history). These restrictions lead us to recognize that the picture is not yet complete. The parts still to be seen seem certain to be at least as exciting as those already known.

Chapter Summary

◆ The biological approach is based on the assumption of *materialism*, which asserts that all behaviour has a physiological basis.

♦ The two primary concerns of the biological approach are the workings of the nervous system, and the role of heredity in behaviour.

♦ The nervous system is composed of billions of individual nerve cells called *neurons*; the most significant component of the nervous system is the *brain*.

♦ Perhaps the most challenging question in the study of the brain is the understanding of the nature of consciousness, and the relationship between the *mind* and the brain.

♦ The effects of the body on the mind have been studied in various ways, including the effects of psychoactive *drugs*, the use of electrical stimulation of the brain (*ESB*) and the effects of severing the corpus callosum (*split brain*).

♦ The influence of mental processes on the body has been examined in terms of the effects of *stress* and *meditation*; more recently, researchers have begun to look at how mental states affect the immune system (*psychoimmunology*).

♦ The study of heredity involves both the direct study of *genes* and how they function, and also looking at interactions between heredity and environment by the study of twins and other groups who have an identifiable genetic relationship (*concordance*).

Key Terms and Concepts

brainstem	localization of function
central nervous system (CNS)	materialism
cerebral dominance	meditation
chromosome	nativism
concordance	nerve impulse
cortex	neuron
electrical stimulation of the brain (ESB)	neuropeptide
empiricism	neurotransmitters
endocrine glands	phenotype
gene	psychoactive drug
genotype	psychoimmunology
heredity	stress
hormone	synapse
limbic system	

Suggestions for Further Reading

Colin Blakemore's *Mechanisms of the Mind* provides a very readable and entertaining history of research on the brain. For a more current overview, see the September 1992 issue of *Scientific American*, which is entirely devoted to the brain. To gain an appreciation of the complexities which doctors and researchers face, read *The Man Who Mistook His Wife for a Hat*, by Oliver Sacks, a neurologist who is both knowledgeable and wise.

Bright Air, Brilliant Fire, by Nobel biologist Gerald Edelman, is a complex book which presents an interesting, if idiosyncratic, view of how physiology and genetics are converging in their understanding of the nervous system.

The Stress of Life is probably the best of Selye's accounts of stress intended for the general reader.

For readers interested in the fast-developing area of psychoimmunology, the most sophisticated overview is provided by Ornstein and Swencionis in *The Healing Brain: A Scientific Reader*. Those seeking a simpler account may prefer Norman Cousins' *Head First: The Biology of Hope*, or Bill Moyers' *Healing and the Mind*, which was written to accompany a US Public Broadcasting Service (PBS) television series.

The awesome promise, and also potential problems, of our increasing knowledge of genetics is knowledgeably presented in Lee's *The Human Genome Project: Cracking the Genetic Code of Life*.

3 The Behaviourist Approach

Mind Doesn't Matter

Psychologist Israel Goldiamond has written a fascinating account of what it is like to suffer from spinal injury (Goldiamond 1973). As a result of a car accident, he spent several months in hospital undergoing treatment. During that period, he had the opportunity to observe his own behaviour, and that of other patients. At one point, he shared a room with a man who had suffered brain damage. This patient was often disoriented, urinating on walls and muttering about 'what the hell am I doing in Panama?' (he wasn't).

Thus far, this story appears unremarkable – after all, we have spent the last chapter exploring how the brain controls behaviour. Yet, rather than focusing on the physiological processes that underlay the brain-damaged man's behaviour, Goldiamond examined the environmental context. He noted, for example, that the man did not act oddly in the hospital cafeteria, a fact which the staff had overlooked. Goldiamond accounted for this by noting that the features of cafeterias are fairly universal, while those of a rehabilitation hospital are not familiar to most people. Hence, the man was only disoriented when he was in an unfamiliar setting. Furthermore, the hospital was located on a large lake, and the patient's room overlooked a naval pier, perhaps accounting for his questions about Panama. Goldiamond suggested that the man's urinating inappropriately could be dealt with by rewarding him with cigarettes for urinating properly – in effect, controlling the behaviour by means of an external incentive. As anticipated, the technique worked.

The point of this story is to show that looking at the brain is not always the best way to understand behaviour. Goldiamond, like other behaviourists, preferred to look at the role the environment plays in behaviour. There is no question that the man in the story had suffered brain damage. But it is equally clear that his behaviour could not be fully understood by looking *only* at the brain damage. In one sense, by placing such a heavy emphasis on *internal* events, the biological approach tends to give too little attention to the *external* context of behaviour – that is, the environment in which behaviour occurs. For example, using drugs to treat anxiety can lead to ignoring the circumstances which trigger the anxiety. In this chapter, we will turn to a consideration of the external influences on behaviour, as seen from the behaviourist perspective.

Introduction

learning a change in behaviour which occurs as the result of experience

The *behaviourist approach* emphasizes the role of environmental stimuli in determining the way we act. In large measure, this means focusing on **learning** – changes in behaviour which occur as the result of experience. Behaviourists have added considerably to our understanding of learning through the study of what is called classical and operant conditioning, but before examining what has been discovered, let us look àt the basic assumptions and methods which distinguish behaviourism from the other approaches.

As with all approaches, the choice of focus is one of the factors which gives behaviourism its uniqueness. In this case, the behaviourist approach is commonly distinguished by its emphasis on the relationship between observable behaviour (*responses*) and environmental events (*stimuli*). Consider the simple interaction involved when a child reaches out towards a glowing fire, and then quickly draws back from the heat: first, the stimulus of the sparkling flame attracts their attention, so that they move their hand forward (stimulus of fire leads to response of reaching). Then, the heat of the fire leads to a reflexive withdrawal (stimulus of heat leads to withdrawal response). This, in turn, might lead the child to throw water on the fire, or take some other action. Thus, from the behaviourist perspective, human experience can be understood in terms of the interrelations between stimuli and responses.

Basic Assumptions of Behaviourism

While clearly differing from the biological approach in the kinds of data it emphasizes, the behavioural approach is also distinctive in terms of its basic assumptions, which are closely related to its historical origins. At the turn of the century, psychologists tended to emphasize either the experimental study of physiological processes, or the introspective analysis of experience (see Chapter 1 for a review). Physiological research was hampered by the available technology for research, and introspectionism frequently foundered on problems of subjectivity. William James argued that psychologists should focus on how behaviour relates to its purpose (called *functionalism*), but he was often better at framing the issues than at doing research to solve them. Thus, none of the available methods was achieving unequivocal success. It was against this backdrop that behaviourism arose. (It should be noted that 'behaviourism', like other approaches, can refer to a number of theories, each with points of uniqueness; however, at the risk of doing minor violence to the views of any one researcher, it is possible to seek some common elements within the approach.)

While the temptation in discussing the behaviourist approach is to emphasize the type of data collected (the observable behaviours which give the approach its name), doing so ignores the broader assumptions which underlie the approach. The most fundamental of these is the scientific principle of parsimony. Sometimes called 'Occam's razor' after the English philosopher who first proposed it, **parsimony** emphasizes seeking the simplest possible explanation for any event. If, for example, one can explain a person's eating a pastry without referring to a non-observable concept like 'hunger' or 'oral personality', then parsimony says one should avoid using such concepts. Thus, behaviourists reacted against introspectionism in part because it seemed to invoke too many vague concepts. Instead, behaviourism placed a heavy emphasis on the use of *operational definitions* (defining concepts in terms of observable events), and this led naturally to the focus on 'stimuli' and 'responses' (for further discussion of operational definitions, refer back to Chapter 1).

A second assumption of the behaviourist approach relates to the mechanism for behavioural change. Like functionalism, behaviourism emphasizes trying to understand the conditions under which behaviour occurs: When does a particular behaviour occur? What conditions lead to it? What changes in the environment result from it? Since relatively few behaviours in human beings are genetically programmed, this leads to a focus on the role of experience, which is expressed through learning. It is easy to say that the way we act depends on our past experiences, but just *how* does learning occur? Since the time of Aristotle, the basic explanation has been that we learn by *association* – that is, by forming connections between ideas and/or events. This concept of **associationism**, which was also favoured by such English philosophers as David Hume and J.S. Mill, has had a fundamental influence on psychology, particularly for the behaviourists. As we shall see, behaviourist theories are essentially theories of how associations form in behaviour.

The third influence which should be acknowledged is the notion of pragmatism. First coined by the American philosopher C.S. Peirce in 1878, **pragmatism** stresses the purpose of thought and behaviour, and emphasizes examining their consequences as a means of determining their significance. Pragmatism influenced William James in his notion of functionalism, but it can be argued that both Peirce and James were reflecting the American cultural tradition of 'Yankee practicality', which values effectiveness over elegance; in other words, a good theory is one which has some practical value.

Taken together, parsimony, associationism and pragmatism formed the foundation from which behaviourism arose. Exactly how, and what the result has been for our understanding of psychology, will form the substance of this chapter.

parsimony in the philosophy of science, the principle that states one should always seek the simplest possible explanation for any event

associationism the doctrine, supported by Aristotle, Hume and others, that mental processes, particularly learning, are based on forming connections between ideas and/or events

pragmatism a philosophical doctrine developed by C.S. Peirce, which argues that the significance of thoughts and behaviour can be found by examining their consequences

Edwin Lynn Thorndike

Edwin L. Thorndike (1874–1949) was born in Williamsburg, a small town in western Massachusetts. After receiving his bachelor's degree from Wesleyan University, he went to Harvard University to study psychology under William James, but was forced to transfer to Columbia University because of financial difficulties. In the newly formed psychology department at Columbia, he studied under James McKeen Cattell, one of the most influential early American psychologists. For his research, he studied problem solving in animals, using a series of puzzle-like tasks (e.g. confining a cat in a box, from which it could release itself by pressing against a lever). His dissertation, published in 1898, had the rather cognitive-sounding title of 'Animal intelligence'. Thorndike is probably best known today for his 'law of effect', which foreshadowed Skinner's concept of reinforcement as a description of the role of consequences in learning. From 1899 he taught at Teachers College at Columbia, where he wrote prolifically on education as well as psychology. He died in New York at the age of seventy-five.

The Pioneers of Behaviourism

Just before the turn of the century, an American named Edwin L. Thorndike was studying for his PhD in the newly formed psychology department at Columbia University (he started at Harvard, under William James, but transferred for financial reasons). For his research, he studied problem-solving in animals, using a series of puzzle-like tasks (e.g. confining a cat in a box, from which it could release itself by pressing against a lever). His dissertation, published in 1898, had the rather cognitive-sounding title of 'Animal intelligence' (Thorndike 1898).

Thorndike's work was influential in many ways, but he is today perhaps best known for what he called 'the law of effect'. In trying to analyse the conditions under which the animals he studied changed their behaviour (i.e. learned), he focused on the relationship between a response and its consequences. Basically, the **law of effect** said that any response which leads to an outcome satisfying to the organism is likely to be repeated, and any response which leads to an unpleasant outcome is not likely to be repeated. This was a form of associationism, in that the organism (animal, person) was seen as making a connection between a response and its consequences. (This is technically called association by *contiguity*, in that it assumes the response and consequence must be closely linked in time and space.) While basically unoriginal – the idea that individuals respond to reward and punishment extends back to the Greeks – Thorndike's version could be said to differ in that *it was supported by experimental data* (Robinson 1979). By framing the issue in experimental (and therefore scientific) terms, Thorndike paved the way for the behaviouristic approach.

Thorndike's law of effect, while significant, was not without problems, in part because it was vague about what made something 'satisfying'. One way to resolve this was to seek physiologically oriented mechanisms for 'satisfaction'. However, given turn-of-the-century knowledge of physiology, this often required

law of effect a principle of learning proposed by Thorndike, which stated that any response which leads to an outcome satisfying to the organism is likely to be repeated, and any response which leads to an unpleasant outcome is not likely to be repeated resorting to non-observable concepts which violated the demands of parsimony. A more radical approach, pioneered by John B. Watson, was to pare theorizing to the bone, restricting theoretical descriptions to factors which could be observed and measured directly.

John B. Watson was both gifted and provocative. As a student at the University of Chicago, he initially trained in introspectionism, but found its approach to psychology excessively vague, especially in its emphasis on mental processes. He began working with animals, and completed his PhD in three years – at the time the youngest such graduate from the university. After teaching for only four years at Chicago, he was offered a full professorship at Johns Hopkins, and shortly after became chairman of the psychology department there – certainly remarkable career advancement!

Watson can only be described as zealous in promoting his ideas. Reading his major work (*Behaviourism*, 1930) today, one is struck by the scorn he heaps on William James and others, and by his willingness to test his ideas whenever possible (even using his own children). Confident that he was correct, he was willing to extend his claims even when he lacked experimental support, as in his famous remark, 'Give me a dozen healthy infants, well-formed, and my own specified world to bring them up in and I'll guarantee to take any one at random and train him to become any type of specialist I might select – doctor, lawyer, artist, merchant-chief and yes, even beggar-man and thief, regardless of his talents, penchants, tendencies, abilities, vocations, and race of his ancestors'. What is often omitted in this quotation is the statement which follows it: '*I am going beyond my facts and I admit it, but so have the advocates of the contrary* and they have been doing it for thousands of years' (Watson 1930: 104; emphasis added). In pursuing his ideas, Watson clearly did not shirk from confrontation. Later, while at Johns Hopkins University, he became interested in human sexual behaviour; when these activities (including participant observation) did not sit well with the prevailing moral views, he was finally dismissed. At this point, ever the pragmatist, he took a job with the J. Walter Thompson advertising firm, becoming perhaps the first psychologist to apply psychological theory to advertising and marketing! Not surprisingly, he did well in his new role, embarking on studies of consumer behaviour, writing psychology articles for the general public, and becoming a vice-president of the advertising firm in less than four years.

Watson's writings and ideas were a lever that moved the world. In the following decades, until the mid-1950s, behaviourism became the dominant force in psychology, particularly in North America. The irony is that while the general approach became highly influential, most researchers never accepted Watson's extreme position, which is sometimes called *radical behaviourism*. Even B.F. Skinner, the spiritual heir to Watson's work, has commented, 'A shortage of facts is always a problem in a new science, but in Watson's aggressive program in a field as vast as human behaviour it was especially damaging' (Skinner 1974: 6). The greatest impact can be traced in three central elements: (1) the emphasis on observable responses and environmental stimuli; (2) the rejection of mentalistic concepts not grounded in direct observation; and (3) the focus on learning and experience as central to the understanding of human behaviour. Some seventy years of research, both basic and applied, has demonstrated that in many ways we are indeed what we learn.

John B. Watson

John Broadus Watson (1878–1958) was the founder of behaviourism. After a brief exploration of the introspectionist approach at the University of Chicago, he continued under John Dewey and James Angell, two of the pioneers of the functionalist approach. Watson was both gifted and outspoken – two characteristics which played a major role in his career. He completed his PhD in only three years and began teaching at the University of Chicago; four years later, he was offered a full professorship in psychology at Johns Hopkins, and shortly after became chairman of the department. In 1913, he began publishing the first of a series of works which outlined his behaviourist approach, and which quickly gained him both fame and notoriety – his statement about shaping a healthy infant in any way desired (quoted in the text) is characteristic of his assertive style. While at Johns Hopkins, he met graduate student Rosalie Rayner, who became his second wife. After collaborating with Rayner on the case of 'little Albert', Watson became interested in human sexual behaviour; his activities in this regard (including participant observation) did not sit well with the prevailing moral views, and he was finally dismissed. At this point, he took a job with the J. Walter Thompson advertising firm, where he soon became a vice-president of marketing. Thus, Watson not only founded an entire approach to psychology, but also was perhaps the first psychologist to apply psychological theory to advertising and marketing! He died in New York at the age of eighty.

Behaviourism, as already noted, has many variants; indeed, some would say it is more appropriate to speak of the behaviouristic approach than the behaviourist approach. Even E.C. Tolman, often regarded as one of the founders of the *cognitive* approach, considered himself a 'behaviourist' (Tolman 1932). However, what all behaviourists share is an interest in how behaviour is learned, and an emphasis on explanations based on observable events. In this chapter, we will see how this approach has been applied to a variety of situations.

For further consideration

As noted, John B. Watson ended his career working in the field of marketing and advertising. As you consider the principles which follow, you might think about how they could be applied to advertising.

Stimuli and Responses

Behaviourism, by focusing on *observable* events, sets its own limits on what can be studied. Thoughts, feelings and other inner mental states cannot be studied empirically, and so have no place in behaviourist theory. Genetic variation, while presumably contributing to differences among individuals, is also largely inaccessible. By contrast, environmental conditions seem open to measurement and study.

Taken as a whole, the environment involves colours, shapes, smells, sounds and many other characteristics. Obviously, it is impossible in an everyday setting to measure every element of a typical environment. However, in most cases, this would be unnecessary, because there are many environmental elements that do not seem to enter our awareness, and consequently typically have little impact (recall the discussion of perceptual processes in Chapter 1). Nonetheless, behaviourists recognize that in order to study environmental influences on behaviour, one must be able to define rigorously the environmental characteristics involved in a situation. In practice, this means that research often involves limiting the complexity of the environment, particularly in laboratory studies. Second, it means that one must be able to define terms clearly. With regard to the environment, sights, sounds and smells are all considered examples of stimuli. A **stimulus** (often abbreviated as **S**) is any event, situation, object or factor that is measurable and which may affect behaviour. Simple examples could include a red triangle, the ticking of a watch or a pinprick.

For a behaviourist, an important element in understanding a particular behaviour is to identify the stimulus (or stimuli) involved. From the examples above, this would seem to be a fairly straightforward task. In reality, however, it can sometimes be quite difficult to define which environmental elements are involved as stimuli in a particular situation. For example, a mother approaches her two-month-old infant, and the baby smiles. The mother seems to be the stimulus which elicits the baby's smiling. But is it the mother as a whole, or her face, or her expression, or her smell, or her touch, or some combination of these and other elements to which the baby is actually responding? In research, it would be necessary to identify the actual stimulus elements in order to understand the situation properly. (In this regard, the desire for operational definitions of terms, including stimuli, becomes understandable as a means of avoiding ambiguity.)

Similarly, it is necessary to describe clearly the behaviour being studied. Normally, the behaviour which is measured is called the **response** (often abbreviated as **R**). Again, this may seem very simple at first glance. For example, a person sitting at a table engages in eating. 'Eating' is obviously a response; however, a moment's thought will show that there can be tremendous variations in the behaviour described as eating. A finicky child may pick reluctantly at a disliked vegetable. A hungry person may ravenously devour a favourite dish. While both are 'eating', there is clearly a large difference in their behaviour. Consequently, researchers must be careful to describe a response in terms that are meaningful to the situation. Often this will require specifying the rate, intensity and/or other characteristics of the response.

One of the distinctions among responses that became evident to the early behaviourists was a distinction between reflexes and voluntary actions. **Reflexes** are unlearned responses that can be triggered by specific environmental stimuli. Examples of human reflexes include withdrawing the hand from a hot surface, or a baby's sucking on an object placed in the mouth. By contrast, **voluntary responses** are emitted – that is, they are not triggered by stimuli in the way reflexes are. Typically, they involve more complex actions, which often require extensive practice. Thorndike, for example, in his studies of problem-solving by animals, found it took repeated trials for learning to occur. Voluntary behaviour can span the range from learning to ride a bike to understanding a new language. Such differences led behaviourists to the separate study of reflexes and voluntary responses. As we shall see, learning occurs in relation to both types of behaviour. Furthermore, the differences between the two types may be less significant than they appear.

stimulus (often abbreviated as S) in general, any event, situation, object or factor that may affect behaviour; for the behaviourists, a measurable change in the environment

response in general, any reaction to a stimulus, whether overt or mental; in research, the behaviour which is measured

reflex an unlearned response that can be triggered by specific environmental stimuli, such as a baby's sucking on an object placed in the mouth
voluntary response a response which is controlled by the individual (i.e. emitted) rather than being triggered by specific stimuli as reflexes are

Ivan Pavlov

Ivan Petrovich Pavlov (1849–1936) was a Russian physiologist who pioneered the study of classical conditioning. Born in Ryazan, Russia, he initially began seminary studies, but then changed to St Petersburg University, where he graduated in natural science, and subsequently received his doctorate in physiology from the Military Medical Academy in St Petersburg. After a few years spent in Germany, he went on to become a professor at the Military Medical Academy. His work on the physiology of digestion, begun in 1879, earned him the Nobel Prize in 1904. He first became aware of reflexes by reading Sechenov's work while still at seminary, but his own research on what became known as classical conditioning did not begin until about 1902. At this time, while still studying digestion in dogs, he noticed what he called 'psychic salivation' – a dog would salivate before it was actually given food. Since Pavlov believed that digestion involved a series of reflexes, he set out to determine what controlled this anticipatory response. Ultimately, his work on conditioning overshadowed the research which had earned him the Nobel Prize. He continued to be intellectually active, forming a genetics institute only a few years before his death at the age of eighty-seven.

Classical Conditioning

classical conditioning the study of learning which involves reflex responses, in which a neutral stimulus comes to elicit an existing reflex response

At the turn of the century, a Russian physiologist named Ivan Pavlov was engaged in a long-term project to understand the process of digestion. Beginning in 1879 and working primarily with dogs, his work earned him the Nobel Prize in 1904. However, sometime around 1902, he noticed a phenomenon which was to lead him in a new and unexpected direction. In order to study digestion, Pavlov measured a number of factors, including how much a dog salivated when it was given food. At some point, he noticed what he called 'psychic salivation' – a dog would salivate before it was actually given food. Since Pavlov believed that digestion involved a series of reflexes, he set out to determine what controlled this anticipatory response. What he discovered became the basis for what is now commonly called **classical conditioning**, the study of learning which involves reflex responses.

Pavlov's original studies have become so well known as to be the object of jokes (like the psychologist who salivates when he hears the name 'Pavlov'!). In simple outline, Pavlov found that by ringing a bell and then immediately giving the dog food, the bell came to evoke the same response as the food itself (i.e. salivation). To understand why this is remarkable, we need to consider the elements of the situation more closely. As Pavlov's lengthy studies of digestion showed, salivating to the presence of food is a basic neural reflex that requires no learning. For example, if you put a piece of chocolate in your mouth, you will salivate. A light shined in the eye will cause the pupil to contract. Reflex responses like these (and they exist in species from worms to humans) are referred to in classical conditioning as **unconditioned responses**. For any reflex, there is some stimulus which will *elicit* the response (e.g. food for salivating, light for

unconditioned response a reflexive response produced by a specific stimulus, such as pupil contraction to bright light

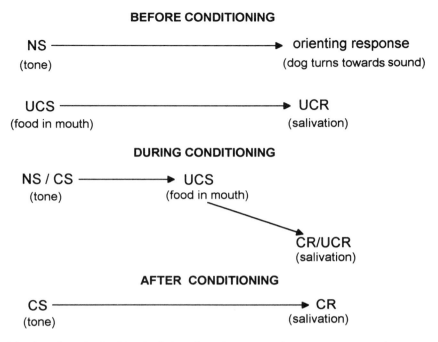

BEFORE CONDITIONING

NS ⟶ orienting response
(tone) (dog turns towards sound)

UCS ⟶ UCR
(food in mouth) (salivation)

DURING CONDITIONING

NS / CS ⟶ UCS
(tone) (food in mouth)
⟶ CR/UCR
(salivation)

AFTER CONDITIONING

CS ⟶ CR
(tone) (salivation)

Fig. 3.1 The Basic Classical Conditioning Procedure In classical conditioning, repeated pairing of a neutral stimulus (NS) with an unconditioned stimulus (UCS) results in conditioning, whereby the NS becomes conditioned (CS) to elicit the same type of response as the UCS did.

unconditioned stimulus a stimulus which elicits a reflexive (unconditioned) response

neutral stimulus in classical conditioning, a stimulus which initially produces no specific response other than provoking attention; as conditioning proceeds, the neutral stimulus becomes a conditioned stimulus

conditioned stimulus a stimulus which by repeated pairings with an unconditioned stimulus comes to elicit a conditioned response

conditioned response in classical conditioning, a response to a previously neutral stimulus which has become a conditioned stimulus by repeated pairing with an unconditioned stimulus

pupil contraction); the stimulus which elicits an unconditioned response is called an **unconditioned stimulus**. Since 'conditioned' refers to *learned*, the term refers to the unlearned nature of reflexes. (Pavlov of course wrote in Russian, and actually used the term 'unconditio*nal*', but an early English translator erred, and the mistake has remained.)

If reflexes are unlearned, then what is the learning that occurs in classical conditioning? Pavlov noted that the learning is based on forming a connection between the bell and the food. Ringing the bell initially had no effect on salivation – that is, with respect to the response under study, it was a **neutral stimulus**. (To be a stimulus, an environmental element must be something which the organism is aware of; normally this is demonstrated by the stimulus provoking attention, called an *orienting response*.) After repeated pairings with the food which was placed in its mouth, the sound of the bell came to elicit drooling. At this point, the sound has become a **conditioned stimulus**, and the salivating which results is called a **conditioned response** (to distinguish it from the response to food alone) (see Fig. 3.1). In effect, the conditioned stimulus has become associated with the occurrence of food (Pavlov 1927).

In order to appreciate the significance of classical conditioning, we must examine its characteristics more closely. Since the response involved is essentially a pre-existing reflex, the learning actually consists of forming a connection (association) between two stimuli (the CS and UCS). In order for optimal conditioning to occur, the conditioned stimulus (CS) must occur a second or so before the unconditioned stimulus (UCS). If the two occur simultaneously, conditioning may occur, but is typically weaker. If the CS is presented *after* the UCS (what is sometimes called *backward conditioning*), then *no* learning occurs. What this tells us is that conditioning is closely linked to the ability of the CS to serve as an advanced signal that the UCS is going to occur. This is further demonstrated by studies which show that conditioning is only likely when the CS *reliably* predicts the occurrence of the UCS. In some sense, what makes classical conditioning a valuable process for the organism is the fact that *it allows one to anticipate environmental events.*

Classical conditioning has been demonstrated in a wide variety of species, from worms to birds to primates. Thus, it appears to be a very fundamental form of learning. But given that much of human behaviour does not depend on reflex responses, it might seem that classical conditioning is of little significance in people. In fact, the reality seems to be just the opposite; examples of classical conditioning seem pervasive in our lives. For example, we respond to stimuli associated with food – smells, pictures in advertisements, words like 'chocolate cake' – in much the way that Pavlov's dogs reacted, by increased digestive activity. In these cases, the food cues, having been associated with food itself (the UCS), are conditioned stimuli. Such food cues are among the most reliable of conditioned stimuli, because the sight and smell of food always precedes the actual eating of it. In movies, directors will use sounds to enhance the emotional content of the story. For example, a particular theme may precede the repeated appearances of the villain in a horror movie; viewers then come to associate the theme to the moments of mayhem that follow. (Of course, film images of violence are *themselves* conditioned stimuli, associated with past experiences of actual injury (UCS). This relates to the process of *higher-order conditioning*, which we will discuss further in this chapter.) Many people, when showering, develop a conditioned response of anxiety to the sound of a toilet flushing (CS), since it often results in a sudden increase in the temperature of the water (UCS)! Classical conditioning is thus a flexible process which allows us to anticipate biologically significant events (UCSs) by making an association to stimuli (CSs) which precede them.

For further consideration

Given the basic principles of classical conditioning, why do you think the advertising of products (from toothpaste to automobiles) typically involves the use of attractive models?

Classical Conditioning Phenomena

Stimulus Generalization and Discrimination

Having established the basic elements of classical conditioning, Pavlov (and later others) began to explore some variations of the original situation. One subject that interested him was the element of stimulus novelty: what would happen if a new stimulus was presented as a CS? Tests with unrelated stimuli quickly established that a neutral stimulus will not elicit a response which has been conditioned (a conditioned response, CR) to a different stimulus (e.g. flashing a light will not elicit a CR if the previous CS was the sound of a bell). However, what would happen if a stimulus *similar to* the CS was used (e.g. a different

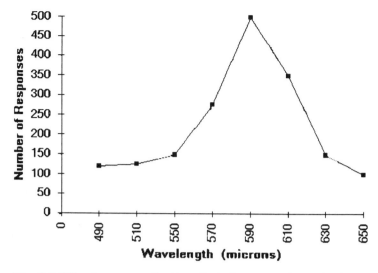

Fig. 3.2 Stimulus generalization Typically, an organism trained to respond to one stimulus will respond in the same way to stimuli which are perceived as similar. In the example, varying the wavelength (colour) from the original greenish stimulus leads to responding which decreases as the test stimuli become less similar. [These data, averaged from Peterson (1962) actually refer to operant conditioning of pigeons, but the basic phenomenon is the same in classical conditioning.]

stimulus generalization in classical conditioning, the tendency to produce a CR to both the original CS and to stimuli which are similar to it in some way

bell)? Tests of this type revealed a new phenomenon, called **stimulus generalization**: stimuli similar to the original CS would tend to elicit the same CR. Research has shown that the degree of response is related to the amount of similarity between the new stimulus and the original CS (see Fig. 3.2).

This may not seem like a very surprising result, but it is very profound in its implications. In everyday life, we seldom encounter the same precise situation twice. Even the appearance of our friends changes, as they wear different clothes, change their hairstyle, etc. Given this reality, it is generally desirable to be able to ignore these minor variations; in other words, to generalize across basically similar stimuli. This is precisely what the studies of stimulus generalization in classical conditioning demonstrate. In practical terms, stimulus generalization results in responding to *a whole class of related stimuli*, after initial learning with a single stimulus. A child who has learned to withdraw after touching a glowing burner on a gas stove will tend to generalize this withdrawal to other stimuli that are similarly bright and hot, for example electric burners, open fires, etc. In this sense, stimulus generalization generally enables organisms to adapt better to their environment.

How exactly can we define or measure 'similarity'? Ideally, we should have some general procedure, operationally defined, to measure similarity for any stimuli. Considerable attention has been given to this problem, but as yet there is no universal standard to determine similarity. Lacking a clear general definition, one must resort to defining similarity by observing the outcome of experimental tests. Thus, if two stimuli elicit essentially identical results, they are highly similar; if CS_1 produces a strong conditioned response, but CS_2 elicits only a weak response, then they are not very similar.

Fig. 3.3 Pure generalization When pigeons were raised under monochromatic light, testing for stimulus generalization with other colours of light yielded essentially no differences in responding; in effect, the animals generalized to *any* colour of light (data averaged from Peterson 1962).

The fact that there is no clear way to predefine similarity may seem a serious weakness, but in fact it may actually tell us something about the nature of stimulus generalization. The typical experiment produces results like those in Fig. 3.2, where response intensity drops off as the stimulus difference increases. However, this is not the only possible outcome. Depending on experience during and prior to training, the results can differ significantly. For example, when two stimuli are randomly mixed as the CS during training, generalization is essentially equal to both (Grice and Hunter 1964). Even more interesting are the implications of experiments on stimulus generalization where the environment of the animals has been carefully controlled prior to conditioning. For example, if pigeons are reared from birth with only yellow light for illumination, and then a light is used as the CS, the pigeons will respond *equally* to *any* colour of light (Peterson 1962; see Fig. 3.3). In this situation, it seems that the absence of prior experience with colour as a stimulus characteristic leads to regarding all colours as similar. Babies show a somewhat comparable response, in that they initially smile at anyone who smiles at them, whether parent or stranger. Thus, it seems that the initial tendency of an organism is to generalize when encountering a new situation. (As a perceptual characteristic, this may also relate to such behaviours as stereotyping, which involve generalizing based on group membership.)

Why, then, do most experiments show the gradients seen in the first example? The answer seems to lie with another phenomenon which Pavlov studied. He noted that a dog conditioned to salivate to the presentation of a black square (CS) also salivated at the sight of a grey square, an example of stimulus generalization. Pavlov then ran a series of trials during which the black square was always followed by food (UCS), but the grey square was never followed by food. After a number of such trials, the dog reliably salivated to the black square, but no

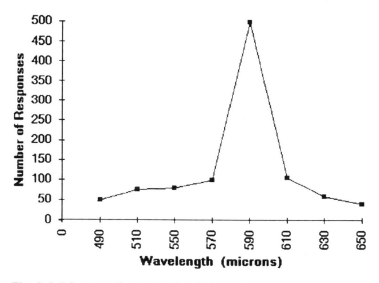

Fig. 3.4 Stimulus discrimination When pigeons are trained in discrimination, the generalization gradient becomes much steeper (cf. Fig. 3.2). Taken with the two previous graphs, this suggests that a 'typical' generalization response actually reflects a degree of discrimination, unlike the pure generalization produced when there has been no prior experience of stimulus variation (cf. Fig. 3.3).

stimulus discrimination
in classical conditioning, selective responding to the CS, but not to stimuli which are similar in some way, as a result of training

longer did so when presented with the grey square. This was a demonstration of **stimulus discrimination**, whereby the organism is conditioned to *distinguish* between two stimuli (see Fig. 3.4). Pavlov subsequently demonstrated that such discriminations can be remarkably precise, if training is continued with stimuli which become progressively more alike. What is notable is that *stimulus discrimination always requires training*; in the *absence* of such training, organisms tend to *generalize*.

If we then reconsider the puzzle of generalization gradients, what seems to emerge is the implication that 'typical' gradients reflect a *combination* of generalization and discrimination. In the everyday world, organisms learn that stimulus variations sometimes are significant, and sometimes are not. Pigeons, for example, may use their colour vision to determine when berries are ripe or not, but not to distinguish between berries and seeds. Typically, the smaller the colour difference, the less significant it would be. Only when they have *no prior experience* with colour variations (as in the unusual experiment described above) will they totally ignore colour differences. According to this analysis, trying to determine a universal standard of similarity is a hopeless task, since organisms will show varying response patterns depending on their past experience. In other words, learning based on classical conditioning is a cumulative process, wherein present behaviour will be influenced by prior conditioning experiences.

While *what* we discriminate may depend on past experience, the *capacity* to discriminate can often be crucial to adaptation. For instance, detecting the difference between food which is safe or spoiled often depends on discriminating particular odour cues. Some occupations are closed to individuals with colour blindness, because job performance requires discrimination based on colour (e.g.

certain types of electrical work, where wires are colour-coded). Thus, in some circumstances, lacking the capacity to discriminate would be a serious obstacle to survival.

Extinction and Spontaneous Recovery

We have seen how classical conditioning, combined with stimulus generalization and discrimination, can lead to learning which is often highly adaptive. However, we have not said anything about how long the effects of conditioning last, or what happens if a conditioned response is *not* adaptive. A Russian researcher, W.H. Gantt, has commented on the possibility that conditioned responses, being persistent once formed, can turn an individual into 'a museum of antiquities' as time goes on. Many reactions would be based on particular past situations, and consequently might be either no longer useful, or even detrimental (Gantt 1966). For example, a person who broke an arm might continue to favour it (because of the pain associated with the original injury) long after healing had been completed. This would represent a form of persistent classical conditioning which, as Gantt suggested, would be maladaptive. Clearly, if *all* conditioning persists indefinitely, then the possibility of inappropriate responses becomes a serious possibility.

In part because of this possibility, Pavlov was also interested in the degree of permanence of classical conditioning. In order to test the limits, Pavlov and his colleagues first conditioned a dog to salivate at the sound of a bell. Once the response was well-established (by pairing the sound of the bell with a UCS of food placed in the dog's mouth), they continued to ring the bell, but no longer provided food. Under these conditions, the conditioned response (salivating) became weaker and weaker, and eventually ceased altogether. Pavlov referred to

> **extinction** in classical conditioning, the cessation of responding when the CS is presented repeatedly *without* being paired with the UCS

this cessation of responding when the CS is presented repeatedly *without* being paired with the UCS as **extinction**. Thus, extinction seems to suggest that what can be learned can be unlearned, and that conditioned responses are not necessarily permanent.

However, there are certain qualifiers that should be added to this conclusion. First, one should distinguish between active training in extinction, such as Pavlov used, and the persistence of conditioned responses in the absence of such training. Potentially, without active extinction, a conditioned response may simply remain dormant until the person encounters the CS again. For example, a fear response associated with the sound of a dentist's drill may persist despite lengthy intervals between visits, because no extinction training occurs. The other qualifier on the effectiveness of extinction concerns the *type* of conditioned response. Work by Gantt and others has indicated that internal responses like heart rate and blood pressure changes, which are frequently associated with stressful or emotional stimulus situations, are more persistent than simple muscle responses like withdrawing from a hot surface. This has implications for the conditioning of emotions, as we will see below.

What effect does time passing have on extinction? One might assume that the effects of extinction in 'erasing' the original conditioning would be as long-lasting as conditioning itself is in the absence of extinction. However, this is not really the case. Pavlov found that if he waited several hours after extinguishing salivation to the bell, ringing the bell tended to elicit the conditioned response again. While the response was weaker than when originally learned, and could in turn be re-extinguished, the most striking point was that it reoccurred *at all*. Pavlov called this return of the conditioned response **spontaneous recovery**, which is defined as the restoration of the response when the CS is presented after some time has elapsed since extinction training. Spontaneous recovery of extinguished responses has been well-demonstrated in a variety of species, sometimes after long time periods. This implies that, in terms of conditioning, what we learn is never really forgotten, but at best is simply overlaid with different experience. Instances in which old fears re-emerge long after we thought we had conquered them (e.g. fear of public speaking, fear of doctors, etc.) may reflect the enduring nature of conditioned behaviour. It seems that conditioned behaviour can be modified, but no conditioning is ever simply 'erased'.

Higher-order Conditioning

We have seen that the principles of classical conditioning provide a mechanism whereby new stimuli can come to elicit a reflex response. In many cases, the conditioned stimulus serves as a signal allowing anticipation of the UCS, which is frequently beneficial to the organism. Sometimes, the sequence involves stimuli like food or water, which are beneficial to the individual. In other cases, the CS may signal something harmful, like heat or electric shock (for example, farm animals typically develop a fear of electric fences after a single experience of getting shocked). However, sometimes we encounter situations in which the conditioned stimulus seems to have no direct connection to an unconditioned stimulus. For example, a child hears the word 'cake' and begins to salivate. How can this arise from the processes we have discussed?

Pavlov proposed a possible mechanism for such remote associations in terms of what he called higher-order conditioning. In **higher-order conditioning**, a previously established conditioned stimulus is used as if it were an unconditioned stimulus to create conditioning to a new stimulus. While the wording may seem complex, the process itself is easy to grasp. In Pavlov's original experiment, he first trained a dog to salivate to the sound of a buzzer (CS_1), using food as a UCS. Once conditioning was established, he then introduced a new stimulus, a black square, which was repeatedly paired with the sound of the buzzer (but not food). After several such pairings, presenting the black square alone tended to elicit salivation (see Fig. 3.5). Not surprisingly, the effect was rather weak, since each trial also functioned as extinction training for the original buzzer-food association. Pavlov called such conditioning *second-order* conditioning, and attempted to extend the sequence by using the black square as if it were a UCS, and attempting to link a new stimulus (*third-order* conditioning). Pavlov found this was not possible when using salivation to food as the original reflex; however, he *was* able to create third-order conditioning when leg withdrawal to electric shock was the response. (This result may actually tell us more about the significance of stimuli like electric shock than it does about higher-order conditioning as such. As with extinction effects, the distinguishing element may be responses associated with emotions.)

Dogs, of course, are not exactly like people, and the everyday world is not exactly like the laboratory. Without the controlled conditions of a laboratory, it can be difficult to prove the existence of higher-order conditioning, but many

spontaneous recovery in classical conditioning, the reoccurrence of the CR when the CS is presented after some time has elapsed since extinction training

higher-order conditioning a form of classical conditioning in which a previously established conditioned stimulus is used as if it were an unconditioned stimulus to create conditioning to a new stimulus

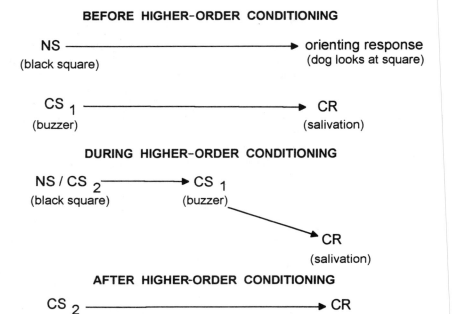

BEFORE HIGHER-ORDER CONDITIONING

NS ————————————————→ orienting response
(black square)   (dog looks at square)

CS $_1$ ————————————————→ CR
(buzzer)   (salivation)

DURING HIGHER-ORDER CONDITIONING

NS / CS $_2$————————→ CS $_1$
(black square)   (buzzer)
                                                      ↘
                                                         CR
                                                         (salivation)

AFTER HIGHER-ORDER CONDITIONING

CS $_2$ ————————————————→ CR
(black square)   (salivation)

Fig. 3.5 Higher-order conditioning Pavlov found that once a conditioned response had been established, the CS could be used as if it were a UCS in order to develop further conditioning (cf. Fig. 3.1 and note where the UCS would be).

researchers believe that analogues exist in human behaviour. For example, the child who salivates to the word 'cake' has likely previously developed a conditioned response of salivating to the sight of cake (the original CS). Then, in the process of learning to talk, the word 'cake' became associated with the sight of the object it described; by repeatedly pairing 'cake' with the sight of cake, higher-order conditioning became established.

It is tempting, certainly, to speculate on how language learning may be closely linked to higher-order conditioning. Parents sometimes verbalize (e.g. 'bad boy!') while physically punishing a child; it is easy to understand how 'bad boy!' would then come to evoke fear and withdrawal, almost like a physical blow. If later, receiving a poor grade on a school report card leads to 'bad boy!', a poor grade could itself become a conditioned stimulus for fear and withdrawal. Precisely how significant this process is everyday life, no-one really knows. Whether such effects are actually due to higher-order conditioning or not, it is clear that classical conditioning does play a role in our everyday lives.

Applications of Classical Conditioning

While deceptively simple at first glance, classical conditioning seems to be a potent process for learning in a wide variety of species. In humans, salivation to food cues, fear arousal in the shower when the sound of a toilet flushing occurs, and a wide range of other instances show how a diverse range of stimuli can come to elicit reflex responses. Sometimes, time itself can be a conditioned stimulus. Most pet owners notice that their pets are sensitive to the timing of daily routines, ranging from meal times to the time a particular family member comes home. Since mammals (and a range of other species) have an internal biological clock, time of day can be an unseen stimulus for various responses, including hunger pangs. If you normally eat meals at a particular time of day, you have probably noticed that your stomach becomes active when that time approaches. This conditioned response enables your body to correctly anticipate the arrival of food (provided you don't skip a meal!). Still, the range of motor responses which are typically conditioned in people is limited in comparison to our overall behaviour. Let us look at some other areas where the role of classical conditioning has been explored.

Conditioned Emotional Responses

Pavlov's work on classical conditioning became known relatively quickly, perhaps because he was already famous for his work on digestion. (By contrast, an American named Louis Twitmeyer, who discovered the same phenomenon almost simultaneously with Pavlov, died essentially unrecognized.) Among those who saw the importance of this new paradigm was John B. Watson, who saw in Pavlov's work a model for the behaviourist methodology he was trying to foster. One area where he saw potential was in the study of emotions, which had previously been the domain of the introspectionists. The introspectionists studied emotions, like other aspects of experience, by trying to describe the mental states involved. Watson instead believed that emotions represented observable responses, and proceeded to study the issue by attempting to create emotional responses experimentally. While he used a number of subjects, including his own children, the best known case was a study done with Rosalie Rayner, using a toddler identified as Albert (Watson and Rayner 1920). (As a side note, Rayner later became Watson's second wife.)

Albert was an eleven-month-old boy who had been admitted to hospital for reasons unrelated to Watson's research. Watson initially observed Albert at play, and tested his responses to various stimulus objects, including blocks, a ball of cotton, some furry material and a white rat. The boy, like most children of his age, seemed curious about these objects, examining and playing with them. Then, Watson and Rayner began systematically to associate the white rat with the noise of a loud metal gong. On the first conditioning trial, Albert approached the animal without fear. Suddenly, the sound of the gong arose behind him. The loud noise elicited a startle response (UCR), and also caused Albert to begin crying. Three times, the same sequence of events was repeated. Each time, Albert began crying at the sound of the gong. After a total of seven conditioning trials on two occasions, the white rat was presented alone – and Albert began crying. Thus, a fear reaction had been classically conditioned to the rat, which previously had been a neutral stimulus. Watson called this fear a **conditioned emotional response**.

About a week later, Watson and Rayner returned to test Albert again. This time, the experimenters showed Albert the objects from the original session. The toddler continued to show interest in the blocks and several masks. However,

conditioned emotional response an emotional response such as fear which is established through classical conditioning certain objects – balls of cotton, a white fur and a Santa Claus mask with a white beard – elicited the same crying and withdrawal as the white rat. In terms of classical conditioning, Albert had generalized his response to any white, fluffy stimulus!

Having established that fear could be classically conditioned, Watson and Rayner then sought to eliminate the fear response. To accomplish this, they used Pavlov's extinction procedure, presenting the white rat without pairing it with the sound of the gong. They tried this several times over a three-week period, but found that, contrary to their expectations, the fear did not extinguish. Unfortunately, before they could pursue the matter further, Albert was discharged from the hospital, ending the test.

With hindsight, we can recognize two factors that contributed to the failure of extinction. One is the fact that fear responses, like various other responses of the autonomic nervous system, are hard to extinguish (Gantt 1966; recall Pavlov's experiences with higher-order conditioning – the conditioned fear produced by electric shock may account for his success in conditioning leg withdrawal to shock, but not salivation to food). In addition, the occurrence of stimulus generalization (common for fear responses) tends to make extinction difficult, since a whole *range* of stimuli must be extinguished. Today, other techniques have been developed to deal with fear responses, since extinction training has such limited impact (see Chapter 9 for a discussion of such techniques).

Before continuing our discussion of conditioned emotional responses, it is appropriate to consider the ethics of Watson and Rayner's study. Not surprisingly, Watson and Rayner have frequently been criticized for the questionable ethics and potential harm of their test. Without attempting to second-guess past actions, it should be noted that the intent was not to harm Albert permanently; at the outset, Watson believed both conditioning *and* extinction would be successful. At the same time, it is clear that the procedure involved suffering for Albert, and it is unlikely that such a test would pass current ethical standards.

Watson and Rayner's demonstration, however questionable ethically, served to illustrate that emotional responses like fear could at least potentially arise from classical conditioning. In fact, most behaviourists would argue that phobias (a clinical category for irrational fears) can best be understood as conditioned emotional responses. Thus, anything from the fear of water to the fear of dogs could result from a traumatic episode in which the stimulus (water, dogs, etc.) was associated with a pain-evoking stimulus.

However, human emotions extend well beyond fear. Could other emotions also be classically conditioned? Behaviourists would assert not only that such conditioning can happen, but also that it is responsible for most of the emotional richness of our lives. A newborn infant may instinctively respond to contact with the mother's body, but later this pleasurable response becomes associated with the mother's face, and still later objects in the home, and maybe even home itself. Couples who experience pleasure at hearing a favourite old song are experiencing emotions which have become associated with the conditioned stimulus of the music. Even when we go to the movies, conditioning is involved (probably through a higher-order process) in our responses to heroes, villains and a variety of plot situations.

Words may even be the most refined of stimuli in terms of emotional conditioning. Words have a literal meaning and an emotional meaning; what is curious is that the two often do not correspond. Terms of endearment may range from the silly to the meaningless (e.g. 'little cabbage' or 'snuggie-poo'). Even more interesting is the emotional response to profanity. For example, what are considered 'dirty words' varies from language to language: in English, most forbidden words relate to sexuality; in French, they usually relate to religion. Such differences relate not to the literal meaning of the words, but to the emotional significance of sexuality and religion in the respective cultures. When Shakespeare noted that 'a rose by any other name would smell as sweet', he recognized that the word is only a label – and labels depend on learning for their meaning. Without classical conditioning, it is likely that all language would be emotionally meaningless!

For further consideration

Most of us have various types of fears. Can you identify one fear which you feel affects you significantly? Can you recall a traumatic event that produced the fear (e.g. a fear of dogs resulting from having been bitten as a child)? If not, do you think this invalidates the idea that phobias are based on conditioning?

Conditioned Drug and Immune Responses

As discussed in relation to the biological approach to psychology, the human body is a highly integrated system, involving neural, hormonal and immunological activity. Although we have not discussed the possible physiological mechanisms underlying classical conditioning, Pavlov believed that the mechanism was neural. Assuming this is true (and the evidence largely supports this idea), one might still ask whether conditioning can influence other bodily processes, such as the response to drugs or disease. The exploration of such possibilities represents perhaps the most exciting area of conditioning research today.

Pavlov himself was interested in how drug reactions might be classically conditioned. In one study, the sound of a tone was repeatedly paired with a drug which induced vomiting (UCS); after several trials, the dog began to vomit to the sound of the tone alone. This suggests that stimuli present when a drug is administered may acquire the power to induce the drug's symptoms. For example, the smell of coffee may trigger the stimulating effect of caffeine.

Interestingly, more recent work has suggested that with some drugs the conditioned response is the *opposite* to the primary effect of the drug itself. For example, rats were conditioned by giving injections of morphine in a specific environment. While morphine normally reduces sensitivity to painful stimuli, the rats after conditioning showed *increased* sensitivity to pain when placed in the conditioning context (Siegel 1976). Similarly, diabetics taking insulin by injection sometimes show a decreased response to the insulin over time. It appears that the process of injection becomes a CS which counteracts the effects of the insulin.

Why would conditioning mimic the effects of some drugs and counteract others? The explanation seems to relate to the type of drug and the body's response to it. For some drugs, like the vomiting agent used by Pavlov, the body reacts by showing a strong reaction, which gradually diminishes as the drug dissipates. By contrast, certain drugs, such as morphine and insulin, interact with the body's natural mechanisms for maintaining equilibrium (called *homeostasis*). In these cases, there is an initial reaction triggered by the drug, which is then followed by an opposite reaction, triggered by the body's homeostatic mechanisms. As a result, the conditioned stimulus becomes associated with the second reaction, which is opposite to that of the drug itself (Siegel *et al.* 1988).

While drugs, being artificially introduced, seem to interact with the body's own equilibrium processes, what about the immune system? Can classical conditioning affect the way our body reacts to disease? Recent research suggests this may be a real possibility. In one study, rats were given saccharine-sweetened water at the same time that they were injected with cyclosporine, a drug which inhibits immune system response. After several such pairings, tests showed that the taste of saccharine alone was able to suppress the immune system of the rats (Ader and Cohen 1975). Other studies have shown similar effects (see Ader and Cohen 1985). These studies imply that stimuli associated with low points of immune system functioning (e.g. gifts received during a major illness, or objects associated with the death of a loved one) may continue to impair immune response at later times. Conversely, researchers have also been able to use conditioning to *enhance* immune system response (Gorcynski *et al.* 1982). While the practical implications have yet to be adequately tested, it may well turn out that conditioning effects can influence our long-term health.

Research on conditioned emotional responses and drug/immune effects indicate that Pavlov's basic paradigm is still providing us with new insights on behaviour. The significance of classical conditioning is easily underestimated, since involuntary responses are often overlooked in our daily experience; this is partly because they *are* involuntary, and operate with no conscious intervention. (Equally, conscious attempts at controlling reflexes have minimal success, as those who recognize that their fear responses are irrational can testify.) While we cannot say at present that all issues related to classical conditioning have been resolved, neither have we reached the limit in terms of finding new applications and insights.

Operant Conditioning

operant conditioning in the behaviourist approach, the form of learning concerned with changes in emitted responses as a function of their consequences

As important as classical conditioning is, it must be recognized that it is only concerned with how new stimuli come to control existing involuntary responses. While reflexes and the 'gut-level' responses associated with emotions play a role in our everyday experience, most of our behaviour is self-generated, or voluntary. Behaviours like driving the car, working at the computer and calling a friend on the telephone are not elicited by conditioned stimuli. Instead, they are *emitted* – that is, they are generated by the individual as a way of influencing the surrounding environment. In order to understand the dynamics of such behaviour, we need to consider a different approach to learning. This approach deals with changes in emitted responses as a function of their consequences, commonly referred to as **operant conditioning**.

To understand the origins of operant conditioning, we need to go back to the work of Edwin Thorndike. Although Thorndike was studying animal behaviour and learning at roughly the same time as Pavlov, his approach was very different. Whereas Pavlov began with an interest in digestion and then became interested in conditioning, Thorndike was initially interested in problem-solving and intelligence. Consequently, instead of focusing on simple reflexes, Thorndike studied situations in which an animal was actively interacting with its environment. In a typical experiment, a cat was confined in a 'puzzle box', a cage-like structure from which it could free itself by pressing a lever. Any cat owner can testify that cats generally dislike confinement, hence the cats were typically eager to escape. However, Thorndike increased the incentive by depriving the animals of food prior to testing, and then placing food outside the puzzle box, where it was visible to the cat. Not surprisingly, the cats learned to press the lever, thereby escaping and obtaining the food (Thorndike 1898).

Two primary conclusions emerged from Thorndike's work. The first was that if one measured *how long* it took a cat to escape, the time gradually declined with repeated trials. This improvement in performance represented a change in behaviour as a result of experience – in other words, *learning*. The other major conclusion concerned the relationship between the cat's behaviour and its consequences. Both escape and obtaining food appeared to be desirable outcomes for the cats, leading Thorndike to conclude that this satisfying outcome was what led to the behaviour being repeated. By contrast, flailing at the walls of the box, and other behaviours which did not lead to escape, declined. From observations like this, Thorndike formulated his *law of effect*: behaviour which leads to a satisfying outcome tends to be repeated, whereas behaviour that leads to an unsatisfactory outcome is unlikely to be repeated. Note that the law of effect makes no reference to reducing hunger, desire to escape, or other mentalistic concepts. The observational nature of the principle was one of the factors which attracted the attention of Watson and later behaviourists.

Thorndike's research laid the foundation for the study of non-reflex behaviour. By emphasizing the connection between an action and its outcome, his law of effect provided a framework for studying such behaviour. In Thorndike's system, responses are initiated by the organism as part of dealing with its surroundings, not as a reflex triggered by an environmental stimulus. Depending on the consequences, a particular behaviour might or might not be repeated in the future. For example, a child who draws a picture and presents it to their mother may receive praise; this will encourage the child to draw more pictures in the future. On the other hand, if the child takes a cookie without permission and is scolded, they are less likely to try this again. In its simplest form, the law of effect reaffirms what might be considered 'common sense'. At the same time, by suggesting an approach to the study of the broad range of non-reflex behaviours, it fits well with the developing behaviourist approach. Yet, while Thorndike's work was acknowledged by Watson, and stimulated a variety of subsequent research, it did not result in a coherent system comparable to Pavlov's paradigm until the work of B.F Skinner in the 1930s.

For further consideration

In Thorndike's terms, what sort of things give you satisfaction? What things produce dissatisfaction? Why?

Skinner and Operant Conditioning

Within behaviourism, B.F. Skinner occupies a position of influence equal to, and in some ways greater than, that of John B. Watson. As the pioneer of operant

B.F. Skinner

Burrhus Frederic Skinner (1904–   ) is probably the best known American behaviourist, and the founder of operant conditioning. His early years were rather peripatetic – educated at Hamilton College and then Harvard (receiving his PhD in 1931), he taught at the University of Minnesota and Indiana University. During the Second World War, he did research with a military flavour, including a programme designed to teach pigeons to direct missiles to targets while flying in the nosecone; the technique was never implemented. In 1947, he returned to Harvard to deliver the annual William James Lectures; in 1948, he was appointed as a full professor at Harvard, where he is currently professor emeritus. Skinner's development of operant conditioning began while training as a graduate student at Harvard. Although his initial work on animal behaviour was somewhat similar to Thorndike's, he became influenced by Watson's ideas, and began a systematic attempt to purge psychology of mentalistic concepts and language. While his theories have remained controversial, the practical applications of operant conditioning have been widespread. Skinner continues to live and write in Cambridge, Massachusetts.

conditioning, he almost single-handedly created a framework for the study of learned behaviour. (He also created his own terms: Skinner coined the term operant conditioning to replace Thorndike's 'instrumental learning'; similarly, he renamed classical conditioning as 'respondent conditioning'.) Skinner's contributions are significant in terms of both research methods and conceptual analysis. To understand this, we need to consider the origins of his work.

While training as a graduate student at Harvard, Skinner was doing studies of animal behaviour somewhat similar to Thorndike's. Influenced by Watson, he found himself frustrated that so much of the vocabulary of psychology seemed clouded by the ambiguities of everyday language. In particular, it seemed that terms referring to mental states were both vague and unnecessary to the understanding of behaviour. For Skinner, the inner workings of the mind (and the body) were a 'black box', inaccessible to direct observation. This point of view was shared by all behaviourists, but Skinner went further, arguing that even if thoughts and other mental states were open to study, they would have no real value in explaining behaviour. The environment in which behaviour occurs, the response itself and the consequence of the action are all that are necessary to understand behaviour. By insisting that mental states are both inaccessible to study *and irrelevant to understanding*, Skinner was advocating a point of view which has come to be called **radical behaviourism**.

Having come to this point of view, he subsequently embarked on a programme of creating new terms for describing and analysing behaviour, which have become the vocabulary of operant conditioning. For example, he refers to emitted behaviours as operant responses, arguing that 'voluntary behaviour' implies undesirable notions about free will. In doing so, he attempted to purge the study of behaviour of all excess conceptual baggage. Skinner (1987) even went so far as to say radical behaviourism is not a part of psychology, but rather an approach to understanding certain issues both inside and outside psychology.

radical behaviourism a position adopted by Watson and Skinner, which argues that mental states are both inaccessible to scientific study and irrelevant to understanding

Operant conditioning has in fact become established as a major form of behaviourism, as we shall see. While Skinner has often argued that his approach is pragmatic, not theoretical (Skinner 1950), in fact it is generally regarded as a *meta-theory* – that is, a theory about what makes a good theory of behaviour. In this sense, his ideas are sometimes deceptive in their apparent simplicity.

A second aspect to consider is the interaction between the concepts of operant conditioning and the procedures used. As a graduate student doing research with rats, Skinner found that the typical tasks, like Thorndike's puzzle boxes, required extensive labour on the part of the researcher, to put the animal in the box, record behaviour, retrieve the animal after each trial, etc. In order to simplify this process, Skinner developed an apparatus which would allow running continuous trials, with behaviour automatically recorded. He called this apparatus an 'auto-environmental chamber', but since it resembled a small box with a lever within, it became known (to Skinner's lasting dismay) as a 'Skinner box'! While it accomplished Skinner's basic goal of automating Thorndike's approach, it also led to other consequences. The most notable of these concerns the measure of behaviour used. Since pressing the lever in the Skinner box could be considered analogous to the cat pressing the lever in Thorndike's puzzle box, counting the number of presses (that is, frequency of response) became the standard measure of operant learning. In some respects, this is unfortunate, since despite Skinner's claims to not having a theory, 'the response' in operant conditioning has largely considered *only* the frequency of behaviour, ignoring such aspects as intensity, duration or quality. While the focus on frequency was a practical consideration, it eventually became part of the overall conceptual framework as well – a case of research methods directing theory.

Although the analyses of behaviour which have resulted have often been highly effective, it should be noted that in everyday life, frequency is not always the most meaningful aspect of behaviour. For example, should we judge the quality of an artist by *how many* works they create, or should we look at the *content* of their work? Thus, operant conditioning, while claiming to be a pragmatic analysis unencumbered by theory, in fact has evolved out of a unique set of assumptions about both theory and methodology. As with other approaches to psychology, recognizing the foundations should help make it easier to understand where it has led in the understanding of behaviour.

Reinforcers and Reinforcement

One of the first issues which Skinner attempted to address was Thorndike's law of effect. While it is intuitively obvious that a response which leads to a satisfying consequence is likely to be repeated, Skinner was bothered by the vagueness of 'satisfying'. To avoid this, he coined a new term, 'reinforcer'. A **reinforcer** is a stimulus which, when it follows a response, results in an increase in the probability of the response recurring. Thus, unlike notions of 'satisfaction', a reinforcer becomes *an observable environmental event*. In everyday terms, a reinforcer is similar to what is often called a 'reward', but of course Skinner would reject such words as being too imprecise for scientific purposes. **Reinforcement** is the process by which a reinforcer increases the probability of a response. (Note that in talking about probabilities, one is implicitly describing how *often* a response occurs, i.e. frequency.)

reinforcer in operant conditioning, a stimulus which, when it follows a response, results in an increase in the probability of the response recurring **reinforcement** the process by which a reinforcer increases the probability of a response

The most basic reinforcers are those which are necessary for survival, notably food and water. Such reinforcers are described as **primary reinforcers**, since they have an innate biological significance. For example, a baby cries because it is hungry. When it receives food, this serves as a reinforcer for the response of crying. As a result of this reinforcement process, the baby is more likely to cry the next time it is hungry. ('Hunger', of course, is a reference to an internal state which cannot be observed directly. To avoid such terms, Skinner would talk about the length of time since the baby was last fed. Any parent who has monitored a baby's feeding schedule can testify that this is a reasonably accurate gauge of 'hunger'!) While food and water are the most common primary reinforcers, items which provide protection from cold, and certain drugs such as nicotine or opiates, also seem to function as primary reinforcers (recent research also suggests that touching can be a form of primary reinforcer). Interestingly, primary reinforcers also typically elicit some form of reflex response – that is, they are also unconditioned reinforcers, in terms of classical conditioning. Food, for example, is a primary reinforcer, but also elicits salivation; this dual nature underlines the fact that primary reinforcers seem to have direct biological significance.

primary reinforcer a stimulus whose capacity to act as a reinforcer is based on an innate biological significance, such as food or water

By contrast, there are a large number of environmental events which seem to act as reinforcers, but are not based on biological survival. For example, attention, praise, money and trophies can all act as reinforcers. Reinforcing stimuli like these are described as **conditioned reinforcers**. As the name suggests, conditioned reinforcers are stimuli which assume reinforcing properties because they have been reliably associated with a primary reinforcer. (This is actually a form of classical conditioning, with the conditioned reinforcer and primary reinforcer related as CS and UCS, respectively.) For example, Skinner has argued that attention becomes a conditioned reinforcer in early infancy because it precedes (and is therefore associated with) receiving primary reinforcers: the baby cries, an adult comes to see what is wrong, and then the adult provides a primary reinforcer like food or a dry nappy. A young child may receive praise for a particular action, and receive a cookie; soon, praise itself becomes a reinforcer, like the cookie. Later, other conditioned reinforcers may develop as stimuli that are associated with existing conditioned reinforcers. (Recall how higher-order conditioning allows new stimuli to become linked to existing conditioned stimuli.) Since conditioned reinforcers are based on learning, not innate factors, the potential range of such reinforcers is virtually unlimited. Perhaps the most powerful conditioned reinforcer in our society is money, which can be used to obtain a wide range of other reinforcers, both primary and conditioned.

conditioned reinforcer stimuli which act as reinforcers but are not based on biological survival, such as attention, praise or money

Reinforcement, the process of increasing the frequency of a response by means of a reinforcer which follows the response, is at once both simple and subtle. One element which is important for proper reinforcement is contiguity – that is, the reinforcer should immediately follow the desired response. If a child does something desirable, then praise should be given *immediately*; if not, one runs the risk that the reinforcer will influence a subsequent response. For example, two-year-old Johnny goes to the potty instead of wetting his pants. Half an hour later, Johnny's mother realizes what has happened, and praises Johnny, who is now engaged in pulling books out of the bookcase. In this situation, the reinforcer is unlikely to be strongly associated with going to the potty, and may in fact reinforce the less desirable current behaviour! Parents sometimes misunderstand the significance of contiguity, but it is a powerful factor in operant conditioning. When the wrong response is reinforced, the tendency is to assume the principles don't work. But Skinner once commented that if an experiment doesn't turn out the way we expect, there is a temptation to tell the animal, 'Behave properly!' However, in such cases, the animal *always* behaves – the error is in our understanding (Skinner 1967).

Particularly when it comes to bad habits, people tend to invoke rationalizations for failing to change. A would-be dieter or a heavy smoker might say, 'I lack willpower'. Skinner would argue that such phrases have no real explanatory value, and in fact obscure the actual dynamics of the situation. A smoker, for example, may worry that they will develop lung cancer some years hence, and thus wishes to quit. When the attempt fails, the person concludes it is because of personal weakness. In fact, they are ignoring the actual reinforcers – the nicotine, the conditioned reinforcement of smoking being associated with enjoyable moments, possibly peer approval, and so forth. Compared with these *immediate* reinforcers for the act of smoking, the perceived value of better health some time *in the future* has much less effect on the response of quitting. Thus, both *what* the reinforcers are, and *when* they are received, is crucial to understanding the dynamics of behaviour.

One point which has been overlooked thus far is the question of negative consequences. Thorndike's law of effect stated that satisfying consequences increases a behaviour, but dissatisfying consequences make the behaviour less likely in the future. How does this relate to Skinner's concept of reinforcers? The fact is that aversive consequences are acknowledged – they are referred to as **negative reinforcers** (the reinforcers we have been discussing thus far, which work to encourage responses, are normally called **positive reinforcers**). Negative reinforcers can be either primary (such as a physical blow or electric shock) or conditioned (such as criticism, deliberate ignoring, fines, etc.). Obviously, negative reinforcers do not affect a response in the same way that positive reinforcers do. In order to understand the differences, let us re-examine the nature of reinforcement.

Contingencies of Reinforcement

As noted previously, reinforcement is a *process* by which the probability of a response is increased. In the cases we have discussed, the response increases when it is immediately followed by a positive reinforcer. In keeping with our previous terminology, this can be termed **positive reinforcement**. Suppose now that a response is immediately followed by a *negative* reinforcer; since this represents an aversive consequence, do you think that it would make the response more likely in the future? Obviously, the answer is 'no'; in fact, the response would become *less* likely. For example, three-year-old Sally pokes a pin in an electric outlet and receives a shock. In the future, Sally is not likely to repeat this action! Since the probability of the response does not increase, this cannot be termed a case of *reinforcement*. Instead, one would likely call it 'punishment', and that is the term used in operant conditioning as well (it is one of the rare cases in which Skinner adopted a term with obvious everyday meaning). **Punishment** is defined as a process whereby a response is followed by a negative reinforcer, which results in a decrease in the probability of the response.

negative reinforcer an aversive stimulus which when it follows a response serves to decrease the probability of the response in the future

positive reinforcer in operant conditioning, a stimulus which when it follows a response serves to increase the probability of the response in the future

positive reinforcement in operant conditioning, a process of increasing the probability of a response by immediately following the response with a desirable stimulus (a positive reinforcer)

punishment in operant conditioning, a process whereby a response is followed by a negative reinforcer, which results in a decrease in the probability of the response

The distinction between reinforcement and punishment gets at the heart of Skinner's approach. Operant responses are freely produced by the individual, but the likelihood of making a response is determined by its consequences in the past. This relationship between a response and a reinforcer is called the **contingency of reinforcement**. In order to understand the dynamics of learning, one must be able to identify the contingency which is involved. For example, parents and teachers often react to a child who is misbehaving by scolding the child. The intent, of course, is to decrease the undesirable behaviour – that is, to use *punishment*. What sometimes happens, however, is that the child continues to misbehave, and may even become more disruptive. The frustrated adult exclaims, 'I don't know what's wrong with that child! The more I punish them, the worse they behave!' Skinner would respond by looking at the situation from the child's point of view (since the child is the one receiving a reinforcer). Given that the disruptive behaviour *increases*, Skinner would say that obviously the child is receiving reinforcement, and so the reinforcer (scolding) is actually a positive reinforcer for the child! At first glance, this may seem silly, but in fact scolding requires paying attention to the child – and attention is a powerful positive reinforcer, especially for a child who feels neglected. What typically happens is that a busy adult ignores the child who plays quietly, but immediately responds to misbehaviour; so, in order to get attention, the child misbehaves more and more. The moral of this example is that the *organism* (i.e. the child) determines the significance of the reinforcer, *not* the environment which delivers the reinforcer (the adult, in this case).

Reinforcement and punishment represent the most common contingencies in operant conditioning; they are roughly equivalent to the old notion of 'the carrot and the stick' to train a mule. However, reinforcers can be related to behaviour in other, more indirect ways. For example, a teenager is nagged by a parent to clean up a messy bedroom. The nagging is, in this case, unpleasant – a negative reinforcer. In order to end the nagging, the teenager eventually (albeit reluctantly) cleans up the room, and the parent stops nagging. If we look at this from the viewpoint of operant conditioning, the desired response is cleaning up the room. As long as the response is *not* made, a negative reinforcer is presented (the nagging). Ultimately, the response is made, and the negative reinforcer ceases! So, in this case, a behaviour has been *increased* by the use of a negative reinforcer – a case of *reinforcement, not* punishment. In order to distinguish this process from reinforcement using a positive reinforcer, it is generally called **negative reinforcement** (to make it even clearer, increases in behaviour produced by use of a positive reinforcer are called *positive reinforcement*).

In the example just given, the teenager reacts to eliminate the nagging – that is, to *escape* from an existing negative reinforcer. It is possible that in the future they will respond at the first hint of parental displeasure, before the nagging actually begins. In this case, they would be responding before the reinforcer is given, in order to *avoid* it. Thus, negative reinforcement actually has two variations, escape and avoidance. Normally, initial learning requires presenting the negative reinforcer until the response is made (i.e. escape); later, the individual anticipates the sequence, and responds before the negative reinforcer is presented (i.e. avoidance). Just how this anticipation is accomplished is something we will discuss shortly.

To recap what has been said about the process of reinforcement, one can

contingency of reinforcement in operant conditioning, a description of the relationship between a response and a reinforcer

negative reinforcement in operant conditioning, a process for increasing the probability of a response in which a response is immediately followed by the removal of an aversive stimulus (negative reinforcer); note that since the response increases in frequency, it is *not* equivalent to punishment understand the dynamics of behaviour by identifying the contingency of reinforcement involved. To do so, one must identify the response, the reinforcer and how they are related. In doing so, one must remember that the value of the reinforcer is determined by the organism, not the environment. An example might help to clarify this. Imagine that you are offered a chocolate milkshake if you will sing a song. Assuming you like milkshakes, you will likely sing; thus, the milkshake is a positive reinforcer. Based on your rousing performance, you are offered a second shake if you sing another song. You do so, but drink the second shake more slowly. When you finish, you are offered a third shake for another song. At this point, the prospect of consuming another milkshake is very unappealing, and you refuse to sing. Thus, what started out as a *positive* reinforcer has now become a *negative* reinforcer. The sodas haven't changed, but their value to the organism has – and that is the crucial point. Thus, one must look at how the behaviour changes in order to identify the contingency involved (see Fig. 3.6). As Skinner said, the organism always behaves, it's our understanding that is sometimes wrong.

For further consideration

The previous question asked what you find satisfying and dissatisfying, and why. Can you better understand your behaviour if you analyse it in terms of the process of reinforcement, as Skinner does?

Operant Conditioning Phenomena

Shaping and the Learning Process

In all the examples we have discussed, the reinforcer was used to alter the likelihood of an existing response. While this shows the power of reinforcement, it also poses a problem. Since one cannot reinforce a response that doesn't occur at all, how do new behaviours arise? How can operant principles explain the development of complex behaviours? For example, how does a child learn to walk, or an adult learn to play the piano? One factor to recognize is that complex behaviours do not suddenly emerge fully formed. Instead, they tend to be formed out of a series of simpler behaviours, which can then be combined. A child learns to crawl, and to pull itself upright, before it takes its first steps. Piano-playing involves a whole set of responses, from learning how to position the hands and body at the piano, to identifying written musical notes, to controlling the pedals while playing. Thus, complex behaviours can be thought of as sequences of simpler responses which are combined; it is only after the whole sequence is established that reinforcement can be applied to increase the behaviour. Thus, a toddler who takes their first steps will be praised and hugged; but no amount of praise will force the behaviour to occur.

While this description can account for complex responses, it still doesn't explain how new responses arise. Such originality is related to what Skinner has called 'behavioural drift'. Operant behaviour, in the absence of reinforcement for a specific response, tends to vary somewhat over time. Much of this variation is simply random, but the fact that drift occurs means that sometimes new responses will occur, and therefore may be reinforced. This means that desired new behaviours can be encouraged through a process called shaping.

Desired Change in Behaviour

Type of Reinforcer	Increase Response	Decrease Response
Positive Reinforcer	POSITIVE REINFORCEMENT	NEGATIVE REINFORCEMENT (witholding pos. reinforcer)
Negative Reinforcer	NEGATIVE REINFORCEMENT (escape, avoidance)	PUNISHMENT

Fig. 3.6 Contingencies of reinforcement Skinner argues that in order to understand how operant responses change, one must look at both the type of reinforcer and its relationship to the response (see text for definitions of forms of reinforcement).

Shaping is defined as the process of reinforcing successive approximations to a desired response. The process assumes that someone (an experimenter, a parent, etc.) has in mind a behavioural goal, and can control the delivery of a reinforcer accordingly. For example, most operant research involves an animal (such as a white rat) pressing a lever in a Skinner box. While rats are capable of pressing a lever, it is not a natural response in the wild. Consequently, the rat must be shaped to acquire the response. As a graduate student working as a lab assistant, I had many experiences of such training. Typically, when one places an untrained rat in the Skinner box, it begins to explore this new environment, looking around and sniffing at everything. In one corner of the chamber, there is a food dispenser which can deliver pellets of dry food. At first, one simply dispenses pellets, one at a time, until the rat associates the click of the mechanism with the arrival of a food pellet. Then, when the rat turns towards the lever, a food pellet is given. After eating, the rat will probably turn back towards the lever. If it moves closer, or lifts a paw towards the lever, another pellet is given. Gradually, the standard is raised, until the rat must actually press the bar to get a food pellet, and at this point the desired shaping has been achieved.

Shaping is a simple concept, but very powerful. Although they might not use the terms of operant conditioning, generations of animal trainers have applied the same principle in their work. There is even a story, probably apocryphal, about a class of psychology students who shaped their professor to stand in the corner. The students used writing in their notebooks as the reinforcer (professors tend to find this reinforcing, since it implies both paying attention and being interested). Whenever the professor, who tended to walk about, moved towards

shaping in operant conditioning, the process of guiding the acquisition of a new response by reinforcing successive approximations to the desired response one corner, the students all wrote furiously. When he moved in the opposite direction, they all put down their pens. By the end of the class, the story goes, the poor professor was wedged into the corner!

The process of shaping has also been applied to more serious purposes, including assisting children with language learning and helping accident victims to re-acquire basic skills (see Chapter 9 for details). Anyone who has watched trained animals, whether at a circus or in a movie, has also witnessed the power of shaping. Having said this, it is also worth noting that shaping is easier to grasp as a concept than to apply in practice. I can still recall my first attempt to shape a rat to press the lever in a Skinner box – it took nearly an hour. Later, after gaining more experience, I could typically do it in fifteen minutes! The difference was one of judgement and timing, deciding when a new approximation was 'good enough' to merit a reinforcer. If I rewarded too often, the rat spent more time eating than learning; if I rewarded too infrequently, the rat lost interest, or seemed to forget what the last reinforced response had been. In this sense, shaping, while clearly consistent with operant principles, is not simply a mechanical process.

Extinction

Shaping uses the variability inherent in responding in order to produce a desired response. Once a response occurs, it can be reinforced, as we have seen. But what happens if the reinforcement is discontinued? Consider a rat that has been reinforced with a food pellet each time it presses the lever, or a child that has been praised each time they pick up their toys. If the situation changes so that reinforcers are no longer given, what will the organism do? An intuitive answer, which is supported by research, would be that the behaviour might continue for a short time, but once it is recognized that reinforcers are no longer forthcoming, the behaviour will decrease in probability. This drop in responding when reinforcement is discontinued is called **extinction**. (One can see a parallel with extinction in classical conditioning, where no longer pairing the CS with the UCS results in the CR disappearing.) Note that while both extinction and punishment produce decreases in responding, they do so in very different ways. Extinction can be considered a passive process, in that it diminishes the value of the response by eliminating the reinforcer which supported it. Punishment, on the other hand, uses an aversive stimulus to actively suppress the (undesired) behaviour.

extinction in operant conditioning, a drop in responding when reinforcement is discontinued

One implication of extinction seems to be that, in order to be effective, reinforcement must be given continuously for every response. Unfortunately, this seldom seems the case in the real world. Students study regularly, but receive reinforcement only after the occasional test. People go to work every day, but may be paid only weekly or even monthly. How, then, can operant conditioning be said to apply to such behaviours?

Schedules of Reinforcement

continuous reinforcement a reinforcement schedule in which every response is followed by a reinforcer; equivalent to a FR 1 schedule

Early in his research, Skinner recognized that in everyday life we rarely experience either true extinction (no reinforcement at all) or **continuous reinforcement** (with every response reinforced). Instead, what we tend to encounter is something in between – some responses get reinforced and some don't. Skinner coined the term **partial reinforcement** to describe situations where reinforcement is given only intermittently. In order to understand what happens under such circumstances, he began a series of studies looking at various forms of partial reinforcement. In order to distinguish various types of intermittent reinforcement, Skinner coined the term **schedules of reinforcement** (see Ferster and Skinner 1957). In general, a reinforcement schedule describes when a reinforcer is given, in much the same way that a train schedule describes when a train departs.

The most straightforward schedule, of course, is continuous reinforcement, since every response receives a reinforcer. By contrast, partial reinforcement can occur under an essentially infinite number of variations. However, a surprisingly large number of situations can be described in one of two ways: according to the number of responses made before a reinforcer is given, or the amount of time that elapses between reinforcers. Schedules which depend on the number of responses made are called *ratio schedules*; those which are time-dependent are called *interval schedules*. Also, such schedules may be very regular (e.g. every third response, every fifteen seconds) or somewhat unpredictable. Regular schedules are called *fixed schedules*, while those which are more unpredictable are called *variable schedules*. Let us look at the different types more closely in order to see how they affect behaviour.

Fixed ratio (FR) schedules are the simplest to understand (in fact, continuous reinforcement is equivalent to a fixed ratio of 1). The ratio is measured as FR x, where x is the number of responses the organism must make in order to get a reinforcer. Thus, FR 5 means that every fifth response would receive a reinforcer (see Fig. 3.7a). In everyday life, this is analogous to piece work, where a person will be paid according to the number of responses made. An example might be a seamstress: each shirt may have seven buttons to be sewn, and completing a shirt earns $1 (this would be FR 7). Skinner found in his experiments that increasing the ratio tended to increase the rate of responding; the animals sought to maintain the total amount of reinforcement received, regardless of the schedule (in the same way, a seamstress might try to work faster if the rate of pay per shirt declined). In the laboratory, pigeons would peck at a key fifty or more times to get one reinforcer! Eventually, however, as fixed ratios increase, behaviour slows, and may even cease. Essentially, if the ratio is too high, the organism reacts as if it were an extinction situation. For example, if it takes 150 responses to produce one reinforcer, it may *seem* as though reinforcement has ceased!

Interestingly, when the ratio is made less predictable, performance tends to be even better. A **variable ratio (VR) schedule** is defined in terms of the *average* number of responses required to receive a reinforcer (e.g. VR 10 means on average every tenth response is reinforced; see Fig. 3.7b). This means that the ratio is predictable in the long run, but in the short run the number of responses required varies. This is much like a slot machine, which pays off on a predefined percentage of plays – but one cannot predict precisely when the next payoff will be. This analogy actually works surprisingly well, for animals on variable ratio schedules tend to perform very steadily, much like the gambler who plays a slot machine for hours, hoping that the next play will be the big payoff. In both cases, the fact that reinforcement occasionally occurs after only a few responses

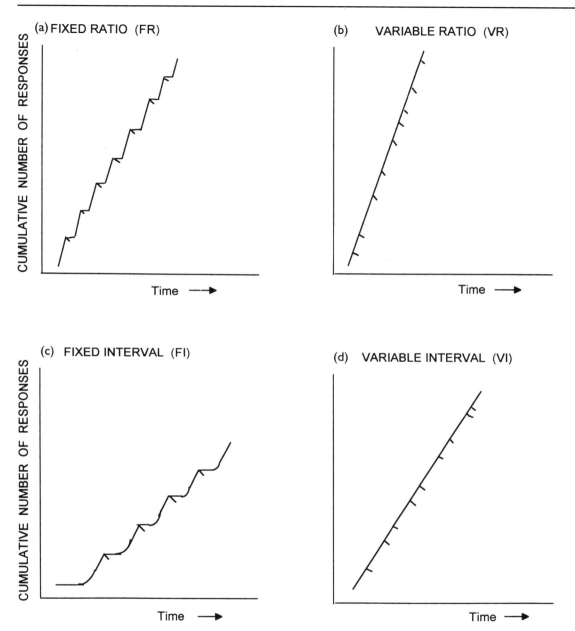

Fig. 3.7 Schedules of reinforcement Using cumulative frequency graphs (where total responses are counted), one can see the differences in response patterns using different types of schedules. Note in particular the lag in responding after a reinforcer (shown by hash marks) under fixed interval schedules, and the relatively fast response rates (steep curve) under variable ratio.

tends to maintain the behaviour over the sequences when no reinforcement occurs. Many other activities also seem to be based on variable ratio reinforcement. In sales jobs, for example, a sales agent might have to make a varying number of client contacts before closing a sale; even so, the occasional sale sustains the behaviour. Sport fishermen don't typically succeed on every outing, and cannot predict when they will catch a 'big one'; even so, they continue to try, knowing the next outing may lead to success. Thus, while both variable and fixed ratios tend to produce very steady responding, variable schedules are slightly better overall.

In ratio schedules, since getting a reinforcer depends on making the specified number of responses, performance tends to occur at a relatively high rate. The situation is somewhat different with *interval* schedules, where time is the crucial factor. In a **fixed interval (FI) schedule**, a timer determines how long it has been since the previous reinforcer was given, and only a response made *after* the required time interval has elapsed will receive a reinforcer (of course, if no response at all is made, no reinforcer is given). Thus, in a FI 15 sec schedule, at least fifteen seconds must pass between delivery of reinforcers (assuming a response is made at the end of the required interval; see Fig. 3.7c). It may seem odd to consider reinforcement as being time-dependent, but in fact there are many situations in which this type of schedule applies. For example, if you are waiting for a bus on a rainy day, you must go out at the appropriate time in order to get the bus. It does not matter how often you go out to check (i.e. make multiple responses), only going out at the appropriate time will get reinforced (by actually getting the bus). Another example is the administering of pain-killers in hospitals. In many cases, a patient will only receive medication for pain (the reinforcer) if they request it (the response). However, to avoid over-doses, the medication will only be given after a certain time interval since the previous dose, such as four hours (the fixed interval); any requests made before this time has passed will be ignored. Another example is work which is paid on an hourly rate rather than on a piecework basis. In this situation, there is an assumption by employers that responses are being made (i.e. that work is being done), but technically the response which is reinforced is arriving for work! (You show up for a week, and you get paid at the end.) Thus, fixed interval schedules are actually a fairly common form of reinforcement.

One special characteristic of fixed interval schedules is that they only *require* a single response in order to receive reinforcement, provided the required time interval has elapsed. The result is that fixed interval schedules tend to produce rather low rates of responding compared with ratio schedules. In fact, even in laboratory studies with animals, as the animal becomes familiar with the situation, one finds a distinctive pattern emerges. Typically, few responses are made immediately after a reinforcer is delivered. Instead, there is a lull, and then a few tentative responses, and finally a brief surge in responding clustered near the end of the time interval. Essentially, the organism comes to recognize that premature responses are wasted, and tries to determine the end of the time interval. (While not as precise as a real clock, most species have a 'biological clock' which provides a sense of time.) On a cumulative record of responses, this clustering of responses produces a distinctive 'scallop' in the graph (see Fig. 3.7c). If the intention is to encourage steady responding, a fixed interval schedule is inappropriate, given the clustering of responses which it produces.

fixed interval (FI) schedule a reinforcement contingency defined by the amount of time that must pass since the previous reinforcer was given, before a response will receive a reinforcer; measured as FI *x*, where *x* specifies the required time interval

**variable interval (VI)
schedule** in operant
conditioning, a reinforcement
contingency defined by the
average time interval which
must elapse since the last
reinforcer before a response
will be reinforced; thus, on a
VI 15 sec schedule, over a
long period the average
duration would be fifteen
seconds

If fixed interval schedules tend to produce irregular rates of response, is there any time-based alternative schedule which remedies this problem? The answer is yes; the trick is to vary the time interval. In a **variable interval (VI) schedule**, the schedule is defined in terms of the average time interval required over the long term, much as a variable ratio is defined by an average number of responses required. Thus, on a VI 15 sec schedule, one interval might be only five seconds, the interval after another reinforcer might be twenty seconds, and so on – only over a long period would the average duration be fifteen seconds (see Fig. 3.7d). From the point of view of the organism being reinforced, this variability means that the availability of a reinforcer is no longer predictable; consequently, the only way to determine if the interval has elapsed is to make a response. The result is that variable interval schedules result in steady behaviour, albeit at much lower rates than ratio schedules. Since the schedule is still time-based, very fast response rates don't really accelerate the process of getting a reinforcer; the purpose of responding regularly is simply to check if a reinforcer is available.

An example which provides an analogy may help clarify the nature of behaviour under variable interval schedules. Imagine someone who works as a quality control inspector on an assembly line; the person's role is to watch items as they pass by, and pick out any which appear defective. In this situation, a person who ignores the task (e.g. to read a newspaper) may not be detected for several months, until complaints about defective products are received from customers. Consequently, the foreman checks the person every two hours, on the hour. Since this is equivalent to a fixed interval schedule, a person intent on goofing off could simply begin working just before the foreman arrives, and then return to loafing after the foreman leaves (this is equivalent to a fixed interval 'scallop'). In order to avoid this, the foreman varies the time of his visits; in effect, a variable interval schedule. Now, since the visits are unpredictable, the worker must work steadily, or run the risk of being caught unexpectedly. The result would be typical of behaviour under variable interval schedules – steady responding! (Compared with variable ratio schedules, where there is a direct incentive for fast responding, variable interval schedules tend to produce slow but steady response rates.)

While these four types of schedules are only a small sample of the possible types of partial reinforcement, they show that intermittent reinforcement can be used to sustain behaviour, and that the behaviour tends to reflect the specific requirements of the schedule. In this sense, both people and animals are adept at recognizing the demands of their environment, adjusting their responses to fit the situation. Beyond that, it is worth noting some other characteristics of behaviour using partial reinforcement. The most obvious difference between continuous and partial reinforcement is that under partial reinforcement, an organism does more work to get a reinforcer. This gap increases as the size of the ratio or length of the interval increases. One might expect that this 'more work, less pay' regimen would result in resistance (reduced responding), yet behaviour tends to occur at a *higher* rate with partial reinforcement than with continuous reinforcement (except with very high fixed ratios, as discussed previously). In addition, variable schedules (ratio *or* interval) tend to produce greater response rates than equivalent fixed schedules. Overall, variable ratio schedules seem to be the most effective in maintaining behaviour. Skinner, of course, would never speculate about *why* this occurs (it would require discussing non-observable events), but the dynamics may involve the fact that primary reinforcers have survival value, and organisms must meet their survival needs, regardless of the effort involved. (Early hunters, for example, probably received only partial reinforcement for their efforts, and still had to hunt when game was scarce.)

Since partial reinforcement tends to produce higher rates of responding than continuous reinforcement, what happens under extinction conditions (when no reinforcement at all is given)? Generally speaking, *behaviour acquired under partial reinforcement is much more persistent than behaviour acquired under continuous reinforcement.* The standard measure is to count how many responses are made once reinforcers are no longer available; this is called 'resistance to extinction', where a larger number reflects more persistent behaviour. Interestingly, one finds that resistance to extinction roughly parallels the hierarchy found when reinforcement *is* available; that is, variable schedules are more resistant to extinction than fixed schedules. This pattern is characteristic of many forms of gambling, which tend to produce very persistent behaviour, despite the fact that individuals are assured of losing in the long run (e.g. slot machines, roulette and craps all fit this description). Again, Skinner does not speculate as to *why* this is true, but a number of researchers have noted that the change in contingency (from reinforcement to extinction) is simply harder to detect with partial reinforcement. That is, with continuous reinforcement, it is immediately obvious if reinforcement ceases, since a reinforcer should follow every response. By contrast, with any form of partial reinforcement, the organism has learned ('expects') to make responses that go unreinforced; the more variable the schedule, the longer it would take to determine that reinforcement has definitely ceased. Consider an analogy: if you play a slot machine for some time without winning, when would you conclude that the machine was broken or crooked, as opposed to your simply being on a losing streak? In studies with college students who used slot machines that either paid off every time or on a variable ratio, a change to extinction was quickly recognized by the first group, while the second group continued playing for lengthy periods without ever winning! Thus, partial reinforcement produces higher rates of responding during reinforcement, and greater persistence during extinction.

Discriminative Stimuli

At this point, it should be clear that contingencies of reinforcement are very diverse, and that individuals seem to be capable of adapting to the requirements of different situations. But how do they *know* what the requirements are in a particular situation? Consider a simple example: five-year-old Johnny likes to eat spaghetti with his fingers. His mother dislikes this behaviour, and slaps his hand when she catches him eating that way. By contrast, his father is relatively indifferent to the behaviour, neither scolding nor praising it. Thus, depending upon who is present, the consequences of Johnny's behaviour differ significantly. Obviously, Johnny is likely to make the connection between who is present and what consequence occurs, and adapt his behaviour accordingly – eating with his fork when his mother is present, but using his fingers if his father is present! In this situation, the parents are **discriminative stimuli**, stimuli which signal the contingency of reinforcement available. In the above case, Johnny's mother is a stimulus which signals *punishment* of eating with fingers, while

discriminative stimulus
in operant conditioning, a stimulus which signals the contingency of reinforcement available

Johnny's father signals reinforcement (i.e. Johnny presumably eats with fingers because it is reinforcing). In general, discriminative stimuli arise when elements of the environment are associated with a particular contingency.

In principle, it is possible for any contingency to become associated with a discriminative stimulus. Researchers have found, for example, that rats will use discriminative stimuli to decide when to press a bar: pressing it when the contingency is highly reinforcing (e.g. continuous reinforcement), and not responding when the contingency is not reinforcing (e.g. extinction). In everyday life, we all make similar distinctions: most people will exceed the speed limit when no police are visible (in which case speeding is not punished), but will immediately slow down when a police car is spotted (a discriminative stimulus that speeding will be punished). Children may react differently with each parent, as in the case above. We act differently at a party than at work, because the environmental stimuli signal that different behaviours will be rewarded in each case. Thus, discriminative stimuli, by indicating the potential consequences of behaviour, tend to influence the responses we make. The behaviour is still operant, not reflex – it is up to the individual what response is produced. For example, some people would rather park a car illegally and risk a ticket, than park in a lot where it is certain they must pay a fee. The fact that discriminative stimuli exist makes it easier to make sense out of a changing environment.

Non-contingent Reinforcement

In all of the situations we have been examining, there has been a clearly identified relationship between a response and a reinforcer, described by the contingency. Depending on the type of contingency, behaviour increases or decreases systematically. But is this really a fair description of what happens in the real world? Is reinforcement always clearly dependent on behaviour, or do consequences sometimes occur randomly? Most people would quickly grant that some events in life are random, at least in terms of our ability to control them through our actions. That means that sometimes reinforcement is also random. Can we say anything about how organisms react to such random consequences?

Skinner has considered this question, and has described such random consequences as **non-contingent reinforcement**, which means that the occurrence of the reinforcer is not related to whether the response occurs or not. Using pigeons as subjects, Skinner did some inventive studies of the issue. In the typical situation, a pigeon that was already familiar with a Skinner box apparatus would be placed in a chamber, and a timer would provide a food pellet every fifteen seconds, *regardless of what the pigeon did*. (Note that since *no* responses are required, this is *not* the same as a fixed interval schedule; in the extreme case, if the pigeon went to sleep, the feeder would still keep dropping food pellets!) After a period of time, Skinner and another observer would return to see what was happening. According to his description (Skinner 1948a), six out of eight pigeons had developed elaborate, stereotyped response sequences. Since these behaviours actually had no effect on the availability of reinforcement, Skinner called such behaviours 'superstitious'. All that was happening, he argued, was that responses were reinforced *by coincidence*, and then the organism maintained the response that was reinforced.

Skinner went on to suggest that non-contingent reinforcement has similar

non-contingent reinforcement in operant conditioning, the occurrence of a reinforcer which is not related to whether the response occurs or not effects on people. Superstitious behaviours, like wearing a favourite shirt while playing a sport, seem to arise in situations in which behaviour is only inconsistently reinforced. (Note that this is not the same as partial reinforcement, because Skinner assumes that the superstitious behaviour has no actual impact on the outcome.) I have noticed, for example, that many people have particular rituals for trying to make elevator doors close – tapping the edge of the door, holding the 'close' button, even jumping to momentarily increase the load on the elevator! Unfortunately, most modern elevators operate on a programmed cycle, and so people are really acting like Skinner's pigeons, engaging in a ritual which makes the time go by! (Not everyone, however, feels that such behaviours are truly non-contingent; it could be argued, for example, that if you *believe* your lucky shirt helps your tennis game, then you will actually play better when you wear it.) At the very least, non-contingent reinforcement shows how sensitive organisms are to environmental consequences.

For further consideration

Having studied the basic principles of operant conditioning, can you apply them to an example of your own behaviour? For example, most of us would like to change the way we behave in various ways. Do you have any 'bad habits'? What is the response? What is the discriminative stimulus that cues the response? What is the reinforcer that sustains it? Can you think of a way to modify your behaviour?

Applications and Implications of Conditioning

behaviour modification
the application of conditioning techniques to altering human behaviour, particularly those behaviours identified as abnormal

One of the striking things about behaviourism is the strong pragmatic element which underlies it. Behaviourists are typically very interested not only in trying to understand behaviour, but in *applying* their understanding in the real world. Watson's claim about raising children, cited at the start of this chapter, is one example of this impulse. Skinner has often been outspoken concerning his ideas for reshaping society, including writing a Utopian novel, *Walden Two* (Skinner 1948b). In more limited ways, behaviourist methods have been applied to dealing with many aspects of human behaviour; these applications are commonly referred to as **behaviour modification**. While more specifics about the application of conditioning principles to therapy will be given in Chapter 9, it is appropriate to consider here some general issues related to conditioning.

Negative Reinforcers and the Aversive Control of Operant Behaviour

As Thorndike noted, not all behavioural outcomes are alike. While positive reinforcers like praise or money are welcomed by individuals, negative reinforcers like criticism or physical punishment are unpleasant. Therefore, positive reinforcement is more attractive than punishment and negative reinforcement, which depend on use of negative reinforcers. Although Skinner would shun descriptions like 'positive reinforcement is more attractive' as being vague and subjective, researchers have found a number of ways to examine the differences between use of positive and negative reinforcers.

The use of negative reinforcers is often referred to as *aversive control of behaviour*, because of the way organisms react to negative reinforcers. One can distinguish two ways in which aversive control is used: punishment is used to reduce the frequency of a response, whereas negative reinforcement is used to increase a response (i.e. the response leads to escaping or avoiding the negative reinforcer).

Punishment is probably the most used – and misunderstood – method of dealing with undesirable behaviour. Parents resort to scolding when disciplining their children. Employers will criticize or threaten hapless employees. Even our legal system is based on punishment for breaking society's rules. Unfortunately, punishment has several limitations. First, as with *any* operant reinforcement, it depends on *contiguity* between the response and the reinforcer; for effective learning, the reinforcer must immediately follow the response. Punishment which is delayed will be ineffective in controlling the response, or worse, may become associated with a different response. For example, five-year-old Sarah breaks a plate, and then later tells her mother what happened. Her mother, upset about the broken plate, scolds Sarah, but in fact this negative reinforcer will tend to be associated with *telling* about the accident, *not* breaking the plate. In the future, Sarah may still break things, but may not be forthcoming about admitting it! In the same way, imagine if your dog soiled the carpet, and two hours later, when you discovered the damage, you yelled at the dog, who was now quietly resting on his blanket! Ignoring the importance of contiguity can seriously hamper the effectiveness of punishment. (One might also note that our legal system, with its typically long delays between crime and punishment, is also poorly designed in terms of contiguity.)

A second limitation of punishment is that it tends to encourage avoidance behaviours. A child in school may be scolded by a teacher for giving a wrong answer. Obviously, the teacher's intention is to get the child to study harder, and thereby give more correct answers, but the real result may be rather different. The child may refuse to answer at all, or even skip the classes taught by that teacher. Because of classical conditioning, any stimulus associated with a negative reinforcer (the teacher, the classroom) may itself become aversive, and trigger avoidance. The avoidance responses may be directed at the situation, or simply finding ways to avoid the negative reinforcer itself. A criminal with a history of robbing banks was once confronted by a prison official who asked, 'After all these years, don't you know robbing banks is wrong?' The criminal's response was, 'Actually, I don't see anything wrong with robbing banks; it's getting caught that I don't like!' Research by criminologists has indicated that most people obey laws because they feel it is the right thing to do (feeling virtuous can be a form of positive reinforcement); it is only a minority of people (mostly criminals) who focus on the punishments for transgressing. As anyone aware of crime statistics knows, having laws with specified punishments does not in itself deter criminal behaviour, since those so inclined will simply seek to avoid getting caught.

This issue of punishment encouraging avoidance is a major concern, because punishment tends to *suppress* behaviour, *not extinguish* it. Any operant response occurs because there is some reinforcer supporting it; applying punishment to suppress the response simply pits one reinforcer against the other. Worse, whereas positive reinforcement can be highly effective with only partial reinforcement, *punishment must be continuous in order to suppress behaviour effectively.* Thus, in situations in which it is possible to avoid the punishment even occasionally, punishment will not be fully effective in suppressing the undesired response. (Consider what this means in terms of our legal system, where arrest and conviction rates rarely approach 100 per cent.) Instead, it would be better to identify the factor which encourages the undesirable behaviour, and try to alter the environment to eliminate that positive reinforcer. For example, children sometimes misbehave because it quickly draws parental attention (a positive reinforcer); to a child starved for attention, the scolding which may follow is less significant than the attention. The result is an increase in disruptive behaviour, followed by more attention (and scolding), etc. The way out of this may be for the parents to *ignore* (extinguish) misbehaviour, and *also* attempt to offer attention when the child is playing quietly or otherwise desirably engaged. In cases like this, the reinforcing of appropriate behaviour is as important as the extinguishing of undesirable behaviour.

Because of the way the contingency operates, negative reinforcement is often more effective than punishment as a form of aversive control. Since the focus is on *increasing* a desired response, one does not encounter the problems of suppression associated with punishment. In addition, the acquired fear which can lead to escaping/avoiding the punishment situation, in negative reinforcement tends to *sustain* the desired behaviour. For example, a child may refuse to dress for school, whereupon the parent scowls, and begins yelling at the child, who finally gets dressed. In the future, a scowl may be sufficient to induce the child to dress. In this sense, negative reinforcement is probably preferable to the use of punishment. In addition, because making the desired response is directly linked to the removal of the aversive stimulus, negative reinforcement is more effective than punishment in signalling what the desired behaviour is (punishment simply indicates what is *not* desired).

Unfortunately, there is one consequence of aversive control which is associated with *any* use of negative reinforcers. By their nature, negative reinforcers represent aversive stimuli, and no organism readily tolerates such events. The use of aversive control therefore tends to promote anxiety, resentment and even aggression, in addition to the problems identified above (Azrin and Holz 1966; Berkowitz 1983). This means that depending on aversive control to regulate behaviour is going to produce a whole range of secondary problems, which may even be less desirable than the original behaviour. Skinner once suggested that a well-designed society would depend on a combination of positive reinforcement (for desired behaviours) and extinction (for undesired behaviours), not aversive control (Skinner 1948b). Given present realities, it is clear that most law-makers have not studied operant conditioning!

For further consideration   Given what has been said about punishment, how would you handle a child that is misbehaving (e.g. using foul language)?

Interrelationships of Classical and Operant Conditioning

For most of this chapter, we have been discussing classical and operant conditioning as if they were totally separate aspects of behaviour. However, it should not be surprising to find there are interconnections between the two; after all, organisms are constantly producing *many* responses, both reflex and operant. In this sense, the distinction between the two types of learning is partly a way of simplifying the analysis of behaviour, by breaking it into reflex and operant components. In the real world, both processes can occur simultaneously. One striking example of this is negative reinforcement. You may recall that negative reinforcement utilizes a negative reinforcer in order to increase the probability of a response. One form of this is *escape*, where a negative reinforcer is presented, and is only removed after the organism makes the desired response. In this circumstance, the removal of the aversive stimulus is effectively like a reward, so the behaviour becomes more likely (hence reinforcement). For example, a dog given a mild shock through an electrified floor grid will learn to jump to another chamber to escape the shock. Now, if a light flashes before the start of the shock, the dog will soon anticipate the shock, and jump *before* the shock begins. This becomes *avoidance* – the dog jumps in order to avoid the negative reinforcer. This leads to an interesting problem: since the dog jumps before the shock, there is no longer any experience of the original reinforcer, a circumstance that would lead to *extinction* of the response if one were looking at positive reinforcement. So why does the dog keep jumping each time the light goes on? The light, of course, has become a discriminative stimulus. Still, why should the dog persist in jumping without at least an occasional experience of shock? The answer seems to be that, through classical conditioning, the light has become a CS associated with the UCS of shock, which is a perfect scenario for creating a conditioned fear. Thus, the dog continues to jump, not to *avoid* the *shock*, but to *escape* from the feared *light* (Mowrer 1956; Rescorla and Solomon 1967).

Recognizing that the two processes are occurring together helps to explain operant avoidance learning, and also adds to our understanding of conditioned fears. Watson, in his demonstration with little Albert, discovered that conditioned fears do not readily extinguish. The reason for this seems to be that the feared stimulus (the CS) *also* triggers operant escape behaviour. This escape response removes the individual from the situation *before* there is an opportunity to determine if the UCS will follow or not. (The same mixture of classical and operant responses happens in the shower when we hear the toilet flush; while we *fear* the sound, we also tend to *jump* away from the water spray to avoid being scalded.) The fact that fear stimuli can evoke an operant response is a very significant point in terms of those everyday fears which are called phobias. If, as Watson argued, such fears are based on classical conditioning, then it is also likely that the fears persist long after the original experience, because we *avoid* the situations that *elicit* the fear. Consequently, there is little opportunity to find out if our fear is realistic or not. For example, a person who is afraid of flying will be reluctant to fly, yet flying would demonstrate that there is nothing to fear. In essence, until we face the fear situation, there is no opportunity to extinguish the fear response.

Autonomic Conditioning and Biofeedback

Consider the following proposal: I will give you twenty dollars if you raise the temperature of your left hand while simultaneously lowering the temperature of your right hand. Short of getting a blanket and ice pack, this may seem like an impossible goal. After all, body temperature is an involuntary (reflex) function. How could I expect to control it with a reinforcer like money? At one time, psychologists would have agreed that such a task was impossible; after all, reflexes are the domain of classical conditioning, not operant conditioning. Even the evidence that shows the two types of learning can occur together (as in avoidance learning) does not challenge the fundamental distinction of reflex versus operant responses. In fact, the boundaries are more ambiguous than the traditional view suggests.

The change was triggered by the work of Neal Miller, a noted researcher in the field of learning, and Leo DiCara, then a graduate student working with Miller. Miller and DiCara wondered if it would be possible to use operant reinforcement with so-called involuntary responses. Although this seemed far-fetched, data on phenomena like meditation (see Chapter 2) suggested that under some circumstances individuals *could* deliberately alter such responses. While the details of the original procedures were rather complex (involving partially paralysed rats, and using electrical stimulation of the brain as a positive reinforcer), the implications of the results were quickly apparent: involuntary responses *could* be operantly controlled!

Miller described the process as 'learned operant control of autonomic responses', or **autonomic conditioning** (Miller 1969). By providing reinforcement which was based on changes in autonomic (involuntary) responses, it was possible to alter behaviours such as heart rate, blood pressure and even the temperature of various limbs (by changes in blood flow). To understand what is involved in autonomic conditioning, it is necessary to consider how operant responses normally function. For all voluntary muscle movements, our brain receives information, called *proprioceptive feedback*, about the execution of the movement. It is proprioceptive feedback which tells you the position of your arm even when your eyes are closed, for example. But for involuntary functions (involving the autonomic nervous system), there is little or no proprioceptive feedback. Consequently, there is typically no direct awareness of autonomic responses. To circumvent this limitation, DiCara and Miller used sophisticated equipment to monitor these hidden processes, and thus determine when to deliver a reinforcer. Since most autonomic functions show natural fluctuations (e.g. heart rate varies slightly even when sitting), the procedure amounted to a process of shaping a desired response.

Thus, the essential element of autonomic conditioning is the ability to measure the response. While the recording of physiological activity dates back to the 1930s, using the procedures in operant conditioning is much more recent. Today, applications of the process are frequently referred to as **biofeedback**, since the process provides an individual with information ('feedback') about physiological processes ('bio') which are normally not observable (see Mercer 1986).

Basically, any biofeedback procedure requires equipment to monitor the response of interest, and a means of conveying information to the individual about changes in their response. (Unlike the original animal studies, in applications with people, informational feedback is often a sufficient reinforcer.) For example, if interested in muscle relaxation, one would use a device called an electromyograph (EMG), which measures the electrical activity in the motor neurons which control the muscles. If interested in the heart, one would use an

autonomic conditioning (also called 'learned operant control of autonomic responses') the conditioning of changes in autonomic (involuntary) responses (such as heart rate or blood pressure) by providing operant reinforcement

biofeedback a general term for applications of the process of autonomic conditioning; the name refers to the fact that in humans reinforcement is based on providing an individual with information ('feedback') about physiological processes ('bio') which are normally not observable

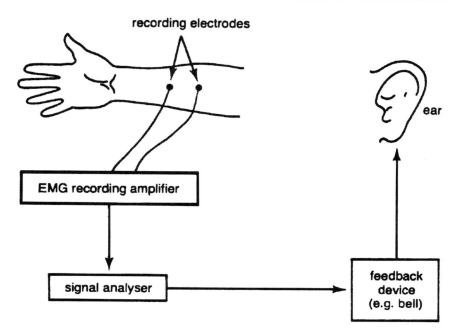

Fig. 3.8 Biofeedback Basically, the procedure for biofeedback requires some means of monitoring the physiological response (in this case a muscle twitch, recorded using an electromyograph), and a means of making the individual aware of changes that occur (in this case, a bell that rings whenever the target muscle twitches). Using this type of procedure, while monitoring several muscles with several bells, subjects actually can learn to play tunes.

electrocardiograph (ECG), and so on. The means of providing feedback might be a buzzer, or a light which flashes, when the desired response occurs (see Fig. 3.8).

The most significant applications of biofeedback are for medical treatment. It has proven very effective for relaxation of voluntary muscles (e.g. arms, legs, neck), which is often utilized for tension control. It has also proven moderately effective for reducing hypertension (high blood pressure) and for regulating the rhythm of the heart (but not very effective for reducing overall heart rate). One of the more interesting uses has been to train individuals to control epileptic seizures, by teaching them to produce a brain-wave pattern which seems to inhibit seizure activity (Sterman 1978).

From a more theoretical point of view, autonomic conditioning demonstrates that the processes of classical and operant conditioning are more closely intertwined than was once believed. While it does *not* imply that Pavlov was wrong about the formation of CS–UCS associations, it raises questions about the definition of 'operant' behaviour. Skinner originally defined operants as emitted responses, in contrast to elicited reflexes. This made sense, in view of how such responses can be used to alter one's environment. Now, however, it seems that operant conditioning can be applied to almost any response, *provided there is a clear contingency of reinforcement* (i.e. connection to consequences). Clearly, this would suggest a widening of the boundaries for operant behaviour. Thus, the study of autonomic conditioning has opened up new areas for operant research. Ironically, at just about the time that research on autonomic conditioning was broadening the horizons, other research was suggesting new limitations of operant learning.

Before leaving the topic of autonomic conditioning, there is a sad side-note to the original discovery. The initial study by DiCara and Miller was very complex, as noted. When it was first reported, it was viewed as so remarkable that other researchers immediately set out to duplicate the results, and failed. Miller himself eventually tried, and also could not reproduce the original findings. While no-one doubts that the general phenomenon is real, and Miller maintained that there was no evidence of fraud in DiCara's work, the younger researcher was discredited by the controversy. Today, the original study goes largely uncited, and DiCara has become a forgotten pioneer. In science, reputation can sometimes make or break a career.

Biological Constraints on Learning

When most people read about conditioning processes for the first time, one of the first things to strike them is the apparent artificiality of the experimental situations. After all, what does a ringing bell, or manipulating a lever, have to do with receiving food in the real world? How can the study of such arbitrary acts tell us about ordinary behaviour? In fact, the situations *are* rather artificial, and deliberately so. Laboratory environments provide a high degree of experimental control, and behaviour is still behaviour, in the lab or out. Consequently, many behaviourists would see the success of their methods as demonstrating just how powerful the basic principles are. However, as with all research, there are inevitably assumptions made when one generalizes from the laboratory to the real world.

One of the assumptions commonly made is called the *equipotentiality premise*. Essentially, this premise says that the principles of conditioning should apply to any response, and any species. (Interestingly, Skinner himself has never endorsed such generalizations. He might be willing to generalize from observations of one pigeon to another, but would hesitate to generalize from one species to another.) For many years, studies of a wide variety of species in the laboratory seemed to demonstrate that the equipotentiality premise was correct.

However, quite independently of behaviourism, other researchers, coming from a tradition of biology rather than psychology, have studied the behaviour of animals in their natural environments. This approach is called **ethology**. The founder of ethology is often regarded as Konrad Lorenz, a German researcher who did pioneering studies of species ranging from fish to wolves (Lorenz 1967). Ethologists like Lorenz have tended to study **species-specific behaviours**, behaviours which are characteristic of all members of a particular species. These response patterns (sometimes popularly called 'instincts') apply to behaviours such as mating, finding food, defence and raising offspring. Typically, the behaviours seem to be genetically shaped, but also responsive to environmental demands. For example, the young of many species identify their parents through a process called *imprinting*, whereby they attach themselves shortly after birth

ethology the study of the behaviour of animals in their natural environments
species-specific behaviour behaviours which are characteristic of all members of a particular species. These response patterns (sometimes popularly called 'instincts') apply to behaviours such as mating, finding food, defence and raising offspring

Degree of Biological Preparedness

Fig. 3.9 Seligman's preparedness continuum Martin Seligman has suggested that not all responses are the same, and that various behaviours can be understood in terms of how physiological factors prepare us to learn easily (prepared) or not at all (contraprepared).

to the nearest moving stimulus. Lorenz at one point had a group of ducklings who followed him around as though he were their mother! Unlike simple re-flexes, species-specific behaviour can involve complex sequences of responses, such as the ritual fighting in some species of tropical fish.

For many years, ethologists and behaviourists pursued their interests separately, but in recent years there has been increasing dialogue between the approaches. One of the prime areas of interest has been the interaction of hereditary and environmental influences on learning. The ethologists have tended to assume that much of behaviour is governed by the genetic make-up of a species, while many behaviourists have tended to see behaviour as completely malleable, based on the principles of conditioning. As with many such issues, the truth seems to be something in between: environmental circumstances affect the expression of many species-specific behaviours, and biological constraints limit the process of learning. Contrary to the equipotentiality premise, not all learning is the same. Some behaviours are easier to acquire than others; for example, learning to clap your hands is easier than rubbing your stomach and tapping your head simultaneously. Also, some behaviours appear to be learned best at particular times during development, called **critical periods**. For instance, a child who is not exposed to language prior to six years of age will generally have great difficulty learning to speak later.

One way to make sense of these variations in ease of learning is the preparedness dimension developed by Martin Seligman (1970). **Preparedness** refers to the degree to which physiological structure influences the occurrence of behaviour (see Fig. 3.9). Some behaviours seem to develop with little or no specific experience required. Seligman refers to these as *prepared* behaviours, because the organism seems physiologically structured to produce the behaviour. Species-specific behaviours would belong to this category; the pouncing behaviour of cats is an example. Dogs, by contrast, do not have a pre-programmed pounce response; it must be learned. In the same way, most human behaviour does not stem from 'pre-wired' origins. For example, while we are capable of the balance and coordination required to ride a bicycle, the specific responses involved are not inborn, and must be learned. Seligman refers to behaviours which must be acquired through experience as *unprepared*, since there is no hereditary predisposition involved. At the other extreme, there are some types of complex patterns of behaviour that we find very difficult, if not impossible, to acquire. In

critical period in development, the concept that there are optimal periods for the learning of certain behaviours

preparedness a concept developed by Martin Seligman to describe the degree to which physiological structure influences the occurrence of behaviour these cases, it seems that the physiological structure is not intended to cope with these situations. Seligman says that we are *contraprepared* to acquire such behaviour patterns. For instance, cats are prepared to lick themselves after eating, but they are contraprepared to use licking as a way of operantly obtaining food. Their physiology is structured for a 'food, then lick' sequence, not 'lick, then food'.

Traditionally, behaviourists focused on those response patterns which depend on learning (i.e. unprepared behaviours). In doing so, they developed the view that all behaviour was alike, as expressed by the equipotentiality premise. As time went on, however, evidence arose which called this concept into question. While unlearned species-specific behaviours are clearly prepared, there are other behaviours which are learned so quickly as to seem prepared as well. One example concerns food-avoidance learning. Food preferences are well-known in both people and animals – but what leads to rejecting a particular food?

In a series of insightful studies, John Garcia and his colleagues (1974) demonstrated that if a rat gets ill after eating a distinctive-tasting food, it will avoid that food in the future. This discovery came about while Garcia was studying the effects of exposure to x-rays. Animals given large doses of x-rays became sick to their stomachs several hours later; if they had eaten earlier, they would subsequently avoid whatever the food had been. Garcia became interested in this behaviour, in much the way that Pavlov moved from the study of digestion to the exploration of classical conditioning.

Garcia recognized that while it was the x-rays (which the rats could not detect directly) which produced the sickness, the rats associated it with the food instead. This would be like a person who, while coming down with the stomach flu, happens to go out for dinner and eats something out of the ordinary (e.g. curried chicken). Later, they get nauseated because of the flu – but the next time they order curried chicken, the reaction re-occurs. Garcia called this behaviour *bait-shyness* (based on fishermen's belief that a fish nearly hooked on a particular bait won't strike it again). Subsequent research, as well as anecdotal evidence, has confirmed that this phenomenon is genuine (Logue 1988).

Exploration of bait-shyness led to the conclusion that many species, including man, have developed in such a way that getting sick is very readily associated with the last food eaten. The link between food and sickness often occurs after a single experience, despite the long delay between eating and getting sick. (Imagine trying to teach a rat to press a bar by reinforcing it several hours after it makes the correct response!) Garcia suggested that this behavioural capacity evolved because it was adaptive: an animal which ate something harmful would do well to avoid it in the future. Through mutation and natural selection, a neural mechanism was created to link taste with stomach upset, hence bait-shyness as a form of prepared behaviour.

Over time, research has shown that food-avoidance learning is only one example of such prepared behaviours. For example, migratory birds are biologically predisposed to learn landmarks on their route (Shettleworth 1972). It has also been suggested that some types of human fears are more easily conditioned than others. Consider fear of the dark: humans are basically daytime creatures. To our ancestors, who depended (as we still do) on vision more than smell or hearing, the night world of darkness was a place of invisible dangers. Consequently, natural selection may have 'prepared' us to be afraid of the dark. (Note this does *not* mean that all people automatically have a strong fear of the dark; it simply implies that very little experience is needed to *develop* such a fear.)

Studies of classically conditioned fears suggest that not all stimuli are equally likely to elicit conditioned fear responses. A few years after Watson's study of little Albert, another researcher found that an infant could be conditioned to fear a rat, but not wooden blocks or pieces of cloth (Bregman 1934). More recently, studies with adults have shown that fear is more easily conditioned to pictures of snakes or spiders than to pictures of flowers or houses (Öhman 1986). Thus, evolutionary factors may partially explain differences in the frequency of occurrence of different phobias, based on certain fears being biologically prepared (note that other factors, including cultural influences, could also be involved).

It is harder to evaluate the possibility of there being contraprepared behaviours in humans. One of the difficulties is that, by definition, what is contraprepared is unlearnable. So if there *is* some behavioural pattern that we cannot learn, would we even be able to recognize it? After many discussions with colleagues, no-one has come forth with a clear example of contrapreparedness in people, despite many known examples in other species (e.g. the 'lick, then food' sequence in cats). Since there is no logical necessity that states there *must* be such behaviours in humans, the absence of examples tells us little. So, at present, the issue is unresolved.

Overall, there seems little doubt that genetic and physiological factors play a role in human behaviour. However, such factors do not seem to play as significant a role in human activity as they do in many other species. This is indicated in part by the long infancy/childhood of human development; whereas many animals may be fully developed at birth, human infants require care and assistance longer than any other species. While this is a disadvantage in terms of survival, it allows for maximum flexibility of behaviour, based on experience. Learning takes time, and with time the helplessness of the infant becomes the diverse and complex behaviour of the adult.

The study of biological constraints, by both ethologists and behaviourists, has enriched our understanding of behaviour, even as it has limited the range of application of conditioning principles. One of the significant lessons seems to be a recognition of the limitations of laboratory research. Whenever one enters the laboratory to study behaviour, one trades the advantages of control for the disadvantages of an artificial situation. It is well recognized that people often react differently when they know they are being studied (see Chapter 1), and even with animals the laboratory setting may give a distorted perspective. This is not to say that the years of research on operant and classical conditioning are invalid; indeed, both methods have added a great deal to our understanding. However, just as each approach to psychology has its limits, so too it seems that a full understanding of behaviour cannot come from the laboratory alone. By exploring biological constraints, it can be argued that behaviourists have enriched their approach, rather than weakened it.

For further consideration

Have you ever developed a sudden aversion to a particular food? Do you recall the circumstances? In what ways does Garcia's work on bait-shyness help you to understand your own taste preferences?

Conclusion

The behaviourist approach is based on the assumption that science must be based on the study of observable events. In terms of behaviour, this means looking at the interactions between an organism and its environment. In adopting this stance, behaviourists forego attempts to study consciousness and internal subjective states. As Skinner has pointed out, behaviourism is a method of analysis rather than simply a theory (Skinner 1987). Critics say that treating the organism like a 'black box' means that one ignores the mental processes that are central to human behaviour. Skinner says that such events are scientifically unknowable, and in any case do not cause behaviour: 'thinking about' something before doing it is simply correlated with the observable behaviour. For example, if a Freudian theorist suggests that adult behaviour can best be understood by looking at childhood experiences, Skinner agrees – but suggests that the connections are based on the reinforcement history of the person, not some vague concept of 'conflicts between id and ego'.

Ultimately, the best criterion for judging behaviourism is not theoretical preference, but the extent to which it helps us to make sense out of behaviour. While many have criticized its restrictions, the reality is that the study of classical and operant conditioning has added to our overall understanding in psychology. The appeal of behaviourism is reflected in the fact that for many years it was the dominant force in North American psychology. Even today, its precepts have influenced other approaches, in that the emphasis on observational processes has become broadly accepted in psychological research. Ironically, this is true even in the study of mental processes, as seen in the cognitive approach. (Many cognitive researchers began their training as behaviourists. Even Edward Tolman, regarded as one of the founders of the cognitive approach, considered himself a behaviourist – though not a radical behaviourist like Skinner.) Where the introspectionists failed in their attempts to make sense out of mental processes, the behaviourists have pointed the way to new possibilities for a scientific psychology.

Although the behaviourist approach has contributed significantly to our understanding of behaviour, it no longer occupies the dominant position it once did within psychology. In part this reflects changes in the discipline, and in part the limitations of the approach. As we have noted, in recent years the distinction between operant and reflex behaviours has become blurred, and the processes of operant and classical conditioning must be viewed as interconnected. More importantly, research by ethologists and others has shown that the principles of conditioning are not as universal as was once asserted. This failure of the 'equipotentiality premise' restricts the generality of behaviourist principles in important ways. Beyond that, interest in mental processes has not diminished simply because the behaviourists have refused to address the issues. Instead, researchers have found new ways to study mental processes, resulting in new interest in the cognitive approach, as we shall see in the next chapter.

Chapter Summary

- The behaviourist approach emphasizes the study of *observable responses*, and rejects attempts to study internal processes like thinking.

- In doing so, behaviourists focus on *learning* as the primary factor in explaining changes in behaviour. Depending on the type of response, this involves either *classical conditioning* or *operant conditioning*.

- Classical conditioning is concerned with how *conditioned stimuli* come to elicit (reflex) *conditioned responses* which are normally elicited by *unconditioned stimuli*.

- Classical conditioning can be applied to a number of aspects of human behaviour, including emotional responses like fears and even activity of the immune system.

- Operant conditioning is concerned with how the probability of a voluntary 'operant' *response* changes as a function of the environmental consequences (*reinforcer*) which follow the response.

- This process of *reinforcement* can be analysed in terms of the *type of reinforcer*, the *contingency of reinforcement* and the *schedule of reinforcement*.

- Operant conditioning has been applied in many different ways to 'real-world' behaviour; these applications, commonly called *behaviour modification*, include studies of the effectiveness of *punishment*, altering behaviour by *biofeedback* and other applications.

- Recent research has indicated that while conceptually distinct, classical and operant conditioning are interrelated in actual behaviour. In addition, research on *biological constraints on learning* has suggested that there are limits to the generality of conditioning principles.

Key Terms and Concepts

behaviour modification	negative reinforcer
biofeedback	operant conditioning
classical conditioning	partial reinforcement
conditioned emotional response	positive reinforcement
conditioned response	positive reinforcer
conditioned stimulus	preparedness
continuous reinforcement	punishment
discriminative stimulus	reinforcement
extinction (classical)	reinforcer
extinction (operant)	schedules of reinforcement
higher-order conditioning	shaping
law of effect	species-specific behaviour
learning	spontaneous recovery
negative reinforcement	stimulus discrimination

stimulus generalization   unconditioned stimulus
unconditioned response

Suggestions for Further Reading

For the reader interested in a more detailed discussion of the principles of learning (both classical and operant), Chance's *Learning and Behavior* is a very readable account.

B.F. Skinner has maintained a distinctive position within behaviourism, not least for his outspoken comments on changing society. One of his clearest presentations of his views on society is *Beyond Freedom and Dignity*.

Despite the early controversy it caused, autonomic conditioning has subsequently moved from the public spotlight. However, Neal Miller's 1985 review in *American Psychologist* shows how this and other forms of conditioning have been used to help people in various ways. For more specific discussion of biofeedback techniques, see Mercer's account of clinical applications in *Biofeedback and Related Therapies in Clinical Practice*.

For an account which shows how the ethological approach differs from laboratory studies of behaviour, Jane Goodall's *Through a Window* provides a highly readable beginning.

4 The Cognitive Approach

Thought and Action

At the turn of the century, a young physicist was working as a clerk in the Swiss patent office. In his spare time, he continued his interest in theoretical physics. Like many other physicists of the day, he was puzzled by discoveries which seemed to challenge many long-held notions about matter and energy. For one thing, the speed of light seemed to be a constant throughout the universe, but no-one could explain why. Then, the young clerk tried reversing the problem, saying one could assume the speed of light was constant. Having made this shift, many aspects of the problem fell into place. Many of his older colleagues were perplexed and even outraged; after all, the proposal contradicted all of their previous training. In the end, his solution became accepted, and his work triggered many changes in science and in the world. The theory is now called the special theory of relativity, and the young clerk was Albert Einstein.

Today, all college physics students, and many others, have a basic grasp of Einstein's insights, expressed as $E = mc^2$. It is one of the marvels of such great ideas that, once formulated, they can be readily understood by many. Yet the first formulation of such solutions is often elusive; many of Einstein's colleagues had difficulty grasping it. What leads to such insights? How do we develop new solutions to old problems?

Consider a simpler example of problem solving: A young child is given a problem in which pointing to a star leads to getting candy as a reinforcer, but pointing to a circle does not. Gradually, the child becomes consistent in choosing the star. However, once the child has learned this discrimination, the child is given a new problem, involving a square and a triangle. On this problem, they are consistently correct by the second trial (on the first trial, of course, they must guess). On other problems with new shapes, the child continues to perform consistently well. Behaviourists would talk about responding to the shape as learning to respond to a discriminative stimulus, a process which requires trial-and-error learning. Yet in this situation, the child seems to develop a *rule* for making choices, rather than being simply reinforced for a particular response. How can conditioning explain such behaviour?

Or consider this: If you have developed a skill, such as playing a piano, does the skill disappear if there is no piano present? Is *knowing* something the same as *doing* something?

To the behaviourists, all human activity can be described in terms of responses to environmental cues. Behaviour, defined as observable responses, is based on conditioned reflexes, reinforcement and other simple processes. By its nature, this approach tends to deny that anything happening *within* the person is significant. Memories, thoughts and feelings are seen as irrelevant to science, and therefore meaningless. Expressed in these terms, all of the above examples become virtually impossible to understand.

Introduction

As the above examples illustrate, much of our behaviour involves not simply actions, but mental processes such as perception, memory, problem solving and language. While these processes cannot be observed directly, that does not seem sufficient reason to ignore their existence, or the ways in which they affect behaviour. Consequently, the *cognitive approach* is concerned with thinking, and the mental processes related to it. Unlike the behaviourists, the cognitive approach sees events within the person as being at least as important as environmental stimuli in the understanding of behaviour. These events within the individual are described as mediational processes or **mediators**, because they come between the stimulus and the response. Thinking processes like memory, problem solving and language are all based on mediators.

mediator a process or event within the individual which comes between a stimulus and a response

This emphasis on mediating processes, and the way they are defined, is central to the cognitive approach. In contrast to the behaviourists, cognitive psychologists believe that one cannot explain behaviour without reference to something more than stimulus–response connections (the child learning a 'rule' for discrimination problems is one example). However, the nature of these mediators is also important. In essence, mediational processes are defined functionally – that is, with reference to how behaviour is altered. These mediators are therefore *conceptual*; one describes the properties of memory, for example, without concern for its physical embodiment. By contrast, the biological approach also deals with mediational processes, but they are defined physiologically, not conceptually (e.g. looking at how the visual cortex is involved in perception). Hence, the cognitive approach is distinct from either of the approaches we have considered thus far.

The development of the cognitive approach is closely related to behaviourism, since in part it developed as a reaction against the behaviourists' emphasis on external events (sometimes called radical empiricism). By the time Watson published the first edition of *Behaviourism* in 1924, he felt that his approach was gaining ground against the ambiguities of introspectionism. Yet at virtually the same point in time, the seeds for a new alternative were being sown. In 1925, a book by a young German researcher named Wolfgang Kohler appeared, called *The Mentality of Apes.* In this book, he reported observations which suggested that animals could show behaviour which was *insightful*, and he rejected behaviourism in favour of an approach called 'Gestalt' psychology. The other challenge to behaviourism came from someone who actually called himself a behaviourist. In 1932, E.C. Tolman published a book entitled *Purposive Behavior in Animals and Man.* In this book, he described research which was difficult to explain in terms of traditional behaviourism, which emphasized associations between stimuli and responses. Instead, Tolman talked about learning as based on relationships among stimuli, referred to as forming **cognitive maps**. In addition, he argued that learning and responding are not the same, and that it is possible to learn without showing a correct response. Taken together, the work of Kohler and Tolman raised basic questions about the validity of behaviourism, and laid the foundations for what has become the cognitive approach. To see how, let us briefly examine each man's work more closely.

While the early behaviourists saw learning as basically a matter of trial and error, Kohler argued that we tend to *organize* experience in particular ways. This is illustrated by the phenomenon Kohler called insight. **Insight** is a sudden change in the way one organizes a problem situation; typically this is characterized by a change in behaviour from random responding to rule-based responding. A child solving discrimination problems can show insight, as mentioned above. In general, insight can be described as forming an appropriate *schema* (or, to use Kohler's term, **mental set**) for a particular situation.

One of the most famous examples of Kohler's work on insight involved an ape named Sultan. Kohler gave Sultan a series of related problems, in which he had to use a stick to reach for a banana which was placed outside his cage, out of arm's reach. After solving such problems on several occasions, Sultan was then presented with a stick that was not long enough to reach the banana. However, outside the cage was a longer stick. After several unsuccessful tries, Sultan threw down the short stick in evident frustration, and retreated to the corner of his cage. A little later, he suddenly went over to the short stick, used it to reach the other, longer stick, and with the *new* stick reached the banana! As Kohler noted, there was no gradual sequence, as one might expect with shaping, nor did it seem to be the result of trial and error. Instead, there was a sudden transformation of the way Sultan organized the elements – insight. Kohler's work thus created a shift away from seeing all behaviour as trial and error, towards a concern with the internal organizing processes which mediate behaviour.

cognitive map Tolman's term for the mental representation of learned relationships among stimuli.
insight a sudden change in the way one organizes a problem situation; typically this is characterized by a change in behaviour from random responding to rule-based responding
mental set in Gestalt theory, a cognitive schema for a particular situation, such as a problem

Wolfgang Kohler

Wolfgang Kohler (1887–1967) was a founder of Gestalt theory. Born in Tallinn, Estonia, he was educated in Germany, attending the universities of Tübingen, Frankfurt and Berlin (where he received his doctorate). While at Frankfurt, he met Max Wertheimer and Kurt Koffka, who also contributed to the development of Gestalt theory. In 1913, Kohler went to Tenerife in the Canary Islands to study the resident apes; in what became an act of serendipity, he was stranded there for the duration of the First World War, unable to leave until 1919. During this period, his studies with the apes led him to a view of problem solving as an active process of insight, unlike the trial-and-error viewpoint advocated by Tolman. Eventually, this work became an important influence on Gestalt theory, which Kohler promoted as a professor at the University of Berlin (he was made chair in psychology in 1921). In 1934, he travelled to the United States to deliver the annual William James Lectures at Harvard; aware of Hitler's rise to power in Germany, he accepted an appointment at Swarthmore University in Pennsylvania, where he remained almost until his death at the age of eighty.

latent learning a term used by Tolman to describe situations in which learning is distinct from the performance of a behaviour

Kohler talked about internal organizing principles, which behaviourists avoided. By contrast, Tolman regarded himself as a behaviourist, in that his data were strictly based on observations of stimuli and responses. But the problems he examined were very embarrassing to the traditional behaviourists of his day. (In fact, some issues he raised were still actively researched and debated almost forty years later!) For instance, behaviourists argued that unless there was a change in behaviour (performance of a new response), no learning had taken place. Tolman demonstrated that animals may learn the pattern of a maze, forming a *cognitive map*, and yet not perform correctly until a reward is given. This **latent learning**, being undetectable as it occurred, suggested that learning is distinct from the performance of a behaviour. In another study, rats explored mazes which had several paths of varying length, all leading to the end; later, if the shortest path to reach food at the goal was blocked, the rats chose the second shortest route. This is similar to a person who finds his normal driving route blocked by construction, and quickly selects the most reasonable alternative route. In both the rat and person, this seems to require a knowledge of how locations are connected, rather than mechanical repetition of a shaped sequence of responses. Thus, Tolman's theory ultimately emphasized the importance of mediational processes.

Both Kohler and Tolman had an important influence in laying the foundation of the cognitive approach. Yet despite their early role, neither has many direct followers today. This does not mean that the cognitive approach is not important (if anything, its influence has grown in recent years). Rather, it means that the impact of these pioneers is diffuse, and sometimes not directly recognized. To a greater extent than in other approaches in psychology, the important aspects are based on the underlying assumptions about behaviour, and the central focus given to internal mental processes. Hence, various elements of the cognitive approach have been transformed or used piecemeal by researchers of various

Edward Tolman

Edward Chace Tolman (1886–1959) was born in Newton, Massachusetts. He received his bachelor's degree from MIT, and his doctorate in psychology from Harvard in 1915. Tolman spent almost his entire career at the University of California at Berkeley. While he considered himself a 'behaviourist', and his own research was done almost entirely with rats, Tolman's work bears little resemblance to the radical behaviourists, such as Watson and Skinner. A contemporary of Watson, he rejected the emphasis on reflexes and trial-and-error learning which were central to Watson's views. Instead, he developed a concept of 'purposive behaviourism', which emphasized the distinction between learning and performance (as seen in latent learning), and viewed learning in terms of the formation of 'hypotheses' and 'cognitive maps'. Both by showing the weaknesses of radical behaviourism, and by proposing concepts which acknowledged the existence of mediational processes, Tolman helped lay the foundations for the cognitive approach. He was seventy-three when he died, just a few years before the blossoming of the cognitive approach in the 1960s.

outlooks. Still, much of the basis of current work can be traced back to the influence of Kohler and Tolman.

Since no single theorist has dominated the cognitive approach in the way that Skinner has operant conditioning or Freud has psychoanalysis, there has been a greater exchange with other approaches, both within and outside psychology. Thus, today one hears about a cognitive theory of social behaviour, or of emotion, or even cognitive behaviour modification. At the same time, cognitive psychologists have borrowed from other fields, including computer science and physiology. In fact, some even refer to 'cognitive science' as a hybrid discipline, incorporating elements of psychology, linguistics, computer science and physiology!

One reason for this broad interchange is the tendency of psychologists to seek new models. Analogies and metaphors have long played a role in scientific thinking, in terms of the desire to describe problems in new ways: In the seventeenth century, Descartes used hydraulically operated statues in the Tuileries Gardens of Paris as a model for the physiology of body movements. At the turn of this century, psychologists compared the brain (as a network of stimulus–response connections) to a telephone switchboard. Today, computers play a large role in our lives, and psychologists have borrowed from the language of computer technology, in the form of 'information-processing' models. Each analogy has benefits and limitations, but the use of such models to aid understanding is a well-established practice.

Consciously or not, those who use information-processing descriptions fall within the tradition of Kohler and Tolman. **Information processing** refers to the intervening events (mediators) which come between input (stimulus) and output (response) of the system (person). In a computer, one cannot predict the output from the input without knowing something about what is going on within the computer. In the same way, a person's behaviour cannot be understood solely by looking at environmental stimuli. There is a further parallel in that the computer

information processing a term borrowed from computer science by cognitive psychologists to describe the mental functions which occur between stimulus and response model emphasizes the concept of processing of information. By *processing*, we mean the output represents a qualitative change in the input, such as combination, analysis, or comparison of input data. This element of active transformation is also seen in behaviour, as Kohler's emphasis on insight as creative, and Tolman's view of cognitive maps as going beyond mere repetitions of previous responses. Thus, information-processing models fit very comfortably within the cognitive approach.

In this chapter, we will look at several aspects of behaviour from the cognitive viewpoint. The most general concern is simply trying to understand how we behave. Generally, cognitive researchers have focused on questions concerning how we remember, why we forget, what leads to effective solutions to problems, and related questions. This emphasis on thinking processes (memory, problem solving, decision making, language) is natural, given that the word 'cognitive' refers to thinking. At the same time, the scope of the cognitive approach has broadened in recent years, and even includes such 'irrational' aspects of behaviour as emotions. Whatever the topic, the key elements of the cognitive approach remain the same: (1) processes within the person are considered central to understanding behaviour; and (2) these mediating processes operate in an organized and systematic way, not by trial and error.

Perception and Cognition

Traditionally, psychologists tried to separate the process of perceiving from thinking – that is, to separate perception and cognition. Perception was used to refer to the receiving of sensory inputs, while cognition referred to mental processes. However, over time, it has come to be recognized that the distinction is hard to maintain. For example, perceiving involves recognizing a stimulus, and recognition of something as familiar requires making use of memory (a cognitive process). In the same way, thinking does not occur in the absence of something to think about, and much of the content of thought relates to present and past sensory stimuli. Hence, while clearly not synonyms, perception and cognition are also not totally distinct terms (Robinson 1979).

One example of this overlap is Gestalt theory, as developed by Kohler and others. Gestalt theory is a theory of perception as well as cognition. For instance, memory for stimuli is related to how they are perceived. In a classic study by Carmichael and his colleagues, subjects were given simple line figures to remember, along with a word cue (Carmichael *et al.* 1932). Later, they were asked to draw each figure when given the appropriate cue. The crucial variable was the word cue used. For example, one figure consisted of a short horizontal line, terminated at each end by a circle. The verbal cue given to different subjects was either 'glasses' or 'barbell'. Later, the drawings produced tended to be distorted in ways that reflected the word cue (e.g. adding extensions for 'glasses', or changing the line to a solid bar for 'barbell'). This study, while complicated by the problem of interpreting subjects' drawings for accuracy, is consistent with a number of Gestalt studies which suggest that perception and memory are interrelated. In the first chapter, we noted how perception is best conceived as an active process of interpreting the environment, based in part on one's mental schemata, which in turn are shaped by one's experiences. This model is similar to Gestalt theory, which sees perception as based on a number of internal organizing principles. While it is beyond the scope of this chapter to provide a full overview of Gestalt theory, we will touch upon various aspects related to memory and problem solving. For the present, it is worth noting that the cognitive processes we will discuss are in fact closely linked to the process of perceiving.

Learning and Memory

Learning as Information Gathering

While behaviourists talk about learning as changes in responses, the cognitive approach focuses on the knowledge which guides those responses. In terms of the information-processing model, learning may be considered as *information gathering*. Information can be any meaningful data. We gather, and store in memory for later use, everything from the names of new business contacts to the location of the washroom in our favourite restaurant. (There is no requirement that what we store has to be 'significant'.) In the process, we all accumulate vast amounts of seemingly useless information. For instance, what were the first names of the Beatles? What does A-OK stand for? What did you have for dinner last night?

At first glance, the gathering and storage of information may seem less efficient as a learning system than the behaviourist notion of associations between stimuli and responses. But learning through information gathering has one great advantage – flexibility. Tolman's concept of cognitive maps illustrates this clearly. For example, if your route to work is represented by a mental map of the city, not a fixed series of responses, then you can detour to go to the drycleaner, take an alternative route when traffic is bad, and so on. Information which was previously not reflected in behaviour thus becomes significant as the situation is altered (for example, knowing that a particular street is one-way affects your choice of alternative routes). Tolman would call this a form of *latent learning*.

For the cognitive psychologist, **learning** represents the process gathering information, and organizing it into mental schemata. The emphasis is on the mediating processes that lead from stimulus to response. Consider again the example of the traffic jam: the stimuli could include your present location, the time of day, the density of traffic and awareness of your goal. Making a detour involves several types of mediators: your knowledge of the street layout (a cognitive map), information from past experiences about where traffic is likely to be lighter (memory) and motivational preferences (e.g. whether you prefer a short route through slow-moving traffic, or a longer route via an expressway). As reasonable as this description may seem, it also raises several questions: How did you develop a cognitive map of the city originally? How do you recall past experiences about traffic patterns, especially if it didn't seem important at the time? And how did you decide the best route, given all of the information? Let us begin by considering the question of how we remember things.

learning in cognitive psychology, the process of gathering information and organizing it into mental schemata

Memory as the Retention of Learning

Effective behaviour often depends on remembering information at the right time. **Memory** can be defined as the retention and use of prior learning. Memory is a mediator of behaviour because, through memory, past experiences influence what we do now. However, there are several ways in which this information can be used.

Usually, we simply remember the information as we need it. This is called **recall**, the active retrieval of information. Answering any of the 'trivia' questions in the previous section would involve recall. Sometimes, however, we can't recall something, but are able to recognize it as correct if it is presented to us. For instance, does A-OK refer to the name of a ranch, hippie slang or astronaut's jargon? This process of identifying information as familiar is called **recognition**. Multiple-choice tests of memory are based on testing recognition, not recall. (What sort of examination would test recall?) While recognition is usually (but not always) easier than recall, there are also circumstances in which we may not be able to recognize something, yet on reviewing it, it quickly seems familiar. For example, a person who hasn't spoken a foreign language for several years adapts more quickly than a first-time learner. Hence, there is still some memory of the prior learning, despite the inability to recall or recognize the information. This type of improvement by reviewing is called **relearning**.

Remembering, then, can take many forms. Although it is easy to say memory refers to the storage of information, such a definition does not tell us very much. To understand how memory functions, we must look more closely at the capabilities of our memories. First, try to answer the following questions: What colour was the house you grew up in? Was your first teacher a man or a woman? Can you recall the teacher's name? These questions may sound like further trivia items, but with a difference. Virtually everyone could answer at least the first two questions. Yet for most readers, those events occurred at least fifteen years ago, and possibly much longer. Such recall is not unusual; many people have recalled personal experiences which happened sixty or eighty years earlier. So we might say that memory is permanent, or at least potentially permanent, since we do seem to forget some things.

Before you ask why we forget, since we can be so good at remembering, let's take another example. Have you ever looked up a telephone number, found it busy on dialling, and then had to look it up again to dial a minute later? Or have you ever been introduced to someone, and then not been able to remember their name at the end of the conversation? Often we forget information almost immediately after we encounter it. How can we forget something which happened thirty seconds ago, and yet remember something from many years ago? To understand these variations, we need to consider what we know about how memory functions.

A Basic Model of Memory

Over time, a consensus has developed about the basic features of memory, which are often expressed in a model based on a computer analogy (i.e. in terms of how information is processed). Since many researchers have contributed to

memory the retention and use of prior learning

recall in memory, the active retrieval of information
recognition in memory, the process of identifying presented information as familiar
relearning in memory, an improvement in performance which occurs by reviewing, despite the inability to recall or recognize the information

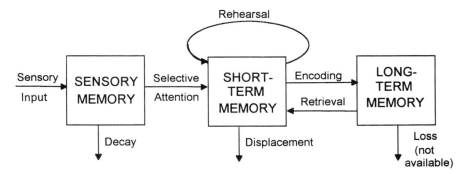

Fig. 4.1 A general model of memory We tend to view memory as consisting of a number of stages, which are linked by processes like selective attention; one of the first models of this type was proposed by Atkinson and Shiffrin (1968).

the development of this model, it is frequently discussed in generic terms (see Waugh and Norman 1965; Atkinson and Shiffrin 1968). This model views memory as consisting of a series of distinct stages, each with its own special characteristics (see Fig. 4.1). While not everyone accepts this description (e.g. Potter 1990), the model is useful for organizing what we know, especially since no other model has yet been broadly accepted.

Information which we gather must be acquired through our senses, and research has demonstrated that there is a form of **sensory memory** which is distinctive for each sense modality. Typically, however, this form of retention is very transient, and serves primarily as a sort of buffer between the senses and our true memory. In fact, we seem to have not one sensory memory, but several – each sense mode (vision, hearing, etc.) seems to involve its own form of sensory memory. Extensive work has been done on the nature of the various forms of sensory memory, especially for vision and hearing (see Sperling 1960; Crowder and Morton 1969); however, for our purposes, it is what happens *after* sensory memory that is most significant.

Since we are continually bombarded by sensory stimuli, we must selectively focus on those elements which are likely to be most significant. This selection occurs through the perceptual process of **attention**, as discussed in Chapter 1. Attention limits our conscious awareness to a small portion of our moment-to-moment environment. Because sensory memory functions at a level *before* the filtering of attention takes place, it is sometimes referred to as being *pre-attentive*. Attention can be redirected, either by deliberate choice or a particularly compelling stimulus (e.g. a sudden loud noise while you are studying); hence, it enables us to shift from one sense mode to another, or even to focus on particular stimuli within one sense mode. A good example of this is the so-called *cocktail party effect*, whereby in a crowded room, you can shift your attention from talking to a person in front of you to suddenly listening to another conversation taking place behind you, without even shifting your head! Attention thus selects the information which becomes available to memory.

While we talk about memory in everyday life as a single process, the evidence suggests that it is more meaningful to consider it as two separate stages. **Short-term memory** (STM), refers to retention over relatively brief intervals, usually

sensory memory a modality-specific transient form of memory which serves as a buffer between the senses and STM

attention the process of selectively focusing on particular stimulus elements, typically those deemed most significant

short-term memory (STM) the component of memory which handles retention over relatively brief intervals of up to approximately fifteen seconds

long-term memory
(LTM) the component of
memory which is involved
with retention over relatively
long periods (hours, days,
weeks or longer)

rehearsal in STM, the
process of repeating
information over and over,
usually silently

fifteen seconds or so. By contrast, **long-term memory** (LTM) refers to retention over relatively long periods – hours, days, weeks or longer. The generally accepted model assumes that the two types of retention reflect different processes. Since both represent mediating processes that cannot be observed directly, it is worth considering the evidence which is used to support this view.

One type of evidence has already been noted – *duration*. LTM is potentially permanent, while STM is very limited. Information held in STM will normally be lost after several seconds, unless it is transferred to LTM (how this might happen will be discussed later) or rehearsed. **Rehearsal** consists of repeating information over and over, usually silently. (Have you ever found yourself rehearsing a telephone number as you dial?)

It may help to understand how STM works if we draw an analogy to a leaky bucket. Normally, water poured into the bucket will gradually dribble away. This is similar to the loss over time from STM. If you use a cup to catch the drips, and periodically pour the cup back into the leaky bucket, this would be like rehearsal. It is worth noting that this is an imperfect process, because the bucket will still be leaking while you are moving the cup. Rehearsal is also an imperfect process, and can lead to gradual loss of information. (Of course, STM is not really a leaky bucket; like most models, this description simply tries to aid comprehension.)

The bucket analogy brings up another distinction between STM and LTM, that of *capacity*. STM is very limited in the amount of information it can retain. In order to see this, try the following test. In Fig. 4.2, you will find a string of letters. Read through them once, then turn the page and immediately try to recall them in correct order. Then, check your accuracy. Only those letters which are correct, and are in the correct sequence, should be counted as correct. If you remembered about seven letters, you are average. Nine or more letters would be very unusual. Now, consider how long you had to retain the letters before writing them down: perhaps four seconds? Yet, on average, people forget about one-third of the letters (assuming ten altogether). Increasing the original number of letters would lower your percentage, because the number seven, not two-thirds, appears to be the best measure of STM capacity, which is often described as being 7 ± 2 meaningful items, or **chunks**. That is, STM appears to be limited to between five and nine independent items, such as random letters, numbers or words (Miller 1956). Telephone numbers, because they have familiar three-digit exchanges, are not really seven independent items. Similarly, letters that spell a word are neither independent nor random, and are therefore easier to remember.

chunk the basic measure of
STM capacity, representing a
meaningful unit, such as
random letters, numbers or
words

Attempts to remember longer sequences of items usually result in greater forgetting of the earlier items. In terms of the bucket analogy, trying to remember a long sequence is like trying to overfill the bucket – the surplus simply spills over.

LTM, on the other hand, appears to be practically unlimited in capacity. At the very least, no documented case of someone 'running out of memory space' has ever occurred. (There is a story of an Oxford zoology professor, an expert on fish, who tried to remember his students' names, but found that each time he learned another student's name, he forgot the name of a species of fish. Since he preferred fish to students, he gave up trying to remember students' names!) You may have encountered speculations about the capacity of the human brain, and statements such as 'Einstein only used 40 per cent of his brain capacity'.

> ## A TEST OF SHORT-TERM MEMORY
>
> To test your STM capacity, read through the list of letters below. Read the list slowly, but only once. Immediately after reading the last letter, try to write down the entire sequence in the correct order.
>
> ### L R X D V C M Q B N
>
> For scoring, give yourself credit only for letters in the correct order, not counting reversals, omissions, or other errors. Typical recall would be about seven correct.

Fig. 4.2 A test of short-term memory To test your short-term memory, follow the instructions in the box.

While provocative, such statements must be taken lightly, since at best they are crude estimates. The problem is that we still know very little about how information is stored in the nervous system, and consequently any estimate of capacity is purely guesswork.

As noted earlier, current models in cognitive psychology are influenced by computer analogies. Thus, in the model presented earlier, STM is like the input buffer, which can handle only a small amount of information at one time. If the buffer is overloaded, information is lost. Once it has processed the information, the buffer has no record of it. Such losses are analogous to STM forgetting. LTM would be like a computer's storage device, which retains information permanently unless there is damage to the system (or, in the case of a computer, a command to erase the information). In order for a computer to be able to retrieve stored information at a later time, processing must occur at the time of storage to create a *retrieval code* – that is, a pointer that tells where in the system the information is located. In the same way, information placed in LTM must be coded for later retrieval.

The nature of *coding* is one of the greatest challenges in research on memory. While capacity and duration can be readily measured using recall tasks, coding is not directly observable, and must be inferred. As already noted, information in STM must be actively rehearsed in order to be retained for very long. Usually we are subjectively aware of this as a form of talking to ourselves. This observation has been supported by research suggesting that coding in STM is *acoustic* (based on sounds). Even when rehearsal is silent, it is like speaking: speech muscles in the larynx are active, and errors made are typically related to the sound of the items (Glassman 1972). An analogy to this process is the game of 'Gossip', in which a message is whispered from person to person in a group. By the time the message has been passed, 'Diane, be quiet' may become 'I am on a diet'! In the same way, errors in STM often involve words which sound alike.

For LTM, understanding coding is more complex, and may be related to both the type of information and the way it is processed. Some researchers believe

procedural memory that
component of LTM which
stores 'how-to' information,
such as how to play a piano
or cook a turkey
semantic memory the
component of LTM which
involves general knowledge
of the world
episodic memory the
portion of LTM which
contains personal
experiences, organized
according to where and
when events happened, such
as what happened on your
last birthday

there may in fact be several different types of LTM, which independently process and store different forms of information. Canadian psychologist Endel Tulving has argued that there are three distinct forms of long-term memory: procedural, semantic and episodic (Tulving 1985). **Procedural memory** stores 'how-to' information, such as how to play a piano or cook a turkey. **Semantic memory** involves general knowledge of the world, such as knowing the capital of Japan, or the temperature at which ice melts. **Episodic memory** contains personal experiences, organized according to where and when events happened, such as what happened on your last birthday. Tulving believes the three systems function independently, a view which is supported by research on specific types of brain damage. For example, it is possible for a patient with brain damage to learn how to solve a puzzle (procedural), and yet not be able to recall having seen it before (episodic). In the same way, a patient may learn a specific fact (semantic), and not know when they learned it (episodic). As an aside, Tulving believes that episodic memory (which is closely involved with our sense of self-identity) is the most recent form of memory in terms of evolutionary development, and consequently is the most vulnerable to traumatic damage. By contrast, procedural memory is likely the oldest form of memory, and the most resistant to damage.

The different forms of storage which Tulving discusses are not the only possible differences in LTM coding. There is also evidence that *visual* information is processed and represented differently than *verbal* information (Paivio 1971). One type of evidence for this point of view is derived from studies which indicate people handle visual information in memory in much the same way that they process direct visual inputs. For example, in one innovative study, subjects were asked to make comparisons of pairs of three-dimensional shapes (Shepard and Metzler 1971). The time required to compare the shapes correlated with the amount of rotation required to match the orientation of the two shapes; this implied that subjects were using something analogous to a visual image. However, these data do not prove directly that the information is represented in memory as an image. All we can really say is that people perform certain memory tasks in ways that are consistent with a visual representation.

The debates about the nature of LTM are not new. In the past, theorists compared LTM to a junk box in the attic, or to a library with many shelves to store individual items. While these models have serious limitations, they do point out the importance of some form of organizational structure in memory. Consider a library having hundreds of thousands of books that had no cataloguing system – imagine trying to find a particular book! In the same way, LTM, with its vast capacity, must process information in some way that permits locating it later. The question is, what sort of coding process creates this structure?

The traditional view of LTM processing is based on *associationism*. Just as learning can be seen as a process of forming ties between a stimulus and a response, so memory is seen as forming ties between new experiences and prior knowledge. These ties, called associations, are typically based on stimulus aspects that have meaning. For instance, to remember the name of someone you meet, you may associate the name with some aspect of their appearance (e.g. *Bob* has a *beard*, *Susan* is *short*).

Sigmund Freud recognized the significance of associations as a tool in psychoanalysis. By using **free association** – that is, simply asking a person to say

free association a
technique originated by
Freud for studying the mind,
based on asking a person to
simply say whatever words
float into their mind, and
then looking for patterns

repression in Freud's theory, a defence mechanism in which impulses, memories or ideas are forcibly blocked from the conscious mind

whatever words float into their mind – he looked for patterns that might reveal their inner conflicts. Consider the example of a teaching colleague who had separated from his wife, Barbara. Shortly after, he met a former student on the street. He remembered having taught the girl, what course she had taken, and even her final grade, but not her name. When he asked her, it was, of course, Barbara! The association of names evoked an unpleasant event for my colleague, leading to a memory failure. Freud referred to forgetting due to inner conflicts as **repression**.

One need not turn to psychoanalysis to recognize that associations can seem obscure, yet are always based on an organizing structure. For example, conversations at a party may wander over many topics, yet if you trace back carefully, you can always find the links between topics. The mind (including memory) does not seem to function as a random structure. One way of describing the structure which underlies memory is in terms of associations.

Although it is easy to see how associations can be useful, nothing has been said about how they are formed. The usual explanation is in terms of *rote repetition*. By repetition, information re-enters STM, and each entry into STM makes it more probable that the information will be stored in LTM. Because rehearsal represents a form of rote repetition, learning based on rote repetition is also sometimes called **maintenance rehearsal** (Craik and Lockhart 1972). (Note, however, that repetition could also be aloud, over a long time period, and so on.)

maintenance rehearsal the retention of material in STM by means of rote repetition

One problem with this view is that the formation of associations is represented as being random. It is impossible to predict what type of association, if any, will be formed to mediate between a stimulus and prior knowledge. In fact, the early behaviourists insisted that the process *was* random, based simply on trial and error. Unfortunately, this does not fit well with the cognitive view of mediating processes as being purposeful or systematic, nor does it seem to account for the evident organization of information in memory.

An alternative to the associationist view exists, and it may be both closer to reality and easier to apply in improving memory performance. According to the concept of **cue-dependent coding**, all information is stored in memory as a set of relationships which are called the *context*. Remembering is dependent on restoring the cues which formed the original context (Tulving 1974). When meeting someone on the street who seems familiar, you may try to recall *where* you met them, or *who* you were with, or *when* it was, since these are all potential parts of the context of the original encounter. Similarly, hearing an old song may bring back a flood of memories related to the situation in which you first heard the song. In this case, the song provides the cues for remembering the events. Even internal body states may provide context cues; for example, an athlete, recalling a performance, may make movements of the same muscles originally used.

cue-dependent coding the concept that all information is stored in memory as a set of relationships called the context; remembering is seen as dependent on restoring the cues which formed the original context

While there is evidence for cue-based encoding in both episodic and semantic memory, not surprisingly, the types of cues may differ in the two cases. Semantic memory, being based on the meaning of information, tends to be structured in logical and conceptual ways (e.g. 'apples' would be related to 'fruits'; a geometry theorem may be related to other maths information). By contrast, episodic memory is situational in nature, and hence coding reflects the context of when, where and what happened.

Just as one can ask why particular associations are formed, one may ask what determines the contextual coding of a specific memory. While there is no absolute answer to this, since it is possible that different individuals develop different organizational structures over time, there is a model which addresses the issue in general terms. Just as associations seem to build up by rote repetition (maintenance rehearsal), it seems that coding for context is related to elaborative rehearsal. **Elaborative rehearsal** involves doing some form of processing of items in STM in order to code the information for LTM (Craik and Lockhart 1972). The argument is that material may be processed in various ways, ranging from an emphasis on sensory characteristics (visual appearance, sound) to a focus on the semantic content ('meaning') of information. For example, an emphasis on *sound* might lead to noting what words rhyme with a given word. Emphasizing *meaning* can involve extracting the 'gist' of a speech, without remembering the specific words used. Overall, the evidence indicates that processing for meaning is the most effective strategy for coding in semantic memory. However, since this type of processing is also the most demanding in terms of cognitive resources, individuals will sometimes resort to faster, but more superficial, forms of coding (e.g. sound or appearance).

In some ways, the notion of cue-dependent coding does not differ greatly from the associationist view. Since both are ultimately trying to explain the same behaviour, the similarities should not seem surprising. However, as with any competing theories, there are also areas of difference which can be used to distinguish between the alternatives. One area in which differences emerge is how the two views deal with forgetting.

elaborative rehearsal the active processing of items in STM in order to code the information for LTM; material may be processed in various ways, ranging from an emphasis on sensory characteristics (visual appearance, sound) to a focus on the semantic content ('meaning') of information

Forgetting

The failure to remember, or *forgetting*, is perhaps the most salient aspect of memory for most people. When we succeed at remembering something, we tend to take the act for granted. When we *can't* remember, we get irritated, frustrated and eager to find ways to remedy the situation. While no panaceas exist, understanding *why* forgetting occurs is important to knowing what one can do to reduce difficulties of forgetting.

As noted previously, the first stage of memory is sensory memory. Since the sensory stores serve primarily to provide an input channel, it should not be surprising to learn that the information held in sensory storage is very transient. Unless selected by attention for transfer to STM, the contents of sensory memory are quickly lost. The spontaneous loss of information from sensory memory is described as **decay**, to note its time-related character. Other than selecting information by means of attention, there is very little one can do to influence sensory memory.

decay in memory, the spontaneous loss of information with the passage of time

Forgetting in STM

By contrast, STM is a more complex system, used both to process incoming information and to retrieve material from LTM. At first glance, STM seems ill-designed for such a weighty role, since it has limited duration and limited

displacement in memory, forgetting in STM due to new incoming information pushing out the previous contents

capacity. In addition, maintenance rehearsal involves minimal processing, at best classifying information by sound. Since information passing through STM leaves no permanent impression (much like water leaves the bucket unchanged in our earlier analogy), one might think that its limited duration is directly responsible for forgetting. Instead, forgetting in STM seems to be related to its limited capacity: new incoming information tends to push out the previous contents. This **displacement** of information is the basic cause of forgetting in STM.

Since the capacity of STM is fixed, one cannot really reduce displacement. On the other hand, awareness of displacement *does* imply that, for remembering important material, one should avoid distractions. How often have you been talking about something, been interrupted, and then been unable to recall the point where you left off? In this situation, an interruption leads to displacement of the previous words spoken. Similarly, forgetting a telephone number you've just looked up involves forgetting by displacement.

While the basic capacity of STM does not seem alterable, we can improve the *use* of STM by better coding of information. As noted earlier, the capacity of STM is about 7 ± 2 *chunks*. A chunk may be a letter in a random series (as in Fig. 4.2), a word (as in an item on a grocery list), or a whole concept (as in the key points of a speech). In general, a chunk represents the minimum meaningful unit. This means that one can increase the *effective* capacity of STM by recoding information into larger chunks whenever possible. Consider a grocery list. By grouping items into categories (e.g. fruits, meats, canned goods), you can focus on remembering the categories. Then, each time you think of a category, the individual items will be easier to recall. The effect of categories on improving learning and recall has been well-established in research. Another approach is to convert meaningless items into meaningful chunks. Telephone numbers are one example: at one time, everyone learned the initial numbers as the name of an exchange (for example, Cherry stood for CH, or 24). Today, the telephone company officially avoids these names, but using letter equivalents can still be helpful. For example, a Canadian bank advertises its telephone number as 980-CIBC (the letters of the bank's name). You may be able to make similar codes for numbers that you need to remember.

As with many activities, practice makes such recoding easier to accomplish. In one well-known study, a student given long sequences of random numbers learned, over several months, to recode them as chunks, and then as chunks-made-up-of-chunks. Over time, he was able to increase his performance to the point that he could recall sequences of *eighty digits* correctly after one presentation (Ericsson and Chase 1982). This feat was a function of developing efficient codes, not somehow stretching capacity by extensive use; in fact, when tested with random *letter* strings at the end of the experiment, his performance was only average. As we will discuss later, such recoding techniques are one example of memory aids called *mnemonic devices*.

The use of recoding to enhance chunking compensates for the limited capacity of STM. However, it would be wrong to believe that chunking occurs independently of LTM. Clearly, the use of any coding method involves drawing on past experience which is stored in LTM. In fact, it can be argued that the *real* function of chunking or other coding is to increase transfer into LTM – that is, recoding represents a form of elaborative rehearsal. To understand this, let us consider forgetting in LTM.

Forgetting in LTM

The first point to note is that not everything blamed on 'forgetting' really is a failure to remember. In order to be remembered, information must first *reach* LTM. Simply being exposed to something does not guarantee that we will retain it, since there is filtering by attention prior to STM. Furthermore, not everything which reaches STM is transferred to LTM, as we have seen. In both of these circumstances, one cannot really speak of 'forgetting' information which never entered LTM! Having said that, it is still clear that there are circumstances which reflect genuine forgetting. Since capacity in LTM appears to be unlimited in any practical sense, clearly forgetting cannot be based on displacement. And despite the limitations on what reaches LTM, information which *does* enter LTM may potentially be available for the rest of our lives. Given this picture of a permanent system, unlimited in capacity, it may seem puzzling that we ever fail to remember.

The traditional explanation offered by associationism is **interference**, or competition between various items of information. As with books in a large library, often the problem in memory is not storage space, but locating what you want. The larger the collection of books, or information, the more difficult it can be to retrieve a particular item. The concept of interference implies that as our store of information grows, it becomes harder and harder to uniquely identify a piece of information. In terms of associations, the associations for a particular item will tend to overlap those for similar items ('Was it *last* summer that I met Harry in Boston, or when I was there two years ago?'). As time goes on, we experience a running together of past experience, and a consequent loss of details, due to interference. If there are too many competing associations, you may end up unable to remember the desired information.

Interference takes two basic forms, which differ in terms of the time relationship between competing responses. The first form to be studied was **retroactive** ('acting backwards') **interference**, which involves the effect of recent experiences making it more difficult to recall something learned earlier (see Fig. 4.3a). One classic experiment concerned testing recall for two groups, one which went to sleep after the original learning session, and the other which went about daily activities (Jenkins and Dallenbach 1924). When both groups were tested after the same interval of time had passed, the sleep group showed better recall. Why? Because daily experiences created more interference than did sleeping! Students often experience retroactive interference when they find that, for example, this semester's physics has interfered with remembering last semester's biology. Similarly, retroactive interference can occur at work when a person changes job responsibilities. The programmer who becomes a supervisor may get rusty at programming skills. In each case, recent experiences and the associations they create can interfere with recall of earlier experiences, particularly if there is some overlap of associations.

The other form of interference, called **proactive** ('acting forwards') **interference**, concerns the effect of prior experiences making learning and recall of subsequent experiences more difficult (see Fig. 4.3b). At first glance, this may seem rather odd – how can old memories disrupt something more recent? The reason, according to interference theory, is that interactions among associations are not directional with respect to time. Consequently, it is just as possible for

interference according to associationism, competition between items which can hamper learning and produce forgetting

retroactive interference in memory, a form of interference in recent experiences make it difficult to recall something learned earlier

proactive interference in memory, a form of interference in which prior experiences make learning and recall of subsequent experiences difficult

(a) TESTING FOR RETROACTIVE INTERFERENCE

Experimental Group   LEARN A ⟶ LEARN B ⟶ RECALL A

Control Group   LEARN A ⟶ (REST) ⟶ RECALL A

When looking at retroactive interference, one is concerned with whether recent experiences can interfere with the recall of material learned earlier. In the above situation, if the experimental group does worse than the control group, that would be evidence of retroactive interference

(b) TESTING FOR PROACTIVE INTERFERENCE

Experimental Group   LEARN A ⟶ LEARN B ⟶ RECALL B

Control Group   (REST) ⟶ LEARN B ⟶ RECALL B

In proactive interference, one is concerned with whether earlier experiences interfere with recall for more recently learned material. If the experimental group recalls less than the control group in the above situation, we would call it proactive interference. Note that what is being recalled differs from the retroactive interference test.

Fig. 4.3 Retroactive and proactive interference Associationism argues that forgetting in long-term memory is based on competing associations, particularly in terms of when information was learned. Retroactive (a) and proactive (b) interference represent the two basic forms of interference.

old information to interfere with new information as vice versa. The concept of proactive interference is expressed in the proverb, 'You can't teach an old dog new tricks', presumably because all the dog's *old* tricks interfere! Interestingly, researchers were slow to recognize the possibility of proactive interference, despite existing evidence of the phenomenon. For example, William James, after spending time learning large amounts of material, found that learning was *slower* than it had been initially, a clear sign of proactive interference from the previous material learned. In everyday life, proactive interference is most likely to arise when two situations show some similarities. For instance, in driving, cars proceed either on the right or the left side of the road, depending on the country. The side makes no difference when one is first learning to drive, as the task is completely new. But an experienced driver will have great difficulty in changing if visiting a country where it is the opposite – the prior learning interferes with behaviour in the new situation. Part of the reason why people are slow to change their attitudes, or learn new technology, as they get older may be due to proactive interference from what they already know. Thus, it may be that proactive interference is more significant in the long run than is retroactive interference.

Tulving (1986) has suggested that interference may be more significant for episodic memory than for semantic memory. Since episodic memory tracks the 'where and when' of our lives, it would be vulnerable to interference, given the continual flow of new experiences. As a trivial example, try and recall what you had for lunch three weeks ago today; in most cases, individuals would find this very difficult, due to the interference from other lunches, both more recent and more distant. By contrast, semantic memory, based on meaning, forms associations based on existing logical concepts, rather than physical context. Consequently, it should be less sensitive to variations in external context. To the extent that the issue has actually been researched, there seems to be evidence to support this distinction.

The precise nature of interference is not fully understood. As already noted, the common view is that similar associations produce competition among responses. An alternative view holds that the build-up of interference can lead to the actual destruction of memories; this notion is referred to as **unlearning**. Basically, unlearning implies that amid the tangles of associations, some ties are broken. While various attempts have been made to test this idea, the evidence favouring it is rather limited. Unfortunately, there is no way to know for certain that something forgotten is truly gone forever. In fact, it may make more sense to assume the opposite, that memories are permanently stored (assuming no physical damage to the brain). Consider the following situation: Suppose someone tries to recall something and, despite every conceivable attempt, cannot remember it. Then, a short time after they have given up, the desired information mysteriously floats into consciousness. This effect is familiar to most people, but how can interference theory account for it? Clearly, the information was not permanently lost, so it is not a case of unlearning. While one could conceive of changes in associations, such a spontaneous change in a short period of time would seem little short of miraculous. Hence, spontaneous recall after forgetting poses a serious challenge to interference theory.

As noted previously, the alternative to associationism is *cue-dependent coding*. According to this view, remembering depends on restoring the appropriate context, in terms of the cues present at the time of learning. If you do not remember something at a particular moment, it does not mean that the information is destroyed (referred to as a lack of **availability**). Rather, the information may not be retrievable, given the cues used to search for the information (that is, it is not **accessible**). Since LTM appears to be largely permanent, most forgetting should be due to problems of accessibility, not availability. Forgetting due to failures to retrieve the desired information is called **context-dependent forgetting**.

The concept of context-dependent forgetting suggests that generally we fail to remember because the cues we use to aid retrieval are inappropriate. For example, a friend once told me of having met a Nobel laureate in physics at a party the previous night. When I asked the physicist's name, my friend could not recall, except to say the last name began with the letter P. He strove to remember, but it was not until a few days later that he told me the name: Dirac. 'Dirac?' I asked. 'But you told me it began with P!' 'Yes, I know', he replied.

unlearning an alternative interpretation of the interference theory of memory, which holds that the build-up of interference can lead to the breaking of associations, and therefore the destruction of memories
availability in memory, the principle that remembering is determined by whether the information exists in LTM or not; forgetting implies that the information is destroyed
accessibility in LTM, the principle that remembering and forgetting are dependent on effective retrieval; without the proper cues, information which exists in LTM may not be accessible
context-dependent forgetting failure to retrieve information from LTM due to the absence of appropriate contextual cues

'But you see, his name is Paul Dirac, and on his name badge it said "P. Dirac". All I could think of was seeing that letter P, until the name popped into my head this morning!' By emphasizing the wrong cue – seeking a last name beginning with P, in this case – it is possible to block retrieval of the desired information. Similarly, in trying to remember someone's name, if you place a previous encounter in the wrong context (e.g. at work, rather than at a party), you may block retrieval of the name. By relaxing, it may be possible to drop the inappropriate context, and allow the proper cues to be generated.

Even when we don't perceive the physical context (i.e. the location) as relevant to what we are learning, it can become encoded as a part of the memory cues. For example, a variety of studies have shown that recall is best if people are tested in the same room where learning takes place. In one unusual variation of this technique, scuba divers were tested either above or under water; as expected, changing environments between learning and testing impaired memory (Godden and Baddeley 1975). Context-dependent forgetting may apply more strongly to episodic than semantic memory, as with interference effects; nonetheless, it might be beneficial, for example, to study where one will be writing an exam!

state-dependent forgetting forgetting related to changes in context associated with internal cues of physical and mental state, as opposed to the context defined by the external environment

Normally, we think of 'context' as being our physical surroundings. But part of the context is actually internal – the thoughts, feelings and state of mind that are part of our moment-to-moment experience. The changes in context associated with physical and mental state are often referred to as *state-dependent coding*, to distinguish these cues from those related to the external environment. Forgetting related to these internal cues is therefore referred to as **state-dependent forgetting**. Many students have experienced the frustration of studying hard, then 'blanking' while writing a test – only to have the information come flooding back shortly after leaving the test. This effect can be explained in terms of state-dependent forgetting. If a student is relaxed while studying, but anxious during a test, the change in mental state makes recall difficult. After the test, anxiety is reduced, and the answers become accessible once more.

Clearly, performance while highly anxious can lead to underestimating of what is known. To reduce this state-dependent forgetting, one must make the study and test circumstances more alike, either by learning to relax during tests, or possibly becoming anxious while studying! Since anxiety can hamper performance in other ways, obviously the former is the preferred solution. Another example of state-dependent forgetting occurs with drugs. A drinker may not be able to remember something read while sober; a user of cocaine may later be unable to remember what happened while 'high', and so on. Such effects have been found in many studies with animals, and they appear to occur in varying degrees in people, depending on the dosage and other factors.

The effects of variations in context should not be underestimated. Successive changes in context can make it difficult to reinstate a particular context. This may be one reason why information that is not used for a long period can be difficult to recall (e.g. foreign language skills). Often in this situation, attempts at *relearning* (such as refresher courses) will quickly restore the context, and hence increase accessibility of the information. Probably such courses should be required for seldom-used job skills; one example of this is the requirement in Canada for annual training in cardiac resuscitation (CPR) by all medical staff.

Context-dependent forgetting also helps to explain the typical differences found between memory performance involving recall versus recognition. Characteristically, people find it easier to recognize something as familiar than to spontaneously remember something – that is, recognition is usually easier than free recall. This can be explained in terms of more cues being provided in the recognition situation (in fact, the information itself is given, which only needs to be compared with what is already in memory). With unstructured recall, there is little contextual support to aid access. (This perhaps explains why most students prefer multiple-choice tests to essay exams.)

At the same time, the superiority of recognition depends on the context. Most people have had the experience of spotting someone familiar down the street, only to discover as they approach nearer that it is actually a stranger. This is an example of **false recognition**, whereby the presence of familiar cues (e.g. hairstyle, colour of jacket, etc.) leads one to believe the stimulus matches an item in memory. This effect is more than anecdotal, having been demonstrated in a number of experimental studies. What is more interesting is that studies have also shown individuals can fail to recognize something they have just recalled – that is, sometimes recall is *better* than recognition! In the classic study, students learned a list of words until they could recall the list perfectly. Then, they were given a longer list, which included some of the previously recalled words. By changing the context of surrounding items, the experimenters fooled subjects into ignoring words they had just recognized. For example, steel, iron and copper appeared in the original list; on the recognition task, the items broom, stove and iron appeared. Given the different context, subjects failed to recognize 'iron' as one of the words they had learned (Tulving and Thompson 1971). Thus, context-dependent forgetting seems to account for a wide variety of memory phenomena.

false recognition a form of memory error whereby the presence of familiar cues leads one to believe the stimulus matches a previously experienced stimulus

Memory as Reconstruction

Forgetting can certainly be frustrating, especially when we sense that the information is available, but we cannot retrieve it. Ironically, the emphasis on forgetting as a failure of retrieval tends to create the impression that memory storage is static and unchanging. Yet this interpretation, with its implication that retrieval is a neutral process of locating the correct item, may not be correct. Although there is little evidence to support unlearning, as previously discussed, it can be argued that remembering is not simply passive retrieval. Instead, it may involve **reconstruction** – that is, creating a whole out of partial information.

The view that remembering is somehow creative was supported by Gestalt theorists, who saw perception and memory as closely linked (see the section on 'Perception and cognition' above). Context not only provides cues for retrieval, but allows us to create information to fill gaps in our recall. For example, if you hear a funny joke, and then later retell it, it is unlikely that you will use exactly the same words as the person who told you the joke originally. Instead, you will remember the outline of the story, including crucial elements like the punchline, and then *fill in* the rest, using both your knowledge of the joke *and* your general knowledge of language and the world to make the joke work. Since semantic memory stores meanings, not the original words, it is inevitable that one will

reconstruction in memory, the process of remembering by actively creating a whole out of partial information reconstruct, not retrieve, most of the details of the joke. (Those who 'don't remember jokes' likely ignore crucial elements, such as noting whether the punchline depends on a particular play on words.)

The idea that *all* recall involves reconstruction as well as retrieval was supported by a classic study by British psychologist Frederick Bartlett. Bartlett read a story based on Native American legend to his subjects, and then later asked them to retell it from memory (Bartlett 1932). He found several interesting results. While the subjects tried to be faithful to the story, minor details tended to be forgotten. In addition, points which were central to the storyline were sometimes exaggerated. Most interestingly, Bartlett found that his subjects (British university students) tended to *change* details which, although consistent with Native American beliefs (e.g. the role of spirits), were not consistent with the students' own beliefs. Typically, the subjects were unaware of making such changes – they were simply trying to reconstruct the story in a way that made sense to them.

Eyewitness Testimony

An area in which the idea of memory as reconstruction has aroused concern is in the legal system. After all, if memory can be constructive, what does this say about the accuracy of eyewitness testimony? Our culture, especially our legal system, tends to place great value on personal testimony when trying to analyse events. 'Seeing is believing' says the old proverb, even though we know perception is not always accurate (see Chapter 1). In much the same way, we tend to assume that testimony about past events will somehow be free from distortion or error. Despite the emphasis on telling the truth, our legal system cannot test the accuracy of witnesses' memories directly except by seeking corroboration from other witnesses. Unfortunately, this is a less than perfect method, since a conflict between two witnesses does not indicate which, if either, is correct.

In order to address this problem in a more controlled manner, American researcher Elizabeth Loftus has done a number of experiments involving the basic elements of courtroom testimony (Loftus 1980; Loftus and Hoffman 1989). In one case, individuals first watched a tape of a car accident. Later, they were questioned about what had happened, in much the way that courtroom witnesses are. During this interrogation, the questioner sometimes asked how fast the cars were going when they *hit*, or how fast they were going when they *smashed into* each other. When 'smashed into' was used in the question, estimates of speed tended to be higher. What's more, when later asked about broken glass at the scene (there was none in the tape), individuals with the 'smashed into' phrasing were more likely to report having seen broken glass! Loftus argues that studies like this call into question the reliability of eyewitness testimony, since the wording of questions can influence both witnesses' interpretations (e.g. speed estimates) and even their subsequent recall (e.g. seeing broken glass when there was none). In other experiments, individuals have been influenced to 'recall' stop signs that were not present, and similar details.

Loftus believes that the person's memory for the events is actually altered by these manipulations. Other researchers have questioned this interpretation, arguing that misleading subjects simply leads them to question their original memories. In effect, it would be like Loftus' subjects thinking, 'Well, if she's mentioning broken glass, I guess there *was* broken glass . . .'. In one study, subjects were shown a series of slides, and then given misleading information about one of the slides (McCloskey and Zaragoza 1985). For the memory test, some were given the chance to choose between the misleading information and the original information. In this circumstance, the misleading information typically was chosen. However, if given a choice between the original information and a neutral alternative (i.e. unrelated to the misleading information), individuals tended to choose the original information. Hence, being presented with misleading information did not apparently cause loss of the original information, as Loftus believes.

The debates about eyewitness testimony are more than academic. Both Loftus and some of her critics have been employed as experts to testify in court about the merits and limitations of eyewitness testimony. While certainly raising concerns about the style of questioning permitted in the courts, the research does not seem to answer the basic question of whether memories are changed by misleading questions. Given that recall is nearly always a combination of retrieval and reconstruction, it is possible for *recall* to be altered without any change to what is *stored*. Since it is impossible to determine what is stored *without* involving the normal processes of recall, there may be no possible experiment that can tell us conclusively whether memories for past events can be modified. Yet, while research may not end the debates about eyewitness testimony, it is probable that increased understanding of how memory functions may allow the courts to perform their function more effectively.

For further consideration

What is the earliest memory you can recall? How can you be sure this is a real memory, as opposed to a construction from stories your parents have told? If you find it hard to determine, what does this say about the significance of viewing memory as reconstruction?

Improving Memory

Clearly, the greatest memory concern for most people is forgetting. Despite advances in our understanding, it may be small consolation to know that something is temporarily inaccessible rather than gone forever. There is no magic potion for improving memory, but there *are* techniques which can make memory more effective. The study and use of such memory aids is called **mnemonics** (from the Greek for 'memory'). The origin of mnemonics is credited to a Greek poet named Simonides. By a strange sequence of events, Simonides was the only survivor when the roof of a banquet hall collapsed. The bodies were so mangled that mourning relatives could not identify them for burial. However, by remembering the seating arrangement, Simonides was able to identify each body. Impressed with his own feat, he began a systematic study of techniques for aiding memory (Yates 1966). Today, a number of mnemonic devices, or memory aids, are known.

mnemonics the study and use of techniques for improving memory (from the Greek for 'memory')

One of the most basic ways to improve memory is by *concentration*. Too often, memory failure is blamed for what is really a lack of attention. For example, many people report difficulty in learning names. When introduced to someone, they are not focusing on the name, but instead worrying about the impression they're making, what to talk about, or some other concern. The result is that the name, never having been processed, is not available (not in memory) later on. By focusing on the name during the introduction, you facilitate storage, and consequently later recall. One memory expert used to advise, 'Look at the person, listen to the name, repeat it in your mind, and then say the name when you shake hands'. The same technique can be helpful for other learning – too often, students 'study' by casually glancing at the page, rather than reading carefully and thinking about the material.

Organization is another important element in improving memory. Taking the time to organize material which you wish to remember can improve retrieval by providing a natural context and set of retrieval cues. For example, outlining the contents of a chapter in a textbook can help show how various concepts are related to each other. Creating a time line for events in a history course can provide both a visual and verbal structure for remembering. Even if material has no natural structure, it is possible to artificially create one by recoding the information in some way (see below).

One unusual technique which can be used even with non-organized material is called the *method of loci* (loci is Latin for 'places'). This was the technique used by Simonides, and later recommended by Cicero, a Roman noted as an excellent speaker. Orators like Cicero would mentally 'place' key points of a planned speech in various locations around the assembly hall. By looking around the room in sequence, they would recall the desired points of their speech. Although it may seem a strange notion, the method of loci is quite effective, even with minimal practice (to try your own hand at this, look at the exercise in Fig. 4.4). A version of the method of loci can also be used to remember tasks you wish to do tomorrow. By vividly associating the task with some routine action, such as taking off your coat at work, you are reminded of the task when you reach the office. In this example, the visualized action provides the cue for recalling the task. By appropriate choice of key action, you can jog your memory at almost any point in the day's routine. Such mnemonic codes work by creating vivid and distinctive associations between new information (the task) and prior knowledge (about daily routine); by providing strong, distinctive links, the technique minimizes interference. At the same time, the cues used in this technique also depend on context, as in the method of loci.

Mnemonic techniques like the method of loci can be helpful by providing prearranged cues for recall. But for non-meaningful material, such as long lists of dates or terms, *recoding* into a more meaningful form may be more effective. As mentioned in the earlier discussion of STM, there are various ways to encode information, but the general goal is to make meaningful chunks. For example, generations of medical students have spent many hours memorizing the body's parts. The sequence of cranial nerves was made easier to remember by the nameless wit who recoded them into, 'On old Olympus' tallest top, a Finn and German vault and hop'. The purpose of the low poetry lies in the first letter of each word, which is also the first letter for a nerve, in proper sequence. This type of recoding, which creates a sentence or similar verbal structure as a cue, is called the *narrative technique*.

Another form of recoding creates a cue by making a word out of the first

Word list: voice, dollar, lake, soldier, library, plant, train, symphony, cup, game, desert, hat, turtle, sofa, moon, wasp, frame, home, eat, navy, pillow, legal

Fig. 4.4 A walk down memory lane If you want to see how mnemonic techniques like the method of loci work, use the 'map' together with the list of words. Take about five seconds for each word, trying to form a mental link to each location in sequence; when you get to the end of the map, go back and start again – hence, you will end up with two words for each location. Then, use the map to trigger your recall of the words. On average, most people get about seventeen words correct!

letters of a set of words. For example, a 'vibgyor' is a device for remembering the colours of the rainbow (violet, indigo, blue, etc.). Such made-up words are called *acronyms*. The US Army (which seems to love such creations), has added *snafu* (*s*ituation *n*ormal: *a*ll *f*ouled *u*p) to our language, as well as *jeep* (*g*eneral *p*urpose vehicle) and many other terms. (Note that the phonetic spelling *jeep* was later trademarked by an enterprising ex-GI – that is, *g*eneral *i*nfantry!)

The most general form of recoding is *elaboration*. This involves any form of recoding which adds to the information in some way which makes it meaningful and/or distinctive. For instance, *key word schemes* introduce one or more words as mediating links. Designed for learning vocabulary in a foreign language, a key word scheme tries to create both a verbal and visual cue as links between an English word and a foreign word. For example, to learn the Spanish word for 'duck', which is *pato*, one might focus on the key word 'pot' as a sound cue, and then picture a duck with a pot on its head! By combining verbal and visual cues, the information becomes more distinctive, and easier to retrieve. *Rhymes* can also be used. 'Thirty days hath September' is the beginning of a rhyme to remember the number of days in each month. 'I before E except after C, or when sounded as "ay", as in neighbour and weigh' is a rhyme which provides assistance with spelling rules. Sometimes *unique recodings* can be particularly useful. At one time, my postal code was M6C 1X1; I eventually remembered this by noting that 6C sounds like 'sexy', and that one times (X) one equals one, and then recoding it as 'my sexy one'!

Whatever the form, such techniques function by creating meaningful connections for information which has no natural structure. This has several advantages: stronger associations, forming larger chunks, and creating a unique context for retrieval. While it might seem that these techniques, especially elaboration, increase memory demands, remember that the problem in LTM is not storage capacity, but retrieval. Although mnemonic techniques add to the information to be retained, they also make access for retrieval easier. The only limits to the use of such methods seem to lie in one's willingness to use them, and possibly in one's creative abilities (see Fig. 4.5 for a review).

Given our increasing understanding of how memory operates, you may ask whether an infallible memory can be acquired. A few observations are worth noting in this regard. First, forgetting is universal, despite occasional reports of people with 'photographic memories'. Although differences in recall performance exist among individuals, experiments have usually indicated that these differences can be accounted for by what happens at the time of learning (if activity between learning and recall is held constant). That is, the likelihood of retrieving the information depends on whether you formed appropriate associations and contextual cues at the time of coding.

While practising mnemonic techniques can lead to more efficient coding, there is little one can do to alter memory itself. Despite periodic newspaper reports about 'memory pills' (such as the role of vasopressin, as mentioned in Chapter 2), there is no clear sign that any such remedy is likely in the foreseeable future. Hence, we must all muddle along, forgetting at least *some* of what we'd like to remember.

Lest you find this disappointing, it might be worth considering the consequences of *never* forgetting: all of life's traumas would remain vividly intact, as would every bit of trivial information, such as grocery lists from ten years previous. Overall, our memory system seems to strike a reasonable balance of benefits and limitations. In any case, in life the crucial factor is usually not how much information one has, but what one does with it.

For further consideration

Do you currently make use of any mnemonics to help you remember things? If you were trying to learn a list of terms for a science course, what technique would you use? What about if you wanted to remember a telephone number?

MAXIMIZING USE OF MEMORY

Most of us experience memory failures at one time or another. Indeed, sometimes it seems the likelihood of forgetting increases with the importance of remembering! What can one do? The following represents a brief guide to some techniques for improving memory. For more detailed information, refer to the accompanying text.

Names—Concentrate when introduced; don't let your mind wander as the name is being given. Repeat it silently. If there are couples, mentally link their names. Note the face—often you can make an association between the name and some physical feature (e.g. 'Tom is tall').

Phone Numbers—The trick is to make the number meaningful, or at least familiar. Is there a sequence (e.g. 1357) or other cue (e.g. 1293 is 'Dec. '93')? Failing that, repeat the number several times, each time saying the person's name.

Aids to Learning
1) Distribute learning time—cramming is not effective (*unless* you only want to recall the material for an hour or two after study).
2) Make the connection—look for links between the current information and what you already know. This may involve finding *similarities* ('how is managing staff like dealing with customers?') or forming *unique associations* ('This is Tom Gordon, whose wife's name is the same as my sister's').

Aids to Remembering
1) Use context cues—they can help both by organizing information while learning (making connections) and for remembering (e.g. using method of loci when giving a speech).
2) Use mnemonic devices—rhymes, acronyms, stories and other techniques can help structure material, which aids both initial learning and also minimizes the chance of omitting items during recall.
3) Relax—anxiety tends to create state-dependent forgetting ('blanking'), and increases the chances of fixating on the wrong context. If you start with the wrong context, the more you try, the less likely you are to remember. Overall, relaxation is surprisingly important for effective recall.

While none of these tips represents a cure-all, our memory works best when we act in ways which recognize its basic characteristics.

Fig. 4.5 Maximizing use of memory

Problem Solving

In many situations, the value of retaining information lies simply in being able to recall it when needed; for example, telephone numbers are a tool for communication. In other situations, information stored in our memory is used instead to help make sense out of the situation, and to overcome obstacles. For example, a person planning a trip from New York to Toronto will be aided by knowing the distance, highway routes, plane schedules, relative cost by car and plane, and so on. Each piece of information is of little value in itself, but is simply an input to the process of choosing the best travel arrangements.

When we are faced with a complex situation like this, the information in memory mediates decisions about what response is most appropriate for the situation. In this sense, memory is the basis of the cognitive maps Tolman described. As Tolman argued, cognitive maps allow the organism to choose different responses at different times. In fact, those situations that we call *problems* nearly always require a response we haven't tried before. Thus, how well we cope with a problem can depend on how much information our cognitive map of the situation contains.

Generally speaking, **problem solving** refers to a process for overcoming obstacles that interfere with reaching a desired goal. That is, a problem is a situation in which we face some sort of obstacle. The challenge becomes finding a way to overcome the obstacle. Apart from the information about the situation which we have stored in memory, our effectiveness in problem solving often depends on how we approach the situation. That is, problem solving is a type of skill, and like all skills, it can benefit from training and practice. Unfortunately, the teaching of such skills has sadly been neglected in our society, even though cognitive psychologists have been studying problem solving since the time of Kohler and Tolman.

problem solving the process of determining appropriate actions in order to overcome obstacles that interfere with reaching a desired goal

Wolfgang Kohler and the other early Gestalt psychologists (including Max Wertheimer, Kohler's teacher) did extensive studies of problem solving as well as perception. As described earlier, some of Kohler's most famous studies were done with chimpanzees. Interestingly, this work was largely a product of necessity; he was stranded on the Island of Tenerife during the First World War, and so began studying the chimps living on the island (Gardner 1985). In a sense, his studies of problem solving emerged as the solution to the problem of what to do with his time! The Gestalt approach to psychology was based on the premise that behaviour is based on organized structures, and is not simply a collection of its elements. For example, a melody is perceived as a particular unity – a 'Gestalt' – which is independent of the notes (e.g. transposing to another key will still preserve the melody).

Similarly, Gestalt psychologists viewed problem solving as a process of changing one's perception of a situation in order to arrive at a solution. This involved a restructuring of the elements in that sudden, spontaneous way called *insight*. Hence, the goal of Gestalt psychology was to understand what creates a particular perception of a situation, described as a *mental set*. (In this context, the term is roughly equivalent to the more modern term *schema*, as defined in Chapter 1.) Thinking was seen as productive and creative, rather than a mechanical process of trial and error. As it turns out, many of the *explanations* which the Gestalt theorists developed were incorrect; but by their observations, and the questions raised, they set the stage for later research on cognitive processes.

Problem Solving as Information Processing

Today, the greatest influence on the study of problem solving is information processing. While many researchers have been involved in the development of this paradigm, among the early pioneers were Allen Newell and Herbert Simon (Simon has made contributions in several fields, and received the Nobel Prize in economics in 1978). In the 1950s, they began working on computer programs which could simulate human thinking processes, foreshadowing what has become known as 'artificial intelligence'. Newell and Simon developed a program called Logic Theorist, which was able to do mathematical proofs – the first such result by a computer. Rather than using uninsightful 'brute force' procedures, Logic Theorist worked by using rules which Newell and Simon saw as analogous to human problem solving. Later, they began work on a program that could do other forms of problems (Newell *et al.* 1958; Newell and Simon 1972).

One of the influential aspects of their work was the emphasis on studying the actual problem-solving behaviour of people. To do so, Newell and Simon would ask individuals what they were doing and thinking as they worked on problems. In some cases, they asked the individuals to think out loud, creating what have

think-aloud protocol a transcript of the comments made when an individual is asked to describe their thoughts and behaviour while working on a task such as problem solving

initial state in problem solving, the situation at the outset of a problem, including any existing constraints (such as time limits or restrictions on permitted actions)
goal state in problem solving, the desired outcome of a problem
operator in problem solving, one of the actions permitted in order to solve a problem

become known as **think-aloud protocols**. Since the researchers came from a non-psychological tradition, they felt no qualms about taking such verbal reports seriously – in direct contradiction to behaviourist methods. Subsequently, a variety of studies, including work by Levine (1976), have demonstrated that verbal reports can be correlated with actual behaviour, validating the use of thinking-aloud procedures.

Beyond the impact of their procedures, Newell and Simon also generated an analysis of problem solving which has subsequently influenced cognitive research. In essence, they argued that effective problem solving requires a clear representation of the problem. In its simplest form, this means that one must know the situation at the outset (the **initial state**), the desired outcome (the **goal state**) and the available options to solve the problem (the **operators**). For example, to solve a multiplication problem, one must know what the starting numbers are (the initial state), what a product is (the goal) and the rules for doing multiplication (the operators). In suggesting a common framework for describing *any* problem, the information-processing approach represented by the work of Newell and Simon has been a significant influence on our current understanding of problem solving.

Stages of Problem Solving

Having sketched the background of the Gestalt and information-processing models, let us consider what we know about the process of problem solving, and what factors contribute to effective performance. To begin with, let us consider the stages involved in problem solving. While various researchers have used slightly different models, the basic stages are:

1. defining the problem;
2. developing possible solutions;
3. selecting and evaluating the best solution.

(Gestalt theorists have also talked about a substage of stage 2, called *incubation*, where one temporarily abandons conscious efforts to solve the problem.)

Defining the problem has several aspects. First, one must recognize that a problem exists in order to solve it. Second, the *way* one defines the problem can influence attempts to solve it. As Newell and Simon noted, it is important to develop a clear representation of a problem. Overly broad statements can hinder by their vagueness. For instance, asking 'How can we end air pollution?' does not point towards any specific solutions. On the other hand, overly specific descriptions can hinder problem solving by restricting possible options. For example, asking 'What is the best way to get sulphur dioxide out of the air?' may inhibit the idea that one reduce the amount going *into* the air (since it is mainly a product of car exhaust fumes). As Edward deBono, a well-known British psychologist, has said, a definition is sufficient 'as soon as it allows one to do something about a situation' (deBono 1976).

The second stage of problem solving is *generating solutions*. The process of developing possible solutions often gives people trouble. In generating possible solutions, one should try to list as many options as possible, rather than just looking for 'the right one'. Studies have shown that when people fail to solve problems, it is often because their set of possible options was too narrow (i.e. they did not include the correct solution as a possibility). Another tendency is to evaluate prematurely possible solutions before exploring the full range of possibilities – this sort of impulsiveness also works against effective performance. Properly, one should try to keep solution generation distinct from evaluation (i.e. keep stage 2 separate from stage 3). Later in this section, we will consider a variety of techniques to aid in the process of developing solutions.

The third stage, *selecting and evaluating the best solution*, has different characteristics for different problems. Some problems (e.g. many mathematical problems) have only a single solution, so evaluation simply involves checking that the chosen solution is correct. Other problems do not have a single ideal solution. In these cases, choosing the best solution depends on what criteria one selects. For example, in 1960 many people saw nuclear reactors as a means to cheap energy production, but today there is concern with the disposal of fuel wastes. Thus, the best solution from one point of view (or at one time) may not be the best from another. Among the factors to consider in selecting the best solution might be: What are the relative advantages of different solutions? Which aspects of the problem is it most important to solve? And what new problems are created by the proposed solution? As in the example of nuclear energy, it is possible that different people will prefer different solutions because they give different weights to these factors.

Convergent Problems

Not all problems are alike in their structure. Various systems have been proposed to distinguish problem types, but one useful approach is to characterize the problem according to the type of goal. Many problems that we face in

WATER JUG PROBLEMS

In each problem, the goal is to use the empty jugs as measures to obtain the desired amount of water. For example, in the sample problem, one would fill jug A, and then use its contents to fill jug B (discarding the amount in B each time). One would then have the desired amount remaining in jug A.

PROBLEM	EMPTY JUGS AVAILABLE			AMOUNT DESIRED
	A	B	C	
Sample	29	3		20
1	21	127	3	100
2	14	163	25	99
3	18	43	10	5
4	6	42	6	21
5	20	59	4	31
6	24	49	4	20

Fig. 4.6 Persistence of set in problem solving Gestalt theorists state that in solving problems we develop a mental set; if this set is not appropriate for a particular problem, we can get stuck. In the above problems, what happens when you get to problem 6? (Adapted from Luchins 1942).

everyday life are **convergent** – that is, they have a single solution, and everything leads towards that solution (Guilford 1967). For example, calculating the cost of a $10,000 loan at 6 per cent over two years has only a single solution. Sometimes, problems with only one solution are called *closed-end* or *well-defined* problems; by whatever label, such problems are frequently used in studies of problem solving because they are easy to evaluate. (The other main type, divergent problems, will be discussed in the next section.)

convergent problem a problem which has a single solution, and all elements lead towards that solution; also called *closed-end* or *well-defined* problems

Gestalt Theory

The Gestalt psychologists developed a number of intriguing convergent problems in the course of their research. In general, their concern was with the organizational characteristics that influence how we perceive, and therefore solve, a problem. In order to solve a problem, one must organize the information in an appropriate way. As noted earlier, the Gestalt psychologists referred to the way we organize the elements of a problem as our *mental set*. To a certain extent, developing an appropriate set is very useful. For example, consider the problems in Fig. 4.6. Once you have figured out the first problem, you can apply the same set to problems 2 through 5. However, you will find the sixth problem impossible to do in this way. This illustrates a hazard called **persistence of set**. The mental set developed in the first problem is no longer appropriate, and tends to interfere with solving the last problem.

persistence of set a phenomenon in problem solving, identified by Gestalt psychologists, in which a mental set developed in a previous problem is maintained even though it is no longer appropriate, and tends to interfere with solving a current problem

This phenomenon is very common, and accounts for many cases of failure in problem solving. Even in everyday life, it can be a hazard. For example, one could argue that executives at IBM were slow to recognize the shift from mainframe to personal computers, because they had been successful in selling mainframe systems for so long. Yet, before concluding that mental sets are always negative, one should note that the availability of sets *also* makes it possible for us to recognize, and solve quickly, the many problems for which existing sets *are* appropriate. It is simply that one needs to be flexible, especially if a particular approach to a problem is unsuccessful.

A related phenomenon which Gestalt researchers identified is **functional fixedness**, which refers to perceiving an object as having only one use. For example, a person moving boxes of belongings into an apartment building may feel frustrated that the front door has no doorstop to keep it open, never realizing that one of the boxes could be used for this purpose! Similarly, many people fail to realize that a coin or knife blade can be used as a screwdriver in an emergency. Obviously, functional fixedness reflects a perceptual rigidity, much like persistence of set.

The first step in avoiding these difficulties is to be aware of the danger. Beyond that, the Gestalt answer to these difficulties was **recentring**, which is developing an alternative mental set for a problem. Sometimes it helps to disengage from the problem, which is one of the functions of *incubation*. The Gestalt theorists believed that a spontaneous restructuring of set was more likely to occur if one ceased active effort when the existing set didn't work. Sultan solving the two-stick problem (described in the beginning of the chapter) shows the effects of incubation. Sometimes, over-familiarity with a problem inhibits original thinking and recentring. The development of the theory of relativity is an example. Since classical Newtonian theory worked well for many physical phenomena, established physicists were reluctant to abandon it; Einstein, as a young physicist, felt no such commitment to the old theory, which made it easier to envision a new approach.

Unfortunately, Gestalt theory is rather descriptive, and doesn't offer many concrete suggestions to improve problem solving. Even Edward deBono, noted for his work on problem solving and thinking, tends to offer fairly broad suggestions (deBono 1976). For example, he notes that rigid thinking can take several forms, from failure to recognize that an old solution is no longer appropriate, to arrogant attachment to one's own ideas. To aid recentring, he promotes the value of humour, provocativeness (especially in what-if scenarios) and novelty. While his writings are highly entertaining ('if you cannot imagine any alternatives, it is easy to be convinced that the only one you have is absolutely right'), his approach still tends to be rather general.

Problem Solving and Information Processing

By contrast, information-processing approaches have tended to be rather detailed and specific. In part, this reflects the influence of computer science, since programming traditionally could not deal with ambiguity. However, similar concepts have evolved in studies of problem solving in adults. One of the most powerful concepts is the notion of specific strategies for solving problems. In a pioneering study in the 1950s, Jerome Bruner and his colleagues at Harvard

functional fixedness in Gestalt theory, perceiving an object as having only one use

recentring in Gestalt theory, developing an alternative mental set for a situation, such as when trying to solve a problem identified two broad categories of strategies – wholist and scanning (Bruner *et al.* 1956). A *wholist* strategy is based on adopting a tentative solution which accounts for all the known information, and then modifying this solution only to the extent that new information requires. Such strategies tend to be logical and systematic; Sherlock Holmes's reasoning in the well-known mystery stories is an example.

By contrast, *scanning* strategies are based on adopting a series of possible solutions, each unconnected to the last. One version of this is the 'shotgun' approach: 'If I try enough things, something has to work'. In its most inefficient form, a scanning strategy can even lead to retrying a previously rejected idea. (Young children often make this mistake in games like 'twenty questions'; adults may revert to it when they feel frustrated or overwhelmed by a problem.) Apart from the inefficiency of repeating previously rejected possibilities, scanning strategies may also prove ineffective. Since solutions are chosen at random, there is no guarantee that a new one is better than previous attempts. Also, the randomness means that there is no guarantee one will *ever* find the solution. (Imagine looking for a particular number in a hat, by drawing one number at a time, and replacing it before drawing another – the chances of drawing the correct one never improve.) Only if one is lucky will scanning lead to a solution more quickly than the systematic wholist strategy.

Algorithms

The need for systematic methods of solving problems is very apparent in computer applications. Computers, by their design, are not well-suited to the 'maybe-I'll-get-lucky' approach of scanning strategies. At the same time, their speed enables them to carry out sequences of actions very quickly. These characteristics have led to particular interest in an area of mathematical logic called algorithms. Basically, an **algorithm** is a procedure which always enables solution of a particular type of problem.

algorithm a procedure for problem solving which always enables solution of a particular type of problem

The most basic type of algorithm is *systematic search*, which involves identifying all possible solution options, and then systematically testing them in sequence. For example, suppose you didn't know the combination on a lock which has a dial with forty numbers, and uses a three-number combination. That means that the total number of possibilities is $40 \times 40 \times 40 = 64,000$! If one began testing these in sequence, never trying the same combination twice, then on average it would take 32,000 tries to get the correct number. (One might get lucky and find it sooner, or be unlucky and find it only after 63,999 tries!) Clearly, this would be a tedious process for a person, and even for a computer the time taken grows exponentially as the number of digits on the dial increases (e.g. with 60 numbers, the total is 216,000!). Ideally, one would like to find a solution which is more efficient than this (and therefore remains practical even if the number of possible solutions increases significantly). Bruner and his colleagues found some individuals used a strategy called *conservative focusing*, which was similar to such an algorithm, since it enabled eliminating several possible solutions at once.

Thus, algorithms always enable one to reach the solution, but some are more efficient than others. Another example may help clarify this point: Suppose there is a tennis tournament, with 101 players competing. If the tournament is based on elimination matches, what is the minimum number of matches necessary? One algorithm, equivalent to systematic search, is to list all the necessary rounds, providing for 'bys' when there is an odd number of players. A shorter algorithm is possible, however; by definition, every player except one (the final winner) must lose once and only once. Thus, the minimum number of matches equals 101–1, or 100 matches! While efficient algorithms are obviously desirable, unfortunately for some problems only inefficient algorithms (like systematic search) exist, and for large problems this approach would tax even a computer. For still other types of problems, theorists doubt that any efficient algorithm is possible. (One example, often called 'the salesman's map' problem, requires finding the shortest total route to connect a number of points, like cities on a map. While systematic search works, it is not efficient, and grows unwieldy as the number of points increases.) For situations where no appropriate algorithm exists, other strategies must be used.

Heuristics

heuristic a guide to thinking; in problem solving, heuristics provide informal strategies which are usually better than random search, but less effective than algorithms

One option is the use of **heuristics**, or guides to thinking. Like algorithms, heuristics save us from the randomness of scanning strategies. Unlike algorithms, they are not precise or formal, and can make use of metaphors, analogies and other intuitive techniques. Unfortunately, heuristics are only guidelines and (unlike algorithms) do not guarantee solving the problem. For example, with the salesman's map problem, the question is in what order to visit the cities in order to produce the shortest overall route. A heuristic which gives a *reasonable* solution (but not necessarily the optimum) is to go to the nearest new city next. Or, consider the heuristic a mechanic once told me for fixing a stalled car: 'A car needs gas and it needs a spark. If one is OK, check the other'. Obviously, such a rule is better than nothing, but equally obviously, it doesn't provide very specific guidance. This is typical of the nature of heuristics.

A number of general heuristics have been identified which can be used for a variety of problems. These strategies include working backwards, creating subgoals, and using metaphors and analogies. *Working backwards* involves backtracking from the goal to one's current situation. For example, when you misplace something, you might retrace your steps from the last point at which you had the item. *Creating subgoals* is designed to break the problem into smaller, more manageable problems. For example, asking 'how can we end pollution?' can be broken down into types of pollution, sources of pollution, and so on. Once one has identified some subgoals, one then tries to deal with them individually. *Using metaphors and analogies* involves looking for similarities between seemingly different contexts. For example, asking how a camera is like the human eye has led to automatic focusing and automatic exposure systems for cameras.

In the end, no single technique will prove useful in all situations. However, it is worth remembering the perils of persistence of set and functional fixedness, identified by Gestalt theorists. The wider the range of techniques one can call on in solving a problem, the less likely these difficulties become.

For further consideration

Given a choice between an algorithm and a heuristic for a particular problem, which would you use? Why?

Divergent Problems

Convergent problems have a single best solution, and all the information ultimately points towards this. **Divergent problems**, on the other hand, do not have a single optimal solution, except according to the criteria one may adopt. For example, asking 'How can I design the perfect car?' depends on what one means by 'perfect'. Because the nature of the problem tends to lead in several different directions, the thinking processes involved were regarded by Guilford (who coined the term 'divergent thinking') as creative.

The term 'creativity' is often abused, with judgements being based on what amounts to personal preference. To avoid this element of aesthetic bias, researchers often define **creativity** as the production of something which has two characteristics: *uniqueness* and *utility*. Uniqueness is significant, because an idea which occurs to everyone is not regarded as creative (for example, suggesting that wheels should be round instead of square is not creative). On the other hand, unique ideas must also be useful for solving a problem (for example, wearing clothes made out of spaghetti would be unique, but not very practical). As Edward deBono has commented, a creative idea is just a new idea that works.

Divergent problems are creative in the sense that they have many possible solutions, not all of which will be equivalent in either originality or practicality. Hence, solving a divergent problem requires selecting the 'best' solution. In this sense, the difference between convergent and divergent problems lies not in the means of developing solutions (stage 2), but only in the means of evaluation (stage 3). Many of the heuristics discussed in the previous section, for example, can be applied equally well to generating solutions for divergent problems. Once one has found a possible solution, however, the two types of problems must be handled differently. Since convergent problems have only a single solution, stage 3 consists of making sure the solution is correct. (How many times have you made mistakes which would have been easily caught if you had taken the time to check your work?) With divergent problems, it becomes necessary to identify the criteria for an acceptable solution, and then apply these criteria to the available solution options. For example, in business, most decisions must involve cost factors, and possibly degree of risk. A promising new manufacturing technique which may not work in real production may be considered a poor solution, even if it is more efficient than the current process. Thus, the process of evaluation becomes very significant in divergent problems.

Ultimately, the distinction between convergent and divergent problems centres on evaluation, not production, of solutions. Unfortunately, social attitudes towards creativity have tended to blur this distinction, and to emphasize the *number* of ideas as the primary indicator of creativity. (Even Guilford was guilty of this simplification, since one of his tests of creativity simply counts how many different uses one can imagine for a common object, like a brick.) We tend to value more highly the person who generates five ideas, only one of which is effective, than the person who describes only one, because they have already recognized that the other four ideas are not workable. Of course, this is the whole point of evaluation in problem solving – to know when something *isn't* a solution as well as when it *is*.

The Formation of Problem-solving Skills

Good problem solvers often make use of many of the techniques that we have been discussing, even when they have not been formally trained in problem solving. Other people seem to flounder when given any type of unfamiliar problem. Since research suggests that problem solving is a matter of acquired skills, not general intellect, it leads us to the following questions: How do people learn how to solve problems? What makes some people more 'insightful'?

Gestalt theory refers to *mental set* as the way one perceives a particular situation, including a problem. Insight triggers a shift in mental set, so that one's perceptions are rearranged in a more appropriate way. The question is, *how* does this occur? One of the difficulties with the Gestalt approach is its tendency to be primarily descriptive. Kohler's concept of insight really only describes the end result, not how one arrives at it. Similarly, the description of incubation does not explain why it is sometimes effective, and sometimes not. These and other aspects of the problem-solving process were left to other researchers to examine – some of whom, ironically, began, like Tolman, within the behaviourist approach.

learning set a learned strategy or set which enables the individual to deal efficiently with problems of the same type; similar in meaning to the Gestalt concept of mental set, except it emphasizes that the set develops as the result of experience

In the late 1940s, an American psychologist named Harry Harlow discovered a phenomenon which he called 'learning to learn'. Working with primates, he found that problem-solving behaviour (such as choosing which of two symbols marked the location of a food reward) was initially trial and error, much as a behaviourist would expect (Harlow 1949). However, given experience with many problems of the same type, the animals would develop a 'set' which enabled them to deal with new problems in an 'insightful' way. Harlow called these learned strategies **learning sets** (in essence, Harlow's term has the same meaning as the Gestalt concept of mental set, except it emphasizes that the set develops as the result of experience).

Later research has shown that young children, and even adults, develop similar learning sets from experience. For example, the story of the child solving problems involving different shapes, presented at the beginning of this chapter, illustrates the formation of a learning set. In this case, the child quickly learns a strategy called win-stay, lose-shift. That is, if the first shape you pick is correct, stay with it; if you choose incorrectly the first time, then this tells you the other shape is the correct one, and should be chosen thereafter. At a more complex level, it can be argued that students in school learn *how* to learn, by learning to select what is most important when studying, by identifying cues to test questions from lecture content, and so on. In this sense, education is a type of problem solving, not simply a passive intake of information. Regardless of the situation, Harlow's work implies that effective problem solving depends on appropriate past experience – not to know the answer, but to know *how* to get the answer. Insight comes, not out of the blue, but to those who are prepared.

Research on the formation of learning sets and their use in problem solving has helped to clarify the role of experience in the development of problem-solving skills. While adult behaviour is usually insightful in terms of the use of strategies, it is based on a foundation of early trial-and-error experience. In this sense, Kohler's emphasis on insight as *distinct* from trial and error appears to be wrong. In the end, though, there is little doubt that cognitive research has increased our understanding of problem solving in ways that have practical benefit.

Language

While animals like chimpanzees have demonstrated some ability in problem solving, there is little doubt that people are more capable of dealing with complex problems. We can do so in large part because we know so much, which in turn is partly due to our ability to learn from experience, and store that knowledge in memory in an organized way. But another important element is our ability to communicate with each other, and thereby benefit from the experiences of others (reading a textbook like this is a clear example!). Without language, we would be largely restricted to learning from personal experience, and there is little doubt that our lives would be the poorer for it.

In many ways, language is a paradox: we learn to use it as a child with very little difficulty, yet as an adult find learning a second language a major challenge. We can use it to understand other people, yet we have very little understanding of the process itself. Psychologists, linguists, philosophers and others have all examined language, but at present there are many unresolved questions.

To start with, not everyone agrees on what language *is*. It is clear that language serves as a communication method and as a symbol system, but not every form of communication is considered language. For example, the innately determined threat gestures used by baboons to warn away rivals are signals, but are not language. In order to qualify as **language**, most researchers would say the symbols or gestures used for communicating must show *variety* within the species, and must be *open-ended* – that is, allowing for new forms and meanings. Baboon gestures show neither of these characteristics, and so would not be considered a true language. Variety is important, in that it implies the influence of learning, and also that symbols are somewhat arbitrary – that is, the same meaning could be communicated using different elements. Interestingly, bird-song is somewhat like language in that it is dependent on learning, and shows intra-species variation, including regional 'dialects' (Marler 1970). However, it is not clear whether bird-song can be considered an open-ended symbol system, as the definition of language requires. For our purposes, we will focus on the role of human language in communication and thinking.

The existence of language is such an obvious human characteristic that even the behaviourists could not ignore it. Traditionally, they have tried to explain it in terms of complex patterns of reinforcers and stimulus–response sequences (Skinner 1957). Beyond accounting for spoken language, the behaviourists showed little interest in its role in thinking, as befits their general point of view. Watson saw thinking as simply muscle movements reduced to small, unobserved twitches; Pavlov saw thought as the product of a 'second signal system', operating in parallel with the process of conditioning. Unfortunately, the behaviourist view of language and thought is challenged by the data. While there is evidence that muscle activity often occurs along with thinking (for example, deaf individuals who know sign language show activity in hand muscles while engaging in

language a system of communication based on symbols or gestures which can vary across individuals and allow for new forms and meanings problem solving), the evidence concerning thinking as *only* muscle activity is mostly negative. As we will see, there are also other problems with the behaviourist view of language.

By contrast, cognitive researchers see language as a symbol system which can mediate a variety of thinking processes, and which is not dependent on 'muscle twitches'. In addition, the cognitive approach views our use of language as based on innate capacities, not simply reinforced responses. To understand the reasons for this viewpoint, we need to consider how we learn to use language.

Language Learning

We all learn to use language, but typically show little concern about how we learn. Children absorb the vocabulary and basic grammar of their mother tongue long before it is formally taught in school. Yet, when closely examined, early language learning is a remarkable process. At about six months of age, a baby will begin babbling, producing a wide variety of speech sounds, only some of which will later be used in their first language. Later on, it is difficult to re-acquire those sounds which are lost. For example, native French speakers have trouble with the 'th' sound in English; similarly, English speakers have trouble with 'û' in French. At about one year of age, the first words appear. By about one-and-a-half to two years, the child produces two-word 'sentences'. These phrases were called *telegraphic speech* by early researchers, but we now recognize that there is considerable complexity in the production and use of these 'simple' phrases. Some examples of telegraphic speech are clear even out of context; for instance, 'that red' for 'that is red', or 'see mummy' for 'I see mummy'. In other cases, what seems meaningless when considered out of context is nonetheless understandable in context. For example, a child, seeing a blue ball roll off a table, may say 'blue fall'. (It is worth noting that in some cases *adult* language is *also* unclear when taken out of context!) By the age of two, the typical child produces about two dozen two-word sentences. From this time on, the growth of language skills is explosive, so that at age three the average child knows almost one thousand words, and this figure may *double* in the ensuing year (Moskowitz 1978). As an adult, it has been estimated that the average person knows over 100,000 words, though only a small fraction of these may be used regularly.

The rapid development of language skills, which does not vary greatly across languages or cultural settings, poses several difficulties for a behaviourist interpretation of language. First, acquisition seems to occur too quickly and too consistently to be based on trial and error. Second, there is evidence that we are best prepared to learn language at the time children normally do. If this 'critical period' is passed, it may be difficult or impossible to learn normal language skills later. (Incidents of children raised in isolation support this view, as do cases of children with correctable hearing deficits which are not recognized until age four or five, which is already past the point when language learning normally begins.) Third, although the evidence is not conclusive, it seems that individuals have less difficulty learning a second language as children than as adults. All of these factors suggest that language learning is based on some innate capacities which are tied to early development. While Skinner might accept such physiological factors as species-based, the evidence also suggests that there are internal rules which govern acquisition and use of language. Noam Chomsky, a linguist at Harvard, was one of the first to propose a model based on innate grammatical rules, and his position has gained many supporters in recent years. Roger Brown, a cognitive psychologist who is interested in both language and child development, favours the notion of internal rules. After reviewing studies of twelve different languages, he feels the evidence is compelling (Brown 1973).

The possibility that language is based on innate capacities is hardly disturbing to a cognitive psychologist. After all, such capacities would represent a form of mediating process for language learning, and hence are consistent with the general assumptions of the cognitive approach. The Gestalt psychologists, in particular, would find this view comfortable, since many of their organizing principles were seen as innate. At the same time, there is a risk in describing language capacity as innate. For one thing, emphasis on innateness minimizes the need to *explain* the process. In addition, there is still great variability among human languages and across individuals, and the notion of innate capacities does not address these details. Also, it may make it too easy to separate our own use of language from any apparent usage by other species, since it can simply be called an innate difference.

Of Apes and Language

The question of language capacity in other species has become a controversial area in recent years. Researchers have long speculated on the possibility of teaching human language to another species, usually primates like chimpanzees. Earlier in this century, several teams of researchers attempted to teach chimps to speak, often by rearing them as if they were human children. Then, in the mid-1960s, a husband and wife team of psychologists, Allen and Beatrice Gardner, tried a new approach. Reasoning that it might be an inability to *speak*, not an inability to *use language*, that led to previous failures, the Gardners decided to try sign language. Using a modified form of ASL (a sign language used by many deaf individuals in the United States), they began training a female chimp named Washoe. To their surprise as well as satisfaction, Washoe began using signs proficiently, albeit with a limited vocabulary (Gardner and Gardner 1969).

The first published reports set off an earthquake in both psychology and linguistics, mostly about what constitutes true language. A rash of studies followed, some using the methods of the Gardners, and some using other methods (including having primates interacting with a computer). Apart from chimpanzees, there have also been studies with gorillas, orang-outangs and dolphins. The ferment generated by these studies has been considerable. Some theorists say the use of ASL and other symbol systems shows chimps have basically the same type of language capacity we do. Others, including Herb Terrace, a behaviourist, have questioned whether the chimps really show awareness of syntax (use of word order to convey meaning), and have also noted the relatively limited vocabulary of the animals (Terrace *et al.* 1979). It is impossible to discuss every study in detail, but it should be noted that some researchers have found evidence for both syntax and the creation of new 'words' (Premack 1983). Even more interesting is the evidence that ASL-trained chimps spontaneously teach signing to other chimps (Fouts *et al.* 1983).

At present, it seems that the controversy is still unresolved, with each side finding some data which support their viewpoint. However, we should be wary of defining language in such a way that only human behaviour would qualify. For example, the limited vocabulary of chimps does not seem a sufficient reason to discount their behaviour as language. Similarly, judgements of creativity seem ambiguous: while it is true no chimp has produced the equivalent of Shakespeare, few humans have either; in this regard, it is interesting that a gorilla named Koko has shown an interest in poetry, and has commented on the death of a kitten in surprising ways (Patterson and Linden 1981; Stone 1988). Communication can range from the mundane to the extraordinary, and it is likely that the study of language-related behaviour in other species will help us to achieve a better understanding of our own linguistic accomplishments.

Language and Thinking

The study of language raises questions about the relationship of language to thinking. Is all thinking based on words? Do the words we use influence the way we think? In many ways, these questions are much deeper than simply asking if thinking consists of muscle twitches. Thinking processes are central to the cognitive approach, and it is obviously desirable to understand what the *basis* of thinking is. At one time, it was assumed that all thinking was verbal, in much the way that memory researchers thought all memory was verbal. One consequence of this view was the tendency to assume that infants, lacking language, could not think. More recently, ingenious experiments have shown that infants are capable of thinking (see discussion in Chapter 7). In addition, research on visual imagery and memory, as discussed earlier, suggests that not all thinking is verbal, even in adults. Yet, few would disagree that the *primary* mode of thinking for most individuals is verbal. And if this is so, then how do the words we use affect the way we think?

One answer to this question was proposed some years ago by Benjamin Whorf, a specialist in Native American languages. Whorf argued that the way a language is structured influences the way that individuals perceive, and think about, the world (Whorf 1956) – this has been popularized as the phrase, 'language shapes thought'. Essentially, Whorf argued that the way we think depends on the words available to us. He based this on the observation that various Native American languages have very different vocabularies, and that it is often nearly impossible to translate from one language to another. A well-known example concerns the fact that the Inuit have many words for different kinds of snow, but the Navajo have only one. Whorf took the strong position that such differences not only affect thinking and communication, but that they also affect perception. That is, he believed that Inuit actually *see* snow differently than other people do.

This view, sometimes called the Whorfian hypothesis, has been the subject of extensive research and debate. At the level of perception, the evidence has been mostly negative; for example, despite variations in colour names across languages, people tend to discriminate colours in similar ways. However, a milder form, that language can influence the categories used in thinking, is still an open question. Certainly, it is true that concepts can be easier to express when there is a specific word available, as opposed to a lengthy description. This is evident in the tendency of English (and other languages) to incorporate foreign words. For example, 'ennui' (borrowed from French) conveys a meaning which is subtly different than 'boredom'. At the same time, the fact that a single word does not exist does not necessarily mean that a concept cannot be expressed in some indirect way.

Since questions of vocabulary seem indecisive in judging Whorf's hypothesis, it is more interesting to consider areas where thinking interacts with the *structure* of a language. For example, some Native American languages do not refer to time in verb tenses; instead, different tenses reflect the degree of certainty the person has about what they are saying. In this circumstance, complex time relationships would be hard to express, and possibly to understand. Another example concerns counterfactual statements. In English, we frequently express ideas which are contrary to fact; for example, after John has a car accident, we might say, 'if he hadn't been drinking, he wouldn't have had an accident'. By contrast, Cantonese Chinese does not have a ready means of producing such statements; instead, individuals are likely to simply say, 'John had an accident because he was drinking'. Based on this linguistic difference, one researcher found that Chinese speakers had more difficulty than American English speakers in understanding arguments involving counterfactual statements (Bloom 1981).

While obviously not conclusive, such findings are certainly intriguing. At what point, one might wonder, do such difficulties in expression lead to different ways of thinking? On the other hand, does the way we think lead to changes in the language we use? For example, one might speculate that our experience of the world has been changed by concepts like Einstein's theory of relativity, with its suggestion that frameworks of perception are always relative. Whorf was likely too extreme in his position, but the issues he raised are likely to be with us for a long time to come.

The relationship between language and thinking is complex and subtle. Certainly, language is the primary symbol system used in thinking, and the specifics of a language can probably influence the way we organize information. Beyond that, there is much that we do not know about language, *including* precisely how it affects our thinking. Words let us think about the world, and communicate those thoughts to each other. At some level, that process is as wondrous as the latest technology. Future research may help us understand the process better, but it is unlikely to rob language of the capacity to amaze.

For further consideration

If you know someone who is fluent in another language as well as English, you might explore Whorf's hypothesis by asking them about their experiences: Are some ideas easier to express in one language or the other? In general, do they notice any ways in which their thinking changes when they switch languages?

The Cognitive Viewpoint in Other Areas

Cognitive psychologists have been active in studying all aspects of thinking, as indicated above. In focusing on these topics, one should not lose sight of the basic viewpoint of the cognitive approach: it is not that thinking processes like memory are the most significant aspect of behaviour, but rather that mediational processes of *some* kind underlie *all* behaviour. As noted in the introduction of this chapter, this approach can be applied to understanding many other aspects of behaviour. For example, early Gestalt psychologists were as interested in perception as in problem solving. Today, one can see cognitive influences in development (as in the work of Jean Piaget, Jerome Bruner and others), computer science (in the area of artificial intelligence) and even applications of behaviourism (where psychologists like Donald Meichenbaum are advocating 'cognitive behaviour modification') (some of these topics will be discussed in later chapters).

Given the many dimensions of human behaviour, it should not be surprising that cognitive interpretations are applied to many aspects of behaviour other than thinking processes. In discussing these areas, it is clear that the underlying assumptions are the same – that is, that there are mediational processes which underlie behaviour, and that these processes provide an organizational structure for guiding behaviour. At the same time, the specific models used often developed independently of either Gestalt or information-processing influences. Regardless of origin, the resulting models are characteristically cognitive in nature, as we shall see.

Attitudes and Cognitive Dissonance

One area in which the cognitive approach has been significant is social psychology. In this case, the influence is probably direct, owing to the work of Kurt Lewin, an early Gestalt psychologist who wrote extensively about social behaviour. Social psychology is concerned with the ways in which behaviour is influenced by social interactions. While this covers a broad territory, one of the primary interests has been **social cognition**, the mental processes involved in the way people perceive and react to social situations. We will look at two aspects of social cognition, beginning with the study of attitudes.

Attitudes represent personal beliefs of an evaluative nature – that is, good or bad, likeable or not likeable, etc. Attitudes are of practical as well as theoretical interest, since they involve such basic concerns as attraction and prejudice. Understanding who likes/hates whom, and why, thus requires an understanding of how attitudes are formed, and how they are altered. In this section, we will look at one approach to the study of attitude change.

One of the best known theories of attitude change is the *theory of cognitive dissonance* developed by Leon Festinger (1957). According to Festinger, we all seek to behave in a self-consistent manner. Our actions should fit with both our words and our attitudes. What happens, however, if our actions don't fit our beliefs, or two beliefs conflict? Festinger argues that whenever there are conflicts of this type, we experience a tension which he calls **cognitive dissonance**. For example, suppose you hate the hustle and bustle of New York City, but have good friends who live there whom you want to see. This creates a conflict between your attitude towards New York and your attitude towards your friends, resulting in dissonance. Festinger's theory deals with the nature of such conflicts, and how we resolve them.

One possibility is to change your attitudes to make them consistent with your

social cognition the mental processes involved in the way people perceive and react to social situations

attitude a personal belief of an evaluative nature, such as good or bad, likeable or not likeable, which influences our reactions towards people or things

cognitive dissonance in Festinger's theory, a state of tension created when there are conflicts between an individual's behaviour and beliefs, or between two beliefs actions. In the example given, you could decide New York isn't so bad, and go, or you could decide you really don't care that much about your friends, and not go. In either case, one of your attitudes would change to become consistent with your actions. Or, you could persuade your friends to come to visit you. In this case, your attitudes remain firm, but the conflict is resolved by adding a new factor. This is analogous to a smoking colleague who once commented, 'Sure, I know smoking causes cancer, but I'd be miserable if I *didn't* smoke!' In effect, the belief that life would be miserable without smoking is invoked to resolve the conflict between the belief that smoking causes cancer, and the desire not to get cancer. Dissonance theory says that conflict (dissonance) can lead to changes in attitudes or actions; if attitudes are changed, usually the weakest belief is the one to be changed.

Dissonance reduction seems to be a common occurrence. Consider the following example: Have you ever waited outside for a movie in the middle of winter, possibly for an hour or more? What was your reaction to the movie afterwards? According to dissonance theory, you very likely thought the movie was good, since it would arouse dissonance to think you suffered outside for a terrible film! In a laboratory analogy to this situation, Festinger found that participants in a purposely dull experiment were more positive about it if they were unpaid than if they had been paid $10 (Festinger and Carlsmith 1959).

Dissonance theory has generated a tremendous amount of research in social psychology. Partly this is because the issues it raises are interesting, and partly because of seeming weaknesses in the theory. One weakness is that the theory does not predict precisely what will happen in a particular situation. For example, a smoker confronted by evidence that links smoking to cancer may react in several ways: they may quit smoking (thereby changing actions); they may reject the evidence as being only correlational (rejecting one belief); or they may justify the discrepancy in some other way, as in the earlier example of the smoker who introduced an additional belief about the consequences of quitting. Festinger himself suggested that we tend to ignore information which creates conflict, a phenomenon called *selective exposure*. More recent evidence suggests that this sometimes does occur (Frey 1986).

A second issue concerns how widespread dissonance reactions are in daily life. While it is possible to produce supporting anecdotes, the evidence suggests that not all conflicts produce dissonance. For instance, a person *forced* to do something inconsistent with their beliefs will usually not experience dissonance. (This may explain why the people who were paid in the Festinger and Carlsmith experiment felt no dissonance about taking part in a boring experience – the money could be seen as the factor 'forcing' them to participate.) Generally, dissonance is most likely to occur when someone *voluntarily* does something which is inconsistent with their attitudes. (Since the people who did the boring experiment without pay were *not* forced to take part, they experienced dissonance.)

In recent years, there has been less research related to cognitive dissonance, since most of the major aspects have been explored extensively. Nonetheless, Festinger's theory shows the influence of the cognitive approach in both name and substance. As a theory of social behaviour, it clearly states that mediating processes are important in understanding how people act. The stimulus situation alone is insufficient to explain social behaviour; rather, one must consider internal processes represented by attitudes and dissonance reduction. In this and other ways, the cognitive approach plays an important role in understanding social behaviour.

Attribution Theory and Emotions

A second area which has been influenced by the cognitive approach is the process by which we interpret the causes of behaviour – our own and that of other people. The inferences we make about the causes of behaviour are called *attributions*, and the model used to explain the interpretations we make is called **attribution theory**. As Fritz Heider, the founder of attribution theory, said, we are all 'psychologists', in that we all try to make sense out of people's actions (Heider 1958). Heider, like Lewin, a Gestalt psychologist, suggested that we tend to interpret behaviour in terms of internal (e.g. physiological) and/or external (e.g. social) factors. If you see someone frowning, you may decide they are angry, and speculate about the source of their anger. Depending on the circumstances and the information you have, you may attribute it to *internal factors*, such as the person having a hostile nature, or you may attribute it to something in the *situation*, such as having received bad news. Sometimes, of course, our interpretations of cause are accurate; however, it turns out that certain types of errors occur quite commonly. One such error, called the **fundamental attribution error**, is the tendency to underestimate the importance of situational influences, and overestimate the importance of internal factors. For example, if we encounter a sales assistant who seems unhelpful, we are likely to assume that the person is unfriendly, rather than consider whether their working conditions or other situational factors might be responsible (for example, the person may have sore feet after standing for seven hours).

The widespread occurrence of the fundamental attribution error suggests there is a basic bias in the way we perceive others. However, attribution theory also applies to the way we interpret our own behaviour. For example, the *self-serving bias* is reflected in our tendency to attribute our successes to our own ability (i.e. internal cause), but blame our failures on situational factors, such as distraction, lack of time, etc. Thus, a student may 'take credit' for a good test grade, but blame a poor grade on having felt ill. In general, attribution theory suggests that such biases play an important role in the formation of our mental schema. Another area in which attribution theory has been applied is in the seemingly unlikely area of the study of emotions.

Emotions

We are all aware of the varied nature of emotions. Fear, anger, sadness and joy are all part of everyone's experience. Yet understanding how emotions arise, and how we interpret them, is a more difficult matter. In part, we know that emotions are based on physiological factors, such as changes in heart rate, breathing and blood pressure. These changes, which are referred to as changes in physiological *arousal*, are easy to recognize subjectively, at least in the extremes. But it is not clear that changes in arousal can account for the *variety* of emotions which we experience. For example, try listing some of the physiological changes you experience when you're very angry and when you're very happy. If you think carefully, you'll probably note a great deal of overlap in the

attribution theory a theory dealing with the inferences we make about the causes of our own behaviour, and that of other people; the interpretations made are called *attributions*
fundamental attribution error the tendency to underestimate the importance of situational influences, and overestimate the importance of internal factors in interpreting the causes of people's behaviour

two cases (heart and breathing accelerate, etc.). If two such different emotions share a number of physiological characteristics, then how can arousal alone account for different emotions? It is this problem that has led to examining the role of cognitive factors in emotional response.

Evidence for a cognitive influence comes from a well-known study by Stanley Schachter and Jerome Singer (1962). These researchers used injections of adrenaline to create physiological arousal in their volunteers, who thought the experiment concerned the effects of vitamin C on vision (as noted in Chapter 2, adrenaline production is part of our normal response to stress or emergencies). Some people were correctly told what to expect (e.g. increased heart rate), whereas the others were either misinformed (told to expect numbness, itching and headaches) or given no information about what to expect. After receiving the injection, each person was then asked to wait in another room, with a fellow 'subject'; the other person was actually a confederate of the experimenter, who had been given instructions on how to act.

The results of this procedure were quite striking. The volunteers given correct information about the injection *did* experience arousal, but attributed it to the drug, and felt no emotion. (A control group given a saline injection experienced no arousal, and also felt no emotion.) This indicates arousal is necessary, but not sufficient, to produce emotion. The volunteers who were given either false information or no information *also* felt arousal, but did not suspect that the drug was the cause. As a result, these people tended to look at their situation for clues to their state (i.e. external rather than internal attribution). Depending on the behaviour of the confederate in the room, who in some cases acted happy and in other cases angry, they tended to experience either euphoria or anger, respectively. Thus, the drug created the arousal, but the subject's *interpretation of the situation* determined the type of emotion they felt.

We can summarize the results of the Schachter and Singer study as follows: Physiological arousal is not always interpreted as indicating emotion. For example, someone who has just run to catch a bus will experience arousal, but will not attribute it to emotion. When arousal *is* seen as due to an emotional state, our interpretation of the situation determines how we define the emotion. William James suggested this basic idea when he argued that we are afraid because we run, not we run because we are afraid! Schachter and Singer extend this idea by suggesting that when we lack an appropriate internal explanation of arousal, we will attribute it to an external cause, which we label as emotion-provoking.

Attribution theory suggests that cognitive factors play an important role in our emotions. In everyday terms, one can see many situations that are consistent with this model of emotion. For example, a driver who has a near-accident may experience a strong degree of arousal. At the moment it happens, the physiological changes may be ignored. On arriving at work, the person may still feel tense and irritable. Not recalling the previous incident, the person attributes these feelings to something in the immediate situation, such as, 'Gee, my job is really getting to me today!'

Subsequent research has both supported and expanded on this model. In terms of the importance of arousal, Hohmann has examined emotions in victims of spinal cord injuries, which result in a loss of sensation below the site of injury, and hence less awareness of many aspects of bodily arousal (Hohmann 1966). Interestingly, the patients also tend to report feeling less emotional after the time of the injury. Thus, in the absence of information about arousal, less emotion is experienced. Conversely, a study by Stuart Valins looked at the effects of providing false information about arousal (Valins 1966). Valins showed male subjects pictures of nude women, while presenting what was supposedly their own heart beat. Actually, the heart beats were a tape-recording, prearranged so that for half the pictures the beats were faster than for the other half. The participants consistently rated more positively those pictures associated with the faster heart rate. That is, when confronted with information suggesting greater arousal, they interpreted it as meaning that they liked those pictures more. Interestingly, this cognitive factor was so strong that the men persisted in their ratings even *after* it was explained that the heart beats were fake! (This may be explainable in terms of cognitive dissonance theory, above.) Taken together, it seems that it is the *awareness* of arousal, rather than the direct effects of arousal itself, which trigger emotions.

The model of emotion which we have been discussing suggests that emotions depend on an interaction of cognitive, situational and physiological factors. This viewpoint has also been applied to the experience of pain. Psychologist Ronald Melzack, in conjunction with a physiologist named Patrick Wall, has developed a theory of pain which is quite consistent with the attribution model (Melzack and Wall 1982). While noting that there are a number of physiological pathways involved in pain, they also assign a role to cognitive factors, such as memory for past experiences and perception of the immediate situation. These cognitive factors (which they believe are mediated by the cortex) help to explain many of the puzzling aspects of pain. For example, two individuals with similar injuries may show significant differences in experienced pain, because they interpret the situation differently (e.g. a soldier may see a wound as removing them from the risks of battle, while a civilian may see a similar injury as a major disruption of a secure life). Similarly, distractions, such as listening to music during dental procedures, can reduce pain by changing our perception of the environment. Thus, the Melzack and Wall model suggests that attributions play an important role in our experience of pain, as they do with other emotions.

Attribution theory has been applied to many aspects of behaviour other than emotion, but its usage in this regard illustrates that the cognitive approach has a surprisingly wide range of application. Still, it is worth noting that attribution cannot by itself account for all of emotional behaviour. For example, it does not directly explain the occurrence of arousal. Also, recent research, such as that of Melzack and Wall, has indicated that emotional reactions may be *bi-directional*, with physiological factors influencing cognitive states, as well as the reverse pattern implied by attribution theory. As with many phenomena, the final understanding of emotion may involve a complex interaction of different factors, of which one will certainly be cognitive processes.

Artificial Intelligence

As noted at the beginning of this chapter, the cognitive approach in recent years has extensively used information-processing models, which are based on analogies to computers. Before leaving the cognitive approach, it is useful to note how psychology and computer science have 'cross-fertilized', primarily through research in artificial intelligence (AI). The term **artificial intelligence** involves two overlapping aspects: building machines which can function intelligently, and using such machines to test our understanding of human intelligent behaviour (Block 1990). The origin of AI is frequently traced to a summer conference held at Dartmouth College in 1956. At that conference, a small group of people (including Newell and Simon, mentioned in the section on problem solving) met to discuss the potential for computer programs to perform in ways that could simulate human intelligence. They set out a number of tasks that such a program would have to accomplish in order to be considered 'intelligent'. The tasks proposed were rather diverse, including language comprehension and translation, speech recognition, visual perception, music composition and chess playing! At the time, they felt these goals could be accomplished in 10–15 years; as events unfolded, twice that time has elapsed, with many goals still incomplete. The point here, however, is not to grade the progress in AI research, but rather to ask what it has to contribute to our understanding of human behaviour.

Intelligence is notoriously difficult to define, for humans or machines. While many theories have been proposed (e.g. Guilford 1967; Sternberg 1985), and a variety of tests designed to measure it, there is no universal consensus among researchers about the validity of any one definition of 'intelligence'. Alan Turing, a British mathematician who made significant contributions to the theory of computing, once proposed a procedure designed to avoid the complexities of defining intelligence (Turing 1950). The proposal has become so well known that it is usually called *Turing's test*. Turing suggested that a human judge be placed in a room, from where they could communicate by keyboard with another person, and also a computer. If, after a reasonable time (e.g. one hour), the judge could not determine which was the machine, then the computer must be assumed to have intelligence. This provocative and imaginative test has generated almost endless debate, in part because it seems so direct, and in part because it is so ambiguous. The difficulties are illustrated by ELIZA, one of the first computer programs to fool people in a form of Turing's test. ELIZA, a 'psychotherapy' program based on a library of stock phrases, was actually designed to show people the *flaws* of Turing's proposal. Instead, the program convinced some observers it was a real psychotherapist (Weizenbaum 1966). In the end, it seems that Turing's attempt to avoid explicitly defining intelligence has been at best a partial success.

In trying to define intelligence, one should be careful to distinguish two types of definitions: one is a definition for the *word*, in much the way that one might define *water* as a colourless, odourless liquid; the other is an attempt to define the underlying *thing*, much as one might analyse the chemical constituents of water. Unfortunately, human intelligence may not even be a 'thing', but simply a collection of processes or characteristics. In this sense, the study of artificial intelligence has been useful, for it demands that one consider what is required for intelligent behaviour, whether in a person or a machine (suffice it to say that the debates continue).

In practical terms, artificial intelligence, as expressed by the goals of the Dartmouth conference, has had significant influence on cognitive psychology. The research has led to an improved understanding of such processes as visual perception, problem solving and language. For example, early attempts at language translation by machine relied on a primitive process of choosing entries

artificial intelligence in computer science, the ⟨...⟩ ⟨...⟩chines ⟨...⟩ intelligently, and the use of such machines to test our understanding of human intelligence in a bilingual dictionary. This quickly led to the recognition that meaning is often dependent on context. For example, a story, possibly apocryphal, relates how a machine translated 'the spirit is willing, but the flesh is weak' from English to Russian, and then back to English. When it was finished, the sentence now read, 'the vodka is agreeable, but the meat is spoiled'! One obvious lesson of this story is that the meaning of words often depends on the context in which they occur, a point that has become basic to the study of language. With time, efforts have become much more sophisticated, and AI research has led to considerable interchange between psychology and computer science.

One of the areas of continuing debate concerns whether information processing is a suitable model for understanding human cognitive processes. ⁣holds that AI is a theory of computation, and that cognition require specific (i.e. biological) model. As Block has noted, if the attempts at intelligence ultimately fail, then it would be clear that a computational r ⁣.el is inadequate. Similarly, Nobel-winning physiologist Gerald Edelman believes AI models will ultimately prove useless, because they ignore the way structure and function are interlinked in the brain (Edelman 1992). At present, however, one cannot yet tell what the outcome will be. What *is* clear is that using a model based on computers (as the information-processing model is) involves various assumptions and implications, just as the choice of any other model does. Certainly, information processing has been productive in inspiring research in the past few decades; it is still unknown whether in the future the cognitive approach will discard it for a different model, much as the Gestalt view has been largely supplanted.

For further consideration

Suppose *you* were the judge in the situation described by Turing's test. How would you seek to distinguish person from machine? What questions would you ask, and what responses would you look for, in order to determine whether you were communicating with a computer? Do you think Turing's test is a reasonable way to determine if a computer has 'intelligence'?

Conclusion

No other approach in psychology considers thinking processes in quite the same way as the cognitive approach. Some psychologists, like the behaviourists, ignore thinking processes, while others accept the existence of thought without examining its nature. One example is psychoanalysis: Freud's theory, despite emphasizing basic drives, would be empty were it not for the emphasis he gave to verbal behaviour (e.g. 'Freudian slips') and to the symbolic meanings of actions. Yet, while he acknowledged the existence of thinking and symbols, he never focused on the processes involved in our *capacity* to use such symbols.

Despite its distinctive stance, and the successes of the cognitive approach thus far, significant challenges remain. One concern is that there is still a great deal of integration to do before the approach can lay claim to being an inclusive perspective on behaviour. While it is clear that problem solving, cognitive dissonance and emotion all involve mediational processes, the descriptions used tend to vary in each area. They are all 'cognitive theories', but as yet there is no *single* cognitive theory which links all of these areas in a coherent manner. One can talk about 'operant conditioning', and use the same terms for any type of behaviour one considers, but this is currently not true of the cognitive approach. While this may be partly due to the lack of a single central theorist, whatever the cause, it remains a limitation.

A second problem concerns the use of the information-processing model. This metaphor is borrowed from computer science, as reflected in terms like *input*, *storage* and *retrieval* of information. With respect to these terms, computers are infallible: errors are always the result of either human programming errors or equipment malfunctions. People, on the other hand, are clearly fallible. People forget; computers don't. People sometimes ignore available information; computers cannot ignore information provided to them. Given that such differences exist, one must remember that the information-processing model is a *metaphor*, and however useful it is in some ways, it also has limitations.

In addition, while we have considered a cognitive approach to emotion, there is not, as yet, an emotional approach to cognition. That is, the *motivation* for actions has been largely ignored. Although Kohler recognized that perception and learning can be influenced by a motivational state (for instance, being highly motivated can increase functional fixedness), this aspect was never well developed in Gestalt theory, and has been largely ignored in information-processing models. Tolman, in fact, was accused of 'leaving the organism lost in thought' – that is, in distinguishing learning from performance, he failed to explain *why* behaviour occurs. By contrast, although Freud tended to minimize the details of cognitive processes, he *was* vividly aware of the importance of motivational processes. (It has been suggested that this split of cognition and motivation goes back to psychology's philosophical roots, in that philosophers viewed cognition as distinct from emotion and motivation: see Eysenck 1993.)

It remains for the future to solve some of these issues, particularly in terms of creating a general theory of behaviour. In this sense, the cognitive approach is no more perfect as a means of understanding human behaviour than is any other approach. With the trend towards 'cognitive science', we are seeing an increasing interchange among disciplines, including psychology, physiology, computer science and linguistics, and it is possible that dramatic changes lie ahead. There has already been tremendous change, from Tolman's cognitive maps to today's information-processing models. Yet even as the metaphors change, the questions remain largely the same. It is characteristic of human behaviour that we seek to understand the world, including our own actions. And it is characteristic of the cognitive approach that we will continue to ask *how* it is that we understand.

Chapter Summary

◆ The cognitive approach emphasizes the role of *mediating processes* in human behaviour. The central assumption is that behaviour can best be understood by looking at the processes which come between an environmental stimulus and the behavioural response.

◆ Models based on the role of mediating processes, such as the *information-processing* model, have increased our understanding of phenomena like *memory* and *problem solving*, and also offered practical insights on enhancing their effectiveness.

◆ Memory is regarded as having three separate stages – *sensory memory*, *short-term memory* (STM) and *long-term memory* (LTM). Each stage has distinctive characteristics, with transfer between stages dependent on *attention*, *rehearsal* and *coding*.

◆ Forgetting from LTM can be interpreted in terms of either *interference* or *context dependence*; each interpretation has been productive, though in recent years the concept of context-dependent forgetting seems to have drawn more attention.

◆ Problem solving, like memory, can be viewed in terms of information processing, with distinct stages.

◆ Defining a problem requires identifying the *initial state*, *goal state* and *operators*.

◆ Generating solutions can involve the use of either *algorithms* or *heuristics*.

◆ Problems can be described as either *convergent* or *divergent*, depending on the number of possible solutions and the process for reaching a solution.

◆ While Gestalt psychologists emphasized the importance of an appropriate *mental set* and *insight*, more recent research suggests that problem-solving skills involve *learning to learn*.

◆ *Language* is an open-ended system of symbolic communication, whose basis may be partially dependent on innate physiological capacities, and partly learned.

◆ Controversy exists concerning studies of language capacities in other species, particularly primates who have learned sign languages.

◆ There is an interactive relationship between thinking and language, with the language we use at least partially influencing the way we think.

◆ The cognitive approach has also been applied to problems of *social cognition* such as *attitude change* and *cognitive dissonance*, and *attribution theory* and the causes of behaviours like emotions; in addition, there are clear links to computer science research on *artificial intelligence*.

Key Terms and Concepts

accessibility	context-dependent forgetting
algorithm	convergent problem
artificial intelligence	divergent problem
availability	elaborative rehearsal
cognitive dissonance	fundamental attribution error
cognitive map	goal state

heuristic
information-processing
initial state
insight
language
learning
long-term memory
maintenance rehearsal
memory
mental set
mnemonics

operator
proactive interference
problem solving
recall
recentring
recognition
reconstruction
retroactive interference
sensory memory
short-term memory

Suggestions for Further Reading

For readers interested in an overview of the cognitive approach in readable form, there are two highly readable accounts. Howard Gardner's *The Mind's New Science: A History of the Cognitive Revolution* provides an entertaining overview, while Bernard Baars allows many of those involved to speak for themselves, via interviews he conducted (*The Cognitive Revolution in Psychology*). For those seeking a more technical account of current research, Osherson and Smith's *An Invitation to Cognitive Science* (3 Vols) provides a good survey.

For an overview of memory, Elizabeth Loftus has written a readable account (*Memory*), which includes a good description of her work on eyewitness testimony.

Edward deBono's books on problem solving are both interesting and entertaining; *Practical Thinking* is perhaps more focused than some of his more recent books.

There have been a number of books written about the use of language by primates, but Patterson and Linden's account of *The Education of Koko* is one of the more interesting.

For readers interested in the implications of AI for psychology, Block's article on 'The computer model of the mind' is thought-provoking reading.

5 The Psychodynamic Approach

Motivation and the Mind

Several years ago, while at a conference, I attended a preview of a new film about the work of Sigmund Freud. At one point, the film discussed Freud's ideas on development, and referred to the concept of identification, which involves a child trying to copy the behaviour of a parent. To illustrate the concept, the film showed a father and his five-year-old son doing chores in the yard. Suddenly, the audience (all psychologists) burst into gales of laughter. The film's producer, himself a psychologist, stopped the film to ask what was funny – clearly, he didn't expect it to be humorous. A member of the audience pointed out that the father was showing the boy how to cut a limb from a dead tree using a saw; in the speaker's view (and also the rest of the audience, including myself), this seemed much too blatant a reference to Freud's concept of castration fear. The film producer, showing a mixture of shock and embarrassment, could only mumble, 'You know, I never thought of it that way – we thought it was just an ordinary activity.'

Even if you know nothing of identification and castration fear, the basic point is clear: the film's content conveyed an obvious meaning of which the film's producer was unaware. One of the central assumptions of Freud's theory is that we often are unaware of the true reasons for our actions. In this incident, the film producer seemed to prove Freud right; ironically, while presenting Freud's ideas!

Introduction

If you were to do a survey in any Western country, asking people who had never taken psychology to name a psychologist, you would likely get more people responding 'Freud' than any other figure, past or present. The image of Freud, stroking his beard and pondering the meaning of his patient's words and actions, has become almost a caricature of psychotherapy. As the founder of psychoanalysis, he has had a profound impact on the study of behaviour. Yet the approach which he pioneered has also spawned many variants, which share many of the same assumptions, but differ in theoretical details. Hence it is appropriate to discuss the larger context of psychodynamic theories, rather than only Freud's theory.

As discussed in the previous chapter, the cognitive approach deals extensively with mental processes within the person. In this sense, it is similar to the psychodynamic approach. However, one of the major limitations of the cognitive approach is its failure to address questions of intentionality – that is, it does not explain what *motivates* behaviour. By contrast, issues of motivation are central to the psychodynamic approach. As Robinson (1979) has pointed out, concerns about motivation are inevitably linked to the psychology of personality, since intentions must be held by *someone* (i.e. a person). Hence, theories of motivation are often also theories of personality. In the case of psychoanalysis, this is certainly true.

The *psychodynamic approach* can then be considered as focusing on the role of internal processes (e.g. motivation) and past experience in shaping personality, and thereby behaviour. In taking personality and motivation as its central focus, it is distinct from any of the approaches we have discussed. To the extent that behaviourism deals with motivation at all, it does so descriptively, in terms of an 'empty organism'. By contrast, inner processes, particularly notions of self and conscious awareness, are central to the psychodynamic approach. By viewing behaviour within the context of personality, psychodynamic theories focus on the whole person, rather than the discrete mental processes characteristic of the cognitive approach. And while Freud himself was trained in neurology, in practical terms psychodynamic theories operate at a very different level of description than do physiological theories. Thus, the psychodynamic approach differs in important ways from any of the approaches we have considered thus far. Since Freud is certainly the main pioneer of this approach, let us begin with him.

Freud and Psychoanalysis

Freud is probably one of the most complex, and most gifted, figures in the history of psychology. A contemporary of both James and Pavlov, he has become better known than either. By his own reckoning, expressed on several occasions, he was one of the three most important figures in the history of

Western science (Copernicus and Darwin being the other two). While this can be considered a form of exaggeration, there is no question that many concepts from Freud's work have become household words, including *ego*, *unconscious* and *Freudian slip*. More so than most of the theories we have considered, the man and his ideas are intertwined (for one thing, his analysis of his own life significantly influenced his theorizing). So let us begin by briefly setting the context of his life.

Sigmund Freud was born in Moravia (now part of the Czech Republic) in 1856, the eldest of eight children in a closely knit, middle-class family. Since his father had remarried, Freud actually had two elder half-brothers; as a result, he had a nephew who was slightly older than he! He was educated in Vienna, and spent most of his life there. Entering medical school at the University of Vienna, he studied physiology with Ernst Brücke, whom he later described as the most influential person in his life (Fancher 1979). Brücke favoured a mechanistic view of both physiology and behaviour, which probably influenced Freud's own later thinking. Freud seemed to relish research in Brücke's lab, but practical considerations (including marriage) led him to finish his medical studies, which offered greater economic rewards and recognition. He finished his degree in 1881, and in 1885 won a six-month fellowship to study with Jean Charcot, a leading French doctor who was interested in hysteria (neurological symptoms with no neurological basis) and hypnosis, both of which were to play a role in Freud's later career.

Upon returning to Vienna to practise, he specialized in neurological disorders, and became a leading figure in the area – a focus which eventually led to his search for new treatments and explanations. In 1919, well after he had become known for his writings on psychoanalysis, he was granted the title of professor at the University of Vienna. In 1923, he underwent the first of a long series of operations for cancer of the jaw. As the cancer ate at his body, he also suffered social torments. Raised a Jew, he became concerned about the anti-Semitism of the growing Nazi party in Germany; his books were burned in a Berlin bonfire in 1933, where he was called an 'enemy of the state'. When Germany annexed Austria in 1938, Freud was reluctantly persuaded by family and friends to move to London, where he died the next year. He was eighty-three, having outlived both James and Pavlov. Given the connections between Freud's life and work, we will return to some details of his life in the course of discussing his theory.

Freud's Assumptions about Behaviour

As with other approaches, it is helpful to note some of the assumptions Freud made in developing his theory. As noted, his early training in physiology under Brücke had a significant influence on his thinking. One of Freud's most fundamental assumptions, psychic determinism, was partially derived from Brücke's ideas. **Psychic determinism** states that all behaviour has a cause (i.e. is determined), and that the cause is to be found in the mind (psyche in Greek). While Freud seemed to believe that ultimately his ideas could be reduced to physiological principles, he recognized that such a goal was not yet attainable, and instead focused on mental constructs (*id*, *ego*, etc.). His work in physiology also converged with another influence – Darwin's work on evolution, which had

psychic determinism the assumption made by Freud which states that all behaviour has a cause, and that the cause is to be found in the mind

Sigmund Freud

Sigmund Freud (1856–1939) was born in Moravia (now part of the Czech Republic) in 1856, the eldest of eight children in a closely knit, middle-class family. He was educated in Vienna, and spent most of his life there. Entering medical school at the University of Vienna, he studied physiology with Ernst Brücke, whom he later described as the most influential person in his life; Brücke's mechanistic views seemed to influence Freud's own later thinking. While Freud seemed drawn to research, practical considerations (including marriage) led him to become a doctor, which offered greater economic rewards and recognition. A post-degree fellowship in 1885 exposed him to the ideas of Jean Charcot, a leading French doctor who was interested in *hysteria* and hypnosis, both of which were to play a role in Freud's later career.

Upon returning to Vienna to practise, he specialized in neurological disorders, and became a leading figure in the area – a focus which eventually led to his search for new treatments and explanations. In 1919, well after he had become known for his writings on psycho-analysis, he was granted the title of professor at the University of Vienna. In 1923, he underwent the first of a long series of operations for cancer of the jaw. The last years of his life were to be darkened by his battles with cancer, and his concerns about the rise of Nazism in Germany (raised a Jew, he fled Austria for London after the invasion by Germany in 1938). These concerns seem to be reflected in the dark tone of *Civilization and its Discontents*, his last major work. He died in London in 1939 at the age of eighty-three.

recently been published (*The Descent of Man*, 1871). The notion of biological continuity across species convinced Freud that human motivation is based on biologically based, *innate drives*. (Note that, writing in German, Freud used the word *Trieb*, which in his usage is best translated as 'drive'; however, early translations into English used the word 'instinct'.)

Another form of assumed continuity is also crucial to understanding Freud's theory: the *continuity of normal and abnormal behaviour*. In this regard, Freud accepted the enlightened view of mental illness pioneered by Phillipe Pinel roughly 100 years earlier. Pinel, while the head of the French asylum at Bicêtre, argued that mental disorders represented an illness, rather than spirit possession or degeneracy, as was then commonly believed. By taking this viewpoint, Freud was not only taking a humane attitude towards his patients, he was also justi-fying the use of clinical data in supporting a theory of normal personality. Since he believed normal and abnormal behaviour differed only in degree, not in kind, he felt justified in mixing the two types of observations in his theorizing.

The third assumption, and perhaps the best known, was Freud's belief that much of behaviour is governed by processes that lie outside the individual's awareness – that is, are *unconscious* (this will be elaborated in the next section).

The last point to consider is that although Freud was trained as an experi-mentalist (in Brücke's lab), most of his career was spent as a clinician, and he used *clinical observations* as his primary data. While he was as gifted an observer as he was a writer, clinical observations (i.e. *case studies*) are inevitably limited in drawing conclusions about causation (see Chapter 1). To the extent that he was aware of this limitation, Freud seemed unconcerned about its potential impact in weakening his theorizing. Taken together, psychic determinism, the biological origins of motivation, the importance of the unconscious and the emphasis on clinical data, are the framework on which Freud built his ideas. (Note that these assumptions are consistent with the general emphasis on motivation and past experience found in all psychodynamic theories, but are more specific.) Having noted these points, we should explore the substance of Freud's work.

Exploring the Workings of the Mind

At the outset of his career, Freud attempted to specialize in cases of organic brain damage, and his work on cerebral palsy in children and on aphasia (a neurologically based language disorder) was met with approval by the medical community. However, treatable cases of neurological disorders were relatively rare, and so he began treating patients with hysterias.

Hysteria refers to disorders in which there are physical symptoms for which there is no apparent physical cause. (The term was used long before Freud; its origin, from the Greek for 'uterus', reflected a common belief that only women could show the symptoms – an idea Freud himself rejected in 1886.) Although neurology had advanced to the point that doctors could rule out conscious deceit (malingering), they were nonetheless confounded by the paradoxical nature of these disorders, and their inability to relieve the evident suffering of their mostly female patients. For example, in the phenomenon of *glove anaesthesia*, the patient complains of loss of feeling in the hand, as if covered by a glove. Neurologically, this poses a problem, since the pattern of nerves extends along the top of the forearm and back of the hand, and along the underside of the forearm and palm of the hand; consequently, it is nearly impossible to have neurological damage which affects the *entire* hand, and *no* part of the forearm.

Like most doctors, Freud tried a number of techniques to treat hysteria, not always successfully. Two events were to lead him in a new direction, which eventually led to the development of psychoanalysis. First, he had studied with Charcot, who used hypnosis in treating hysteria. Second, a Viennese colleague, Joseph Breuer, had reported successfully treating a case of hysteria using hypnosis to prompt for recall of experiences associated with the onset of symptoms. Breuer found that re-experiencing the situation, which was usually emotional or even traumatic, produced relief from the associated symptom. In one case, a patient had developed a squint while trying to hold back tears at the bedside of her dying father. When she later was able to re-experience the situation, and express the grief she had hidden at the time, her symptom disappeared. While Breuer himself did not routinely deal with hysterias, his report intrigued Freud, who began his own explorations of the method. He quickly concluded that hypnosis was merely a tool, and that the process of recalling emotionally charged experiences produced a release of emotional tension called **catharsis**. The striking thing about this discovery, easily overlooked from today's perspective, was that Freud was proposing that the *body* could be affected by processes within the *mind*! How was this possible? Freud began an exploration of the relations between mind and body which was to occupy the remainder of his life – over fifty years.

hysteria a disorder characterized by physical symptoms for which there is no apparent physical cause; the term was used by Freud but actually predates him

catharsis the release of drive energy in indirect form, either through the process of recalling emotionally charged experiences or involvement in symbolic activity

free association a
technique originated by
Freud for studying the mind,
based on asking a person to
simply say whatever words
float into their mind, and
then looking for patterns

conscious in Freud's theory,
that aspect of the mind
which contains those
thoughts and feelings of
which we are immediately
aware at a given moment
subconscious in Freud's
theory, the portions of the
mind which are below the
level of conscious awareness
preconscious in Freud's
theory, that part of the
subconscious mind which can
be accessed by conscious
choice
unconscious in Freud's
theory, that portion of the
subconscious which cannot
be accessed directly by the
conscious mind; nonetheless,
impulses and thoughts from
the unconscious can 'leak
out' in fragmentary intrusions
into conscious awareness,
either directly or in symbolic
form

Abandoning hypnosis, he developed the technique of **free association**, in which the patient says aloud whatever thoughts come into mind. Such thoughts were often jumbled and fragmentary, with no apparent patterns; however, listening to these thoughts, and occasionally asking questions, Freud would gradually see a pattern emerge, which typically climaxed in a highly emotional recall of forgotten events. The memory of these events had been *repressed*, blocked from conscious awareness. In turn, these repressed events were expressed through physical symptoms that were either directly *or symbolically* connected with the blocked memories. (Since Freud believed behaviour always had a cause, a lack of *direct* connection would not be taken as implying no connection existed.) Frequently, recall of a traumatic memory would produce relief, though in some cases symptoms were *over-determined* – that is, there were multiple events contributing to the symptom, each of which had to be uncovered and re-experienced.

Freud's Theory of Consciousness

The discovery of a connection between repressed memories and behaviour led Freud to propose a novel concept: that awareness is not unitary, but rather divided into different levels of consciousness. Those thoughts and feelings which we are aware of at a given moment are part of the **conscious** mind. Much like William James' 'stream of consciousness' (a phrase coined at about the same point in time), the conscious mind, in Freud's view, is filled with a passing parade of ideas and emotions. Yet there is much more to the mind than this window of awareness; much of the contents of the mind are **subconscious** – that is, below the level of conscious awareness. The subconscious is divided into two levels – the preconscious and the unconscious. The **preconscious** contains all those thoughts, memories and emotions which we are not presently aware of, but which can be brought into the conscious mind by choice. By contrast, the **unconscious**, which may be much larger, contains all those ideas, experiences and feelings which are blocked from conscious awareness by power of *repression*. The unconscious cannot be accessed directly by the conscious mind, but its contents 'leak out' in fragmentary intrusions into conscious awareness, either directly or in symbolic form. And, of course, the contents of the unconscious can cause pathology, as Freud found in treating hysteria.

The notion of consciousness being divided has become so widely known as to become integrated into general usage, as when someone says, 'I did it unconsciously'. In fact, in our society, the validity of the concept has become almost a given, despite the absence of any *direct* evidence. Equally significant, there are cultures in which the notion of the unconscious does not traditionally exist, notably in Asia. Pointing this out is not meant as a challenge to Freud, but simply to point out what a remarkable idea it was when he first proposed it. The unconscious was a powerful concept, and a powerful force in behaviour. Thoughts and feelings which we don't even realize exist may manifest themselves in physical symptoms. While Freud found gaining access to the unconscious helped his patients, he was still faced with a problem: How do thoughts have such power to distort behaviour? To understand how Freud solved this question, we need to return to the cases he dealt with.

Initially, almost all his patients were middle-class women, living in the rather repressive culture of the Victorian age, in which women had rigidly prescribed roles as wives and mothers. Freud found that many of the experiences that they recalled were sexual in nature, often of assaults by family members or friends. This led him to propose that hysterias were the result of traumas which were always sexual in origin. Breuer could not accept this, and Freud reported later that most of his colleagues greeted the concept with shock and rejection. (It is difficult in this context to separate the realities from Freud's perception. In point of fact, the idea of pathology having a sexual origin was not new with Freud, having already been proposed in the work of Kraft-Ebbing and Havelock Ellis: see Robinson 1979.) Freud himself found it difficult to accept that sexual abuse could occur on the scale suggested by his patients' reports. His own doubts, combined with the lack of support from his colleagues, gradually he came to the conclusion that the events recalled were not true memories at all. (Interestingly, recent trends in research on sexual abuse would make it seem more likely that the reports may have been true; see, for example, Faller 1988.) But this posed a further dilemma – if they were not true, what were they? And how could false memories have such a powerful effect on the body?

Dreams and Symbolic Expression

The answers to Freud's questions about false memories came from his research on dreams. He was already aware of his patients' dreams, and had been interested in his own dreams from an early age. In *The Interpretation of Dreams*, he reported a dream which first occurred when he was about ten, portions of which later appeared in his adult dreams (Freud 1900). As he analysed these dreams, he came to the conclusion that dreams operate on two levels: the manifest content and the latent content. The **manifest content** is what the conscious mind is aware of, both during sleep and on waking. For example, one of Freud's female patients dreamt that she was holding a banquet, but had to cancel it because she had no food. However, this manifest content is not the true meaning of the dream. The true meaning is given by the **latent content**, which is expressed *symbolically* as the manifest content. In the above case (reported in *The Interpretation of Dreams*), the patient was recently married, and very jealous of other women. One woman in particular was of concern to the patient, but her husband had reassured her that the rival was too thin to be attractive. By dreaming of a banquet with no food, Freud explained, she was expressing the desire that the other woman remain thin, and therefore non-threatening.

This dream expresses two characteristics of Freud's theory of dreams. First, he believed that dreams were basically motivated by **wish fulfilment**, expressing fantasies that were not acceptable or even possible in real life. Second, it shows how the actual nature of the dream (the latent content) is transformed into something which is less threatening to the conscious mind (the manifest content). The mechanism of this process was what Freud called the **dream censor**, whose function is to ensure that sleep is not disturbed by the unconsciously expressed desires that are the basis of dreams. To accomplish this, the dream censor converts the content of the dream into *symbolic* form (the manifest content). Thus, in order to understand a dream, one must interpret the symbolism expressed in what the person recalls. In therapy, this was rendered easier by the other knowledge Freud had of the patient, from direct report, from free association and other observations. In addition, Freud came to believe that many

manifest content the symbolic content of a dream (disguised by the dream censor) which the conscious mind is aware of, both during sleep and on waking

latent content in Freud's theory of dreams, the true meaning of a dream, which is transformed by the dream censor into symbolic form as the manifest content

wish fulfilment in Freud's theory, the symbolic expression of drives in fantasty form, as in dreams

dream censor the psychic mechanism whose function is to ensure that sleep is not disturbed by the unconsciously expressed desires that are the basis of dreams; to accomplish this, the dream censor converts the content of the dream into symbolic form (the manifest content) symbols are nearly universal (e.g. swords as phallic symbols, money as faeces). Recognizing common symbols was helpful to Freud when colleagues (or even strangers on the street) challenged him to interpret dreams. Still, Freud viewed dream interpretation not as a parlour game, but as a serious technique for gaining insight into the unconscious mind. (The issue of symbolism will be further examined later in the chapter.)

Having decided that dreams were based on wish fulfilment, Freud returned to the subject of hysteria, and decided that, in a similar way, his patients' vivid descriptions were fantasies, not real traumas. This had at least two advantages: First, it produced a theoretical symmetry, in that both phenomena (hysteria and dreams) were now based on the same process (wish fulfilment). Second, it tended to placate his critics, who were incensed at his suggestion that sexual abuse was the source of all hysterias. Coupled with successes in treating a number of patients, this theoretical advance led Freud to feel that he was indeed on the right track in understanding the mind. His biggest question still remained, however: What was the force that *motivated* these processes?

For further consideration

Do you ever remember your dreams? You might try keeping a pad of paper and a pencil by your bed for a week, and try writing down dream images as soon as you awaken. Do they make sense to you? How do you think Freud felt when he first explored dreams?

Drives and the Psychodynamics of Behaviour

As noted previously, Freud's own training in physiology, coupled with the ideas of Darwin, led him to believe that there was a biological continuity between humans and other species. This meant that the basic forces driving human behaviour were not greatly different from those driving animal behaviour. Survival needs, including the need for food, water and shelter, were obviously basic. In addition, the demands of species survival made procreation (and therefore sexuality) a powerful force. As he worked with his patients and strove to understand both their behaviour and his own, he wrestled with the question of how to describe these biological forces. At first, he thought that motivation could be described in terms of the desire to maximize pleasure (*Lust* in German), and to avoid that which was unpleasant (*Unlust*). This concept, which he dubbed the **pleasure principle**, was similar to the well-known philosophical concept of *hedonism* (a term coined by Jeremy Bentham in 1789). (One might compare the pleasure principle to Thorndike's law of effect, proposed at about the same time, and likewise influenced by Bentham.) Of the basic biological forces, Freud felt that sexuality was the most powerful, and for many years he conceived of it as the central force in behaviour. (It is worth noting, however, that Freud conceived of sexual energy in broader terms than simply adult sexual behaviour; all forms of physical, sensuous pleasure were based on the sexual drive.)

Freud first expressed this view in a set of essays in 1905, but continued to reassess his thinking as time went on. By 1920, he had come to the conclusion that pleasure (sexuality) alone could not account for the behaviours and phenomena he observed (including sadism and masochism). This led him to propose

pleasure principle an early description by Freud of the basis of human motivation, which stated we are driven to maximize pleasure (*Lust* in German) and to avoid that which is unpleasant (*Unlust*) two basic drives, commonly referred to as sexuality and aggression; the change was described in *Beyond the Pleasure Principle* (Freud 1920).

As psychoanalyst Charles Brenner, and many other writers, have noted, Freud's writings sometimes pose a problem for those who wish to describe 'Freud's theory' (Brenner 1957). In grappling with the puzzles of motivation, he was forced to *infer* the nature of the underlying drives from the observed effects on behaviour. Given the complexity of human behaviour, this is a difficult and uncertain process. Not surprisingly, therefore, Freud himself sometimes had doubts about his descriptions, and would revise his thinking. In terms of discussing his work, the difficulty comes from the fact that he was a prolific writer (his collected works fill 24 volumes), and in writing, did not always make explicit when he was repudiating his earlier work. In addition, not all Freudian psychoanalysts necessarily agree with his later work, making it harder still to determine what is the 'true' version of Freud's thinking. In the end, it seems best to acknowledge the variations, and let readers draw their own conclusions.

By the time Freud wrote *Beyond the Pleasure Principle*, he had gone through many experiences, both professionally and personally. Between 1906 and 1920, not only had he received greater recognition for his work, but he had gone from middle age to the gateway of old age (he was 64 when *Beyond the Pleasure Principle* was published). In addition, the First World War had occurred, with horrors previously unimaginable. To the rationalist culture of the late nineteenth century, this was a stunning shock. It was in this context that Freud introduced aggression as being equal to sexuality as a basic drive. For most Freudians, this stage of his thinking represents the main form of his theory.

However, Freud was to approach the issue of motivation yet again, ten years later. In *Civilization and its Discontents*, he offered a sombre analysis of the nature of human society, and the drives which direct all human activity (Freud 1930). The First World War, and the signs of growing Nazi sentiment in Germany, led him to be somewhat pessimistic about the future of mankind (we will return to this issue later, in discussing defence mechanisms). At the same time, he again revised his description of the motivating forces, referring now to Eros (named after the Greek god of Love) and Thanatos (the Greek representation of Death). *Eros* was seen as a positive, life-affirming force, expressed in human creative activities, including procreation (hence the link to earlier notions of a sexual drive). *Thanatos*, as its name implied, was a destructive energy, expressed both in aggression towards others, and in self-destructive behaviour. (It is interesting that Freud came to this view after witnessing the First World War, and discovering he had cancer of the jaw – a condition possibly linked to his passion for smoking cigars.) Like his earlier concepts of motivation, Eros and Thanatos were seen as seeking continual expression and satisfaction. However, for the first time, he saw the two drives as also conflicting with each other. In fact, Freud ends *Civilization and its Discontents* by referring to Eros struggling to assert himself against his adversary Thanatos – and wondering what the outcome will be. Such comments suggest not simply a shift in theoretical viewpoint, but also a profound sadness and possibly despair. Whether that means the theoretical shift is simply due to personal bias is hard to say. Zangwill, a psychologist but not a psychoanalyst, and an admirer of Freud the man, has simply said, 'though some of his [later] ideas are of great interest, their empirical foundation [is] decidedly weaker (Zangwill 1987: 269).

Clearly, there are difficulties in discussing Freud's conception of motivation, but the difficulties are also inherent in the underlying problem: we can *observe* behaviour, but must *infer* the reasons for it. (Even the behaviourists, in opting for a descriptive model based on stimuli and responses, are making inferences about the causal nature of such connections.) Without getting into issues of Freud's intent, we will adhere to the generally accepted form, using the terms *sexuality* and *aggression* when discussing how the expression of drives fits into Freud's theory.

Thus far, we have seen how Freud dealt with two fundamental issues: the structure of consciousness and the nature of the drives that motivate behaviour. This still leaves the large question of how these forces are expressed in behaviour. What determines, for example, whether something becomes repressed? And how do the basic drives result in the wondrous variety of human behaviour? For Freud, these questions were answered by developing a psychodynamic model of personality.

Freud's Psychodynamic Model of Personality

Freud's early theorizing was closely linked to his clinical observations, dealing with hysteria and neuroses (a *neurosis* is a disorder in which high levels of anxiety are a primary symptom). As such, his initial model was a model of pathological behaviour, not a general model of personality. However, by the time of writing his *Three Essays on Sexuality* in 1905, he was discussing general human behaviour, not just pathology. The fullest formulation of his model came with the publication of *The Ego and the Id* in 1923. Much as in his analysis of the structure of consciousness, Freud conceived of personality in terms of a three-part structure: the id, ego and superego. The **id** (Latin for 'it') was the source of all basic drives; from the moment of birth, we are driven to try to obtain gratification of our needs. Motivation was seen as based on *tension–reduction*: when a drive is active, we experience it as a form of tension, which we seek to reduce by obtaining the appropriate form of gratification. In Freud's view, a young infant is concerned only with obtaining what it needs; for example, if it is hungry or wet, it cries until its demands are met. To the infant, there is no right or wrong, no past or future, simply the pressing immediacy of its desire for gratification. The id lacks any sort of conception of reality, and consequently cannot distinguish between reality and fantasy; in this form of thinking, called **primary process thinking**, a wish and its fulfilment are equivalent, with no reference to reality. Thus, a hungry infant may conjure up an image of its mother's breast as a way of reducing the tension associated with hunger. Of course, since the image cannot provide food, such primary process thinking provides only a limited form of tension reduction.

In an adult, the demands of id normally operate outside conscious awareness – we may experience the tension, but be unable to identify the source. In other cases, the focus of gratification may shift. For example, hunger may be satisfied by making a sandwich, going to a restaurant for a steak, or a range of other behaviours. The specific food, and the process for obtaining it, can vary; what remains constant is the tension induced by hunger. Some years ago, a popular song had the line, 'If you can't be with the one you love, then love the one

id (Latin for 'it') in Freud's theory, the element of the psyche which is the source of all basic drives

primary process thinking in Freud's theory, a form of thinking characteristic of the id in which no distinction is made between a wish and its fulfilment you're with'. Like many song lyrics, this can be seen as supporting Freud's view.

Opposing the demands of id is the **superego** ('over the ego'), which is governed by moral constraints. Roughly speaking, it is the 'conscience' of the person (not to be confused with 'conscious'). Superego represents the moral demands of family and society, and opposes the desire of id for immediate gratification (sometimes this is referred to as the 'morality principle', but Freud did not use the term). Not surprisingly, Freud saw id and superego as being fundamentally in conflict, since they attempt to direct behaviour in very different ways.

Mediating between the id and superego is the **ego** (Latin for 'I'), which provides the integrating of personality, and also mediates the links with the outside world. Ego provides the sense of self which is central to personality, yet it must also cope with the demands of ego, superego and the external world. Because it must contend with constraints imposed by the real world, ego is described as governed by the **reality principle**. Ego's task is not an easy one, since it must deal with three very different sorts of demands, two of which (id and superego) are fundamentally irreconcilable. This means that conflict is a fact of life within personality, and the varying demands of id, superego and external world require a continuing balancing act by ego. The ways in which it does so are what determine behaviour. For example, a teenage boy sees an exotic sports car sitting parked, with the keys visible within. Id will see an opportunity to race around in a fast and powerful vehicle. Superego will insist that such behaviour would be stealing, and is morally wrong. Ego may note that people are walking on the street, and therefore the chances of being caught are very high. Thus, in this case, the outcome would likely be to *not* steal the car.

There is no hard and fast rule determining how ego resolves the ongoing conflicts within personality. Freud suggested, for example, that sometimes individuals will respond to the moral demands of superego even when this conflicts with external reality, as when a person risks their life to help another person. In other cases, ego may allow id's demands for gratification, despite the opposing demands of superego, as when a child impulsively steals a candy bar from a supermarket.

Ego is capable of rational thought, which Freud refers to as **secondary process thinking**. Unlike the primary process thinking of the id, in which a wish and its fulfilment are synonymous, ego perceives gratification in terms of the constraints of the external world. Secondary process thinking also differs from primary process thinking in that it is accessible to the conscious mind, whereas primary process thinking cannot be accessed directly in conscious awareness. Only in limited circumstances, such as dreams, the physical symptoms of hysteria and the symbolism of artistic expression, does our conscious awareness make contact with the primitive nature of primary process thinking.

As suggested by the preceding, the relationship between the three aspects of personality and consciousness is rather complex. The development of the psychodynamic model of personality came much later than Freud's ideas about levels of consciousness. In fact, even the assignment of secondary process thinking to ego was a late development; originally, it was associated with the conscious mind, while primary process thinking was seen as characteristic of the unconscious mind. However, the descriptions in *The Ego and the Id* make it

superego in Freud's theory, that portion of the psyche which represents the moral demands of family and society, and is therefore governed by moral constraints

ego (Latin for 'I') in psychoanalysis, the element of the psyche which provides the integrating of personality by mediating between the id and the superego, and also mediates the links with the outside world

reality principle in Freud's theory, the constraints imposed on the ego by the recognition of the demands of the environment

secondary process thinking in Freud's theory, a form of thinking used by the ego to direct the gratification of drives; unlike primary process thinking, secondary process thinking is accessible to conscious awareness, and recognizes constraints imposed by the external world clear that he believed ego was largely conscious, and that much of the contents of superego were also available to the conscious mind.

The complex relationships in Freud's psychodynamic model have often led to attempts to represent the theory visually. For example, the observation that ego and superego are largely conscious, while id is not, has led to a frequently used analogy, in which ego and superego are at the top of an iceberg, with id at the bottom (see Fig. 5.1a). The part of the iceberg which is above water is the conscious mind; that which is *visible* under the surface of the water is the preconscious; while the very bottom of the iceberg, where id lurks, cannot be seen from the surface – this is the unconscious mind. Like any analogy, this image has its limitations, not the least of which is the tendency to see the mind as discrete boxes, instead of dynamic processes. It may be more appropriate to describe personality in terms of the forces which press on ego, as in Fig. 5.1b. Here, one can see that ego is at the centre of the mind, with the forces of drives (id), morality (superego) and reality all converging – and conflicting. It is ego's responsibility to maintain the integrity of personality. This task is not easy, but as ego interacts with the world, it continues to develop. To understand this, we need to look at Freud's model of personality development.

Psychosexual Stages of Development

While the notion that our lives pass through stages was not invented by Freud (for example, even Shakespeare referred to 'the stages of man'), Freud was the first to offer a detailed psychological model of human development based on stages. In one sense, stages are a counter intuitive concept, since we experience our lives, day-to-day, as a more or less continual progression. Birthdays, graduations and other landmark events occur, but their timing is largely social, and bears no necessary relationship to underlying psychological processes. So what led Freud to conclude that there are discrete stages?

To understand Freud's model of development, one must bear in mind the importance he placed on biological drives. Throughout life, our behaviour is motivated by the need to satisfy our basic drives; however, Freud believed that the expression of these drives changes during the course of our lives. The objects which are the focus of gratification change, and so does the *mode of gratification* – that is, the area of the body which is the centre for gratification. As you may recall, sexuality is not simply genital stimulation. It is also expressed through many parts of the body, called *erogenous zones*. Even as adults we can derive pleasure from our skin – a cool cloth applied to our neck on a hot day, a light touch on the arm to reassure us, and many other experiences. But at particular points during development, drive energy will be particularly focused on specific body regions (erogenous zones). It is the shifts in mode of gratification, associated with different erogenous zones, which defines the stages of development. Since these stages reflect differences in the expression of (sexual) drive energy, associated with changes in the functioning of the mind (psyche), they are called *psychosexual stages of development*. Altogether, Freud concluded that there are five stages, the first four of which occur in childhood. These stages also play a central role in the development of personality.

(a)

(b)

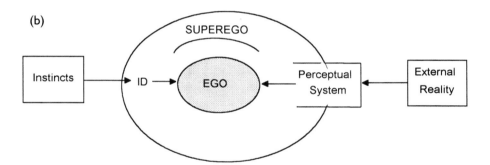

Fig. 5.1 Graphic representations of Freud's theory Many people have sought to present Freud's ideas in graphic form. The iceberg model (a) emphasizes that the id is unconscious, whereas the ego and superego are mostly conscious. Freud himself proposed a vector model (b) emphasizing the various forces which bear on the ego (b adapted from Fancher 1979).

Oral Stage

The first stage is the **oral stage**, when the focus of gratification is on the mouth. An infant is gratified by the pleasures of nursing; it cries to express its anger and frustration. In this context, nursing is not just a means of obtaining food, it is a primary source of pleasure, through oral stimulation. The newborn infant is governed by its drives – that is, only id is present at birth. It is a world dominated by immediate gratification and the magical powers of primary process thinking, where wish and fulfilment merge. Yet the child also has an interest in its surroundings, and its explorations are also linked to oral gratification; for

oral stage in Freud's theory of development, the first stage, extending from birth to about 15 months, when the focus of gratification is on the mouth example, if a six-month-old infant is given a new object, the first thing they are likely to do is try to put it in their mouth. As they develop teeth, biting becomes a way of expressing anger, but is also used to gain pleasure; my niece, for example, used to chew on the rails of her crib! From observations like these, Freud concluded that oral activity is so dominant because it provides the primary means of gratification – hence, the oral stage.

Anal Stage

anal stage in Freud's theory of psychosexual development, the second stage (15 months to 3 years); during this stage, the focus of drive energy shifts to the lower end of the digestive tract, and the major conflict is toilet training

At around fifteen months of age (the time boundaries of the stages are not precise), the focus of drive energy begins to shift. This shift of drive energy from the mouth and upper digestive tract to the lower end of the digestive tract characterizes the **anal stage**. Given the shift in mode of gratification, pleasure comes primarily from the process of elimination, and activities related to it (including handling of faeces). This stage also sees the emergence of ego, based on the child's experiences with their surroundings.

The beginnings of ego are seen in the development of body image – the recognition that one's body is distinctly different than the rest of the environment. For instance, if an angry toddler hits the wall with a hand, their hand will feel the impact, but they are not aware of how it affects the wall. By contrast, if they hit their own face with a hand, both the hand and the face register the impact. Through such experiences, the child begins to recognize the boundaries of self. A second type of experience involves delays in receiving gratification. Id is responsive only to the inner drives, and when gratification is sought, the child wants it *now*! However, even the most attentive parent cannot respond so fully that the child never has to wait; so, inevitably, the child learns that gratification is not immediate. At first, the child will use primary process imagery to try to cope; for example, conjuring up the image of the mother's breast while waiting for mother to answer its cries. This is ultimately inadequate, but the child does gradually come to realize that it can initiate actions which lead to gratification. Infant specialists sometimes speak of babies 'settling', around two months of age. Before this time, their crying often seems purposeless, as if the infant itself doesn't know why it is crying. After this period, they begin to be calmer, and their crying seems more connected to specific wants. This change may well reflect the realization that crying can be used productively, to call attention to specific needs (parents can often distinguish between a 'hungry' cry and a 'wet' cry, for example). Thus, delays in gratification ultimately lead to the realization that behaviour can be directed towards obtaining gratification.

By the time the child enters the anal stage, these experiences have initiated the beginnings of ego. As the infant becomes a toddler, they gradually exert greater control over both their own body and their surroundings – crawling, walking, grasping objects of interest, and so on. By the age of two, they have made dramatic advances, including the first beginnings of language. At this stage, they are likely to encounter another major challenge – toilet training. (Again, the timing is not exact; in the Victorian era when Freud made most of his observations, the tendency was probably to toilet train somewhat earlier than is the norm in our culture today.)

Toilet training poses the first major conflict between the demands of id and the external world. For the child, bowel movements are intensely pleasurable (remember the focus on the anus as an erogenous zone at this stage). As well, their own faeces are of significant interest – after all, they are produced by the child's body, so there is an intimate connection. Many a parent has witnessed a two-year-old who wishes to play with their faeces, or is dismayed at the prospect that their faeces will simply be flushed away. Parents, of course, take a very different view of the situation, seeing faeces as smelly, messy and germ-laden (of course, it will be much later before the child will understand about germs). To the extent that the parents impose demands about toilet training, the child for the first time is faced with a major conflict between the demands of id and the external world: the choice is between heeding the demands of id and heeding the demands of the parents. Heeding the id means risking the negative reactions of the parents, who are the most closely linked figures in the child's world; heeding the parents means denying the demands of id, which is the source of all motivation. The resolution of this conflict may be gradual and relatively untraumatic, or intense and stormy, depending on both the timing of the process and the parents' method of handling the situation. If the child tries to accommodate, and the parents are moderate, the child may gradually learn that self-control is valuable, and that there can be value to order and cleanliness. If the parents place too much value on this outcome, the child may become excessively concerned about cleanliness and discipline, laying the pattern for compulsive neatness and related behaviours in later life. On the other hand, if the child decides to heed the demands of id rather than parents, the conflict is likely to be more intense. If the parents use harsh punishment, the child will eventually comply, but at the cost of a weakened sense of self (it is the parents, not ego, controlling the situation), and possibly a life-long resentment towards authority figures (for which the parents are the prototype). On the other hand, if parents give in when the child resists, the child may never fully learn to balance the demands of id against the realities of the external world. Not only could this lead to a sloppy, self-indulgent adult, but it may seriously hamper the development of ego.

These scenarios point out one of the significant features of Freud's model of development: while the order and approximate timing of the stages is fixed, each individual will have different experiences, and will respond to them differently. To varying degrees, all childhood experiences affect the shape of personality in the adult; those most laden with emotion are likely to be the most influential, particularly if the conflicts involved are not adequately resolved. As the old saying has it, 'the child is the father to the man'. This aspect of development will be discussed further after we have considered the other stages.

Phallic Stage

phallic stage in Freud's theory, the third stage of development, extending from about three to five years of age, during which gratification is focused on the genitals, although not in the form of adult sexuality

As the ego grows stronger, through dealing with the conflict of toilet training and other experiences, the child begins to move into the third stage, which again is marked by a shift in the mode of gratification. In the **phallic stage**, from about three to five years of age, gratification is focused on the genitals. In Freud's day (and sometimes even today), the concept of childhood sexuality was seen as shocking, in part because it was interpreted in adult terms. Obviously, young children are still physically immature, and the expression of the drive is not the same as in an adult. However, they do seek gratification, and genital stimulation, for example, is experienced as pleasurable. Parents often find that children show an increased awareness of their body, including genitals, at this age, and a curiosity about other people's bodies. For example, four-year-olds may take off their clothes to 'play doctor' with each other. A boy may ask his mother if she has a penis, or may want to see her body. Boys, like adult males, will sometimes have erections while sleeping. A girl may suddenly become jealous when her father is affectionate to her mother. All of these behaviours indicated to Freud that the genitals have become a focus of gratification – hence the *phallic* stage (after the Greek word for penis).

As with the anal stage, the phallic stage is associated with a major conflict which challenges the developing ego. This conflict is called the **Oedipal conflict**, and is named after the Greek story of Oedipus, who unknowingly killed his father and married his mother. While the dynamics of the conflict are somewhat different for boys and for girls, Freud used the term Oedipal conflict to refer to both sexes; early on, some analysts proposed calling the female variant the 'Electra conflict' (after Oedipus' sister), but Freud himself did not use the term (see Freud 1924). The central focus of the Oedipal conflict is the attachment to the parents, who as care-givers have become the focus of drive energy (and therefore attraction). Depending on family circumstances, the mother is typically the primary care-giver, and hence becomes a strong source of gratification for both boys and girls. However, as the child grows, the awareness of sexual differences increases, and with it, an increased sense of sexual identity. It is this difference which begins to alter the dynamics for boys and girls.

For the boy, his mother, who is already the primary source of gratification, becomes more intensely desired, in what is the prototype for all future love relationships. The father is a source of gratification, but now also becomes the focus of jealousy and rivalry; hence the boy's feelings towards his father are ambivalent. In primary process terms, the id wishes to unite with the mother, and eliminate the father as a rival. At the same time, ego is aware that the father is larger and more powerful, and may retaliate against the boy's feelings. This becomes expressed as a fear that the father may take away the boy's source of gratification, through cutting off the genitals – called castration fear. (Of course, it is irrelevant to say such fears are not rational – it is precisely the point that these feelings are at an instinctive level.) Thus, there is an intense conflict created, which ego is poorly equipped to resolve. To deny the attraction to the mother is to prevent the experiencing of feelings that will later be crucial to forming love relationships. To attempt to act on the jealousy towards the father is to risk an emotional and possibly physical split.

The resolution of this conflict comes through adopting two *defence mechanisms*, techniques used by the ego to cope with anxiety. The first is **identification**, which involves incorporating an object of conflict as part of one's own ego. This process is expressed in the old phrase, 'if you can't lick 'em, join 'em'. By adopting the values and behaviour patterns of the father, the boy seeks to reduce the threat associated with castration fear; in effect, 'if I'm like Dad, he won't want to hurt me'. The mother, too, is identified with, as the model for future attractions. As the old song says, 'I want a girl just like the girl that married dear old Dad!' Identification is important in reducing the conflict the boy experiences, but also in triggering the development of superego; the earliest values of the superego are those derived from one's parents (later, other social values can

Oedipal conflict in Freud's theory of development, the major conflict associated with the phallic stage which challenges the developing ego; named after the Greek story of Oedipus, who unknowingly killed his father and married his mother

identification a defence mechanism which involves incorporating characteristics of a drive object into one's own ego

repression in Freud's theory, a defence mechanism in which impulses, memories or ideas are forcibly blocked from the conscious mind

also be incorporated). The second mechanism used by the ego in dealing with the Oedipal conflict is **repression** – forcing the conflict into the unconscious, so that the conscious mind is unaware of the fears and attractions. When adults would scorn his notions about the Oedipal conflict, saying they never experienced such things as a child, Freud would note that this was simply evidence of repression.

In support of his conception of the Oedipal conflict, Freud used both evidence from clinical cases and also observations of normal behaviour. One observation he made in this regard continues to tantalize researchers – the phenomenon of *childhood amnesia*. Typically, individuals recall very little of their life before about age five, other than a few fragmentary memories and stories that were likely heard from parents at a later age. Freud argued that childhood amnesia was due to the repression associated with coping with the Oedipal conflict. While other theories have been offered, ranging from changes in the myelination of brain neurons to changes in cognitive structure, no mechanism has been universally accepted; what *is* accepted is that Freud was correct in describing the basic phenomenon. *Sibling rivalry*, the conflicts frequently seen among children in a family, was also seen by Freud as representing a redirection of the Oedipal conflict to a different object.

For girls, the Oedipal conflict involves the same sense of attraction and rivalry, though the objects are reversed – now the mother is the rival, and the father is the object of attraction. Despite the basic similarity, the dynamics are rather different, for several reasons. First of all, the mother promotes greater ambivalence, since the mother is typically the first object to which drive energy is attached by the growing infant. Also, while the girl fears discovery of her jealous impulses towards her mother, the increased awareness of body features leads her to recognize that both she and her mother lack a penis. While a boy may fear the possibility of losing his penis (castration fear), the girl feels a sense of devastation at having *already* lost hers, leading to feelings of guilt and loss described as *penis envy*. The girl realizes that her mother, too, has been castrated, and this enhances the sense of identification with her mother. Faced with this attraction towards her father and ambivalence towards her mother, the girl's ego, like the boy's, seeks some way of resolving the conflict. As with the boy, this involves *identification* (the father as prototype for future lovers, the mother as role model) and *repression* (blocking conscious access to the underlying impulses).

While the use of identification and repression occurs in both sexes, the dynamics are somewhat different. These differences, related to the mother's position as primary love object as well as rival, and penis envy versus castration fear, make the Oedipal conflict more difficult for girls, and can result in greater submissiveness and lower self-esteem in adulthood.

Freud's description of penis envy, and of the female Oedipal conflict more generally, has been heavily attacked in recent years for its negative view of women. This view was apparently based on Freud's observations of both his patients (who were primarily female) and his society (which generally kept women in a submissive role). However, modern evaluations have questioned his emphasis on biological, as opposed to social, causes of such patterns, an issue which will warrant further discussion later on.

In both sexes, the Oedipal conflict is crucial both in the development of the superego and in establishing the basis for sexual identity and formation of love relationships. Prior to this stage, the child has awareness of moral principles, but they are regarded as part of the environment (Brenner 1955). For example, if a child wants a cookie, they may look to see if the mother is nearby. If she is, the child will refrain from taking the cookie; if she is not present, the child will proceed. That is, morality is evaluated in terms of getting caught, not right or wrong. As values become *internalized* through identification, they form the basis of superego. Without identification, superego development will be weak or absent; Freud saw this as the origin of psychopathic behaviour (anti-social behaviour unaccompanied by a sense of wrong-doing). Identification is also necessary for developing a clear sense of sexual identity, and for the creation of a prototype love object as the basis for later relationships. Problems of identification can lead to an inability to form love relationships, or repeated difficulties with authority figures, who are seen as surrogate parents. If the conflict is not adequately resolved (that is, too much emphasis is placed on repression rather than identification), the consequences can be severe in later life: excessive guilt and anxiety (as seen in many of Freud's patients).

The Oedipal conflict is the greatest crisis in the development of personality. Failing to resolve it can result in a distorted ego which sees all relationships in terms of the unresolved conflicts of the phallic stage. Freud saw the problems of many of his patients (sexual conflicts, guilt and anxiety) as stemming from this source. As a result, he came to the conclusion that most people fail to resolve the Oedipal conflict in a psychologically (as opposed to socially) satisfactory manner (Freud 1924). As we will see, the issue resurfaces in the genital stage.

Latency Stage

latency stage in Freud's developmental theory, the stage which begins at about age five and extends until puberty, during which the drives appear to be relatively inactive

Whether the Oedipal conflict is successfully resolved or not, the imperatives of development push the child from the phallic stage to the stage of latency at around age five. In the **latency stage**, which extends until puberty, the drives appear to be relatively inactive – hence the concept of them being 'latent' or hidden. In part, the change is due to the use of repression in resolving the Oedipal conflict. Because this results in blocking conscious access to the id, gratification hereafter is related to secondary process thinking, and hence is never as direct or as immediate as the gratifications of early childhood. In latency, the repressed impulses are redirected into new activities, with new objects of gratification. Thus, sports, hobbies, school and friendships all provide opportunities for satisfaction of the drives. Problems during latency, such as excessive aggression, can be related to inadequate repression and/or the ego being unable to redirect drive energy into socially approved outlets.

Genital Stage

genital stage in Freud's theory, the final stage of psychosexual development (from puberty onward), when drive energy is focused on the genitals, with adult expression of sexuality

At the onset of puberty, there is a resurfacing of drive energy, triggered in part by the physiological changes involved in sexual maturation. At this point, the individual enters the adult phase of development, called the genital phase. In the **genital stage**, drive energy is focused on the genitals, with adult expression of sexuality. The term genital is somewhat misleading, however, for the expression of drive energy is very different from the primary expression of id seen in the phallic stage. Ego's use of *secondary process thinking* has become well developed, allowing possibilities for *symbolic* gratification in a variety of ways. Symbolic expression is also encouraged by social influences, which direct the person towards new types of behaviours, including forming a love relationship, having children and assuming responsibilities in other socially approved ways.

Curiously, given that the genital stage represents the major portion of life, Freud gave comparatively little attention to it. Primarily, he saw it as a period of trying to come to terms with the unresolved residues of childhood. The primary task for this stage was to separate oneself from one's parents. 'Only after this detachment is accomplished can he [the individual] cease to be a child, and so become a member of the social community' (Freud 1924: 346). Freud saw many instances of problems at this stage, including the hysterias and neuroses of his patients, but said relatively little about what successful development might lead to. This has been one aspect of psychodynamic theory that other theorists, such as Erik Erikson, have attempted to address, as we shall see.

For further consideration

In part, Freud defined his stages of development (especially the early stages) based on his behavioural observations. If you can, you might observe young children to see if their behaviour fits his descriptions. Could Freud be right about *what* children do, without being correct about *why* they do it?

Fixation and Regression During Development

The failure to resolve the challenges of development result in **fixation**, the incomplete release of drive energy associated with a particular stage. This can occur if, during a particular stage, the child receives either too little or too much gratification. Under-gratification denies the individual the opportunity for drive satisfaction, leading to a desire for what was missed. For example, a newborn who is denied opportunities to suckle the breast will later be orally fixated (Freud saw weaning as the origin of the story of being cast out of Eden, with its plentiful food). On the other hand, a child who is over-indulged will not face the challenges associated with each stage, making them reluctant to move ahead in their development. For example, a two-year-old who is still nursing, or a child who is given a bottle or pacifier at any indication of upset, will later be orally fixated. Fixation in turn is associated with **regression**, the tendency to revert to an earlier mode of gratification, usually under stress. Since repression has cut off direct access to the id in the adult, regression is seen in symbolic forms of gratification. For example, a person who is orally fixated may binge on ice cream, or smoke, or chew their nails, or get drunk, etc. (the list of possibilities is obviously quite long). Fixation can also be expressed through *denial* of gratification, as when someone becomes a fanatical anti-smoker, or a teetotaller.

fixation the incomplete release of drive energy associated with a particular stage
regression in Freud's theory, a defence mechanism in which the individual reverts to an earlier mode of gratification

Each stage manifests its own forms of fixation, representative of the focus of drive energy at that stage. Freud argued that many aspects of adult behaviour are based on early fixations. For instance, at the anal stage, either overly rigid *or* overly permissive toilet training can result in fixation. In later life, this will be seen in excessive sloppiness of either dress or living areas, a preference for activities that involve messes (e.g. cooking or painting), or a preoccupation with money (seen by Freud as a symbol for faeces). Anal denial may be seen in compulsive neatness of clothes and surroundings, a preference for activities that involve order (such as cataloguing books), stinginess, or an aversion to financial matters. Phallic fixations are associated with failures to resolve the Oedipal conflict, which later results in not detaching from the parents. A man who continually fights with his boss, traffic officers and other authority figures, is showing a phallic fixation – he is trying to dominate the father figure. The man who is overly submissive is still complying with the father he dared not challenge. Problems of sexual identity may lead to homosexuality. For a woman, phallic fixation may be expressed as seductiveness and a preference for older men (seeking to replace the mother), or as a desire to dominate men (symbolically castrating the father who rejected her). In latency, where direct expression of the drives is repressed, fixation results in behaviours which do not seem to involve drives – acts of altruism, for example.

One interesting aspect of the role of fixation is the way that Freud related it to career choices. Like many subsequent theorists, Freud believed that career decisions reflect personality at least as much as ability. Oral fixation, for example, would lead to careers that involve oral behaviour – wine tasters, writers, salespersons, even university professors, are engaged in a symbolic form of oral behaviour. Fixation at the anal stage, with its emphasis on cleanliness and bowel movements, leads to careers that involve messiness, order and/or money. Thus, bankers, accountants (keeping money organized!), painters, sanitation workers, all are reflective of an anal fixation. Laboratory research in chemistry or biology, with its requirements for precision combined with messy procedures, seems to offer both indulgence and denial! The phallic stage tends to lead to careers in which body image, sexuality and/or authority figures are involved. Thus, professional models (and the photographers who work with them) have made a choice based on phallic fixation, as have career soldiers, police officers and even prostitutes. In latency, the influence of repression means that drives must be expressed indirectly. Consequently, careers which seem unrelated to drive satisfaction, such as clergyman, charity organizer or social worker, are likely choices for a person who is fixated at the latency stage.

One aspect of these descriptions that often bothers people is the non-obvious nature of many of the connections. This is inevitable, according to Freud, since the conscious mind of the adult is cut off (by repression) from direct access to the underlying drives. Consequently, the drives are always expressed in *symbolic* form, whether in the manifest content of dreams or the choice of a career. In fact, from a Freudian viewpoint, adult actions and interests, being based on secondary process thinking, can *only* be regarded as symbolic. What differs is the degree to which the behaviour is adaptive or pathological. The man who collects swords (phallic symbols) may have an unresolved Oedipal conflict, but his method of dealing with it is more functional than the person who develops a psychogenic form of impotence.

There are other points that should be made concerning fixation and regression. First, in suggesting that these patterns exist, Freud was not making a value judgement. For example, he did *not* say that because a career reflects a particular form of fixation, it is therefore undesirable. His basic point was that behaviour is never random, and consequently behaviours like career choices simply reflect the developmental history of the individual (and, in instances of pathology, may give clues to the nature of the underlying conflict). Second, he saw such relationships as evidence that all behaviour is ultimately related to the basic drives – even those actions which seem remote from any connection with such motivating forces. Since expression in adults is symbolic, the fact that we have no *conscious awareness* of what motivates the behaviour in no way invalidates the connection. In fact, it is *necessary* that such connections be unconscious, in order to protect the ego from the threatening implications of recognizing what motivates us. To understand this, let us look at the concept of anxiety, and the methods the mind uses to cope with it.

Anxiety and Defence Mechanisms

As discussed earlier, adult personality is comprised of id, ego and superego. Ego, as the central element, must contend with the divergent demands of id, superego and the external world. Meeting these demands is not simple at the best of times, and many circumstances, including unresolved conflicts from earlier stages and external threats, can make ego's task even more formidable. In such circumstances, the ego may experience anxiety. **Anxiety** arises when the ego is faced with an influx of stimuli with which it cannot cope. This may be the result of an external danger, such as a civilian living in wartime conditions, or it may be due to an internal threat, related to the demands of id or superego. Since ego is unable to acknowledge the drives within the id, the breakthrough of unsatisfied id impulses into conscious awareness can trigger anxiety. Similarly, the moral demands of superego can be excessive, producing guilt and anxiety at the least suggestion of id gratification. Thus the various forms of demands can threaten the integrity of the ego, which must protect itself.

Freud considered anxiety at several points in his writings, trying to find a way to understand this phenomenon. In *The Problem of Anxiety* (1926), he presented his mature views on the issue. Freud believed that anxiety was biologically based, and was intended as an adaptive mechanism – anxiety serving to warn the ego of a potentially overwhelming situation. However, ego has limited options: it cannot completely deny id's desire for gratification, nor can it allow superego to make all decisions, without regard to either id or external reality (for example, it may be wrong to hurt others, but what if one's life is in danger?). Thus, ego must somehow cope with both the conflicting demands, and the anxiety produced by awareness of them. Some forms of coping involve a reversion to primary process thinking, such as dreams and the physical symptoms of hysteria. However, such methods were seen as signs of a weak ego, in that they involve ignoring external reality.

More commonly, ego will invoke various defence mechanisms, a term actually coined by Freud's daughter, Anna (herself a distinguished psychoanalyst) (A. Freud 1936). **Defence mechanisms** are techniques used by the ego to protect itself from anxiety and the threats which give rise to it. There are a number of such techniques, and frequently the ego will use a combination of them, rather than a single mechanism. There are several basic points to note about the defence mechanisms. First, the defence mechanisms operate unconsciously; otherwise, they would fail to protect the ego from awareness of the conflicts which produce anxiety. Second, most defence mechanisms (with the significant exception

anxiety a negative emotional state associated with threat to the self; in Freud's theory, it arises when the ego is faced with an influx of stimuli with which it cannot cope, as a result of either external danger or the demands of id or superego

defence mechanism in Freud's theory, a technique used by the ego to protect itself from anxiety and the threats which give rise to it; many psychologists use the terms as descriptions of behaviour patterns, without endorsing the Freudian interpretation of their origin of repression) operate by allowing gratification in some indirect way, typically involving either symbolic gratification or a substitute object. Third, to the extent that defence mechanisms succeed in protecting the ego, they do so by distorting reality (since gratification is redirected). Before considering the implications of these factors, let us consider some of the specific defence mechanisms, several of which have already been mentioned in passing.

Repression. This is the blocking of id impulses at the unconscious level, and is the most primitive of all defence mechanisms. While universal (in the transition from phallic to latency stages), it is extremely limited, in that it fails to resolve the demands which led to its use (no gratification occurs). Even worse, it can absorb significant amounts of mental energy to maintain the blockage against the increasing pressures for gratification. One can use an analogy to a boiling pot of water: As steam is generated, it starts to lift the lid off the pot. Putting a weight on the lid will help, but eventually the pressure will increase, until either a larger weight is needed, or the lid blows off. Similarly, maintaining repression, in the absence of any other response, will require more and more of the mental energy that should properly go into other life activities. Since the ego is unaware of the underlying pressures, it experiences only the fatigue. Thus, depression is seen by Freudians as a result of excessive repression. A distortion of reality can also occur, as when memories are blocked which could trigger the leakage of underlying conflicts into conscious awareness.

Displacement. One of the most common defence mechanisms, displacement is the redirection of drive energy towards a substitute object. Whenever the direct expression of drives would be too threatening – either because of the disapproval of superego or a realistic threat associated with the original object – we tend to seek a substitute object. For example, yelling at the boss when you are asked to work overtime could result in being fired; instead, you complete the work, then cut someone up while driving home! Or, a teenage boy is attracted to Mary, but when she rejects him, he asks out Sally (in whom he initially had no interest). In a classic cartoon, a man receives a speeding ticket while driving. Rather than yell at the officer, he goes home and yells at his wife; she in turn yells at their son; the boy then kicks the family dog, who goes out and bites a police officer! In each case, there is displacement of drive energy onto a substitute object. The problem with displacement, of course, is that the substitutes are unrelated to the original object. Thus, while displacement allows release of drive energy, it clearly involves a distortion of reality in the process of doing so.

displacement in psychoanalysis, a defence mechanism which involves the redirection of drive energy from one object to a substitute object

Identification. As seen in the discussion of the Oedipal conflict, identification involves incorporating characteristics of a drive object into one's ego. Typically, this occurs with individuals who are either admired or feared. For instance, hostages will frequently come to adopt some of the values of their captors. More benignly, a young child may try to act like a superhero seen on television. When we are unable to express sexual or aggressive impulses directly, we can adopt the guise of a figure in whom such impulses are acceptable. In movies, books or plays, identification with a character can provide a form of release called *catharsis*, the vicarious release of drive energy. While identification is necessary to resolve the Oedipal conflict, and may be a source of learning social values, it still poses the risk of distorting reality, since the values incorporated are not freely generated by the ego. In extreme form, such as in delusional disorders, the identification may destroy the ego's own identity, for example when someone believes they are Christ.

Regression. Regression, reverting to behaviour characteristic of an earlier stage under conditions of stress, is closely associated with fixation, as noted earlier. Like repression, regression is a fairly primitive defence mechanism. A four-year-old child who has been toilet trained, for example, may begin wetting the bed after the birth of a sibling: faced with the stress of a rival for parental attention, the child regresses to an earlier stage. Working to meet a deadline, a smoker may begin smoking more heavily, a form of oral regression. (It is interesting to note that Freud himself was a heavy smoker of cigars. When once asked about the symbolic meaning of this, he apparently replied to the effect, 'Sometimes a cigar is a phallic symbol, and sometimes it is only a cigar. This is only a cigar!') Another person, faced with the same situation but being anally rather than orally fixated, may spend time rearranging everything on their desk as a means of getting some gratification. These behaviours allow for some gratification, but since the behaviours are to some extent inappropriate, they represent a distortion of reality. Freud argued that the seriousness of regression depends on both the stage of regression and the primitiveness of the response. For example, disaster victims will sometimes curl up in a ball, like an infant in the foetal position – a severe form of regression. Ultimately, regression is of limited value; since there is an inevitable shift of erogenous zones as one goes through stages, it is impossible to re-experience the satisfaction of an earlier stage in the original way.

Rationalization. Perhaps one of the most interesting defences, rationalization involves offering an *acceptable* reason for behaviour in place of the true reason (acceptable to the ego, though the reactions of other people may be a concern as well). When we rationalize, we try to justify our actions. For instance, a person engaging in flirtatious behaviour may say, 'I was only being friendly'. Rationalization may be combined with other defences as well, providing a justification for the behaviour. For example, a person who wastes time organizing their desk may say, 'Oh, but I work better when everything is neat'. This may, in fact, be generally true, but the real reason for doing it *when facing the stress of a deadline* is in order to get some gratification through regression to the anal stage! 'White lies' offer an analogy to this form of defence. When a white lie is generated, both the liar and the person lied to may recognize that it is untrue, but may find it socially convenient to let the lie stand. Since rationalization prevents the person from recognizing the true motives for their actions, it represents a form of distortion of reality. It also suggests one should be wary of the 'rational' analyses people make of their own behaviour: while the ego is capable of rational thought, the potential for rationalization means that logic can serve reasons other than objectivity, and yet the ego will not recognize when that happens.

Sublimation. This is one of the few defences which Freud saw as potentially positive. Sublimation occurs when drive energy is redirected towards a socially desirable creative activity. While similar to displacement in mechanism, it differs in terms of the restriction on outcomes. An artist, for example, may rechannel sexual energy into creating a beautiful statue of the desired person. A musician may create a patriotic anthem in a time of war, rechannelling aggressive energy. While sublimation is useful, because it results in a socially valued product, it is

rationalization a defence mechanism in which one explains behaviour by offering a reason acceptable to the ego in place of the true reason

sublimation in Freud's theory, a defence mechanism in which drive energy is redirected towards a socially desirable creative activity also limited; since gratification is very indirect, it cannot fully satisfy the demands of id. In addition, since it requires particular skills to be a painter, musician or other creator, it is not a universally available mechanism. Still, it is unique, in that Freud believed that the creative activity which sublimation supports makes it more than simply a response to neurotic anxiety.

There are a number of other defence mechanisms, but by this time the basic point should be clear: defence mechanisms exist to protect the ego from anxiety, but they do so at the cost of distorting reality. To the extent that defences work, they pose the risk of isolating the person from reality; in extreme form, Freud saw this as the basis of the major mental disorders which he called *psychoses*. By contrast, to the extent that ego is aware of using a particular defence, distortion of reality is reduced, but anxiety will increase. Freud defined *neuroses* as disorders in which excessive anxiety is a primary symptom; in these circumstances, defence mechanisms are not adequately protecting the ego. When I was in graduate school, the joke was, 'a neurotic worries about going crazy (distorting reality), but never will; a psychotic *is* crazy (distorts reality), but doesn't worry about it!' While obviously glib, it does capture the essence of the Freudian distinction between neuroses and psychoses.

In his later years, Freud was very interested in how the demands of society affect the growth of ego. In *Civilization and its Discontents*, he gave extensive attention to this issue (Freud 1930). One basic point was that living in society has its psychological price – coping with the arbitrary demands of society, as represented by the superego. Without a superego, one would face fewer conflicts, since there would only be id and external reality to satisfy. (Note that asking 'what is possible?' is not the same as asking 'what is right?') Interestingly, psychopathic individuals, who are regarded by Freudians as having little superego development, show no guilt (moral anxiety) for their anti-social behaviour. For the rest of us, being 'civilized' requires dealing with the demands of superego. This means that the opportunities for id gratification become largely symbolic and indirect. Freud once commented to the effect that 'civilization began the first time an angry person cast a word instead of a rock'. In addition to the demands of id, one must cope with the demands of superego itself, which may also conflict with reality. As a result, Freud believed that anxiety levels were increased by living in a civilized society.

At the same time, Freud was pessimistic about the possibilities of ego protecting itself from these threats to its integrity. He saw only two possible solutions that might satisfy society while permitting a healthy development of ego. One was sublimation, which, as we have discussed, is unlikely to be an adequate solution. The other (which is seldom mentioned in discussions of his theory) was love (Fancher 1979). *Love* is a defence mechanism, but it allows the drives to be gratified in the context of concern for another being, while meeting both moral and reality demands. Yet, while he believed love had the potential to benefit the ego, Freud also saw it as fraught with peril, since the *loss* of a loved one could leave the ego vulnerable to catastrophic pain.

Society, Freud concluded, creates a paradox for the individual: sublimation and love are only *possible* within the group structures which society provides, but it is also society that creates the constraints on id which make sublimation and love *necessary*! Unfortunately, in looking at the world as the Second World

War was approaching, Freud felt that society was placing greater restrictions on love, while at the same time directing aggressive energy into ever more dangerous forms. As quoted earlier, the conclusion to *Civilization and its Discontents* strikes an uncertain and pessimistic tone. To what extent this view was influenced by adverse circumstances (both personal and social), and to what extent it remains an accurate description of the ego's plight, is difficult to say.

For further consideration

The behaviours associated with defence mechanisms seem relatively common – Woody Allen has often used them to comic effect in his films. What examples can you find in your everyday experience? Do you ever rationalize? Does finding the behavioural patterns mean that the causes are related to unconscious conflicts?

Evidence of the Unconscious in Behaviour

One of the basic elements of Freud's theory is that id will always seek gratification, but that in adults its expression is usually symbolic and indirect. This leads to the question of how one can provide supporting evidence. Since the id is by definition unconscious, one cannot simply analyse one's own actions to assess the validity of this conception. So how did Freud support his view? The key lies in one of his other basic assumptions, *psychic determinism*, which states that there is always a cause for behaviour, which can be found within the mind. This assumption meant that potentially *any* form of behaviour could provide evidence of the workings of the unconscious, especially the id. While we have already noted many examples of supporting evidence, it is worth reviewing some of the most significant forms.

Freudian slips. Perhaps the best known type of Freudian evidence are the everyday errors and slips of the tongue which he called *parapraxes*, but which have generally become known as *Freudian slips*. Since all behaviour has a cause, errors and slips are never accidental. While Freud conceded that fatigue and distraction could sometimes lead to errors and slips, he argued that the majority of cases reflected the workings of the unconscious. In arguing for this point of view, he made extensive use of examples from both his clinical cases and from everyday observation. In *Psychopathology in Everyday Life*, he offered detailed analyses of many such cases, for example the newspaper misprint 'His Highness, the Clown Prince' (Freud 1904). In one case, a paper printed an apology for having said 'a battle-scared veteran', but the apology appeared as 'a bottle-scarred veteran'! In such a case, Freud would argue the errors reflected a latent hostility on the part of the writer. In general, Freudian slips can best be understood when they fit into a broader pattern of behaviour, which can help in interpreting the underlying dynamics.

Free association. Asking patients to say whatever came to mind was used as a therapeutic technique very early, when he began to abandon hypnosis as a tool. Since even 'random' thoughts have a pattern, listening to what his patients said (as well as what they *didn't* say in some cases) could provide a means of accessing the unconscious mind. While free association quickly demonstrates the organized nature of cognitive structure, its use as a tool in analysis is slow

(a)

(b)

Fig. 5.2 Ambiguous stimuli and projective tests Projective tests use the individual's interpretation of ambiguous stimuli to access the unconscious mind. Two popular tests are the Rorschach, which uses inkblot stimuli (a), and the Thematic Apperception Test, which asks individuals to tell a story about the people in a picture (b).

projective test a type of personality test used by psychodynamic theorists in which an individual is asked to interpret an ambiguous stimulus; since the stimulus itself is ambiguous, the assumption is that whatever the person says reveals the workings of their own unconscious mind

and painstaking, requiring considerable attentiveness by the therapist. A technique which Freud himself never used, but has subsequently become associated with psychoanalytic and psychodynamic approaches, is the use of projective tests. A **projective test** presents the person with an ambiguous stimulus, which they are then asked to interpret. Since the stimulus itself is ambiguous, the assumption is that whatever the person says reveals the workings of their own unconscious mind (examples of projective test materials are given in Fig. 5.2).

Dreams. As previously discussed, dreams operate on two levels, the *manifest content* and the *latent content*. The manifest content is symbolic, having been created out of the original forms by the *dream censor*. Thus, a dream must be analysed closely to determine what the latent content actually is. While Freud believed that certain symbols were fairly universal (e.g. guns and knives as phallic symbols, money as faeces, tunnels and flowers as vaginal symbols), he also recognized that sometimes symbols have a meaning which is particular to the individual, a point sometimes overlooked in popular accounts and 'dream guides'. As with other techniques, proper analysis requires placing the dream within a larger pattern of the person's behaviour.

Cross-cultural studies. In keeping with his belief that all behaviour is significant, Freud had a deep curiosity about similarities and differences across cultures. At the time of his death, he had amassed a considerable collection of primitive art (mostly carvings), which he valued both aesthetically and scientifically. One of his major attempts at cultural interpretation was *Totem and Taboo*, in which he noted the prevalence of incest taboos across many cultures, and explained such taboos in terms of the Oedipal conflict (Freud 1913).

Self-analysis. In keeping with his willingness to find evidence in any behaviour, Freud also used examples from his own self-analysis, which began after the death of his father in 1896. This event was terribly emotional for him; he later described the death of one's father as 'the most important event, the most poignant loss, in a man's life' (Fancher 1979: 227). Faced with this loss, he had anxiety, depression and trouble concentrating on work; as a result, he embarked on an analysis of his own behaviour at a point when he was still grappling for a framework for understanding the dynamics of behaviour. As a form of theoretical validation, self-analysis represents a potentially treacherous endeavour: one can never be certain that what is discovered is genuine, rather than a distortion based on defence mechanisms (actually, at the time he began his self-analysis, Freud had not yet developed the concept of defence mechanisms). In addition, self-analysis raises the danger of increasing anxiety, since it may impair the effectiveness of defence mechanisms before the underlying conflicts have been recognized and dealt with. Freud apparently found this was true, since he told friends and pupils that during this period he was sometimes afraid to cross the street, for fear of discovering some unexpected meaning in the act! Still, Freud had long been interested in his own dreams and frequently used examples of his own dreams, as well as his other behaviours, in his writings.

Art. As discussed previously, Freud came to believe that art was the product of sublimation, and therefore was based on a healthy coping mechanism for the ego. At the same time, art is symbolic and can be probed for unconscious meanings. While Freud was interested in art, particularly from other cultures, he rarely used analyses of art in his writings. Instead, this has become a popular extension of his work. One of the most interesting aspects of this notion is the ease with which analysis can be applied to pre-Freudian artistic creations. For example, the art of Hieronymus Bosch, a fifteenth-century Dutch painter, has frequently been cited for its Freudian imagery. Similarly, Herman Melville's *Moby Dick*, written about fifty years before Freud began developing his theory, has been extensively analysed; typically, the white whale is seen as a phallic symbol, representing Melville's latent homosexuality. It is more difficult to evaluate art created since Freud's time, since any symbolism could reflect either conscious or unconscious awareness of Freud's work. While psychoanalytic interpretations have become popular in relation to art, it poses problems similar to dream analysis – there is a danger that when too little context is available, the analysis may become a projective test, telling more about the analyst than the artist. (For examples of visual symbols which have significance in Freudian theory, see Fig. 5.4.)

For further
consideration

You may want to look for your own examples of Freudian symbols in everyday life. Alternatively, go back to your dream notes (if you tried recording your dreams). Whether you consider everyday symbols or dreams, how can one be sure the interpretations are correct?

Assessing Freud's Work

Attempting to evaluate Freud's work is a challenging endeavour, given both the range of his efforts and the impact which his work has had. As we will see in the next section, one way to evaluate his work is by examining what others have done subsequently. For the moment, though, let us deal with Freud in his own right.

Freud was a remarkable person: gifted intellectually, a keen observer, a fluid writer and, by some accounts, a very humane person (Zangwill 1987). While many of his basic assumptions were influenced by the work of others (e.g. Brücke, Darwin, Pinel), he was a tremendous synthesizer, and typically explored the implications of ideas more effectively than many of his predecessors (Robinson 1979). These are all admirable traits, but still they do not really tell us much about the validity of his work.

One of the most basic criteria for a scientific theory is **falsifiability** – that is, one should be able to conceive of circumstances where a theory could be proven wrong. Typically, one of the most common criticisms of Freud's theory is that it is not falsifiable. There are several reasons for this criticism. First, Freud's assumptions dictate that many terms refer to variables that must be inferred rather than observed directly, which makes them harder to validate. Second, the large number of interrelated concepts, and the lack of precision associated with many of them, makes it very difficult to set up critical tests. In many cases, the evidence used to *support* the theory is also *dependent* on the theory for its validity (e.g. demonstrating the symbolic meaning of dreams is dependent on accepting the concept of latent content). In addition, the theory is primarily descriptive rather than predictive, which makes it more difficult to test its valid-

falsifiability a criterion for evaluating a theory, which states the theory should specify circumstances wherein it could be proven wrong

ity (see Chapter 1). For example, the theory does not predict which defence mechanisms a person will use in a particular situation, nor does it specify which experiences will be repressed. In some cases, there is also a problem of determining what exactly is the appropriate theory to test, since Freud frequently revised his ideas without repudiating earlier work (see Brenner 1957).

All of these considerations make it difficult to test Freud's ideas directly. At the same time, his work has generated considerable attention, and there have been many attempts to test specific aspects of his work. It is impossible to review all such studies here, but a few examples will help to clarify what is involved in such tests. One of the most systematic attempts to explore Freud's ideas experimentally was the work of John Dollard and Neal Miller (1950). Dollard, an anthropologist who became interested in psychotherapy, and Miller, an experimental psychologist (see autonomic conditioning in Chapter 3), attempted to 'translate' Freudian concepts into behaviourally based terms. Given that Freud's theory is expressed in terms of mental events, this is not an easy task. Some of their formulations were both creative and insightful; for example, they suggested that aggression could be described in terms of the circumstances that trigger it (see Chapter 7). In other cases, they found it difficult to provide behavioural definitions, for example distinguishing fear from anxiety (the fact that Freud offered different interpretations at different times perhaps contributed to this confusion). They *did* suggest, however, that the problems of anxiety seen in clinical practice involve more than the simple fear conditioning proposed by Watson and other behaviourists. Their work caused a considerable stir at the time it was published, but has declined in influence subsequently. Whatever its limitations, one important element of their work was that they treated Freud seriously, rather than dismissing his work as most behaviourists have done.

More recent studies have focused on the testing of specific Freudian concepts, most notably repression, but also Freudian slips. One example of an experimental approach to evaluating repression is a study by D'Zurilla (1965). Using male college students, D'Zurilla first manipulated anxiety by falsely telling subjects in the experimental group that they had just scored nine out of ten on a test for latent homosexuality. Then, the participants were asked to recall words from the 'test'. Consistent with repression, the experimental subjects recalled less than the control group, who had not been given any information about the nature of the test. After the memory test, the experimental subjects were told (correctly) that the 'homosexuality test' was simply an experimental ploy; following receipt of this information, these subjects were able to improve their recall of the test items. This outcome may be explained by the lifting of repression; but, unfortunately, it can also be explained in other ways, such as state-dependent forgetting. More recently, Gary Schwartz and his colleagues have done a series of studies on repression, based on first classifying individuals as likely to use repression or not. When exposed to sexual or aggressive written material, those classed as repressors claimed not to feel anxious, but showed higher physiological arousal than non-repressors (Weinberger *et al.* 1979). In a related study, repressors spontaneously recalled fewer emotional experiences from childhood than non-repressors (Davis and Schwartz 1987). These results seem consistent with Freud's theory, and thereby provide some experimental support, but do not provide direct proof for Freud's interpretation of repression.

Experimental studies of Freudian slips have typically involved verbal slips, in part because they are easier to produce in the lab, and in part because there are alternative theories to Freud's. The study of verbal slips from a cognitive (linguistic) standpoint was initiated by Victoria Fromkin of UCLA (Fromkin 1973). Based on several thousand naturally occurring verbal slips collected by Fromkin and her colleagues, she noted that slips are not random with regard to the linguistic units of words. For example, phonemes may be transposed *within* a phrase (as in 'queer old dean' for 'dear old Queen'), but not *across* phrases (e.g. 'the red ten on the pable' is not a likely result from 'the red pen on the table'). This approach has been extended to the laboratory by Michael Motley and his colleagues (Motley 1985). In one study, subjects were asked to read aloud word pairs that were presented on a screen. In order to manipulate anxiety, the subjects in one group were told to expect a painful electric shock at some point during the experiment (aggression drive condition). In another condition, the experimenter was 'an attractive and provocatively dressed woman' (sexual drive condition). A control group was treated normally. Consistent with the Freudian view, each group made errors related to the type of drive stimulated; for example, 'varied colts' was read as 'carried volts' in the aggression condition, and

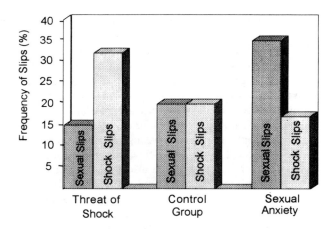

Shock Slips—transposition errors related to electricity
(e.g. 'cursed wattage' for 'worst cottage')

Sexual Slips—transposition errors related to sexual attraction
(e.g. 'bare shoulders' for 'share boulders')

Fig. 5.3 Studying verbal slips A study by Motley compared the frequency of verbal slips made by subjects who were either fearful of electric shocks or aroused by an attractive woman. Errors were typically Spoonerisms, in which syllables of two words are transposed, as indicated in the figure (data from Motley 1985).

'past fashion' became 'fast passion' in the sexuality condition (see Fig. 5.3). In addition, a pre-test of subjects in the sexual drive condition showed that those who scored highest on a test of sexual anxiety later made the greatest numbers of slips. While these results are consistent with Freud's theory of slips as anxiety-related, Motley, like Fromkin, notes that there are linguistic constraints on the types of errors that subjects make; he also argues that some errors, particularly in children, are not anxiety-related at all. For instance, my three-year-old son, returning from a historical site, called it 'pineapple village' rather than 'pioneer village'; the word 'pineapple' was already familiar to him, whereas the word 'pioneer' was not. However, as already noted, Freud himself suggested that not all slips are significant. Thus, the evidence for linguistic constraints does not seem to contradict Freud's view, and overall the research seems to support his theory.

Obviously, these studies do not provide an adequate basis for judging the overall body of Freud's work. However, it is worth noting that there are some aspects which are well accepted at the *descriptive* level (that is, without reference to the specifics of Freud's *explanations*). For example, childhood amnesia is an accepted fact, though its origin is still unclear. Similarly, therapists ranging in orientation from psychoanalytic to humanistic to even behaviouristic accept the utility of defence mechanisms as shorthand descriptions for particular behavioural patterns; where the approaches tend to differ is in the explanation offered for the existence of these patterns. As already discussed, repression and Freudian slips are recognized as behaviours, though alternative explanations of the causes exist. These examples point out that Freud was a sensitive observer, who noted a number of behavioural phenomena that had previously been ignored. Similarly, his written descriptions of his case studies are vivid and detailed, often giving insights into his own thinking as well as the specifics of the cases. In this sense, they still make interesting reading. So at the descriptive level, there is no doubt that Freud made major contributions to the observational base of psychology.

This raises a second criterion for judging theories: generality. **Generality** refers to the range of application of a theory; a good theory should apply to a wide range of situations. For example, a theory which only explains the behaviour of a particular species of rat in T-shaped mazes, and nothing else, is likely to be seen as trivial, no matter how accurate it might be. By contrast, Freud's work addresses almost the entire range of human behaviour. For example, he explicitly argued for the continuity of normal and abnormal behaviour. In addition, he discussed issues related to memory, art, cultural patterns, mythology and a wide range of other topics. Indeed, the assumption of psychic determinism meant that in principle the theory could be applied to understanding the motivational aspect of *any* behaviour. In this regard, Freud's theory still stands as probably the most comprehensive account of human behaviour produced by a single individual. (Skinner, who has written on everything from superstitions to Utopian societies, may be a strong second.) The difficulty, of course, is that, without falsifiability, it is difficult to tell if it is a *correct* theory. Just as a trivial but accurate theory is of little value, so, too, is a broad but false theory. But is Freud's theory necessarily false?

generality a criterion for evaluating a theory, which refers to the range of application of a theory; a good theory should apply to a wide range of situations

Without the objective standard of falsifiability, it becomes hard to evaluate Freud's theory (or *any* theory). While *no* theory can be *proven* true, a theory which cannot be tested also cannot be proven to be *false*. Instead, one tries to determine if it is self-consistent, and looks for evidence of distortions in the observations. A good theory should not be contradictory, and there should be no indication of bias or other distortions in interpretations of the data. Both of these points have been matters of controversy with regard to Freud's work. In terms of consistency, he frequently revised his thinking, as already noted. This was perhaps inevitable, given the difficulties of forming a theory based on inferred variables. Hence, one could argue that, rather than worry about the possible contradictions, one should simply consider his latest work as reflecting what he ultimately thought.

In terms of distortion or bias, however, the situation is much more complex. Freud himself believed he had many opponents, as his letters and comments to friends indicate. Yet some authors have suggested that much of this opposition existed in his own mind (e.g. Roazen 1975; Sulloway 1979; Masson 1984). Freud seemed to thrive on challenge, according to Sulloway, and was at his best in defending his views from attack. But he also seems to have been very intolerant of real critics, which ultimately became a factor in his relationships with several colleagues and disciples. While his ventures into psychoanalysis began with his collaboration with Joseph Breuer, the two parted company when Freud developed his seduction theory of hysteria. Later, he had acrimonious splits with Carl Jung, Alfred Adler and Wilhelm Fleiss, all one-time protégés.

Two issues – the seduction theory and his views of women – have perhaps generated the greatest controversy concerning Freud's work. Early in his career, Freud proposed that hysteria arose from the trauma of sexual assault; this was the seduction theory of neurosis. Later, he decided that in fact the traumas were imagined assaults, not real attacks (see earlier discussion). However, Masson (1984) has argued that Freud's shift was a mistake, and that Freud, like his contemporaries, was unwilling to acknowledge the realities of sexual abuse of children. Masson based his argument in part on letters and documents accessed during his brief stint as project director of the Sigmund Freud Archives, a position from which he was abruptly terminated, and later won a wrongful dismissal suit. No stranger to controversy, Masson has been embroiled in a lengthy lawsuit against Janet Malcolm and *The New Yorker* magazine over an article about him published in 1984. It is difficult to assess the issue fairly. Masson's point about the reality of child abuse is certainly consistent with modern research, but that does not prove that fantasy cannot cause trauma, as Freud came to believe. Interestingly, the disorder which Freud most closely associated with the seduction theory – hysteria – is today a rare phenomenon. (The term *hysteria* is not common usage today; the expression of psychological conflicts through physical symptoms is called *conversion disorder*. However, by whatever name, this type of problem is uncommon.)

Critics have also argued that Freud's views of women – especially the feelings of inferiority which he associated with penis envy – were based on the cultural attitudes of his time. Again, there is no doubt that attitudes have changed in the past hundred years, and it is possible that Freud's ideas were influenced by both the cases he considered and prevailing social norms. Later analysts (notably Karen Horney) have addressed the issue in different terms, suggesting that women's feelings of self-worth have nothing to do with biological mechanisms, inferior or otherwise (Horney 1950). Hence, at the very least, one can argue that alternative interpretations exist for explaining personality dynamics in women.

These disputes seem inevitably to interweave the man and the theory. In part, this is probably because he dominated the field for so long, and in part because of the difficulties of evaluating the theory in more conventional ways. However, claims of bias also raise an interesting conundrum: Does bias prove Freud was wrong, or that he was right? If Freud was biased, then it seems that he was *unaware* of the distortions to his thinking, since in most respects he adapted his thinking to fit new information. That means that he was *unconsciously* distorting his interpretations, which is precisely what his theory says: no person can ever fully understand their own behaviour, or be free of distortions induced by unconscious processes. So if Freud's thinking (e.g. about women) was biased despite his efforts to be objective, then that proves that his basic assumptions about the dynamics of the unconscious mind are correct! By the same reasoning, one would have to conclude that no-one can offer a purely rational analysis of Freud's work – or of anything else in the world (this possibility has in fact been suggested by some philosophers of science: see Kuhn 1970).

It is precisely this 'catch-22' nature of the theory that bothers some critics. If you accept the basic assumptions, then it is nearly impossible to invalidate the theory. Consequently, some have argued that Freud's work is more of a story than a theory, weaving together the threads of human experience into a fictional tapestry (e.g. Robinson 1979). Others see such a view as too negative – a case of seeing the faults, but not the contributions, of psychoanalysis (Wachtel 1977). There is no doubt that Freud broke new ground in both his observations and his ideas. Given his pioneering role, it would seem unreasonable to expect him to have found the final answers to all questions – others could surely follow in his path. In this regard, a statement by psychoanalyst Charles Brenner, writing in a selected volume of Freud's writings, is apt: 'If the history of psychoanalysis is like the history of the other natural sciences, and we have no reason to doubt that it will be, the time will come when the theories Freud elaborated in the 1920s will be incorporated into and superseded by other more complete and more precise hypotheses which will be based on more extensive data and perhaps on different ways of viewing psychic phenomena' (Brenner 1957). That, indeed, is the way of science. Let us see just what Freud's successors have achieved.

Neo-Freudian and Non-Freudian Psychodynamic Theories

As his ideas became known, Freud attracted the attention of a number of doctors who were interested in his methods and theory. Several individuals became part of a closely knit group of followers, who were to help Freud spread his ideas. Unfortunately, the relationships were not always amicable. Just as Freud perceived opposition from the greater medical community, so too he had limited tolerance for dissent within his group of followers. As a consequence, several early protégés either left or were cast out of the group. Wilhelm Fleiss, who influenced Freud's thinking about the sexual origins of hysteria, was eventually relegated to the shadows (Masson 1984). More significant were the departures of Alfred Adler and Carl Jung, who split from Freud in the years just before the First World War. Both men disagreed with various aspects of Freud's evolving theory, and ultimately became well-known for their own theories. Interestingly, G. Stanley Hall, the American psychologist who sponsored Freud's first lectures in the United States, commented in 1924 that he hoped Freud would not make the mistake of making 'too abrupt a break with his more advanced pupils like Adler and the Zurich group' (Hall 1924: 7).

Even among those who stayed relatively close to Freud's basic views, a number of variants arose. The publication of *The Ego and the Id* in 1923 led Freud's followers in two different directions, called the 'ego psychology' and 'object relations' schools. *Ego psychology*, promoted by Freud's daughter Anna, emphasized the mechanisms used by the ego to deal with the world. Later, Erik Erikson, who worked with Anna, was to extend the conception of developmental stages over the entire lifespan, in the process placing greater emphasis on social influences. The *object relations* school, which became popular in England, focused on the relationships between the individual and those to whom there are significant emotional ties (particularly the mother, due to early rearing). Melanie Klein and Donald Winnicott were among the pioneers of this approach, which later influenced John Bowlby (for an overview, see Padel 1987).

Thus, Freud's work spawned a number of approaches, some closely related to his original ideas, some markedly different. Over time, the degree of divergence and variety of viewpoints has expanded. Thus today one finds a number of viewpoints which are 'analytic', but clearly not Freudian, such as *transactional analysis* (Berne 1961). In addition, the humanistic approach, which differs in many ways from the psychodynamic perspective, was founded by individuals who were initially trained in analysis, as we shall see in the next chapter.

Given this diversity, and the considerable period that has elapsed since Freud's death, it is appropriate to reconsider Brenner's observation, quoted at the end of the last section: Has the psychodynamic approach advanced, in the manner of the natural sciences, or are the ideas of Freud's successors simply variations on a theme? To get some sense of an answer to this question, let us consider briefly some major contributors.

Carl Jung and the Collective Unconscious

Carl Jung was born in Switzerland in 1875, the son of a Lutheran pastor. As a boy, he struggled to reconcile the religious differences between himself and his father. In his autobiography, he contrasts his own ideas, based on the immediate experience of spirituality, with his father's, which were based on intellectual adherence to doctrine (Dourley 1992). These feelings, which sometimes led him to feel isolated in childhood, were later to influence his ideas about psychological growth. In university, he studied medicine, and in 1900 did a psychiatric internship at a major institute in Zurich. By 1905, he was lecturing in psychiatry at the University of Zurich, and conducting a psychiatric practice.

At this time, he contacted Freud to express interest in his work, and the two men met in Vienna – talking together on their first visit for thirteen hours! They had regular contacts after that, and Freud came to consider Jung as his protégé and successor (Fadiman and Frager 1976). For example, when Freud was invited to speak in the United States in 1909, Jung was prominent among those who accompanied him. Despite their personal rapport, the two men differed on matters of theory – Jung disagreed with Freud's emphasis on sexuality, and Freud questioned Jung's interest in spirituality, among other issues (Jung saw psychic energy as being much more general than Freud's emphasis on sexuality). As a result, they broke contact in 1912, and Jung gradually evolved his own theory.

Apart from de-emphasizing sexuality, Jung's approach differed from Freud's primarily in two areas: the process of development and the nature of the unconscious. Jung's conception of development, which he referred to as the process of **individuation**, was related to his conception of personality, which in many respects was more complex than Freud's. It is not possible to provide a complete treatment here, but some general comments may help to suggest the nature of the differences. At the conscious level, Jung talked about the **ego**, which provides the conscious direction of our lives (much like Freud's conception), and the **persona**, which is the character or role we assume in presenting ourselves to the world. Both of these are distinct from the **self**, which comprises the totality of the person, both conscious and unconscious. The goal of human development, in Jung's view, was to expand conscious awareness by the ego making contact with the unconscious portions of the self.

Jung perceived human growth and development as more open-ended than Freud's description of the genital stage, which was characterized primarily in negative terms. For Jung, individuation was a life-long process. For the *ego*, which reflects the conscious sense of identity, growth involves expansion of one's awareness of the world and of oneself. But for the *self*, which is the whole

individuation Jung's conception of the goal of development, which he described as the expansion of conscious awareness by the ego making contact with the unconscious portions of the self.

ego in Jung's theory, the element of the self which provides the conscious direction of one's life

persona in Jung's theory, the conscious character or role we assume in presenting ourselves to the world

self in Jung's theory, the self comprises the totality of the person, both conscious and unconscious, and is distinct from both the ego and the persona (conscious aspects of personality)

Carl Jung

Carl Jung (1875–1962) was born in Kesswil, Switzerland, the son of a Lutheran pastor. Despite his vocation, Jung's father seemed more intellectual than spiritual, and his detached attitude led Jung as a child to feel isolated by his own spiritual interests. The feelings he experienced were later to influence his ideas about psychological growth. Jung was educated in Basel, and received his medical degree from the University of Basel in 1900; he then did a psychiatric internship at the Burgholzli in Zurich under Eugen Bleuler (who coined the term 'schizophrenia'). By 1905, he was lecturing in psychiatry at the University of Zurich, and conducting a psychiatric practice. At this time, he contacted Freud to express interest in his work, and the two men developed a quick rapport; Freud came to consider Jung as his protégé and successor. However, by 1912 they had clashed on a number of issues, and Jung left Freud's circle to evolve his own theory and techniques. In later years, he continued to live in Zurich, where he conducted a private practice as well as wrote. Faced with heart problems that underlined to him the frailty of human life, he remained interested in the issues of individuation and growth until his death at the age of eighty-seven.

of one's being (including the unconscious), the goal is to transcend egotistical interests, achieving a union of the conscious with the unconscious.

At this point, it is necessary to describe Jung's view of the unconscious, which differed significantly from Freud's. Jung believed that part of the contents of the unconscious are personal, related to the experiences of the individual; he called this portion of the unconscious the **shadow**. But, in addition, there is a portion of the unconscious which reflects universal, not individual, themes and ideas; this portion, which he called the **collective unconscious**, was biologically based, not the product of experience. While sometimes the collective unconscious is caricatured as a sort of 'race memory', Jung's actual intent was to suggest that just as the body has an evolutionary history, so does the mind (in biological terms, one might say the way the brain functions reflects its evolution).

One important element of the collective unconscious is the existence of organizing structures called archetypes. **Archetypes** contain no content of their own, but instead serve to organize our experiences, almost like cognitive schema. As such, they are the basis of many fantasies, myths and symbols. For example, Jung explained the story of Oedipus as an expression of an underlying archetype, in contrast to Freud's view that it reflected a developmental conflict. At the same time, Jung agreed with Freud that the unconscious expresses itself in symbolic form, and he had a great interest in how certain symbols recur across different cultures (Jung and von Franz 1964; see Fig. 5.4). Like Freud, Jung also believed that analysing the meaning of symbols was helpful to understanding the dynamics of the mind. By exploring symbols, the individual can make contact with, and come to terms with, the unconscious portions of the self.

Taken as a whole, Jung's theory is rich in detail, and complex. The theory often deals with pairs of opposites, such as conscious and unconscious, ego and shadow. (Another pair which has become well known is his description of personality in terms of *introversion*, being inwardly oriented, and *extraversion*,

shadow in Jung's theory, that part of the contents of the unconscious which are personal, related to the experiences of the individual

collective unconscious in Jung's theory, a biologically based portion of the unconscious which reflects universal themes and ideas, not individual experience

archetypes organizing structures within the collective unconscious which serve to organize our experiences, providing the basis of many fantasies, myths and symbols

Fig. 5.4 Symbolism in psychoanalytic theories Both Freud and Jung believed symbols had meaning, although for Freud they represented the personal unconscious, as in the figures in (a); Jung saw symbols as expressions of the collective unconscious, as in the figures in (b), which represent archetypes. (Try to figure out what drives the Freudian symbols represent.)

being focused on the outer world.) Like Freud, he was a prolific writer, and the large body of his writings makes it difficult to summarize all of his thinking. Like Freud, he often returned to the same themes and issues, seeking to clarify his earlier work. For example, late in his life, after a heart attack at the age of sixty-nine, Jung returned to the issue of growth, relating it to his youthful concerns about the role of spirituality in human life. The increasing awareness associated with individuation, he concluded, was an affirmation of the meaning of human life. In his autobiography, he wrote, 'the sole purpose of human existence is to kindle a light in the darkness of mere being' (Jung 1963: 326).

Evaluating Jung's work is difficult. His theory has drawn many adherents, and provides a distinctive perspective on psychodynamic processes. His ideas about the collective unconscious raise interesting questions about the use of symbols in areas such as religion, mythology and children's art. However, as with other observations, it is also possible to offer alternative interpretations (for example, children's art may be influenced by the development of perceptual and motor skills: see Kellogg 1967). In the end, the metaphorical nature of many of Jung's concepts has led critics to argue that his theory, while different than Freud's, comes no closer to being scientifically testable. As we shall see, this remains a concern when considering other psychodynamic theories.

For further consideration

Compare the symbols which Jung would call archetypes in Fig. 5.4 with the Freudian symbols given. Which do you find easiest to interpret? Is this a reasonable standard for determining their validity?

Alfred Adler and Individual Psychology

Born in Vienna in 1870, Alfred Adler had a more challenging childhood than most individuals. For one thing, his younger brother died in the bed they shared when Adler was three years old. In addition to this tragedy, he suffered from serious health problems, including a near-fatal bout of pneumonia at the age of five. Despite such difficulties, he struggled to overcome their impact, and was popular among his peers. These events seem to have influenced his later theorizing, with its emphasis on social factors and the importance of childhood experiences.

When he survived the pneumonia, thanks to the interventions of a dedicated doctor, Adler decided to make medicine his career goal. He enrolled in the University of Vienna in 1888, and received his medical degree in 1895. After initially practising as an ophthalmologist, he gradually shifted to neurology and psychiatry. Although he had already begun his own theoretical work, he was drawn to Freud, who was becoming known in Vienna for his approach to hysterias. He became one of the first members of Freud's inner circle in 1902, three years before Jung, and was very active in the group. Like Jung, Adler was an early heir-apparent, as shown by Freud nominating him as the first president of the Viennese Psychoanalytic Society in 1910.

Unfortunately, Adler's favoured relationship with Freud was not to last. Even when they first met, Adler had difficulty accepting Freud's views of the nature of drives, and the notion of the Oedipal conflict. As time went on, their disagreements became more evident, and more vehement. By 1911, the matters had come to a head, and Adler resigned as president of the society, just a year after taking the post! He went on to found his own organization, called the Association for Individual Psychology; some of the founding members were ex-members of the Viennese Psychoanalytic Society. The group flourished in Europe, helping the spread of Adler's ideas. When Nazism began to threaten (like Freud, Adler came from a middle-class Jewish family), he moved to the United States, accepting a teaching post at Long Island Medical College. He died in Scotland in 1937, while on a lecture tour (Fadiman and Frager 1976).

Adler's early views were shaped by his interest in organic dysfunctions and

Alfred Adler

Alfred Adler (1870–1937) was born in Vienna in 1870. He had a difficult childhood, marked by the death of his younger brother when Alfred was three, and a near-fatal bout of pneumonia at the age of five. Such traumas led him to struggle for success, which probably helped to shape his later ideas about inferiority and compensation. He received his medical degree from the University of Vienna in 1895. After initially practising as an ophthalmologist, he gradually shifted to neurology and psychiatry, and became one of the first members of Freud's innner circle in 1902, three years before Jung. Like Jung, Adler was an early heir-apparent, as shown by Freud nominating him as the first president of the Viennese Psychoanalytic Society in 1910. Unfortunately, Adler's favoured relationship with Freud was not to last, as they repeatedly clashed on theoretical issues. By 1911, the matters had come to a head, and Adler resigned as president of the society, just a year after taking the post! He went on to found his own organization, called the Association for Individual Psychology; some of the founding members were ex-members of the Viennese Psychoanalytic Society. The group flourished in Europe, helping the spread of Adler's ideas. When Nazism began to threaten (like Freud, Adler came from a middle-class Jewish family), he moved to the United States, accepting a teaching post at Long Island Medical College. He died while on a lecture tour in Scotland in 1937 at the age of sixty-seven.

inferiority for Adler, the notion that all children experience a sense of helplessness because of their size and dependence on others; this feeling can also be intensified by real or imagined physical defects, social rejection and other factors

compensation in Adler's theory, a process of engaging in activities intended to produce a feeling of superiority over others, in order to overcome feelings of inferiority

inferiority complex in Adler's theory, an intense feeling of insecurity based on a failure to resolve the feelings evoked by childhood experiences of helplessness

superiority complex in Adler's theory, a response to feelings of inferiority in which the individual attempts to mask their weakness by adopting an attitude of exaggerated self-importance

the implications of Darwinian theory. These influences led to the notion of *inferiority*, and subsequent attempts at *compensation*. While originally meant in a physical sense, these concepts gradually shifted towards the psychological, as Adler grew more interested in social relations. Gradually he evolved the notion that all children experience a sense of **inferiority** because of their size and dependence on others. Inferiority can lead to attempts at overcoming the perceived weakness (**compensation**); this process is motivated by the generalized drive which Adler called *striving for superiority* (this was a later view; in his early work, he interpreted motivation in terms of aggression and striving for power; see Ansbacher and Ansbacher 1956).

For Adler, the experience of childhood inferiority is the most important influence on the development of personality. Some individuals are so overwhelmed by the sense of helplessness that they develop a lifelong feeling of inferiority, called an **inferiority complex**. Others attempt to mask their weakness by pretending to feel superior, when inwardly they lack self-esteem; this is called a **superiority complex**. Early experiences like major illness, being overly pampered, or neglect can have a major impact on how the child views their own capacities, and on the child's social interactions (one can see in pampering and neglect a parallel to Freud's view of how over- or under-gratification create fixations).

As adults, the individual is best understood as a whole, rather than individual behaviours; each person has a unique **style of life**, a way of adapting and interacting, which is an expression of the person's life history and goals (the contemporary term 'lifestyle' is really a corruption of Adler's concept). For a healthy individual, unmarred by either inferiority or superiority complexes, the goals

style of life a term used
by Adler to describe an
individual's unique way of
adapting to and interacting
with the world, which is an
expression of the person's
life history and goals

will include love, friendships and a commitment to society. Individuals who lack
self-esteem will instead divert their energy into behaviours which are productive
neither for the person nor society. Thus, Adler's approach to personality places
much more emphasis on social factors than does Freud's.

Adler's ideas have had a broad, but rather diffuse, impact. His emphasis on
social interactions and self-esteem has influenced both other psychodynamic
theorists like Karen Horney and Erich Fromm, and also the humanistic approach
of theorists like Carl Rogers. In addition, his focus on childhood led him and his
colleagues to pay considerable attention to educational processes, and 'Adlerian'
school programmes still exist. In addition, terms like 'inferiority complex' and
'style of life' have been used by many with no real connection to Adlerian
theory. In this sense, one must acknowledge his significance.

At the same time, it is not clear whether his theory should be considered a
revision of psychoanalytic theory or an alternative. The disagreements which led
to the split between Freud and Adler (about the nature of basic drives and
childhood complexes) clearly show the differences in the two theories. However, there is little evidence which addresses the issue of which view is more
correct. Salvatore Maddi has argued that Freud's concepts can be applied to his
own life (Maddi 1974); the same might be said of Adler and *his* theory. The
difficulty with this sort of comparison, as Maddi notes, is that this is not a valid
means of establishing scientific truth. Lacking proper evidence, one can only
view the theories and draw one's own tentative conclusions.

Other Psychodynamic Theorists

Many other psychodynamic theories have been developed in the last hundred
years, and it is not possible to review all of them here. A few, however, are
worth noting briefly for the ways in which their work highlights the areas of
contention in Freud's work.

Karen Horney (1885–1952) began as a psychoanalyst in Berlin; along with
Anna Freud, she was one of the first female analysts. Right from the beginning,
she was critical of what she saw as male-centred ideas in Freud's theory, particularly the concept of penis envy. Despite these differences, she agreed with
Freud (and Adler) about the significance of early childhood in shaping personality. For Horney, the development of personality involved the fundamental
need for security, This need is experienced right from birth, as part of the *basic
anxiety* experienced by a newborn child. In general, her theory, like Adler's,
placed much greater emphasis on self-esteem than did Freud's work (Horney
1950). Her distinction between the *real self* (who we actually are) and the *ideal
self* (an image of what we should be) also influenced the work of Carl Rogers
(see Chapter 6). In addition, by examining how women's experiences, rather
than their anatomy, shape their behaviour, she was a precursor to more recent
feminist theories. In all these respects, her contributions have been significant.

Erik Erikson (1902–1994) originally studied under Anna Freud in Vienna,
and later began to do research and child therapy in the United States. He developed his own theory of development, which differed significantly from Freud's
in both the nature of developmental stages and also the drives which underlie

COMPARING FREUD AND ERIKSON'S THEORIES OF DEVELOPMENT

AGE	FREUD	ERIKSON
0 - 1½	Oral stage–development of ego through body image, delaying gratification	Trust vs. mistrust–developing trust in others and self
1½ - 3	Anal stage–development of ego through toilet training	Autonomy vs. shame–learning self-control
3 - 5	Phallic stage–Oedipal conflict	Initiative vs. guilt–learning to plan and initiate new actions
5 - 12 (puberty)	Latency–drives repressed, little conscious conflict	Industry vs. inferiority–absorbed in activities like school; developing sense of competence
12 - 20 (adolescence)	Genital stage–development complete; gratification largely symbolic in form	Identity vs. role confusion–forming clear sense of self-identity
Young Adult (20 - 25)		Intimacy vs. isolation–learning commitment and sharing in relations with others
Middle Adult (25 - 65)		Generativity vs. stagnation–making contributions to family and society
Late Adult (65 +)		Integrity vs. despair–developing sense of completeness towards life, accepting past

Fig. 5.5 Erikson's and Freud's models of development While the timing of early stages is nearly identical, Freud defined his stages in psychosexual terms, whereas Erikson defined his in psychosocial terms.

them. First, he defined stages in *psychosocial* terms, not in terms of sexuality and aggression. To Erikson, the basic drives are social ones, which are biologically based. Development involves resolving a series of problems or conflicts which concern the individual's sense of self and relationships to other people. For example, infants must resolve their fears of helplessness by learning to trust their primary care-giver. Second, whereas Freud's theory never elaborated on adult behaviour (the genital stage), Erikson's theory has eight stages, four of which focus on the years after puberty (see Fig. 5.5). In this regard, his focus on adult personality, from mid-life changes to retirement and ageing, foreshadowed modern issues in the study of human development (Erikson 1963). In addition, with his biographical analyses of historical figures like Martin Luther, he pioneered the application of psychological analysis to the writing of biographies, an approach now sometimes called *psychohistory* (Erikson 1962). In some sense, his own life mirrored his theory, as he continued to be active well into his eighties, and was ninety-one when he died in 1994.

Eric Berne, an American psychiatrist, developed an approach to personality and therapy which he called *transactional analysis*. He based his theory on three 'phenomenological ego states' – the *Child*, the *Adult* and the *Parent*. Berne argued that these three states are distinct and identifiable in the behaviour of adult individuals, and referred to the work of Penfield (see Chapter 2) as partial support. These ego states were seen as having their origins in the experience of the individual; in effect, the Child ego state is a form of regression to childhood behaviour, while the Parent is based on having internalized the attitudes of one's own parents (or other care-givers). The Adult is the rational, reality-testing capacity present in all individuals. Berne argued that both personal problems and social interactions could be seen in terms of the interactions (*transactions*) of these ego states. These transactions can become elaborated into ritualized inter-personal exchanges which he called *scripts*, because of their predictable nature. For example, casual encounters often involve an exchange of greetings which includes asking, 'How are you?' Yet everyone recognizes that among casual acquaintances this question is *not* meant as an honest inquiry, and should not be given an honest response. The Parent demands that one observe the social ritual, while the Adult recognizes that the inquiry is not meant literally. The Child, however, receives some gratification from the brief social exchange.

Berne wrote both technical and popular accounts of his theory, and it has been adopted by a variety of other therapists (Berne 1961, 1973; Steiner 1974). The most interesting aspect of his work, in relation to Freud's, is the apparent similarity of their three-part divisions of the mind, and yet the very different conceptual terminology used. It is clear that Berne saw his theory as an alternative to Freudian and other psychodynamic theories, not just as a modification. However, we have little evidence on which to make a comparative assessment. In its intuitive appeal (we are all familiar with children, parents and adults), it is somewhat like the humanistic approach, which also appeals to experience as a form of validation. Unfortunately, intuitive appeal is not equivalent to scientific validation.

In the end, each of these theories, both neo-Freudian and non-Freudian, seems to emphasize different concepts and structures. Yet it is not easy to determine if they are simply variations on a theme, as Robinson (1979) suggests, or whether one or more represent clear advances over Freud's pioneering theory. However they might disagree with Freud's concepts and theory, they clearly share the same difficulties of falsifiability.

Conclusion

The psychodynamic approach attempts to understand behaviour by analysing how personality is shaped by past experience and the workings of the mind. In one sense, it is like the cognitive approach, in that both focus on processes which cannot be observed directly. At the same time, it is rather different than the cognitive approach, for it attempts to deal with the individual as a person, including what motivates behaviour. By contrast, the cognitive approach currently offers no integrated conception of the individual, and is essentially silent on the question of motivation. In the same way, the biological approach also offers explanations of the mind, but its theories operate at a very different level of description, and cannot be compared directly. (Ironically, Freud himself hoped that ultimately his theory could be supported by reference to physiological processes.)

Within the psychodynamic approach, there is no question that Sigmund Freud occupies the central place. His position as pioneer has made his work the standard, rightly or wrongly, against which other psychodynamic models must be judged. Freud's theorizing, which is marked by numerous modifications over the course of his career, highlights the challenges posed in trying to infer the unobservable (the dynamics of the mind) from what can be seen.

At the same time, Freud's approach has inspired many others to develop psychodynamic models of behaviour, including some of his own close associates. Viewed together, it is possible to identify many kinds of similarities among these theories, and also many differences. One such similarity is the emphasis placed on early childhood experiences in understanding adult personality. Yet overall, the similar-yet-different nature of the theories makes it hard to decide which is the most accurate. To some extent, this seems unavoidable, given the goals and methods of the psychodynamic approach.

Ultimately, all psychological theories, psychodynamic or otherwise, are attempting to account for actual behaviour; in that sense, it is inevitable that there should be agreement on some aspects. At the same time, the necessity of inferring processes from observed behaviour makes it likely that different observers will create different organizing structures. This in turn can help to explain the wide diversity of conceptual structures found in psychodynamic theories. Seen this way, the theories represent different ways of viewing the same thing; as one analyst put it, 'Most conflicts in analysis are definitional' (Arlow, quoted in Karen 1992: 49). Thus, one is left with the sense that psychodynamic models are like cognitive schema – each is shaped by the experiences of the person who developed it.

While this might be reasonable in literature, science seeks to avoid such ambiguities by subjecting competing theories to experimental test. Unfortunately, the same factors that lead to *differing* psychodynamic theories also result in *complex* theories which involve a large number of factors. This poses a difficulty, since in any scientific model, the more factors one must deal with, the more difficult it becomes to evaluate the model. (As a graduate student, I once proposed a model of short-term memory which had no less than nine variables; when I showed it to my research adviser, he commented, 'Even if it's true, there's too many variables'. His point was that such a model could never be tested adequately.) This difficulty is clear in Freud's theory, which can *describe* almost any aspect of human behaviour, but *predicts* very little. In general, there is no way to determine empirically which psychodynamic model is the most accurate, since they generally lack *falsifiability*.

Still, there are other ways to judge a theory. One way is in terms of *generality*: Does a theory address the full range of human behaviour? Evaluating generality requires considering both what a theory covers *and* what it *doesn't* cover. One of the apparent omissions in Freud's work which has drawn criticism is the lack of a clear conception of the goal of development. Indeed, the genital stage, which represents the long final phase of life, is the stage which he elaborated the least.

Interestingly, this omission helped to trigger the development of the humanistic approach. Humanistic psychologists have developed a conception of healthy growth which views development in terms of reaching one's maximum potential. In this sense, the approach is very different to the 'brutal pessimism' of Freud, and closer to the views of Adler and Horney.

One example which seems to illustrate this is the recent interest in *shame* (Karen 1992). Freud seldom wrote about shame, apparently seeing it as less important than guilt as the source of anxiety (especially Oedipal guilt). Guilt, however, is solitary; it need not involve another person. Shame and esteem, by contrast, involve our perceptions of ourselves *in relation to* other people (as Adler noted). Today, there seems to be increasing interest in shame, and less concern about guilt. Hence, the difficulties of dealing with shame within Freudian theory have been interpreted recently as a significant limitation.

Whatever their differences and limitations, all psychodynamic theories share certain basic assumptions, such as the belief that it is possible to understand an individual's personality objectively. By contrast, the humanistic approach assumes that each person is in the best position to know their own self, and so humanistic theories focus on the individual's own subjective perceptions. In this respect, we are led back to the fact that different approaches to psychology make different assumptions, and therefore emphasize different aspects of behaviour. In the next chapter, we will see how the humanistic approach starts with many of the same concerns about personality as does the psychodynamic approach, but proceeds to frame its explanations in a very different way.

Chapter Summary

◆ The psychodynamic approach attempts to understand behaviour in terms of the workings of the mind, with an emphasis on motivation and the role of past experience. The approach was pioneered by *Sigmund Freud*, who developed *psychoanalytic theory*.

◆ Psychoanalytic theory emphasizes the importance of *innate drives*, the *continuity* of normal and abnormal behaviour, and the role of the *unconscious* mind.

◆ Freud's theory of personality accounts for behaviour in terms of the dynamic relationships of the *id*, *ego* and *superego*.

◆ Freud described development in terms of five psychosexual stages distinguished by shifts in the underlying mode of gratification: *oral*, *anal*, *phallic*, *latency* and *genital*. Each stage is marked by particular challenges and conflicts; of these, the *Oedipal conflict* (in the phallic stage) is perhaps the most significant in terms of later development.

- Psychoanalysis, by making the assumption of psychic determinism, views all behaviour as having meaning; consequently, Freud looked at everything from *dreams* to *everyday* (Freudian) *slips* to art as expressions of the dynamics of the mind.

- Anxiety, which results from conflicts within the individual, is handled by the use of various *defence mechanisms*, such as *displacement* and *repression*, which reduce anxiety by distorting reality rather than resolving the conflict.

- While seemingly very inclusive, Freud's theory has limitations (including problems of *falsifiability*), and even in his lifetime spawned competing theories, including several by his former students.

- The best-known of Freud's disciples are *Carl Jung* and *Alfred Adler*, who are considered *neo-Freudian* theorists; other psychodynamic theorists, such as *Karen Horney*, *Erik Erikson* and *Eric Berne*, are generally regarded as *non-Freudian* psychodynamic theorists.

- Carl Jung's theory expanded on the nature of the unconscious, particularly by including a conception of a *collective unconscious* whose *archetypes* influence our interpretation of experiences. Jung rejected Freud's emphasis on sexual motivation, and instead emphasized the importance of *individuation*, the enhancing of awareness, as a motive for development.

- Alfred Adler, while less well known to the general public, was influential in the emphasis he gave to issues of *esteem*, and many of his terms, like *inferiority complex* and *style of life*, have become common usage.

- Psychodynamic theories provide a distinctive approach to the understanding of behaviour; the primary difficulty is finding an effective way to evaluate the differences among the theories within the approach.

Key Terms and Concepts

anxiety	Oedipal conflict
archetypes	pleasure principle
catharsis	preconscious
collective unconscious	psychic determinism
conscious	psychosexual stages of development
defence mechanism	reality principle
ego	regression
fixation	repression
id	subconscious
identification	superego
individuation	style of life
inferiority complex	unconscious

Suggestions for Further Reading

For the reader interested in more information on psychodynamic theories in general, both Cramer's *Personality and Psychotherapy* and Pervin's *Personality: Theory and Research* provide good general references.

The best way to get the flavour of Freud's work is by reading his own writings. *Psychopathology in Everyday Life*, with its many examples of 'Freudian slips', provides an interesting starting point for the general reader. For those seeking a brief summary of Freud's theory, Brenner's *An Elementary Textbook of Psychoanalysis* is still a good brief guide, written by a Freudian analyst.

Paul Roazen's *Freud and His Followers* places Freud's work into historical context, and also explores his relations to Jung, Adler and others.

To explore Jung's ideas in more detail, *Man and His Symbols*, an edited collection of his writings, is a useful source.

6 The Humanistic Approach

Keeping the Person in 'Personality'

Freud's explorations of personality were initially driven by the suffering of his patients, and his desire to help them. In the same way, the origins of the humanistic approach can be traced to the desire to aid those in distress. Carl Rogers, one of the founders of humanistic psychology, has described an experience he had as a counsellor, while working with a young man who suffered from schizophrenia, a serious form of psychosis. The man was hospitalized in a state institution, and Rogers had been working with him for some time, with little evident progress. Then one day, something happened:

> [The man] made a few remarks about individuals who had recently left the hospital; then he remained silent for almost forty minutes. When he got up to go, he mumbled almost under his breath, 'If some of *them* can do it, maybe I can too.' That was all – not a dramatic statement, not uttered with force and vigour, yet a statement of choice by this young man to work toward his own improvement.
>
> (Rogers 1969: 265–6)

Eight months later, the man was in fact discharged from the hospital. To Rogers, this represented, not a triumph for him as a therapist, but an 'experience of responsible choice' by the young man. In this event, as in all of life, 'It is the *meaning* of the *decision* which is essential to understanding the act' (Rogers 1969: 268).

This story is striking both for the improvement in the man's condition – which is remarkable in itself – but also for the way Rogers describes it. One can scarcely imagine Freud interpreting the events in this way – a cure by *choice*? In what sense do choices determine our lives? And how can the meaning people give to their actions be incorporated into a psychological theory? To Freud, it was the therapist, not the patient, that determined meanings. In the humanistic approach, personal meanings are central to the understanding of behaviour – which itself is only one part of the person as a whole. In the end, the goal is to understand the whole person. To grasp what this means, we must look at the origins of the approach.

Introduction

In the 1950s, the field of psychology, particularly in North America, was dominated by psychoanalysis and behaviourism. Clinically oriented practitioners favoured psychoanalysis, while experimental researchers tended to follow the precepts of behaviourism. Supporters of each approach viewed it as a comprehensive system for understanding human behaviour. Not surprisingly, however, not every psychologist felt comfortable with these approaches. Some found behaviourism too limited, because it focused on specific responses, while ignoring the person as a whole. Others found psychoanalysis both too rigid and too pessimistic. (Some of the pioneers of the humanistic approach started their careers in the psychoanalytic tradition.) Out of these concerns emerged the humanistic approach.

The *humanistic approach* encompasses a variety of theorists, who have often applied other labels to their theoretical perspective, such as 'existential' or 'phenomenological' psychology. Abraham Maslow, one of the pioneers of the approach, has referred to humanistic psychology as a 'Third Force', opposing the dominant perspectives of behaviourism and psychoanalysis (Maslow 1968). While each label, and the associated theory, conveys a slightly different meaning, collectively the various theories embody certain common elements which justify treating them together. These common elements are the assumptions which define the humanistic approach.

phenomenological
pertaining to the way things appear or are experienced; in the humanistic approach, a reference to the emphasis on an individual's perceptions and feelings as defining the meaning of their behaviour

The basic assumptions of the humanistic approach are that behaviour must be understood in terms of the subjective experience of the individual, and that behaviour is not constrained by either past experience or current circumstances. Human behaviour is not simply a response to an immediate stimulus. If you wish to understand behaviour, the humanists argue, you must understand the person producing the behaviour, *including* how the person sees the world (this is sometimes described as a **phenomenological** viewpoint).

These assumptions contrast with those of the other approaches we have considered, particularly behaviourism and psychoanalysis. While obviously different in their details, behaviourism and psychoanalysis share two basic characteristics: both believe in determinism, and both see little explanatory value in subjective experience. Let us briefly consider each assumption.

determinism the assumption that all behaviour has specific causes

Determinism is the assumption that all behaviour has specific causes. While both behaviourism and psychoanalysis both assume some form of determinism, they differ in what *types* of causes they consider. For the behaviourist, behaviour is dictated by environmental factors, such as reinforcers. For the psychoanalyst, the individual is governed by innate drives whose influence is largely unconscious. Ultimately, both see the individual as a kind of puppet, at the mercy of largely uncontrollable forces.

By contrast, the humanists do not see behaviour as determined by either the immediate situation or past experience. While both types of factors can influence behaviour, the crucial element, in the view of the humanists, is that individuals are able to respond based on their subjective assessment of a situation – that is, they can make *choices* (sometimes this is referred to as 'free will').

The justification for this stance is complex, and has been a source of debate between the two sides (see Rogers and Skinner 1956). In large part, the humanist position is connected to the view that the way we think affects our behaviour, independently of external factors. Note that the humanists are *not* saying that causes do not exist in the world. Instead, they disagree with their opponents about what the primary causes of behaviour are. Without trying to settle the dispute, let us point out that both determinism and choice represent *assumptions*, neither of which is open to proof.

The second humanistic assumption is that behaviour must be understood in terms of the individual's subjective experience. Only the individual can explain the meaning of a particular behaviour. Psychologists have long been wary of dealing with subjective reports, as we have seen in earlier chapters. The behaviourists have tried to handle the issue by arguing that what people think or say is irrelevant to the explanation of behaviour. Instead, their explanations focus on the role of the environment. Psychoanalysis also claims that individuals cannot explain their own behaviour, because the causes are largely unconscious. Consequently, conscious explanations will be distorted by rationalization or other defences. The result is that both approaches devalue the significance of subjective experience. The explanation of behaviour ends up depending not on the person who is behaving, but on the assessment of an observer (the researcher/theorist).

The humanists reject these interpretations, and instead suggest that subjective experience is an important aspect of behaviour, *and* that it can be studied scientifically. Essentially, the argument is that *all data*, being gathered by human beings, are inherently *subjective*, and must be regarded as such. (Recall what has been said in previous chapters about the nature of perception.) The traditional insistence on an objective observer is meaningless, since no one is objective. As a result, there is no reason to reject subjective experience in favour of third-party observations.

In favouring this view, Carl Rogers argued that, rather than making science impossible, the recognition of subjectivity establishes new criteria for legitimate scientific observations (Rogers 1964). Basically, any event or observation which can be agreed upon by two observers is a valid observation, even though each person is reacting out of their own subjectivity. This process of agreement, which Rogers called **intersubjective verification**, is seen as ultimately the basis of all science, as well as all human relationships. Since science depends on agreement among observers (e.g. in using replicability as a test for the accuracy of experimental results), intersubjective verification is fundamentally no different than other methods. In this sense, rather than endorsing a dangerous form of subjectivity, the humanists are simply making explicit how intersubjective verification is the basis of traditional methods.

intersubjective verification a process for validating observations based on agreement by two observers; proposed by Rogers as a means of making subjective impressions useful as scientific data

A third characteristic of the humanistic approach, which emerges from the first two assumptions, is an emphasis on *meaning* – the purpose or value that a person attaches to their actions and experience. Traditionally, psychology has tended to ignore any notion of meaning or purpose to behaviour. At first glance, this seems strange, since questions of meaning lie at the heart of much of human experience – the myths we create, the stories we tell, the questions we ask ourselves about our lives, and so on. So why has psychology not tried to deal with the issue?

One reason psychology has ignored meaning has to do with the nature of science. Questions of meaning seem too closely tied to value judgements, and traditionally science has been regarded as 'value-free' – that is, science is neither intended nor equipped to talk about such questions. Today, of course, we recognize that *no* human activity, *including* science, is truly value-free. What we choose to study, and the consequences of what we learn, have moral implications. Richard Feynman, one of the developers of the atomic bomb, acknowledged the existence of this moral dimension in an essay on values in science (Feynman 1988). Hence, one cannot justify ignoring meaning as part of human experience by saying that science should not deal with values.

Like Feynman, many of the founders of the humanistic approach came to recognize the importance of meaning in behaviour because of personal experiences. The Second World War led to an exodus of thinkers and therapists from Europe to North America, a number of whom became significant figures in the development of the humanistic approach. Many were psychoanalytically trained, and some, like Viktor Frankl, were survivors of the concentration camps. For these individuals, a value-free stance was inadequate to comprehend the atrocities of the war. Instead, questions of the meaning and value of human activity were central for these theorists, and their concern was a factor which shaped the nature of the humanistic approach (e.g. Viktor Frankl's best-known work is *Man's Search for Meaning*, 1992).

Despite the obvious appeal of studying the issue, there is still the practical problem that dealing with meaning is even more difficult than dealing with subjective experience. Meaning cannot be observed directly, and often can be inferred only incompletely. (To take a trivial example, if I go to the refrigerator, look in, and then close the door without removing anything, what can you infer?) Yet, if we accept that subjective experience is relevant to understanding behaviour, we cannot ignore the value that people place on their experiences. To do so is to once more exclude part of behaviour from study, the way Skinner tried to do with mental processes. As Gordon Allport, a personality psychologist, has said, psychology must deal with all aspects of the individual: 'If present-day psychology is not fully equal to the task, then we should improve the science until it is' (Allport 1955: 5). The humanists have responded to this challenge by accepting that questions of meaning – and the answers individuals identify – are central to understanding the way people behave. Of course, *acknowledging* meaning is not the same as *understanding* it, and ultimately the issue is whether the humanistic approach succeeds in constructing an effective framework for understanding. Only by looking closely at the theories will it be possible to evaluate them fairly in this regard.

To summarize, then, the humanistic approach evolved out of the analytic tradition, but was also a reaction to the deterministic viewpoint found in psychoanalysis and behaviourism. It is also unique in emphasizing the importance of subjective experience in the understanding of an individual. Conscious awareness, the process of choosing and evaluating one's actions, and the meaning one gives to experience, are all part of this 'phenomenological' view.

By necessity, this introduction has been somewhat longer than that for the other approaches, precisely because the underlying assumptions of the humanistic approach are so different. As the humanists suggest, one cannot understand a person's point of view without trying to place oneself in their position. By examining closely the origins of the humanistic approach, we have tried to make that shift of perspective easier. In some ways, the humanistic approach is the most accessible of all the approaches, because it tries to connect to personal experience. At the same time, it is perhaps the most difficult of all the approaches, for it does not permit one to take the relatively comfortable position of a third-party observer in understanding behaviour. To be valid within their own framework, the theories must be useful not only for understanding other people, but also for understanding one's *own* life. Hence, studying the humanistic approach should not be considered a spectator sport; as you read, you should think about how the concepts relate to your own experience.

Carl Rogers' Theory

Carl Rogers was born in Oak Park, Illinois, a suburb of Chicago, in 1902. He came from a large family, and was reared in a rather strict religious atmosphere. In his later writings, he has talked about his boyhood, and indicated that the rather rigid beliefs he grew up with contributed to feelings of loneliness and being an outsider (Rogers 1973). He sought refuge in his studies, and was an excellent student in high school. Only when he left home to attend the University of Wisconsin did he begin to develop wider horizons. In his second year, he began to study for the ministry, and the following year went to China in conjunction with a Christian student organization. The trip gave him new confidence, as well as an appreciation for other perspectives on life. He started graduate studies at Union Theological Seminary, but then decided to continue in psychology at Columbia University instead. The shift occurred partly from increasing doubts about his religious commitment, and partly through the realization that one could take a counselling role *outside* the church. After obtaining his PhD, Rogers began working in the area of therapy and counselling, and also began developing his theoretical ideas. Over a long and active career, he taught at several universities before founding the Centre for the Studies of the Person in La Jolla, California. He died in 1987.

As he told it, Rogers was drawn to psychology because of his interest in counselling, and after completing his PhD, he began his career working in a child guidance centre in Rochester, New York. Over time, he worked with many types of individuals, including both children and adults who suffered from a wide variety of problems. He found himself challenged both intellectually and emotionally by their suffering, and it led him to seek better ways of understanding and helping. In this sense, his experiences were like those of Freud (and all

Carl Rogers

Carl Rogers (1902–1987) was born in Oak Park, Illinois, a suburb of Chicago, in 1902. He came from a large family, and was reared in a rather strict religious atmosphere. In his later writings, he talked about his boyhood, and indicated that the rather rigid beliefs he grew up with contributed to his feelings of loneliness and being an outsider (Rogers 1973). He sought refuge in his studies, and was an excellent student in high school. Only when he left home to attend the University of Wisconsin did he begin to develop wider horizons. In his second year, he began to study for the ministry, and the following year went to China in conjunction with a Christian student organization. The trip gave him new confidence, as well as an appreciation for other perspectives on life. He started graduate studies at Union Theological Seminary, but then decided to continue in psychology at Columbia University instead. The shift occurred partly from increasing doubts about his religious commitment, and partly through the realization that one could take a counselling role *outside* the church. After obtaining his PhD in 1931, Rogers began working in the area of therapy and counselling, and also began developing his theoretical ideas. By 1945, he had become a professor at the University of Chicago, and was elected President of the American Psychological Association in 1946. Over a long and active career, he taught at several universities and lectured widely. His later years were spent at the Centre for the Studies of the Person in La Jolla, California, which he founded. He died in 1987 at the age of eighty-five.

those who seek to combine theory with treatment): the practical challenge of relieving suffering leads to a journey of theoretical discovery. However, the path for Rogers was very different from that of Freud.

Rogers spent twelve years in Rochester, and during this time he began developing his own ideas about personality and therapy. Circumstances favoured this process, in that his superiors provided minimal constraints in terms of treatment orientation. Along the way, he encountered Otto Rank (a student of Freud's who, like Jung and Adler, had parted ways with his mentor), and found that Rank's techniques (though not his theory) seemed similar to the direction Rogers himself was moving in. His early thinking was summarized in *The Clinical Treatment of the Problem Child*, published while he was in Rochester (Rogers 1939).

The book was well-received, and led to Rogers receiving an offer of a full professorship at Ohio State University. In later years, Rogers observed that this chance to start at the top of the academic hierarchy freed him from the pressures and politics of academic life, and made it possible for him to move in new theoretical directions without fear of censure. In this sense, he encountered the 'conditions for growth' which he eventually emphasized in his theorizing. To understand what this means, let us look at his theory.

Self Theory and Personality

As noted at the beginning of this chapter, humanistic theories emphasize understanding behaviour by understanding the way a person experiences the world.

Rogers was a strong advocate of this view. As a consequence, his thinking is sometimes referred to as a **self theory**, since his ideas about personality focus on the notion of self (the concept of self has a long history, which had already been documented by G.H. Mead some fifty years before Rogers; see Mead 1934). Rogers himself saw the theory as evolving out of his clinical work. Since the time of Freud, it had been assumed that it was the therapist's role to determine the direction and goals of therapy; this concept reflected the traditional view of medical practice, including the linguistic usage of calling a person seeking treatment a *patient*. By contrast, Rogers, consistent with his ideas about the importance of self, came to believe that the person seeking treatment, not the therapist, should direct the process of therapy. To reflect this, the person seeking help was termed a *client* (implying a relationship of equals, not the subordination of the term *patient*); the process itself came to be called **client-centred therapy** (Rogers 1951). While Rogers, like Freud, developed his ideas largely out of a clinical context, his theory of personality, like Freud's, was intended as a general theory of behaviour.

self theory a general term for theories of behaviour which focus on an individual's self-concept and subjective experience of the world; pioneered by G.H. Mead, and adapted by many humanistic theorists

client-centred therapy an approach to therapy developed by Carl Rogers, in which the person seeking treatment (termed a *client*), not the therapist, is seen as directing the process of therapy; later called person-centred therapy

The Organism and the Actualizing Tendency

Rogers' theory is grounded in experience, and this includes his ideas about the basic aspects of personality. One of the most fundamental aspects of human experience is the fact that we are living creatures – we are born, we grow, and eventually we die. These basic realities are true for all individuals, regardless of race, creed or social status. In turn, our capacity for self-awareness tells us that however long we live, and however much we wish otherwise, we will in fact die. Cultures develop elaborate rituals to cope with death, but can do nothing to alter its finality. Yet what about what happens while we are alive? What needs must be fulfilled? What directs the path we walk through life? For Rogers, the answers to these questions stem from the biological reality of our existence: as living creatures, we need food, water, shelter, and so on. These needs arise out of our biological being, termed the **organism**. At the same time, Rogers believed there is a broader motive that directs our lives. This motive, called the **actualizing tendency**, reflects the desire to grow, to develop and to enhance one's capacities; Rogers saw this as an intrinsic property of life. It is the actualizing tendency that stimulates creativity, that leads us to seek new challenges and skills, and that motivates healthy growth in all the myriad aspects of our lives. The actualizing tendency motivates the baby to learn to walk. It nurtures our curiosity and our appreciation for beauty. It even underlies our desire for human contact, from sex to friendship to love. When a person is 'in touch' with the actualizing tendency, it becomes a powerful guide for directing behaviour into ways that foster positive growth and happiness. As we shall see, individuals can also be influenced by other forces, often to the detriment of healthy growth.

organism in Rogers' theory, the biological being which is the source of basic needs (such as food and water), and also the source of a growth motive termed the *actualizing tendency*

actualizing tendency in Rogers' theory, an innate drive which reflects the desire to grow, to develop and to enhance one's capacities

The Phenomenal Field and the Self

If awareness of being alive is the most basic of human experiences, shared by all, there are also many ways in which individual experience differs. Fundamentally, we each live in a world of our own creation, formed by our processes of perception. Rogers referred to an individual's unique perception of the world as their **phenomenal field**. As we saw in Chapter 1, perceptual processes structure our experience of the world according to our individual cognitive schemata; the way we perceive a situation is influenced by our past experiences, our needs and our expectations. In many respects, our perceptions match the external world, but as Rogers noted, 'We live by a perceptual "map" which is never reality itself' (Rogers 1951: 485). Some aspects of what we experience are internal, including thoughts and feelings. For each of us, the world we experience is personal and private. Hence, external reality is not what shapes our lives – our *perceptions* of it, expressed through our phenomenal field, are what guide our behaviour.

phenomenal field for Rogers, an individual's unique perception of the world

The way in which each of us sees the world affects the way we interact with each other. Very often, misunderstandings arise because two individuals perceive a situation differently, and are each unable to see the other's point of view. A teacher looks at the course material in terms of what 'should' be in the course; a student may look at the content in terms of whether it relates to their personal interests. A pregnant woman sees her body changing, and fears that her husband will no longer find her attractive; her husband may welcome the changes as positive signs of a much-desired child, and never imagine his wife needs re-assurance. Such differences can lead to disagreements, but they can often be resolved when we make a deliberate attempt to see the other person's point of view; Rogers believed this process of *empathy* plays an important role in healthy growth, as we shall see later. In more extreme cases, distortions of reality as expressed in our phenomenal field can lead to inappropriate behaviour: desire may lead to misinterpreting a friendly smile as a flirtatious invitation; a driver frustrated by pressures at work may see an unintentional error by another driver as a deliberate act of aggression. Whether it is consistent with the external world or not, the phenomenal field *is* the reality that we experience.

Overall, our phenomenal field reflects the way we see the world, and often how we act. Within this framework, the most significant element is our sense of self. While we all tend to perceive our self as a stable entity, in fact it is a fluid, changing thing, a unity comprised of many elements. Rogers called the **self** 'an organized consistent gestalt, constantly in the process of forming and reforming' (Rogers 1959: 201). The sense of constancy and stability which we experience is largely derived from the fact that, in order to observe the self, we must focus on a particular moment, much the way time becomes frozen in a photograph. Since we are inclined to see our own being as constant, we often selectively attend to those elements of the 'snapshot' that seem consistent with prior 'snapshots'. (This notion that constancy is a product of the mind, not of reality, was familiar even in ancient Greece; the philosopher Heraclitus said, 'We can never cross the same river twice. The water changes, and so do we.') In this sense, Rogers' use of the term self is rather different from many other theorists, who tend to describe it as a central, unchanging core of personality.

self for Rogers, an organized cognitive structure based on our experience of our own being

The self reflects our view of 'who we are' are at a given moment, and is influenced by all those factors which shape perception in general, including past experiences, the present situation and our expectations for the future. If we are in touch with our own being, then the self will be guided by the actualizing tendency as it relates to the present situation. Whereas psychoanalytic theory sees personality as the product of past experience, Rogers argued that the past is only relevant to the extent that we *perceive* it to be relevant. If I believe that the way I act is based on my childhood, and I perceive certain childhood experiences (positive *or* negative) as highly significant, then my behaviour at this moment will be strongly influenced by those experiences. On the other hand, if I 'let go' of the past, and emphasize my current needs and aspirations, then the past will play a much less significant role. Rogers related how, in therapy, a young man came to focus on how his life had been 'distorted and spoiled' by his parents. Then, as he reflected on his own analysis, he said, 'Maybe now that I *see* that, it's up to *me*' (Rogers 1969: 266). The self may well reflect the past, but it is not constrained by it; it is always possible for a new pattern to emerge, even based on a seemingly minor alteration of the phenomenal field (Rogers 1959).

The Ideal Self, Congruence and Incongruence

Apart from the self, there is another aspect of the phenomenal field which relates to our sense of our own being. The **ideal self** refers to our notions of who we would *like* to be, the goals and aspirations we have for our lives. Depending on what these goals and aspirations are, the ideal self may either be quite similar to the real self, or radically different. However, like the self, the ideal self is not a stable entity, but a dynamically changing construct, reflecting both the actualizing tendency and external forces. When we talk of a dying person who is 'at peace with himself', we are implying that their ideal self is consistent with their self. By contrast, when we perceive our behaviour as falling short of our desired goals, we can experience it as powerfully negative. I encountered a vivid example of this a few years ago. While I was returning papers to a class of university students, a young woman burst into tears. Since I knew she had received an excellent grade (94 per cent), this seemed a very strange response. When I discussed it with her after class, she explained that she had seen the grade for the person seated near her, which was 97 per cent. Since she had always tried to be the best, to discover that someone else had done better than her was a source of considerable distress – *regardless* of the objective quality of her own work. While I tried to console her, and suggest that her standards were perhaps unrealistic, this aspect of her ideal self was not something she could easily relinquish.

Obviously, the relationship between the self and the ideal self is an important factor in how we view ourselves, and consequently it formed a central issue in Rogers' theory of personality. To the extent that the self and ideal self match, the individual experiences a sense of **congruence**. (The sense of similarity which the term implies is also found in geometry, where *congruent figures* are ones which are identical in size and shape.) It is further expressed as consistency between what one experiences (phenomenal field) and what one expresses (communicates to others). On the other hand, if the person experiences contradictions in their sense of self and surroundings, then this will produce a feeling of incongruence. **Incongruence** represents a mismatch between self and ideal self, between what we experience and what we communicate. Imagine going to a party which you thought was casual, only to find everyone else dressed formally. The discomfort and embarrassment you would feel would reflect incongruence.

Obviously, no-one deliberately tries to feel out of place, and it seems equally obvious that incongruence is a very unpleasant experience. So why does it arise?

ideal self in Rogers' theory, a dynamically changing construct which represents an individual's goals and aspirations

congruence in Rogers' theory, a feeling of integration experienced when the self and ideal self match

incongruence in Rogers' theory, a feeling of conflict or unease experienced when there is a mismatch between the self and ideal self

Wouldn't it make sense to shape our perceptions so that such discrepancies don't arise? To some extent, we *do* in fact engage in such perceptual filtering. As we have seen, our perceptions can be influenced by our needs and expectations. Freud described this process in terms of defence mechanisms, and while Rogers disagrees profoundly with Freud's theory, he would acknowledge that perceptual distortions like those Freud described certainly can occur. However, he would disagree with Freud's explanation of their basis. In addition, Rogers would disagree with his more general assertion that conflict (or incongruence) within personality (the trigger for using defences, in Freud's view) is inevitable. Hence, the question becomes, how does incongruence arise?

For further consideration

Can you think of any ways in which your self and ideal self differ? Are there particular situations that make this discrepancy particularly distressing to you? Why do you think this occurs?

Personality Development and Conditions for Growth

Positive Regard

Philosophers and social theorists have long noted that people like company – very few people seem to welcome long periods of isolation. Rogers, too – perhaps influenced by his own experiences of loneliness as a boy – believed that social contact and positive relationships are essential to human growth. Contact with others can provide us with a feeling of belonging, of being valued and loved. Rogers referred to the need for such love and caring as the need for **positive regard**. He saw this need as universally expressed, and was not concerned about how it originates: 'Whether it is an inherent or learned need is irrelevant to the theory' (Rogers 1959: 223). Any form of attention and praise is positive regard. Little Johnny does a picture, and Mummy gives him verbal praise and a hug. Mary tells a funny story, and Daddy laughs and smiles. Such incidents provide positive regard.

positive regard love and caring which satisfy a need which Rogers regarded as universal

At first glance, this may seem very reminiscent of the behaviourist concept of positive reinforcement. However, behaviourism places the emphasis on the way that reinforcement is related to *behaviour*, while Rogers emphasized the *feelings* that positive regard induces, and how these affect our sense of self.

Conditions of Worth and the Would–Should Dilemma

Positive regard is so important that finding ways to obtain it can lead to ignoring other aspects of self. For example, if Mary finds that telling funny stories makes people laugh, she may begin finding other ways to make people laugh, even if at heart she feels her actions are foolish and inappropriate. Earning positive regard becomes the measure of self-worth, and pleasing others can become an end to itself. The restrictions imposed on self-expression in order to earn positive regard are called **conditions of worth**. Sometimes, these conditions are self-created, as in the example of Mary trying to be funny all the time. However, conditions of worth can also be created by others (such as parents or teachers). If Tommy hurts his knee and starts to cry, but is told that big boys don't cry, then crying may later be suppressed as a possible emotional expression. If Jane

conditions of worth restrictions imposed on self-expression in order to earn positive regard gets angry, but is told ladies don't show a temper, then she may come to suppress all feelings of anger. Rogers encountered many individuals in counselling who seemed out of touch with their emotions; typically, this could be related to parental demands in early childhood. As we internalize conditions of worth into the ideal self, we lose touch with our actual perceptions and emotions – with who we really are.

In accepting various conditions of worth, we also incorporate the values represented by these conditions into our ideal self, a process Rogers described as **introjection of values**. (The term *introjection* was first used by Freud to refer to a defence mechanism; hence this is a case where Rogers has implicitly accepted the behavioural pattern, but not the underlying explanation.) As the ideal self comes to represent the values and standards of other people, it is likely to become more and more discrepant with one's real nature (the self). This in turn creates the basis for incongruence. When pleasing others becomes more important than satisfying one's own actualizing tendency, then healthy growth is threatened. Thus, conditions of worth, and the resulting introjection of values, result in the negative experiences of incongruence.

In one sense, conditions of worth are unavoidable: parents and society inevitably set standards for conduct, and at least some of these standards will be arbitrary, or at least conflict with personal needs. As a teacher, I have sometimes encountered students who are pursuing a career goal which does not seem to suit them. When probed, they often say, 'Well, my mother's a nurse, so I feel I should be one, too', or 'My parents want me to be an engineer', or similar statements. In such cases, the individual often has other aspirations – art, or accounting, or whatever – which are being submerged in order to maintain parental approval. The result, of course, is incongruence, and feelings of being in conflict with oneself.

The conflict between one's own needs, expressed through the actualizing tendency, and the demands of others, expressed through the ideal self, is referred to as the **would–should dilemma**. While the values represented by the ideal self may have *originated* with other people, once they are introjected as part of the ideal self, they are *experienced* as internal in nature. Hence, rather than seeming to be a conflict between oneself and another person (who might reasonably disagree), the conflict is experienced as internal, between two parts of one's own being. This type of internal conflict is much more threatening and anxiety-provoking than disagreements with another person. This conflict can take many forms: When a student *would like* to study art, but feels they *should* study nursing, this is experienced as a would–should dilemma. Two adolescents *would like* to engage in sex, but feel they *should* wait until they are married. A parent *would like* to spend time playing with their children, but feels they *should* spend extra time at work.

In the would–should dilemma, there is a conflict between personal needs and goals, and perceptions of expected behaviour. Freud described this in terms of the conflicts between superego (parental values) and id (one's own needs), and believed that such conflicts were inevitable. By contrast, Rogers saw such conflicts, described as the result of incongruence between self and ideal self, as both undesirable and avoidable. Furthermore, he did not see them as reflecting a simple conflict between personal needs and society, because concern for others is an inherent part of the self. That is, a healthy person is naturally motivated

introjection of values for Rogers, the incorporation of values into the ideal self due to accepting conditions of worth imposed by others; the term was first used by Freud to refer to a defence mechanism

would–should dilemma the conflict between one's own needs, expressed through the actualizing tendency, and the demands of others, expressed through the ideal self to consider the impact of their actions on other people when choosing how to act. Still, if conflicts like the would–should dilemma are *not* inevitable, then how do they arise? To understand this, we must look at the distinction between conditional and unconditional positive regard.

Conditional and Unconditional Positive Regard

As noted earlier, the need for positive regard, in the form of approval and love, was seen by Rogers as universal. Ideally, we would all receive such regard on a free and open basis, both as children and adults. Such **unconditional positive regard** is acceptance and caring extended simply because the person is a human being. Religions have traditionally urged individuals to adopt this attitude, but we all recognize how difficult it is to put into practice. For example, in their best moments, all parents value their children; unfortunately, it is harder to maintain a feeling of unconditional regard if Jimmy has just broken an heirloom vase while trying to get at the cookie jar. Instead, we tend to give love and praise based on the child doing things of which we approve. When regard is given only for meeting certain standards of behaviour, it is called **conditional positive regard**. If Sean cleans up his toys, he gets praised; if he leaves them scattered about, he is likely to get scolded, or at least ignored. In later life, we find that regard is given for good performance at school or at work; we may even find friends welcome some actions, and heap scorn on others (peer pressure is an example of such forces in operation). In all these cases, positive regard is given for certain actions, but not for others. The problem with this is that conditional positive regard often leaves the person feeling that it is their *self*, not their *behaviour*, which is unacceptable: For example, Jimmy's father reacts to the broken vase by saying, 'Jimmy, you idiot! How could you break that vase? You know better than to take cookies without asking! Honestly, I don't think you ever listen to me!' While remarks like this may deter future incidents, they may also leave Jimmy feeling that any error is bad and unacceptable.

Ideally, it should be possible to value a person as a human being without implying that one accepts all of their actions – that is, regard for the *person* would be unconditional, but regard for their *actions* would be conditional. This would mean that one could withhold regard for particular actions – such as when a child has a tantrum – and yet still show regard for the person. In practice, however, both the person *giving* regard and the person *receiving* it often find the distinction between person and action hard to maintain. A scolded child tends to feel rejected, even if the mother says, 'I love you, but . . .'; the criticism of the child's behaviour tends to overshadow the expressed regard. When one's performance at work is criticized, it is hard not to take it as a criticism of one's general competence and worth. When too much conditional regard is given, it undercuts the person's sense of self, and contributes to the development of incongruence. To avoid this, one must focus on the conditions which instead foster congruence.

Congruence and Conditions for Growth

Rogers believed we are all born congruent, because the discrepancies which create incongruence arise through life experiences. Thus, his theory implies that

unconditional positive regard acceptance and caring given to a person as a human being, without imposing conditions on how the person behaves
conditional positive regard acceptance and caring given to a person only for meeting certain standards of behaviour

conditions for growth
the conditions under which
healthy development of
personality occurs; defined
by Rogers as unconditional
positive regard, openness
and empathy

it should be possible to develop in a way that *maintains* this sense of congruence. What fosters congruence, and how can one avoid incongruence? The answer
to this question lies in recognizing the conditions under which healthy development of personality occurs, the **conditions for growth**: unconditional positive
regard, openness and empathy. Let us consider each of these separately.

As discussed in the preceding section, *unconditional positive regard* is based
on accepting that each person has value, without any reference to what they do
or don't do:

> It is an acceptance of this other individual as a separate person, having
> worth in his own right. It is a basic trust – a belief that this other person
> is somehow fundamentally trustworthy. Whether we call it prizing, accept-
> ance, trust, or by some other term, it shows up in a variety of observable
> ways.

(Rogers 1969: 109)

By not imposing external conditions of worth, unconditional positive regard
makes it possible for the individual to develop a sense of self based on their own
actualizing tendency and their individual perceptions and experiences. Without
the distortions introduced by external demands, the values which develop as part
of the ideal self are likely to be self-consistent, and hence to maintain congruence. Thus, receiving unconditional positive regard is the most basic requirement for healthy growth and congruence.

While truly unconditional regard is extremely rare, it can help if we distinguish between the person and the action, as seen in the following incident.
Several years ago, I was meeting some friends for dinner. The husband was on
time at the restaurant, but his wife was nearly an hour late. Since this had
happened on other occasions, the husband was furious when she finally arrived.
Quickly recognizing this, she attempted to defuse his anger by saying, 'Oh,
sweetie, don't you love me any more?' The message implied by this was, 'If you
love me, you'll overlook my being late' – clearly setting up conditional regard.
Instead, the husband replied, 'Of *course* I love you, *but that has nothing to do
with it*: you shouldn't be late!' In effect, he distinguished between loving her,
and yet not accepting her action.

Obviously, though, most of the time we encounter a mixture of conditional
and unconditional positive regard. Yet Rogers believed growth was possible
even if not all the regard we receive is unconditional (otherwise, *no-one* would
be likely to grow!). Basically, it requires an opportunity to interact with at least
one person who can provide primarily unconditional positive regard, whether a
family member, a friend, a counsellor, a co-worker, or whomever (in counselling, Rogers called this *client-centred therapy*; see Chapter 9). For instance, in
a healthy relationship, spouses accept each other even though each has faults
(indeed, sometimes the 'flaws' become points of endearment rather than friction,
much the way parents complain of noisy children for years, and then miss the
noise when they leave home). Unconditional positive regard allows the individual to take chances with their feelings and behaviour – and in the process to
explore and develop their sense of self.

The second condition for growth is **openness**, which refers to a person freely
expressing their own sense of self, rather than playing a role or hiding behind
a façade. Like unconditional positive regard, openness can be found in potentially

openness behaviour
characterized by a person
freely expressing their own
sense of self, rather than
playing a role or hiding
behind a façade

any situation. For example, consider a person who attends a dull party. When approached by the host, the person musters a forced smile, and insists the party is 'wonderful'. Politeness dictates the verbal response, which differs significantly from the person's actual feelings; this contradiction creates incongruence. However, this could change, depending on the host's response. Suppose the host were to respond by saying, 'It's nice of you to say so, but I really think I've been to livelier *funerals*!' By expressing his own feelings instead of relying on social conventions, the host is exhibiting openness. In doing so, the host may open the door to a more honest assessment by the guest, whereby both host and guest gain. It's not that the party is no longer a disaster, but at least the two individuals have been able to make real contact with each other, free of social constraints. Rogers believed that this quality of openness (which he also called 'realness') opens the way to greater self-awareness, and personal growth. By contrast, when we adopt a façade which is based on our social role or other external constraint, we deny the possibility of genuine expression of feelings – either for ourselves or those we interact with. For example, Rogers noted 'the tendency of most teachers to show themselves to their pupils simply as roles', not real persons with doubts, fears and other human limitations (Rogers 1969: 107).

The third condition which can foster growth is **empathy**, the ability to understand the other person's point of view. Ideally, this encompasses their perceptions, thoughts and feelings. This concept is expressed in a proverb popular in the prairie regions of Canada, which says, 'Never judge someone until you've walked ten miles in their boots'. If you meet someone who seems rude (for example, in a store), does this mean they are always rude? Are they having a bad day? Could they have a headache or other problem? While we are often quick to jump to the conclusion that the person is simply rude, the reality is that we cannot properly judge from a brief interaction like this. (As noted in Chapter 4, this tendency to explain behaviour in terms of personality when situational factors are more likely is a *fundamental attribution error*.)

Like unconditional positive regard and openness, empathy is a quality that is readily recognizable, but not so readily found. Teachers, for example, are supposed to empathize with their students, but differences in background, as well as situational factors, can make such understanding difficult to achieve. Faced with this difficulty, teachers will sometimes adopt a smiling, tolerant façade – not empathy, but a pretence of it. Rogers believed that this compounds the problem of not understanding with the problem of not being real. Faced with students one doesn't understand (and may even dislike), Rogers believed that 'it is almost certainly more constructive to be *real* than to be pseudo-empathic, or to put on a façade of caring' (Rogers 1969: 113). Note that being real may sometimes imply expressing negative feelings. For example, a teacher faced with a messy room might say, 'I can't function when things are a mess!' While clearly disapproving, the response reflects the teacher's feelings, not simply disapproval of the students. This is probably more honest – and also more productive – than saying, 'You kids don't know how to be tidy!'

In the end, the three conditions of growth tend to be interwoven – experiencing one factor involves the others as well. Rogers noted this when he commented, 'To be genuine, or honest, or congruent, or real, means to be this way about *oneself*. I cannot be real about another, because I do not *know* what is real for him. I can only tell – if I wish to be truly honest – what is going on in me'

empathy the ability to understand another person's perceptions and feelings; seen by Rogers as a condition for growth

(Rogers 1969: 113). In effect, empathy results from openness and congruence, which are themselves closely connected.

The conditions for growth are meant to allow the individual to evaluate their experiences in terms of their own internal standards, based on the actualizing tendency. Like most things in the world, the conditions exist on a continuum, not as either/or alternatives. Consider, for example, empathy. At first glance, the statement by Rogers quoted in the previous paragraph seems to imply that empathy is impossible: we can never truly know what another person feels. In fact, the reality is more complex. First, when he speaks of empathy, he means the *attitude* of *trying* to empathize, even if the effort doesn't fully succeed. Second, since the same basic elements underlie all human existence (we are all 'siblings under the skin'), empathy may often result from being open to our *own* experience of the situation. The conditions which foster personal growth are also the conditions that will foster positive interactions with others. It is this fact – that what favours my growth will also favour yours – that made Rogers optimistic about the possibilities for growth in everyday life.

For further consideration

Rogers' analysis of the circumstances which promote growth places great emphasis on the interactions we have with other people. Do you find that what you look for in friends is consistent with what Rogers considered the conditions for growth?

Human Potential and the Fully Functioning Person

In describing personality, Rogers' theory repeatedly contrasts the factors which foster healthy growth, and those factors (such as conditional positive regard and conditions of worth) which obstruct growth. But what exactly *is* a healthy personality? One could say that a healthy person is living up to their potential, but what would indicate that a person is fulfilling their potential?

The idea that there is some sort of optimal result for personality development is one of the unique features of the humanistic approach. In this respect, the approach is very different from psychoanalysis. Freud's theory was based largely on his clinical observations, dealing with people who often showed severe problems, including physical symptoms. Perhaps as a consequence, his theory tended to emphasize the negative aspects of development. While Freud's ideas on pathology were very detailed, his conception of healthy development was never fully elaborated; overall, he seemed pessimistic about the possibilities for growth unburdened by fixations and neurotic conflict. By contrast, Rogers argued that personality development naturally moves towards healthy growth, and it is only negative external factors which lead to distortions of personality.

Rogers described the ideal of growth as being a **fully functioning person**. The term itself suggests that anything less than optimal growth is a deviation from proper functioning – that is, healthy growth should be considered the *norm*, not some super form of development. In many respects, being fully functioning is equivalent to being congruent. Congruence produces self-confidence and high self-esteem, which in turn make possible the openness to feelings and experiences that Rogers sees as central to growth. The individual trusts their own ability to deal with the world, and consequently shows a high degree of spontaneity, compassion and self-direction.

fully functioning person described by Rogers as the ideal of growth, closely related to congruence; healthy growth is characterized by openness, a high degree of spontaneity, compassion and self-direction

One characteristic which is *not* part of being fully functioning is aggression. Aggression for Rogers is a result of unhealthy growth, in contrast to Freud's view of aggression as an innate drive. Rogers sees aggression as one of the consequences of too much conditional positive regard. When a person is offered only conditional positive regard, they will often alter their behaviour to meet the imposed standards, since the need for positive regard is so powerful. However, this will often mean denying one's own preferences and feelings, which results in both incongruence *and* frustration. Aggression then arises as a natural response to the denial of one's own needs and feelings. If aggression seems widespread in the world, it is presumably because the use of conditional positive regard is so common. Unconditional positive regard contributes to healthy growth, and also reduces the likelihood of aggression.

If this seems abstract, consider an example. Harry is an only child whose parents were very strict and demanding when he was young. As a result, he incorporated their standards into his ideal self, and as a teenager has become a very rigid, argumentative person who criticizes and challenges all those whom he sees as making errors, whether peers or authority figures like teachers. At the same time, he is dissatisfied with his own behaviour, which cannot meet his own high standards. This combination of being highly critical and having low self-esteem leads Harry to get into many disagreements, resulting in his being rejected by others. His peers see Harry as a loner with a chip on his shoulder, and generally avoid him. Inside, Harry feels frustrated and lonely. Rogers would see this as a typical example of how excessive emphasis on conditional positive regard during Harry's childhood has led to incongruence and aggressive behaviour. Depending on the circumstances (e.g. a social environment in which drug-trafficking is prevalent), Harry could end up expressing his frustrations in criminal form, while being scornful of the society that he sees as having failed him.

Healthy development thus depends on the conditions for growth: where these are basically provided, the individual will move towards being a fully functioning person; in their absence, incongruence and aggression will arise. In one sense, this conception of human potential is very specific, in that it implies a fully functioning person will show little anxiety, an ability to evaluate situations independently, an openness in dealing with other people, and so on. At the same time, it is very broad and vague, in that it implies very little about the specific behaviours, or even values, of a congruent person.

The issue of values is a significant one to humanists like Rogers. Whereas modern science has generally argued for a 'value-free' approach to theorizing, humanistic psychologists believe one cannot understand human behaviour without understanding the values which often direct a person's choice of actions. Rogers addressed this issue in an essay in 1964, and then revised it five years later (Rogers 1969). He noted that infants value food, security, human contact and new experiences, while clearly disliking aversive events like pain, bitter tastes and sudden loud sounds. He noted that as we grow, however, we begin to incorporate values dictated by society, such as 'disobedience is bad' and 'making money is the highest good'. These values may be reinforced by various sources, ranging from parents to advertising. These values often seem directed towards social acceptance, and are rigidly held, without being open to question. Not surprisingly, the result is that the person is often out of touch with their own feelings and internal sources of satisfaction.

VALUES IN THE MATURE PERSON

Characteristics Which Are Negatively Valued

Valuing genuiness—pretence and defensiveness are negatively valued.

Moving away from 'ought'—acting because one values the action, not because one feels one 'ought to' do it.

Moving away from others' expectations—pleasing others *as an end in itself* is negatively valued.

Characteristics Which Are Positively Valued

Being real is positively valued—being 'who one is' and expressing one's feelings honestly.

Self-direction is positively valued—taking pride and confidence in making choices in one's life.

Valuing one's own being—viewing one's self and one's feelings positively.

Focusing on life as a process—instead of valuing the goal, one values the process of living, without concern for reaching a particular goal.

Valuing openness—being open to both one's inner and outer experiences, recognizing one's own feelings and those of other people. This is a particularly important value.

Valuing other people—accepting other people and appreciating them for what they are, just as one accepts oneself for what one is.

Deep relationships are valued—to be close to another person, able to fully communicate and share, is a very basic need.

Fig. 6.1 Values in the mature person Rogers believed that healthy individuals who had reached a mature stage of development would be likely to hold particular types of values (adapted from Rogers 1969).

By contrast, Rogers believed that a fully functioning person will be self-directing in forming values, and will tend to evaluate choices according to the immediately experienced situation. While this sounds like a form of situational ethics, Rogers also argued that the importance of the actualizing tendency will imply certain criteria for making values choices. Life is seen as a process, not as a series of goals to be reached. Relationships, especially to family and close friends, become more important than material accomplishments (this is reflected in the old quip, 'Nobody ever died wishing they'd spent more time at the office'). A more detailed description is given in Fig. 6.1.

While seemingly consistent with his overall conception of the actualizing tendency, Rogers' ideas about values in the fully functioning person are otherwise hard to evaluate. He seems to believe that there is a biological basis for these characteristics, as when he says that mature persons share 'an organismic commonality of value directions' (Rogers 1969: 252). At the same time, he wants to leave individuals free to make their own choices, unrestricted by him or anyone else: 'I do not expect that every [person] would agree with what I have to say here' (p. 239). In the absence of any hard evidence that these characteristics are innate, Rogers' position creates a dilemma, in that it seems to argue for a universal framework of values, while making the individual the ultimate arbiter of morality. If individuals are free to decide their values, how can he be sure that all individuals, even those who are fully functioning, will value the same things? This contradiction can also be seen in the larger issue of defining the ideal of healthy development: How can one have an objectively defined model of ideal development within a phenomenologically based approach which sees each individual as the ultimate arbiter of the nature of self? Rogers himself apparently never saw the contradiction, or at least never addressed it directly. If the actualizing tendency *is* universal, and if it *does* in fact favour certain characteristics (such as valuing immediate experience over long-term goals), then the answer may ultimately be that there *is* no contradiction in Rogers' interpretation. Alternatively, his view may represent a distortion of his own phenomenal field, whereby certain values of his culture were interpreted as being universal.

At present, no-one can really prove whether Rogers' theory fails on this point or not. What *can* be said with certainty is that his ideas have been influential both within the domain of humanistic psychology and beyond it, in fields like education and social work.

Abraham Maslow's Theory

Rogers was not alone in pioneering the humanistic approach. Others, working independently but with similar assumptions, have also shaped the development of the approach. One of the main figures in this regard was Abraham Maslow. Like Rogers, he rejected the psychoanalytic and behaviourist approaches, which he saw as ignoring the positive aspects of human life, such as creativity and love. Instead, Maslow believed that there is an internal force which directs human development towards its highest potential. In describing this motivating force, called 'self-actualization', he focused on the potential for human growth, and the characteristics of healthy individuals. While this emphasis, too, seems reminiscent of Rogers' work, Maslow's perspective differs from that of Rogers in a number of ways, as we shall see.

Abraham Maslow was born in New York in 1908, the son of Jewish immigrants. He received both his undergraduate and graduate training at the University of Wisconsin, where he studied with Harry Harlow, an eminent expert on primate behaviour, and with Clark Hull, a behaviourist theorist, among others. After receiving his doctorate in 1934, he went back to New York to teach psychology at Brooklyn College. At this point in time, New York had become a gathering place for a number of European intellectuals, many of whom were fleeing the increasing Nazi persecution in the years leading up to the Second

Abraham Maslow

Abraham Maslow (1908–1970) was born in New York in 1908, the son of Jewish immigrants. He received both his undergraduate and graduate training at the University of Wisconsin, where he studied with Harry Harlow, an eminent expert on primate behaviour, and with Clark Hull, a behaviourist theorist, among others. After receiving his doctorate in 1934, he went back to New York to teach psychology at Brooklyn College. While his graduate studies focused on primate behaviour, as time went on Maslow became more interested in human concerns, in part because of events related to the Second World War. In the late 1930s, New York had become a gathering place for a number of European intellectuals, many of whom were fleeing the Nazi rise to power. At this time he met such distinguished psychoanalysts as Alfred Adler, Karen Horney and Erich Fromm. In addition, he encountered scholars from a range of other perspectives, including Max Wertheimer, one of the pioneers of Gestalt psychology. The Second World War seemed to emphasize for him how little psychology had contributed to solving social problems, and he began to focus on social psychology and personality theory. His emphasis on real-world issues was also expressed in his interest in applying psychology to business, a domain often disdained by research-oriented psychologists. In 1951, Maslow moved to the newly established Brandeis University near Boston; as first chairperson of the psychology department, he fostered the school's growth until 1968. In 1967–68, he also served as President of the American Psychological Association, an indication of the influence of his work. He died in 1970 at the age of sixty-two.

World War. While teaching, Maslow also continued his studies at Columbia University, where he met such distinguished psychoanalysts as Alfred Adler, Karen Horney and Erich Fromm. In addition, he encountered scholars from a range of other perspectives, including Max Wertheimer, one of the pioneers of Gestalt psychology.

While his graduate studies focused on primate behaviour, as time went on Maslow became more interested in human concerns. The Second World War seemed to emphasize for him how little psychology had contributed to solving social problems, and he began to focus on social psychology and personality theory. His emphasis on real-world issues was also expressed in his interest in applying psychology to business, a domain often disdained by research-oriented psychologists. In 1951, Maslow moved to the newly established Brandeis University near Boston; as first chairperson of the psychology department, he fostered the school's growth until 1968. In 1967–68, he also served as President of the American Psychological Association, an indication of the influence of his work. He died in 1970.

Maslow's ideas evolved significantly over the course of his career. His early training under Harlow taught him the importance of scientific methodology and observation, and exposed him to the work of social anthropologists. His contacts with Wertheimer and other Gestalt psychologists, however, led him to see the importance of viewing the whole person, not just single responses. (*Toward a Psychology of Being*, his major work, was dedicated to Kurt Goldstein, a Gestalt psychologist who had coined the term 'self-actualization'.) He was also influenced heavily by psychoanalysis, both through his contacts with neo-Freudians like Fromm and Horney, and his own experience of psychoanalysis. In fact, in the early 1950s, he saw psychoanalysis as the best therapeutic approach available. However, he gradually became disenchanted with the emphasis on innate influences and past experience in the Freudian approach; by the late 1960s, he had rejected the gloomy determinism of Freud. In a well-known quote, he stated, 'To oversimplify the matter somewhat, it is as if Freud supplied to us the sick half of psychology, and we must now fill it out with the healthy half' (Maslow 1968: 5).

'The healthy half' in fact became the primary focus of Maslow's work, describing and understanding the limits of human potential. He referred to this potential in terms of *self-actualization*, the full utilization of a person's talents and capacities (self-actualization will be discussed in detail below). To Maslow, this focus on healthy people, in contrast to Freud's emphasis on pathology, was the proper subject for psychology. While he preferred to avoid doctrinaire disagreements between approaches, he commented in an interview not long before his death, 'We shouldn't have to say "humanistic psychology". The adjective should be unnecessary' (Hall 1968: 57). This was said not as a rejection of other approaches, but with the conviction that psychology must ultimately concern itself with the betterment of human life – that is, 'humanistic' as a concern with humanity. In his writings, most notably *Toward a Psychology of Being* (1968) and *Motivation and Personality* (1970), Maslow developed a theory of personality based on his ideas and experiences.

Motivation and the Hierarchy of Needs

At the core of Maslow's theory is a description of basic human needs, which he saw as influencing every aspect of our behaviour. This emphasis on motivation seems to reflect the influence of psychodynamic models on Maslow's thinking. However, unlike the two basic drives which Freud described, Maslow saw a whole constellation of needs which could influence our behaviour. Before considering these needs in a formal way, let us consider an example.

In our society, work is a central part of our lives. Every now and then, most of us entertain fantasies of receiving a monetary windfall, and quitting our job. Yet, studies show many lottery winners keep working. Why? If people buy lottery tickets to feed fantasies of quitting, why don't they quit when they win? In order to understand, Maslow would suggest we look at the person's needs. The most basic need fulfilled by working is having the money to buy food, shelter, clothing and the other necessities for survival. At the same time, working can fulfil other kinds of needs. Most people work in jobs that involve various kinds of human interaction; often, co-workers become friends. In this sense, working can satisfy social needs for contact with others; some lottery winners may continue working because they want to preserve these relationships. In addition, successful job performance (whether as a custodian or a neurosurgeon) provides feelings of competence, which can foster both self-esteem and recognition from others. Lottery winners, like many retirees, often fear the loss of meaning in their lives if they no longer have a job to perform. In some cases, a person may even *enjoy* their job – it may provide opportunities for creative challenge and self-expression (this can be as true of a salesperson or electrician

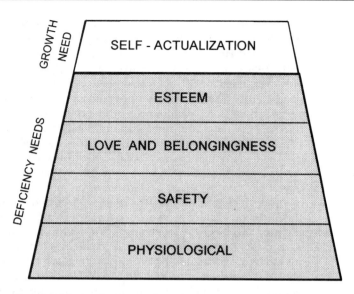

Fig. 6.2 Maslow's hierarchy of needs Maslow's theory states that more basic needs must be fulfilled before higher needs become significant; hence the pyramid, with the most basic needs at the bottom. The higher up the pyramid one goes, the more advanced the needs, and the more variable their expression. Self-actualization, unlike the other needs, is not triggered by a deficit, but is growth-oriented instead.

as an artist or writer; it is only the *form* which creativity takes which differs). If this is the case, a lottery winner may see no reason to stop an activity which gives them satisfaction. Thus, what seems a very simple situation on the surface, may in fact be very complex. Ultimately, only the individual can determine what course of action will best fulfil their needs.

Maslow recognized the complexity of motivation, and sought to describe it in terms of a **hierarchy of needs** – a hierarchical structure of different types of needs (see Fig. 6.2). The most basic needs are those which are linked to basic survival: the *physiological needs* for food, air, sleep, and so on. When these needs are unfulfilled, nothing else matters. As Maslow put it, 'It is quite true that man lives by bread alone – when there is no bread' (Maslow 1970: 38). Once these needs are fulfilled, other types of needs are experienced. The next level of needs is *safety needs*, which relate to both physical (freedom from danger) and psychological (stability, order) safety. Thus, earthquake victims will continue to feel safety needs, because of the disruption of their ordinary routine, long after the quake itself is over. Similarly, a worker who feels that their job is threatened by a corporate restructuring will experience a high safety need. However, when these needs are being met, we begin to focus on needs related to *love* and *belongingness*: giving and receiving acceptance and affection (sex would be a physiological need, but can play a role in the development of love). These needs are normally met through our interactions with family and friends; however, it requires little insight to recognize that not all family relationships are fulfilling. So, too, there are many people, especially in large cities, who often feel lonely and isolated. Dating clubs, 'personal' ads and similar phenomena are an expression

hierarchy of needs
Maslow's model of basic human needs, which he saw as organized in a hierarchical structure; needs range from physiological (most basic) to self-actualization (top of hierarchy)

of such needs. Assuming the needs for love and belongingness are fulfilled, then the individual will experience *esteem needs* – a feeling of self-respect and the sense of being competent at what one does, as well as receiving regard from others. It is interesting to note that Maslow regarded love as more basic than self-esteem; perhaps this is why individuals sometimes seem drawn into relationships which offer acceptance only at the cost of self-respect. In any event, esteem needs are secondary to love and belongingness, and consequently less likely to be satisfied.

All of the above needs reflect **deficiency motives** – that is, we are driven to satisfy them by the *absence* of the underlying requirements. In this sense, they are similar to behaviourist notions of drive motivation, and also psychodynamic concepts of motivation, both of which assume that behaviour is triggered by an underlying deficiency. However, many human activities seem to involve no intrinsic need; hobbies, for example, may have no clearly defined function other than 'having fun'. Freud attempted to deal with this problem by suggesting that drives can be satisfied in *symbolic* ways; for example, collecting stamps may reflect an anal fixation. Maslow rejected both the convoluted nature of such explanations, and also the underlying assumption that all behaviour must be based on fulfilling a deficiency. Instead, he argued for **metaneeds**, based on a *growth motive*, which he called **self-actualization**. As noted earlier, self-actualization is based on using one's capacities to their fullest. Much like Rogers' actualizing tendency, self-actualization is an expression of the potential for growth which is part of all life. Not being based on a deficiency, it can also never be fully satisfied; unlike other needs, the expression of self-actualization is a process, not a goal. It is expressed through the moment-to-moment experiences of living, of facing challenges to one's abilities, and of interacting with the world in all its diverse aspects.

As noted, the structure of needs was seen as a hierarchy, rather than as simply a collection of equally important motivational states. Maslow believed that the needs differed in several ways: the more basic the need (e.g. physiological), the more powerfully it is experienced, and the more difficult it is to suppress or ignore. For this reason, the most basic needs, like hunger, are universally experienced, whereas the higher needs (esteem, and particularly self-actualization) are less commonly experienced (see Fig. 6.2). To put it in practical terms, a person who is starving is not likely to worry about whether they are being creative. Hence, a person will only experience higher needs when the more basic ones are reasonably satisfied.

Taken in the most literal form, the notion of a hierarchy of needs seems to contradict reality; for example, it cannot explain why a parent would sacrifice their own life to save the life of their child, since physiological survival should be more potent than love. Maslow attempted to deal with such contradictions by suggesting that the hierarchy is not completely rigid: different needs may vary in intensity across individuals, and more than one need can be experienced at a given time. Normally we do not experience higher needs until more basic ones have been fulfilled; but, once experienced, the higher needs may become salient for a particular person. This qualification would account for parental sacrifice, as well as an artist who would rather live in poverty than compromise their creative aspirations by producing 'popular' art. Even so, most people will rarely, if ever, experience a strong need for self-actualization, because the

deficiency motives in Maslow's theory, needs whose motivating power is triggered by the absence of the underlying requirements, such as the physiological or esteem needs

metaneeds in Maslow's theory, need states which are based on a desire to grow rather than an underlying deficiency; expressed as the need for *self-actualization*

self-actualization for Maslow, self-actualization is the most advanced human need, and is based on the desire to grow and use one's capacities to their fullest; as such, it is process-oriented, not based on an underlying deficiency circumstances of life prevent the lower needs from ever being satisfied. Whether one considers poverty in under-developed countries, or loneliness in major cities, the complexity of our deficiency needs can be hard to satisfy. Even if the basic needs *are* satisfied, the relative weakness of the need for self-actualization can make it easy to ignore.

For further consideration

What needs are important to you at this point in your life? What category or categories do they fit? Do you perceive needs which *don't* fit within Maslow's hierarchy?

Needs and Self-development

Maslow saw understanding the nature of our needs as an important element of self-development, since the various needs can affect all aspects of our lives. For instance, deciding to make a career change can involve physiological needs ('Will I have money to live on if I don't get a new job?'), safety needs ('Will I have to move?'), belongingness ('What about my friendships at my old job?'), esteem ('Will I be recognized for my abilities?') and self-actualization ('Will this alleviate the boredom I've been feeling at work?'). Given the wide-ranging impact of our needs, it should not be surprising that they influence all aspects of our lives, including our perceptions. Maslow suggested that when deficiency needs are dominant, we tend to see the world in terms of objects that can satisfy the dominant need. Hence, a hungry person will pause before a restaurant and see only the food; a person concerned with esteem will focus on the decor and perceived status of the restaurant. In each case, perception is distorted according to the dominant need (compare this notion with Freud's view of how distortions of reality arise). By contrast, a person experiencing the need for self-actualization is likely to see the world more accurately, because objects are seen in relation to themselves, not as a means of fulfilling a deficiency.

In the same way, the frustrations we experience depend on which needs are dominant. A person with unsatisfied safety needs may complain about unsafe working conditions and a lack of job security; a person who 'has everything' (in terms of deficiency needs) may nonetheless feel unfulfilled, and see life as devoid of meaning – an expression of the self-actualization need. In fact, Maslow saw such complaints as an indication of a basically healthy state, since they imply that the deficiency needs are more or less fulfilled. Like Rogers, Maslow did not view aggression as an innate drive, but rather as a possible response to frustration of one's needs; in a healthy person living in a benign environment, aggression should not occur.

The relationship between needs and the environment is an important element in understanding the behaviour of an individual. For example, a person may be irritable and antagonistic at work, despite being well-paid and secure in their position. How are we to make sense of this? Maslow would suggest that it is only possible to understand the dynamics of this behaviour by exploring the situation thoroughly. Is the job itself boring? Are there unfulfilled aspirations at play? How do co-workers react to the person? If it turns out that significant needs are not being met in the work situation, then one could argue that the environment is at fault. However, this does not mean that the individual should passively accept the situation.

Although the environment may be the source of the problem, Maslow did not see individuals as simply victims of circumstances. Whereas the deterministic notions of the behaviourists might lead to saying 'it's not my fault' and giving up, Maslow believed an individual has a responsibility to strive for growth and self-actualization, regardless of circumstances. Self-actualization is not simply a natural unfolding, but an active process which often involves making choices and overcoming obstacles. In this sense, his views echo Carl Rogers' ideas about individual autonomy. In the case above, the individual must assess the situation carefully, to determine an appropriate course of action: Can the job conditions be changed? Should the person change jobs? Only by identifying what needs are not being met, can the person hope to find a workable solution.

One of the things which can interfere with recognizing, and therefore satisfying, one's needs is *cultural conditioning*. In our society, we are taught to focus on material sources of satisfaction which are associated primarily with physiological and safety needs. By comparison, love and esteem are seen as secondary, and personal growth has been almost completely ignored. (To the extent that esteem is acknowledged, it also tends to be addressed in material terms, i.e. 'status symbols'.) As a consequence, we have been conditioned to interpret the behaviour of others through a schema which emphasizes the lower needs. For example, employee relations are often seen by managers in very limited ways. Consider the case of an airline which several years ago was going through financial difficulties, and was seeking cooperation from the employee unions for various cutbacks. At the same time that the management was seeking employee support, they informed employees of layoffs by posting lists on company bulletin boards! Not surprisingly, the efforts to win union support for cutbacks failed, sending the airline into bankruptcy. The company president spoke of the 'greed' of the employees, while completely ignoring the issues of esteem raised by the way the layoffs were handled.

The tendency to view satisfaction of needs in material ways can be seen in other forms. For example, someone who has just been rejected by a lover may go shopping to try to ease the pain. In the same way, we tend to view a person who is well-off financially as 'having everything', but in Maslow's view this could still mean that many needs are unmet – the person may be going through a marital crisis, or suffer from low self-esteem, for example. Even if the individual's love and esteem needs are met, self-actualization may be completely lacking.

Having been raised to focus on material sources of satisfaction, which originally were associated only with the lower needs, we tend to evaluate needs in these terms, both for ourselves and in perceiving others. Unfortunately, while money can buy food and shelter, it cannot really buy love or respect, and so these needs can continue to go unsatisfied. Ironically, in emphasizing material forms of satisfaction, and successfully finding ways to fulfil them, Western society has actually made it more likely that people will satisfy material goals – only to end up asking themselves, 'Is that all there is to life?'

Self-actualization and Peak Experiences

Self-actualization is a complex need, whose nature sometimes seems hard to grasp. Kurt Goldstein, from whom Maslow borrowed the term, saw it as a drive to actualize one's capacities, found in every organism (Goldstein 1939). Unlike basic drives like hunger, which seem focused on reducing tension, Goldstein noted that self-actualization often involves *increasing* tension, as when we seek out new situations to master. Rather than representing a tranquil state of rest, self-actualization can be a painful process of struggle to grow. Despite this, we are driven to stretch ourselves, to reach new limits, whether they be physical (like an athlete) or mental (like a novelist). As Maslow said, in words that echo Goldstein, 'capacities clamor to be used' (Maslow 1968: 152).

While struggle seems to be a common circumstance in life, self-actualization is not. Indeed, Maslow estimated that only one per cent of people ever really experience the need. Yet, for those who do, it can alter profoundly the individual's perceptions of the world, and the way they relate to others. How can the rest of us understand this type of experience? One way that Maslow used was to discuss peak experiences.

Peak experiences represent moments of deep intensity in which we feel ourselves most fully alive. Such moments may occur when a parent first sees their newborn child, while viewing a great work of art, enjoying the beauty of nature, or in any of a myriad of other ways (Maslow 1964). Maslow believed that such experiences provide a glimpse of what it really means to be self-actualized. In contrast to the sense of routine and drabness that sometimes seems to pervade everyday life, peak experiences represent moments of intense joy and excitement, coupled with a sense of fully living, of being truly *part* of the world. Lovers in the first glow of romance often have this feeling, as do religious mystics; Maslow saw both as examples of peak experiences. Curiously, such moments can even come in the face of adversity, as in the aftermath of a natural disaster, or following the death of a close friend. Whatever the circumstances, peak experiences are perceived as moments of insight into the potential of life.

Peak experiences by nature are both unexpected and relatively short-lived; they seem to come and go unexpectedly, regardless of the individual's desires. While they last, they are typically very intense, clearly distinct from ordinary living. Yet these characteristics also set these experiences apart from self-actualization, which is a less intense, on-going process. Instead, peak experiences are more like a mystical rapture, reminiscent of the Zen experience of *satori*, or enlightenment. Zen practitioners may discipline themselves for years, seeking the moment of enlightenment, without any assurance about when, or even if, it will come. When it does, it is often experienced as an intense rapture, a feeling of suddenly being fully awake for the first time. Yet, like peak experiences, this feeling often fades somewhat after the initial rapture.

A more enduring form of heightened awareness occurs in what Maslow called plateau experiences. A **plateau experience** is a more enduring but less intense state of awareness than a peak experience. One of the primary characteristics of a plateau experience is a change in one's perceptions of the world. The experience produces an intensified awareness of the world, and a heightened appreciation for life (Maslow, in Krippner 1972). Maslow came to this point of view as a way of accounting for more enduring changes than those of peak experiences, but also because of his own experience. After suffering a heart attack late in life, he found himself more deeply aware of the transience of human life, and this led to a profound change in his own view of the world. Commenting on this, he once remarked, 'If I could teach a person only one thing, it would be to live

peak experience for Maslow, a transient experience of deep intensity which involves enhanced awareness, often accompanied by feelings of being 'fully alive'

plateau experience for Maslow, an experience which produces an intensified awareness of the world, and a heightened appreciation for life; a more enduring but less intense state of enhanced awareness than a peak experience each day as if it were the last day of their life'. The point, of course, is not that if we're dying, nothing matters; rather, it is that if we are about to die, how we spend our last moments matters *very much*.

The transcendence of ordinary perceptions which occurs in peak and plateau experiences is not always part of self-actualization. All three concepts emphasize the sense of living to the fullest, but some people seem to live productive, self-actualized lives without ever experiencing the shift of awareness characteristic of peak and plateau experiences. Conversely, some people seem to have peak experiences, without ever being able to integrate this insight into a process of self-actualizing. In essence, self-actualization requires an overall balance and satisfaction of lower needs, not just a sudden insight (this view obviously contradicts the idea, expressed in some books and workshops, that brief experiences can transform one's life). Hence, the transcendent awareness of peak and plateau experiences is neither a requirement, nor a defining characteristic, for self-actualization. Even so, Maslow believed that those self-actualizers who had such experiences were more likely to be creative, and to see life as magical or miraculous. At the same time, such transcendence does not preclude involvement in everyday affairs: 'You can run a grocery store and pay the bills, but still carry on this sense [of the mystical] . . .' (Maslow, in Krippner 1972: 115).

Characteristics of Self-actualized People

Self-actualization refers to making full use of one's talents and capacities (Maslow 1970). Yet, in order for such a description to be meaningful, one must have some idea of what constitutes 'full use' – that is, one must have a conception of the *goal* of growth and development. Maslow recognized this, and over time tried to describe this goal by studying the lives of individuals whom he regarded as highly self-actualized. He began with the examples of two of his own teachers, Ruth Benedict and Max Wertheimer, both of whom seemed to show high levels of fulfilment in both their professional and personal lives. Over time, he expanded the study, eventually basing his description on eighteen people, nine of whom were contemporaries and nine of whom were historical figures. Among the latter were Jane Adams, Albert Einstein, Abraham Lincoln and Eleanor Roosevelt. (It should be noted that one does not have to be famous to be self-actualized; Maslow chose historical examples in part because they would be familiar to most readers.)

Maslow's rationale for this methodology was that he was interested in the psychology of healthy people, and that outstanding individuals would provide the best possible indicator of what it means to fulfil one's potential (this is in marked contrast to Freud, who dealt primarily with pathology, and never developed a clear model of the ideal of adult development). Based on seeking common characteristics in the lives of the eighteen individuals, Maslow proposed a list of characteristics of self-actualized people (see Fig. 6.3). The list is rather daunting, and is apt to make one question whether *any* person could meet such standards. However, in proposing this description, Maslow was offering an ideal, which no individual would fully achieve – each would show some characteristics more strongly than others. Indeed, in describing these characteristics, Maslow commented, 'There are no perfect human beings! Persons can be found who are

CHARACTERISTICS OF SELF-ACTUALIZED PEOPLE

1) More efficient perception of reality

2) Acceptance (of self, others and world)

3) Spontaneity and naturalness

4) Problem-centred rather than ego-centred

5) Need for privacy and being detached from situations

6) Independence from both cultural and environmental influences

7) Freshness of appreciation of all experience

8) Having mystical or peak experiences

9) Feelings of kinship to others

10) Deep relationships with others

11) Democratic attitudes

12) Distinguishing between means and ends, good and evil

13) Philosophical, not hostile, sense of humour

14) Self-actualizing forms of creativity

15) Forming attitudes and values independently of culture

Fig. 6.3 Characteristics of self-actualized individuals Like Rogers, Maslow believed that healthy individuals would come to show certain characteristics. This list is based on his study of a group of famous individuals (see text for details) (adapted from Maslow 1970). Compare this list with Fig. 6.1.

good, very good indeed, in fact, great . . . And yet these very same people can at times be boring, irritating, petulant, selfish, angry, or depressed'. For example, Oskar Schindler, the subject of a popular book and movie, sacrificed his considerable wealth to save the lives of over a thousand Jews during the Second World War – yet he was also a womanizer and con-artist (Keneally 1982).

While suggesting that these characteristics represent a sort of ideal for human growth, Maslow also noted that an ideal is a static concept, and self-actualization is itself not a static thing. Rather than being an *end*, a fixed goal which one can reach, Maslow emphasized that in fact self-actualization is a *process*, for which there is never an end. Like a journey, our lives can encompass detours and even moving backwards; what matters is what we do along the way, not the destination. Seen in this way, it is understandable that no one person will show all of these characteristics all of the time.

Nonetheless, the attempt to define the ideal of human development has drawn many criticisms. One obvious concern is that in selecting individuals for his sample, Maslow was selecting those who exhibited the traits he hoped to find, and that therefore the process was both biased and circular. Maslow himself claimed to be surprised at the similarities he found, but one cannot rule out unconscious bias. Even without assuming such bias, there are concerns. Maslow wished to believe that the named characteristics, and the values associated with them, somehow stem from the very essence of human nature: 'Some values are common to all [healthy] mankind' (Maslow 1970: 150). Yet, he also recognized that individuals differ in many ways, which could affect their actions and values: 'To the extent that capacities differ, so will values also differ' (Maslow 1970: 152). Hence, he was caught in the conundrum of arguing for a universal ideal, while simultaneously acknowledging that great variability exists among individuals.

This is not a trivial issue, and it is one which all the humanistic theories encounter in one form or another (Rogers, for example, faces the same difficulties in describing the fully functioning person). For example, Maslow proposes that *resistance to cultural influences* is one of the characteristics of self-actualized persons. Thus, Oskar Schindler, by not accepting the Nazi view of Jews, was showing a form of self-actualization. But if acceptance by the majority (i.e. the overall culture) is not a requirement, then what makes *any* characteristic an indicator of self-actualization? Could it not be argued that self-actualization is whatever each person thinks it is? And if this is the case, then is Maslow's definition anything more than a reflection of his own values? Obviously, this line of reasoning poses a problem for Maslow's views, and he tries to avoid this conclusion by pointing to cross-cultural commonalities for certain characteristics and values; at best, however, this evidence is incomplete. As one critic put it, 'The question of just what is "natural" to man is, of course, the most vexed in the history of thought, and cannot be settled even by something as lofty as "the universal experience of clinicians"' (Robinson 1979: 257). At the same time, it is striking that Rogers and others have argued independently for similar values and characteristics as those advocated by Maslow; whether this is truly an expression of 'human nature', or simply a consensus of like-minded people, is still unclear.

In the end, Maslow's ideas have proved influential more because of their capacity to inspire than for their empirical foundation. If one compares his work to that of Carl Rogers, one finds that Rogers has made a more concerted effort to validate his ideas through research. This is somewhat ironic, since Maslow began as an experimental psychologist, while Rogers began as a divinity student! Maslow also poses a contradiction when compared to psychodynamic theorists. While he rejected the pessimism and determinism of Freud, his own theory, like Freud's, rests on a foundation of analysing fundamental human needs. In one sense, he incorporated and extended the psychodynamic approach:

Freud's id would represent physiological needs, Horney's work would focus on safety and love, while Adler emphasized esteem needs. To this structure, Maslow then added self-actualization. In doing so, he clearly made a shift from pathology to growth, as he intended. However, to reach the level of self-actualization, one must satisfy the lower needs, and clearly there are echoes of the psychodynamic approach in the lower needs of his hierarchy.

In one sense, the similarities between Maslow's theory and the psychodynamic approach should not really surprise us; while each approach to psychology has its own perspective, the subject matter – human behaviour – is common to all. Consequently, some convergence of descriptions would seem inevitable. At the same time, the distinctive elements of Maslow's work – the hierarchical conception of motivation, the emphasis on self-actualization – place it clearly within the humanistic approach. In domains as disparate as personality theory and diplomacy, Maslow's ideas live on.

For further consideration

Do you know anyone personally whom you would consider highly self-actualized? What leads you to think so? Do their values seem consistent with Maslow's description?

Extending the Humanistic Approach

As noted at the beginning of this chapter, the humanistic approach has no single theoretical founder. Instead, it encompasses a number of theorists, of whom Rogers and Maslow are simply the best known. Within the approach, each theorist uses a somewhat different vocabulary, and tends to emphasize slightly different concepts and issues. What lends coherence to the approach is the set of basic *assumptions* which the various theories make, notably the rejection of determinism and the emphasis on a phenomenological approach to understanding behaviour (i.e. based on subjective experience). In order to better understand this unity-within-diversity, we will briefly consider two other viewpoints which fit within the humanistic approach: *Frankl's logotherapy*, and a more amorphous framework which is often referred to as *the recovery movement*.

Frankl's Logotherapy

Viktor Frankl was born in Vienna in 1905, the son of Orthodox Jewish parents. He was educated at the University of Vienna, where he distinguished himself by earning doctorates in both philosophy and medicine. In medical school, he initially trained in neurology, but found himself drawn to concerns about mental illnesses. In this sense, his training mirrored an earlier Viennese physician – Sigmund Freud. While exposed to Freud's ideas during his early training, he gradually evolved his own framework, which rejected many of the assumptions of Freudian analysis. Like Freud, he faced a threat from the rise to power of the Nazis, and in fact was granted a visa to go to the United States shortly before the USA entered the Second World War. However, since his parents were still

Viktor Frankl

Viktor Frankl (1905–   ) was born in Vienna in 1905, the son of Orthodox Jewish parents. He was educated at the University of Vienna, where he distinguished himself by earning doctorates in both philosophy and medicine. In medical school, he initially trained in neurology, but found himself drawn to concerns about mental illnesses. In this sense, his training mirrored an earlier Viennese physician – Sigmund Freud. While exposed to Freud's ideas during his early training, he gradually evolved his own framework, which rejected many of the assumptions of Freudian analysis. Like Freud, he faced a threat from the rise to power of the Nazis, and in fact was granted a visa to go to the United States shortly before the USA entered the Second World War. However, since his parents were still living in Vienna, and unable to emigrate with him, he chose to stay instead. Consequently, he was imprisoned after the Nazi takeover of Austria, and spent three years struggling to survive in various concentration camps (primarily the notorious camps at Auschwitz and Dachau) until the end of the war. Only one person in twenty-eight survived in the camps, and the experience was to play a significant role in Frankl's later theorizing. After the war, he became a professor of neurology and psychiatry at the University of Vienna, where he has continued as a teacher and therapist.

logotherapy Viktor Frankl's theory of development and therapy, which is based on the argument that finding a meaning for life is central to individual growth and happiness

living in Vienna, and unable to emigrate with him, he chose to stay instead. Consequently, he was imprisoned after the Nazi takeover of Austria, and spent three years struggling to survive in various concentration camps (primarily the notorious camps at Auschwitz and Dachau), until the end of the war. Only one person in twenty-eight survived in the camps, and the experience was to play a significant role in Frankl's later theorizing. After the war, he became a professor of neurology and psychiatry at the University of Vienna, where he has continued as a teacher and therapist.

Frankl is probably best known for his book *Man's Search for Meaning* (1992). Originally, he intended to publish it as an anonymous memoir of his experiences in the concentration camps, but ultimately decided it required a personal framework to be meaningful. Even so, it was not initially meant as a full exposition of his theoretical ideas (its original English title was *From Death-camp to Existentialism*). However, the book proved remarkably popular, and over four editions, the theoretical background, which he refers to as **logotherapy**, was gradually expanded.

To understand Frankl's theory, and how it fits into the humanistic approach, let us consider his view of some of the basic assumptions. Like Rogers, Frankl argues against the determinism found in both behaviourism and psychoanalysis: 'Man is *not* fully conditioned and determined but rather determines himself' (Frankl 1992: 133). While he grants that there are conditions which limit this freedom, the real issue 'is not freedom from conditions, but it is freedom to take a stand toward these conditions' (p. 132). Even in the concentration camps, individuals could 'choose one's attitude in a given set of circumstances' (p. 9). In this sense, Frankl's views are similar to other humanistic theorists.

A second assumption concerns the value of a *phenomenological framework* in understanding behaviour. At the very outset, he distinguishes between 'facts' and 'experiences'. Facts are objective observations, devoid of subjective context and meaning, while experiences are descriptions which are anchored in an individual's perspective – that is, subjective meaning. While he acknowledges that psychology as a science has traditionally emphasized detached objectivity, he suggests that in trying to understand experiences like those of concentration camp survivors, a detached observer 'is too far removed to make any statements of real value' (Frankl 1992: 20). The meaning of human experience can only be determined by the individual having the experience; like Rogers, Frankl sees the understanding of meaning as central to understanding behaviour. Thus, his framework is essentially phenomenological.

As the early title of his book (*From Death-camp to Existentialism*) suggests, Frankl's views are also heavily existential. Like Jean-Paul Sartre (1948) and other existentialists, he sees the basic issue of life as the challenge of finding meaning in a world which often seems meaningless. For Frankl meaning, however, is not an abstract philosophical issue, nor is it based on some universal principle. Rather, meaning is viewed as a personal outcome, which is related both to the immediate context of one's experiences, and the attitudes one takes towards those experiences. That is, rather than there being a general meaning to life, there is only 'the specific meaning of a person's life at a given moment' (Frankl 1992: 113). In this sense, Frankl emphasizes the need to focus on the here-and-now of experience (in contrast to psychoanalysis, which tends to emphasize the person's past). While meaning may refer to future possibilities, it can only be derived from the present moment. Like life itself meaning is changing and transient. (Such a view, as discussed earlier, is a familiar feature of humanistic theories.)

Apart from these assumptions, largely shared with other humanistic theories, logotherapy has its own specific structure and concepts. Not surprisingly, Frankl places issues of meaning at the centre of his theory. Whereas Freud saw concerns about meaning as being a rationalization of instinctual drives, Frankl argues that 'striving to find a meaning in one's life is the primary motivational force in man' (Frankl 1992: 104). In emphasizing the motivational role of meaning, Frankl rejects drive-reduction as being the goal of motivation (as Freud believed). In fact, he suggests that 'mental health is based on a certain degree of tension . . . between what one is and what one should become' (p. 110). This view also places him in seeming contradiction to Rogers, who suggests optimal functioning occurs when there is congruence (i.e. no conflict) between the self and the ideal self. The open-ended nature of the search for meaning is more like Maslow's conception of self-actualization (which, like Frankl's view of motivation, is not based on tension reduction). However, he sees self-actualization as a 'side-effect' of seeking meaning, 'not an attainable end' in itself (p. 115).

noögenic neuroses in Frankl's theory, conflicts within an individual which are based on existential frustrations, rather than the conflicts of id, ego and superego which Freud saw as the source of anxiety

Meaning or its absence has profound effects on a person's life, in Frankl's view. In fact, issues of meaning produce what he calls **noögenic neuroses**, conflicts based on existential frustrations (rather than the issues of anxiety which underlie traditional neuroses). Frankl believes that such problems are more common than anxiety neuroses, and criticizes psychodynamic theories for ignoring issues of meaning. In one case, he encountered a diplomat who had been through an extended period of therapy, and had been told that his concern about his work reflected unresolved feelings about his father. After only a few sessions with Frankl, the man recognized that his problem was really a dislike for his current career. As a result, he decided to change careers, and five years later had shown no recurrence of his former problems (Frankl 1992: 107).

While existential concerns are not themselves pathological, they can *result in* pathology, and Frankl cites examples ranging from aggression to alcoholism. The interaction is seen most clearly in cases of depression (Frankl 1992). At one point, Frankl was working with unemployed individuals (in the economic downturn of the 1930s) who suffered from depression. While he could do nothing to change the economic conditions, Frankl found that those patients who began doing volunteer work for community groups also showed mood improvement. Unemployed individuals, he suggests, may be given social assistance to acquire food and shelter, but this is not the real issue: 'people have enough to live by but nothing to live for' (Frankl 1992: 142). (Unfortunately, like most clinical studies, this result is correlational, and consequently one cannot be certain the volunteer work was the cause of improvement; it may be that only the healthier patients were willing to volunteer, or the result could be coincidental.)

Frankl's view of the interactions between an individual and their surroundings is also different from other humanistic theorists. Ultimately, life has meaning only in terms of the way we relate to others: 'being human always points, and is directed, to something, or someone, other than oneself . . . The more one forgets himself . . . the more human he is and the more he actualizes himself' (Frankl 1992: 115). Yet, at the same time, the circumstances of living can be the source of concerns about meaning. This is clearly evident in the case of those living in the concentration camps, but Frankl also suggests that cultural beliefs can influence the search for meaning in less obvious ways. He is very critical of modern Western culture, suggesting that its belief in determinism (both in science and therapy) has encouraged a feeling that life has no meaning: 'Existential vacuum is the collective neurosis of the present time' (p. 131). In this sense, he goes beyond Rogers' view (which emphasizes how conditional regard given by others affects growth), suggesting that the factors which distort development can be *cultural* rather than individual.

One of the most interesting differences in Frankl's theory is his position on the nature of human values. As has been discussed, both Rogers and Maslow argue that certain types of values are intrinsic to any healthy human being. By contrast, Frankl resists any such notion. Instead of advocating particular values, he argues that part of finding meaning in one's life is based on making choices about what matters in life:

> Logotherapy tries to make the patient fully aware of his own responsibleness; therefore, it must leave to him the option for what, to what, or to whom he understands himself to be responsible. That is why a logotherapist is the least tempted of all psychotherapists to impose value judgements on his patients.
>
> (Frankl 1992: 114)

Rather than imposing values or other beliefs, the therapist's role is seen as helping the individual to discover their own values; in some sense, the *process* (though clearly not the concepts used) seems very much like Rogers' notion of providing the appropriate conditions for growth. The person must discover the truth for themselves, but the therapist can help, much the way an ophthalmologist 'tries to enable us to see the world as it really is . . . so that the whole spectrum of potential meaning becomes conscious and visible' (Frankl 1992: 114–15).

It is possible that Frankl's unwillingness to assert particular values is a reaction to his experiences in the concentration camps; after all, could anyone who lived through such horrors really believe that all people are fundamentally good? Even to survive required suspending conventional notions of morality: when selections were made of those who were to be killed next, 'All that mattered was that one's own name and that of one's friend were crossed off the list of victims, though everyone knew that for each man saved another victim had to be found' (Frankl 1992: 18). In such circumstances, it seems hard to claim the high ground of moral superiority; indeed, many survivors were haunted by the implications of having survived. Frankl alludes to this when he says, 'We who have come back . . . we know: the best of us did not return' (p. 19).

Although Frankl does not argue for a particular meaning to life or a particular set of values, he *does* suggest three ways in which meaning can be *discovered* in life: (1) by achievement; (2) by a transcendent experience (e.g. love or an appreciation of nature); or (3) by the attitude one takes to unavoidable suffering (e.g. a concentration camp prisoner, or someone facing a terminal illness). The first is fairly straightforward: Frankl himself found the will to live when he was in the concentration camps by focusing on his desire to complete a book about his ideas. The idea of transcendent experiences, like the desire to achieve, seems very reminiscent of Maslow's concept of self-actualization. While Frankl suggests self-actualization should not be the *goal*, the *process* of finding meaning seems to lead in the same direction.

For most people, it is likely that the notion of finding meaning through suffering seems rather strange. As Frankl notes, our culture seems to emphasize pleasure-seeking and the avoidance of suffering. While this fits well with drive-reduction notions of motivation, it has the consequence of encouraging denial of unpleasant realities, and even makes the experience of suffering degrading. However, there are clearly individuals who face death – such as terminal cancer or AIDS patients – with grace and calm; for Frankl, their attitude bears witness to 'the uniquely human potential . . . when we are no longer able to change a situation . . . to change ourselves' (Frankl 1992: 116). In his view, 'life has a meaning up to the last moment' (p. 118).

Like other existential thinkers, Frankl's ideas are grounded in some of the harshest realities of life – suffering, death and the apparent pointlessness of some events. In this sense, his theory strikes a very different emotional tone than the sometimes Pollyanna-like optimism of Rogers and Maslow, who talk of 'unconditional regard' and 'peak experiences'. Consequently, it is all the more interesting that his thinking leads to a similar result – that life is worth living, and we have both the freedom and the responsibility to determine our own actions and their meaning. In the end, Frankl, too, is optimistic – and if *he* can be, should we not, too?

The Recovery Movement

The **recovery movement** is a term used to refer to a variety of approaches which share certain similarities in concepts and assumptions. It traces its origins

recovery movement a term used to refer to a variety of humanistically oriented theories and therapies which share certain similarities in concepts and assumptions; its origins are often traced to the Twelve Step programme of Alcoholics Anonymous back to the formation of Alcoholics Anonymous in 1935. Alcoholics Anonymous (AA) is a programme for the treatment of alcoholism which was founded by Dr Robert Smith and Bill Wilson. Over the years, it has grown rapidly, so that by 1990, the organization claimed to have over 93,000 local groups, comprising over 2 million members, spread across 131 countries.

Wilson, an alcoholic who had previously been unsuccessful in dealing with his drinking problem, developed an approach which combined self-help with social support, based on the notion that alcoholism is both a disease and a spiritual problem. Its philosophy is expressed in the *twelve steps to recovery*, which begins with acknowledging that the individual is powerless over their problem (step 1), seeking help from a Higher Power (step 2), and ends with trying to both practise the principles of the twelve steps, and to bring the message to others (step 12).

While no available treatment for alcoholism (or any other form of addiction) has a 100 per cent success rate, AA's approach has claimed many successes, and has certainly proven very popular. Its philosophy of emphasizing the possibility of personal renewal, bolstered by both social and spiritual supports, has been adapted by a variety of groups, from Overeaters Anonymous to Gamblers Anonymous. While many such groups have no formal connection with AA, the original group did lead to the creation of groups to support families of alcoholics, notably Al-Anon. It is the concerns of such individuals which have become a major focus of the recovery movement.

According to the general view, a child growing up with an alcoholic parent will suffer a variety of developmental traumas. The most significant of these is a sense of self-blame for the problems of the parent. As a result, the child experiences very low self-worth, and a personality which is based on a strong sense of shame. Any successes in life are seen as flukes, unrelated to sense of self, while failures are seen as reaffirming the sense of low self-worth. Initially, attention was focused on the idea that these characteristics were particular to the children of alcoholics, since the pattern was frequently found in such individuals (Cermak 1985; Borysenko 1990). In particular, it has been suggested that the very low sense of self-esteem leads to forming relationships (often with addicts of some sort) which are based on co-dependency. In **co-dependency**, individuals form relationships in which one surrenders one's self-esteem to the partner's control (Cermak 1985). Since neither individual can act out of a positive sense of self, what results is a pathological interaction of two dependent individuals.

Concern over self-worth is, of course, a central theme of both Rogers and Maslow. However, the underlying model of the recovery movement is different in significant ways from either theory. Central to the recovery approach is the belief that each person, no matter how traumatized, retains a hidden core which can be the basis of growth. This hidden core is often referred to as the **inner child**: 'The inner child is both a developmental actuality and a symbolic possibility' (Abrams 1990: 1). The inner child represents the full potential of the individual to grow and be creative; in this sense, it is the source of what Rogers called the actualizing tendency. However, it is seen as having a phenomenological reality, such that as adults we can *re-experience* the feelings and desires of childhood; in this sense, it is somewhat like Berne's Child ego state (see Chapter 5). In its symbolic sense, the inner child is also a form of archetype, as described by Carl Jung (1958). Although the inner child is freely expressed at birth, over

co-dependency in the recovery movement, a pattern of behaviour triggered by low self-esteem, such that individuals form relationships in which one's sense of self-esteem is dependent on one's partner

inner child in the recovery movement, a term referring both to the phenomenological re-experiencing of the feelings and desires of childhood, and also the symbolic representation of the full potential of the individual to grow and be creative time, experiences (both normal socialization and pathological traumas) lead to the individual adopting attitudes and behaviour which no longer reflect the natural tendencies of the inner child. (One can easily draw a parallel to the gap between self and ideal self found in Rogers' concept of incongruence.)

The most serious problems are those pathological traumas which lead to feelings of **shame**, a perceived loss of self-esteem associated with some action. John Bradshaw, a counsellor and well-known advocate of the recovery movement (himself an alcoholic), has suggested that feelings of shame, when applied to one's whole being rather than specific actions, destroy any sense of self-worth. Such reactions, which he calls **toxic shame**, are seen as the fundamental problem, not just for children of alcoholics, but for everyone grappling to reach their full potential (Bradshaw 1988). In effect, what conditional positive regard is to Rogers' theory, shame is to the recovery movement – that is, it represents the primary source of distortions in development.

Interestingly, shame has been a relatively recent concern in the study of behaviour. Freud, for example, largely ignored it in preference to its close cousin, guilt. Later psychodynamic theorists like Adler and Horney used shame-related concepts like inferiority, but shame never became a central concept. In other cultures (such as Japan), shame is openly recognized as a factor in behaviour, but in the last 50 years it has been largely absent as an acknowledged concern in our culture. In part, this probably reflected Freud's influence, and in part the seemingly vague nature of shame (many circumstances seem to elicit it), and its close connection with guilt.

Robert Karen has described **guilt** as a response to behaviour which we recognize as harming others. For example, if a child steals money from a parent's wallet, guilt is likely to arise. In such cases, it is the behaviour which is seen as improper. In *shame*, the emotion is directed at one's sense of self – 'it's not my *behaviour* that's bad, I am bad' (Karen 1992). Obviously, both guilt and shame have a role to play in shaping ordinary social behaviour. Without guilt, there is no concern over morality; shame often accompanies guilt, and thereby reinforces the negative significance of the action, but it can arise whenever when one feels outside the circle of social acceptance. Giving a wrong answer in school can evoke shame; so can being in public with a friend who acts badly. Shame, with its averted eyes and submissive posture, appears to be based on an instinctive reaction; instead of blood flowing to the muscles, as in fear, it rushes to the skin, producing the characteristic blush of shame (Borysenko 1990). Bradshaw argues that the basic response of shame is present in infancy, while guilt develops only around the age of four, as moral concepts are acquired (Bradshaw 1988).

Both guilt and shame can also be pathological, however. Pathological guilt arises when one feels responsible for harmful acts one never committed (Karen 1992). Freud saw such guilt as playing an important role in various forms of pathology, including depression. By contrast, pathological shame (equivalent to Bradshaw's toxic shame) arises when one internalizes feelings of being worthless. While one can make amends for harmful acts (the basis of guilt), how can one make amends for feeling worthless?

Dealing with the enormous deficit of self-esteem which such shame creates is not easy. Rogers believed that when the outward conditions for growth are met, congruence will follow, but this assumes the individual believes it is possible to feel self-worth. Alcoholics who have 'hit bottom', and others who feel

shame a negative feeling evoked by a perceived loss of self-esteem associated with a particular behaviour
toxic shame in the recovery movement, feelings of shame which are applied to one's whole being rather than specific actions, resulting in severe loss of self-worth

guilt in the recovery movement, a feeling of negative worth in response to behaviour which we recognize as harming others; for Freud, guilt is a form of anxiety associated with behaviours which violate the standards of the superego completely worthless, may simply perceive unconditional positive regard as undeserved. For example, John meets Mary, and she seems attracted to him. Instead of regarding this as evidence of his own worth, John assumes she either doesn't yet see his 'obvious' shortcomings, or else she does, but her feelings are pity, not love. When shame comes to permeate the individual's perceptions, no outward event can prove their worth. Indeed, defending against outward events that might elicit shame simultaneously leads to blocking any awareness of one's true self. As Bradshaw puts it, 'A shame-based person will guard against exposing his inner self to others, but more significantly, he will guard against exposing himself to himself' (Bradshaw 1988: 10). Without any self-awareness, changing the evaluation of the self seems impossible, or at least very unlikely.

This conundrum is perhaps related to the emphasis on personal transcendence in the recovery movement: it is not me (the adult) that must change, it is me as I once was (the inner child) that must be released or healed (Bradshaw 1988; Borysenko 1990). In Alcoholics Anonymous, a similar attitude is expressed through the focus on a Higher Power, a spiritual domain which extends beyond the self. By shifting the focus away from the self as immediately experienced (by definition, a self which is worthless), the intention is to allow the individual to re-experience the positive aspects of living, and open the door to healing and growth. As Jeremiah Abrams, a Jungian therapist who is part of the recovery movement, has put it, 'The child, by whatever means we achieve contact with it, is the key to our achieving fullest expression as individuals' (Abrams 1990: 2).

In summary, the recovery movement focuses on the role of *shame* as a factor which thwarts individual development by destroying the sense of *self-worth*. This process is seen as the cause of various behavioural problems, including addictions like alcoholism. By contrast, the path to growth, and to healthy development, involves making contact with the *inner child*, a concept which refers to both our earliest experiences and the symbolic expression of human potential.

Assessing the Recovery Movement

When one compares these ideas with those of the other humanists, it is not difficult to draw parallels, as has been noted already. However, this in itself tells us little about the relative validity of the different theories. After all, differences also exist, for example the emphasis on a spiritual component seen both in AA and in many accounts of the recovery movement (Abrams 1990; Borysenko 1990). Ideally, we would like to determine which model provides the most accurate understanding of behaviour. However, making such judgements is never easy, and comparison is particularly difficult among humanistic theories, because of the phenomenological nature of the evidence used. However, there are some issues which seem unique to the recovery movement.

One concern is the diverse backgrounds of advocates of the recovery movement, ranging from Jungian analysts (like Abrams) to mainstream psychologists (like Borysenko) to lay counsellors (like Bradshaw). Given this diversity, it is hard to be sure that all are applying comparable standards to the task of formulating and evaluating theoretical ideas; without some methodological consistency, the problems of subjectivity become even larger.

This brings us to another concern. The recovery movement has become very popular in the past few years, and major figures like Bradshaw earn large sums for appearances and books aimed at a popular audience. Given the financial attractions of such popularity, and the diverse backgrounds of recovery movement advocates, one must allow the possibility that some may have questionable credentials. This concern is heightened when one encounters claims which seem to have little foundation in reality. For example, Charles Whitfield, a medical doctor who deals with issues of the inner child, argues that *80–95 per cent* of all children grow up in dysfunctional families, resulting in shame-based personalities (Borysenko 1990: 44). Such a claim seems either highly exaggerated, or else based on a definition of 'dysfunction' which is so broad as to be meaningless.

At the same time, no theory should be judged simply by its weaknesses. In some aspects, the ideas of the recovery movement seem on solid ground. For example, suggesting that individual development is strongly influenced by the family is a concept endorsed by most theorists, from Freud to Skinner. Beyond that, the recovery movement tends to address the relationship of the individual to society in a way that most psychological theories don't. In broad terms, it suggests that cultural pressures can work to undercut self-esteem, and that most individuals are unable to resist those pressures. Robert Karen, a therapist who has studied the new interest in shame, believes that culture plays a role in the expression of shame-related pathology (Karen 1992). If this is true, then what cultural changes underlie the recent prominence of shame? The answer suggested by the recovery movement is that our society no longer offers individuals a point of orientation, and that individuals find it difficult to develop a sense of self-worth in isolation from some larger reference. Hence, the recovery movement emphasizes a sense of connectedness not just to the inner child, but to something beyond the individual, which it argues is best expressed as the spiritual. Bill Wilson, the founder of Alcoholics Anonymous, felt it was necessary to acknowledge a Higher Power, however defined, in order to heal oneself. Psychologist Joan Borysenko has supported that concept in her own approach to therapy and development (Borysenko 1990). While it is not clear that this explanation is correct, there is little doubt that ours is an increasingly secular society. It remains to be seen if the interpretations of the recovery movement, on this point and others, are vindicated in the longer run.

For further consideration

When was the last time you felt ashamed? How does it compare to Rogers' concept of incongruence? Are the two terms different labels for the same experience?

Conclusion

The humanistic approach encompasses a number of theorists and theories, all of which (as the name implies) seek to understand behaviour in human terms – that is, as it is experienced by the individual. Behaviour itself is only one aspect of human experience, and the humanists believe one can only understand human experience in terms of the meaning an individual gives to it. This emphasis on subjective experience, often referred to as a *phenomenological* viewpoint, distinguishes the humanistic approach from all the other approaches to psychology, which seek to eliminate subjectivity by emphasizing objective observation. However, humanists like Carl Rogers suggest the distinction is more apparent than real, and question whether it is possible for *any* observations by humans to be free of subjectivity.

Evaluating the humanistic approach by traditional scientific criteria is difficult, because of its phenomenological emphasis. The sources of evidence used to support the theories are almost entirely *correlational* (case histories and interviews), which (unlike experiments) do not produce *falsifiable* predictions. While humanistic theorists would argue that prediction is ultimately irrelevant to understanding behaviour, without it evaluation of a theory becomes very difficult. What one is left with is basically two principles: *plausibility* ('does it make sense?') and *utility* ('is it useful?'). Unfortunately, both criteria can be very personal. What 'makes sense' may depend on one's prior experience, and what is 'useful' can depend on one's purposes. For example, many beginning students of psychology prefer the humanistic approach; its optimistic tone and use of subjective experience can be more appealing than the complex concepts of other approaches. Does this mean humanistic theories are better as an explanation of behaviour? For a scientist, plausibility and utility must relate to *accuracy* (how well does the model fit reality), yet when dependent on subjective judgements, this is hard to determine. Only when individual preferences are reflected in a common consensus do scientists trust personal judgements. On this basis, there is some ground for supporting humanistic theories; for example, one can see many points of agreement between Rogers and Maslow. However, when differences exist between theories, it becomes hard to determine which theory (if any) is actually correct.

In the end, judgements about the value of a given set of concepts involve very broad issues: What aspects of behaviour and experience does one wish to emphasize? How can one describe and/or categorize what one observes? And how can one evaluate the accuracy of the resulting view of human behaviour? All psychological theories (not just humanistic ones) face these questions; the only real difference is in how the humanists evaluate accuracy.

Within the humanistic approach, there are several areas that require further consideration. For example, how are *values* related to defining human development? Both Rogers and Maslow suggest there is a common set of values for healthy individuals, yet Frankl rejects this view. Even if one supports the notion of innate values, identifying what they are is not easy; as Robinson (1979) has pointed out, such formulations tend to be either circular or self-contradictory. Hence, this question deserves further consideration.

A second problem concerns the relationship between self-esteem and healthy development. In different ways, Rogers, Maslow and the recovery movement all suggest a connection, but the details differ in each case. Is shame a neglected concept, or an oversold catchphrase? For that matter, how do shifting cultural patterns relate to changing concepts of behaviour? Viktor Frankl has commented that 'every age has its own collective neurosis, and every age needs its own psychotherapy to cope with it' (Frankl 1992: 131). Further, he suggested that the increase in secularism in our society has changed the accepted source of help: 'Some of the people who nowadays call on a psychiatrist would have seen a pastor, priest or rabbi in former days' (p. 119). The notion that attitudes and expectations have changed has been echoed by Perry London, a clinical psychologist. London (1974) has remarked that to Freud a patient was someone who felt bad (i.e. suffered from an obvious problem), while for the humanists it is sufficient that a person doesn't feel good (i.e. is not reaching their full potential). Whether this reflects refinements in our understanding, or simply a cultural shift, is not clear. It is impossible to discuss fully the relationship of theory to culture at this point (although the issue will recur in Chapter 10), but it would seem that humanistic theories, with their emphasis on subjective experience, are particularly likely to be influenced by culture.

Both by its assumptions and the content of its theories, the humanistic approach has enlarged psychology's domain. By emphasizing the importance of meaning in the lives of individuals, it has challenged other approaches to provide their own answers to such questions. Our capacity to be self-aware, to reflect on our own existence, and even to imagine its ending, is as much a part of human life as our capacity to learn or to feel emotion. The answers given by current humanistic theories may be incomplete or even inaccurate, but until the role of meaning in human experience is understood, psychology must not shrink from exploring the issue.

Chapter Summary

◆ The *humanistic approach* is characterized by two basic assumptions which distinguish both its methodology and its theories from other approaches: the focus on subjective experience (*phenomenological* viewpoint) and a rejection of *determinism* in favour of individual *choice*. Among the humanistic theorists, the ideas of *Carl Rogers* and *Abraham Maslow* are certainly the best known.

◆ Rogers developed a model which focuses on the relationship between what we feel we are (the *self*) and what we feel we should be (the *ideal self*). When the two are experienced as being similar, the individual is *congruent* or *fully functioning* – the goal of development. When a gap exists between the self and the ideal self, the person will experience this as *incongruence*.

◆ Being congruent depends on encountering people who provide the *conditions for growth: empathy, openness* and *unconditional positive regard*. Incongruence results from other people setting up *conditions for worth*, expressed through *conditional positive regard*.

◆ Like other humanistic theorists, Rogers was optimistic about human growth. In describing the potential of human development, he described the characteristics of *fully functioning individuals*, including the *values* which he felt such individuals were likely to hold. His ideas have been very influential in counselling and therapy, where his theory forms the basis of *client-centred therapy*.

◆ Abraham Maslow attempted to understand behaviour in terms of the needs which motivate an individual. The recognition that not all needs are alike led him to formulate his *hierarchy of needs*, which ranged from basic *safety needs* to the creative desires represented in *self-actualization*.

◆ Unlike other needs, self-actualization is based on the desire to grow, not on some form of deficit. Maslow believed that individuals can experience self-actualization during peak. Like Rogers, Maslow tried to describe the nature of optimal human growth; to do so, he used historical examples of *self-actualized individuals* (both men and women).

◆ While Rogers and Maslow are the best-known humanists, the approach can also include *existential theories* like that of *Viktor Frankl*. Frankl argues that issues of *meaning* are central to all human experience. Unlike Rogers and Maslow, he rejects the view that particular values are necessary for human growth.

◆ The *recovery movement*, while often not labelled as explicitly humanistic, nonetheless shares many of the same basic assumptions about human behaviour.

◆ Individuals who develop a *shame-based personality*, characterized by low self-worth, lose touch with the *inner child*, which represents both early experiences and the symbolic potential of human development. Because society often fails to provide individuals with social support; the solution is for the individual to seek support in spiritual terms.

◆ Among the approaches, the humanistic approach is unique in emphasizing questions like the role of meaning and spirituality in human life. It remains a challenge to find ways to evaluate effectively the differences among theories and the approach itself.

Key Terms and Concepts

actualizing tendency
client-centred therapy
co-dependency
conditional positive regard
conditions for growth
conditions of worth
congruence
deficiency motives
fully functioning person
hierarchy of needs
ideal self

incongruence
inner child
intersubjective verification
logotherapy
peak experience
phenomenological
self
self-actualization
unconditional positive regard
would–should dilemma

Suggestions for Further Reading

Rogers wrote a number of books on different aspects of his work, but perhaps the best for a reader seeking a general overview is *Freedom to Learn*, which discusses his ideas of personal growth in the context of education.

Maslow's best-known book, *Toward a Psychology of Being*, is also one of his best in terms of conveying an overall view of his ideas.

For the reader interested in Viktor Frankl's ideas, *Man's Search for Meaning* is the primary source.

The recovery movement has been the subject of a large number of books in recent years, of varying quality. For a general sampling of related ideas, the edited collection by Jeremiah Abrams, called *Reclaiming the Inner Child*, is a good choice. For a critical evaluation of the movement by a non-psychologist, Wendy Kaminer's *I'm Dysfunctional, You're Dysfunctional* is an entertaining choice.

7 Perspectives on Development

Observing the Journey of Life

As I have been writing this book, I have also been taking part in an age-old drama – the forming of a new life. Early on in this project, I learned that my wife was expecting our second child. As the writing progressed, so too did the life within the womb. And now, I see and hold my new son, and take joy in the many changes as he grows. A new baby seems an affirmation of life and its potential; it simultaneously leads us into thoughts of the future, and into recollections of the past. Sometimes I watch and am reminded of similar moments when his older brother was a baby. And, like any parent, I see glimmers of my own life journey in the lives of my children.

The start of a new life is a remarkable process. We are conceived as a joining of sperm and ovum, each of which bears only a half set of DNA, but which together provide the genetic pattern for a new being. Nine months later, we emerge from the womb as an infant – small, frail, dependent on others for survival, but still recognizably human. This, of course, is only the beginning of an ongoing process of growth and development, from infant to toddler to child to adolescent, and onward through adulthood and ageing. The process by which we reach our full potential is a slow one: altogether, it takes nearly two decades for physical and intellectual capacities to mature. Thus, given a lifespan of approximately seventy-five years, we spend about *a quarter of our life* simply to reach our full size and skills!

This prolonged developmental period is remarkable; few animals spend such a large portion of their life reaching their full capacities. In fact, it has been suggested that our nature in many ways can be seen as based on a kind of delaying of the developmental timetable. For example, compared with the most genetically similar species, chimpanzees, we are more like a foetal chimp than an adult; like human adults, foetal chimps show a relative absence of body hair, no brow ridges, and a spine–brain connection which makes an upright posture possible (Campbell 1982). By contrast, the appearance of mature (adult-like) capacities in a newborn is generally found only in lower species. It almost seems as if slow development is *necessary* to forming the capacities we do.

Comparing human development with that of other species can pose many difficulties, but the desire to compare is driven by a basic question: *Why* do we develop the way we do? The question quickly leads to a host of other questions: What guides our development? What kinds of factors can influence it? Such questions – and there are many others that are closely related – are basic to the study of developmental psychology.

Introduction

In its most general form, *developmental psychology* is concerned with the processes that produce changes in behaviour over time. These changes are most dramatic in the first two decades of life, so it is not surprising that early researchers tended to focus on this period of human life. Hence, for many years, 'developmental psychology' really meant 'child development'. More recently, the field has broadened to consider events during the ensuing years as well. While the changes that occur in adulthood are generally less obvious, it is clear that we do not simply remain static after childhood and adolescence. Indeed, the long period of 'preparation' would seem to be pointless if nothing important followed! So today researchers are interested in questions of growth and change as related to the whole span of life, from birth to death.

The study of developmental psychology represents a different sort of division within psychology than do the approaches we have considered thus far. What unites the area is the emphasis on the processes of growth and change, not a particular theoretical perspective. In fact, the questions of development can be looked at from each of the approaches (as we will see). At the same time, developmental researchers (of whatever perspective) are all concerned with asking certain types of questions about behaviour, and it is the focus on these questions that gives the area a thematic coherence.

The most basic question in development has already been raised: What makes us the way we are? While simple to ask, it is exceedingly difficult to answer. For one thing, one could ask it about one individual (e.g. what makes Sarah different from Jill), or about humans as a species (as in the earlier comparison to chimpanzees). Long before psychology emerged as a distinct discipline, philosophers asked similar questions – and often disagreed about the answers. As far back as ancient Greece, Plato argued that all human knowledge and virtue was innate – that is, we are what we are born to be. By contrast, John Locke, a seventeenth-century English philosopher, suggested that a newborn child is like a blank slate, on which experience writes its messages; in essence, we are what we experience. In modern psychological terms, these polarities would be represented by the factors of *heredity* and *environment*, and debates about the importance of each are a long-standing issue. But trying to answer this age-old question requires first answering some more basic questions.

Methods of Studying Development

The first thing that is required is to come to some understanding of what exactly development involves. That is, what *are* the changes that go on during a person's life? The physical changes of childhood may seem very obvious, but as with many phenomena, the interesting parts lie in the details. To take a simple question (one which concerns nearly all parents): At what age does (should) a child begin talking? To answer this question, we might study language acquisition in a representative sample of children; this provides us with a description in terms of what is typical – that is, a *norm*. In all likelihood, there will be some noticeable variability across the group; this, in turn, may spawn a whole new series of questions, aimed at understanding *why* such variability occurs. [To answer the 'simple' question, children typically say their first words before their first birthday, but even this generalization ignores many details; for example, not all speech sounds (called *phonemes*) are acquired at the same age, as Prather *et al.* (1975) noted.]

Determining norms for basic aspects of development is an important element in describing the process of development as a whole. However, even this task becomes complicated when one wishes to find relationships between events. For example, do children who are slow to begin talking also lag behind in other respects, such as learning to walk? Or are the behaviours independent of each other? And do children who begin talking early continue to show superiority in language skills later on? While in principle one could establish norms for any single behaviour by selecting a representative sample, it becomes more complicated when one wants to make comparisons at different ages (e.g. as in looking at the pace of language acquisition). One way to answer the question is to select a group of individuals who are all the same age, and then continue to study them during the period of interest (e.g. from six months up to age six). This approach is called a **longitudinal study**, since it represents a long-term study of a given group. While highly informative, such studies are also difficult to do. The most obvious problem is the time required – the study takes at least as long as the time period of interest. This requires a tremendous commitment on the part of the researcher (whose own life is passing along with those of the subjects), as well as the cooperation of the subjects (in the case of children, obviously this means their parents must *also* be supportive). Even so, participants sometimes move away, die or drop out for other reasons. If too many of the initial group fail to complete the study, the representativeness of the results can be jeopardized, eroding the value of possibly years of work. Despite these obstacles, there are instances in which subjects have been studied for decades or longer, providing a remarkable extended portrait of lives unfolding (one example is a study of patterns of adult personality which continued for over two decades: see White 1975).

Longitudinal studies, however useful, represent only a small percentage of all developmental studies. In many cases, neither researchers nor subjects are willing or are able to make the commitment required. As a result, most research which seeks to compare behaviour at different ages is based on selecting representative

longitudinal study a research design in which a group of individuals are studied over a period of time

cross-sectional study a research design based on selecting representative groups who vary on a particular characteristic; when the characteristic is age, this design provides a means of drawing developmental comparisons

groups of each age. This approach, which then draws comparisons across time by looking at different groups, is called a **cross-sectional study**. For example, the study of speech acquisition referred to earlier (Prather *et al.* 1975) used a cross-sectional design. Cross-sectional studies have the obvious advantage of minimizing the time required for the study. For example, one could simultaneously study changes across adulthood by selecting groups of individuals who are age 20, 30, 40, 50, etc. This advantage is one of the primary reasons for the popularity of cross-sectional studies.

Unfortunately, this advantage can often be offset by the disadvantages of the design, particularly when studying individuals across wide age ranges. The problem is that such studies cannot control for any factors that change along with age; for example, the fact that the subjects of different ages were born at different points in time. Such differences can be very important in terms of the role of cultural and historical influences; for example, comparing the attitudes of teenagers today and their parents (who were likely teenagers in the 1970s) would have to contend with differences associated with the spread of technology like television and video games, as well as differences in school curricula. When such outside influences (called **confounding variables**) are present, they can sometimes dramatically alter the interpretation of development. By their nature, confounding variables represent something which has been overlooked in planning the research, and it is often only after the fact that they can be identified. For example, cross-sectional studies have suggested that intelligence test scores begin declining by age 50; however, when a longitudinal design is used, it becomes clear that scores typically remain constant up to the 70s (Labouvie-Vief 1985). Such differences mean that cross-sectional studies require careful assessment, particularly when attempting to compare behaviour over wide age ranges. In this sense, cross-sectional studies are not as helpful as longitudinal studies in clarifying the processes which underlie development.

confounding variable a factor in research which varies jointly with a variable of interest, making it impossible to identify properly the role each variable has in affecting behaviour; typically, a confounding variable represents something which has been overlooked in planning the research, and is only identified after the data have been collected

sequential design a research design which combines features of both longitudinal and cross-sectional studies by selecting groups of different ages (like a cross-sectional design), and then following them over a period of time (like a longitudinal study) sufficient to create overlap in the ages represented by different groups; comparing the behaviour of individuals from different groups at the same age then allows an evaluation for possible confounds or other problems which sometimes arise in simple cross-sectional studies

One way of compensating for the risks of cross-sectional studies is to use a hybrid design which has features of *both* longitudinal *and* cross-sectional studies. This approach, called a **sequential design**, uses groups of different ages, which are then observed for some period of time, such that the groups eventually overlap. For example, a study of adolescents might select four groups, aged 12, 14, 16 and 18. All subjects would then be followed for two years. At this point, those who were originally 12 would now be 14, and their behaviour could be compared with that previously recorded for the group who were *initially* 14. If no differences exist based on this comparison (and similar comparisons for the other groups), the researchers would be more secure in suggesting that no confounds are present. (The problem would come, of course, if the results based on the age-matching were *not* similar; one is then left to ponder whether the difference represents a confound, or simply sampling variability.) Thus, the sequential design would allow study of behaviour over a ten-year span, but would only require two years to complete – in some sense, the best of both worlds!

Issues in the Study of Development

Obviously, one cannot understand development without knowing something about what actually occurs. However, getting accurate information about behaviour at different ages is only part of the puzzle. As discussed in Chapter 1, description is only the starting point in understanding behaviour. Understanding also requires explaining *why* things happen as they do, and this requires *interpreting* what we know, in terms of a theory. In the case of development, the goal is to understand the changes that occur over time. However, we recognize that time itself is not the active force; it is processes going on *within* time that account for the changes. Hence, the task becomes one of identifying and describing these underlying processes. To formulate a theory, one must identify patterns in the observations, and propose mechanisms to account for them. But how can one identify patterns, if one is uncertain what is important? Surely one must have a theory in order to know what to look for? The reality, of course, is that researchers do both; they draw inferences from their observations, and also use their own cognitive schema to guide what they observe. As a result, the same events may be interpreted differently by different researchers. This, of course, is characteristic of psychology. As we have seen in considering the various approaches, each is dealing with the same subject, human behaviour, yet often the interpretations that are made differ significantly.

What are the differences in viewpoint which arise in interpreting development? There are several, but the most basic in terms of how one describes behaviour is concerned with the **continuity** of development. It is obvious that many changes occur over the course of life; for example, the reasoning skills of a three-year-old are dramatically different than those of a twenty-year-old. At what point are these differences so great that they represent a new skill (a *qualitative* change), rather than simply more of the same (a *quantitative* change)? To put it another way, are there distinct **stages** in development, with clear boundaries, or is development a more or less continuous process? (Sometimes this issue is described as one of *continuity* vs *discontinuity*, and sometimes as *gradualism* vs *stages*).

While strikingly different in their implications, the concepts of continuity and discontinuity are nonetheless hard to evaluate in practice. In one sense, it is obvious that development is continuous – physical growth is a gradual process, and many skills, like walking or talking, are acquired only gradually.

At the same time, it is tempting to categorize behaviour into stages, just as we form other sorts of categories. The physical changes which occur at puberty, while gradual, nonetheless seem to herald a new stage of life. Similarly, we talk about 'adolescence' *vs* 'adulthood', implying that the two periods are distinct. Are these stages really distinct in the way that pre- and post-puberty are? Asserting that stages exist implies several things about the underlying processes; most importantly, that each stage is characterized by *distinct underlying mechanisms*. In addition, discontinuity frequently implies that there is a specific *order* to the stages, and possibly even specific *timing* of the occurrence of each stage. (Freud's theory of personality development, for example, involves all three aspects – changing mechanisms underlying stages, a specific order of stages, and specific timing of stages.) As we consider some of the specifics of development, the issue of continuity *vs* discontinuity will arise repeatedly.

A second issue which arises concerns the *generality* of theories of development. A basic principle in science is the notion of *parsimony* – that is, a simpler theory is preferable to a complex one, assuming both can explain a particular set of results. In the same way, having a single theory which can be broadly applied is preferable to using several narrower ones to account for the same range of phenomena. Ideally, we would like to have one general model to describe all

continuity in developmental theory, the view that changes occur through a continuous gradual process, rather than as a series of discrete stages; continuity is an assertion about the processes which underlie development, as well as the changes observed in behaviour

stages in developmental theory, the belief that development is based on distinct periods with clear boundaries, with behaviour at each stage governed by different underlying processes; Freud's theory of psychosexual stages is one such theory

domain-general model a theory which attempts to account for many aspects of behaviour in terms of a single set of principles

domain-specific model a theory which focuses on only a single aspect of behaviour in the belief that different aspects of behaviour involve different processes, and therefore require different theoretical explanations

developmental processes, although at present, this goal seems out of reach. However we can still ask whether specific aspects of development (e.g. cognitive development or social development) can be explained in terms of a single set of principles. A broad theory which attempts to encompass many specific areas or 'domains' of behaviour is sometimes called a **domain-general model** (Rosser 1994). In contrast, a theory which focuses on only one function or domain is called a **domain-specific model**.

For example, the Swiss theorist Jean Piaget (1954), one of the great pioneers in the study of cognitive development, believed that a single set of principles could account for the development of all sorts of cognitive skills, from understanding numbers to spatial reasoning and moral judgements. His work has been highly influential, and his theory represents an example of a domain-general model; that is, he emphasized certain general principles which he believed were applicable to all aspects of cognitive development. The most fundamental of these principles was *equilibration* – the desire to maintain a balance between our surroundings and the mental structures we use to represent those surroundings. To Piaget, this search for balance was the process underlying all cognitive activity. Piaget's theory of cognitive development is also an example of a model based on discrete stages, as can be seen in Fig. 7.1.

Despite its significant influence, Piaget's work has also been criticized, often because the broad picture of cognitive processes which it paints seems wrong in some of its details. This weakness is not unique to Piaget's theory – getting the details right often represents the biggest difficulty in trying to develop a comprehensive or domain-general model. Partly in response to these concerns, other researchers have put forward theories which deal with only limited aspects of cognitive development. For example, Lawrence Kohlberg has developed a theory of moral development (how we make judgements of right and wrong); his work grew out of Piaget's, but its narrower focus on moral thinking makes it an example of a domain-specific model (Kohlberg 1966).

The differences between the theories of Piaget and Kohlberg illustrate the dilemma which developmental theorists face. Basically, the problem is a conflict between principles of parsimony (a general model would be simpler than invoking several different models) and accuracy (a general model may fail to do justice to the complexities of development). In practice, the issue is often not as clear-cut as this, but we nonetheless have to recognize that there are often competing demands involved in deciding what is a good theory.

The broadest issue in forming a theory of development, and in some ways the most contentious, concerns the *origins* of the changes which occur over the span of life. In some ways, development represents a paradox; there is the obvious sense of change, while at the same time, there seems to be a central thread of constancy. For example, parents of grown children often recall ways in which the infant or child foreshadowed the adult. Is this constancy real or imagined? And if real, what is it based on?

The traditional answer to the question of constancy has been to assert that the basic characteristics of a person are innate; that is, the constancy is due to the influence of heredity. In essence, this is the modern version of Plato's nativist theory. The role of heredity is evident in the development of a foetus, whereby cells differentiate to form the various parts of the body. Even after birth, the regularity of growth strongly suggests the influence of genetic timetables.

PIAGET'S THEORY OF COGNITIVE DEVELOPMENT

Age	Stage	Major Characteristics
Birth - age 2	Sensorimotor	Egocentric thinking — inability to conceive of the world as existing apart from one's own experience of it Development of object permanence — understanding that objects exist independent of one's sensory experience
	Preoperational	Development of language skills
2 - 4 years	Preconceptual (sub-stage)	Use of symbols — using words as category labels
4 - 7 years	Intuitive (sub-stage)	Using concepts — sorting objects by size, shape, or colour
7 - 11 years	Concrete operations	Mastery of principles of conservation — understanding that mass, volume, and number remain constant despite perceptual changes in grouping or form
11 - adult	Formal operations	Mastery of abstract thinking — ability to use inductive and deductive reasoning, using symbolic representations to analyse problems and formulate ideas

Fig. 7.1 Piaget's theory of cognitive development Piaget viewed cognitive development as consisting of four distinct stages, which were characterized by qualitatively different thinking processes; these stages were seen as age-related, and as always occurring in the same order.

The alternative to explanations based on heredity is to look for environmental influences. At first glance, it may seem hard to account for either constancy over time in an individual's behaviour, or for the developmental similarities found across individuals, but as Skinner (see Chapter 3) and others have noted, it is possible to talk about environmental constancies and similarities. Thus, one has the two extreme poles of the issue; is development based on *heredity* (the nativist view) or *environment* (the empiricist view)? (Note that the terms *nature* vs *nurture*, and *innate* vs *learned*, are generally synonymous with 'heredity *vs* environment'.)

As with most such questions, the truth seems to lie in between the extremes. For example, as we gain a greater understanding of the genetic mechanisms which are the basis of heredity, we recognize both the tremendous influence of those mechanisms – and also their limitations. Genetic mechanisms do not operate in a vacuum; they must be expressed in the context of the individual's environment – and while one can speak of an impoverished environment, there is always *some* environment. In a similar vein, while the language one speaks depends on early experience – that is, the environment – it appears that the *timing* of language learning is governed partly by genetic programming. (A number of researchers have argued that there is an optimal interval, called a *critical* or 'sensitive' *period*, during which language learning proceeds most effectively (Chomsky 1988). Deprivation at this time – for example, because of an undiagnosed hearing impairment in a three-year-old – may have long-term repercussions for language learning.) Thus, the proper question is not whether development is based on heredity *or* environment, but rather how, and to what degree, the two *interact*. Donald Hebb, a noted Canadian psychologist, once suggested that the interaction is akin to the way the area of a field is determined by its length and width; one can have fields of different shapes, but every field always has some length and width (Hebb 1953).

reaction range in genetics, the limits on the variability of a phenotype (observed characteristic) determined by the genotype; in essence, the limits set by the genes on how environmental influences (whether deprivation or enrichment) can affect the trait

One form of interaction is seen in the **reaction range** of the genotype – that is, the genes set the limits on how environmental influences (whether deprivation or enrichment) can affect the trait (Hirsch 1963). This interaction can occur in various ways, and the outcome will depend on both the specific genetic make-up and the specific environment. For example, on average, white American males are taller than Japanese males; this difference appears to be based on genetic factors. At the same time, however, there is overlap between the two groups; and within each group, variations are associated with differences in nutrition, an environmental factor. Hence, height depends on an interaction of heredity and environment.

A different form of interaction has been suggested by Sandra Scarr. She argues that individuals tend to create their own environment (by their activities, interests, etc.), and that these *active choices* are influenced by heredity. That is, individuals with different genotypes are likely to choose different environments. Evidence which is consistent with this view comes from studies of intelligence test scores, where typically as children get older, their score becomes less like that of their parents and siblings; in effect, older children exert more control over their environment than do younger children (Scarr and McCartney 1983). Assuming Scarr's explanation of these results is correct, this means that the genotype will influence the environment, as well as the environment affecting the expression of the genotype.

Identifying the boundaries for the influence of heredity and environment can be very difficult. For example, most people probably think of environmental influences as beginning at birth, when the infant emerges from the womb into what William James called a 'booming, buzzing confusion of sights and sounds'. In reality, environmental influences exist *within* the womb as well. One reflection of this is that maternal behaviour and health have measurable effects on the unborn child. For example, smoking and drinking by the mother have both been shown to adversely affect the developing foetus. Exposure to certain drugs in the womb can even affect the development of sex characteristics (Money and Tucker 1975). Thus, interactions of heredity and environment must be assumed to occur right from the time of conception.

Similarities between twins are often cited as examples of genetic influence, and studies of identical twins in particular are popular because one can be certain of the genetic relationship between the twins. More generally, researchers may compare the behaviour of individuals with any known degree of genetic relationship. This approach, called the study of *concordance*, is not without problems, especially in terms of evaluating environmental differences. For example, it must be noted that fraternal twins (conceived from separate zygotes) often seem more similar than other siblings in part because they share a common prenatal environment (see Chapter 2 for a related discussion). Thus, simply knowing the genetic relationship between two individuals is insufficient to determine the relative role of heredity and environment.

Some aspects of development seem to occur without any specific environmental conditions. Such processes, referred to as **maturation**, seem to be relatively independent of environmental influences. For example, most mammals (including human infants) are able to perceive depth by the time they are able to move about in the world (Richards and Rader 1983). Obviously, this has adaptive value in terms of avoiding falls, and seems to arise as a result of normal visual experience. Yet, even in such seemingly straightforward situations, making assumptions about genetic mechanisms and/or experience can lead to unexpected outcomes. Psychologist Neil Carlson tells a story about his six-month-old daughter being tested for depth perception using the 'visual cliff', a well-known test in which the toddler is confronted with a glass-covered surface, beneath which there is an obvious drop-off. Typically, infants old enough to crawl will not venture over the apparent 'edge', despite the support of the glass. This is interpreted as evidence of depth perception, whereby vision (the perceived drop) overrides touch (the support of the glass surface). However, when tested, Carlson's daughter went unhesitatingly across! Since it seemed impossible that the toddler could not perceive depth, the perplexed researcher, a colleague of Carlson's, could not understand this result – until it was explained that the family had a glass-covered coffee table, and the child had often crawled on it. Rather than indicating a failure of depth perception, the results reflected the difference in her prior environment (Carlson 1990).

To recap, there are three major issues which underlie the study of development, and the interpretations made by each approach. These issues are: (1) Is development a continuous process of gradual changes, or a series of distinct stages? (2) Can one theory describe the processes which underlie all development (domain-general theory), or are specific models needed to account for different aspects of development (domain-specific theories)? (3) What is the relative importance of heredity (genetic make-up) compared with the environment (especially learned experiences) in explaining the outcome of development? As we consider selected aspects of development, you may want to think about the possible answers to these questions.

Ultimately, one cannot discuss issues of development without considering the specifics of the process – that is, what we actually know about growth and change over the course of life. After all, the questions raised by the preceding issues, as well as the theories which attempt to answer them, have meaning only with regard to the actual events of development. It is beyond the scope of this chapter to discuss fully what is currently known. Instead, we will focus on one aspect of development: the behaviours which we see as characteristic of an individual. We tend to perceive any individual in terms of broad patterns, not single actions. Some of these patterns seem distinctive to the individual, and represent what we call the person's 'personality'. Another pattern, which is both part of personality and separate from it, is the tendency to show gender-related behaviours (called 'sex roles'), as expressed in sayings like 'boys will be boys'. How do these patterns arise? In the remainder of this chapter, we will look at these issues from the point of view of each of the five approaches. In so doing,

maturation a term referring to processes in development which seem to be relatively independent of environmental influences; depth perception and walking are examples of behaviours which seem to depend on maturation; implied in the term is the assumption that the characteristics are governed by heredity we will try to create a sense of both the issues of development and the way the various approaches perceive the process.

For further consideration

Ask a parent, grandparent or some other older adult about their experiences at your age – what were they doing, what they were interested in, and so on. Then ask them about their current preferences in music, books, etc. Assuming their current preferences are different than your own, can you decide whether the difference is due to the age difference, the difference in prior experience, or some other factor? What does this tell you about the difficulties of interpreting developmental research?

Personality and Sex-role Development

Personality and its Origins

Recently, I had the chance to get together with college classmates at a reunion. Some of those present I hadn't seen since our graduation, twenty-five years ago. Not surprisingly, it was a bittersweet occasion, with many shared laughs about long-ago incidents, but also more muted reflections on the passage of time, and of those friends whose lives have already ended. But what struck me most of all was the sense that most people seemed to be 'still the same', that apart from bodily changes (greying/thinning hair, weight gained or lost), much was unchanged. Tom was still shy, Cathy was still extroverted; in other words, there seemed to be a strong sense of consistency in their behaviour, even after twenty-five years. As a psychologist, how can I account for this?

personality patterns of behaviour which are characteristic of an individual and which tend to be consistent across situations and over time

trait a behaviour pattern which occurs consistently across a range of situations; a specific personality characteristic

Traditionally, we talk about such consistency in terms of the individual's personality. **Personality** refers to those behaviour patterns which are characteristic of an individual and which tend to be consistent across situations and over time. At the same time that we use 'personality' to refer to consistency *within* the behaviour of an individual, we also use the word to refer to differences *between* people. In this regard, we often refer to specific characteristics, called personality **traits**. We say 'he's shy' or 'she's outgoing', and people nod knowingly, accepting the terms as a way of both describing the individuals and of predicting how they might act in a particular situation, such as at a party.

To the average person, the study of personality may be the most interesting issue in psychology; indeed, it has been suggested that we are all 'personality theorists', since in our interactions with others, we make interpretations based on our cognitive schemata about what people are like. These schemata are sometimes called **implicit personality theories**. In this sense, ideas about personality may stem from our own perceptions, rather than external reality (see also Chapter 1).

implicit personality theory a general cognitive schema about human behaviour which is used in making interpretations of the behaviour of other people

At the same time, most people, and even most psychologists, would argue that at least *some* of the perceived consistencies are real, just as some of the perceived differences between individuals are real. Each individual is a unique combination of genes and experiences, and both heredity and environment represent potent sources of influence. What is the role of each? What shapes the *person* in the 'personality'?

The study of the origins of personality is one of the most basic, and also broadest, aspects of development. Extensive research has examined how we form our individual identity, our 'sense of self', and the many factors which contribute to it. Despite the volume of work, there are still many unanswered questions. In order to develop some perspective on the basic issues, in this section we will look at how each of the five approaches views the origins of personality, and then focus on one specific aspect of personality in more detail – the development of sex-roles.

For further consideration

In what ways do you think you are consistent? Try to identify four or five personal traits; then, ask a friend to list what they perceive as your major traits. How do the lists compare? What does this tell you about implicit personality theories?

Perspectives on Personality

At the start of this chapter, we noted that there are three major issues which arise when considering theories of development: (1) the role of heredity *vs* environment; (2) whether development is continuous or based on discrete stages; and (3) whether development involves a single process that can be understood in terms of a single model (domain-general), or involves different processes that require separate models (domain-specific). These questions are equally relevant when it comes to considering personality development, so let us examine briefly how each of the five approaches would view the issues.

The Biological Approach

The biological approach, as the name implies, places heavy emphasis on the role of heredity and physiological structure in shaping behaviour. In looking at personality, the approach has tended to focus on those aspects of personality associated with temperament. **Temperament** refers to basic behavioural tendencies, such as emotionality, sociability and fearfulness, which are believed to be determined by heredity (Rothbart 1981). Two types of evidence support the view that temperament is largely innate. One approach is research involving twins; comparisons of fraternal and identical twins indicate identical twins are more alike in activity level, irritability and sociability than fraternal twins (Plomin *et al.* 1988). Of course, such studies can be difficult to evaluate, especially since body structure (itself genetically influenced) and the reactions of others to physical attributes like attractiveness may influence these aspects of behaviour. In a study

temperament behavioural tendencies which are believed to be determined by heredity; examples include emotionality, sociability and fearfulness

which has followed a group of children from the age of three months until adulthood, Thomas and his colleagues have found there are interactions between the temperament of a child and the caregiver, which over time can affect behaviour. For example, mothers may tend to respond more favourably to babies who are not irritable (Thomas and Chess 1977).

In general, longitudinal studies seem better suited than twin studies to determining the stability of traits, hereditary or otherwise. Jerome Kagan has used this approach to look at a trait he calls *behavioural inhibition* – that is, the tendency to withdraw from unfamiliar people or situations. Those children who were either inhibited or uninhibited at twenty-one months of age tended to remain so when followed up to age seven or more (Kagan 1989). Thus, studies of temperament support the biological perspective in suggesting that important components of personality are due to heredity.

In terms of the other two issues, the biological approach is less consistent. *Maturation*, the genetically-programmed development of characteristics over time, often involves the idea of critical periods for development. A *critical period* refers to the idea that the individual is maximally sensitive to particular forms of experience at a particular time. As such, a critical period represents a discontinuity in development – the individual will react differently depending on the timing of experience. While difficult to prove in humans, many researchers believe that there are critical periods for both social attachment and language learning during the first few years of childhood. According to this view, a child who does not form close emotional ties or receive exposure to language, at this time will show a permanent deficit in these behaviours (Lenneberg 1967; Bowlby 1969). While the notion of a critical period suggests that discontinuities or stages exist in development, in other areas, such as temperament, the biological approach emphasizes the continuities of development. Hence, one cannot make a simple generalization about how the biological approach views the issue of continuity *vs* discontinuity.

In terms of the third issue, the validity of domain-general *vs* domain-specific models, the biological approach seems to favour domain-specific models. As suggested in the previous paragraph, different aspects of development are seen as having different characteristics, and this implies different underlying subprocesses. At the practical level, no-one has suggested a comprehensive, domain-general model of development within the biological approach. Thus, it seems reasonable to describe the biological approach as advocating domain-specific models of development.

The Behaviourist Approach

Compared to the biological approach, the behaviourist approach takes a polar-opposite view of the importance of heredity *vs* experience. In fact, Skinner has suggested that physiological processes within the organism are of no concern, provided one can find meaningful links between stimulus conditions and behavioural responses (Skinner 1974). All behaviour is seen as determined by experience, based on the principles of *classical* and *operant conditioning*. Rather than being based on discrete stages, the approach views behavioural change (development) as a continuous process. Since the principles of conditioning are seen as applicable to all behaviour, the behaviourist approach represents a domain-general model.

The main problem this approach faces, in terms of explaining personality, is how to account for the apparent consistency of behaviour. After all, the principles of learning would seem to imply that change is as probable as consistency, since there is no explicit factor pushing for constancy. Skinner and other behaviourists have responded to this problem by suggesting that 'personality' is simply a perceived pattern, with no basis within the individual. Instead, they suggest two factors which could produce the consistencies which are ascribed to personality. One factor is the cumulative effect of reinforcement. Each time we are

history of reinforcement
in operant conditioning, the sum of all prior reinforcement for a particular behaviour; behaviourists assert that the cumulative history of reinforcement is more important than any single reinforcement in determining behaviour

reinforced, the influence of that reinforcer is *in addition to* all prior reinforcement in the same or similar situations. Rarely is one experience so significant as to override our entire past **history of reinforcement** (this is one reason that attempts at changing behavioural patterns like bad habits 'overnight' rarely succeed). Hence, the consistency of behaviour, particularly in adults, is largely a product of prior patterns of reinforcement.

The other factor which behaviourists point to in explaining behavioural consistency is the role of *environmental consistency*. Skinner has argued that in trying to explain behaviour, we tend to give credit to the individual, not the environment, especially when we are unaware of the contingencies which govern the behaviour (Skinner 1971). In the case of the consistencies which we attribute to 'personality', we tend to overlook the degree to which the typical person's environment is consistent. For example, most of us have daily routines which are quite regular, we associate primarily with the same group of friends and acquaintances, we tend to live in the same place for relatively extended periods, and so on. All of these things contribute to an environment which is relatively consistent, in terms of both discriminative stimuli and reinforcers. In such circumstances, it would be surprising if our behaviour were *not* fairly consistent. (Note that the behaviourist is *not* obliged to suggest a mechanism for *perfect* consistency, since nearly every study of personality shows that consistency is generally far from absolute.) Thus, the combination of the cumulative effects of reinforcement, together with overlooked sources of environmental consistency, are viewed by behaviourists as the basis of 'personality'.

The Cognitive Approach

In one sense, cognitive theory does not offer a theory of personality, only a theory of how cognitive processes influence behaviour. In this sense, cognitive psychologists are as interested in why we *believe* in the concept of personality as in the factors that promote behavioural consistency. As noted earlier, cognitive theory assumes that we actively interpret our experiences, forming mental schema about both people and situations. *Attribution theory* is concerned with the kinds of inferences we make about the causes of behaviour – both our own and that of other people. In general, the theory argues that we place too much emphasis on internal characteristics ('personality') and too little on environmental influences ('the situation'); this is called *the fundamental attribution error* (Ross 1977). In this sense, perceived consistencies may reflect a form of mental bias rather than true characteristics. Such bias would lead to overestimating the actual consistency of behaviour. Walter Mischel has criticized trait concepts, arguing that while consistencies in behaviour may exist, they are much more situation-specific than most people realize (Mischel 1968).

cognitive social learning theory (sometimes simply 'social learning theory') a theory derived from the cognitive approach, which asserts that behaviour can be learned from observing other people, and that behaviour is mediated by cognitive schemata

If 'personality' does not represent inherent traits, then how do the consistencies arise? The answer proposed by Mischel and others is based on **cognitive social learning theory**, which looks at behaviour from a cognitive and social perspective. Cognitive social learning theory is based on two premises. First, it argues that much of our behaviour is learned from observing others (hence the 'social learning' component). Second, it asserts that the mental constructs that we form (values, expectations and other schemata) mediate our behaviour in ways that produce our 'personality' (hence the 'cognitive' component). Since constructs are generally closely tied to specific situations, the theory argues for the kind of limited behavioural consistency cited by Mischel.

Cognitive social learning theory traces its origins to two areas which were originally distinct: the study of social perception and the study of observational learning. *Social perception* is concerned with the social dimension of perception – how we see others, and ourselves in relation to others. *Observational learning* (also called imitation or modelling) is concerned with learning based on observing others, as opposed to direct experience. Obviously, there is a social component to both domains, and without retracing the whole history, it should be noted that over time there has been a convergence, so that today the leading proponents use the hybrid term, or some variation of it (Berkowitz 1984; Bandura 1986).

Not surprisingly, the approach is strongly environmentalist, and largely ignores the role of heredity in behaviour. This is evident in the rejection of trait concepts of personality, which typically assert that traits are based on innate factors. In terms of the issue of continuity *vs* discontinuity, the theory largely favours continuity. For example, studies in which children are allowed to observe adults doing Piagetian tasks have been used to challenge Piaget's concept of cognitive stages (Rosser 1994). And in terms of the issue of domain-specificity, the theory appears to be domain-general, in that it has been applied to many aspects of development, from cognitive development to personality and moral development. However, this conclusion is largely tied to the two previous points: if development is seen as a continuous process of learning, it is therefore open to a domain-general model. As yet, however, no-one has attempted to use cognitive social learning theory as a general developmental framework.

The Psychodynamic Approach

While the psychodynamic approach encompasses a number of theorists, Freud is still the dominant figure. The psychoanalytic theory which he developed provides a framework for interpreting nearly every aspect of behaviour, including the origin and nature of personality. In Freud's view, all behaviour is motivated by innate drives, whose mode of expression changes over the course of development. These changes in expression of the drives define the *stages of development* which shape the formation of adult personality: the oral, anal, phallic, latent and genital stages. Personality is based on the three components of *id*, *ego* and *superego*, which dynamically interact to direct behaviour. Id, the source of the drives, is present from birth. By contrast, ego and superego are formed over time, with the first five years of life being of central importance.

While the drives determine the sequence and timing of the stages of development, Freud believed that *experience* was an important factor in the shaping of personality. In particular, the way the individual learned to handle the expression and gratification of the basic drives would determine the conflicts and coping strategies which defined much of adult personality. Unfortunately, by emphasizing early development as the source of personality formation, Freud had little to say about possible changes during adult life. Later neo-Freudian theorists, notably Erik Erikson, have addressed this issue; in the case of Erikson, by creating a model of personality development with stages across the entire life-span (see Chapter 5).

Freud's theory is fairly explicit in terms of the basic issues of development. His emphasis on innate drives clearly argues for the role of heredity; indeed, his view of aggression as innate has been a frequent focus of criticism. At the same time, he clearly recognized the importance of nurture, particularly in terms of the effects of early experiences. Consequently, it is appropriate to classify Freud as an interactionist in relation to heredity *vs* environment – he clearly saw both factors as important to development. With respect to the issue of continuity, it is apparent that Freud saw development as discontinuous. His stages were biologically defined by the expression of the innate drives, and hence fixed in both sequence and timing. In terms of domain specificity, Freud's theory is clearly domain-general. Freud did not invoke different processes to distinguish the development of cognitive capacities (largely connected to ego) from the development of personality. In his view, all of behaviour could be understood in terms of the same basic processes. Indeed, while the specifics of his theory have frequently been challenged, his work still stands as one of the most remarkable attempts at creation of a comprehensive theory of behaviour.

The Humanistic Approach

The humanistic approach includes a large number of specific theories, which share certain basic assumptions, but differ in many details. One respect in which they differ is the degree of attention paid to questions of development. Some, like Rogers' theory, are fairly detailed in discussing the origins of personality. Others, like that of Viktor Frankl, scarcely use the word 'personality'. Hence, in order to provide a useful basis for comparison in this context, we will focus on the work of Carl Rogers (1959).

Rogers sees all of growth and development as motivated by the *actualizing tendency*, a biologically based drive to reach one's full potential. However, the primary factors which influence the process of growth are cognitive and experiential, not biological. Like other humanists, Rogers emphasizes the way individuals see themselves in relation to their surroundings; hence, behaviour can only be understood in terms of the meaning the individual gives to it. In Rogers' theory of personality, each person comes to define a sense of their *self* and their *ideal self*.

The self stems largely from the actualizing tendency, and reflects innate tendencies, but the ideal self is strongly influenced by experience, particularly our interactions with other people. This influence is expressed largely through the type of *positive regard* we receive. Rogers sees the outcome of healthy development as a *fully functioning person*, in whom the self and ideal self are largely consistent. Rather than being a static end state, this represents an on-going process. Thus, Rogers sees development as a life-long process.

In terms of the nature–nurture issue, Rogers supports aspects of each view. For example, he acknowledges the importance of the innate actualizing tendency, and has gone so far as to suggest that particular values are embedded in the actualizing tendency. He also sees our need for positive regard as having an innate basis. Thus, the forces which motivate growth are largely reflective of heredity, but the same is not true of the factors which shape personality. The most significant aspect of personality functioning for Rogers is the relationship between the self and the ideal self. This relationship is largely dependent on encountering the conditions for healthy growth. The *conditions for growth* which Rogers has specified (openness, empathy and unconditional positive regard) are all provided by other people; hence, in this respect, his theory emphasizes the importance of experience. Overall, we must consider his theory as reflecting an interactionist view of heredity and environment.

Rogers sees personality development as a continuous process of growth; his theory makes no reference to possible stages or discontinuities. Thus, his position on this issue seems clear. The remaining question is whether he views development as domain-specific or not. Overall, he seems to present a domain-general model, since he does not explicitly divide development into different aspects or processes. However, one must also note that he says very little about some aspects of development, such as physical and cognitive development. Given these omissions, one can only really evaluate his theory in terms of what it *does* consider, personality development. Within this domain, it does seem to present a general model, but as a theory of behaviour it is clearly not as comprehensive as the theories of Freud and Skinner.

In summary, the five approaches view personality very differently, ranging from the biological interpretation that personality is innate to the behaviourist assertion that personality does not exist. Ultimately, it may be the case that no single approach is adequate to explain the complex behaviour patterns which we call personality. Before trying to make a general assessment, let us look at the more specific issue of sex-role development.

For further consideration

Children are often compared to their parents in terms of personality; for example, 'he has his father's temper' or 'she has her mother's stubbornness'. How would each approach explain such similarities?

The Development of Sex Roles

'Boys will be boys', states an old saying. Unfortunately, this simple statement belies the complexity of the questions which underlie it. What *are* boys like? Do they really act differently than girls? And if so, *why*? We know there are differences associated with sex – for instance, males are typically larger and stronger than females – but do these differences account for why, for example, boys play with trucks and girls play with dolls?

The existence of two physical sexes is one of the most obvious characteristics of human beings. This biological fact is often regarded as equivalent to a psychological imperative – that is, that behaviours *associated with* sex (sex roles and sexual identity) are *determined directly by* gender. However, the realities are not as simple as this view implies. For one thing, **sex roles** refer to the behaviours which a culture considers appropriate for each gender, and obviously differences exist across cultures (Mead 1935; Ford and Beach 1951). That is, there is no universal definition of 'male' and 'female' sex roles; instead, the definition depends on what culture one lives in. In addition, there is also variation within a culture, including differences in *sexual orientation* – that is, whether the individual is attracted to the same (*homosexual*) or opposite (*heterosexual*) sex. Hence, in talking about behaviours related to sex, we encounter the same kinds

sex roles patterns of behaviour which a culture defines as being appropriate for each gender of questions of individuality and causation that are part of the larger domain of personality in general. To try to understand such behaviour, let us consider how each theory interprets the development of sex roles and sexual identity.

The Biological Approach

The physical differences in body structure which are associated with gender are obviously rooted in heredity. Chromosomally, males have an XY pattern, whereas females have an XX pattern. In turn, the expression of this genetic pattern is dependent on the actions of hormones, which affect the development of physical sex characteristics. In particular, the presence or absence of **androgens**, the male hormones, determines prenatal physical development: if androgen is present, the foetus develops male characteristics; if it is not, the foetus develops female characteristics. Normally, the amount of androgens present is determined by the genes associated with the sex chromosomes. However, there are cases in which the process goes awry, either because of genetic defects or environmental factors (such as the presence of drugs which affect androgen levels). In such cases, the development of physical characteristics, including genitalia, can be affected. Thus, at the level of the physical characteristics associated with gender, the nativist position of the biological approach is well supported.

androgens hormones whose functions are related to masculine characteristics; the most important is testosterone

The crucial question, though, is whether *behaviour* is determined in the same way. The biological approach would say it is, and the cultural stereotypes of males and females certainly imply behaviour is connected to gender. For example, males are typically seen as more aggressive than females. Since stereotypes may influence behaviour in ways unrelated to heredity, we need to ask if there is any direct evidence for innate behavioural differences based on gender. A number of studies have found that boys are typically more physically active than girls, even in early infancy (Eaton and Enns 1986). The early appearance of this difference suggests an innate factor, which might be mediated by hormonal influences. John Money, a specialist in hormonal processes, has reported cases of androgenized females (genetic females exposed to high levels of androgens prenatally) (Money and Tucker 1975). Money reports that in these cases not only is physical development affected, but also behaviour – the girls are typically more physically active and 'tomboyish' than their peers. Hence, physical activity level may be a sex difference which has a hereditary origin.

If such differences do exist, what is their basis? The most common answer is that hormones affect development of the brain as well as the body, and that this results in gender-related differences in behaviour. Research has clearly demonstrated such effects in other mammals, and apparent differences in the brains of men and women have been interpreted in the same way (Kimura 1992). As examples, Kimura cites the tendency for men to outperform women on certain spatial tasks, while women outperform men in fine-motor coordination. While this research does not prove directly that gender identity is based on hormones, it certainly can be seen as supportive of such a position.

A similar argument has been made with regard to sexual orientation, particularly the origins of homosexuality. Within our culture, homosexuals have often been maligned and regarded as 'unnatural'. Given the social hostility implied in this view, why would someone choose to be homosexual? In fact, most homosexuals assert that their sexual orientation is not a choice, and was fixed well before puberty (Bell *et al.* 1981). This interpretation is consistent with the view that sexual orientation is innately determined, as the biological approach would argue. Support for this view comes from research indicating that the brains of homosexual men are more like women's than those of heterosexual men (LeVay 1993). Assuming that these findings are reliable, what would account for such differences? One theory is that hormonal variations alter the brain in ways related to sexual orientation. One mechanism for such hormonal variations is maternal stress during the second trimester of prenatal development (Ellis *et al.* 1988). More recently, support for a genetic factor has come from a study suggesting a link between homosexuality and genes on the X chromosome (LeVay and Hamer 1994).

These studies, while supporting the biological view, are not without problems of interpretation. As discussed earlier, experience can influence the development of the nervous system, so finding differences in the brains of adults does not necessarily prove that the cause of the differences is genetic. While studies of hormonal effects in animals provide clear data, the evidence provided by Ellis *et al.* (1988) is both retrospective and correlational. In addition, Byne, in a reply to LeVay and Hamer, has argued that the available evidence is too limited to support the assertion that sexual orientation is genetic (Byne 1994). At present, the question of a biological origin of sexual orientation seems unresolved.

Even if this issue is settled, it does not explain all aspects of sex roles and gender identity. One fact which tends to work against the biological view, at least in the simple form that sex determines behaviour, is the tremendous variation in behaviour *within* each sex, which results in overlap *between* the sexes. Compared to this, the overall differences which can be associated with one's sex are fairly small; Deaux (1985) has estimated that only 5 per cent of individual differences among children can be attributed to sex. This leaves the question of how such small differences can produce a stable and well-differentiated gender identity. In essence, if boys and girls are so similar, how can their gender identities be so different? In this regard, John Money and his colleagues have argued that socialization, not hormones, determines an individual's sense of gender identity (Money and Tucker 1975). Hence, gender identity seems to involve more than simply biological sex; to understand this, we must look at how other approaches explain the development of sex roles.

The Behaviourist Approach

Behaviourists like Skinner argue that all behaviour is shaped by reinforcement, so if differences exist across individuals, this implies differences in reinforcement history. In terms of sex roles, this view is supported by research showing that right from birth, boys and girls are treated differently (Maccoby and Jacklin 1974). These differences persist, and possibly increase, in later childhood (Huston *et al.* 1986). Thus, the behaviourist approach would argue that the behaviours associated with sex roles are shaped by reinforcement and hence are learned, not innate.

This approach is consistent with the observation that sex roles differ across cultures, for both men and women (Mead 1935). Such variations are easier to explain in terms of learning than in terms of heredity. The behaviourist approach also makes it easy to explain individual differences, since experiences can differ for each individual. One disadvantage of the behaviourist view, however (a problem shared by all environmentalist theories), is the difficulty of explaining the *origin* of sex roles. If the patterns are entirely learned, then where did they come from in the first place? *Why* should males and females be treated differently? The behaviourist approach gives no specific answer to this question, but would seem to suggest two possibilities: (1) small biological differences are selectively amplified over time by differential reinforcement; or (2) the pattern is random, somewhat in the way different pigeons respond differently to the same schedule of non-contingent reinforcement (see Chapter 3). If the first explanation is true, then in fact there is a biological component to sex roles. The second interpretation seems less plausible, since it is not clear how random reinforcement would result in differences based on sex, as opposed to simply random variation across individuals. While testing these proposals would seem to require going back in time, in terms of plausibility it seems more likely that biological differences became elaborated by reinforcement. Before accepting this explanation, let us consider the interpretations of the other approaches.

The Cognitive Approach

The cognitive approach emphasizes the role of mental schema in directing behaviour, and also the effects of social influence through social learning. Both elements seem relevant to the understanding of sex-role development.

The existence of sex roles, from the cognitive viewpoint, implies that individuals have a mental schema which tells them what is appropriate behaviour for their sex. This is supported by the evidence that sexual stereotypes exist (see Fig. 7.2). The formation of such schemata seems to begin very early: two-year-olds are able to identify the gender of individuals based on clothing or hairstyle. (Thompson 1975). By the time children are five or six, their memory for events differs based on whether what they are asked to recall is gender-consistent or not (Martin and Halverson 1983). At the same time, the development of such schemata is gradual, and often children as old as five have not yet grasped that gender is a permanent attribute; they may, for example, believe that someone can change gender by changing clothes (Marcus and Overton 1978).

How do children form such concepts, either about others or about themselves? Cognitive theory argues that the behaviour of others, particularly adults, provides an example which is imitated, through the process of social learning (once children enter school, peers are also significant as models to be imitated). Any parent can readily cite examples of children attempting to copy adult actions, ranging from Daddy using a screwdriver to Mummy cooking. Albert Bandura has suggested that such observational learning provides a major factor in sex-role development (Bandura 1977). However, other researchers have indicated that children are more concerned with gender-consistency of behaviour than with the sex of the model until at least about age six. (Masters *et al*. 1979). For example, boys will still play with a truck, which they regard as a 'boys' toy', after watching a girl play with it. It is not until the concept of gender as a permanent attribute of a person is established (around age seven) that the sex of models seems to influence children's behaviours. Although it does not rule out other forms of learning (such as direct reinforcement) as a factor in sex-role development, this finding does suggest that social learning by itself is not a sufficient explanation.

ATTRIBUTES PERCEIVED AS MASCULINE AND FEMININE

MASCULINE	FEMININE
Aggressive	Gentle
Ambitious	Considerate
Competitive	Devotes self to others
Not easily influenced	Aware of others' feelings
Likes maths and science	Enjoys art and music
Self-confident	Needs approval
Skilled in business	Likes children
Stands up under pressure	Excitable in a crisis

Fig. 7.2 Stereotypes of male and female sex roles In a study of university students done about ten years ago, clear differences in the perceived attributes of male and female roles were found. Do you think the same would be true today? (List adapted from Ruble 1983.)

In general, by suggesting how mental concepts and categories interact with social experience, the cognitive approach seems to offer a more specific model for the role of experience in sex-role development than does behaviourism. Indeed, since many of the reinforcers which children receive are social (such as praise from a parent or teacher), the approach in some ways incorporates the behaviourist notion of operant learning. Despite this, there are still many details unresolved and competing models within the cognitive approach (e.g. Kohlberg 1966; Martin and Halverson 1987). In addition, since schemata related to sex roles obviously include the recognition of sex, the biological reality of sex distinctions cannot be ignored. Having said this, it still seems that some variant of cognitive theory is likely to play an important role in the further understanding of sex-role development.

The Psychodynamic Approach

As noted earlier, Freud's theory of development acknowledges both biological and experiential factors. Biological influences are reflected in the innateness of the sexual drive which motivates much of our behaviour, and in the biologically determined *stages of psychosexual development*. The existence of the sexual drive cannot itself explain sex roles or sexual orientation, however, since Freud did not see the drive itself as gender-oriented. Instead, he saw the development of sex roles as a product of the child's attempt to resolve the *Oedipal conflict* during the *phallic stage* of development. For a boy, the mother is the prototype for future relationships, while the father is a rival for the mother's attention. In order to cope with the anxiety created by the Oedipal conflict (including fears that the father will retaliate by castrating him), the boy uses the defence mechanism of *identification*, thereby modelling his behaviour on that of his father. This process of identification establishes both the boy's sex role and sexual orientation. Although the dynamics are somewhat different for girls, ultimately identification still provides the basis for the formation of sexual identity in both sexes. Freud believed that the absence of the same-sex parent would distort the normal process of development, with consequent effects on sex-role development and sexual orientation. In particular, he saw failure to identify with the father (or a surrogate father figure) as the origin of homosexuality in males.

In some ways, Freud's theory is consistent with the available evidence. For example, he correctly identified the period around ages three to five as being significant in the formation of gender identity. In addition, there is some evidence that when boys have no father figure to identify with, their sex role behaviour is often less masculine (Stevenson and Black 1988).

Beyond these points, Freud's theory doesn't fare very well. Since identification, like social learning theory, predicts that children will imitate parents, one might expect that any studies indicating imitative behaviour would therefore support Freud's theory. However, identification is seen as based on anxiety and fear, not positive feelings. Instead, the evidence suggests that nurturance produces more imitative behaviour than does parental dominance (Hetherington and Frankie 1967). Furthermore, the extensive survey by Bell *et al.* (1981) found that a poor relationship with the father was modestly linked to homosexual orientation in *both* sexes (not just males, as Freud would predict), while the maternal relationship was not related to sexual orientation in *either* sex (again, contrary to Freud's view). Overall, the evidence, while not extensive, is not very supportive of Freud's theory as applied to sex roles and sexual orientation.

The Humanistic Approach

The humanistic approach is perhaps the most difficult to evaluate in the present context, since little is said about development. Even Rogers' theory is problematical, since he did not address the issue of sex roles and sexual identity directly. As an aspect of the *ideal self*, sex roles would seem to arise from the *conditional positive regard* that a child receives. That is, parents and others would set *conditions of worth* related to sex roles, which then would be introjected into the ideal self as conceptions of what is appropriate behaviour. For example, a five-year-old girl who shows an interest in playing with blocks may be told, 'Oh, blocks are for boys. You should play with your doll instead!' Similarly, a boy may be told that 'cooking is for girls'. Such messages can easily be incorporated in the ideal self, effectively instilling cultural norms for sex roles.

In some respects, Rogers' theory seems consistent with interpretations offered by other approaches. Since positive regard in Rogers' theory functions in ways that are similar to positive reinforcement in behaviourist theory, it reflects a similar emphasis on learning and experience. One can also draw a parallel between the Rogerian view of *self* as based on the individual's perceptions and experiences, and the cognitive concept of a mental schema.

Sexual orientation would also be seen as related to the self, rather than societal standards as expressed through the ideal self. Since the self reflects the underlying nature of the *organism*, Rogers would suggest that sexual orientation may well be biological, and is certainly self-defined. Thus, Rogers' theory seems consistent with LeVay's biological position, and also Bell's finding that the best predictor of homosexual orientation is experiencing homosexual feelings prior to adolescence (Bell *et al.* 1981; LeVay 1993). Rogers would also understand the conflict that many homosexuals feel about 'going public' in our culture. In essence, it represents a conflict between the feelings of the self, and introjected social standards that are often hostile to homosexuality. As in other such conflicts, Rogers believes the self is the true nature of the individual, not the ideal self.

Beyond such general points, Rogers' theory offers few insights into the process of sex-role development. In large part, since he never addressed the issue of sex-role development directly, there has been no research to explore the issue from within the Rogerian framework. Given that other humanistic theorists have said even less, it is very difficult to apply, or evaluate, the humanistic approach in terms of understanding these developmental issues.

Overall, the two most plausible approaches for understanding sex roles and sexual identity are the biological and the cognitive. While very different in their interpretations, each is well-developed theoretically and supported by a wide range of relevant research. The theories of Rogers and Freud, as representative of the humanistic and psychodynamic approaches, are largely inadequate, albeit for different reasons: Freud's theory does not seem consistent with the available evidence, and Rogers' theory is not sufficiently specific to be evaluated seriously. The behaviourist model of reinforcement, while relevant, seems like a limited version of cognitive social learning theory, with no specific advantages of its own in this area. However, there are still many aspects of this topic, like development as a whole, which are not resolved. It will be interesting to see how the differences between the biological and cognitive approaches are dealt with in the future: by the triumph of one approach over the other, or by some yet unknown model which incorporates elements of both approaches.

For further consideration

Suppose that the parents of a new child, in order to avoid gender-bias, decide to raise their new baby as an 'it' rather than as a boy or girl. What would each theory predict in terms of the effects this would have on the development of a gender-based sex role?

Conclusion

Developmental psychology is concerned with the changes that occur over the course of human life. This interest in understanding the course of life is not unique to psychology; for example, biographers also try to capture the span of life. What distinguishes the study of development in psychology are the questions asked and the methods used. A biographer seeks to understand a single person's life, and in doing so tends to emphasize the events which are unique to that person; for instance, how their place of birth, family, or particular experiences shaped their development. By contrast, developmental psychologists are interested in the principles which are common to *all* lives – the processes which describe development in general. The challenge is to identify and understand these common principles.

As we have seen, there are several basic issues which arise in the study of development. For example, is development a continual unfolding, or a series of discrete stages? Asking about *continuity* vs *discontinuity* is not just a matter of how we *describe* development, but also of identifying the *processes* which direct it.

An equally major concern is the role of heredity and environment. The issue is not whether development is controlled by one factor *or* the other, but rather *to what extent* does each influence a given behaviour, or *in what way*? Phrased in this way, the role of heredity and environment become the foundation for all developmental research.

The challenges of developmental research are clearly seen in the way each of the five approaches views the process of development, and the fact that, at present, no approach seems capable of offering a comprehensive model. This may partly reflect the limitations of each framework, but also suggests that development is not a single process, but many.

This complexity is seen even when one looks at specific aspects of development, such as sex roles. While the explanations proposed by the various approaches are relatively clear, the evidence is very difficult to interpret. It is easy to recognize that human beings are divided into two sexes, but the relationship of behaviour to gender is less clear-cut. Models which emphasize only one type of factor, such as the role of heredity, seem inconsistent with the available data. In the end, it seems that what is needed is a multi-process model which can *combine* the effects of heredity and learning. Possibly the work of John Money and his colleagues will lead in this direction, but there are still large gaps in our understanding.

Overall, the study of development can be the most frustrating area in psychology. In writing this chapter, I was struck, not for the first time, by its seeming lack of coherence. The number of questions to contend with, and the diversity of answers offered, seems to defy attempts at theoretical integration. Given the desire for a full understanding, this fragmentation seems an obvious failing. Yet, one should not be too hasty in blaming developmental theorists for failing to provide a cohesive framework. In some sense, the study of development is a microcosm for all of psychology, since in various ways it touches on nearly every aspect of behaviour and experience. Since at present there is no comprehensive theory of psychology, it should not be surprising that there is no comprehensive theory of development. Yet, by pointing out what is *needed* for a successful theory, the study of development may in fact help to clarify issues for the field as a whole. In that sense, the lack of coherence currently found in developmental psychology may ultimately prove to be a benefit. In the meantime, it provides us with glimpses of insight into the remarkable journey which we are all taking: the journey of life.

Chapter Summary

- *Developmental psychology* is concerned with understanding the changes that occur over the course of human life, and the processes which govern the changes.

- In order to study changes over time, researchers tend to use *longitudinal studies* or *cross-sectional studies* involving groups of different ages; in some cases, researchers will use a *sequential design*, which combines elements of both.

- Three general issues pervade the study of development: *continuity* vs *discontinuity* in the developmental process, the relative importance of *heredity* and *environment*, and the value of *domain-general* vs *domain-specific models*.

- The *biological approach* emphasizes the role of *temperament* in development, as being based on heredity.

- The *behaviourist approach* emphasizes the importance of environmental influences, particularly the role of *environmental consistency* and the person's *history of reinforcement* in accounting for the consistencies which are attributed to *personality*.

- The *cognitive approach* interprets development in terms of cognitive social learning theory, which emphasizes the role of imitation in learning and the importance of cognitive schemata in structuring behaviour.

- The *psychodynamic approach*, as represented by Freud's psychoanalytic theory, favours an interactionist interpretation, which incorporates both physiologically based *psychosexual stages of development* and the role of early experience in explaining personality.

- The *humanistic approach* seems to offer the least detailed analysis of development, in part because developmental researchers tend to seek common principles based on objective observation, while the humanistic approach emphasizes individual experience and subjective perceptions. To the extent that it can be evaluated, Rogers' theory seems to favour an interactionist interpretation of development.

- The study of *sex-role development* presents a clear example of the challenges of developmental research. At present, no one approach seems to offer a fully satisfactory model of the origin of sex roles, though the biological and cognitive approaches in particular have provided some interesting insights.

- Overall, developmental psychology represents the field of psychology in microcosm, since development involves virtually all aspects of behaviour. To the extent that currently no single model seems adequate, it reflects the realities of the current limits of our broader understanding of behaviour.

Key Terms and Concepts

continuity

critical period

cross-sectional study

domain-general *vs* domain-specific

   models

history of reinforcement

implicit personality theory

longitudinal study

maturation

personality

reaction range

sequential design

sex roles

stages

temperament

trait

Suggestions for Further Reading

While not the most current text available, Bower's *Human Development* provides an excellent analysis of the issues in developmental research, as well as clear discussion of the basic findings.

For a detailed discussion of the role of heredity and environment in development, Plomin and co-workers' *Nature and Nurture during Infancy and Early Childhood* provides an authoritative account, albeit with an emphasis on the hereditarian position (Plomin is a behavioural geneticist).

For an example of the potential of longitudinal studies, White's *Lives in Progress* is a fascinating demonstration of what can be learned by a researcher who has both patience and sensitivity.

For a readable overview of sex-role development, Money and Tucker's *Sexual Signatures* presents an interactionist view, including information on the influence of both nature and nurture.

In various ways, all the approaches touch upon development; readers interested in a particular approach should refer back to the suggested readings in the appropriate chapter.

8 Perspectives on Social Behaviour

The Individual and Society

As a teenager, I remember seeing a science fiction drama on television in which a man was the only survivor of a cataclysmic disaster. In his case, he relished being alone, because it freed him from the incessant chatter of other people. He looked forward to the quiet, to being able to sit and read as he pleased – until he broke his only pair of glasses. The story, of course, was meant to be ironic, but it also raised an interesting question: What would it be like to be the only person in the world? To me (and, I suspect, most people) it would be a calamity, not a blessing; part of being human is being involved with other people.

It is an oft-repeated truism that human beings are social creatures. Almost four hundred years ago, the English poet John Donne observed that 'no man is an island, entire of itself'; instead, he said, we are all bound together, each of us 'a piece of the continent, a part of the main'. At birth, we are linked to others by our dependence on them for survival. Later, when we have become physically independent, we still seek others for companionship, affection and mutual support. Indeed, even when we are alone, we are influenced by others – in the memories we carry, in the way we think, and in our perceptions of both ourselves and our surroundings.

Thus far, we have been focusing primarily on the understanding of individual behaviour. That, after all, is what psychology is all about; other fields, like sociology and anthropology, look at the behaviour of groups and cultures. Yet, we also recognize that one cannot study individuals without acknowledging that they interact with, and are influenced by, other people. We have seen examples of this in examining the various approaches; for example, we are reinforced by the praise we receive from others (behaviourist), we learn from observing others (cognitive), and so on. In the end, no study of psychology can be complete without a consideration of the social dimension of individual behaviour.

Introduction

The study of the social aspects of behaviour is the focus of *social psychology*. The subject is traditionally divided into two sub-areas: the study of social cognition and the study of social influence. *Social cognition* refers to the mental processes involved in understanding ourselves, other people and the world. For example, the way we form impressions of other people, and the factors that influence our attitudes, are both matters of social cognition. Not surprisingly, the cognitive approach has been an important contributor to the understanding of these issues; in fact, we have already touched on social cognition in our previous discussions of attribution theory and social perception.

social influence a general term for the various ways in which an individual's behaviour is affected by others, such as conformity pressures and social expectations and norms
conformity the tendency to adjust one's behaviour to comply with group norms
altruism behaviour intended to help others, independently of any self-interest

Social influence is concerned with how an individual's behaviour is affected by others. Social influence is involved, for example, when a person dresses in a particular way in order to 'fit in' with their peers. This tendency to go along with group norms is referred to as **conformity**, a form of social influence. Interestingly, social influence can arise even when we are alone; for example, in shopping for clothes, a person may think about how other people would react to a particular style or colour. Social influence also deals with forms of behaviour which are basically social in orientation. For example, **altruism** (helping others) has no meaning except in a social context. Together, social cognition and social influence touch on virtually every aspect of the relations between an individual and society.

Like development, social psychology is defined by its subject matter, not a theoretical framework. That is, its unity stems from its emphasis on behaviour in a social context, just as the study of development is unified by the emphasis on changes over time. Whereas developmental research uses time-based methods (such as longitudinal studies), in social psychology research is based largely on doing experiments. Other methods, including case studies and participant observation, are sometimes used, but experiments predominate. (This methodological emphasis also helps to distinguish the sometimes fuzzy boundary between social psychology and sociology, which emphasizes non-experimental methods. In the end, the boundary cannot be defined in absolute terms, and there is considerable exchange between the two fields.)

At first glance, this emphasis on doing experiments may seem puzzling. After all, many of the interesting questions about social behaviour arise out of everyday events. For example, in Chapter 1 we discussed the death of Kitty Genovese, an incident in which thirty-eight people observed the fatal attack on a young woman, but did not intervene. Why didn't they help? One can speculate on possible reasons, and her death did in fact generate considerable conjecture at the time, but ultimately no amount of speculation can ever provide the evidence necessary for sound explanations. Instead, social psychologists prefer to do experiments, which provide the kind of controlled conditions necessary for making clear interpretations of causation.

Doing experiments involving social behaviour can pose a number of challenges. Directly or indirectly, these challenges all relate to the conditions required for doing experiments. One of the advantages of the experimental method is that it allows the researcher to control the situation – manipulating the desired variable(s) and keeping other factors constant. Such control is important to the interpretation of the causes of behaviour. However, experimental conditions can sometimes interfere with the very behaviour one is interested in studying. For one thing, when people know they are being observed, they may react differently than they would otherwise, a phenomenon called *reactivity*. Concerns about reactivity are not unique to social psychology; the problem can occur in many kinds of psychological research. Consequently, a number of techniques have been devised to deal with it, including deliberately withholding information, or using deception (see Chapter 1 for a further discussion of reactivity).

A second problem which is more specific to social behaviour is the need to create a convincing situation. In everyday life, social interactions elicit emotional as well as cognitive responses, and these emotions can sometimes be intense. For example, a person may feel 'stage fright' about speaking before a group; two drivers involved in a car accident may get into an angry confrontation; a person may become embarrassed by a social slip. In order to provide meaningful results, an experimental situation must be sufficiently involving that participants will react genuinely. If the person thinks, 'Oh, well, this is just an experiment', then that perception will probably lead to behaviour which is very different from 'real' situations. Elliot Aronson, a well-known social psychologist, has referred to the importance of natural reactions as the need for **experimental realism** (Aronson 1976). This is not quite the same as saying that the situation must be 'life-like' in the sense that it is familiar from daily life. Stanley Milgram's study, in which a 'researcher' encouraged participants to give apparently dangerous electric shocks to another person, was not a situation which most people encounter in daily life; in this sense, it was not 'realistic' (see Chapter 1 for a description of Milgram's study). However, the subjects found the situation highly involving (not to say emotionally distressing), and there is little reason to doubt that their responses were genuine. In this sense, Milgram's research satisfied the need for experimental realism. Essentially, a realistic experiment tells us 'the way people would react if a similar set of events *did* occur in the real world' (Aronson 1976: 292).

Creating a convincing situation often requires considerable ingenuity. In essence, the experiment must be sufficiently complex to be involving, yet sufficiently simple to allow proper experimental control. In addition, because people would probably not behave naturally if they knew the true purpose of the study, it typically requires *deception*. This poses a continual ethical dilemma for researchers – can the knowledge gained justify the process? Most researchers in social psychology believe that deception is a necessary procedure, even given its disagreeable implications (presumably, if they did not feel this way, they would not do any research involving deception!). At the same time, serious researchers agree that one should try to minimize the manipulative aspects of research, and any possible negative consequences of experimental procedures. One way of mitigating harm is to discuss the true nature and goals of the research with the participants when the experiment ends; this is called **debriefing**. Alternatively, a researcher may use observational techniques (such as non-obtrusive measures

experimental realism a quality of involvement whereby research participants respond without regard for the laboratory context, as they would in an ordinary situation

debriefing discussing the nature of a research study with participants at its conclusion, in order to explain the true nature and goals of the research and to answer any questions or concerns of participants, especially in experiments which involve the use of deception or surveys) which do not require the use of deception. Unfortunately, this option *also* precludes the possibility of identifying causal relationships. Thus, the potential conflict between methodological requirements and ethical concerns remains. Ethical issues, obviously, can arise in most psychological research, but they are particularly vivid in social psychology precisely because social interactions are so central to human experience.

Whatever the method, social psychologists are interested in the many aspects of social behaviour, from self-esteem to prejudice, from love to aggression. These issues are obviously very diverse, as are the theories for interpreting them. Consequently, it should not be a surprise to find that each of the five approaches has relevance to the study of social psychology, particularly the area of social influence. Rather than attempt a superficial survey of all aspects of social behaviour, we will focus on the ways in which we hurt and help each other – that is, aggression and altruism. Can we understand what causes aggression, and if so, can we use that knowledge in positive ways? By considering the research and the interpretations offered by the various theoretical approaches, hopefully we can gain a better understanding of the nature of social behaviour.

Aggression

There is little question that aggression represents one of the darker aspects of human behaviour. We seem to be both able and willing to hurt each other, despite our social orientation. Aristotle once described humans as 'the social animal'; given the history of aggression, some would suggest the emphasis should be on 'animal' rather than 'social'. Today, it often seems that the news media provide daily reminders of the human capacity for violence. Not long ago, all of England, and indeed the world, was horrified by the story of two boys, not yet in their teens, who kidnapped and tortured a two-year-old, and then left him to die on the railroad tracks. As I am writing this chapter, the local paper has reported the story of a man in the United States who killed his wife with a shotgun. The reason? She was talking too much during a television programme! In several places in the world, civilian populations are under attack by military forces. Both individually and in groups, we seem only too capable of causing harm to each other.

Such incidents cast a bleak picture, and the past includes many comparable examples. The long history of such violence has led many to assume that such actions represent an intrinsic part of human character. However, we must not be too quick to label 'aggression' as an innate drive; in part, because doing so presumes that we already have the *answer* before we have really posed the *question*. The question, of course, is 'what is the origin of aggressive behaviour?' Unfortunately, before we can attempt to answer this question, we must be clear about what we mean by 'aggressive behaviour'.

Defining Aggression

Most people would say that if someone deliberately harms another person, that this is undesirable behaviour. But is it therefore *aggressive* behaviour? And what if someone *intends* to harm another person, but does not succeed? Is aggression the same as violence? Can there be aggression if there is no actual violence? Although we use (and seem to understand) the terms 'aggression' and 'violence' in everyday language, like many words their meaning can be somewhat ambiguous, shifting according to the context. In order to be useful in the context of scientific explanation, we need to define the terms unambiguously.

The basic problem in defining aggression is whether the focus should be on the behaviour, the intention, or both. *Violent* behaviour is that which causes harm to other people – some researchers, like Moyer (1983), would also include damage to property. However, violence is not necessarily the same as aggression, in that violence may occur accidentally. For example, a golfer's errant ball may hit someone on the head, causing serious injury; given that there was no intent to cause harm, most people would not view it as an aggressive act.

In our culture, we are accustomed to considering a person's intentions, as well as the outcome, in evaluating behaviour. For example, judgements of guilt in our legal system emphasize the consideration of a person's motives. In the same way, researchers have often sought to consider the motivational component of behaviour in defining aggression. For example, Elliot Aronson has defined aggression as 'behaviour aimed at causing harm or pain' (Aronson 1976: 143). By focusing on the *intention* of the behaviour, Aronson is able to make some seemingly useful distinctions. For example, a football player who inadvertently injures another player is not being aggressive, although it results in harm (and is therefore violent behaviour). By contrast, a football player who deliberately sets out to injure an opponent *is* being aggressive, even if he fails to actually cause harm.

The trouble with focusing on intentions in defining aggression is that, like any form of motivation, aggressive intent is difficult to measure. Among other things, one has to consider whether intentions can be expressed symbolically. Freud was willing to talk about symbolic forms of aggression which seem unconnected to violent acts, but this is because he *assumed* aggressive intent is always present (after all, he believed aggression was an innate drive). If one doesn't make this assumption, then it must be acknowledged that measuring aggressive intentions is a difficult task. For example, if a writer lampoons a real-life critic in a story, is that aggression? Who is to judge the intent?

It seems that defining aggression is very much tied up with our assumptions about its origins. Those who believe aggression is a learned behaviour (like Aronson) typically emphasize behaviour in defining aggression (i.e. it must result in harm). By contrast, those who believe aggression is an innate drive (like Freud) prefer to emphasize intentions (which may be expressed symbolically). There is no simple resolution to this dilemma, because the word 'aggression' has many connotations. In this chapter, we will generally try to adhere to a compromise definition which includes both components – that is, **aggression** is behaviour which causes intentional harm to another person (Berkowitz 1975). This definition probably excludes some forms of aggression, but at least has the virtue that nearly every theorist would agree that such behaviours *are* aggressive.

The very fact that it has taken a full page simply to try and define aggression – and then, only with partial success – gives an indication of how complicated it is to explore this topic with some semblance of objectivity. The notion of aggression strikes a very deep chord for most people; in some sense, it goes to

aggression behaviour which causes intentional harm to another person the heart of our beliefs about human nature. In a very similar way, the different approaches to psychology make very different assumptions, and as we will see, these assumptions lead them to very different viewpoints on aggressive behaviour.

Methods of Studying Aggression

Before considering the interpretations offered by the approaches, it is useful to return to the question of research methods: How can one study aggressive behaviour scientifically? Normally, psychologists prefer experimental research when studying any type of behaviour, because experiments allow one to make interpretations about the causes of behaviour. Yet experimental studies of aggression face several hurdles: individuals may act differently in a laboratory than in everyday life, raising concerns about distortion and bias in the results. As noted earlier, the need for *experimental realism* is a concern in all social psychology experiments. However, aggression is a particular concern because researchers cannot ethically explore the full range of aggressive behaviour in the laboratory (to give an extreme example, no-one would do an experiment about murder). Yet restrictions on the types of aggression used may limit the *external validity* of a study – that is, the extent to which one can generalize to other situations involving other forms of aggression. For example, does punching an inflatable doll really tell us whether someone would punch another person? This is not to say that laboratory studies are irrelevant to the study of aggression; but they are difficult to design well, and there are limits to their generality.

In order to avoid these problems, researchers sometimes prefer to avoid laboratory research when studying aggression; instead, they may opt either to perform field experiments or else to use correlational designs based on real-world observations. A *field experiment* involves doing an experiment in a real-world setting, such that the subjects are not aware of participating in a research study. As discussed in Chapter 1, field experiments pose the two-fold problem of trying to maintain proper controls in a natural setting, along with concerns about the ethics of doing research without the informed consent of participants. This is particularly troublesome when dealing with aggressive behaviour and, consequently, relatively few field experiments have been done, compared with either lab experiments or correlational studies. *Correlational studies* involve some form of observation of variables in a natural setting (e.g. naturalistic observation, longitudinal studies) in which one tries to find patterns between particular variables, for example viewing violence on television and aggressive behaviour. Because the aggression observed is 'the real thing', not a laboratory analogue, correlational studies often seem more convincing than laboratory experiments. Unfortunately, this advantage is offset by the fact that these studies, like all correlational studies, do not allow one to draw clear conclusions about cause and effect.

In the end, there is no single research design which can optimally address the issue of aggression. Ideally, one would like to employ all three types of studies, since if one finds similar patterns of results in all three types of studies, it enhances one's confidence that the underlying hypothesis may be valid. As you consider the explanations of aggression offered by the five approaches, ask yourself what sort of evidence is being used, and what limitations there may be.

For further consideration

Can you think of any examples of symbolic aggression, where no actual harm occurs? What convinces you that the behaviour is aggressive? Would you be willing to make similar interpretations about other forms of behaviour, such as love? If yes, why? If no, why not?

Theories of Aggression

The most basic issue in the study of aggression is trying to explain its origin. As with many aspects of behaviour, the various theories tend to split into two groups: those that see aggression as innate and those that see aggressive behaviour as learned. While the nature–nurture controversy runs through all of psychology, it has particular significance for aggression, because explanations of its origin *also* imply specific ways of trying to *limit* it. Since society has an interest in limiting at least *some* forms of aggressive behaviour, understanding its causes is a matter of more than theoretical interest. In general, other areas where there is dispute about heredity *vs* environment, such as personality, do not have the same sense of social immediacy. Hence, in looking at the theories proposed by the various approaches, one should consider both how they explain the causes of aggression, and also how they suggest society could or should deal with it.

The Biological Approach

Given the emphasis the approach places on heredity, it should not seem surprising that aggression is viewed as an innate characteristic of human beings. Several theories have been put forth, and various forms of evidence used to support them. Given that no specific genetic or physiological mechanism has been identified, the arguments often depend on analogies to animal research. Among these, one of the best known is the work of Konrad Lorenz.

Lorenz (1903–1989) was one of the founders of **ethology**, an approach to the study of animal behaviour which originated as an offshoot of zoology, not psychology. Lorenz and other ethologists studied behaviour primarily in natural settings, not in the laboratory; this difference in methodology, along with theoretical differences, led to early disputes with behaviouristic psychologists. Both in the study of animals and in drawing analogies to human behaviour, Lorenz was influenced by Darwin's work on evolution. Like Darwin, he believed that many human characteristics were based on inherited mechanisms. Aggression to Lorenz served an evolutionary function, promoting selective survival of the strongest individuals; in other words, it evolved as a biologically useful characteristic. In his best known work, *On Aggression*, Lorenz reviewed his research on animals and extended his argument to humans (Lorenz 1967).

ethology the study of the behaviour of animals in their natural environments

Lorenz viewed aggression as a biologically-based drive which must be periodically satisfied through behavioural expression. This concept, sometimes referred to as a 'reservoir' model, states that the drive level builds up over time, like a reservoir filling with water; the expression of associated behaviours reduces the drive level, much like draining water from the reservoir. Normally, the expression of aggressive behaviour is controlled by environmental cues called **sign stimuli**. Some stimuli are signs for the initiation of aggression. In many species, such as cichlid fish, the intrusion of one individual into the 'territory'

sign stimuli in ethology, environmental cues which regulate the expression of behaviours related to innate drives

Konrad Lorenz

Konrad Zacharias Lorenz (1903–1989) was one of the founders of ethology, an approach to the study of animal behaviour which originated as an offshoot of zoology, not psychology. Lorenz was born and educated in Vienna; he attended the University of Vienna, receiving both a medical degree and a PhD in zoology. The study of animal behaviour attracted him more than did the practice of medicine, and he began to focus on the role of genetic factors in animal behaviour. Together with Nikolaas Tinbergen and Karl von Frisch, he developed a new approach to the study of such behaviour, which became known as ethology, and culminated in the three sharing the 1973 Nobel Prize in Physiology or Medicine. Like other ethologists, Lorenz studied behaviour primarily in natural settings, not in the laboratory; this difference in methodology, along with theoretical differences, led to early disputes with behaviouristic psychologists. Both in the study of animals and in drawing analogies to human behaviour, Lorenz was influenced by Darwin's work on evolution. Like Darwin, he believed that many human characteristics were based on inherited mechanisms. Aggression to Lorenz served an evolutionary function, promoting selective survival of the strongest individuals; in other words, it evolved as a biologically useful characteristic. In his best known work, *On Aggression*, Lorenz reviewed his research on animals, and extended his argument to humans. While sharply attacked by some critics, the book drew wide popular attention. Lorenz died in Vienna at the age of eighty-six.

of another is a sign stimulus for attack. At the same time, other sign stimuli serve to control the aggressive behaviour so that normally encounters are not fatal to either individual. For example, a wolf which is losing a fight will roll over on its back, averting its eyes and exposing its jugular to the other wolf's teeth. While this makes the wolf physically vulnerable, the gesture actually serves as a sign stimulus which *inhibits* further aggression by the victor. Thus, Lorenz viewed the existence of sign stimuli as a crucial factor to understanding aggression. By regulating the nature of aggressive encounters, sign stimuli allow the expression of aggression while also enabling members of a species to establish stable social hierarchies and to minimize fatal violence.

In Lorenz's view, this analysis of aggression has several implications for human aggression. First of all, it implies that since aggression is innate, it is also unavoidable. If society simply attempts to suppress all forms of aggression, then the reservoir will simply 'overflow', resulting in random acts of violence referred to as **vacuum activities**. Lorenz was also concerned that human technology had outstripped biology, in that the sign stimuli that inhibit most fatal aggression require close contact between aggressors (for example, averting the eyes). Methods of killing at a distance, such as bombs dropped from planes and even guns, render such inhibitory stimuli inoperative. Hence, activities like war, while channelling aggression into socially sanctioned forms, bypass the controls that should limit excessive violence.

Given the potential for either random violence or mass destruction, what is society to do? Lorenz argued that society should encourage specific forms of substitute activity, such as sports. Such activities allow expression of aggression

vacuum activities in ethology, behaviours which arise in the absence of appropriate environmental stimuli when drive levels are very high in limited ways, and thereby reduce drive levels. This process, often referred to as *catharsis*, is a solution frequently proposed by advocates of nativist theories of aggression (both biological and psychodynamic). Presumably, Lorenz would be neither surprised nor alarmed at the violence expressed by soccer fans or ice hockey players; instead, he would probably argue that such limited expressions of aggression are preferable to more extreme forms. Aggression will always exist; all society can do is try to channel it into minimally damaging forms.

The work of Lorenz and other ethologists has been important to our understanding of animal behaviour. The concept of sign stimuli, for example, is recognized as a significant contribution. At the same time, his ideas on human aggression are seriously weakened by the absence of supporting human evidence. In essence, the basic assumption that aggression is innate is also the point which must be proved. Generally speaking, finding analogous behaviours in different species does not mean that they have the same cause. For example, showing that aggression is innate in wolves does *not* prove it is *also* innate in humans.

There are also problems in applying the concept of sign stimuli. Lorenz argues that sign stimuli gradually evolved as specific cues in each species; the fact that no-one has identified a stimulus which categorically inhibits aggression in humans suggests that, at the least, the control mechanisms must be somewhat different than in other species. Lorenz's view has an understandable appeal. There is no doubt that humans *do* have an evolutionary heritage, and seeing aggression as innate fits well with many cultural beliefs (what Klama (1988) has called 'the myth of the beast within'). Nonetheless, there are still many gaps in Lorenz's argument, and given the implications for how we seek to deal with aggression, we must be wary of accepting his view without further evidence. (It is worth noting that other ethologically-oriented researchers have also taken the view that aggression is innate. *Sociobiology*, an offshoot of ethology, offers similar arguments; see Konner 1982.)

A second way that biological theorists have approached aggression is through the study of the physiological system. One of the great success stories of physiological research has been the mapping of the human brain to identify the areas responsible for specific aspects of behaviour (see Chapter 2 for further details). Based on this idea of *localization of function*, some researchers have argued that there are areas of the brain, notably in the evolutionarily older regions of the limbic system, that control aggressive behaviour (Delgado 1969; MacLean 1990). In fact, some have gone so far as to suggest that certain violent criminals might be better handled by brain surgery than by imprisonment (Mark and Ervin 1970). As with the ethological argument, it turns out on close examination that much of the argument depends on analogy to animal studies, and consequently the theories seem to go further than the evidence warrants.

A more limited physiological approach has been to look at the connection between pain and aggression. As Moyer has noted, there is a large body of research suggesting that stimuli which cause pain will often trigger aggressive behaviour (Moyer 1976). There is probably a strong defensive component to such behaviour – that is, it seeks to stop the painful stimulation. However, this appears to be only part of the picture, since many factors affect the likelihood of pain-mediated aggression, not all of which have a biological foundation. Since much of the work in this area has involved animals, Leonard Berkowitz has examined the issue in a human context, and notes that there is evidence to suggest that aversive (painful or unpleasant) stimuli can also trigger aggression in people (Berkowitz 1983). However, he is qualified in his support, suggesting that there is also strong evidence that aggressive responses to such stimuli are cognitively mediated, not simply a reflexive response.

Like the ethological research, the physiological evidence seems more suggestive than conclusive. Minimally, it supports the position that *some* forms of aggressive behaviour have a physiological foundation which is largely independent of learning. While some researchers advocate the stronger view that *all* aggression is rooted in the structure of the brain, at present some form of interaction between nature and nurture seems more probable.

For further consideration

The argument offered by Lorenz is based largely on analogy to animal behaviour. In what ways do you think such analogies are appropriate/inappropriate in talking about aggression? That is, are people really like animals?

The Behaviourist Approach

Unlike Lorenz and other biological researchers, the behaviourists view aggression as a form of learned behaviour. 'Aggression' refers not to an internal drive, but to a particular class of voluntary responses, which are acquired and modified by the process of reinforcement. While this general interpretation can be applied to any particular example of aggression, there are really two aspects of aggressive behaviour which have been emphasized by behaviourist theorists: instrumental aggression and the role of frustration in aggression.

Instrumental aggression is aggressive behaviour which is maintained because it is positively reinforced. For example, suppose Mary sees that her younger brother Tommy has a candy, and takes it away from him so as to eat it herself. In this case, her aggressive behaviour (taking someone else's possession) is reinforced by the outcome (having the candy to eat). Although later Mary may be scolded or otherwise punished for her misdeed, the most immediate consequence is positive reinforcement. In effect, Mary will learn that some desired outcomes can be achieved by the use of aggression. Behaviourists describe this as instrumental aggression because the aggressive behaviour results in acquiring the desired reinforcer; the only difference between this situation and any other case of positive reinforcement is that we label the particular response as 'aggressive'. In the same way, behaviourists would argue that many forms of anti-social behaviour represent instrumental aggression. For example, although we may be dismayed to read that a well-dressed person has been attacked and robbed, we are not likely to be *surprised* by the event – the money simply represents a tempting reinforcer to a thief.

instrumental aggression
aggressive behaviour which is maintained because it is positively reinforced

Examples of instrumental aggression like those above are all too familiar in life. Whatever our *moral* perspective, in *pragmatic* terms force sometimes works. Consequently, the behaviourist perspective would suggest that such aggression will be common enough to be mistaken for 'innate'. To prevent such aggression, one must alter the environmental conditions so that such behaviour no longer pays off. For example, a child who hits other children in order to get something will alter this behaviour if adults intervene, ensuring that hitting not only does not lead to the desired outcome, but in fact is punished instead. On the broader level of society, preventing all instrumental aggression would require similar interventions, a requirement which is not easy to fulfil (for example, in Canada, only about 30 per cent of bank robberies lead to arrests, which means that to someone desperate enough, robbing banks can often be reinforcing).

Despite the pervasive nature of instrumental aggression, we also have to recognize that some instances of aggressive behaviour do *not* appear to be instrumental. Consider an athlete who yells at a referee, or a homeowner who kicks a lawnmower that won't start, or a child who, having been embarrassed at school, then misbehaves at home; in each case, the behaviour seems unlikely to lead to a positive reinforcer (a favourable ruling by the referee, a working lawnmower, expressions of affection). In fact, in most cases, we would expect the behaviour to *worsen* the situation. So if such aggressive acts cannot reasonably be viewed as instrumental aggression, how can we explain them? The answer given by the behaviourists is to look at the role of frustration in aggressive behaviour, in terms of what is called the frustration–aggression hypothesis.

The frustration–aggression hypothesis traces its origins to work by John Dollard and his colleagues at Yale in the 1930s (Dollard *et al.* 1939). Consistent with the behaviourist ideas of Watson, they sought to operationalize, and thereby render precise, the everyday concepts of 'frustration' and 'aggression'. In part, this work was intended as a response to Freud's theory, which argued that aggression was innate (later, this work was extended by Dollard and one of the original group, Neal Miller, as an attempt to 'translate' Freudian concepts into behaviourist terms; see Dollard and Miller 1950). What resulted was the **frustration–aggression hypothesis**, which stated that *frustration* (defined as blocking a goal-oriented response) was the sole cause of aggression. If circumstances create frustration, then this will arouse a drive which motivates aggressive behaviour. The intensity of the aggressive response is determined by the intensity of the frustration, and also by prior punishment of aggressive behaviour (the stronger the punishment, the weaker the aggressive response in the future). For example, if a soccer player is blocked from scoring a goal, this may result in aggression against another player. If, however, this results in a heavy penalty for the offending player, such behaviour is likely to be inhibited in the future. Instead, the aggressive tendencies aroused by frustration may be channelled into expending more effort in legitimate ways. An example of this occurred in North American ice hockey, which in the 1980s experienced a trend towards bench-clearing brawls. When a rule change led to stiff penalties to the third person to enter a fight, such brawls were virtually eliminated. These examples illustrate the basic elements of the frustration–aggression hypothesis: frustration leads to increasing the potential for aggression, but punishment does seem to affect the expression of aggression.

The notion that frustration can elicit aggression has an intuitive appeal – after all, we have all felt frustrations which have led to some form of 'letting loose', whether verbally or physically. Researchers, too, have found the hypothesis interesting, and for about twenty-five years it was the dominant framework for research on aggressive behaviour. While the basic idea that frustration could lead to aggression received some support (e.g. Miller 1941), over time the evidence also indicated weaknesses in the original hypothesis. In its strongest form, the hypothesis states that frustration *always* results in aggression, and aggression *only* occurs as a result of frustration. Both of these principles have been challenged.

frustration–aggression hypothesis a theory of aggression developed by Dollard and Miller, which states that *frustration* (defined as blocking a goal-oriented response) is the sole cause of aggression

For example, aggressive behaviour can be produced by reinforcement, even without frustration (Berkowitz 1978). Even when frustration *does* seem to elicit aggression, the relationship has been interpreted as due to the instrumental value of the aggression (Buss 1963).

The issue is further complicated by the fact that a particular frustrating situation may elicit different types of aggressive response in different people. For example, if a soft drink machine accepts money without giving the selected beverage, one person may kick the machine, another may write an angry letter to the company, and a third may walk away depressed, wondering 'Why does it always happen to *me*?' Thus, aggression may be directly expressed towards the immediate source of frustration, or *displaced* towards another object. Displacement extends the frustration–aggression hypothesis to situations in which there is no *immediate* source of frustration, and may also account for some instances of aggression that instrumental aggression cannot explain. Nonetheless, the weaknesses of the hypothesis remain, which leads to the conclusion that frustration is *one* possible cause of aggression, but not the *only* cause.

Taken together, instrumental aggression and the frustration–aggression hypothesis can account for many cases of aggressive behaviour. While each has weaknesses and limitations, they are at least partially complementary, as suggested above. Most importantly, both suggest ways in which aggressive behaviour can be *learned*, and hence pose an alternative to the nativist stance of Freud and the biological approach. If aggression really *is* learned, then no amount of catharsis is going to solve the problem, despite Lorenz's assertions. Indeed, behaviourists would argue that activities intended to reduce the 'aggressive drive' are likely to *increase* aggression by *teaching* aggressive responses. Instead, the behaviourist perspective suggests that we need to focus on identifying those elements of the social environment that encourage aggressive responses, and alter them so as to produce more socially desirable behaviour.

The Cognitive Approach

Like the behaviourists, cognitive theorists see aggressive behaviour as learned, not innate. They also accept that reinforcement can influence learning, and hence that some aggression is instrumentally based. However, the cognitive perspective sees the behaviourist viewpoint as too limited, because it ignores the role of mental processes in learning. Cognitive theorists point to two ways in which mental processes seem to affect behaviour: first, we are capable of learning by observing what others do (imitation); second, our thoughts and perceptions may influence behaviour directly, as opposed to behaviour depending on external stimuli. Let us consider how each of these factors is applied to the understanding of aggression.

The role of **imitation** (or modelling) in learning is the focus of *cognitive social learning theory*. According to the theory, much of what we learn is based on observing the behaviour of others, rather than direct experience and reinforcement. For example, if I see someone who has just jumped into a swimming pool suddenly show a stunned expression and howl, 'Yipes! It's freezing!', I do not have to touch the water to know it is cold. In the same way, we can learn aggressive behaviour from observing others.

Albert Bandura is one of the theorists who has argued for a social learning

imitation the learning of behaviour by observing the behaviour of others; sometimes called 'modelling' or 'observational learning'

Albert Bandura

Albert Bandura (1925–   ) was born in the small town of Mundare in Alberta, Canada. After receiving his bachelor's degree from the University of British Columbia, he emigrated to the United States, receiving his PhD in psychology from the University of Iowa in 1952. The next year, he received a position at Stanford University, where he is currently the David Starr Jordan professor in social sciences. Bandura's interests in social psychology and development led him to the study of learning in children, which led to several ground-breaking studies on the role of imitation in human learning. Together with Leonard Berkowitz, he has been one of the pioneers of the social learning approach, which emphasizes the importance of imitation and cognitive mediation in learning. His influence has been recognized on many occasions, including a Distinguished Scientist award from the American Psychological Association and a Guggenheim Fellowship. He lives with his family in Stanford, California, where he continues to teach and write.

interpretation of aggression (Bandura 1973). In a well-known series of studies, Bandura and his colleagues examined the effects on children of observing aggressive behaviour by an adult. In one typical study, children individually observed an adult who either acted aggressively (e.g. hitting and kicking an inflatable doll) or non-aggressively (playing quietly with toys). Later, the experimenter frustrated the children by taking away a toy they were playing with, saying a child in another room needed it. Aggression was measured by observing the child's behaviour after the experimenter left the room (note that this procedure implies acceptance of the frustration–aggression hypothesis!). The results indicated that exposure to an aggressive model significantly increased imitative aggressive responses, and somewhat increased non-imitative aggressive behaviour (such as verbal remarks or hitting other toys). Interestingly, the effects tended to be stronger for both boys and girls when the adult model was the same sex as the child (Bandura et al. 1961). Although there are flaws in this experiment (including the use of frustration, and the obvious differences between punching an inflatable doll and hitting a person), the study illustrates the basic premise of social learning theory in this context: aggressive behaviour can be learned from observing aggressive acts by others. Later studies both by Bandura and others have extended the original study to a variety of contexts (for a review, see Bandura 1973).

The implications of the theory are both broad-ranging and serious: exposure to aggressive behaviour, in whatever form, is likely to increase the potential for aggression in observers. For example, parents who use physical punishment to discipline their children are likely to make the children more aggressive, since it teaches them that physical force is an appropriate means to control others. This interpretation is supported by a variety of studies which find a correlation between the use of physical discipline by parents and levels of aggression in children (McCord et al. 1961; Eron et al. 1971; Maccoby 1992).

While there have been a tremendous number of studies exploring cognitive social learning theory, support for the theory does have certain limitations. Most significantly, the crucial links to serious human aggression typically are either correlational (as in the case of punishment), or else arguments by analogy (if children can imitate one form of aggression, they will imitate others). In neither situation can one draw direct conclusions about the causes of serious forms of aggression. This is not a trivial concern, and we will return to it in relation to the debate about violence in the media later in this chapter. Nonetheless, cognitive social learning theory clearly represents a *possible* explanation of the origins of many forms of aggressive behaviour.

Apart from social learning, the cognitive approach would argue that the *cognitive schemata* which guide individuals' behaviour can also affect the possibilities of aggressive behaviour. As was discussed in Chapter 1, we each develop a variety of schemata which influence both the way we perceive the world and the way we act. For example, we develop schemata that tell us how to act in a restaurant – waiting to be seated, selecting from a menu, and so on (Schank 1984). These schemata are in turn influenced by the experiences we have. For example, people who watch large amounts of violent programming on television are more likely to perceive their surroundings as dangerous than those who don't watch such programmes. But can such schemata account for aggressive behaviour?

One example of a cognitive schema which relates to aggressive behaviour is what sociologist Elijah Anderson has called 'the code of the streets' (Anderson 1994). This code is a set of norms which govern interpersonal relations in the inner cities of the United States, particularly for black teenagers. In turn, this code is internalized as a cognitive schema which guides behaviour. The most basic premise is that self-esteem is dependent on receiving 'respect' (defined as deferential behaviour) from others. 'Dissing' (expressions of disrespect) must be dealt with in kind, to prevent erosion of self-esteem. Since self-esteem is vulnerable to perceived insults, the code results in aggressive posturing, and quick, violent responses to even imaginary wrongs. Unfortunately, since both parties operate on the same tit-for-tat premise, the violence can quickly escalate, even to fatal levels. Thus, Anderson argues that the assumptions of the code are a contributory factor to inner-city violence. The code, however, is not universal: 'decent' kids (those trained in mainstream values) use the code only when necessary to minimize confrontational situations; by contrast, 'street' kids, imbued with the code, have no alternative schema. In this sense, what is most striking about Anderson's observations is the implication that different cognitive schema can have a very real effect on the likelihood of aggressive behaviour.

Apart from such specific schemata, it is possible that violent thoughts may elicit violence through a kind of **priming** effect, the notion that any thought or memory is capable of increasing the activation of associated thoughts or memories. Leonard Berkowitz, one of the early supporters of cognitive social learning theory, has endorsed this idea to account for non-imitative forms of aggression. Berkowitz refers to the underlying model as *cognitive neo-association theory* (Berkowitz 1984). Whereas social learning theory requires that a particular aggressive behaviour must be observed in order to be learned, neo-association theory suggests that violent cognitions can increase the potential for *any* related behaviours. For example, Berkowitz notes that suicide rates go up after highly publicized airplane crashes; while both represent violent events, it is clearly not a case of imitation. In one experiment, Berkowitz looked at the effects of

priming a phenomenon whereby a thought or memory increases the activation of associated thoughts or memories (the term is analogous to 'priming a pump' by using a small quantity of water to enhance the flow of water) violence-related stimuli on subsequent aggression by angry individuals. Individuals who were shown pictures of weapons were more willing to punish another person (with electric shocks) than those shown neutral pictures, such as a badminton racquet.

As with social learning theory, much of the evidence for neo-association theory depends on broad extrapolations of experiments, with only correlational data for 'real-world' aggressive behaviour. (Although it should be evident, it is worth mentioning that a primary reason for the lack of more direct evidence is the ethical concerns when doing research involving aggression.) Despite this difficulty, the data suggest that the way we think *can* influence the way we act.

In summary, the cognitive approach suggests that aggressive behaviour is learned, and can be influenced both by what we observe (imitation) and by the way we think (the role of schemata). These assertions have been the focus of extensive research, most of which is consistent with the underlying hypotheses. Nonetheless, critics have been quick to point out the technical limitations of the research for explaining the wide range of aggressive behaviour found in society. By asserting that aggressive behaviour is *learned*, the cognitive approach suggests that such behaviour is not inevitable. In fact, it implies that the same principles can be applied to fostering pro-social behaviour. In essence, humans are neither inherently evil, nor inherently good; how we act depends on what we have learned.

The Psychodynamic Approach

The psychodynamic approach traces its roots to Freud, and psychoanalysis is still probably the best known theory within the approach. While the cognitive and behaviourist approaches see aggressive behaviour as learned, and therefore avoidable, Freud viewed aggression as an innate drive, and therefore an unavoidable reality of human life. Although he gave the underlying drive various names at various times (destrudo, aggression, thanatos), he never wavered in his belief that the urge to commit aggressive acts was innate. In his studies of behaviour, both of his patients and of other times and cultures, he found ample indications of the prevalence of aggressive behaviour.

The aggressive drive was seen as part of the *id*, that aspect of the mind and personality which motivates our behaviour. As we grow, *ego* emerges to mediate our interactions with the world; later, our moral sense, represented by the *superego*, is formed. Ego and superego often oppose the aggressive impulses of the id, creating conflict within the psyche. To cope with this conflict – and the aggressive tendencies – we use defence mechanisms. *Defence mechanisms* block conscious awareness of the underlying conflicts, and attempt to ameliorate the tensions in various ways, for example by *displacing* the aggression onto a substitute object (a man who plays a hard game of squash after having a disagreement with a colleague at work could be viewed as engaging in displacement as he bashes the ball).

In Freud's view, we can never eliminate aggression, we can only seek to control it by channelling it in particular ways which involve *symbolic* gratification. The most desirable form of release is through *sublimation*, the creation of socially approved products like art or music. Since most of us are not proficient in such activities, a more common form of coping is the use of displacement, as noted above. *Fantasy*, seen in both dreams and other activities, is another possible outlet for aggressive energy. For example, imagining that the driver who just cut you off gets stopped by the police is an expression of aggression through fantasy. Underlying these and other defence mechanisms is the principle of *catharsis*, the release of drive energy through indirect gratification. For example, catharsis implies that if one watches violence (e.g. a war movie), then one will symbolically release aggression through one's involvement with the characters (note that Lorenz also advocated catharsis, although the details of his theory are somewhat different). Unfortunately, the evidence regarding the value of catharsis is rather mixed. For example, a study by Feshbach aroused aggressive tendencies by insulting the participants, and then provided one group with the opportunity to engage in fantasy activities. When compared to a control group, this group showed a significant reduction in aggressive impulses, as measured by projective tests (a measure of symbolic aggression) (Feshbach 1955).

However, when looking at more direct forms of aggression, other studies have been less favourable. For example, in one study, participants were first given electric shocks during a learning task (arousing aggressive tendencies), and then half the subjects were allowed to retaliate against their tormentors, which presumably would reduce aggressive tendencies (Geen *et al*. 1975). Instead, in a follow-up to this situation, those subjects who had retaliated subsequently gave *more* intense shocks than those in the group which had no chance to retaliate previously. Hence, rather than reducing aggression, the initial opportunity to retaliate *increased* subsequent aggression, a result more consistent with social learning than catharsis. Aronson (1976), in reviewing the literature on aggression, has argued that the evidence for catharsis is minimal.

Like the biological perspective, psychoanalysis asserts that aggression is innate. For the most part, Freud used case studies and anecdotal observations to support his theory; in addition, by emphasizing the symbolic nature of behaviour, he was able to ascribe even non-violent actions to aggressive motives. Unfortunately, the dependence on case studies and symbolic interpretation can only be considered weak evidence for the innateness of aggression; attempts at experimental validation by later researchers have met with mixed results. Furthermore, it is worth noting that some of Freud's early disciples, including Adler and Jung, disagreed with his interpretation that aggression was innate. As Freud clearly recognized, aggressive behaviour is a common human phenomenon – but explaining *why* is the issue, and its pervasiveness does *not* constitute direct proof that it is innate. Given these realities, we can only conclude that the case for Freud's view seems open to serious doubt.

The Humanistic Approach

A number of humanistic theorists, including Maslow and Rogers, explicitly reject the idea that aggression is an innate drive. As Freud's theory shows, such an assumption leads to a pessimistic view of human potential, and the humanistic approach views human experience in far more optimistic terms. At the same time, even the greatest optimist must acknowledge that aggressive behaviour exists. So how can humanistic theories account for it? To understand, let us look at the theories of Maslow and Rogers.

Maslow, in developing his *hierarchy of needs*, was attempting to describe the basic factors which motivate human behaviour. His model points out that a number of different needs exist, and that for any individual, different needs will be more pressing at different points in time. Conspicuously absent from his hierarchy is any mention of aggression. Instead of being an innate drive which must be satisfied, aggression arises in response to circumstances in which fulfilment of one of the basic needs is obstructed. In this sense, Maslow's view of aggressive behaviour is somewhat akin to the frustration–aggression hypothesis: aggressive behaviour is a possible response to particular circumstances. However, Maslow does not endorse the strong form of the frustration–aggression hypothesis, which states that frustration (blocking satisfaction of a need, for Maslow) *always* results in aggression. Instead, he sees aggressive behaviour (particularly instrumental aggression) as only *one* possible option among many.

To understand this concept of aggression as only one possible response, let us consider an example. If an intruder broke into my home, thereby arousing my need for security, I might grab a baseball bat and attempt to knock the person senseless. Clearly, this would be an aggressive response; however, even in this situation, other options exist. I might, for example, barricade the bedroom door, and warn the intruder that I have telephoned the police. A friend once had the experience of an intruder entering his house, and coming to the bedroom. As the intruder entered the bedroom, Tony's wife woke him, just in time to see the stranger lunging at him with a knife. Fortunately, Tony (who was trained in the martial arts) disarmed the intruder, *without retaliating*, and held him until the police arrived. While they waited for the police, Tony talked with the teenage intruder, who had been driven by economic desperation to commit this offence. Despite nearly being killed (the knife tip came close enough to scratch his chest), Tony felt sorry for the teenager, and almost regretted having telephoned the police! As this example shows, even threats to the need for physical safety do not inevitably require aggressive behaviour as a response. Hence, aggressive behaviour may arise in relation to the deprivation needs, but is only one possible response. In the absence of any deprivation, Maslow would see aggressive behaviour as highly unlikely. Hence, in his portrayal of self-actualized individuals, aggressive behaviour is largely absent; since self-actualization is not a deprivation need, it does not provide even this minimal reason for aggression.

Carl Rogers' theory uses a different set of concepts than does Maslow's, but leads to a similar conclusion concerning aggression. Rogers sees human development as based on the *actualizing tendency*, which is a positive force for growth. Aggression, therefore, is not an innate drive. Instead, aggressive behaviour is one of the possible consequences of a state of incongruence. *Incongruence* occurs when the individual experiences a conflict between their sense of self and their ideal self. Typically, this arises when, as a requirement for providing positive regard, other people impose *conditions of worth*. For example, teenagers frequently resent the rules of conduct which their parents attempt to impose, resulting in various forms of resistance, including acts of aggression. In Rogers' terms, there is a conflict between the teenager's own values (part of the self) and the parental values on which they were raised (part of the ideal self). As awareness of their own values grows, it results in resentment at the parents, who use conditional regard to try to maintain the prior values. Aggressive behaviour can be one response to this situation.

Another possible way in which aggressive behaviour might arise is if a person adopts aggressive norms due to the need for positive regard. For example, an adolescent exposed to the type of 'street code' which Anderson (1994) has described may be reluctantly drawn into aggressive behaviour in order to get peer approval. Note that in both of the preceding examples, Rogers would not see aggression as inevitable, or even as the most appropriate response; it is simply a *possible* response.

Given that conditions of worth are frequently encountered in everyday life, we should not be surprised that aggressive behaviour is relatively common. However, Rogers believes that when individuals are in touch with the actualizing tendency, they will recognize aggressive responses as inappropriate. This is reflected in his description of the values which are associated with healthy growth, which make no mention of aggression, but include 'sensitivity to others and acceptance of others' (Rogers 1964: 166). Rogers notes that under the conditions which foster growth, 'I do not find, in such a climate of freedom, that one person comes to value fraud and murder and thievery, while another values a life of self-sacrifice' (Rogers 1964: 167). In other words, given the conditions for healthy growth and the development of congruence, aggressive behaviour will not occur.

While the interpretations of aggression offered by Maslow and Rogers are consistent with their overall theories of behaviour, neither theorist provides much in terms of direct empirical support for their views. In part, this is due to the humanists' methodology, which emphasizes the subjective nature of experience rather than traditional experimentation. As a consequence, much of the evidence involves case studies and anecdotal observations drawn from their experiences with individuals in therapy; Maslow also emphasized the study of historical figures. As noted with Freud, such data are very limited as a means of proving causation.

Ultimately, the humanistic assertion that aggression is not innate depends on two assertions: first, that aggressive behaviour is based on thwarted development; second, that some individuals function largely without resorting to aggressive behaviour. The first point, as already noted, is problematical at best, since no direct proof is given. The second point is interesting, but equally ambiguous. Since no-one is *fully* self-actualized or *fully* congruent, and definitions of aggression differ, how one interprets aggressive acts is likely to be influenced by one's assumptions. For example, instances of aggressive behaviour in a supposedly self-actualized individual might be seen as refuting the humanistic view, or simply as an indication that the person is less than perfect. Even if someone showed no real sign of overt aggression, such as Mahatma Ghandi (the father of passive resistance as a form of political protest), some critics might say his behaviour reflected indirect or symbolic aggression. In the end, judging the appropriateness of the humanistic view of aggression seems (like other aspects of experience) dependent on one's own perceptions.

Comparing the Approaches

Having considered the interpretations of aggression which the five approaches provide, where does this leave us? What can we conclude about the origins of aggression? The research, while not definitive, does point towards certain conclusions (see Fig. 8.1 for a summary of the approaches' interpretations).

PERSPECTIVES ON AGGRESSION

APPROACH	EXPLANATION OF CAUSE	METHOD OF REDUCING
Biological	Ethology – innate drive	Catharsis (e.g. via sports)
	Physiology – response to aversive stimuli	Minimize aversive stimuli
Behaviourist	Instrumental aggression – using aggression to reach a goal is reinforcing	Change contingencies so aggressive responses not reinforced
	Frustration – aggression hypothesis frustration leads to aggression	Minimize sources of frustration
Cognitive	Social learning theory – aggressive behaviour is imitated	Reduce opportunities for observing aggression
	Neo-association theory – aggressive events trigger related thoughts and actions	Reduce exposure to aggressive stimuli
Psychodynamic (Freud)	Aggression innate drive (in id)	Catharsis (especially sublimation)
Humanistic (Rogers)	Aggression is one response to distortions of growth due to conditions of worth	Provide more unconditional positive regard

Fig. 8.1 Perspectives on aggression This chart provides a comparison of the five approaches in terms of how they view the origin of aggression, and the means by which it can be controlled.

In terms of innate factors, the research on physiological aspects of aggression suggests that there is a relationship between *pain* and aggression; that is, painful or unpleasant stimuli often elicit aggressive behaviour. To the extent that this reaction is governed by particular brain pathways (as some assert), it represents an innate source of aggression. One interpretation of this relationship is that the behaviour is a defensive response, intended to eliminate the aversive stimulus. However, not all situations involving pain can be explained in this way, so the proper conclusion seems to be that painful stimuli can provoke aggression, but do not always do so.

Theories which propose an *innate drive* – both Lorenz's ethological theory and Freud's psychoanalytic theory – have little direct supporting evidence. The argument that aggression is common, and therefore must be innate, is really only circular reasoning. Furthermore, the mechanism which both theories propose for reducing aggression (i.e. *catharsis*) also has only weak experimental support. Consequently, one must conclude that the notion of an innate drive is largely unfounded.

The alternative to assuming aggression is innate is to explain it in terms of learning, and several theories have done so. The behaviourist concept of *instrumental aggression*, which says that aggression is reinforced by experiences in which it is effective in accomplishing a goal, is plausible, and has received some experimental support. It can also be related to other theories. For example, aggression as a defensive reaction to pain can be seen as a form of instrumental aggression if the person succeeds in eliminating the painful stimulus. Hence, it is a likely cause of aggressive behaviour.

The *frustration–aggression hypothesis*, by contrast, has weaker support. There seems no question that frustration can elicit aggression, but there are many qualifiers on the relationship, including the perceived likelihood of retaliation. Indeed, it may well be that frustrating circumstances simply represent a particular form of aversive stimuli, in which case the hypothesis really reduces to a special case of the pain–aggression relationship. In its strong form, which suggests that frustration accounts for *all* aggression, the hypothesis no longer seems justified. Given that its weak form requires so many qualifiers, the frustration–aggression hypothesis has limited explanatory value.

The humanistic approach, as represented by Maslow and Rogers, rejects the nativist interpretation of aggression. Rather than being inevitable, aggressive behaviour is a result of experiences which interfere with healthy growth. That is, healthy individuals (*self-actualized* or *fully functioning*) are unlikely to respond aggressively. While each theory suggests circumstances in which aggression might arise, they suffer from the relative absence of supporting research. Given that the humanistic approach favours subjective analysis of experience over experimentation, the lack of evidence is largely inevitable. While the absence of conventional evidence does not prove the approach is wrong, it does mean that most researchers see it as untestable, and hence of limited value.

The approach which has perhaps the most support, in terms of the volume of research which has been done, is the cognitive approach. While accepting the principle of instrumental aggression, the approach adds two further mechanisms to account for aggressive behaviour: social learning and cognitive schemata. *Social learning theory*, as described by Albert Bandura and others, argues that behaviour is acquired through imitation. Consequently, if children observe violence, then they will in turn act aggressively. This relationship applies not only to direct experience (for example, discipline by parents), but also to vicarious experiences, such as watching television.

Cognitive schemata can influence aggression in two ways: by providing norms to guide behaviour and by priming. We each have various *norms* related to social situations; if a person has acquired, through social learning or otherwise, a schema which states aggression is acceptable, then that person will show aggressive behaviour (as in the case of street gang members). *Priming* suggests that observing violence causes activation of related cognitive schemata, resulting in a greater likelihood of a wide range of aggressive behaviours. As Leonard Berkowitz has noted, this theory can account for rather unexpected relationships, such as increases in the suicide rate after a plane crash. One of the chief difficulties with these theories is that much of the evidence is either correlational or else based on extrapolation from laboratory studies involving relatively mild forms of aggressive behaviour. As a consequence, it is hard to demonstrate that the explanations offered actually apply in everyday life. One case which has proven particularly contentious is the application of social learning theory to predicting the effects of observing violence in the media; we will consider this more closely as an illustration of the difficulties involved in social research.

Aggression and the Media

For many years now, there has been a debate about the relationship between observing violence portrayed in the media and aggressive behaviour. Whether one considers the news media or the entertainment media, there is no question that images of violence are readily encountered. However, the issue is not whether such portrayals occur, but rather what effect they have on society. To a large extent, the debate concerns whether media violence increases aggressive behaviour (as the cognitive approach argues) or not.

At an intuitive level, many people favour the social learning view. For example, after seeing a film like 'Die Hard', in which a lone policeman takes on a group of terrorists who have seized an office building, most people feel some degree of arousal, not relaxation. Does this mean that they will then scour the streets looking for terrorists? Probably not. Yet, occasionally, reality *does* imitate fiction. Nearly everyone is aware of the threat terrorists pose to airline flights; what most people *don't* realize is that the first documented attempt to highjack an airliner came *after* a television drama by Rod Serling in which the idea was proposed. Such instances are disturbing, but in a case like this one cannot rule out coincidence, or the possibility that a highjacking would have occurred eventually even if the Serling drama had never been shown. Nonetheless, the issue tends to emerge whenever reality and fiction meet.

The debate is largely between the cognitive approach and those theories which see aggression as innate (the biological approach and psychoanalysis). The cognitive approach argues that observing violence may increase the potential for aggression, through both imitation and priming. The nativist theories, drawing on the concept of drive-reduction, suggest that observing violence can lessen aggressive energy through catharsis. It is also possible that, in the real world, no consistent relationship exists between observing violence and aggressive behaviour. This could happen if both theories are wrong, or even if the two kinds of processes somehow offset each other, producing no net change in the potential for aggressive behaviour.

Given the limited evidence for catharsis, most of the research has focused on the hypothesis that observing violence *increases* aggressive behaviour. Much of the research has been based on social learning (imitation of observed violent acts), although in practice researchers often measure both imitative and non-imitative forms of aggressive behaviour. (It should be noted that while researchers often refer to 'observing *television* violence', this is a shorthand descriptor for all forms of observed violence: one need not distinguish television from movies, or fictional dramas from news footage, since all provide the basis for modelling. However, much of the research has focused on television dramas, since it is arguable that most individuals are exposed to more violence via such shows than either news shows or movies.)

Exploring the Evidence

Over the past three decades, there have been hundreds of laboratory experiments on social learning of aggressive behaviour, and even several reviews of the published literature. While the details of the studies vary, they have looked at modelling of aggression by both sexes over a wide age range, and using a number of measures of aggressive behaviour (including willingness to give electric shocks to other people). Within the laboratory context, it appears quite clear that observing violence will increase the likelihood of aggressive behaviour (for reviews, see Bandura 1973; Geen 1976; Freidrich-Cofer and Huston 1986). The difficulty with these studies is that laboratory findings may not generalize very well, for several reasons. One obvious concern is that individuals are aware of taking part in an experiment, so they may not react as they would in everyday situations. In addition, ethical considerations limit the forms of aggression that can be used in a laboratory, further reducing the generality of results.

Because of the limitations of laboratory experiments, researchers have also tried to look at the effects of observing television violence in natural settings. One way that this can be done is through the use of correlational studies, which involve making observations without the controls required for experiments. Indeed, one of the earliest studies to report a link between observing television violence and aggressive behaviour in children was based on an incidental finding from a broader study of child-rearing practices (Eron 1963). Subsequently, a positive correlation between observing violence on television and aggressive behaviour has been confirmed in a large number of studies (e.g. Belson 1978; Singer and Singer 1981; Eron 1982).

While these studies have shown a link for a variety of groups in several different countries, the results are nonetheless limited, in that no correlational study can identify the *cause* of an observed pattern. That is, on the basis of the correlational data alone, one could argue that aggressive children choose to watch more violent television (reversing the direction of causation), or that an unidentified third variable accounts for the link (possibly family influences), or that the pattern is simply coincidental (unlikely, given how common the pattern is). Ideally, one would like to gather experimental evidence in a natural setting – in other words, do a field experiment.

One interesting study was conducted by a group of Canadian researchers who took advantage of serendipitous circumstances in order to pursue the issue. Dubbed 'a natural experiment', the study examined the impact of the introduction of television in a Canadian town (Joy *et al.* 1986). A number of small towns in Canada did not have access to television until the 1970s because of their isolated locations. One such town, identified in the study as Notel (for 'no television'), did not have television until 1974. The investigators examined behaviour in this town both before the advent of television and for two years after its introduction. As a control comparison, they also examined behaviour in two other Canadian towns which, while similar in size and demographic profile, already had access to television. Aggressive behaviour was measured in two ways: by direct observation of children's verbal and physical aggression during play periods at school, and by student and teacher ratings of aggressiveness. Compared to before the advent of television, aggressive behaviour for both boys and girls in Notel was significantly higher two years after its introduction; over

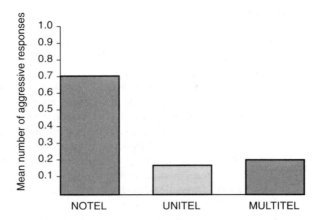

Fig. 8.2 Effects of the introduction of television The graph shows the results of a field experiment in which physical aggression by children was compared as a function of the introduction of television to the Notel community. Unlike in the two communities which already had television at the time of the study, the children in Notel showed a significant increase in physical aggression (adapted from Joy et al. 1986).

the same period, there was no significant increase in such behaviour for children in the other two towns (see Fig. 8.2). What is particularly striking is that the increases occurred for a wide range of children: both sexes, those who were initially high *or* low in aggressiveness, and those who watched large *or* small amounts of television. Hence, the study suggests a strong link between exposure to television and aggressive behaviour. The primary difficulty with the study is that the experimenters did not have direct control over the *content* of what the children watched. This means that the effects cannot specifically be linked to observing violent television programmes, although one might assume that some portion of the viewing (and the results) involved violent programming. This illustrates the difficulty of doing field experiments (and natural-setting research in general) – one cannot control all elements of the situation.

A slightly different approach to a field experiment was reported by Leonard Eron and his colleagues (Eron 1982). As part of an on-going correlational study, Eron and co-workers designed an experiment aimed at reducing the aggressive behaviour of a group who had already been identified as viewing high levels of violence. These 169 boys were randomly divided into two groups: one group was given training intended to reduce aggression by altering attitudes towards television violence; the other group was a control group that engaged in comparable activities (discussing television, writing essays) without reference to the issue of violence. Based on peer ratings of aggression collected four months after the end of the training, the experimental group showed significant reductions in aggressive behaviour, while the control group showed no change. Unfortunately, interpretation of the results is complicated by the mixing of several types of training, which make it unclear precisely which aspect of the training was most significant. However, the general pattern of results suggests that *attitudes* towards what is viewed, not simply the *content* of what is viewed, can be a factor in determining the impact of observing violence. This is a significant finding, because it suggests that it is not simply the viewing of violence which increases aggressive behaviour; instead, it depends on how the viewer interprets the meaning of what they watch. Support for this conclusion comes from other studies which suggest that parental guidance can alter both children's perceptions of violence *and* subsequent aggressive behaviour (Mattern and Lindholm 1985).

Interpreting the Evidence

Taken as a whole, all three types of research point to a connection between observing television violence and aggressive behaviour. However, none of the studies we have mentioned is without its flaws, and critics continue to challenge the conclusion that a relationship exists. Jonathan Freedman, for example, has carefully scrutinized almost all of the above studies and offered objections in each case (Freedman 1984, 1986). In the end, Freedman acknowledges that the correlation between viewing TV violence and aggressive behaviour *is* likely to be genuine. However, he *also* concludes that the effect is small (a correlation coefficient of 0.10–0.20), and that weaknesses in the experimental research suggest that the evidence for a *causal* connection is minimal. He suggests that alternative explanations exist, such as the possibility that aggressive children simply like to watch violent TV (in effect, reversing the direction of causation). Should we accept this interpretation?

In part, Freedman is justified in being sceptical, since each of the studies we have discussed *does* have flaws. However, it should be noted that they are not the *same* flaws in each case, and that the general nature of the results remains the same in all cases. Technically, in science we must assess the evidence on a case-by-case basis, unlike the 'preponderance of probability' criterion that is used in law. Since each study does have flaws, we have no unequivocal outcome on which to base the conclusion that observing violence increases aggression. Yet, given the vast literature, including the experimental studies (both laboratory and field) which point towards the conclusion, it seems reasonable to believe that *some* relationship does exist. At the same time, it is important to note what is *not* being said: no-one is suggesting that observing violence on television is the *only* factor in aggression. Even those who oppose nativist theories would acknowledge that instrumental aggression and other forms of social learning (for example, attitudes of parents and interpersonal skills) play a role in the likelihood of aggressive behaviour (for replies to Freedman, see Freidrich-Cofer and Huston 1986; Liebert and Sprafkin 1988).

The debate raised by Freedman's analysis goes to the heart of our understanding of social behaviour. Psychology has traditionally (but not exclusively) modelled its methods on those of the physical sciences, a domain where many of the phenomena are relatively simple compared to human behaviour. Within psychology, social behaviour may well be the most complex area, since it involves interactions of complex individuals. Beyond this, social psychologists are often limited in their research methods by ethical considerations. All of these factors create constraints on the effectiveness of research. Consequently, it seems unlikely that one could conceive of *any* one study in social psychology which would adequately satisfy the conflicting needs for experimental control, experimental realism, external validity and ethical responsibility. Thus, one must proceed, hesitantly, by exploring the problem from as many angles as possible. Looked at in this way, Freedman's analysis seems overly critical, and possibly disingenuous, in that it seems unlikely that any generally accepted finding in psychology would meet his standard of proof.

One can draw a parallel here to research on the relationship between smoking and lung cancer. Technically, no direct experimental evidence for the relationship exists, yet the convergence of results from animal experiments and human epidemiological studies has led to wide acceptance that there *is* a relationship. [This parallel is also somewhat ironic, it that it was the 1964 Surgeon General's report (claiming a link between smoking and lung cancer) which triggered the first major study of television violence and aggression, the 1972 US Surgeon General's report.] In scientific terms, we must always look at the quality of the evidence, yet questions like the impact of television violence on behaviour also have social implications, which involve elements having little to do with science.

More than any other area of psychology, social psychology seems to invite extrapolation to everyday life. Thus, if one *does* accept that there is a causal connection between observing violence and aggressive behaviour, then shouldn't society do something about it? And if so, what? Ban all violence in television and movies? Prohibit all violence in sports? Such prospects can evoke strong feelings among both advocates and detractors. The problem is, psychological research may help us *understand* behaviour, but it cannot address directly the moral questions of what behaviour *should* be. In this sense, psychological research cannot be the sole criterion for framing social policy.

At the same time, to ignore what psychology has learned when we consider social issues (either individually or collectively) seems equally undesirable. To do so implies that the search for understanding has no bearing on our lives. As a parent, for example, I am concerned both with the upbringing of my children, and with the kind of society in which they live; in both respects, I feel it is important to be as well-informed as possible. To this end, it seems desirable to try to understand the factors that affect aggression, and also socially desirable forms of behaviour.

For further consideration

What conclusion do *you* draw about the relationship between observing violence and aggressive behaviour? How do you feel about movies which vividly portray acts of violence? Should all violence in the media be regarded as alike?

Encouraging Prosocial Behaviour

Thus far, our examination of social behaviour has focused on one of the most negative forms of behaviour, aggression. While not demonstrating that *all* aggressive behaviour is learned, the research on observing violence certainly suggests that the potential for aggressive behaviour can be enhanced through learning. What about behaviour which is socially desirable? How does *it* arise? And are there ways to encourage such behaviour? For example, does reading stories about people who help others (such as the Good Samaritan) have any impact on actual helping by children?

```
          CATEGORIES OF PROSOCIAL BEHAVIOUR


    ATRUISM – sharing, helping, and cooperation with people or animals

    CONTROL OF AGGRESSION – behaviours intended to prevent or
        eliminate aggression by self or others

    EXPLAINING FEELINGS – communicating with another person about
        thoughts, feelings or actions with intent of increasing
        understanding and fostering positive outcomes

    REPARATION FOR WRONGDOING – behaviour which is clearly intended
        to make amends for previous wrongful actions

    RESISTANCE TO TEMPTATION – resisting temptation to engage in
        socially prohibited behaviours (e.g. stealing)

    SYMPATHY – expressing concern for others and their problems

    TASK PERSISTENCE / DELAY OF GRATIFICATION – actions intended
        to fulfil commitments by persisting at a task or delaying gratification
```

Fig. 8.3 Categories of prosocial behaviour Just as various forms of aggression exist, there are also various forms of prosocial behaviour. This chart shows some categories suggested by Rubenstein *et al.* (1974; adapted from the original).

prosocial behaviour
behaviour which is socially desirable; that is, behaviour which is beneficial to another person or to society as a whole

Prosocial behaviour can be defined as behaviour which is socially desirable, and which in some way benefits another person, or society as a whole. While *altruism* is the most frequently studied category of prosocial behaviour, it also includes a number of other kinds of behaviour (see Fig. 8.3). In day-to-day life, we all engage in prosocial behaviour when we play a team sport, when we offer sympathy to a friend who is upset, or when we refrain from littering. Hence, the working of society is largely dependent on the occurrence of prosocial behaviour.

As with aggression, each of the five approaches has an interpretation of how socially desirable behaviour arises. In terms of the biological approach, sociobiologists like Melvin Konner (1982) have suggested that prosocial behaviours like altruism occur only in very narrow contexts, which relate to the transmission of one's genes. Thus, a parent might sacrifice their own life to save their child, because the child carries half of their genes and can in turn preserve them by procreating. For similar reasons, one would be less likely to help a more distant relative like a cousin, and very unlikely to help a total stranger, whose genetic similarity is unknown. By contrast, Freud saw altruism resulting from a defence mechanism, whereby one engages in good deeds in order to block awareness of one's own aggressive nature. In his view, such behaviours have social value, but their occurrence is dependent on the dynamics of the psyche, particularly in terms of how ego handles the competing demands of id and superego. The humanists see helping others as a kind of reciprocity; just as we each need to be accepted and loved by others, we recognize their need to be accepted (and helped) by us. To the behaviourists, prosocial behaviours, like aggressive behaviours, are acquired through reinforcement; if parents and others reinforce such actions, then the child will learn to help others. Like the behaviourists, the cognitive approach views prosocial behaviours as based on the same processes as antisocial behaviours; both types of behaviour are learned by imitation, and are influenced by the schemata we form concerning social interactions.

The converse of altruism is *bystander apathy*, the failure to intervene in an emergency. As discussed in Chapter 1, the study of this issue was stimulated in part by the unfortunate death of Kitty Genovese in New York in 1964. Here was a young woman being repeatedly attacked on the street, and screaming for help, to no avail. As it turned out, none of the thirty-eight individuals later identified as having observed the attack had even telephoned the police. The event shocked many people, and was seen by many as a sign of the callousness of modern urban life. After all, in doing nothing to help, the bystanders had indirectly contributed to her death.

Bystander apathy obviously fails to meet the definition of prosocial behaviour, although it is not as antisocial as aggressive behaviour. The possible reasons for failing to aid someone in distress are many, and include fears to one's own safety, legal barriers and social dynamics. For example, in some jurisdictions, bystanders are not legally compelled to intervene in an emergency, but may be held liable for consequences if they do intervene; clearly, this legal stance can serve as a deterrent to becoming involved. In the present context, we will focus on the social processes that either hinder altruism or serve to encourage it.

As Latané and Darley (1969) noted in their research on the problem, the failure to intervene may reflect social processes that have little to do with a lack of caring. Emergencies, by their nature, are both rare and unpredictable; in addition, some emergencies may call for special training, whether swimming, medical treatment, or other skills. Consequently, many people are unsure what to do when faced with a situation in which someone needs help. In such circumstances, individuals may look to others for clues as to how to act – a form of *social influence*. Thus, if others are present and do nothing, one might conclude that there is no reason to intervene. Even if no-one else is present, social influence may play a role, in terms of calling upon previously learned social schema. For example, a teenager might think, 'What would my Dad do in this situation?' Consequently, social influence is a major factor in determining altruism or its converse, bystander apathy. (When others are present, there can also be a perceived lessening of the onus to act, called **diffusion of responsibility**. To avoid ambiguity, much of the research on enhancing altruism has utilized situations involving single individuals.)

diffusion of responsibility
a lessening of an individual's feeling of responsibility in a situation which involves other people

Research on Prosocial Behaviour

Many early studies of bystander behaviour simply sought to identify the circumstances under which people do or do not intervene; Latané and Darley's work took this approach. More recently, researchers have attempted to increase intervention through social influence. In one study, a variant of Latané and Darley's 'lady in distress' scenario was used; the difference was that in this version the confederate did not ignore the sound of someone falling in the next room (Staub, reported in Goleman 1993). In one case, the confederate said, 'That probably has nothing to do with us'. In this condition, fewer than 25 per cent of subjects intervened to offer help. In the other condition, the confederate said, 'That sounds pretty bad – I'll go get the experimenter and maybe you should go check what's happening next door', and proceeded to leave the room. In this case, 100 per cent of subjects moved to render aid. In effect, the comments of the confederate served to define what was appropriate behaviour in the situation. Hence, one way to enhance altruism is by creating situational interpretations which encourage intervention.

Other research suggests it is also possible to enhance prosocial behaviour by means of exposure to media examples. Sprafkin and her colleagues tested this possibility by exposing first-grade children to one of three television shows: one conveyed a message to help others even at personal cost, while the other two represented control conditions with no such message (Sprafkin et al. 1975). Subsequently, over 90 per cent of children exposed to the helping message chose helping a puppy over a chance for personal gain; in neither control group did more than 50 per cent similarly intervene. One way to explain this result is in terms of imitation, since the helping message also involved rescuing an animal. However, Berkowitz has suggested that these and similar studies involving media exposure can be explained better in terms of *priming* – that is, exposure to concepts of helping serves to activate related schema in the individual (Berkowitz 1984). The activation of these prosocial schemata then makes it more likely that the person will intervene if an emergency – even one dissimilar to the original example – arises. For example, if I hear on the radio that a young child has given their allowance to a charity, I may be more likely to help a stranded motorist while I am driving to work.

Both priming and social learning are consistent with the conclusion that it is possible to enhance prosocial behaviour by exposing individuals to examples of prosocial concepts. However, they do differ in significant ways. One difference is that priming is generally seen as relatively transient, lasting hours or days (Berkowitz 1984). By contrast, social learning effects can often be detected months or years later (e.g. Eron 1982).

Based on current research, we cannot unequivocally explain the origin of prosocial behaviours like altruism. While sociobiologists like Konner assert that such behaviour is biologically determined, the argument is based on analogies to animal behaviour, and must be considered tentative at best (Konner 1982). At the same time, the studies of bystander apathy and priming effects suggest that prosocial behaviour can be modified. Such results support the cognitive approach, in terms of social leaning and the role of mental schema. Of course, the existing research does not prove that *all* prosocial behaviour is learned, nor does it imply that no limits exist to modifiability. Hopefully, over time, we will develop a clearer understanding of prosocial behaviour, and may even find ways to apply that understanding in our communities.

Interestingly, compared to the debates about aggression, the study of prosocial behaviour has been relatively non-controversial. This may be due to differences in the amount of data available – thousands of studies on aggression, but relatively few on prosocial behaviour. It may also reflect differences in how people view the implications. For example, if one believes aggression is innate, then attempts to eliminate it might be seen as not only fruitless, but also possibly dangerous. However, if one believes that prosocial behaviour is innate, then attempts to enhance it would be seen as fruitless, but also harmless. By contrast, theories which emphasize the learning of social behaviour would argue that society must accept responsibility, and develop policies for both discouraging aggression and enhancing prosocial behaviour. In many respects, it comes down to the basic assumptions one makes about behaviour, and how those assumptions interact with one's values.

For further consideration

Have you ever encounterd an emergency? Did you intervene? Can you relate your behaviour to the principles discussed above? Does knowing these principles seem likely to affect how you react to future emergencies?

Conclusion

Social psychology is concerned with the social dimensions of individual behaviour. As such, it deals with both the way we think about ourselves and others (*social cognition*) and also the way social factors affect the way we act (*social influence*). Interest in social behaviour is not restricted to psychology, of course; indeed, it has been studied within the disciplines of biology, sociology and anthropology. What distinguishes social psychology from these other fields is largely its focus on the individual, and its emphasis on experimentation as a methodology.

In some ways, social psychology is the most appealing area within psychology. In a very basic sense, it touches on the social concerns that are basic to our lives. By exploring questions of how we respond to, and are influenced by, other people, it seems to be both 'real' and 'relevant'. This is evident, for example, in the debates about aggression. Yet, one cannot consider social psychology closely without also recognizing the limitations of the area in terms of both what we know, and how we know it.

One of the basic difficulties is the complex nature of social research, and the limits it places on finding hard answers. Experimental *control*, *reactivity*, the need for *experimental realism*, *external validity*, *ethics*, all of these factors (and others unmentioned) place constraints on how one does social research, and on the quality of the answers one obtains. Consider the problem of observing violence: after almost thirty years and hundreds of studies, there is still controversy over what one should conclude. At some stage, this inexactitude can frustrate even the most dedicated researcher. Leon Festinger, at one time one of the most noted social psychologists in the world, suddenly stopped doing social research, and shifted his attention to the study of colour vision. Perhaps (and this must be considered speculation) he concluded that it was better to pursue an area where hard answers are more attainable. If this *was* his reason, it is easy to feel empathy for him.

In the end, the problem may be too *much* emphasis on scientific rigour, rather than too little. As British psychologist Colin Fraser has suggested, the desire for rigorous methods has led to defining social behaviour in terms that can be addressed experimentally (Fraser 1987). This can result in limiting attention to those questions that can be answered (e.g. 'Will children imitate an adult who hits an inflatable doll?'), while being unable to answer broader questions which may be of greater interest. In effect, anything which doesn't fit the mould becomes ignored (such as the effects of social structures on individuals), or else subject to the endless doubts of empirically-minded critics (as with the issue of observing violence). It may be too grandiose to ask 'Whither social psychology?', but it is a concern that social psychology has not yet found satisfactory ways to answer the questions which people find most interesting. Without that ability, its contributions to our understanding of behaviour are likely to remain far less than its potential.

Chapter Summary

- *Social psychology* is concerned with the social dimensions of individual behaviour. As such, it deals with both the way we think about ourselves and others (*social cognition*) and also the way social factors affect the way we act (*social influence*).

- Research on social behaviour faces many challenges, including the need for *experimental realism* and *external validity*. While researchers prefer the controlled conditions of laboratory experiments, it can be difficult to meet these requirements convincingly in a laboratory, due to participants' awareness of being in a study. Consequently, researchers also use *field experiments* and *correlational research* (such as *naturalistic observation*). In the end, the three methods each have advantages and limitations.

- Perhaps the most intensively studied aspect of social behaviour is *aggression*. As with other issues, each approach has its own interpretation of the origins of aggressive behaviour.

- The biological approach sees aggression as physiologically based, in the form of an innate drive (ethology) or as a response to aversive stimuli.

- The behaviourist approach views aggression as learned behaviour. In particular, it is seen as behaviour which is sometimes reinforced as a means to a desired goal (*instrumental aggression*), or as the response to frustration (*frustration–aggression hypothesis*).

- The cognitive approach also sees aggression as learned, but emphasizes the role of *imitation* (*social learning theory*) and *priming* (*neo-association theory*). Because it does not view aggression as innate, the cognitive approach emphasizes the possibilities for avoiding aggressive behaviour.

- The psychodynamic approach, as expressed in Freud's theory, views aggression as an innate drive, which can be redirected by *catharsis* and *defence mechanisms*, but cannot be eliminated.

◆ The humanistic approach sees aggressive behaviour as a response to circumstances which threaten the individual's ability to satisfy needs (Maslow) or as a reaction to arbitrary conditions of worth (Rogers). However, the humanists argue that even in adverse circumstances, aggressive behaviour is only one *possible* response, and is not inevitable.

◆ *Prosocial behaviour* (such as *altruism*) and its absence (such as *bystander apathy*) has also interested social psychologists, though it has been less intensively studied than aggression. The available research suggests that *social influence* (such as cultural norms and the actions of others during an emergency) and *priming* play a role in determining prosocial responses.

◆ Social psychology is an appealing area, but the difficulties of doing research on complex social issues means that at present it is very hard to draw clear conclusions about the causes of social behaviour.

Key Terms and Concepts

aggression	instrumental aggression
altruism	priming
catharsis	prosocial behaviour
diffusion of responsibility	sign stimuli
experimental realism	social influence
frustration–aggression hypothesis	vacuum activities
imitation	

Suggestions for Further Reading

For readers wishing to explore social psychology in general, Aronson's *The Social Animal* is highly readable.

There have been many books about aggression, expressing various points of view. One of the most interesting is an overview by John Klama, *Aggression: Conflict in Animals and Humans Reconsidered*. The authors ('John Klama' is a pseudonym for *John* Durant, Peter *Kl*opfer and Susan O*yama*) provide a history of the concept of aggression as an innate drive, as well as a critique of theories.

The relationship between observing television violence and aggressive behaviour has been studied extensively. In *The Early Window: Effects of Television on Children and Youth*, Liebert and Sprafkin (two social learning researchers) provide an excellent review of both the history of the problem and the evidence.

9 Perspectives on Abnormal Behaviour

Who and What is Normal?

When I was a graduate student in psychology, I had an experience which made a deep impression on me. Even now, years later, it still seems fresh and vivid. On a summer evening, I was standing on a quiet residential street, talking to a friend. As we talked, we noticed a young man, perhaps twenty-four years old, wandering down the street in our direction. He halted periodically, peering intently, and then would continue. His movements seemed erratic, weaving left and right as he went. It was difficult not to notice him on the quiet street, and at first I thought he was inebriated, or possibly on drugs. I commented to my friend that he seemed to be acting strangely, and she agreed. Then, as he neared us, she spoke to him. The conversation went something like this:

'Can we help you?'

'No', he said, then added, 'Yes. Umm . . .', looking around, 'can you tell me where the garbage is?'

'You need a garbage can?', I asked.

'No, no, it's . . .', he said, 'Where does the garbage go?' As I pondered this, he abruptly changed the subject, turning to my friend and asking, 'What's your name?'

'Hope', she said. (It really was her name!)

'That's what I need', he replied, still looking around.

I was beginning to suspect that he was neither drunk nor on drugs, but rather suffering from a mental disorder. Before I could decide how to proceed, however, my friend addressed him.

'Have you ever been to the Clarke?', she asked, referring to a local psychiatric hospital.

'Umm, yeah'.

'When?'

'Janitor . . .' I wasn't sure if this was his job, or if it somehow connected to the earlier query about garbage.

'Well', Hope continued, 'would you like to go there now?'

'Yeah . . . okay'.

With that, we led him to my car, and drove him to the psychiatric hospital. On the way, Hope was able to elicit his name, and confirm that he lived in our city. At the hospital, we explained the situation, and the staff checked their records, which confirmed that he had been a patient there on several occasions. The diagnosis: schizophrenia. They agreed to admit him, and we left.

I think of this experience whenever I consider abnormal psychology. It represents one of my few encounters in everyday life with an individual classed as 'abnormal'. Taking him to the hospital made me feel I was doing him a kindness; but it also served to alleviate. my own distress at dealing with someone who acted very differently than most people.

Consider another episode: In my second year of high school, a new student arrived. By the standards of my peers, he was rather strange. He was a vegetarian, and also refused to wear animal products – meaning he wore plastic belts and plastic shoes, even in midwinter. He had wavy blond hair that by the standards of the day was very 'girlish'. He had no interest in sports, instead preferring to study foreign languages. On many occasions, he would go through the school singing operatic arias, while most students' taste ran to the Beatles and similar groups. Needless to say, he was not very popular. The question is, was he abnormal?

In everyday life, when we describe someone as 'abnormal', we are saying that their behaviour violates our expectations in ways that we find difficult to comprehend. In this sense, both of the individuals described above might be called 'abnormal'. But is that the same as saying someone has a mental disorder? What defines a mental disorder? And what can be done to help someone suffering from such a disorder?

Introduction

abnormal behaviour
behaviour which is regarded by society as deviant or maladaptive; according to DSM-III-R, an individual must be suffering or show maladaptive functioning in order for behaviour to be described as abnormal

Abnormal psychology is concerned with the understanding and treatment of mental disorders. However, defining the boundaries of the field can be difficult: many of those who treat such disorders are doctors, not psychologists; in other cases, help is provided by social workers, clerics or other counsellors. Even the term 'mental disorder' is not universally accepted; other terms include *mental illness*, *psychopathology* and *abnormal behaviour*. For our purposes, we will use the terms *mental disorder* and **abnormal behaviour** as interchangeable, and largely avoid the other terms.

Defining abnormal behaviour is a complex issue which can involve a number of different criteria. Literally, the word 'abnormal' means 'away from the norm'; hence, abnormal behaviour is behaviour which departs from the norm. In turn, norms can be defined in two ways: *statistical abnormality* refers to behaviour which is rare, while *unconventionality* refers to behaviour which departs from social standards. The boy who sang operas in high school would probably be considered 'abnormal' in the sense that he was unconventional. Historically, the standard of conventionality was often a significant element in judgements of abnormality; not conforming was viewed with suspicion, or worse. Today, however, standards of conformity are somewhat looser, and someone who does not 'fit in' is not automatically viewed as having a mental disorder. Behaviour which is unconventional is also often statistically rare, in that most people behave according to the social standards of the culture they live in. However, statistical rarity, like unconventionality, poses difficulties as a criterion for mental disorders. It is true that many mental disorders are relatively rare, as the statistical criterion would imply. Yet there are many rare forms of behaviour which we would not consider indicative of mental disorder – for example, musical genius. Hence, *neither* of these standards is today commonly used by psychologists as part of the definition of abnormal behaviour.

The ambiguities in defining abnormal behaviour are partly due to the complexity and diversity of human behaviour, but also reflect how easily value judgements can creep into the process of evaluation. To see this more clearly, let us consider briefly the history of concepts of abnormality.

Abnormal Behaviour in Historical Perspective

Throughout history, there have been reports of individuals who acted in aberrant ways. In early pantheistic cultures, whose members believed spirits permeate the world, abnormal behaviour was often explained as possession by evil spirits. The notion of mental disorders as demonic possession has also been common in our own culture. As recently as 1692, in Salem, Massachusetts, twenty young women were executed as being 'bewitched by the Devil' because they exhibited visions, sensory distortions and other odd behaviours. Today, scholars believe they were actually suffering from poisoning from ergot, a fungus which sometimes grows on rye (and is related to LSD) (Caporeal 1976). Spirit possession is also central to the origin of the term *hysteria* (used by Freud and others to describe physical symptoms of paralysis and pain of unknown origin). The disorder, whose name comes from the Greek word for 'uterus', was attributed in the Middle Ages to the devil controlling a woman's uterus!

Even when abnormal behaviour was not attributed to spirits, the sense of moral condemnation was often strong. Those with mental disorders were commonly seen as degenerates, less than human. Consequently, common forms of treatment included beatings and imprisonment. This attitude slowly began to change as doctors began to conceive of the behaviour as having physical causes. One of the early pioneers in this regard was Phillipe Pinel, a French doctor who in the latter part of the eighteenth century ran the Bicêtre asylum in Paris. Contrary to the notions of demonism and degeneracy, Pinel saw his patients as *ill*, suffering from physical disorders, and argued for treating them like other patients. By suggesting that abnormal behaviour was like other forms of illness, Pinel's work marked a shift towards more humane and rational treatment.

At the same time, by suggesting that mental disorders have physical causes, Pinel helped introduce what has become known as the **medical model** of abnormal

medical model a theory of abnormal behaviour which assumes that all such disorders have physiological causes behaviour (today, this approach is closely linked to the biological approach, as we shall see below). The medicalizing of abnormal behaviour led to doctors becoming the *de facto* authorities on the treatment of such disorders. This trend lasted well into the middle of this century, and in some ways the medical viewpoint is still the dominant one.

One consequence of the medical model was a move towards rational systems of diagnosis. Doctors, like scientists, had learned the value of classification systems as a means of understanding the world. Diagnosis of illness was based on matching symptoms to known diseases; now, the same approach began to be applied to the understanding of mental disorders, with behaviour representing the symptoms.

The most broadly recognized classification system is the Diagnostic and Statistical Manual of Mental Disorders (DSM), published by the American Psychiatric Association. (**Psychiatrists** are medical doctors who specialize in treating mental disorders). To understand how classification works, and its value and limitations, let us look more closely at the nature and use of the DSM system (the current version is DSM-III-Revised; DSM-IV is due for release as this is being written).

psychiatrists medical doctors who specialize in treating mental disorders; by comparison, clinical psychologists typically have a PhD rather than a MD degree

Classifying Abnormal Behaviour

The most basic concern of diagnosis is to define what we mean by abnormal behaviour. This is not always easy, especially since many theorists (including Freud) believe there is a continuum between 'normal' and 'abnormal', with no absolute dividing line. As discussed earlier, defining abnormality in terms of social norms or frequency of occurrence seems questionable. Instead, DSM-III-R uses two primary criteria to determine whether a person's behaviour warrants being described as a mental disorder: suffering and maladaptiveness.

Suffering implies that the behaviour causes the individual distress or anxiety; *maladaptiveness* implies that the person is hindered from functioning effectively in significant ways. For example, a person who experiences intense anxiety at the prospect of venturing out of their home would be viewed as suffering; this type of anxiety reflects a disorder called *agoraphobia*. Maladaptiveness could take many forms: drinking which interferes with work performance, disordered thinking which prevents communication with others, uncontrollable outbursts of rage, and so on. Most psychologists and other mental health professionals agree that behaviour must fit one or both of these criteria in order to be considered abnormal. However, exceptions exist even to these criteria. For example, an individual with **antisocial personality disorder** may show a history of acts of violence towards others, unaccompanied by guilt. These individuals may not report either suffering or unsatisfactory functioning, yet their behaviour is still deemed abnormal.

antisocial personality disorder a behaviour pattern in which an individual shows a history of acts of violence towards others, unaccompanied by guilt; although these individuals may not report either suffering or unsatisfactory functioning (the generally accepted standard for abnormality), their behaviour is still deemed abnormal because it violates society's norms in such significant ways

The intent of using suffering and maladaptiveness as criteria is to free the definition of abnormality from arbitrary social judgements (such as unconventionality). However, even these criteria can be open to interpretation. For example, if a person prefers beachcombing to banking, does this suggest maladaption? Need one have a fixed address to be well-adapted? In the extreme, the standards are quite obvious (e.g. someone who complains of intense anxiety is obviously

CLASSIFYING ABNORMAL BEHAVIOUR USING DSM-III-R

AXIS I	CLINICAL SYNDROMES	Primary classification of disorders, based on behavioural symptoms.
AXIS II	PERSONALITY AND DEVELOPMENTAL DISORDERS	Personality disorders—long-standing patterns of maladaptive behaviour. Developmental disorders—disorders which affect learning, language and other intellectual skills.
AXIS III	GENERAL MEDICAL CONDITIONS	Any physical problems which may be relevant to the person's condition.
AXIS IV	PSYCHOSOCIAL AND ENVIRONMENTAL FACTORS	A 6-point rating scale for the severity of stressors which contribute to the person's condition.
AXIS V	GLOBAL ASSESSMENT OF FUNCTIONING	A general evaluation of functioning during the past year in terms of work, leisure and social relationships.

Fig. 9.1 Classifying mental disorders As noted in the text, DSM-III-R classifies behaviour using five dimensions or 'axes' (categories copyrighted by American Psychiatric Association 1987).

suffering); it is the grey areas in between that sometimes cause difficulties in assessment.

Assuming that a person's behaviour *is* regarded as abnormal, DSM-III-R tries to identify the particular form of disorder, using five major dimensions ('axes') for assessment (see Fig. 9.1). Axes I–III represent the basic types of disorders (e.g. depression, schizophrenia, antisocial personality disorder, etc.). Axis IV looks at the stressors in the person's life which may contribute to a problem (e.g. the recent death of a family member). Axis V looks at the person's general adaptation in three areas of daily life (social relations, work and leisure); this helps in determining the severity of the current problem, as well as influencing the prognosis for recovery. For example, someone diagnosed as depressed will have a better prognosis if their general life history suggests a high level of functioning than if they have a history of mood problems, poor social relationships and an erratic employment record. By making such assessments part of the overall diagnosis, DSM-III-R tries to provide a more detailed, individualized description.

Not surprisingly, not all disorders are equally common. In a large-scale study done in five cities in the United States, researchers attempted to identify the incidence rates for various disorders using DSM-III criteria (Regier *et al*. 1988). The researchers evaluated the number of cases diagnosed for each disorder over a one-month interval; lifetime risks are typically regarded as about twice as high

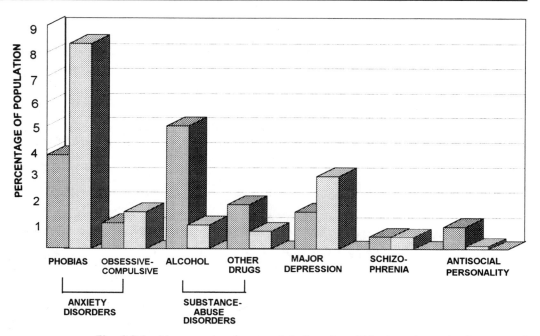

Fig. 9.2 Incidence rates for mental disorders This chart shows the frequency of occurrence of some of the most common disorders. The percentages are for incidence rates over a one-month period in the United States; lifetime risks are roughly twice as high (data from Regier et al. 1988). The left bar in each category represents the rate for men; the right bar, the rate for women.

(see Fig. 9.2). There are several points to notice about these results. First, there are significant differences in the frequency of occurrence of different disorders, and in most cases, the rates for men and women also differ (this has sometimes led to charges of sex bias in diagnosis). In addition, one should note that many of these disorders are not very rare; if one extrapolates to lifetime rates, then about 12 per cent of the population will suffer from a serious phobia at some time in their lives, and roughly the same number of people will experience a mood disorder meriting treatment.

Classifying mental disorders, as with other forms of medical diagnosis, is intended to help identify the cause of a problem and to guide treatment. This is more problematical for mental disorders than for other forms of illness, because we do not yet know the causes of most mental disorders (as we will see in the next section, this is a major source of disagreement among the five approaches). In fact, some critics have focused on this lack of knowledge as part of a challenge to the entire concept of classification. In effect, the argument is that we cannot identify the causes because there is no such thing as a mental disorder. Thomas Szasz, himself a psychiatrist, has argued that mental disorders are a 'myth' (Szasz 1961). To Szasz, identifying behaviour as abnormal is simply a way for society and clinicians to justify interfering in an individual's life. In a similar vein, the British psychiatrist R.D. Laing has argued that mental disorders are a reaction to pathology in the family or society (Laing 1967). That is, the problem is in the environment, not in the person.

Most clinicians reject such claims, although in recent years there has certainly been increasing recognition by professionals that classifying behaviour as abnormal can have adverse consequences. Within our culture, the term 'mental disorder' has a negative connotation; as a consequence, diagnosis assigns a label to someone which identifies them as being different, or *deviant*. Such labels serve as a form of **stigma**, a marking which is used by society to treat someone as an outsider (Goffman 1963). In the case of mental disorders, this results in problems of social rejection which often make recovery more difficult (Clausen 1981). To some extent, this problem has been recognized in DSM-III-R, which recommends referring to an individual *having* a disorder, in contrast to the earlier common practice of equating the disorder with the person. For example, one should refer to 'a person with schizophrenia', not 'a schizophrenic'.

stigma a mark or label which identifies an individual as deviant, resulting in social rejection

Labelling effects illustrate the ultimate dilemma involved in defining abnormality: balancing the benefits and detriments of the classification of behaviour. Advocates of diagnostic systems tend to believe that mental disorders are purely objective phenomena, like a tumour or tuberculosis, while critics of such systems argue that abnormality is simply a reflection of arbitrary social norms. The truth is probably somewhere in between. On the one hand, stigmatizing and even misdiagnosis are possible, as critics have charged. However, diagnostic categories seem useful in understanding an individual's behaviour, and may aid in treatment. The basic standard of abnormality employed in DSM-III-R – that the individual shows significant distress and/or maladaptive functioning – is one that most people would probably find reasonable. Indeed, the autobiographies of those who have suffered from disorders like schizophrenia and depression suggest that they view their disorders as real, not as an arbitrary social conceit (Vonnegut 1975; Endler 1982).

At present, there are no final answers to this debate. In part, disagreements over the issue of classification reflect differences in assumptions about the underlying causes of abnormal behaviour. In the end, the central issue always seems to come back to the causes of abnormal behaviour: if we could be certain of the origin of particular disorders, many of the questions of bias, misdiagnosis and arbitrariness of standards would be resolved. For now, most clinicians, faced with what they see as real suffering, simply do their best to help.

For further consideration

As Fig. 9.2 indicates, various forms of abnormal behaviour are more common than many people think. Do you know anyone who suffers from a serious phobia? Or, someone who has had a mood disorder such as depression? Would your reaction differ in the two cases? What does this tell you about your own attitudes towards abnormal behaviour?

Perspectives on Treatment

aetiology the study of the causes of a disease or mental disorder

To a large extent, treatment methods tend to be linked to ideas about the causes of abnormal behaviour. Consequently, one cannot discuss theories of treatment without also discussing theories of **aetiology** (the study of the causes of a disorder). What makes this difficult is that many types of factors can contribute to a particular behaviour. When one speaks of 'cause', one may actually be referring to *predisposing factors* (genetic inheritance, prior experiences and beliefs), *precipitating factors* (immediate stressors like loss of a family member) or *sustaining factors* (consequences of a disorder that help to perpetuate it, such as reactions of family or society). In addition, there may be more than one factor of a given type; for example, children of individuals with schizophrenia may be at risk both because of genetic factors and also because of growing up with parents who provided a faulty model for behaviour (both of these would be predisposing factors). Consequently, the search for a single cause may often be fruitless. Nonetheless, each of the five approaches tends to emphasize particular types of causal factors, and given the current state of evidence, each feels justified in utilizing the treatment techniques which it does. To see how they differ, let us consider how each approach views aetiology and treatment.

The Biological Approach

As noted earlier, the biological approach to abnormal behaviour is based on the *medical model*, which assumes that disorders are based on physical causes. Given the role of the brain in the control of behaviour, the causes are usually attributed to abnormalities in either the structure or functioning of the brain.

The strongest justification for this approach has come from advances in *psychopharmacology* (the study of drugs which affect mental processes and/or behaviour). Although the use of drugs to alter behaviour has a long history (alcohol, for example, has been used in some form in nearly every culture), the greatest advances have come in the last few decades. Today, a large and growing range of drugs exist to deal with many forms of disorders. For example, tranquillizers are used to relieve anxiety, anti-depressants help relieve depression, and anti-psychotics relieve hallucinations and mental confusion. In addition, sedatives often take the place of physical restraints like strait-jackets. Not only do drugs frequently seem to alleviate symptoms, but drug therapy also seems relatively efficient – compared with alternative treatments like psychoanalysis or behaviour modification, it is relatively low cost, fast-acting and requires comparatively little of the doctor's time. For all of these reasons, the use of psychoactive drugs has become extremely common both in the formal treatment of mental disorders and as part of the practice of many family doctors.

This popularity has not come without criticism. First, treatment using drugs is still largely based on symptom relief, and does not address the issue of causation directly. While our understanding of how drugs work is becoming much more precise, this is not necessarily the same thing as identifying the cause of the disorder. Indeed, many aspects of the available data suggest that drugs may not be addressing the root causes of disorders. For example, one of the unsolved problems of anti-depressant use is why, since the drug reaches the brain in a matter of hours, there is often a considerable time lag between the onset of usage and improvement of mood (intervals of two weeks are not uncommon). In addition, individuals who show comparable symptoms often do not respond equally to a particular drug. Even more troublesome is the possibility that many problems for which drugs are prescribed may be self-limiting. For example, according to its manufacturer, Xanax (alprazolam) is a drug which is designed to alleviate panic disorder (frequent attacks of intense anxiety and panic). The clinical trials which led to its approval showed that after four weeks, 50 per cent of patients taking Xanax were completely free of symptoms, compared with 28 per cent of those taking a placebo. Interestingly, however, after *eight* weeks, there was no significant difference between the two groups (Editors 1993).

At present, there are still many questions associated with using drugs to treat abnormal behaviour. Drugs often *do* seem to be useful in alleviating symptoms, but that does not mean they are addressing the causes of disorders. Nonetheless, drug therapy is consistent with the medical model, and as we shall see in examining schizophrenia, may very well hold important clues to the understanding of abnormal behaviour.

Another application of the biological approach to the study of mental disorders is genetic research. For example, researchers have used concordance studies to examine the role of genetics in disorders like schizophrenia and bipolar mood disorder. The results of such studies are often very variable, and open to conflicting interpretations. For example, reports of a genetic link for bipolar disorder, announced in the late 1980s, were later found to be flawed (Kelsoe *et al.* 1989). The available evidence does not show conclusively that any major form of abnormal behaviour is *solely* genetic. In addition, genetic analysis at present can only indicate an individual's risk – there are no current treatments designed to address mental disorders at the genetic level. If genetic analysis eventually does prove fruitful, it will provide strong support for the medical model.

In summary, drug therapy does prove of benefit, but until we understand more about the causes of abnormal behaviour, it is not clear if it addresses the root of such disorders, or simply masks the symptoms. Genetic research may eventually prove useful, *provided* the primary causes of disorders are in fact genetic in origin. For the biological approach, as for all the approaches, the only criterion for testing a theory at present is to try to evaluate its success in alleviating the misery associated with mental disorders.

The Behaviourist Approach

As one might expect, the behaviourist approach interprets abnormal behaviour in terms of faulty learning. Like all behaviours, abnormal behaviour is acquired through a process of conditioning and learning. In the absence of known organic problems, this explanation does not assume there is any underlying causal factor, as the medical model does; instead, the behaviourists say the behaviour *is* the problem. As a consequence, this means that behaviourists have relatively little interest in classification, since learned behaviour is too variable to make categories very meaningful. To the extent that classification is seen as at all useful, it is as a shorthand description – for example, phobias represent learned fears. This emphasis on the behaviour itself as the central concern also places the behaviourists in opposition to the other three approaches, all of which suggest that cognitive processes of various sorts mediate the behaviour. In addition, the behaviourist approach to treatment is largely ahistorical, since what matters is not the circumstances under which abnormal behaviour was acquired in the

systematic desensitization
a technique based on
classical conditioning which is
designed to treat phobias
(unrealistic fears) and related
anxiety disorders by gradually
diminishing the undesired
response

past, but the need to identify ways to modify it in the present. Because of the emphasis on changing the undesired behaviour, therapy based on the behaviour-ist approach is generally referred to as *behaviour modification*. Often, practition-ers abbreviate this to 'behaviour mod'.

Several forms of behaviour modification exist, based on either classical or operant conditioning. One of the earliest techniques, derived from classical conditioning, is **systematic desensitization**, which is designed to treat phobias (unrealistic fears) and related anxiety disorders. As noted in Chapter 3, Watson had demonstrated with little Albert that it was possible to develop a fear by classical conditioning. Although he was subsequently unsuccessful in eliminat-ing Albert's conditioned fear, the notion that phobias could be explained in terms of classical conditioning was established. Eventually, Joseph Wolpe de-veloped systematic desensitization, which seeks to eliminate the fear response by replacing it with a competing response of relaxation (Wolpe 1973).

In conception, systematic desensitization is very simple, being based on two basic principles of conditioning. First, an individual cannot produce two com-peting reflex responses at the same time (such as fear and relaxation). Second, classical conditioning often involves stimulus generalization. In practice, the procedure requires elements of timing and judgement, which make it more than a mechanical process. Typically, the clinician works with the individual to iden-tify the type of stimuli which trigger the phobia – that is, the conditioned stimu-lus or CS. For example, someone afraid of bees might panic if a bee buzzed near their head. Next, the individual is taught relaxation-inducing techniques, often related to a cue for relaxing. Then, the clinician and individual develop a list of fear-evoking stimuli, ranging from very mild to very intense. This list is called a **hierarchy of fears**, since stimuli are listed in order of the intensity of fear which they elicit. Then, working gradually, the therapist attempts to recondition the person so that the stimuli in the hierarchy become associated with relaxing rather than fear. For example, the person might think of driving by a beehive in a closed car; once they can imagine this without fear, they would proceed to the next stimulus, seeing a bee outside the window, and so on. Once the person can confront the stimulus which originally evoked the greatest fear (imagining a bee buzzing near their head) and yet remain relaxed, then the phobia has been eliminated (see Fig. 9.3).

hierarchy of fears in
systematic desensitization, a
list of fear-evoking stimuli,
ranging from very mild to
very intense, arranged in
order of the intensity of fear
which they elicit

Systematic desensitization has been successfully employed for a wide variety of fears, ranging from the fear of snakes or heights to more unusual fears like a fear of music (Wenrich 1970; Wolpe 1973). Airlines have even sponsored desensitization sessions for individuals who fear flying, based on the very reason-able premise that such individuals otherwise will not be potential customers! Although often effective, rarely does the success rate for treatment reach above 70 per cent. This has prompted concerns about how to improve the effectiveness of systematic desensitization, and also criticisms of its underlying premises. In looking at the other approaches, we will return to this issue, but one should not overlook the fact that systematic desensitization is relatively time- and cost-efficient, as well as frequently successful.

The underlying principle of systematic desensitization – substituting a com-peting response for the undesired response – is sometimes referred to as *counter-conditioning*. Just as it can be used to eliminate a fear, it has also been employed to *induce* an aversive response to stimuli which are associated with existing

---

APPLYING SYSTEMATIC DESENSITIZATION

1) IDENTIFY FEAR-AROUSING STIMULUS (CS) – e.g. person is afraid of snakes

2) PERSON PRACTISES RELAXATION TECHNIQUES (relaxation is an unconditioned response which is incompatible with fear)

3) DEVELOP HIERARCHY OF FEARS – list of stimuli which arouse fear, arranged from least fearful to most fearful
  Ex: seeing a picture of a snake in a book (least fearful)
       seeing a snake on television
       going to a zoo and seeing a snake in a cage
       walking in the woods and seeing a snake
       approaching a snake
       holding a (harmless) snake (most fearful)

4) GRADUALLY PROCEED THROUGH HIERARCHY – at each step, person must imagine the fearful stimulus (from hierarchy), and deliberately relax; once person can imagine the weakest stimulus and remain relaxed, proceed to next stimulus, etc.

ORIGINAL SITUATION: CS (snake) ELICITS CR (fear)

AFTER DESENSITIZATION: CS (snake) ELICITS NEW CR (relaxation)

Fig. 9.3 The basic procedure for systematic desensitization

aversive conditioning a form of behaviour modification which is designed to induce an aversive response to stimuli which are associated with existing undesirable behaviours

undesirable behaviours. This procedure, called **aversive conditioning**, has been applied in dealing with a range of disorders, from sexual fetishes to alcoholism. For example, an alcoholic might be given a drug called *antabuse*, which when present in the body reacts with alcohol to cause extreme nausea and vomiting. Then, if the person drinks, they will get sick, thus establishing an association that alcohol leads to sickness rather than pleasure. In practice, this procedure is only moderately effective, in part because drinkers quickly realize that by not taking the antabuse they can drink with impunity (Forrest 1985). More than other forms of behaviour modification, aversive conditioning is controversial, since it involves deliberately causing pain or discomfort. Consequently, objections have been raised, even by psychologists who support more positive forms of behaviour therapy (McConnell 1974).

Operant conditioning has also been used in therapy, albeit with more limited success. Direct attempts to alter operant behaviour through conditioning are dependent on controlling the availability of reinforcers. Since people can potentially respond to a wide range of reinforcers, this can be a difficult task. Indeed, one writer has suggested that failures of conditioning derive from the individual getting more reinforcement from making the therapist look foolish than from the *intended* reinforcers (Carlson 1990). Thus, the use of shaping and operant reinforcement has generally been most effective in situations which are highly structured.

One major application has been the establishment of institutional programmes where conditioned reinforcers are given for specific behaviours. Such programmes, called **token economies**, allow individuals to earn 'tokens' (conditioned reinforcers) for doing things like making their bed, arriving at meals on time, or similar simple tasks. In turn, the tokens can be exchanged for desired items like candy or cigarettes, or used to buy privileges like television viewing or day passes. In effect, the tokens become a form of 'money' (which is itself a conditioned reinforcer), for which individuals will perform 'work'. Since access to such reinforcers can be readily controlled in an institutional environment, and the desired behaviours easily monitored, token economies can be very effective in establishing behavioural goals (Ayllon and Azrin 1968). Their primary disadvantages are the careful planning required, the requirement for a structured environment and, like other forms of behaviour modification, the ethical problems which some perceive. With regard to the latter point, Skinner has noted, somewhat ironically, that if we seek directly (and efficiently) to modify behaviour, people get concerned, but if we seek to do it indirectly (and thereby less efficiently), then that is considered acceptable (Skinner 1971). While token economies do seem to work, their practical limitations are such that they are nonetheless relatively uncommon today.

Thus, behaviour modification techniques reflect the assumption that the goal of treatment in abnormal behaviour is to change the undesired behaviour. As indicated, these techniques often show relatively high success rates, and the course of treatment is often very brief. Despite these advantages, behaviour modification has been assailed by other approaches on both ethical and theoretical grounds. Certainly, the focused nature of behaviour therapy makes informed consent very important; but the same thing could be said of *any* form of therapy. At the same time, other approaches have also challenged the assumption that abnormal behaviour has no underlying causes. This issue has already been discussed in relation to the biological approach; let us see how the other approaches explain the origins of abnormal behaviour.

token economy a form of behaviour modification based on operant conditioning; most commonly used in institutional settings, it involves giving conditioned reinforcers ('tokens') for doing specific behaviours

For further consideration

Critics have sometimes charged that behaviour modification is manipulative. Assuming that the individual decides what behaviours they want to modify, how do you view this criticism?

The Cognitive Approach

cognitive behaviour modification an extension of behaviour modification which uses cognitive mediation (such as observing a model) in addition to basic conditioning techniques

Cognitive theorists reject the behaviourist assumption that abnormal behaviour has no underlying cause. Instead, they view it in terms of underlying mediational processes – either symbolic mediation of conditioning, or the influence of faulty cognitions. The possible role of symbolic mediation has already been alluded to in the previous section, and therapy based on this premise (called **cognitive behaviour modification**) is really an extension of behaviour therapy. By contrast, interest in *faulty cognitions* has emerged purely from the cognitive tradition, as seen in the work of Albert Ellis. Theorists like Ellis (Aaron Beck is another example) focus on how behaviour is affected by distortions in *how* we think and *what* we think – such as false assumptions about ourselves and the world, inappropriate schema, and unrealistic expectations of life.

Cognitive behaviour modification can be traced back to the work of Albert Bandura, one of the pioneers of cognitive social learning theory. Bandura's experimental research on imitation had already led him to recognize that imitation can often be more effective for learning than being reinforced. He began applying this concept to the use of behaviour modification for treating phobias.

As noted earlier, systematic desensitization rarely has a 100 per cent success rate; one factor which may account for this is the dependence on *imagining* fear-evoking stimuli, rather than dealing with actual stimuli. Imitation, of course, would involve actual stimuli. One way to separate out this component is by comparing the effects of observing a model (an individual who acts out the desired behaviour) with actually imitating the behaviour of the model. This can be seen in a study in which Bandura compared the effects of systematic desensitization, observing a model, and *participant modelling* (where the individual actually does what the model does) in the treatment of a snake phobia (Bandura 1970). Individuals using systematic desensitization and those using simple modelling showed similar improvement when compared with a control group; thus, simply using real stimuli did not enhance treatment. However, those who used participant modelling did significantly better than either of the other treatments, with eleven of twelve individuals showing complete elimination of the phobia in follow-up tests. Thus, active imitation of the desired behaviour seemed more effective than either observing a model or conventional behaviour modification.

More recently, Donald Meichenbaum has extended this approach to the imitation of thought processes (Meichenbaum 1977). The individual and therapist work together to identify problem areas, and then develop new self-statements that will be more effective. For instance, a person who has given a speech thinks, 'I was really boring; nobody will want to invite me again'. This negative assessment is self-defeating, in that it does not focus on any ways to improve behaviour in the future. Instead, the therapist might encourage the person to frame the assessment in more productive ways, such as thinking, 'That talk was pretty dry; I'll have to plan a better opening next time, and vary the pacing more'. By observing and imitating alternative ways of thinking, the individual can develop alternative strategies that lead to more effective behaviour.

The emphasis which Meichenbaum places on thought patterns is very similar to the work of Albert Ellis, although Ellis works within a different theoretical framework. Ellis focuses on the relationship between thoughts and emotions, using what he calls rational-emotive therapy (Ellis 1993). **Rational-emotive therapy** argues that negative emotions arise from people's faulty interpretations of experiences, not from the experiences themselves. Using what he calls the *ABC principle*, Ellis says an activating event (A) triggers a faulty belief (B) which in turn triggers an emotional consequence (C). While we tend to assume that A causes C, it is really the belief (B) that is responsible for our emotional reactions. For example, Bob meets someone for the first time at a business conference, and comes away feeling the person did not like him (the activating

rational-emotive therapy
a form of therapy developed by Albert Ellis, which focuses on the relationship between thoughts and emotions, particularly negative emotions which arise from an individual's faulty interpretations of experiences

event). He then feels unhappy (the emotional consequence). Ellis would point out that this emotion was triggered by the irrational expectation (belief) that everyone he meets should like Bob. Realistically, there are always people whom we don't get along with; while this is unfortunate, a realistic attitude is to accept this, rather than feeling devastated. Similarly, people who focus excessively on negative events are engaging in what Ellis humorously calls *awfulizing*.

cognitive restructuring in Ellis' rational-emotive therapy, a process for modifying faulty beliefs and the negative emotions they produce, in order to develop realistic beliefs and self-acceptance

Thus, Ellis works in very directive ways to modify the beliefs which lead to negative emotions. This process, called **cognitive restructuring**, is designed to develop realistic beliefs and self-acceptance. At first glance, Ellis' emphasis on self-worth and developing beliefs which foster growth seems similar to the humanistic approach. However, his technique is much more directive, and he believes that the therapist should focus on the individual's cognitive patterns, rather than being concerned about empathy.

In terms of evaluating cognitive techniques for treating abnormal behaviour, the evidence is generally less specific than for either behaviour modification or drug treatments. Overall, the evidence is strongest for cognitive behaviour modification, as discussed above. By contrast, the work of Ellis has been significant primarily in making clinicians aware of the role cognitions play in abnormal behaviour. Overall, the evidence on efficacy of treatment is somewhat limited, and the outcomes somewhat mixed (Emmelkamp *et al.* 1978; Ellis 1993).

Perhaps the most interesting question concerning the cognitive theories is *why* focusing on cognitions sometimes seems more effective than focusing on the behaviour itself. This question is particularly interesting given the bidirectional links between cognition and behaviour. While cognitive theorists emphasize how thoughts mediate behaviour, from a practical standpoint we recognize that changing behaviour can *also* affect cognitions, making the direction of causation less than clear. Cognitive therapists frequently suggest that emphasizing the cognitive mediators produces broader-scale changes (i.e. more generalization) than does modifying specific responses. While this may in fact be true, at present our understanding of this question is still quite limited. The relationship between thoughts and behaviour remains an important issue when we look at psychodynamic and humanistic techniques, both of which emphasize the importance of cognitive insight in changing abnormal behaviour.

The Psychodynamic Approach

The various theories which make up the psychodynamic approach all assume that abnormal behaviour is the product of some form of inner conflict. For Freud, this was seen in the dynamics of id, ego and superego. For other theorists, the conflicting elements vary (for example, Jung emphasized the relations between the ego and the collective unconscious). However they view the source of conflict, all psychodynamic theorists agree on two points: first, that abnormal behaviour is only the *symptom*, not the *cause* of the problem; and second, that treatment requires gaining awareness and understanding of the underlying conflicts which represent the true cause of disorders (Jones and Pulos 1993).

In asserting that behaviour is a symptom, not the problem itself, psychodynamic theorists have been critical of behaviour therapy. Since the behaviour is only an expression of the problem, they assert that trying to change the behaviour without addressing the underlying cause will prove ineffective. Instead, it will simply lead to **symptom substitution**, the expression of the problem in a new way. For example, if a person complains of a fear of snakes, and this reflects denial of sexual impulses, then eliminating the fear of snakes without addressing the sexual conflict will only lead to some other problem – possibly a different phobia, possibly a very different manifestation. However, this concept has found little experimental support. For example, bedwetting might be interpreted by a Freudian as reflecting Oedipal conflicts, yet behaviour therapy can successfully eliminate it while simultaneously increasing self-esteem (Baker 1969). Overall, the evidence suggests that symptom substitution is not a consequence of successful behaviour therapy (Kazdin and Wilson 1980).

symptom substitution in psychodynamic theory, the assumption that changing overt behaviour without addressing the underlying dynamics will lead to the expression of the problem in a new way

The second point, that successful treatment requires awareness of the underlying conflicts, is basic to the therapeutic techniques used by psychodynamic theorists. The development of **insight** into the causes of behaviour represents the basic goal of treatment. Using a variety of techniques, the therapist analyses the underlying conflicts, and helps the individual to understand how they are related to outward behaviour. Once the individual understands the causes of their behaviour, then change in the behaviour should follow.

insight in psychotherapy, awareness of the underlying conflicts which are regarded as the causes of behaviour

At first glance, the psychodynamic approach's emphasis on insight seems similar to both the cognitive and humanistic approaches to treatment. However, there are differences among the three in both the process and the types of cognitions emphasized. As noted earlier, the cognitive approach is largely present-oriented, whereas psychodynamic theories tend to look at how present behaviour is related to past experience. In addition, cognitive theories like Ellis' see faulty beliefs as being the direct cause of disorders, while psychodynamic theorists see unconscious conflicts as the actual cause. While both psychodynamic and humanistic therapy emphasize insight, the types of conflict involved are different, as is the role of the therapist. In psychodynamic therapy, it is the therapist's responsibility to analyse the behaviour and identify the underlying causes; in humanistic therapy (as we shall see shortly), the individual, not the therapist, is the final judge of what is significant or not. Hence, while all three approaches utilize insight, there are differences as well as similarities.

The prototype for all psychodynamic therapies, and still probably the best known, is Freudian psychoanalysis. Since the development of his theory of personality was largely related to his clinical practice, Freud in fact began with a desire to treat abnormal behaviour. His experiences with patients shaped not only his ideas about how the mind works, but also his views on treatment techniques. One of his basic assumptions was the value of *catharsis* – that is, the release of emotions associated with the underlying conflict, often through remembering traumatic experiences. This emotional release, in turn, could help to foster insight.

Freud used a number of techniques to identify the underlying causes of conflict, all based on analysing various aspects of the individual's behaviour. Among the most important were free association, transference and resistance. *Free association* involves having the person relax, and say whatever comes into awareness – thoughts, feelings, even bodily sensations. Freud would then seek to interpret the contents of such reports by looking for patterns and symbolic meanings. Freud also believed that the relationship between the individual and the therapist could come to represent other past relationships, often between the

transference in psychoanalysis, the displacement of drive energy from past relationships, often between the individual and a parent, to the relationship between the individual and the therapist

resistance in psychoanalysis, the rejection by an individual of the analyst's interpretations of the meaning of behaviour; regarded as a defence mechanism

individual and a parent. The analysis of the emotions involved in this **transference** could then provide an important tool for understanding the development of current conflicts. In the same way, if a patient rejects the analyst's interpretations of the meaning of behaviour, this **resistance** can represent a defence against acknowledging the identified conflict. Thus, in various ways, all aspects of the therapeutic situation become relevant to analysing the underlying dynamics which produce the disorder.

Critics have often pointed out that Freud's approach to therapy places the therapist in a position of great power. Only the analyst can determine what is significant and what is not; in fact, if a patient objects to a particular interpretation, that is simply taken as evidence of resistance! Another limitation is that traditional psychoanalysis is a very open-ended process, potentially lasting several years (partly in response to this limitation, more recent theorists have worked on developing forms of brief psychodynamic therapy). In fairness, one must evaluate these criticisms in the context of the overall effectiveness of Freud's therapeutic techniques.

One concern in evaluating Freudian therapy is finding appropriate measures of efficacy, since psychoanalysts seek not simply symptom relief, but also broader changes in the awareness and functioning of the individual. To a large extent, other psychodynamic therapies would make the same claim. Consequently, comparing psychodynamic techniques to alternatives which emphasize narrower goals, such as behaviour therapy, can pose difficulties. In addition, since real-world evaluations involve individuals who are suffering, there are also ethical limits on doing comparisons. These difficulties have not diminished the enthusiasm of researchers, however; in the past three decades, literally hundreds of studies have assessed psychodynamic and other forms of therapy.

One well-controlled study, done at a clinic in Philadelphia, randomly assigned individuals suffering from anxiety disorders to either behaviour therapy or psychoanalytic therapy (Sloane *et al.* 1975). A control group consisted of those on a waiting list for treatment. After four months, all three groups had shown some improvement, although the results were much better for those in treatment than for the control group (see Fig. 9.4). Interestingly, in this study, there was no significant difference between psychoanalysis and behaviour therapy. Obviously, this represents only one study, and it involves a type of disorder for which psychoanalysis may be fairly well suited. Interestingly, a study at the Meninger Foundation suggests that much of the benefit may come from the empathy and concern which the therapist shows, rather than from the specific insights (Wallerstein 1989). Since this is potentially a factor in all forms of therapy, we will return to it when discussing the general issue of evaluating the treatment of abnormal behaviour. For now, it is sufficient to suggest that psychodynamic therapy, including psychoanalysis, produces some benefits – though the reasons for improvement may not be those cited by the theorists.

The Humanistic Approach

The humanistic approach argues that the meaning of behaviour can only be understood in terms of an individual's own perceptions and experience. This *phenomenological* emphasis, as it is referred to, is central to all of the various

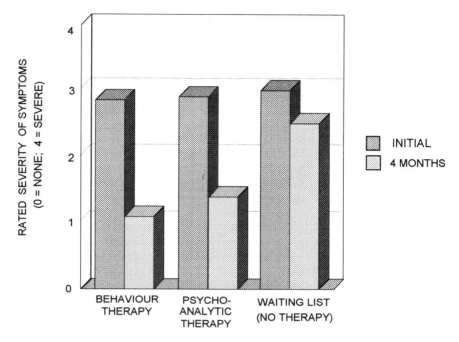

Fig. 9.4 Comparing the efficacy of behaviour modification and psychoanalysis In a carefully controlled experiment of individuals who sought treatment at a psychiatric outpatient clinic in Philadelphia, most suffered from anxiety disorders. Since the clinic had a waiting list, this group was used for a control comparison for the initial condition and at follow-up four months later (data from Sloane *et al.* 1975).

humanistic theories, and has particular significance when considering abnormal behaviour. Since only the individual can assess the appropriateness of their own behaviour, objective definitions of 'abnormal' are meaningless. Instead, the humanists focus on describing the potential for human growth. In effect, it is a psychology of health, not a therapy for abnormal behaviour.

Although the emphasis is rather different, humanistic therapy is still dealing with the same human beings as other therapists, however the process is described. That means that the humanistic therapist must still deal with the reality that individuals seek help because they are suffering in some way. This suffering is interpreted as due to distortions of growth, usually caused by the demands of other people. The desire to meet these demands can result in frustration and despair, as well as loss of awareness of one's own feelings and preferences. Consequently, humanistic therapy tends to focus on creating conditions under which the individual can increase self-awareness and begin to make choices which will enhance the process of growth.

Although each humanistic theorist uses slightly different concepts and techniques, in practice the different therapies tend to be similar in several respects: the emphasis on the individual's own perceptions and feelings, the importance of self-awareness or *insight* as a tool for growth, and the responsibility of the

person-centred therapy
(also called 'client-centred therapy') a form of therapy developed by Carl Rogers, which emphasizes the responsibility of the individual to determine the direction of change within therapy

therapist to respect the individual's autonomy. Among the various therapies, however, the work of Carl Rogers has become perhaps the best known.

As noted in Chapter 6, Carl Rogers developed his approach to therapy partly as a reaction against the pessimistic image of human growth which psychoanalysis offered. Over time, he developed a technique which was initially called 'client-centred therapy', and later **person-centred therapy** (Rogers 1951; Meador and Rogers 1979). (The early emphasis on the term 'client' was meant to contrast with the traditional usage, by both psychoanalysts and other therapists, of the term 'patient'.) In Rogers' view, the therapeutic relationship was between equals; the therapist's role was to provide a sounding board, not to make judgements as an authority figure. Hence, 'client' seemed preferable to 'patient'; the later shift to 'person-centred' was simply a further step towards acknowledging that the therapeutic relationship is essentially an interaction between two human beings.

Rogerian therapy is based on the therapist trying to provide the *conditions for growth*: empathy, openness and unconditional positive regard. The therapist must act in an *open* and genuine way, not hiding behind a professional façade. By trying to understand the individual's perceptions and feelings, the therapist provides *empathy*. *Unconditional positive regard* comes through demonstrating caring and acceptance of the individual and their concerns. By showing these qualities, the therapist can help the person to become more self-aware and more self-confident.

Despite the seemingly subjective nature of person-centred therapy, Rogers was very concerned with the importance of demonstrating that therapy actually helps people. Consequently, very early on he began keeping detailed transcripts of therapy sessions, and used them as a tool for evaluating therapeutic change (Rogers and Dymond 1954). Typically, as therapy progressed, an individual would make more statements relating to feelings, wishes and having a sense of control over life. For example, a person might go from saying, 'I'm a failure; I always disappoint my parents', to saying, 'I realize how important my parents are to me; but I also realize I have to make my own career decisions'. Changes like this are consistent with what the theory would predict, and suggests Rogerian therapy is effective. Unfortunately, we recognize that what people *say* is not always what they *do*, and the data provide no direct evidence of behavioural change. Indeed, a study by a psychologist who was allowed to observe Rogers conducting therapy found that *only* statements indicating progress regularly led to positive comments by Rogers (Truax 1966). In effect, Rogers' comments provided a form of social reinforcement for the individual to make appropriate statements. Based partly on this finding, Rogers abandoned the term 'non-directive therapy' as a description of his therapeutic technique; while the therapist tries to be neutral, the reality is that *any* human interaction is influenced by the attitudes and preferences of each person. Nonetheless, Rogers continued to assert that the process of therapy must emphasize the individual's own potential for growth, not the judgements of the therapist. In this respect, the dynamics of Rogerian therapy seem very different from psychoanalysis.

This issue of implicit control is one basis on which person-centred therapy has been criticized. Another criticism is that, as an insight-oriented therapy, it requires a high level of verbal interaction. As such, critics suggest, it works best for problems of living – anxiety, depression and, in particular, self-esteem. There is some evidence to support this view, although Rogers himself also worked with individuals with more serious disorders, including schizophrenia (Rogers 1967).

As with other forms of 'talking cures', which seek large-scale changes in the individual, Rogerian therapy is very difficult to evaluate. While it may be that its primary effects are due to social reinforcement and the empathic support which the therapist provides, one thing is clear: Rogers has been highly influential on other clinicians. When a survey in the 1980s asked American therapists who had had the greatest influence on their work, Rogers was cited more frequently than anyone else (Smith 1982). More recently, a similar study of Canadian therapists (completed four years after Rogers' death) found him still in second place (Warner 1991). As a personal model of a caring and compassionate therapist, Rogers seemed to fit his own theory very well indeed.

For further consideration

Recall the question raised earlier about whether behaviour modification is manipulative. Suppose the same criticism was made of person-centred therapy. How would you respond?

Evaluating Therapeutic Techniques

In describing how each of the approaches views abnormal behaviour, we have made reference to the apparent effectiveness, or **efficacy**, of the treatment techniques. The issue of efficacy is important, because obviously a treatment which doesn't help is worthless. To the average person, though, the question would probably be expressed in terms of 'which one is *best*?' As simple as it seems, this is a very difficult question to answer.

efficacy the measured effectiveness of a treatment technique in medicine or psychotherapy

Diversity is part of the problem: not only are there five broadly recognized approaches, but within each many possible variants of treatment exist. This diversity of choices can create confusion, what behaviour therapist Joseph Wolpe has called 'the babble of conflicting voices' (Leo 1985: 39). Not surprisingly, one result has been an increased interest in comparative evaluations of the various types of therapy.

Unfortunately, it is not easy to design comparative studies. Therapeutic approaches often have different goals (e.g. modifying personality *vs* eliminating a specific behaviour), which can make it difficult to define a common standard of evaluation. Indeed, some suggest that standardized assessment is meaningless, since it ignores these differences in goals (Persons 1991). Nonetheless, most researchers and clinicians accept that there must be at least some minimal common standard, since *all* techniques seek to alleviate the distress which leads people to seek treatment.

spontaneous remission in medicine or therapy, improvement in an individual's condition in the absence of treatment

A further problem in doing evaluation studies of therapy is the possibility that an individual may show improvement even *without* treatment – what is referred to as **spontaneous remission**. Obviously, if spontaneous remission is not considered, then some apparent improvements will be credited to treatment, instead of coincidence! Yet, there is an obvious ethical problem in deliberately denying treatment simply to create a control group. As a result, control groups are usually either based on soliciting informed consent to delay treatment, or else created by selecting individuals from waiting lists for treatment (unfortunately, many treatment centres are unable to meet immediate demands).

Having noted these difficulties, let us consider some of the findings of evaluation studies. One of the best-controlled comparative studies was conducted by the National Institutes of Mental Health, a US government agency (Elkin *et al.* 1989). In this study, twenty-eight clinicians of various orientations worked with 240 individuals diagnosed as having major depression. Individuals were randomly assigned to treatment using either an antidepressant drug (imipramine), psychodynamic therapy (not psychoanalysis) or cognitive therapy. In addition, a control group was given a placebo pill, along with brief weekly meetings with a psychiatrist. The placebo/drug groups were conducted as a *double-blind* design, so that neither the doctor nor the individual knew which was which. All individuals were assessed at the start, after sixteen weeks of treatment, and again eighteen months later. The results of the study are complex, and don't point to the type of clear-cut result one might hope for. For example, all three types of treatment produced greater improvement than did the placebo. Drug therapy produced faster improvements than did the insight therapies, but was also associated with higher rates of relapse of symptoms. Even in the placebo group, some of the individuals with only moderate depression showed improvement (this improvement is not evident in the final results, because these individuals tended to drop out before the study was completed). In addition, of course, this study only looked at efficacy in treating *depression*; while relatively common, depression is obviously only one form of disorder.

A different approach to comparing treatment techniques was used by Mary Lee Smith and her colleagues (Smith *et al.* 1980). Drawing on the hundreds of previously published evaluations of various forms of therapy, Smith did a *meta-analysis* of 475 studies, statistically analysing the combined results according to various factors, such as theoretical orientation and type of disorder treated (a partial summary of results is shown in Fig. 9.5). The major finding was that, overall, *all* of the various approaches seemed to produce significant improvement, and that there was little difference in these ratings of overall effectiveness. However, when the analysis was broken down in terms of *types of disorders*, there were significant differences between approaches. For example, humanistic therapy seemed the *least* effective approach for treating anxiety, but was the *most* effective approach for problems of self-esteem.

The type of analysis used by Smith and her colleagues, while interesting, poses many difficulties. For example, different studies would use different assessment criteria, different durations of treatment, and possibly differences in accuracy of diagnoses and assessments of severity, among other variations. In addition, this study did not include treatment based on the medical model (i.e. drugs), which limits the possibility of complete comparisons. Overall, the finding that *all* methods show *some* efficacy suggests there may be factors which are common to all types of treatment.

The idea that there are *non-specific factors* associated with treatment has been recognized for many years. In a classic book entitled *Persuasion and Healing*, psychiatrist Jerome Frank suggested that the common factors in all forms of treatment are the clinician's commitment to helping, and the belief in improvement which this instils in the individual (Frank 1963). More recently, this has been echoed by other researchers; one study suggested that the primary non-specific factors are *support* and *hope* (Stiles *et al.* 1986). The importance of support has been affirmed by psychodynamic therapist Hans Strupp, who states

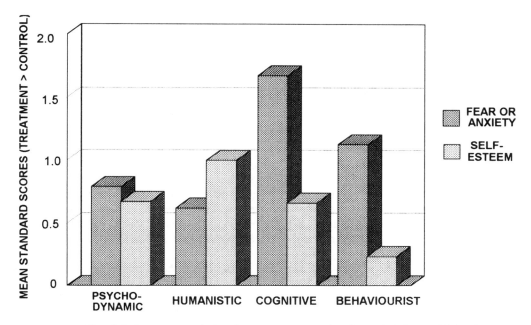

Fig. 9.5 A meta-analysis of treatment results By statistically combining the results from 475 different studies, researchers were able to do a comparative study of four approaches to the treatment of anxiety and self-esteem. The scores are 'standard scores', which are expressed in units of the standard deviation. A score of 1.0 would mean approximately 84 per cent of those in the treatment group improved more than those in the control group; any positive score indicates greater improvement among treatment than in control groups (data adapted from Smith et al. 1980).

that creating an atmosphere of acceptance and empathy is itself of great therapeutic value (Strupp 1989). Hope, which may be created by the therapist's attitude or even a placebo, also seems to be a general feature of effective therapy.

Given the welter of results, and the absence of clear-cut findings that one method is consistently superior, should one conclude that all therapies are the same? Probably not. As noted in Smith's review, some approaches work better than others for certain problems. In part, this may reflect the reality that abnormal behaviour does not have a single cause. Instead, genetic predisposition, prior experiences and current circumstances all probably play a role. In addition, the relative importance of each factor is likely to vary across disorders and even across individuals. Consequently, the finding that each approach has *some* benefit may reflect the realities of complex causation, as well as the non-specific treatment factors discussed above. One reflection of this reality is that a significant number of practitioners describe their approach to treatment as *eclectic* – that is, they draw upon a range of techniques on a case-by-case basis, rather than adhering to a single theoretical model. In a study of therapeutic orientations, between 30 and 40 per cent of Canadian and American psychologists described themselves as eclectic in orientation – more than any single approach (Warner 1991). This seems a reasonable attitude, although we still need to learn more about what works best with whom – and why.

For further consideration

Suppose that you had a problem such as severe depression. What type of therapist would you go to? Why? What questions would you want to ask them before beginning therapy?

Understanding Schizophrenia

multiple-personality disorder a severe form of dissociative reaction which can result in several independent personalities being manifested

schizophrenia a severe form of mental disorder in which there can be distortions of perception, thought, language and emotions

delusions false beliefs which are maintained in the absence of clear evidence to the contrary

hallucinations false perceptions in the absence of relevant sensory stimuli, such as hearing voices or seeing objects which are not present

thought disturbances in abnormal psychology, distortions of thinking processess such as violations of logic, incoherent speech and inappropriate shifts in word usage

negative symptoms in abnormal psychology, particularly with reference to schizophrenia, the absence of expected behaviours; negative symptoms include bodily immobility, limited speech, flattened affect (absence of emotional expression) and social withdrawal

At the beginning of this chapter, we described the case of a young man who had been diagnosed as having schizophrenia. The symptoms he manifested – confusion, incoherent speech, possible delusions – are common in schizophrenia. Although it is relatively uncommon (about 1 per cent of the population are affected, compared with a lifetime risk of serious depression of about 12 per cent), schizophrenia and its stereotypes are closely associated with the popular conception of abnormal behaviour as 'madness'. Of all the forms of mental disorders, schizophrenia is perhaps the most frightening to the average person, and the most difficult to understand.

What we now call schizophrenia has been recognized in various forms for centuries. Even in ancient Greece, Hippocrates described its basic symptoms. The term *schizophrenia* was first used by a Swiss psychiatrist named Eugen Bleuler. Drawing on the Greek words for 'split mind', Bleuler coined the term to refer to disorders in which there seemed to be a separation of cognitive and emotional functions, resulting in mental confusion and either inappropriate emotions or the absence of emotional expression. (It should be noted that schizophrenia, despite the connotation of 'split personality', is *not* the same as **multiple-personality disorder**, a severe form of dissociative reaction which can result in several independent personalities being manifested.)

Schizophrenia represents a severe form of disorder in which there can be distortions of perception, thought, language and emotions. While no two cases are likely to be identical, DSM-III-R requires that there be cognitive or perceptual distortions which impair the person's contact with reality, and also significant deterioration in general functioning (as in working and caring for oneself). In addition, DSM-III-R lists several categories of symptoms which may occur: delusions, hallucinations, thought disturbances and negative symptoms. **Delusions** are false beliefs which are maintained in the absence of clear evidence to the contrary. For example, psychologist Milton Rokeach once encountered three individuals with schizophrenia, each of whom believed himself to be Jesus Christ (Rokeach 1981). **Hallucinations** are false perceptions – most commonly, hearing voices. When asked to describe the source of such voices, individuals typically say they come from within their own head. Interestingly, one study suggests the perceived voices originate by the same process as ordinary silent verbalizations, but are instead perceived as actual voices (Bick and Kinsbourne 1987). **Thought disturbances** can take many forms – apparent violations of logic (called *paralogic*), incoherent speech and shifts in word usage (as when the young man in the Introduction responded to the name Hope as 'that's what I need'). **Negative symptoms** involve the absence of expected behaviours. Negative symptoms can include bodily immobility, limited speech, flattened affect (absence of emotional expression) and social withdrawal, among other forms.

Although not all of these types of symptoms occur in all patients, the predominance of one type is often used to characterize the sub-type of schizophrenia: *paranoid schizophrenia* involves delusions of grandeur (as in the three Christs) and persecution; *catatonic schizophrenia* is characterized primarily by negative symptoms, particularly non-responsiveness to environmental stimuli; and the *disorganized* type shows disturbances of thought and flattened or absent emotional expression. In addition to these three types, there is a fourth category, *undifferentiated schizophrenia*, for those cases that meet the primary criteria (cognitive or perceptual distortions, and generally poor functioning) but do not fit one of the three specific sub-types.

The definition of schizophrenia, and the description of sub-types, is still a matter of some controversy. In part, this reflects the complex mix of possible symptoms, and the necessity of defining the condition (at least at present) purely symptomatically. This is a serious issue, because if the categories are invalid, then classification may actually impede our understanding of aetiology. To give an example, excessive use of amphetamines can result in a disorder called **delusional amphetamine disorder**, which is *symptomatically* identical to paranoid schizophrenia. While circumstances usually allow speedy resolution of the ambiguity, the point is that symptoms are not always a direct indicator of cause. In addition, some critics, like Szasz, continue to assert that schizophrenia is nothing more than society's way of handling perceived deviancy (Szasz 1961).

Despite these difficulties, there is little question that there are individuals with these general symptoms who experience significant distress, and who often seem unable or unwilling to function effectively. In recent years, the estimates of its frequency have tended to centre on 1 per cent of the population (lifetime risk), with men and women equally likely to be affected, but with men often showing an earlier age of onset (late teens to early twenties *vs* late twenties or later for women). Since most clinicians *do* accept that the behaviours associated with schizophrenia do exist, it is worth considering what we know about its origins and possible treatment.

delusional amphetamine disorder a form of mental disorder resulting from the excessive use of amphetamines; its primary symptom, extreme delusions, can make it appear *symptomatically* identical to paranoid schizophrenia

The Medical Model and Schizophrenia

Of the many theories of the causes of schizophrenia, perhaps the best known is the idea that it is biologically based. This concept seems consistent with its apparent severity and generally poor prognosis for permanent recovery. In addition, by suggesting there is a fundamental physiological difference between those with schizophrenia and those who don't have it, it may also be reassuring to people who want to believe that 'it can't happen to me'. As we have discussed, the medical model used by the biological approach interprets abnormal behaviour in precisely this way.

In the case of schizophrenia, there have been hundreds of studies, and a general pattern has emerged. Studies of concordance rates for family members suggest that there is a genetic predisposition for schizophrenia (Nicol and Gottesman 1983; Gershon and Rieder 1992). These findings indicate that for relatives of individuals with schizophrenia, the closer the genetic relationship, the greater the risk. In cases where family members separated early in life have been examined, they suggest that the observed pattern cannot be accounted for by environmental influences.

Still, there are limits on what these findings tell us. First, they do *not* mean that schizophrenia is purely genetic – even identical twins reared together show no more than a 50 per cent concordance rate. Second, assessments of environmental influence are somewhat limited, since we cannot be sure that the factors which lead to family separation are not also factors which contribute to abnormal behaviour in general (such as poverty or marital breakdown). As Nicol and Gottesman (1983) note, there are very few cases involving separated identical twins with schizophrenia, and those cases may not be representative of the general population. Most importantly, while a genetic factor *does* seem implied, no-one knows exactly what it is, despite years of searching. Consequently, in recent years, most research has focused on identifying possible physiological mechanisms to account for the occurrence of schizophrenia.

Over the years, various studies have suggested a number of physiological differences between individuals with schizophrenia and the normal population. For example, scans of the brain using positron emission tomography (PET) have shown that there is less frontal lobe activity during attention tests (Gershon and Rieder 1992). The ventricles (fluid-filled chambers in the brain) are often slightly enlarged, and the tissues surrounding the ventricles – notably in the hippocampus and temporal lobe – are often slightly shrunken.

While such studies are promising, they still do not offer a clear explanation of the basis of schizophrenia. Indeed, the evidence is weakened by several factors. Most damaging is the fact that no single factor is consistently found in the majority of individuals diagnosed with schizophrenia (Heinrichs 1993). The picture is also complicated by the fact that, when looking at differences in the brains of adults, one cannot rule out the role of environmental factors in producing some of the changes, since we know that experience modifies brain structure (see Chapter 7). Environmental influences could include early rearing, malnutrition, social isolation and treatment-related factors like drug effects and institutionalization. While the physical evidence may be confirmed and refined over time, history suggests we should be cautious, since there have been previous claims to having found 'the cause of schizophrenia' (see Brown and Herrnstein 1975, for a scathing review of the history).

The explanation which has attracted the greatest attention in recent years has been the **dopamine hypothesis**, the theory that schizophrenia is related to overactivity in neural pathways which depend on dopamine as a neurotransmitter. The primary evidence in favour of this hypothesis comes from clinical experience with drugs which disrupt the activity of dopamine in the brain. Beginning in the 1950s, doctors found that a family of drugs called *neuroleptics* were of great benefit in reducing many of the most severe symptoms of schizophrenia, particularly hallucinations, delusions and disorganization (Wender and Klein 1981). As research into the mechanism of action of these drugs progressed, it was discovered that their clinical action seemed related to their ability to block the activity of dopamine in the brain. Additional evidence came from studies of amphetamine-induced psychosis, since amphetamines also stimulate dopamine levels. There is also evidence that the drug commonly used to treat Parkinson's disease, a muscle-control disorder whose treatment involves elevating dopamine levels, can worsen the symptoms of schizophrenia (Kendell 1987). Conversely,

dopamine hypothesis a theory which argues that schizophrenia is based on overactivity in neural pathways which depend on dopamine as a neurotransmitter it has been found that a side-effect of neuroleptic drugs can be muscle tremors reminiscent of Parkinsonism. Hence, in various ways, the clinical evidence points to a link between dopamine and schizophrenia.

When one looks for direct physiological evidence, there is greater controversy. Based on the available evidence, some researchers believe that the dopamine hypothesis is correct (Carlsson 1978; Gershon and Rieder 1992). However, many of the studies which have found abnormalities in dopamine receptors in individuals with schizophrenia have depended on post-mortem analyses. Since most individuals with a lengthy history of schizophrenia also have a long history of taking neuroleptics, one cannot rule out drug-induced changes in the neural pathways. A further problem is that the drugs usually reach the brain very shortly after ingestion, yet there is typically a lag of days or weeks before clinical improvement occurs.

The picture is also muddied by recent research on a newer drug, *clozapine*. Clozapine appears to be even more effective clinically than the earlier neuroleptics (notably chlorpromazine), yet it affects *non*-dopamine pathways more than dopamine pathways (Tandon and Kane 1993). These difficulties have led to modifications of the original hypothesis, suggesting that the key is either selective effects on particular receptors, or some sort of stabilizing of activity in dopamine *vs* non-dopamine pathways (Gershon and Rieder 1992). By contrast, given the methodological problems and inconsistencies, some researchers have concluded that there is no compelling evidence for the dopamine hypothesis at present (Cooper *et al*. 1991).

Where does this leave us in terms of understanding the aetiology of schizophrenia? At present, no clear conclusion is possible in terms of theories based on the medical model. There appears to be a genetic risk factor, but no-one has yet identified a specific mechanism. The pragmatic evidence concerning the clinical benefits of neuroleptic drugs is impressive, but our understanding of the physiological underpinnings is far from complete. Indeed, at present there is no direct proof that observed physiological differences are the *cause*, rather than the *result*, of schizophrenia. Given this, and also the possibility that multiple factors contribute to schizophrenia, let us consider some alternative explanations.

Alternatives to the Medical Model of Schizophrenia

The biological approach uses the medical model to explain schizophrenia in terms of genetic and physiological processes. In contrast, the other four approaches all emphasize environmental influences. While the specific factors emphasized differ, each approach offers theories to explain the aetiology of the behaviour, and also treatment techniques derived from theory. In comparing these various theories, we face a basic problem of evaluation. While we can attempt to measure the effectiveness of the treatments, this does *not* prove directly that the associated theory is correct in explaining the cause of schizophrenia. The problem, for both the environmental theories and the medical model, is that nearly all of the evidence is *retrospective*. That is, we are unable to do controlled experiments to test the theories; instead, researchers have to work backwards, after the disorder has already been diagnosed. At best, one can try to identify individuals who are defined as being at risk, and observe whether they in fact develop schizophrenia; but even in this case, the results are technically correlational, and prone to errors such as sampling bias. The problems of evaluation are further complicated by the disputes about the validity of current diagnostic categories, since evidence favouring several theories may either mean that multiple factors contribute to the occurrence of schizophrenia, or simply that we are currently lumping together disorders with very different origins. With these difficulties in mind, let us consider how each of the other approaches views schizophrenia and its treatment.

The Behaviourist Approach

As previously discussed, the behaviourist approach interprets abnormal behaviour as simply maladaptive learning. In this regard, schizophrenia is not regarded any differently than other forms of abnormal behaviour. Indeed, behaviourists would regard the term 'schizophrenia' as having no aetiological value; even viewed descriptively, the term would be seen as useful only to the extent that it reliably describes particular patterns of behaviour.

As an explanation of the origin of schizophrenia, the behaviourist view has several weaknesses. First, although reinforcement is a well-demonstrated general principle, there is no direct evidence for the acquisition of *schizophrenic* behaviour. There are also several ways in which the model seems inconsistent with the available evidence. For example, while it is possible to use learning to suggest why children of individuals with schizophrenia are at greater risk, it is hard to see how this applies in cases where children are reared *apart* from the parent with schizophrenia. Also, although one can conceive of a particular symptom being learned, it is not clear why particular *combinations* of symptoms should occur so regularly (e.g. delusions coupled with hallucinations). It has been argued that by regarding all behaviour as alike, behaviourists give little attention to the *kinds* of problems people tend to develop (Wachtel 1977). Given the lack of specifics, the model does not seem to contribute greatly to our understanding of the causes of schizophrenia.

At the same time, a number of studies have shown that reinforcement can be effective in modifying the behaviour of individuals with schizophrenia. For example, in one case, a forty-year-old man had been hospitalized for nineteen years, and had not spoken to anyone in all that time. The researchers discovered that he loved chewing gum, and used it as a reinforcer to successfully reintroduce speech, by a process of shaping (Isaacs *et al.* 1960). Other studies have focused on shaping the behaviour of entire wards, by establishing a *token economy* (Schaefer and Martin 1966; Atthowe and Krasner 1968). These studies have typically reported success in improving specific behaviours (such as dressing and going to meals), and also improvements in overall functioning. What is most striking is that these studies involved individuals who had already been institutionalized for long periods; in the Atthowe and Krasner study, the median age of the patients was fifty-seven, and the median duration of hospitalization was *twenty-two years*. Despite the negative prognosis this implies, 90 per cent of the eighty-seven men on the ward participated actively in the programme, and showed improvements over a two-year period.

Token economy programmes represent one of the most frequent applications of the behaviourist approach within mental institutions (Ayllon and Azrin 1968). One obvious reason for this is that the institutional environment makes it possible to control reinforcers sufficiently to make tokens meaningful. However, these programmes also raise questions about the effects of an institutionalized environment on behaviour. Schaefer and Martin note the passivity of the patients, a characteristic noted by many observers (Schaefer and Martin 1966; Rosenhan 1973). Indeed, concern about the negative effects of institutionalization partially explains the shift from hospitalization to out-patient treatment which followed the discovery of drugs like chlorpromazine. This shift led to dramatic drops in hospitalization rates; from a peak in the early 1950s, hospitalization rates in the United States for mental disorders (of which schizophrenia represented a large proportion) dropped almost four-fold over the following twenty years (Bassuk and Gerson 1978). To some critics, the shift to minimal hospitalization (supplemented by out-patient services) has not been entirely positive. As negative as most hospital environments were, the failure to create appropriate community-based supports for individuals with schizophrenia and other disorders has often led to even greater neglect (Thomas 1981).

The reason for engaging in this digression is two-fold. First, it indicates that many of the behaviours modified in the above studies may have been related to institutionalization, not schizophrenia. Consequently, they may tell us little about the validity of the behaviourist model in terms of schizophrenia proper. Second, the emptying of institutions described above (a pattern repeated in most Western countries) has meant that there are fewer opportunities to apply the behaviourist approach, particularly token economies. This, at least in part, accounts for the paucity of studies since the late 1960s. (However, many of the *principles* of behaviour modification, if not the name, have been integrated into the repertoire of 'eclectic' therapists; see Krasner 1976.)

Overall, then, the evidence suggests that certain forms of maladaptive behaviour can be modified by reinforcement, and this may have some benefit for overall functioning of individuals with schizophrenia. Beyond that, there seems little basis to suggest that maladaptive learning based on reinforcement is the sole, or even primary, *cause* of schizophrenia.

The Cognitive Approach

In dealing with schizophrenia, the cognitive approach has tended to focus on analysing the various types of symptoms, and suggesting explanations based on *faulty cognitive processing*. While these models do not represent a coherent whole, they nonetheless suggest interesting insights into the nature of schizophrenic behaviour. There are three aspects that we will focus on: delusions, language and thought disturbances.

At first glance, *delusions* are easy to define – they represent beliefs which seem contradictory to reality. The difficulty with this, as Roger Brown has pointed out, is defining what constitutes reality (Brown 1972). When Milton Rokeach encountered three individuals who each believed himself to be Jesus Christ, he thought that confronting them with each other would be an effective therapeutic tool (Rokeach 1981). In fact, each remained steadfast in his belief, convinced the *others* were deluded. (Ultimately, Rokeach came to regret his own actions, which did little to help the three men, citing his own 'Godlike delusion that I could change them by omnipotently and omnisciently arranging and re-arranging their daily lives'.)

While the three Christs fit the stereotype of delusions, in practice most individuals show much more limited delusional beliefs; for example, out of 25,000 patients in Michigan, Rokeach found only a handful who had delusional identities. Moreover, delusional individuals typically recognize as false the delusions of *other* patients (Brown 1972). That is, there is not a complete loss of commonly defined reality, but only in specific content areas. For the moment, let us leave aside the question of *why* this might occur.

At one time, the *language* of individuals with schizophrenia was regarded as an incoherent babble, a 'word salad' or regression to infantile speech. However, in recent years, a number of analyses have suggested that this picture, like the stereotype of delusions, is inaccurate. Roger Brown, who is a specialist in the development of language, has declared that he has never encountered evidence of child-like utterances in individuals with schizophrenia (Brown 1972). Instead, words are simply used in ways that other individuals find strange. Often, it seems that particular words will have private significance to the individual, which can only be interpreted by a patient observer (Maher 1972; Forest 1976). Sometimes the difficulty seems to be a looseness of *connotation* – the associations which a word suggests, rather than its specific meaning. For example, the word 'life' might conjure up human birth (a new life), a magazine (*Life*), a party ('the life of . . .'), and so on, leading to 'the baby came in the magazine and the noise was too much'. Unfortunately, developing a consistent model to explain such utterances on a case-by-case basis is a near impossible task (Rochester 1977). What is needed is an understanding of *why* individuals with schizophrenia sometimes use language in such idiosyncratic ways.

Similarly, *thought disturbances* can seem very puzzling. Two aspects that have garnered attention are faulty reference and logical errors. **Faulty reference** (sometimes considered a form of delusion) involves misinterpreting the significance of stimuli and events. For example, if a person on the street is observed frowning, the individual assumes that it is directed at them. A branch knocks against a window, and it is taken as a sign from God. In such cases, the person attributes a meaning to the event which most people would not. *Logical errors* – apparent lapses in reasoning – are a matter of some contention. Some theorists, like Silvano Arieti, believe such errors are based on the individual using a different form of reasoning (Arieti 1974). For example, the person may say, 'The Virgin Mary is a virgin. I am a virgin. Therefore I am the Virgin Mary'. In this case, the person is creating an identity based on the predicates of the first two statements being alike; in conventional logic, this is considered improper. However, if the person reasons this way consistently, then it could still be considered 'logical', albeit using unconventional rules. On the other hand, other theorists reject the idea that individuals with schizophrenia reason better, worse or differently when compared with normal individuals (Brown and Herrnstein 1975).

Considered together, these various phenomena can seem very puzzling, and somewhat bizarre. Yet one must remember that not all individuals with schizophrenia show all of these behaviours; in fact, even those that do manifest these symptoms tend to do so in limited ways. This leaves the question, how can these behaviours be explained? From a cognitive standpoint, one explanation suggested

faulty reference an error involving misinterpreting the significance of stimuli and events; while sometimes considered a form of delusion, it can also arise through faulty perceptual processing is that individuals with schizophrenia have a problem of **defective attention**, a difficulty in selecting and attending to the relevant stimuli in a situation (McGhie 1970). Even Bleuler, in first defining schizophrenia, noted that individuals with schizophrenia seemed unable to keep their thoughts focused. Many individuals who have developed schizophrenia have described their early symptoms in terms of behaviours like memorizing trivial details, being distracted easily or misinterpreting instructions (Chapman 1966). What is particularly striking is that they describe these behaviours not as personal preferences, but as something which they are *unable to control*.

If looked at in this context, many of the above symptoms seem understandable. Typically, we assume two people focus on the same 'evidence' when evaluating beliefs; if a person holds an anomalous belief, it is clearly a 'delusion'. Instead, delusions and faulty reference may arise from idiosyncratic selection and/or interpretation of information. Similarly, 'word salads' and other language problems could arise because of an inability to ignore the connotations of words. The cumulative effect of such attention deficits could be to develop atypical beliefs (delusions), and to have difficulty with language and thought in ways that would hamper social interactions. In turn, the negative responses of other people would aggravate the social impact of the initial problem of defective attention. This interpretation is supported by the finding that children at risk of developing schizophrenia (in genetic terms) often show similar attention deficits (Green 1993).

While no specific treatment technique has emerged from the defective attention theory, it does pose some interesting implications. One obvious attraction is that it suggests a common mechanism underlying many seemingly disparate symptoms, as discussed above. Also, it provides an explanation for why individuals with schizophrenia can function normally in some respects, while other behaviours seem very bizarre. While it is premature to say with certainty, it is also possible that this model can ultimately be connected to research on the effects of neuroleptic drugs. The neural pathways for attention are complex, and in some respects broadly distributed in the brain, but two areas involved in the selection and processing of stimulus information are the brainstem and the frontal lobes, both of which seem implicated by the studies of drug actions. It will be interesting to see if future research brings at least a partial convergence of the two models.

The Psychodynamic Approach

The psychodynamic approach views schizophrenia as a severe distortion of psychological functioning, a disintegration of ego functions which results in the loss of reality testing. To Freud, for example, schizophrenia reflected a regression to the oral or anal stages, during which the ego first develops. Because the child fails to develop a clear sense of the boundaries between the self and the outside world, the ego is later unable to effectively maintain reality testing, or cope with the demands of id. The result is the variety of symptomatic behaviours which we associate with schizophrenia. For example, the self-neglect and behavioural passivity found in schizophrenia, particularly the catatonic form, can be attributed to the distorted body image of a damaged ego. Similarly, the incomprehensible language is interpreted as infantile regression.

Objectively, there is little evidence to support the Freudian interpretation. For example, Roger Brown has challenged the notion that the language behaviour found in schizophrenia bears any resemblance to children's speech (Brown 1972). Even in terms of treatment, the picture is not encouraging. As with other disorders, Freud viewed therapy as involving the analysis of the underlying conflicts; once the person could develop insight into these unconscious processes, it was possible to alleviate the symptomatic behaviour. The difficulty is that psychoanalysis, like other insight therapies, has a strong verbal component. As a result, its record of success in major disorders like schizophrenia is poor (Luborsky and Spence 1978).

Other psychodynamic theorists have also offered interpretations of the origins of schizophrenia. One common focus is the effects of early relationships (a factor implicit in Freud's interpretation as well). For example, Margaret Mahler, a neo-Freudian theorist who has focused on personality development in infancy, suggests schizophrenia develops from the child being unable to separate from the mother. Mahler views this separation process as difficult for all individuals: 'not even the most normally endowed child, with the most optimally available mother, is able to weather the separation . . . process without crisis' (Mahler *et al.* 1975: 229). In the case of schizophrenia, the mother and child form an intense interdependency, called a **symbiotic attachment**, which prevents the child from developing a healthy, distinct ego. Other theorists have focused on parent–child communication patterns, as in Bateson's **double-bind hypothesis** (Bateson *et al.* 1956). Bateson's model, which suggested that the mother gives contradictory messages (like 'come closer', but then shrinks from physical contact) has been attacked for depending largely on retrospective analysis of communication patterns. This makes it impossible to know if the way family members communicate is the *cause* of schizophrenia, or a *result* of trying to cope with the behaviours associated with schizophrenia. After many years, the issue is still not fully resolved, but in general the evidence to support models based on family interactions is not compelling. Whatever successes it may claim for lesser disorders, the psychodynamic approach does not fare well in dealing with the complexities of schizophrenia.

symbiotic attachment an intense interdependency between a mother and child which prevents the child from developing a healthy, distinct ego; seen by psychodynamic theorist Margaret Mahler as the basis of schizophrenia

double-bind hypothesis a theory of schizophrenia developed by anthropologist Gregory Bateson and his colleagues, which argues that faulty communication patterns within the family are the cause of schizophrenia

The Humanistic Approach

Like the psychodynamic approach, the humanistic approach emphasizes distortions of development. However, it interprets the origins of the distortions very differently than Freud or other psychodynamic theorists. The behaviours which are labelled as 'schizophrenia' represent the individual's response to the world, however distorted it may seem to other people. For the therapist, the essential concern is to try to understand *what* the person is experiencing. As Rollo May has said, focusing instead on the *how* and *why* of the individual's condition will result in understanding 'everything except the most important thing of all, the existing person' (May 1961: 25).

What is it that the person is experiencing in schizophrenia? In some sense, it seems that the person sees the demands of the environment as intensely conflicting with the needs of the self. R.D. Laing, a psychoanalytically-trained British psychiatrist who came to adopt a humanistic view, talked about it as 'the divided self' – a split created by the need for 'compliance with the other person's intentions or expectations for one's self' (Laing 1965: 98). In Rogerian terms, externally imposed conditions of worth lead to an extreme lack of congruence. If the external demands are sufficiently threatening, then withdrawal from social interaction can seem a reasonable option in order to preserve some part of the self. This withdrawal, accompanied by a 'splitting off' of the self, is sometimes called **depersonalization** by clinicians; such reactions are at least occasionally experienced by most people under stressful circumstances. As Brown and Herrnstein (1975) have noted, it is a sense of looking at the situation from outside, accompanied by the feeling that 'this isn't really happening to *me*'.

However the process is described, it seems that the threats to the self produce a profound sense of distress and loss of self-awareness, which results in the characteristic behaviours seen in schizophrenia. Since withdrawal from social interaction is often part of the response, it seems hard to fathom how humanistic therapy could proceed. Yet in fact, Rogers and other clinicians have successfully applied person-centred therapy to working with individuals with schizophrenia (Rogers 1967). As he noted, the process depends on the therapist first convincing the individual that the therapist is concerned, and is not a threat. Often, this may require long periods of sitting quietly with the person, waiting for a sign of possible interaction. In one case, Rogers worked with a twenty-eight-year-old man named Jim who had been hospitalized for two and a half years. After months of weekly meetings which passed mostly in silence, Jim finally began to speak. After several more sessions, he began to reveal feelings of bitterness, mistrust and worthlessness. Near the end of one session, Jim, expressing his frustration, said, 'I want to go, 'cause I don't care what happens'. Rogers responded to this by saying, 'I'd just like to say – I care about you. And I care what happens' (Rogers 1967). The conversation in which this exchange occurred marked a turning point in the therapeutic process; several months later, Jim was discharged from the hospital and began a job. Eight years later, he spontaneously wrote to Rogers to say that he was still employed, had friends and felt content with his life (Meador and Rogers 1979).

While this example typifies the Rogerian approach, and suggests that it may be useful with schizophrenia, there are possible limitations. Some would suggest that, like other insight therapies, person-centred therapy is not likely to have a very high overall success rate in such cases. It is even conceivable that, given the poor reliability of diagnostic standards in the early 1960s, Jim would not be diagnosed as schizophrenic under current criteria. While insufficient information exists to answer these criticisms, some conclusions do seem possible. First, it seems clear that individuals with schizophrenia experience a distortion of self (e.g. Vonnegut 1975). Second, Rogerian techniques clearly emphasize the caring which has been identified as a beneficial factor in all therapies (Frank 1963; Stiles *et al.* 1986).

The humanistic approach suggests that schizophrenia is an expression of the vulnerability of the self. Faced with demands from others that contradict the self, yet needing the positive regard which others provide, the individual can find no resolution; the final result can be a virtual dissolution of the individual's sense of self. By contrast, caring and acceptance by others seems to open the door to growth and rediscovery of the self.

depersonalization a type of dissociative reaction in which the individual psychologically withdraws from a situation, often accompanied by feeling that their body is not real or belongs to someone else

Evaluating Our Understanding of Schizophrenia

As we have seen, each of the approaches has something to say about the nature of schizophrenia, and how to help those who suffer from it. The explanations offered differ significantly, however, and so do the attitudes which are implied. In this sense, schizophrenia provides perhaps the clearest example of how the approaches differ in their views of abnormal behaviour.

Resolving these differences requires a better understanding of what schizophrenia *is*. Is it a physiological disorder? A form of learned dysfunction? An arbitrary social construct? All of these? One way of gaining some perspective on the issue is by looking at how other cultures view it. A major study by the World Health Organization in the 1970s looked at schizophrenia in ten countries, reflecting both industrialized and developing societies (Jablensky *et al.* 1992). Using agreed-upon diagnostic criteria, the researchers in each country identified new cases of schizophrenia, and followed the course of treatment for two years; altogether, they considered almost 1400 cases. In terms of overall incidence rates, types of symptoms and even average age of onset, there was remarkable similarity across cultures. This tends to suggest that there *is* some common cause which is unrelated to culture – in other words, a physiological factor. However, the results of treatment were startling: over two years, the rate of recovery in industrialized countries was only 37 per cent, whereas in developing countries it was 63 per cent, almost double!

Given that we tend to view medical care as superior in industrialized countries, how can one account for this disparity? While individuals in the developing countries were more likely to seek folk remedies and less likely to receive drugs, the primary difference may be one of attitudes (Lin and Kleinman 1988). People in developing countries typically have less rigid conceptions of abnormality, and are less likely to view the behaviour as permanent. Differences in family structures and possibilities for useful work in a family setting may also play a role. Whatever the explanation, the differences in recovery rates cannot easily be explained if one assumes that schizophrenia is purely physiological. Instead, it seems that environmental factors, including culture, play a role as well. This conclusion perhaps helps to explain why each of the approaches has *some* benefit as therapy, but leaves us with questions about how our own culture views schizophrenia, and abnormal behaviour in general.

For further consideration   Does it surprise you that recovery rates differ across countries? Do you think this supports the view of critics like Thomas Szasz, who argues that mental illnesses like schizophrenia are a 'myth'?

Conclusion

Abnormal psychology is concerned with the understanding of *abnormal behaviour*. The question of what constitutes 'abnormal' behaviour is a difficult one. While it always implies some form of *deviance* from expected norms of behaviour, deviance is not in itself a reasonable basis for defining mental disorders, since it is too dependent on cultural values. Instead, the generally accepted definition today is that abnormal behaviour involves significant *suffering* and/or *maladaptive functioning*. While these criteria seem intuitively reasonable, they still pose problems of *who decides* what is maladaptive and what represents significant suffering.

Viewed conceptually, abnormal psychology involves three aspects: diagnosis of the problem, understanding the cause of the problem and therapy to treat the problem. In practice, the three elements are closely intertwined, making it hard to assess one element independently of the others. Hence, while each of the five approaches has its own interpretation of the origins of abnormal behaviour, at present the primary means of assessing the various theories is by examining their *efficacy* as therapies.

Evaluating the various approaches to therapy is a difficult task, in part because they often have different goals and criteria for measuring improvement. In addition, there is the problem of how to do experimental evaluations without violating the ethical rights of those who seek help. To the extent that it is possible to determine, the evidence suggests that *all* the approaches have some value, but that *no* approach is equally effective with all forms of disorders. One explanation for this outcome may be that there are *non-specific effects* of therapy in general, such as emotional support provided by the therapist and the individual's belief that therapy can help.

Another possible reason for the partial effectiveness of most therapies is that most patterns of abnormal behaviour may have multiple causes. For example, a particular disorder may be triggered by a physiological imbalance, which can be treated with drug therapy. However, in trying to adapt to that imbalance, the individual may have developed other maladaptive behaviours which drugs will not change. To deal with these aspects, other forms of treatment may also be of benefit.

Whatever the reason, the apparent advantages and disadvantages of each approach have resulted in a tendency for most clinicians to become eclectic, utilizing different techniques on a case-by-case basis. While this seems a desirable thing in principle, we still know too little about causes, and consequently about which technique works best in a given circumstance. Without this knowledge, eclectic approaches could conceivably result in the *worst* of all methods, rather than the *best*. Clearly, we need to know more about what works, and *why*.

The limitations of our current knowledge are particularly evident when considering *schizophrenia*. While neuroleptic drugs have proven effective in alleviating delusions, hallucinations and other primary symptoms of the disorder, the *medical model* on which drug therapy is based has not yet produced a clear explanation of the mechanism of action. The *dopamine hypothesis*, which attributes schizophrenia to the effects of excessive dopamine in the brain, has attracted considerable interest, but is still controversial.

In contrast to the biological approach, all the other approaches interpret schizophrenia in terms of maladaptive learning. While each has had some limited successes, none has been proven to be more effective than drug treatments, although all may be useful as adjuncts to drug therapy. As a theoretical model, the *defective attention theory* of the cognitive approach comes closest to integrating our understanding of the various symptoms associated with schizophrenia. To some extent, it is also consistent with the medical model, and may eventually lead to a multi-level theory of the origins of schizophrenia. At present, though, the model has not led to any significant therapeutic initiatives, so its value is primarily as a theoretical device.

In the end, we must admit that we still have no clear understanding of the causes of schizophrenia, or how to treat it. Interestingly, some cultures seem to deal with it better than we do – a reminder that there is a social dimension to abnormal behaviour. While most clinicians believe that normality and abnormality are part of a continuum, too many people still view mental disorders as something strange and frightening. Not only does this hamper the understanding of abnormal behaviour, it also hampers treatment by encouraging the stigmatizing of individuals with mental disorders. Consider this example: Suppose that schizophrenia really is based on defective attention, which leads people to behave in idiosyncratic ways. In itself, this defect may hamper the individual in some ways, but if the quirkiness of their behaviour (or society's perception of it) leads to the person being stigmatized and rejected, then the effects of social isolation will create further problems. The challenge is to understand the core problem, but respond to the *person*, not simply the problem.

In the end, behaviour, whether normal or abnormal, is still *human* behaviour. As travellers on the human journey, we are all alike, and ignoring this reality ultimately diminishes our capacity to understand *any* aspect of human experience. As R.D. Laing said in *The Divided Self*, there is still too much talk of Them, and not enough of Us (Laing 1965).

One may argue that this is a social issue, not a scientific one. Yet the whole premise of this book is that psychology is the product of human beings, and is therefore influenced by the processes which affect all human behaviour. Each of us brings to the study of behaviour our own perceptions and cognitive schema, based on our past experience. Part of that past experience, of course, is the culture we live in. If our culture encourages us to view abnormal behaviour as Us *vs* Them, then that perception will influence our theories as well. This is *not* to suggest that everything is a construction of our minds – the behaviour we seek to explain is real. Instead, it is simply meant to point out that we each tend to see only part of the overall picture, and this partial vision tends to be reflected in our theories. In this sense, the struggle to understand abnormal behaviour, and the perplexities that surround it, reflect the larger challenges which face psychology as a whole.

Chapter Summary

- ◆ *Abnormal psychology* is concerned with the understanding of *abnormal behaviour*. While definitions have varied historically, it has typically been defined in terms of *deviance* from society's norms. Today, *DSM-III-R* identifies significant *suffering* and/or *maladaptive functioning* as the primary criteria.

- ◆ Critics have questioned the value of classification systems like DSM-III-R, citing problems of misdiagnosis and the *stigmatizing* effects of labels, but most psychiatrists and other clinicians find classification useful.

◆ Each of the five approaches has its own interpretation of the origins of abnormal behaviour; evaluation of these theories is closely tied up with assessment of the *efficacy* of therapies based on the theories.

◆ The *biological approach* emphasizes physiological and genetic factors, in terms of the *medical model*. The use of drug therapy, based on this approach, has made great progress as our knowledge of psychopharmacology has grown in recent years.

◆ The *behaviourist approach* sees abnormal behaviour as based on learning of inappropriate responses. Techniques of *behaviour modification*, such as *systematic desensitization*, have been used to treat a variety of problems.

◆ The *cognitive approach*, consistent with its general view, emphasizes the role of cognitive mediators in abnormal behaviour. Social learning theory has been applied to the use of behaviour modification, resulting in *cognitive behaviour modification*. Other cognitive theories, such as Ellis's *rational-emotive therapy*, have focused on the faulty beliefs which accompany maladaptive behaviour. Like psychodynamic and humanistic therapies, cognitive therapy places an emphasis on *insight* into one's behaviour.

◆ Within the *psychodynamic approach*, Freud saw abnormal behaviour as the result of unconscious conflicts within the psyche; therapy was based on helping the individual gain awareness of the underlying dynamics. While differing in specifics, other psychodynamic theorists also emphasize the importance of insight. Psychodynamic therapy can be difficult to evaluate, since its goals are often fairly global, involving modifying the whole structure of personality.

◆ The *humanistic approach* rejects classification in favour of trying to understand how the individual experiences the world. Abnormal behaviour is regarded as a distortion of growth, with the maladaptive behaviours representing an attempt to cope with a threatening environment. Rogers' *person-centred therapy* often results in changes in how individuals express their feelings and goals, but it is harder to assess behavioural change.

◆ *Schizophrenia* is one of the most challenging forms of mental disorder, and has been the focus of considerable research. Though the term itself is less than 100 years old, the primary symptoms of *delusions, hallucinations, thought disturbances* and *distortions of emotional expression* have been recorded since ancient times.

◆ The *dopamine hypothesis* has drawn considerable attention as a theory of schizophrenia, and is supported in part by the effectiveness of neuroleptic drugs in treating the primary symptoms. However, difficulties still exist with both the theory and the use of drugs in treatment.

◆ The other approaches interpret schizophrenia in terms of maladaptive learning of various types. Of these, the *defective attention theory* of the cognitive approach seems to offer the greatest potential to enhance our understanding, possibly in conjunction with the medical model. However, it has not yet resulted in any specific therapy.

◆ In the end, the study of abnormal behaviour, including schizophrenia, challenges our perceptions of ourselves and our relationship to other people. In this sense, progress in understanding abnormal behaviour is likely to depend on our progress in psychology in general.

Key Terms and Concepts

abnormal behaviour
aversive conditioning
behaviour modification
cognitive behaviour modification
cognitive restructuring
defective attention theory
delusions
depersonalization
dopamine hypothesis
efficacy
hallucinations
hierarchy of fears
insight

medical model
negative symptoms
person-centred therapy
rational-emotive therapy
resistance
schizophrenia
spontaneous remission
stigma
symptom substitution
systematic desensitization
thought disturbances
token economy
transference

Suggestions for Further Reading

For readers wondering what it is like to have a mental disorder, Dale Peterson's *A Mad People's History of Madness* provides a remarkable collection of auto-biographical accounts. For an individual account of schizophrenia, read Mark Vonnegut's *The Eden Express*.

For a fascinating exploration of society's attitudes towards abnormal behaviour in the past thirty-five years, *Back to the Asylum*, by LaFond and Durham, covers legal and social as well as scientific aspects.

The biological approach to mental disorders is captured well in a brief, readable book by Samuel Baronides, *Molecules and Mental Illness*. Approaches *other* than the biological are well represented in *The Evolution of Psychotherapy* by Jeffrey Zeig; it is based on an extraordinary conference that brought together twenty-six well-known therapists to discuss their ideas.

10 Psychology in Perspective

Searching for Answers

There is an old story about a man who had accomplished many things in his life – inventing new products, acquiring a great fortune, and becoming famous. Yet still he felt a sense of incompleteness, as though somehow the real meaning of life had eluded him.

One day, he heard of a hermit who lived on a far-off mountain. Despite the remoteness of the location, many people journeyed to visit the hermit, because he was reputed to know the secret of life. Like these travellers, the dissatisfied man decided to seek out the hermit.

After a long and difficult journey, the man finally located the hermit. He lived in a simple shack, with no running water or electricity – yet his eyes glowed with what seemed great joy. Sensing that the rumours might be true, the man pressed the hermit for the secret of life. The hermit looked at him, with his fine clothes and belongings, and said, 'If you wish to know the secret, you must first give away all your money and possessions'. At this, the man hesitated. He thought about it for some time, and finally agreed, having realized that his possessions had not made him happy anyway. Finally, the hermit spoke. 'The secret of life is . . .'. He paused, drawing out the suspense, and then whispered, 'there *is* no secret!'

Introduction

Like the man in the story, you have been on a journey. Rather than crossing unfamiliar terrain, you have been venturing into a domain of new ideas. In some ways, such journeys are more difficult than physical journeys, because they challenge us to think in new ways. Having gone through the previous chapters, you should have a better understanding of what psychology is, and what research has been able to tell us about human behaviour. Hopefully, you have found the experience both interesting and challenging. Interesting, in that psychology is concerned with who and what we are, and most of us would like to understand more about both ourselves and other people. Challenging, because psychology is full of unanswered questions and controversies, and in this book we have tried to explain those controversies, rather than hide them behind a mass of 'facts'. Exploring ideas *is* a kind of adventure, and psychology is fertile territory for such adventures. In much the way that a hired guide helps explorers, I have tried to guide your experience and to help you past the worst difficulties and confusions. While I hope you will venture further in the future, it seems an opportune moment to look back over the ground we've covered, and try to get some sense of what may lie ahead.

Approaches Reconsidered – The Many and the One

In the preceding chapters, we have explored five major approaches to the study of human behaviour. Each approach seems to offer its own interpretation, and on many issues there seems to be significant disagreement – for example in explaining the origins of aggression. Consequently, it is understandable if at this point, like the man in the above story, you are tempted to ask for a simple answer to a basic question: 'Which one is right?' Like the man in the story, you may be disappointed at the response.

The answer, of course, is all of them and none of them. All of them, in that each approach has had a significant impact on our view of ourselves and has many adherents. None of them, in that no one approach has been able to successfully explain the full range of human behaviour and experience. As we have discussed, each approach still has gaps and unanswered major questions. Interestingly, however, each sees *different* questions as awaiting answer. In this respect, as in so many others, they continue to disagree.

The diversity of approaches poses a contradiction: while the approaches differ in assumptions, methods and explanations, each claims to be offering the appropriate basis for psychology. Normally, a discipline is defined by its assumptions and methods, as well as its subject matter. How can one speak of psychology as a single discipline, when there is no single framework which underlies it? One answer, suggested by cognitive psychologist George Miller, is to assert that what unites psychology is the faith that eventually a common framework will be found (Miller 1985). This framework will provide 'a science of immediate experience', Miller's description of psychology's central focus. But why isn't there such a framework *already*? And if no such framework exists after more than a hundred years, is it reasonable to hope for one in the future? In order to answer these questions, we need to return to the subject of how different approaches originate.

For further consideration

Which of the five approaches do you prefer? Why? Try to poll some of your classmates, to see their preferences. What do you conclude from these results?

Perception and Theory Formation

In Chapter 1, we looked at some of the basic principles of perception, and noted that the way we see the world depends both on what is 'out there' to be experienced, and also on what is 'inside' – that is, perception depends on the interaction of external stimuli and our internal processes of selection and interpretation. Hence, in any situation, what we experience is influenced by what we *expect* to experience. In the extreme case, our perceptions may depend more on our interpretation than on the actual stimulus. Not long ago, a Japanese exchange student in Louisiana was seeking directions to a party. He approached a house to get information; the owner, perceiving him as a threat, shot and killed the student before he even spoke. We can call it a tragedy, which it certainly is, but we must also acknowledge the power of the processes that led to that tragedy. Given the vast range of stimuli we encounter, we select certain elements, and then interpret them using our current cognitive schemata. In this sense, the 'reality' we experience is individually constructed.

As human beings, psychologists inevitably are also dependent on the processes of perceptual selection and interpretation. This is reflected in the differences in starting assumptions and methods which are central to the various approaches. As Sigmund Koch, a psychologist noted for his interest in such issues, has commented, 'Different theorists will – relative to their different analytical purposes, predictive or practical aims, perceptual sensitivities, metaphor-forming capacities, and pre-existing discrimination repertoires – make asystematically different perceptual cuts upon the same domain' (Koch 1985: 93). In effect, different theorists, with differing interests and differing expectations, will perceive the world differently, and will develop their theories accordingly. Philosopher Bertrand Russell had this in mind when he commented that animals in psychological research seem to match the theories of their experimenters: American (behaviourist) animals use trial and error, while German (cognitive) animals are reflective! (cited by Skinner 1974: 18).

Hence, the origin of any approach is dependent on processes which are partly subjective. Failing to recognize this can lead to becoming blind to the limitations of one's own approach, what Koch has called **cognitive pathology**. Cognitive pathology is reflected in practices like making simplifying assumptions that lead to restrictions in what one observes, and then developing 'total amnesia' for those assumptions and restrictions (a limited example would be when a researcher defines aggression as the willingness to shock people in a laboratory, and then assumes that the results of a study can be applied to homicide). Indeed, it can be argued that without recognizing the role of underlying assumptions and methods, it is impossible to evaluate any conclusion properly. In this regard, the tendency for many authors to present psychology as a collection of 'facts' has questionable value, and may even be hostile to the possibility of real understanding.

Because our assumptions affect our judgement about what is relevant in interpreting a situation, different approaches may view the same event differently. For example, suppose two researchers examine the same experiment, dealing with the effects of television viewing on children's aggressive behaviour. One asserts that the results can be generalized to everyday life, while the other insists that the laboratory study lacks realism and cannot be applied to the real world.

cognitive pathology a phenomenon whereby researchers selectively ignore simplifying assumptions and other limitations which are part of the foundations of their theories and methods

If the argument actually reflects differing assumptions about the causes of aggression, but this is not acknowledged, then no real dialogue is possible. It is not simply the validity of generalizing, but the entire meaning of the evidence that is at issue.

The idea that our assumptions affect the way we reason was supported in a study conducted by Eric Amsel (Amsel *et al.* 1991). In conjunction with a lawyer and another psychologist, Amsel studied the way that lawyers and psychologists evaluate the causes of events. They found that lawyers are trained to reason mechanistically, using counterfactual arguments, whereas psychologists are trained to reason statistically, using covariance arguments. As a result, the two groups tend to explain behaviour differently. For example, consider this situation: David was watching TV, and the picture was poor. He kicked the set, and the picture improved. Given this scenario, a lawyer might justify David's behaviour by suggesting that if he had not kicked it, the picture would not have improved (a counterfactual argument). By contrast, a psychologist might explain it by noting that on several past occasions, kicking the set led to the picture improving (a covariance argument). The point here is *not* that one argument is necessarily better than the other, but that they depend on different assumptions about what makes an argument convincing. In the same way, advocates of different approaches make different assumptions about behaviour. Understanding those assumptions can help to clarify the ways in which the approaches disagree.

While perceptual processes help us to understand how different approaches can arise, they do *not* answer the question of whether one approach is better than another. After all, the fact that advocates of various approaches perceive the world differently does not automatically mean that all see it *equally accurately*. Instead, it is *logically* possible for one theory to be superior at explaining the world. Does it therefore follow that one approach actually *is* better? And how do we decide?

Objective Evidence *vs* Shifting Paradigms

Traditionally, psychology has been founded on the premise of logical empiricism, a principle shared with the sciences in general. **Logical empiricism** says that it is possible to evaluate theories in terms of how well they account for the evidence (Savage 1990). This principle is an extension of the basic belief in *empiricism*, which states that observing the world is the way to gain knowledge. However, accepting the importance of observation does not necessarily imply that observational evidence is a *sufficient* basis for evaluating a theory. Indeed, statistical theory tells us that observations cannot directly prove a theory to be true (see the Appendix for further discussion of this point). Hence, logical empiricism is a probable, but not inevitable, result of accepting the importance of observations.

Logical empiricism says that theories are evaluated, and either accepted or discarded, on the weight of the evidence. An alternative interpretation for why theories are accepted rests on the role of social processes. One of the earliest and best known expressions of this view was a book entitled *The Structure of Scientific Revolutions*, by philosopher of science Thomas Kuhn (1970). Kuhn

logical empiricism in philosophy of science, the assumption that it is possible to compare and evaluate theories in terms of how well they account for the evidence

paradigm in Kuhn's analysis of science, a superordinate framework or world-view accepted by a group of researchers, which shapes both theories and evidence; since the paradigm influences the observations one makes, no observations can ever be used to evaluate the paradigm

asserts that science operates in terms of **paradigms**, frameworks which are endorsed by a group of adherents. Rather than being simply a theory, a paradigm represents an entire way of seeing the world. As Kuhn states, in a new paradigm, 'old terms, concepts, and experiments fall into new relationships with each other' (p. 148).

As a basic framework for our concepts, a framework is more basic than a theory; indeed, different theories can exist within the same framework (for example, Pavlov and Skinner both developed theories within the behaviourist approach, each dealing with different types of responses). However, theories exist in any paradigm, and sometimes a new or competing theory actually is based on a different paradigm. For example, Einstein's theory of relativity required physicists to adopt a new paradigm as a way of seeing the structure of the universe. Instead of space and time being independent as in Newton's framework, space and time became inseparably linked in the new paradigm represented by Einstein's theory.

The crucial element of Kuhn's view is his conception of how one framework replaces another. Paradigms change not because a new one proves better at explaining the evidence than the old paradigm, but because the new one becomes more *popular*. Citing the shift from a Newtonian to an Einsteinian universe, Kuhn argues the change came because the newer paradigm came to be preferred to the older one. Indeed, he cites a famous remark by physicist Max Planck (who helped shape the 'Einsteinian revolution'), that '. . . a new scientific theory does not triumph by convincing its opponents and making them see the light, but rather because its opponents eventually die, and a new generation grows up that is familiar with it' (Kuhn 1970: 150).

In Kuhn's view, because a paradigm is an entire way of seeing the world, observations cannot be made independently of the paradigm. Any piece of evidence only makes sense in terms of the underlying framework which generated it. As a result, observations cannot be used as the basis of choosing between paradigms. This conclusion, which is in direct contradiction to logical empiricism, means that the reasons for preferring one paradigm to another are not simply the result of a better fit to the data. While one may refer to the 'simplicity' or 'elegance' of a model, Kuhn argues that ultimately the choice is more social than rational.

To anyone accustomed to thinking of science as rational and objective, this is a rather startling notion, and Kuhn's argument has not gone uncriticized. Indeed, the very term 'paradigm' is a slippery one, and Kuhn has been attacked for not defining it sufficiently precisely. However, as Baars points out, Kuhn was writing in reaction to the notions of logical empiricism, and in that sense, most readers have little trouble grasping his intended meaning (Baars 1986). Still, Kuhn's view is disturbing, because it suggests that a paradigm is essentially an arbitrary framework. This limits the value of evidence in science, because observations will have completely different meanings depending on the paradigm. For example, consider how a behaviourist and a humanist would interpret someone saying, 'I feel depressed'. In the former case, the statement is simply a verbal response which has been previously reinforced; in the latter case, it is a valid description of an internal emotional state.

While Kuhn's analysis has been both controversial and influential, it has not led to the complete abandonment of empiricism. Most philosophers of science still seem to believe rational choices can be made between theories, and assume that observations *can* be made independently of a theoretical framework. In this view, theories may be subjective structurings of the world, but observations are still useful in evaluating theories (Savage 1990).

Paradigms in Psychology

Whether Kuhn's notion of paradigms is correct or not, it has frequently been applied to psychology (e.g. Berlyne, 1975; Baars 1986). However, unlike physics, psychology has never had a single paradigm; instead, there have been several paradigms, denoted by the different approaches we have discussed in this book. Hence, we cannot talk of 'paradigm shifts' in the sense of a complete reorientation of the discipline. Instead, psychology has several competing paradigms, none of which has complete dominance. Over time, though, the approaches have varied in their level of acceptance, and it is interesting to look at the changes in their *relative* popularity as paradigms.

With the exception of the humanistic, all of the approaches can trace their origins back to at least the early decades of this century. Within that time frame, there have certainly been indications of shifts in popularity. From the 1930s until the early 1960s, the dominant paradigms were the psychodynamic (mainly psychoanalytic) and behaviourist approaches. The former was favoured by clinicians and the latter by experimentalists. As has already been discussed earlier in the book, these two approaches differed in many of their assumptions and methods, and were frequently highly critical of each other. However, over time, both have lost influence, and have largely been supplanted by the biological and cognitive approaches.

Many authors have talked about the striking shift from behaviourism to cognitivism (e.g. Berlyne 1975; Baars 1986), whereby mental processes have gone from being essentially irrelevant to being the central concern. Although the change involved new experimental techniques and results, the primary factor was the shift in interests of a new generation of researchers. The parallel shift from the psychodynamic to the biological is not as simple to describe. While the development of new drugs has certainly altered clinical practice, the increasing popularity of the biological approach is also evident among experimentalists. In addition, the cognitive and biological approaches are not completely at loggerheads, as the earlier pair of approaches were. Indeed, some researchers see an increasing fusion of the two in what is called 'cognitive science'.

Does this change suggest that the long turmoil of conflicting approaches is coming to an end? While it is dangerous to make predictions, the answer is probably not. The basic reason is that, no matter how popular it may become, cognitive science has different interests to those of psychology. It includes elements of philosophy and computer science, and largely ignores some of the questions which have always been central to psychology, such as the role of motivation in behaviour. Hence, it does not promise to resolve the basic disputes within psychology.

Whether Kuhn's argument about how paradigms change is correct or not, it is clear that psychology is very different from most disciplines, in that there is significant disagreement about what paradigm is most appropriate for the discipline.

Psychology has been defined in different ways by different people, but the most widely accepted view, reflected in this book, is that psychology must deal with *both* behaviour *and* experience. It is not, as the behaviourists suggest, purely the study of overt responses, nor is it solely concerned with inner experience (thoughts, feelings, etc.). This duality has always been a source of difficulty. Wundt's attempts to analyse experience in terms of sensory inputs ultimately came to little, and the awkward position of the humanists in contemporary psychology shows that dealing with subjective experience is still problematical. As Robinson has suggested, it seems we are forced to choose between a psychology which is non-scientific, and a science which is not psychology (Robinson 1985). That is, Robinson believes that questions of inner experience are central to psychology, but that they cannot be addressed scientifically.

To understand this comment, one need only consider some of the ways in which researchers have tried to handle inner experience and the questions of thought, feeling and desire which it raises. The introspectionists tried to reduce conscious experience to objective sensory properties, to little avail. Radical behaviourists like Watson and Skinner have sought to side-step the problem by insisting that inner experience is irrelevant. The humanists have pointed to the failures of others, and have argued for significant changes in how we conceive of science. However, the methods they advocate have not been widely accepted. Even the middle ground – trying to adapt the methods of natural science to address in some limited way the questions of mind – faces serious obstacles. All of these responses acknowledge that 'inner experience' and 'science' seem hard to combine. It is this dilemma which has prevented the acceptance of a single approach as the universal paradigm. In this regard, the approaches differ in their emphasis: the biological and behaviourist approaches emphasize science, the psychodynamic and humanistic emphasize inner experience, and the cognitive approach is somewhere in between.

For further consideration

Assuming Robinson is right, would you rather see a scientific psychology which ignored inner experience, or a non-scientific psychology which included the study of inner experience? Why?

Psychology and Science

Depending on how one chooses to look at it, the fault for this continuing fragmentation lies either with the limitations of science, or with our expectations of psychology. Let us consider the second point first. Our experience as human beings leads us to ask about the causes of behaviour. In everyday life, we generate such explanations constantly, invoking our individual and collective notions of personality, motivation, and so on. Science, including psychology, often charges that these notions are not really explanations at all, but simply muddled generalities. However, unless science is itself willing to tackle the task of explaining experience, its criticisms lack credibility (Robinson 1985). Hence, saying psychology should not address these issues (as Watson and other radical behaviourists have said) seems to miss the point.

Limitations of the Scientific Method

Indeed, it can be argued that the problem lies not with the subject matter of psychology, but with the scientific method. Critics have suggested that science has two limitations when it comes to addressing inner experience. One limitation involves science's search for causal explanations. While this has proven highly successful in dealing with many phenomena in the natural sciences, when applied to mental states it encounters difficulties. The crucial difficulty is that mental states are not directly observable, and neither they, nor the behaviours which are used to indicate them, can be uniquely associated with particular causes (Robinson 1985). Instead, the result is often a kind of circularity, like pulling oneself up by the bootstraps: inner experience is used to explain the behaviour which is meant to indicate inner experience. For example, John says he is unhappy. We then examine John's facial expression, tone of voice and other behaviours as a means of validating this statement. In turn, we then 'explain' the behaviour by referring to the fact that he is unhappy! While this is a simplified example, it points to the difficulties involved in trying to explain inner experience independently of behaviour. In this regard, the traditional model of causation which is used in science seems ineffective when dealing with inner experience.

The second limitation concerns the use of the experimental method. The logic of experiments, with their need for strict control and assumptions of objectivity, falters when applied to complex behaviour (as opposed to simple behaviours, like isolated muscular responses). The central difficulty is that human beings are *aware* of being studied, which makes it difficult to obtain an objective assessment of behaviour, particularly when awareness is part of what researchers hope to explain. Thus, as medical ethicist Richard Zaner has commented, an experiment is really an interaction: even as one tries to study the behaviour of individuals, they will be studying the experimental situation (Zaner 1985).

This tendency for behaviour to be altered by the experimental context is emphasized by the concept of **demand characteristics** in research settings. Martin Orne uses the term to describe how participants in experiments respond to both the overt and covert cues of the situation (Orne 1962). Orne suggests that participants will attempt to figure out what is expected, and will use this information in guiding their behaviour. Consequently, he suggests, the only reliable experiment is one which produces a different outcome than what people expect. Otherwise, one can't be sure if the results obtained are a result of natural behaviour, or simply self-fulfilling prophecy by the participants. At the very least, one must acknowledge that individuals in laboratory experiments are aware of being in an experiment, and this can obviously affect their behaviour. Reflecting this, Berlyne suggests researchers should 'form the habit of asking what a subject would do without a psychologist at his elbow' (Berlyne 1975: 77).

demand characteristics
the overt and covert cues present in an experimental situation which can influence how participants behave

As discussed in Chapter 8, concerns about how individuals react to being studied are particularly strong in dealing with social behaviour. Indeed, social psychologist William McGuire suggests that 'our social psychological knowledge is a delusional system which represents reality only poorly, the representation being distorted by our limited intellectual apparatus and distorted by our cognitive systems and our wishes, values, and expectations' (McGuire 1985: 585). In one sense, he is offering an indictment of the traditional experimental method; but at the same time, he is not advocating the wholesale abandonment of observation and inquiry. Rather, he argues for recognizing the limitations of scientific knowledge, and working to minimize distortion and oversimplification. Paul Meehl, a former president of the American Psychological Association, has argued that psychology places too much emphasis on experimental methods and the search for causes. Other methods may not give direct information about causation, he notes, but are nonetheless empirical, and therefore scientifically useful (Meehl 1971).

The Search for a New Methodology

The difficulty of applying the scientific method to inner experience has been a problem throughout psychology's history, and has contributed to the existing diversity of approaches. While it seems unlikely that any one of the approaches we have discussed will suddenly be universally adopted, we may still wonder what the future holds.

One thing we *do* know is this: both the theoretical tools we have, and the empirical methods we use to generate and evaluate them, have limitations. As human creations, both current and future theories are influenced by the limitations of human perception. Hence, it does not seem likely that some new framework will suddenly arise which will resolve all of the theoretical shortcomings of the current approaches.

Just as the theories seem limited, so too does the process for evaluating them. Logical empiricism seems to fail, in that no theory can ever be evaluated *purely* in terms of the evidence. There are logical constraints, as we have alluded to, and also observational constraints: evidence cannot be totally objective and theory-free, since the decisions of both *what* to observe and *how* to observe it are rooted in the very kinds of processes we are trying to understand (the workings of mind and behaviour).

Given these challenges, it may seem tempting to abandon the attempt to understand behaviour. Yet to do so is equivalent to saying that our awareness and capacity to think are of no use in understanding who and what we are. This seems a singular surrender, as well as unreasonably pessimistic. Consequently, we must seek a resolution to the problems, instead of abandoning attempts at understanding.

Redefining 'Understanding'

One approach is to develop new criteria for what 'understanding' means. As noted above, science has traditionally defined understanding in terms of identifying the causes of events. In this regard, the use of prediction has been a basic tool for evaluating our understanding (as represented by our theories). Typically, it has accomplished this through the study of simple experimental situations, which allow generating predictions, and then generalizing the conclusions to the larger world (Hunt 1991). Unfortunately, applying such methods to psychology has resulted in the problems which we have already discussed. Since the methods required for prediction create the difficulties, it may be time to reconsider the appropriateness of prediction as the criterion for evaluating our understanding.

One relatively recent development in basic science which challenges the appropriateness of prediction is the study of non-linear dynamics associated with chaos theory (Hilborn 1994). **Chaos theory** tells us that many physical systems are non-linear; that is, they are not predictable, because very small changes in initial conditions can result in radical differences at a later point. This phenomenon is sometimes called 'the butterfly effect', since something as small as the flap of a butterfly's wing could ultimately affect something as large as weather patterns over a large area. Similarly, a small measurement error could radically alter the expected outcome of an experiment. Hence, while still subject to the laws of causation, chaotic systems defy any serious attempts at predictability. Today, applications of chaos theory are just developing, but it is likely that some aspects of human behaviour (such as the brain's functioning, which in turn affects behaviour) are chaotic. Contrary to the deterministic model of the world on which psychology has often depended, non-linear systems may be the rule, not the exception.

Abandoning prediction (or at least de-emphasizing it) would not be a death blow to psychology. Indeed, there are already precedents: Freud's theory is essentially non-predictive, as is the phenomenological framework of the humanistic approach. Even in the biological approach, non-predictive models have sometimes been met with acceptance; the best current model of pain phenomena, developed by psychologist Ronald Melzack and physiologist Patrick Wall, is largely descriptive (Melzack and Wall 1982).

The danger, of course, is that without prediction it is harder to reject a faulty theory, particularly one which is vague enough to describe almost any observed outcome (Freud's theory has frequently been criticized in this regard). In simple systems, it may still be possible to talk about descriptive accuracy, but at present it is not clear what criterion could be used to evaluate chaotic theories of human behaviour. Still, we must also recognize that it is possible for new answers to be posed for old questions.

Other models besides chaos theory may also prove influential. For example, both Hunt (1991) and McGuire (1985) see systems theory as a potentially productive approach to psychological issues.

Embracing Pluralism

A second way of resolving the contradictions which psychology faces is to endorse the notion of pluralism. Koch has argued that psychology can never be a coherent field, and that we should welcome the diversity of approaches (Koch 1985). In some sense, this brings us back to a metaphor which was mentioned in Chapter 1: the story of the blind men and the elephant. Just as each of the blind men comprehends only part of the whole elephant, so, too, each approach has limitations. Rather than engaging in a divisive – *and* fruitless – attempt to seek the triumph of one approach, Koch suggests that psychology should acknowledge the value of multiple approaches.

One virtue of multiple approaches, each with its own constraints, is that the domain of phenomena to be explained is thereby limited, and therefore becomes

chaos theory a branch of mathematics dealing with non-linear functions which has been applied to the modelling of situations such as the weather and stock markets; non-linear systems are not predictable, because very small changes in initial conditions can result in radical differences at a later point potentially more manageable. That is, one can explicitly decide to focus on only limited aspects of the world. (The radical behaviourists like Watson and Skinner have in fact done this, except they then proceed to declare that the rest of the world is irrelevant, anyway. What is being discussed here is a decision to set limits, but *without* suggesting that what lies *outside* the limits is without value or relevance to a broader understanding.)

Although this idea of setting limits on the field of study (the *domain*) contradicts the goal of developing a comprehensive theory, it may be a more realistic way to proceed. Somehow, we expect a psychological theory to answer everything, yet we don't expect the same of other sciences. For example, Berlyne has pointed out that botany largely ignores the existence of animals, the geology of soils and the astrophysics of the sun (Berlyne 1975). Instead, botany deals with a world of plants – even though we know that animals, soils and the sun exist, and in various ways do affect the way plants function (for example, birds and other animals help distribute seeds). No theory is likely to explain everything, particularly if the domain is a large one. Even physics, with a much longer history than psychology, has not achieved a single uniform theory of forces. Indeed, as noted in Chapter 1, physicists invoke the concept of *complementarity* to deal with the existence of two models which are both useful but not directly reconcilable. If psychology were to be seen as a set of complementary domains, each with its own value, then possibly there would be less concern over the differences and disagreements.

Constraining the domain may be useful, *provided* researchers do not set such narrow limits as to make the enterprise worthless (recall Koch's comments on cognitive pathology). Most psychologists see this as a mistake of the radical behaviourists (like Skinner), though not necessarily of behaviourism more generally; for example, Tolman, who is often seen as one of the pioneers of the cognitive approach, considered himself a behaviourist. The problem of where to set the limits is essentially one of context: creating an artificially simple situation often leads to overlooking elements of the situation which are actually crucial to understanding. This is particularly tricky in psychology, given the complexity of behaviour. An example of the pitfalls of oversimplification concerns the study of memory, and the role of contextual cues. For almost sixty years, the use of nonsense syllables (meaningless combinations of letters) in studying memory was seen as a way of stripping memory processes to the essentials. With little opportunity to utilize meaning, subjects performed in ways that seemed to reflect rote associations. When researchers finally began to study more realistic tasks, it was instead recognized that memory is context-dependent, and that this reality was largely obscured by using 'nonsense' materials.

It may well be that simultaneous exploration of different approaches is the best way to be sure the limits are not set too narrowly. For example, the cognitive approach became dominant over behaviourism not simply as a change of taste, but because people who insisted on pushing the limits of the framework (like Tolman, Krechevsky and Levine) demonstrated that there were phenomena that the old approach could not explain.

Koch's call for pluralism seems reasonable, at least given current realities. In some ways, acceptance of the validity of multiple approaches is already the case; for example, most counsellors view themselves as eclectic, not bound to one approach. Indeed, contrary to Koch's criticism that many researchers show cognitive pathology, most psychologists seem aware that there are limits to their chosen approach. Along with this awareness of limitations goes a (sometimes grudging) acceptance of other approaches. For example, even John B. Watson, the founder of behaviourism, seemed to harbour the tiniest of doubts in his attacks on psychoanalysis. Near the end of *Behaviourism*, he commented that if he ever developed a symptom like paralysis for which no physical cause could be found, 'I should hasten to my psychoanalytic friends and say, "Please, in spite of all the mean things I've said about you, help me out of this mess"' (Watson 1930: 301).

Conclusion

Amidst these criticisms of the past and worries about the future, one should not lose sight of psychology's accomplishments. Even if one restricts the assessment to simply observing behaviour and cataloguing the results, there have been impressive accumulations of information. In some areas, the results have in fact added greatly to our understanding; examples include, the functions of the brain and the workings of memory. Even in complex areas like social behaviour, there have been important insights. For example, consider a problem we discussed in Chapter 1 – social intervention in emergencies. The work of Latané and Darley, and others, has put the lie to the 'common sense' notion that people don't help because they simply don't care. Instead, the factors that govern intervention are often related to social influence – and knowing that may help us find ways to increase intervention in emergencies. Hence, even when our understanding is incomplete, it can be argued that psychology has increased our awareness of possibilities.

Whether the future is one of pluralism or paradigm shift, it is sure to be both interesting and challenging. As Stephen Chorover has suggested, the ferment in psychology in some ways is interconnected to the ferment in society (Chorover 1985). We are living in a world in which large problems exist, involving population growth, environmental degradation, and conflicts between nations and also cultures. At the same time, our intellectual traditions are also being challenged. While science has long been based on the premise that knowledge can aspire to objective absolutes, this view has been challenged by notions of knowledge as a social construction. (Kuhn, of course, has contributed to this.) The study of the human dimensions of science has been useful, for it has helped us recognize points of weakness in the scientific process. However, like many ideas, the notion of knowledge as a social construct can be dangerous if carried too far. When taken to the extreme, it leads to the conclusion that no absolutes exist in the world. The framework for psychology then becomes just one more arbitrary choice in a world of arbitrary choices – and therefore meaningless. To conclude that, however, seems far too pessimistic, and ignores what we *have* learned about behaviour.

In this book, we have taken pains to point to the limitations of what we know, and where possible to suggest what the difficulties are. Yet, however limited our understanding, it should be clear that this book does *not* accept the view that the search for understanding is either completely arbitrary or meaningless. While our understanding of reality can be affected by our personal beliefs and biases (i.e. our cognitive schemata), there *is* something 'out there' to be explained. The existence of human behaviour is not simply a construct of the mind, nor is its nature purely imaginary. Indeed, our desire to understand ourselves is an affirmation of our existence and our capacity for awareness. Consequently, far from being arbitrary or meaningless, the search for understanding is central to our being.

Psychology, like the behaviour it studies, is rich and diverse, and full of unanswered questions. If we can proceed with an appreciation for the wondrous complexity we are seeking to explain, and a suitable humility before that complexity, then psychology should bring us closer to a proper understanding of what we are, and why.

For further consideration

This book, as an introduction to psychology, is of course limited in many ways. What question about behaviour would you like answered which this book has not discussed? Try looking for an answer through the references given, a library, etc.

Chapter Summary

- One of the most basic issues in psychology is how to deal with the existence of different approaches.

- The formation of a theory, and the gathering of evidence, cannot be fully understood without considering the processes of *perception*.

- Whereas *logical empiricism* asserts that theories can be judged by seeing how well they fit the available evidence, Kuhn's theory of *paradigms* suggests both theories and observations are influenced by the broader frameworks (paradigms) which we use to view the world.

- The various approaches within psychology can be seen as examples of paradigms, but this does not resolve the disagreements among them about the nature of behaviour.

- The application of traditional scientific methods to psychology faces two limitations: (1) it is very difficult to talk about the causes of mental events, and (2) the fact that participants are aware of their surroundings makes it difficult to maintain control and objectivity in experiments.

- In the face of these difficulties, various psychologists have called for either redefining 'understanding' to not require causal predictions, or accepting the existence of different approaches/paradigms as a form of *complementarity*.

Key Terms and Concepts

cognitive pathology
complementarity
demand characteristics

logical empiricism
paradigm

Suggestions for Further Reading

For a better understanding of the concept of paradigms in science, Thomas Kuhn's pioneering book, *The Structure of Scientific Revolutions*, provides an authoritative view. While it is not light reading, Kuhn proposes some provocative ideas.

One of the most interesting sources for assessments of all aspects of psychology is Koch and Leary's edited collection, *A Century of Psychology as a Science*. Written to commemorate the centenary of Wundt's first laboratory, it contains chapters written by a variety of eminent modern psychologists. While it is not the type of book one sits down to read cover to cover, it makes fascinating browsing.

Appendix: Research Methods and Statistics

Making Sense of the Evidence

Most people initially think that the study of research methods and statistics is both dull and meaningless, something that only professional researchers should be concerned about. In fact, however, we all have to make sense of the information that we encounter. Sometimes this is presented as research results (for example, in a newspaper report), and sometimes it may appear unrelated to research issues. Consider the following situations:

◆ A politician running for re-election claims that the average family income has risen by $3000 in the past two years. Does this really mean that most people are better off than they were?

◆ A friend goes on a business trip to France. Before leaving, she expresses concern that the French are not friendly to foreigners. On her return, she reports several instances of situations where people were rude and hostile to her. Does this mean that her preconception was correct?

◆ Your doctor proposes to do a diagnostic test to find out why you don't feel well. When it comes back positive, he says you should go for exploratory surgery. What do you need to know about the test before agreeing to surgery?

In none of these situations have we used the words 'research methods' or 'statistics', but all of them are in fact examples of basic issues in the design and analysis of research. As we explore these issues, think back to the situations mentioned here, and see how you can apply the principles you encounter. Far from being dull and irrelevant, the material in this appendix can lead you into a number of challenging insights.

Introduction

Throughout this book, we have emphasized that psychology is an *empirical* pursuit – that is, the knowledge gained is based on the observation of behaviour. The process of gathering observations is commonly referred to as 'doing research'. Research provides the basic information that is used to formulate and test theories. Although the various approaches differ in the kinds of research methods used, all agree on the importance of observation.

In Chapter 1, we talked about the basic methods, both correlational and experimental, which are most commonly used in psychological research. At various points, we have focused on particular aspects of research methods; for example, the use of time-based studies in developmental psychology, and the difficulties of doing experiments on social behaviour. Regardless of the problem studied or the method used, there are some basic considerations that apply to all psychological research. In this section, we will look briefly at some of these points.

The Logic of Research

Making Observations: Measurement and Sampling

One basic concern in research is how to describe what we observe. It takes very little insight to recognize that people vary in many ways. For example, people differ in size, age, education, and so on. Obviously, they also differ in the way they behave. Any characteristic which shows variation can be called a *variable*, and so in essence the information we collect is based on observing different variables. The choice of variables is one of the things which distinguishes the approaches – for example, the behaviourists' use of reflex responses or the humanists' use of subjective reports of feelings.

Unfortunately, not all variables are alike. For example, variables may be simple descriptive labels, as when we refer to eye colour as green, blue, brown, and so on. Such labels are very limited when it comes to making comparisons between individuals. We can put people in groups (e.g. all those with blue eyes), but we cannot really say how *much* they differ. For example, is the difference between blue and green greater than the difference between blue and brown? Whatever our intent might be in asking the question, there is no meaningful way to answer it from the information provided by the labels.

ratio variable a characteristic whose measurement is based on a continuous scale, with an obvious zero point

In order to make relative comparisons, we must use variables which provide more information. The most detailed information is provided by **ratio variables**, which use measurements based on a continuous scale, with an obvious zero point. For example, we can measure age in years, weight in kilograms (or pounds), and so on. Ratio variables are highly useful, because they allow a wide variety of comparisons. For example, one can say John and Bob together weigh as much as Jim, or Mary is three times as old as her daughter Jane, and so on. As implied in the examples, ratio variables are fairly common when measuring physical characteristics. They are less common in dealing with psychological variables, many of which don't have a clear zero point. For example, what would it mean to say someone has 'zero intelligence'? Without a clear zero point, we cannot say that someone who has an IQ of 140 is 'twice as intelligent' as someone with an IQ of 70. Thus, one concern in making observations is deciding what kinds of comparisons are appropriate for particular variables.

Another way in which variables can differ is how easy they are to measure. Variables which refer to physical characteristics are relatively simple to measure (although errors can still occur), but measuring psychological variables like 'intelligence' or 'aggressiveness' is more difficult, since they cannot be observed directly. Hence, in gathering data, we have to be concerned about the measurement process. Basically, we want our measurements of any variable to be both reliable and valid. **Reliability** means that the measuring process gives consistent results; **validity** means that the variable measures what it claims to, as opposed to some other characteristic. That is, the measurement process should be both consistent (reliable) and accurate (valid). There are several effective ways to measure reliability, all of which basically compare the consistency of repeated measurements of particular cases. Validity is more difficult to assess, because one must have an independent means of measuring the same property (called the validity criterion); this means you cannot measure the validity of any characteristic for which you don't already have an accurate validity criterion. To take a simple example, you can't determine whether a ruler is accurate unless you already have an accurate ruler (or other measuring device) with which to compare it! Having measurements which are reliable and valid is important to effective research; without dependable observations, the whole enterprise is threatened.

reliability a criterion for evaluating a measurement process, which assesses the consistency of measurements; often measured by comparing the correlation between repeated observations

validity a criterion for evaluating a measurement process, which assesses whether the variable measures the intended property, as opposed to some other characteristic

Assuming one has confidence in the measurement process, there is still the question of *who* to observe and measure. In practical terms, a researcher can only observe a limited number of individuals, yet would like to draw conclusions about all human beings. That is, we make observations of a limited group (the *sample*), but we wish to generalize about the larger group from which the sample is selected (the *population*). This leads to concerns about **sampling**, the process by which one selects observations. In sampling, the goal is to select a *representative sample*, one which can be assumed to be a fair reflection of the population.

sampling the process by which one selects observations for research (the sample)

There are normally two ways to obtain a representative sample: random sampling and cross-sectional sampling. A **random sample** is one in which everyone in the population has an equal chance of being selected. In the case of an election poll, suppose the researcher went to a large shopping centre in Toronto at lunch time, and stopped every third person that went by. Would that be a proper random sample of Canadian voters? No, since not every Canadian voter is likely to be found at that site. Similarly, if survey forms were mailed out

random sample a sample obtained through a selection procedure in which everyone in the population has an equal chance of being selected

self-selected sample a sampling procedure which allows members of the population to decide whether to be included or not, as when a survey has a low rate of response

based on voter registration lists, the researcher would have to be concerned about how many were actually returned. Although the initial mailing might be random, if only a small percentage actually responded, the results would no longer be random, due to possible differences between those who answered and those who didn't. With a low response rate, the sample becomes **self-selected** rather than random. This point – the need to ensure a high response rate in the target sample – is sometimes overlooked. A few years ago, a book was published based on a survey of women's attitudes towards men (Hite 1987). The author made much of the fact that almost 5000 women had responded; unfortunately, since over 100,000 survey forms had been distributed, the response rate was so low as to make the results of questionable value.

The primary alternative to random sampling is a cross-sectional sample. As the name implies, a **cross-sectional sample** is deliberately selected so that the sample matches the population for particular characteristics. For example, in an election survey, one would want the sample to reflect the age, income, sex and geographic origin of the population among other things. For example, if 20 per cent of the population live in Ontario, one would want 20 per cent of the sample to come from Ontario. For a voter survey, such data could be obtained from census figures; for other types of survey, depending on the focus, other sources might be used to determine population data.

cross-sectional sample a sample which is deliberately selected in such a way that the sample matches the population for particular characteristics, such as age and income

The primary limitation of using cross-sectional sampling is the problem of determining the population characteristics to be matched. Sometimes, a factor that is important may be overlooked; for instance, the above example neglects native language, which would be a relevant factor in surveying Canadian voters, since differences probably exist between English- and French-speaking voters. At the same time, it is obviously impossible to match a population for every known characteristic. Even more importantly, it is impossible to create a proper cross-sectional sample if the population characteristics are *unknown*.

In doing research, the goal of sampling procedures is to avoid serious *bias*, or systematic error. For example, if I am interested in how children react to watching violence on television, it might make a difference if I study children in a university day care centre or children in a home for delinquents. In this case, either sample would be biased; that is, neither sample is likely to be typical of the larger population (all children in the world). In terms of the logic of research, there is one thing to keep in mind: even when using generally accepted procedures for sampling, it is still possible to get a set of observations which are not actually representative of the population. This potential for **sampling error** is one of the main reasons we use statistical analysis in interpreting the results of research.

sampling error an error caused by having a non-representative sample, due either to using a biased sampling procedure, or the inherent variability associated with the sampling process

For further consideration

If a researcher were to do a survey of people's favourite television programme by randomly dialling listings from the telephone book, would this be a representative sample of the population of television viewers? If yes, why? If no, why not?

Designing Research

The concerns about types of variables, measurement procedures and sampling apply to all psychological research. In this sense, they are independent of both the question being asked and the research method used. Nonetheless, doing research always involves a number of choices, which begin with the question one seeks to answer, and end, hopefully, with the results providing the answer. In between, one must consider how the question is to be stated, in terms of the *hypothesis* to be tested, what *research method* is to be used to collect the observations and how the *variables* are to be measured. All of these choices are part of the general domain of *research design*.

The decisions involved in designing a study are not cut and dried. In practice, one could give the same question to several researchers, asking each to design a relevant study, and find that each one produces a different design for addressing the question (consider, for example, the many studies which have looked at the relationship between observing television violence and aggressive behaviour, as discussed in Chapter 8). In each case, the reasons given for the resulting design could be very sensible, despite the differences.

Research design is a creative activity, and like other forms of creation can be both challenging and gratifying. We cannot deal with all of the complexities here, but it is important to realize that designing and doing research is not a dry and mundane task; it is an inventive process for exploring the unknown. There are rules, to be sure, but within those rules there is tremendous opportunity for the mind to imagine new possibilities.

Pitfalls in Experimental Research

internal validity the assessment of the degree to which the design and execution of an experiment are free from bias, confounds and other sources of error

In general, using experiments to gather information can be more complicated than using non-experimental observational procedures. In order to draw clear conclusions, one must maintain consistent conditions in the experimental situation, and ensure that no unwanted factors distort the results. The issues of proper design and execution of an experiment are part of the issue of **internal validity**. (You may recall that concerns about the ability to generalize from the results, particularly with laboratory experiments, are related to *external validity*.)

Confounds

confound in experimental research, a situation where two variables change simultaneously, making it impossible to determine their relative influence

Broadly speaking, there are two kinds of factors that can detract from internal validity: confounds and bias. A **confound** represents a situation where two variables change simultaneously, making it impossible to determine their relative influence (i.e. there is a *confounding variable*). For example, suppose that in Latané and Darley's field experiment (see Chapter 1), it turned out that all the subjects in one group were male and in another group were all female. In this situation, one could not tell whether differences in helping behaviour were due to the independent variable or the sex of the subjects. Similarly, if an experiment designed to compare two teaching methods used two classes which met at different times of day (one early morning, one mid-afternoon), then differences in results (e.g. student grades) might be due to the teaching methods, the time of day, or a combination of both factors. Such situations are undesirable, because they represent a confound of two variables.

Basically, there are two ways to avoid confounds. The most common approach is to hold constant factors which are not of direct interest; this is a key feature of experimental design. For example, in the experiment on teaching methods, one would plan it so that the groups met at the equivalent times (e.g. morning or afternoon on alternate days). The other approach to avoiding confounds, used when the variables involved are of direct interest, is to use multiple *independent variables*. In Latané and Darley's field experiment, the number of customers and the number of robbers were both intended to be independent variables; by using four groups (which reflected all possible combinations of the independent variables), they were able to avoid the difficulties of confounding. Generally, careful planning of the experiment should be able to prevent most confounds, although in research, as in everyday life, the unexpected can still create surprises. In this regard, the greatest risk is that an unrecognized variable will turn out to be confounded with a planned independent variable, resulting in the kind of ambiguities we have noted.

While confounds can make it difficult to interpret the results, various forms of *error* can affect directly the results obtained. So-called **random error**, produced by natural variability in sampling or other processes, is an inevitable part of research. For example, in doing a survey, no two samples of a population will be identical; the differences represent a form of random error. Generally speaking, random error can be dealt with in the analysis of results, and does not threaten the basic legitimacy of the research. By contrast, systematic forms of error, called *bias*, are a more serious concern.

random error non-systematic error produced by the variability in sampling or other natural processes

Bias

Systematic error, as its name implies, means that some factor is at work which consistently influences the results in a particular way; since this influence is not a planned part of the research design, its intrusion is undesirable. Systematic error (bias) can arise in many ways. Suppose that Latané and Darley had told their subjects the purpose of the research; do you think that people would react differently if they knew the researchers were interested in helping behaviour? One possibility is that more people would intervene, in order to create a better impression of themselves. If this were true, the results would be biased, since the information led people to intervene more than would otherwise be the case.

To consider a different example, suppose an experiment was designed to test a new drug; the independent variable will be the presence or absence of the drug. In its simplest form, this would mean that some subjects would receive medication and others would receive nothing. Unfortunately, this would mean that the subjects in the control group would know they were not getting treatment, since they were not given anything. As in Latané and Darley's example, this could distort the results by creating a confound (see Fig. A.1a). In both of these examples, bias is created because of what the subjects know; consequently, this form of bias is commonly called **subject bias**. In order to prevent subject bias, experimenters usually try to set up an experiment in such a way that the participants do not know anything which might lead to bias. An experiment planned in this manner is commonly called a **single-blind design**, since the subjects are kept uninformed or 'blind' to the purpose. Sometimes this is done by withholding information or by active deception, as in Latané and Darley's experiments. In drug studies, those not given a real drug are usually given a placebo, an inert substance which they believe is a drug (see Fig. A.1b). (In

subject bias in an experiment, systematic error created because the subjects in different groups have different information (for example, knowing whether they are in the control group or experimental group)

single-blind design an experiment set up in such a way that subjects are kept uninformed of any details which might lead to bias

The Effects of Subject Bias in Experiments

Standard Design		Single-blind Design	
Experimental Group	Control Group	Experimental Group	Placebo Group
Gets drug	Gets nothing	Gets drug	Gets placebo
Expects Drug effect	Expects No effects	Expects Drug effect	Expects Drug effect
(a)		(b)	

Fig. A.1 Subject bias in experiments In doing drug research, experimenters normally use a placebo with the control group, rather than giving nothing, in order to prevent subject bias. As (a) and (b) show, providing a placebo changes the expectations of those in the control group so that they are consistent with the expectations of those in the experimental group.

some cases, both those receiving the drug and those receiving the placebo are kept in doubt; in this case, the expectation in both groups is one of uncertainty.) Since bias is particularly likely in social situations (due to reactivity), nearly all social psychology experiments use some form of single-blind design.

The behaviours that create subject bias are very understandable: subjects are simply reacting to the situation as they perceive it; when the information available changes, their behaviour changes as well. While such reactions complicate the task of the researcher, they also represent part of the complexity which makes human behaviour fascinating; studying behaviour would certainly be less interesting if people were not so responsive to their environment.

Unfortunately, it is harder to find redeeming value in a second form of bias, called **experimenter bias**. The term was coined by a social psychologist, Robert Rosenthal, who was interested in how people's expectations affect their interactions with others. To understand experimenter bias, we must clarify how it differs from simple perceptual interpretation. As we have already discussed, perception depends in part on our existing schemata – hence, what we perceive is influenced by our expectations. For instance, a **halo effect** occurs when our knowledge of *one* characteristic which is positive or negative about a person leads to similar expectations of *other* characteristics. For example, people are likely to perceive someone who is 'intelligent' as honest rather than dishonest,

experimenter bias systematic error created when an experimenter's knowledge and expectations about the experiment influences the behaviour of subjects

halo effect a form of perceptual bias which occurs when our rating of a person on *one* characteristic as being positive or negative of a person leads to similar expectations for *other* characteristics of the individual.

sincere rather than insincere, and so on. Note that a halo effect refers only to the perception; it does *not* specify what the person perceived is actually like.

While perceptual effects like the halo effect could pose a threat to scientific objectivity, experimenter bias takes this process one step further. In exploring experimenter bias, Rosenthal was asking if our expectations can alter the way others actually *behave* (as opposed to our *perception* of them). To explore this idea, he did a study with Lenore Jacobson in which they looked at the influence of teachers' expectations on the behaviour of their students (Rosenthal and Jacobson 1968). The teachers were told that certain students had been identified as 'late bloomers', who could be expected to blossom during the school year. Sure enough, those students actually did improve, not only in the eyes of their teacher, but according to independent assessments as well. What made this surprising was that the only *real* difference between these students and their classmates was the label 'late bloomers', which Rosenthal and Jacobson had applied to randomly chosen students. That is, other than the teachers' expectations, nothing was different about the 'late bloomers'! Rosenthal subsequently called this expectancy effect a **self-fulfilling prophecy**. That is, we tend to produce in others the type of behaviour which our expectations lead us to predict. For example, if I visit a foreign country with the expectation that the people are unfriendly, my own behaviour is likely to lead to experiences which justify my original expectation. While there has been considerable subsequent research on how expectations affect behaviour, it is not clear how significant the phenomenon is in everyday life – in part, because it is so difficult to identify in non-experimental situations.

In experiments, however, such expectancy effects raise a real concern about the objectivity of research. If an experimenter's knowledge and expectations about the experiment could alter the behaviour of subjects, this would be a form of bias (hence the term *experimenter bias*). For example, by unconsciously smiling or frowning, the researcher might lead subjects to respond in ways consistent with the experimental hypothesis (we assume, of course, that there is no conscious intent to bias the results). Rosenthal went on to do a number of experiments, which suggested the risks were potentially very significant. How can a researcher cope with this risk? By analogy to subject bias, where one uses a single-blind design, one would seek to keep the experimenter uninformed about the details of the experiment; when both the subject and experimenter are kept uninformed, the experiment is called a **double-blind design**.

Unfortunately, the requirements of a double-blind design can pose considerable difficulties to the execution of the research. In medical experiments, it is possible to use placebos and complex procedures so that neither the person giving nor the person receiving a 'drug' know whether it is a placebo or a real drug; but it requires careful record-keeping to ensure everything proceeds properly. Other situations, particularly those involving social variables, can be even more problematical. For example, in Latané and Darley's field experiment, the independent variables dealt with the number of people present. Since anyone involved – whether the store clerk or an observer recording the results – would be aware of this, there would be no simple way to conduct a double-blind study. Consequently, while Rosenthal would argue that ideally all research should be double-blind, in practice only the minority of psychology experiments are actually designed in this way. Instead, most researchers would suggest that

self-fulfilling prophecy a phenomenon whereby our expectations about other people leads to acting in ways which elicit the expected response from them; the everyday equivalent to experimenter bias

double-blind design a rigorous form of experimental control, whereby both the subject and experimenter are left uninformed about details of the experiment which could result in bias (both subject bias and experimenter bias) replication provides a check on possible experimenter bias: if someone does a study which seems inconsistent with previous research, others who disbelieve it are likely to try to repeat the experiment; if the results come out the same, it tends to suggest the result is genuine, not a product of the original researcher's bias. Still, no-one would dispute that the use of a double-blind design is desirable when circumstances make it possible.

For further consideration

Have you ever created a self-fulfilling prophecy? What was the result? In what ways are self-fulfilling prophecies related to our cognitive schemata?

Going from Observation to Interpretation

Whatever the question and whatever the research design, one ends up with a set of observations – the *data*. (The word *data* sometimes confuses readers, because it is a *plural* noun (borrowed from Latin). One should say, for example, 'The data *are* clear'. The singular, used to refer to a single observation, is *datum*.) One must then look at the results in terms of the original question, to determine if the hypothesis is supported or not. For example, suppose that one wanted to know if there are differences in the attitudes of men and women towards violence in sports. A survey is done, and the results show that 55 per cent of women say there is too much violence, 34 per cent say it is not a problem and 11 per cent have no opinion. In contrast, 38 per cent of men say there is too much violence, 58 per cent say it is not a problem and 4 per cent have no opinion. Does this mean that women are more opposed to violence in sports? How can we decide?

This example highlights the problem of how to *interpret* the results of research. The research design is intended to produce observations which are relevant to the original question; once we have those observations, however, we must still decide whether they support the hypothesis or not. This is actually not as simple as it seems. At first glance, it may appear that we have two choices: to conclude that the results support the hypothesis, or that they contradict it. It turns out, however, that **falsification** (proving a hypothesis is wrong) is much simpler than **confirmation** (deciding that a hypothesis is true). For example, if I visit a remote tropical island, and the first seagull I encounter is black (instead of the usual white), I may be surprised. If the next several seagulls I see are also black, I may be tempted to propose a hypothesis: on this island, all the seagulls are a mutant form which is black. Now, all it would take to *falsify* this hypothesis would be seeing one white seagull. That is, one clearly contradictory observation is enough to prove it wrong. On the other hand, what would it take to be sure the hypothesis is *true*? It would seem that I would have to observe every seagull on the island (the entire population) in order to be absolutely sure. If I depend on a sample, even a large one, there is still the chance that I will miss one or more white seagulls.

Thus, it turns out that proving a hypothesis is false is a lot simpler than proving it is true. In large part, this is because of the need to depend on samples; if we could observe every relevant case (the entire population), in theory we could prove a hypothesis to be true. In practice, psychologists wish to generalize

falsification in research, the process of using observations to prove that a hypothesis is wrong
confirmation in research, the process of determining that observations are consistent with the hypothesis being true

null hypothesis in research, a hypothesis which asserts that any differences observed between groups are random rather than representing an experimental effect; normally the contrary of the experimental hypothesis, it is used for statistical purposes to evaluate results

about such large populations (e.g. all human beings) that observing everyone becomes impossible. As a result, researchers end up framing the original question in terms of a **null hypothesis**, which essentially says the results are random. If one can prove this is *false*, then it implies that there *is* a difference. For example, in the survey mentioned above, the null hypothesis would say, 'There is no difference between the attitudes of men and women towards violence in sports'. If we can show that this statement is false, then we can show that there *is* a difference. In order to do that, we use *statistics*.

Statistics – Making Sense of the Data

statistics the branch of mathematics that is concerned with the description and interpretation of sets of scores, such as scientific data
descriptive statistics the branch of statistics which is concerned with describing and summarizing sets of scores
inferential statistics the branch of statistics which deals with the interpretation of data, particularly in terms of generalizing from the observed sample to the larger population

The very word 'statistics' seems to strike fear into many students. The reasons for this are varied, but may include a fear of mathematics and an aversion to things which are 'boring'. While it is true that statistics is a form of applied mathematics, it need not be boring. When properly understood, many of the questions it tries to answer are very provocative and challenging. This section will try to show that the fears are largely unjustified, and that the issues are in fact both understandable and interesting.

In essence, **statistics** is concerned with the description and interpretation of scientific data. That is, it is used to describe and summarize research results, and to assist in understanding what the results mean. The first function, describing and summarizing results, is referred to as the domain of **descriptive statistics**. The second function, the interpretation of the results, particularly in terms of generalizing from the observed sample to the larger population, is the domain of **inferential statistics**. Since one must know what the results are before one can decide what they mean, we will first consider descriptive statistics.

Descriptive Statistics – Describing the Data

In doing psychological research, one gathers information about behaviour, in the form of observations of one or more variables. These observations then comprise a set of data; typically, numbers of some sort. For example, one could measure students' performance on a test, with performance represented by grades expressed as percentages. In Fig. A.2a, the results of an actual test are given. The results are listed in the order in which they appeared in my grade book, though I have substituted letter codes for student names. If you look at them, you will note that there is considerable variation. The question is, what do these grades tell us? As they stand, they present a rather random picture. In order to make sense of them, we need some way to summarize the information.

Frequency Distributions

One way to approach the task is to try rearranging the scores in order of size, and then see how many people got each score. If we do this for the numbers in Fig. A.2a, we would end up with the result shown in Fig. A.2b. This is called

Fig. A.2 Analysing the frequency distribution for a set of data The three tables are as follows: (a) the original scores, expressed in the order they appeared in my grade book; (b) a frequency analysis of the original scores, arranged in order of score value; (c) a frequency analysis based on combining scores into intervals of five.

TEST GRADES

CA	67
DB	74
FC	58
GC	70
YC	64
ED	78
SD	69
LE	58
JE	69
SF	70
PG	63
YG	64
DH	52
RH	52
SI	73
LJ	84
NJ	79
FL	68
RL	49
AM	64
LM	70
TM	66
BN	63
EN	46
CO	54
LO	73
SQ	84
FR	81
TR	78
AS	89
KS	55
PS	63
MT	60
RT	77
WT	58
AV	69
DY	48
TOTAL NUMBER OF SCORES	37

(a)

FREQUENCY DISTRIBUTION (RAW SCORES)

SCORE	FREQUENCY
46	2
49	1
52	2
54	1
55	1
58	3
60	1
63	3
64	3
66	1
67	1
68	1
69	3
70	3
73	2
74	1
77	1
78	2
79	1
81	1
84	2
89	1
TOTAL NUMBER OF SCORES	37

Note: scores with zero frequency omitted in order to simplify table.

(b)

FREQUENCY DISTRIBUTION (USING INTERVALS)

SCORE RANGE	MIDPOINT	FREQUENCY
40-44	42	0
45-49	47	2
50-54	52	3
55-59	57	4
60-64	62	6
65-69	67	7
70-74	72	5
75-79	77	4
80-84	82	3
85-89	87	1
90-94	92	0
TOTAL NUMBER OF SCORES		37

(c)

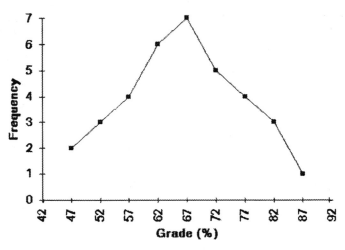

Fig. A.3 A frequency distribution graph which shows the data listed in the table in Fig. A.2.

a **frequency distribution**, because it tells us how frequently each value occurs. As you can see, a few scores are repeated, but most occur only once. So it is still somewhat difficult to make much sense out of the data.

If we group the scores into *intervals* (for example, 45–49, 50–54, etc.), then we might simplify the overall frequency distribution (there will be fewer categories), and also perhaps get a clearer picture of where scores are clustered. The result for this is shown in Fig. A.2c. Now we get a clearer idea of overall performance; looking at the frequencies, it is evident that more people are near the middle than at either extreme. If we want to visualize this, we can represent it graphically, as in Fig. A.3. In making a graph like this, the convention is to put the frequency scale on the vertical axis, and place data points based on using the midpoint of each interval. In effect, the graph assumes all the people in any interval scored at the midpoint. If you look at the original data, you'll see that this is an over-simplification, although not a very extreme one. This points out one of the basic principles of descriptive statistics: *whenever we seek to summarize data, we inevitably lose a little of the information we started with.* Thus, the challenge in descriptive statistics is to not lose anything that seems *essential.* In the example above, it doesn't seem to distort things very much to use the intervals as we have.

Measures of Central Tendency

While a frequency distribution, particularly in graphical form, gives us a general sense of the data, it still is rather limiting. For instance, it suggests that most people scored near the middle, but doesn't tell us how the typical student did. To describe what is typical of a group of scores, we use a type of statistic called a *measure of central tendency* (a *statistic* is a number which results from some sort of statistical calculation on a set of data, while *statistics* is the name for the discipline). In everyday terms, a **measure of central tendency** tells us what is an 'average' score. However, the term 'average' is avoided in statistical discussions, because the word can be used to refer to *any* measure of central tendency; and as we shall see, they are not all the same.

The simplest measure of central tendency (particularly if one already has a frequency distribution) is the **mode**, which is the most frequently occurring score (or interval). Looking at the graph in Fig. A.3, it is clear that the peak, representing the most frequent value, occurs in the interval 65–69; using the simplification of the midpoint of the interval, we get a mode of 67 per cent. Note, however, that this does *not* prove that the single score of 67 per cent occurred most often – only that scores were most common in the interval 65–69 per cent. If we were to determine the mode directly from the original data, we would find that the most frequent single score is actually 64 per cent. While this is close to the value of 67 per cent calculated from the interval data, it *also* shows how some information gets lost when we summarize. In general, the mode is a measure of popularity – what occurs most frequently defines what is typical.

A second measure of central tendency is the **median**, the score which is in the *middle* of the frequency distribution. This is actually easier to calculate using the raw frequency data, since we need to find the value which is the midpoint of all the ranked scores. In the current case, the actual value is 67 per cent. (It could also be calculated for interval data, if the original data were not available, but doing so sometimes requires a bit of estimating within the interval. In the present case, it would not be necessary, since the median is the midpoint of the interval.) The median reflects what is typical in the sense of being middle-of-the-road, rather than an extreme. Indeed, one way to remember its meaning is to think of the divider found in the middle of some highways – it is called a 'median'!

The most commonly used measure of central tendency is the **mean**, which is the sum of all the scores divided by the number of scores. In our example, the mean is 66.5 per cent. The mean is commonly used because of two characteristics. First, it does not require rearranging the scores in rank order, or creating a frequency distribution, in order to calculate the mean. In many situations, this is a real advantage. Second, unlike either the median or the mode, the mean reflects *all* of the scores; if you change one score, the mean will change, too. By contrast, the mode tells us nothing about any score except itself, while the median tells us only that half the scores are above it and half below it. In both cases, it would be possible to alter one (or more) scores without altering the value of the central tendency as these measures define it.

If we compare the three values in the current example, they are in reasonably close agreement: using the original scores, the mode is 64 per cent, the median 67 per cent and the mean 66.5 per cent. Since the three measures seem to correspond fairly well, why should we be concerned about differences in how each is derived? The reason is that not all situations are like this example. Consider the data in Fig. A.4 and the associated graph (Fig. A.5). These data are hypothetical, representing the salaries of employees of a large company (totalling 1000 employees). This 'lop-sided' frequency distribution is characteristic of income data, both for companies and nations; in effect, the large majority of individuals have relatively low incomes, while very high incomes are very rare. In analysing the data in this example, we will use the interval data exclusively, because of the large numbers involved (as the number of scores increases, the

mode a statistic measuring central tendency, calculated as the most frequently occurring value (or interval) in a set of scores

median a statistic measuring central tendency, calculated as the middle score in a frequency distribution

mean (also called 'arithmetic mean') a statistic measuring central tendency, calculated as the sum of all the scores, divided by the number of scores

FREQUENCY DISTRIBUTION
FOR SALARY DATA

SALARY RANGE	FREQUENCY
$0	0
$12,500	250
$37,500	500
$62,500	125
$87,500	60
$112,500	35
$137,500	18
$162,500	6
$187,500	3
$212,500	2
$237,500	1
TOTAL NUMBER OF EMPLOYEES	1000

Fig. A.4 A frequency distribution for salaries in company 'X' A hypothetical set of data for salaries.

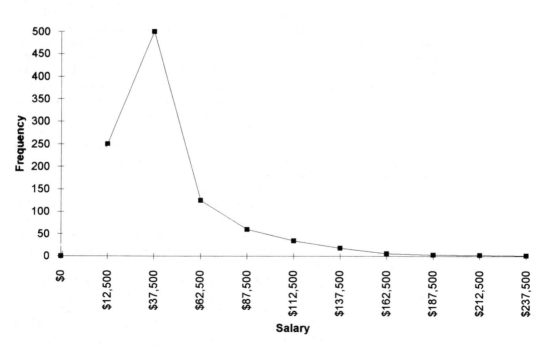

Fig. A.5 A skewed frequency distribution which shows the data listed in the table in Fig. A.4.

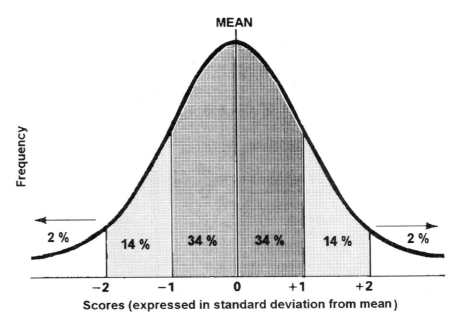

Fig. A.6 A normal distribution In a normal distribution, the mean is the same as the median and the mode; hence it also represents the peak of the frequency curve, and the point at which 50 per cent of scores lie on either side. As discussed in the text, in a normal distribution one can also predict what percentage of people fall into a certain score range by expressing scores in units of the standard deviation. When this is done, the percentages falling within certain regions are as shown in the graph.

distortions resulting from simplification typically get smaller, not larger). In this case, both the mode and the median salary are $37,500. The mean, however, is $43,438, almost $6000 higher! Now, if one says the 'average' salary is $43,438 (referring to the mean), this sounds pretty good, until one realizes that at least half the people (those who are at or below the median) earn appreciably *less* than this. Consider further: suppose that the top thirty executives each receive a $25,000 rise. This will raise the 'average' (mean) salary by almost 2 per cent – and yet 97 per cent of employees will have received no increase! Obviously, the word 'average' can be very misleading.

There are two points worth remembering in relation to this example. The first is that one should always be clear on what someone is referring to when they use the term 'average'. The second is that descriptive statistics have limitations, and they are only helpful when used appropriately.

How can one determine when the mean is appropriate or not? Although it is possible to give a technical answer to this, one helpful guide is to look at the shape of the frequency distribution. Very often, the shape is a symmetrical curve that looks something like a bell in profile; this bell-shaped curve is called a **normal distribution** (see Fig. A.6). As you can see, the distribution in our example of test grades (Fig. A.3) is approximately normal shaped. In a true normal distribution, the highest point occurs at the middle of the distribution – that is, the mode (the highest frequency) is the same as the median (the middle

normal distribution a type of frequency distribution which resembles a bell-shaped curve; among its special properties, first identified by Gauss, is that its measures of central tendency are all the same score); in addition, the mean will have the same value. Thus, in a normal distribution, it doesn't matter which measure of central tendency one uses, because they all produce the same result. (Even though our grade example is not perfectly symmetrical, the values come out to be very similar.) By contrast, the frequency distribution in the salary example (Fig. A.5) is distinctly lop-sided; this is referred to as a **skewed distribution**. Whenever one encounters a very skewed distribution, the mean is unlikely to be representative of the majority of scores. In such circumstances, most researchers prefer to use the median as a way of describing the 'typical' result.

Measures of Variability

Even when one deals with an approximately normal distribution, as in Fig. A.3, measures of central tendency do not give us a full picture of the data. To understand why, let us look at another example. In this case, we will consider two simple distributions of test grades (see Fig. A.7a). If you look at the two groups, you will note that they have the same mode, the same median and the same mean. Yet, in some sense, they are different. One way to recognize this is by considering the following questions: If you were writing this test, and you were told that you had scored 'below the mean', would you care which group it was? Alternatively, if you were told your performance was 'above the mean', would the group matter? (Look again at the scores.) Most people, asked the first question, would prefer Group 2, because most of the low scores are actually close to the mean. If asked the second question, most people would choose Group 1, because most of the high scores are much higher than the mean. Thus, in a very real sense, these two sets of data are different, even though they have identical measures of central tendency. How is this possible?

The answer to this paradox lies in their **variability**, which tells us how the scores are distributed around the centre. One simple indicator of variability is the **range**, which is the difference between the highest score and the lowest score. Interestingly, the range in *both* of these groups is the same – that is, 30 percentage points. Because the range only reflects the two most extreme scores, it is only a crude measure of variability; by ignoring where scores fall *in between* these extremes, it ignores a great deal of information available in the original data. What we would ideally like is a measure of variability that takes into account every score, somewhat the way the mean does as a measure of central tendency.

One way to look at this is to determine *how far away* from the centre each score is. This could be done by subtracting the mean (defined as the centre – in a normal distribution it will be the median as well) from each score. To see how this works, consider Fig. A.7b, in which we have calculated the deviations for both groups. You will note that the deviations (ignoring signs) tend to be larger in Group 1 than in Group 2; this tells us that the scores tend to lie further from the mean in this group. Now, if we consider these *deviation scores* as data in themselves, we could ask, 'What is the typical deviation in each group?' If we then proceed to calculate the mean, we will find a strange thing – the mean of these deviation scores is zero in both groups! While this may seem like a strange coincidence, in fact it is an inevitable result, since it turns out one can *define* the mean of a distribution as being the number for which the mean of the deviation

DATA FOR TWO SAMPLE GROUPS

GROUP 1	GROUP 2
55	55
58	64
60	68
62	69
63	69
70	70
70	70
70	70
77	71
78	71
80	72
82	76
85	85
MEAN 70	70

(a)

DATA FOR TWO SAMPLE GROUPS

GROUP 1	DEVIATION SCORES	GROUP 2	DEVIATION SCORES
55	-15	55	-15
58	-12	64	-6
60	-10	68	-2
62	-8	69	-1
63	-7	69	-1
70	0	70	0
70	0	70	0
70	0	70	0
77	7	71	1
78	8	71	1
80	10	72	2
82	12	76	6
85	15	85	15
MEAN 70	0	70	0

(b)

Fig. A.7 Comparing groups Table (a) shows the original scores for two groups which have the same central tendency and range; in table (b), the deviation scores are also calculated (see text for discussion).

scores is zero! So although the deviation scores *do* tell us something about variability, we cannot simply use these scores to measure mean variability.

If you look closely at the examples, you'll see that the difficulty is partly related to the plus and minus signs; if we could focus on just the size of the numbers (what is called the *absolute value*), then we could perhaps get somewhere. Early statisticians recognized this, but found it was cumbersome to extract the signs when doing calculations. However, they also recognized that one could accomplish something similar by *squaring* all the deviation scores, since the squares of both positive *and* negative numbers are positive. The mean of these 'squared deviations' could then be calculated as a measure of variability (which is called the *variance*). While the variance is used in a number of ways by statisticians, in terms of our original question ('How can we describe the typical variability of these groups?'), it gives an inflated number, since it is based on the *squares* of the deviations, *not* the deviations themselves. To circumvent this, one can take the *square root* of the variance, which in one sense scales things back to size. This value is called the **standard deviation**, and it provides us with our goal – a measure of variability which reflects the position of every score within the group, expressed in the same units as the original scores. (As we will see below, there are additional reasons why the standard deviation is preferred to the mean deviation.) If we were to define the standard deviation in a single sentence, it would be as 'the square root of the mean of the squared deviations of the scores from the original mean'. Quite a mouthful, to be sure, but if you go back to Fig. A.7 and try taking it step-by-step, it is actually fairly straightforward.

Taken together, the mean and standard deviation tell us a great deal about a set of data. For instance, in the previous example, although the means are identical, the standard deviations are quite different: for Group 1 it is 9.8 per cent, while in Group 2 it is only 6.7 per cent (note the standard deviation, like the mean, is expressed in the same units as the original data). This is consistent with our earlier intuition that the scores are more widely scattered in Group 1. In general, the larger the standard deviation, the greater the variability of the scores.

standard deviation a commonly used measure of variability, calculated as the square root of the mean of the squared deviations from the mean of a set of scores

Properties of Normal Distributions

As mentioned earlier, the normal distribution is a symmetrical frequency distribution, with an overall bell-like shape, whose measures of central tendency are all identical. These properties are themselves distinctive, but when combined with the standard deviation, they yield even more surprising results. Because it goes beyond the scope of this overview, we will not try to prove the following points. However, the conclusions have been well-established by statisticians.

If you return to the normal distribution in Fig. A.6, you will see that the mean has been indicated by a vertical line, which passes through the peak of the curve – hence it is the mode as well. In addition, since this line marks the median, we know that 50 per cent of the scores will lie on either side of this line. Now, if we also mark a line at a distance equal to the standard deviation on either side of the mean, then we break up the 50 per cent into two portions, one of which is larger in area than the other (note that it is marked in Fig. A.6 as '±1 standard deviation units'). In fact, it turns out that approximately 34 per cent (34.13 per cent if one wishes to be a bit more precise) of the scores lie between the standard deviation and the mean (as noted on the graph). If we continue this process, marking lines at a point equal to twice the standard deviation from the mean, we further subdivide the remaining area. The larger portion will be about 14 per cent (13.59 per cent), leaving about 2 per cent (2.28 per cent) beyond this point.

At this point, you probably have two questions: How do we know this, and why should we care? The first question is too technical to answer in full here, but is well-established, as noted earlier. What we *can* say is that normal distributions are found in many aspects of the real world, and they always have these same characteristics. For example, the height of all men in the world is a normal distribution, as is the waist size of all women, as is the weight of travellers' suitcases taken on airplanes, and many other things. Consequently, knowing something is 'normally distributed' immediately tells us some very specific things, including that most scores are near the mean, and that very few scores (only about 2 per cent) lie more than two standard deviations from the mean.

For example, consider IQ test scores, which have a mean of 100 and a standard deviation of about 15 (depending on the test used). This means that just over two-thirds of all people have IQs between 85 and 115 (these scores represent the dividing lines for ± one standard deviation). Similarly, it also tells us that only about 2 per cent of all people score higher than 130 on this test. This leads to the answer to the second question ('who cares?'), at least in part: knowing these properties of normal distributions becomes very useful in making predictions about scores, and in our ability to interpret the results of research. For example, airlines depend on statistics about the weight of suitcases in order to plan cargo capacity. Knowing how many people will be on a particular plane, they can also make predictions about the total weight of all luggage. This follows from knowing the mean weight of suitcases, and also the likelihood that unusually heavy ones will occur. To understand how this works, we need to consider how statistics are used in the interpretation of data – that is, *inferential statistics*. However, before doing so, let us take a look at a different type of descriptive statistic, which is used to identify relationships between two sets of observations.

Correlations

As discussed in Chapter 1, there are many situations in which a researcher is unable or uninclined to do an experiment. When using non-experimental research methods such as surveys or naturalistic observation, any relationships perceived between variables are *correlational*, and do not identify causal factors directly. Nonetheless, correlational data can be very useful in identifying patterns or relationships which merit further research.

While Chapter 1 discusses the logic behind the use of correlations, it is worth considering further how statistics are used to describe correlational data. Correlational patterns typically fit one of two types: a positive correlation or a negative correlation. A **positive correlation** occurs when increases in one variable are associated with increases in the other variable. For example, if we were to record the height and weight of a group of people, we would find a positive correlation – generally, taller people also weigh more. A **negative correlation** occurs when increases in one variable occur as the value of the other variable decreases (in mathematics, this is called an inverse relationship). For example,

positive correlation a relationship observed between two variables in which increases in the value of one variable are associated with increases in the value of the other variable

negative correlation a relationship observed between two variables in which increases in one variable occur as the value of the other variable decreases

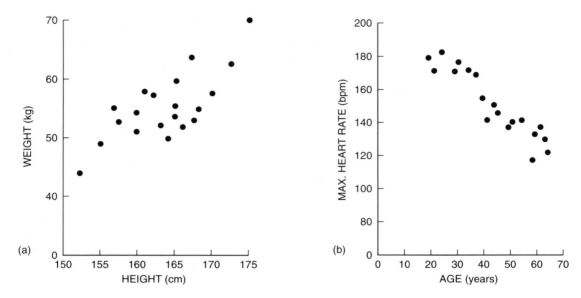

Fig. A.8 Correlational patterns Correlations are relationships observed between two variables which do not directly tell us about causation. In (a), there is a *positive* correlation between height and weight; in (b), there is a *negative* correlation between age and fitness, measured by maximum heart rate.

there is a negative correlation between age and fitness – that is, as age increases among adults, fitness level (measured by maximum heart rate) generally declines (see Fig. A.8). Typically, correlational patterns are measured using a statistical measure called a *correlation coefficient*. A correlation coefficient is a number which varies between 0.0 and +1.0 for positive correlations, and between 0.0 and –1.0 for negative correlations. In both cases, as the value moves from zero towards the maximum, the degree of relationship between the variables becomes stronger. For example, the correlation between height and political success is about + 0.20 (tall individuals are slightly more likely to be elected than shorter individuals); by comparison, the correlation between IQ test scores and grade average in high school is about +0.60 (people with above average IQs tend to do well in school). In these examples, there is a stronger relationship between IQ and grades than between height and political success.

Technically, the examples in Fig. A.8 represent what is called a linear correlation, where the underlying relationship between the two variables is linear (that is, it can be represented as a straight line function). In principle, it is possible for two variables to be related in more complex ways, represented by curvilinear functions (curved lines). For example, the relationship between motivational level and performance is frequently curvilinear, and can be represented by an upside-down U-shape: people tend to perform badly when motivation is very low or very high, and perform best when motivation is moderate. If one were to calculate a linear correlation for the variables of motivation and performance, it would appear to be very low, because a straight line does not accurately represent the relationship between the variables. It is beyond the scope of this Appendix to pursue this issue in detail, but it is worth noting that not all relationships observed in the world are simple straight lines.

For further consideration

Make a hypothetical graph of the motivation–performance relationship by drawing an inverted U-curve and placing 'data points' on it. Would either a positive or negative correlation fit these points very well? What would happen if you considered only the points on the left (or right) half of the curve? Does the type of relationship observed depend on the range of the observations?

Inferential Statistics

As noted, inferential statistics are used for making inferences about the meaning of our observations – that is, they aid us in interpreting a set of data. In essence, this involves making some assumptions, and then seeing what one can conclude based on those assumptions. In a way, using inferential statistics is like being a detective who tries to interpret a set of clues.

Sampling and Variability

Psychologists almost always depend on observing samples when doing research, even though they want to draw conclusions about a larger population. Ideally, proper sampling procedures will lead to a representative sample. However, even when proper procedures are used, one cannot be absolutely certain that the sample will match the population. To understand why, we must return to the idea of variability. Suppose that the local candy store has a contest: a large barrel is filled with red and yellow jellybeans, and one must guess the ratio of the two in the barrel. As part of the contest, you are allowed to buy a handful, which can then be examined as a way of determining the contents of the barrel. If you examine a handful, and find 8 red and 5 yellow jellybeans, what does this tell us about what is in the barrel? It *might* mean that there are more red ones than yellow ones. But could one get a sample like this if the ratio is actually equal? And what are the chances that a second sample (another handful) will be identical to the first sample?

Intuitively, we recognize that not all samples will be alike, and that any particular sample may differ from the population. Both of these facts are the result of **sampling variability**, the fact that samples randomly drawn from the same population will tend to vary. As a result, using a sample to decide what the population is like can be filled with uncertainty. While this is relatively easy to understand in an example like the jellybean contest, the same thing holds true in *any* sampling situation, such as doing research. For example, a cognitive psychologist may test the short-term memory capacity of a group of thirty individuals. The mean capacity is 7.2 chunks of information. Does this mean that people in general would show the same result? Could this be a fluke result, either higher or lower than the proper value in the population? How can one decide? Inferential statistics are concerned with providing guidelines for evaluating situations like this.

sampling variability
variability due to chance variations among samples randomly drawn from the same population

Drawing Inferences from a Normal Distribution

Perhaps the simplest situation for making inferences involves looking at a single score in relation to a set of data. Suppose that as a teacher I discover that I have overlooked recording a grade for one particular student on a test. Approaching the student directly, I ask what the grade was, and the student says it was 92 per cent. Now, this strikes me as unlikely, but I am reluctant to accuse the student of lying without reasonable grounds. What can I do? As it happens, I know that the mean for the rest of the class is 66 per cent, with a standard deviation of 7 per cent. Furthermore, I know that the grade distribution is approximately normal. Can this information help me to evaluate the student's claimed grade?

Thanks to what we know about the normal distribution, it is possible to ask about the likelihood of *anyone* receiving a grade of 92 per cent. Knowing the mean and standard deviation, I can refer back to the normal distribution, and note that only about 2 per cent of all students would receive a grade of even 80 per cent or better; the chances a of grade of 92 per cent are much less. (If our graph in Fig. A.6 were more detailed, it would show that the chance of such a grade, given the mean and standard deviation, is less than one in a thousand.) Faced with this information, I conclude that the grade is probably false, and I would insist that the student produce the test as corroboration.

In this situation, I have made an **inference**, a logical conclusion based on what I know (in this case, I have used the observed results to generalize about grades). Note that I can only say the grade is *probably* false; in making inferences, one can never have absolute certainty. In using inferential statistics, we try to generalize from our sample to the population. In doing so, the characteristics of the sample are considered *estimates* of the characteristics of the population. Thus, in the case above, my known values of the mean and standard deviation are based on the sample (i.e. the class with one score missing), while the population would be represented by the total class. In effect, by using the estimates, I can ask how probable it would be to find a score of 92 per cent in the total class.

inference the process of drawing a conclusion based on logical analysis of what is already known

Inferences about the Significance of Results

In similar ways, one can make other kinds of inferences about observational data. For example, a medical researcher does an experiment designed to evaluate a new cold remedy. Sixty people who come to a clinic seeking a cold remedy are randomly assigned to either the experimental group (who receive the new drug) or a control group (who receive a placebo) (we will assume that the experiment is a proper double-blind design, and is conducted properly). All individuals are monitored, and it is found that the mean time to recovery for the experimental group is 4.2 days, and for the control group is 6.4 days; the standard deviation of the combined groups is 1.1 days. Does this result represent a real effect of the drug, or is the difference between the groups simply a result of sampling variability, like getting different handfuls of jellybeans? In this situation, the experimenter could use a procedure called Student's *t*-test. [Ferguson (1981) has noted that 'Student' was a pen name for W.S. Gossett, who developed the *t*-test while working for the Guinness Brewery. Since the problems he dealt with concerned quality control in the brewing process, one might say that we owe current beer quality to statistics!]

t-test in inferential statistics, a procedure for determining the significance of observed differences; a common use is to decide whether the difference between the means of two groups is due only to sampling variability

significance tests in statistics, the general name given to inferential statistical procedures which are used to determine whether observed results reflect real differences rather than chance variations

significance level in inferential statistics, a statement of the probability that an observed outcome is due only to chance

In essence, the *t*-test asks how likely it is to find the observed difference between the means, if only sampling variability is at work; in terms of our example, this would mean that the drug is ineffective. Without going into the technical details, the *t*-test compares the observed results with a normal distribution of possible sample results. In this case, the probability of finding such a difference purely by chance is less than three in a hundred, which would normally lead a researcher to conclude that the drug probably works. Results which are interpreted as based on a real effect (i.e. *not* due to chance) are referred to as 'significant'; the statistical tests for evaluating chance *vs* real effects are therefore sometimes called **significance tests**. The conclusion one draws, expressed as the probability that the outcome is due to chance, is called the **significance level** of the results.

Thus, inferential statistics use sample data to try to make inferences about a population which cannot be known directly. In doing so, significance tests evaluate the possibility of obtaining a given result based solely on the chance variations associated with sampling variability. This is reflected in the *null hypothesis*, which always asserts that only chance is at work. If one can *reject* the null hypothesis as being *false*, then this makes the desired hypothesis more likely (but does *not* directly *prove* it to be true, for the reasons mentioned earlier in discussing the logic of research). Although various significance tests exist, they always lead to a probability statement, indicating the likelihood that the observed results would occur if the null hypothesis were true. Thus, statistical inference is always a matter of probabilities, never certainty.

In judging these probabilities, there is no magical cut-off where one can say, '*Now* I can be *sure* of my conclusion'. Instead, the commonly accepted standard is that the probability of obtaining the results by chance must be fewer than five in a hundred, although even lower probabilities are more comforting (often, this value will be printed as '$P < 0.05$'). This means that researchers are actually quite conservative, since less than five chances of being wrong implies better than ninety-five chances of being *right*; imagine a gambler who wouldn't bet unless the chances of winning were greater than ninety-five out of a hundred!

Decision Errors in Interpreting Data

Despite this conservative attitude, researchers must still face the possibility that sometimes a result *is* due to chance, and that therefore their interpretation of the results is wrong. This leads to the basic problem of all inferential reasoning – trying to make statements based on incomplete knowledge of the world. To return to the drug experiment, the doctors want to determine if the drug works or not; their basis for deciding is their examination of the experimental data. However, as we have discussed, sampling variability implies that if they did the experiment again, the results would be different. So how can they be sure if the drug works or not?

In essence, the situation implies four possibilities, which involve the relationship of the observed results to the underlying reality (see Fig. A.9). The results will either suggest the drug works or that it doesn't work. Similarly, the underlying reality is either that the drug works or that it doesn't. This leads to four possible decision outcomes, two of which are correct decisions and two of which are errors. If the drug actually works, and the statistical analysis says it

DECISION TABLE FOR EVALUATING HYPOTHESES

REALITY IN POPULATION

DECISION FROM SAMPLE	DRUG WORKS	DRUG DOESN'T WORK
REJECT NULL HYPOTHESIS (CONCLUDE DRUG WORKS)	CORRECT DECISION	TYPE 1 ERROR (FALSE–POSITIVE)
ACCEPT NULL HYPOTHESIS (CONCLUDE DRUG DOESN'T WORK)	TYPE 2 ERROR (FALSE–NEGATIVE)	CORRECT DECISION

Fig. A.9 Errors in evaluating hypotheses No statistical procedure can ensure that researchers never make an error in interpreting what the results of a study mean. This chart shows the various ways in which either correct or incorrect decisions can be made (see text for discussion of the various types of error).

false-positive in inferential statistics, concluding that an observed outcome is significant when in fact it reflects only chance variability; also called a Type I error

false-negative in inferential statistics, concluding that the observed results are due only to chance variability when in fact a significant effect exists; also called a Type II error

works, then this is obviously a correct decision. Similarly, if the drug doesn't work, and the analysis does not lead to rejecting the null hypothesis that it doesn't, then this is also a correct decision. The potential problems arise with the other two possible outcomes, which reflect different types of errors. If the drug does not work, but chance factors in the results lead to a *conclusion* that it does, then rejecting the null hypothesis is really an error. This type of error is variously called a *Type I error* or a **false-positive**. If the drug actually works, but the results are *not* strong enough to conclude that it does, then accepting the null hypothesis is an error. This second form of error, which leads to overlooking genuine effects, is called either a *Type II error* or a **false-negative**. In each case, the errors are due to the uncertainty inherent in the process of interpreting results. In a world where sampling variability did not exist, such problems would also be non-existent. But sampling variability is a reality, along with random variations like measurement errors, all of which make it more difficult to get unambiguous results in doing research.

These effects may seem rather abstract, but in fact they can be all too real. In the case of drug research, false-negatives can lead to abandoning the development of a potentially useful drug, while false-positives can lead to wasted effort pursuing an ineffective drug. This type of situation can also arise in situations remote from research; indeed, wherever we must make decisions based on imperfect information.

Increasingly, individuals are faced with making decisions in situations like health care. For example, in the past few years, a blood test has been developed for pregnant women which is designed to detect defects called *neural tube disorders* in the developing embryo. While the test is simple to do, its interpretation is more difficult. Since neural tube disorders are rare, the test results are mostly negative (meaning the embryo is normal). However, of those which are *positive* (suggesting a defect in the embryo), 19 out of 20 are false-positives! When a test is positive, the mother must undergo further tests over several weeks. The uncertainty created can cause significant distress, while some of the additional tests (like *amniocentesis*) themselves pose risks. After all this, 95 per cent of those initially told the test is positive will discover that in fact there is nothing wrong with the embryo. In addition, while they occur much less often, the test can also occasionally give false-negatives; such a result would lead to the conclusion that the embryo is normal, even when a neural tube disorder exists. Given these realities, many prospective mothers, if informed, might ask whether the test is worth taking.

The dilemma which decisions of this nature create cannot be avoided by simple refinements of technology – the limitations are inherent to the process of interpreting the meaning of samples. What one *can* do, if so inclined, is decide which type of error is more serious, and therefore more important to avoid. Traditionally, the preference in science is to avoid false-positives (i.e. Type I errors), which would lead to concluding there is support for a theory when in fact it is false. That is why the *minimum* criterion (i.e. *significance level*) for rejecting the null hypothesis is a less than 5 per cent chance that the null hypothesis is correct. In the extreme case, one could avoid *all* false-positives by *never* concluding that the results are significant; of course, this would lead to many false-negatives, since some data due to real effects would *also* be rejected as inconclusive (similarly, the only way to avoid *all* false-negatives is by calling all results significant). Ultimately, uncertainty is an inherent part of the interpretation of data; it is part of the reason that we never can speak of absolute proof in science. To most researchers in psychology, living with such uncertainty is simply part of the larger challenge of understanding behaviour.

For further consideration

Suppose that your doctor proposed doing a new test as a means of diagnosing why you don't feel well. What would you want to know about the accuracy and interpretation of the test?

Conclusion

Doing research is a complex and challenging process, involving many possible ways that things can go wrong – from the design of the study, to the process of gathering data, to the interpretations that are made once the data have been collected. At the same time, research offers the chance to ask new questions, to be creative in developing a research design, and ultimately, to experience the thrill of discovering something previously unknown. For many people, the rewards far outweigh the risks.

While some individuals reading this book may go on to become professional psychologists, and make discoveries of their own, most readers probably won't. So what value does this material have? In part, this Appendix is intended to appeal to a sense of curiosity, to the desire to understand a bit more about what is actually involved in doing research. Beyond that, it also has a more practical intent: in today's world, we all encounter the results of research, whether in news reports or in our personal lives (as with medical tests). By understanding something about the process which underlies research and statistical analysis, one can be better equipped to evaluate the information we receive. In this sense, the old saying is true: knowledge *is* power. May the knowledge included here add to the power of your understanding as you continue in psychology, and in your life.

Chapter Summary

◆ As a science, psychology makes use of systematic methods for doing research and analysing the resulting data; these topics are referred to as *research methods* and *statistics*.

◆ In planning research, researchers must consider how observations are made (*measurement*), what observations to make (*sampling*) and how the hypothesis is to be tested (*research design*).

◆ In experimental research, the researcher must pay particular attention to the possibility of *error* due to *confounds* or *bias*.

◆ Statistical analysis involves summarizing the data (*descriptive statistics*) and interpreting the meaning of the results (*inferential statistics*).

◆ Descriptive statistics include *frequency distributions, measures of central tendency, measures of variability* and *correlations*.

◆ The most important form of frequency distribution is the *normal distribution*, which is useful both for its particular characteristics and its relevance to many everyday types of data.

◆ Inferential statistics are necessary in evaluating results because of the occurrence of *variability* when sampling.

◆ *Significance tests* like the *t-test* are used to estimate the likelihood of obtaining the observed results by chance.

◆ In using inferential statistics, there is never absolute certainty about one's interpretation; instead, *decision errors* (*false-positives* and *false-negatives*) can arise.

◆ Despite the challenges, research provides opportunities to be creative and to explore the unknown.

Key Terms and Concepts

confound	double-blind design
correlation coefficient	experimenter bias
cross-sectional sample	falsification
descriptive statistics	frequency distribution

halo effect   range
hypothesis   reliability
internal validity   sample
mean   sampling error
median   sampling variability
mode   self-fulfilling prophecy
negative correlation   significance tests
normal distribution   single-blind design
null hypothesis   standard deviation
population   subject bias
positive correlation t-test
random sample   validity

Suggestions for Further Reading

For an entertaining exploration of the ways in which scientific evidence can be misused in everyday life, read Peter Huber's book, *Galileo's Revenge: Junk Science in the Courtroom*.

While statistics is not likely to be considered a topic for light reading, for those who wish to investigate the subject further, Ferguson's *Statistical Analysis in Psychology and Education* is a well-known text which has survived through several editions.

Glossary

abnormal behaviour behaviour which is regarded by society as deviant or maladaptive; according to DSM-III-R, an individual must be suffering or show maladaptive functioning in order for behaviour to be described as abnormal.

accessibility in LTM, the principle that remembering and forgetting are dependent on effective retrieval; without the proper cues, information which exists in LTM may not be accessible.

actualizing tendency in Rogers' theory, an innate drive which reflects the desire to grow, to develop and to enhance one's capacities.

adrenal glands endocrine glands, located just above the kidneys, which play an important role in arousal and stress; the outer layer (the cortex) secretes corticosteroids, and the *medulla* (the inner core) secretes *epinephrine* (adrenaline) and *norepinephrine* (noradrenaline).

aetiology the study of the causes of a disease or mental disorder.

aggression behaviour which causes intentional harm to another person.

algorithm a procedure for problem solving which always enables solution of a particular type of problem.

altered state of consciousness any state of awareness which differs from normal waking awareness; examples could include meditation, sleep, drug states and psychosis.

altruism behaviour intended to help others, independently of any self-interest.

ambiguous figure any stimulus which can be perceived in more than one way.

anal stage in Freud's theory of psychosexual development, the second stage (15 months to 3 years); during this stage, the focus of drive energy shifts to the lower end of the digestive tract, and the major conflict is toilet training.

androgens hormones whose functions are related to masculine characteristics; the most important is testosterone.

antisocial personality disorder a behaviour pattern in which an individual shows a history of acts of violence towards others, unaccompanied by guilt; although these individuals may not report either suffering or unsatisfactory functioning (the generally accepted standard for abnormality), their behaviour is still deemed abnormal because it violates society's norms in such significant ways.

anxiety a negative emotional state associated with threat to the self; in Freud's theory, it arises when the ego is faced with an influx of stimuli with which it cannot cope, as a result of either external danger or the demands of id or superego.

archetypes organizing structures within the collective unconscious which serve to organize our experiences, providing the basis of many fantasies, myths and symbols.

artificial intelligence in computer science, the attempt to build machines which can function intelligently, and the use of such machines to test our understanding of human intelligence.

association areas areas of the cortex which have no primary function (such as receiving direct sensory data), but rather play a role in integrating activity from other brain areas.

associationism the doctrine, supported by Aristotle, Hume and others, that mental processes, particularly learning, are based on forming connections between ideas and/or events.

attention the process of selectively focusing on particular stimulus elements, typically those deemed most significant.

attitude a personal belief of an evaluative nature, such as good or bad, likeable or not likeable, which influences our reactions towards people or things.

attribution theory a theory dealing with the inferences we make about the causes of our own behaviour, and that of other people; the interpretations made are called *attributions*.

autonomic conditioning (also called 'learned operant control of autonomic responses') the conditioning of changes in autonomic (involuntary) responses (such as heart rate or blood pressure) by providing operant reinforcement.

availability in memory, the principle that remembering is determined by whether the information exists in LTM or not; forgetting implies that the information is destroyed.

aversive conditioning a form of behaviour modification which is designed to induce an aversive response to stimuli which are associated with existing undesirable behaviours.

axon the relatively elongated portion of a neuron between the cell body and the terminals which provides the signal pathway for a nerve impulse.

behaviour modification the application of conditioning techniques to altering human behaviour, particularly those behaviours identified as abnormal.

bias a source of error which results in a systematic distortion of results.

biofeedback a general term for applications of the process of autonomic conditioning; the name refers to the fact that in humans reinforcement is based on providing an individual with information ('feedback') about physiological processes ('bio') which are normally not observable.

brain the portion of the central nervous system which lies within the skull.

brainstem the region at the top of the spinal cord, composed of three primary structures: the medulla, the pons and the midbrain.

bystander apathy the failure of onlookers to intervene in an emergency; despite the label, the cause is often unrelated to apathy.

case study a detailed description of a single individual, typically used to provide information on the person's history and to aid in interpreting the person's behaviour.

catharsis the release of drive energy in indirect form, either through the process of recalling emotionally charged experiences or involvement in symbolic activity.

central nervous system (CNS) the brain, together with the nerve pathways of the spinal cord.

cerebellum ('little brain' in Latin) two small hemispheres located beneath the cortical hemispheres, at the back of the head; the cerebellum plays an important role in directing movements and balance.

cerebral dominance the tendency for one hemisphere to be superior for particular functions.

cerebral hemispheres two half spheres, made up of the cortex and underlying structures, which comprise the major portion of the brain.

chaos theory a branch of mathematics dealing with non-linear functions which has been applied to the modelling of situations such as the weather and stock markets; non-linear systems are not predictable, because very small changes in initial conditions can result in radical differences at a later point.

chromosomes thread-like genetic structures composed of double strands of DNA and proteins, containing the genes; in humans, there are twenty-three pairs of chromosomes.

chunk the basic measure of STM capacity, representing a meaningful unit, such as random letters, numbers or words.

classical conditioning the study of learning which involves reflex responses, in which a neutral stimulus comes to elicit an existing reflex response.

client-centred therapy an approach to therapy developed by Carl Rogers, in which the person seeking treatment (termed a *client*), not the therapist, is seen as directing the process of therapy; later called person-centred therapy.

closure in perception, the tendency to fill in incomplete patterns to produce a coherent whole.

co-dependency in the recovery movement, a pattern of behaviour triggered by low self-esteem, such that individuals form relationships in which one's sense of self-esteem is dependent on one's partner.

cognitive behaviour modification an extension of behaviour modification which uses cognitive mediation (such as observing a model) in addition to basic conditioning techniques.

cognitive dissonance in Festinger's theory, a state of tension created when there are conflicts between an individual's behaviour and beliefs, or between two beliefs.

cognitive map Tolman's term for the mental representation of learned relationships among stimuli.

cognitive pathology a phenomenon whereby researchers selectively ignore simplifying assumptions and other limitations which are part of the foundations of their theories and methods.

cognitive restructuring in Ellis' rational-emotive therapy, a process for modifying faulty beliefs and the negative emotions they produce, in order to develop realistic beliefs and self-acceptance.

cognitive social learning theory (sometimes simply 'social learning theory') a theory derived from the cognitive approach, which asserts that behaviour can be learned from observing other people, and that behaviour is mediated by cognitive schemata.

collective unconscious in Jung's theory, a biologically based portion of the unconscious which reflects universal themes and ideas, not individual experience.

compensation in Adler's theory, a process of engaging in activities intended to produce a feeling of superiority over others, in order to overcome feelings of inferiority.

complementarity a concept developed by physicists to deal with the existence of two models which are both useful, but not directly reconcilable.

computerized imaging techniques for studying brain function which use computers to convert information into a three-dimensional model of the brain which can be viewed on a television monitor.

concordance a technique for studying inheritance by examining characteristics of individuals whose genetic relationship is known.

conditional positive regard acceptance and caring given to a person only for meeting certain standards of behaviour.

conditioned emotional response an emotional response such as fear which is established through classical conditioning.

conditioned reinforcer stimuli which act as reinforcers but are not based on biological survival, such as attention, praise or money.

conditioned response in classical conditioning, a response to a previously neutral stimulus which has become a conditioned stimulus by repeated pairing with an unconditioned stimulus.

conditioned stimulus a stimulus which by repeated pairings with an unconditioned stimulus comes to elicit a conditioned response.

conditions for growth the conditions under which healthy development of personality occurs; defined by Rogers as unconditional positive regard, openness and empathy.

conditions of worth restrictions imposed on self-expression in order to earn positive regard.

confirmation in research, the process of determining that observations are consistent with the hypothesis being true.

confirmation bias a form of cognitive error based on the tendency to seek out information which supports one's beliefs, and ignore contradictory information.

conformity the tendency to adjust one's behaviour to comply with group norms.

confound in experimental research, a situation where two variables change simultaneously, making it impossible to determine their relative influence.

confounding variable a factor in research which varies jointly with a variable of interest, making it impossible to identify properly the role each variable has in affecting behaviour; typically, a confounding variable represents something which has been overlooked in planning the research, and is only identified after the data have been collected.

congruence in Rogers' theory, a feeling of integration experienced when the self and ideal self match.

conscious in Freud's theory, that aspect of the mind which contains those thoughts and feelings of which we are immediately aware at a given moment.

context-dependent forgetting failure to retrieve information from LTM due to the absence of appropriate contextual cues.

contingency of reinforcement in operant conditioning, a description of the relationship between a response and a reinforcer.

continuity in developmental theory, the view that changes occur through a continuous gradual process, rather than as a series of discrete stages; continuity is an assertion about the processes which underlie development, as well as the changes observed in behaviour.

continuous reinforcement a reinforcement schedule in which every response is followed by a reinforcer; equivalent to a FR 1 schedule.

convergent problem a problem which has a single solution, and all elements lead towards that solution; also called *closed-end* or *well-defined* problems.

corpus callosum a wide band of nerve fibres which connect the two hemispheres.

correlation a pattern or relationship observed between two variables.

correlation coefficient a descriptive statistic measuring the degree of relationship between two variables; for positive correlations, it is a number which varies between 0.0 and + 1.0, and for negative correlations between 0.0 and –1.0; in both cases, the closer the value is to 1, the stronger the relationship between the two variables.

cortex the pink, somewhat wrinkled outer layer of the brain which controls many of our higher functions like speech and perception; from the Greek for 'bark' (as on a tree).

creativity the capacity to produce something which is both unique and useful.

critical period in development, the concept that there are optimal periods for the learning of certain behaviours.

cross-sectional sample a sample which is deliberately selected in such a way that the sample matches the population for particular characteristics, such as age and income.

cross-sectional study a research design based on selecting representative groups who vary on a particular characteristic; when the characteristic is age, this design provides a means of drawing developmental comparisons.

cue-dependent coding the concept that all information is stored in memory as a set of relationships called the context; remembering is seen as dependent on restoring the cues which formed the original context.

debriefing discussing the nature of a research study with participants at its conclusion, in order to explain the true nature and goals of the research and to answer any questions or concerns of participants, especially in experiments which involve the use of deception.

decay in memory, the spontaneous loss of information with the passage of time.

deception in research, the deliberate misinforming of participants concerning the nature of the study and of their role.

deduction the process of drawing specific conclusions from a set of general principles.

defective attention theory a theory which argues that schizophrenia is due to difficulties in selecting and attending to the relevant stimuli in a situation.

defence mechanism in Freud's theory, a technique used by the ego to protect itself from anxiety and the threats which give rise to it; many psychologists use the terms as descriptions of behaviour patterns, without endorsing the Freudian interpretation of their origin.

deficiency motives in Maslow's theory, needs whose motivating power is triggered by the absence of the underlying requirements, such as the physiological or esteem needs.

delusional amphetamine disorder a form of mental disorder resulting from the excessive use of amphetamines; its primary symptom, extreme delusions, can make it appear *symptomatically* identical to paranoid schizophrenia.

delusions false beliefs which are maintained in the absence of clear evidence to the contrary.

demand characteristics the overt and covert cues present in an experimental situation which can influence how participants behave.

dependent variable in an experiment, the behaviour measured in order to evaluate the effects of the independent variable.

depersonalization a type of dissociative reaction in which the individual psychologically withdraws from a situation, often accompanied by feeling that their body is not real or belongs to someone else.

depressant a drug which reduces CNS activity; in large doses, depressants can cause coma and even death.

descriptive statistics the branch of statistics which is concerned with describing and summarizing sets of scores.

determinism the assumption that all behaviour has specific causes.

diffusion of responsibility a lessening of an individual's feeling of responsibility in a situation which involves other people.

discriminative stimulus in operant conditioning, a stimulus which signals the contingency of reinforcement available.

displacement in memory, forgetting in STM due to new incoming information pushing out the previous contents; in psychoanalysis, a defence mechanism which involves the redirection of drive energy from one object to a substitute object.

divergent problem a problem which does not have a single optimal solution, except according to the criteria one may adopt; rather, the problem tends to lead in several different directions; equivalent to an ill-defined problem.

domain-general model a theory which attempts to account for many aspects of behaviour in terms of a single set of principles.

domain-specific model a theory which focuses on only a single aspect of behaviour in the belief that different aspects of behaviour involve different processes, and therefore require different theoretical explanations.

dopamine hypothesis a theory which argues that schizophrenia is based on overactivity in neural pathways which depend on dopamine as a neurotransmitter.

double-bind hypothesis a theory of schizophrenia developed by anthropologist Gregory Bateson and his colleagues, which argues that faulty communication patterns within the family are the cause of schizophrenia.

double-blind design a rigorous form of experimental control, whereby both the subject and experimenter are left uninformed about details of the experiment which could result in bias (both subject bias and experimenter bias).

dream censor the psychic mechanism whose function is to ensure that sleep is not disturbed by the unconsciously expressed desires that are the basis of dreams; to accomplish this, the dream censor converts the content of the dream into symbolic form (the manifest content).

dualism the view, first attributed to Descartes, that mind and body are distinct; Descartes believed the two could interact via the pineal gland in the brain.

efficacy the measured effectiveness of a treatment technique in medicine or psychotherapy.

ego (Latin for 'I') in psychoanalysis, the element of the psyche which provides the integrating of personality by mediating between the id and the superego, and also mediates the links with the outside world; in Jung's theory, the element of the self which provides the conscious direction of one's life.

elaborative rehearsal the active processing of items in STM in order to code the information for LTM; material may be processed in various ways, ranging from an emphasis on sensory characteristics (visual appearance, sound) to a focus on the semantic content ('meaning') of information.

electrical stimulation of the brain (ESB) artificial stimulation of neurons by means of a current applied through an implanted electrode.

electroencephalograph (EEG – 'writing the electricity of the brain') a device for recording the electrical activity of the brain.

empathy the ability to understand another person's perceptions and feelings; seen by Rogers as a condition for growth.

empirical based on making observations, as in an *empirical* theory.

empiricism the philosophical position, first attributed to John Locke, that all knowledge is based on experience; hence, the basis of the view that behaviour is learned.

endocrine glands ('ductless glands') glands which secrete chemicals called **hormones** directly into the bloodstream.

endorphin (*end*ogenous – 'naturally occurring' – m*orphine*) a neuropeptide which plays a significant role in pain and mood states.

episodic memory the portion of LTM which contains personal experiences, organized according to where and when events happened, such as what happened on your last birthday.

ethology the study of the behaviour of animals in their natural environments.

evolution a theory to account for the development of species diversity; while various theories have been proposed, Darwin's theory based on natural selection is the most broadly recognized.

experiment a procedure whereby a researcher systematically varies one or more factors (called independent variables) in order to see what effect the changes have on behaviour.

experimental realism a quality of involvement whereby research participants respond without regard for the laboratory context, as they would in an ordinary situation.

experimenter bias systematic error created when an experimenter's knowledge and expectations about the experiment influences the behaviour of subjects.

external validity an assessment of the degree to which one can generalize research results beyond the specific situation.

extinction in classical conditioning, the cessation of responding when the CS is presented repeatedly *without* being paired with the UCS; in operant conditioning, a drop in responding when reinforcement is discontinued.

false-negative in inferential statistics, concluding that the observed results are due only to chance variability when in fact a significant effect exists; also called a Type II error.

false-positive in inferential statistics, concluding that an observed outcome is significant when in fact it reflects only chance variability; also called a Type I error.

false recognition a form of memory error whereby the presence of familiar cues leads one to believe the stimulus matches a previously experienced stimulus.

falsifiability a criterion for evaluating a theory, which states the theory should specify circumstances wherein it could be proven wrong.

falsification in research, the process of using observations to prove that a hypothesis is wrong.

faulty reference an error involving misinterpreting the significance of stimuli and events; while sometimes considered a form of delusion, it can also arise through faulty perceptual processing.

field experiment an experiment done in a natural setting, usually without the explicit awareness of participants; as contrasted to experiments done in a laboratory setting.

fixation the incomplete release of drive energy associated with a particular stage.

fixed interval (FI) schedule a reinforcement contingency defined by the amount of time that must pass since the previous reinforcer was given, before a response will receive a reinforcer; measured as FI x, where x specifies the required time interval.

fixed ratio (FR) schedule a reinforcement contingency defined by the number of responses the organism must make in order to get a reinforcer; the ratio is measured as FR x, where x is the required number of responses.

free association a technique originated by Freud for studying the mind, based on asking a person to simply say whatever words float into their mind, and then looking for patterns.

frequency distribution a statistical analysis of a set of data which tells how frequently each value occurs.

frontal lobe the area of the cortex in front of the central fissure, and above the lateral fissure; it is involved in the interpretation of emotion and experience.

frontal lobotomy an operation, popular in the 1940s and 1950s, which involved cutting off or removing portions of the frontal lobes, in an attempt to treat cases of manic depression or chronic pain; later shown to be largely ineffective as a therapeutic procedure.

frontal motor area the area of the frontal lobes just before the central fissure which controls all voluntary movements of the muscles.

frustration–aggression hypothesis a theory of aggression developed by Dollard and Miller, which states that *frustration* (defined as blocking a goal-oriented response) is the sole cause of aggression.

fully functioning person described by Rogers as the ideal of growth, closely related to congruence;

healthy growth is characterized by openness, a high degree of spontaneity, compassion and self-direction.

functional fixedness in Gestalt theory, perceiving an object as having only one use.

functionalism an approach to the study of behaviour pioneered by William James, which emphasizes the analysis of the processes by which the mind works, as opposed to the study of the mind's contents advocated by structuralism.

fundamental attribution error the tendency to underestimate the importance of situational influences, and overestimate the importance of internal factors in interpreting the causes of people's behaviour.

gene the basic unit of heredity, made up of strings of 'building blocks' called amino acids; it is estimated that humans possess about 100,000 different genes, each regulating a different process.

general adaptation syndrome a model of stages of stress identified by Hans Selye, ranging from acute stress (alarm) to outward coping (resistance) and, finally, to depletion of bodily resources (exhaustion).

generality a criterion for evaluating a theory, which refers to the range of application of a theory; a good theory should apply to a wide range of situations.

genital stage in Freud's theory, the final stage of psychosexual development (from puberty onward), when drive energy is focused on the genitals, with adult expression of sexuality.

genotype the genetic code which an individual carries in the DNA of their cells.

Gestalt theory a theory of behaviour pioneered in the early part of this century by Kohler, Wertheimer and others, which emphasized the active, creative nature of perception and learning (*Gestalt* is German, and means roughly 'organized whole').

goal state in problem solving, the desired outcome of a problem.

guilt in the recovery movement, a feeling of negative worth in response to behaviour which we recognize as harming others; for Freud, guilt is a form of anxiety associated with behaviours which violate the standards of the superego.

habituation a reduction in neural response due to continual stimulation.

hallucinations false perceptions in the absence of relevant sensory stimuli, such as hearing voices or seeing objects which are not present.

halo effect a form of perceptual bias which occurs when our rating of a person on *one* characteristic as being positive or negative of a person leads to similar expectations for *other* characteristics of the individual.

heredity the biological transmission of characteristics from one generation to another.

heritability index a measure of the influence of heredity within a group based on comparing the estimated genetic variability for the particular characteristic to the overall variability within the group.

heuristic a guide to thinking; in problem solving, heuristics provide informal strategies which are usually better than random search, but less effective than algorithms.

hierarchy of fears in systematic desensitization, a list of fear-evoking stimuli, ranging from very mild to very intense, arranged in order of the intensity of fear which they elicit.

hierarchy of needs Maslow's model of basic human needs, which he saw as organized in a hierarchical structure; needs range from physiological (most basic) to self-actualization (top of hierarchy).

higher-order conditioning a form of classical conditioning in which a previously established conditioned stimulus is used as if it were an unconditioned stimulus to create conditioning to a new stimulus.

hippocampus a structure within the limbic system which is important to memory function.

history of reinforcement in operant conditioning, the sum of all prior reinforcement for a particular behaviour; behaviourists assert that the cumulative history of reinforcement is more important than any single reinforcement in determining behaviour.

hormone a chemical secreted by an endocrine gland; hormones are involved in many aspects of metabolism and long-term functioning of the body.

hypothalamus one of the most important elements in the limbic system, the hypothalamus both regulates behaviours associated with hunger, thirst, sex and other basic drives, and also plays a role in regulating hormonal functions.

hypothesis a statement describing a proposed relationship between two types of variables; a conclusion derived from a theory which can be evaluated by making further observations.

hysteria a disorder characterized by physical symptoms for which there is no apparent physical cause; the term was used by Freud but actually predates him.

id (Latin for 'it') in Freud's theory, the element of the psyche which is the source of all basic drives.

ideal self in Rogers' theory, a dynamically changing construct which represents an individual's goals and aspirations.

identification a defence mechanism which involves incorporating characteristics of a drive object into one's own ego.

illusory correlation a cognitive error in which an individual perceives a relationship between variables where none actually exists.

imitation the learning of behaviour by observing the behaviour of others; sometimes called 'modelling' or 'observational learning'.

implicit personality theories a general cognitive schema about human behaviour which is used in making interpretations of the behaviour of other people.

incongruence in Rogers' theory, a feeling of conflict or unease experienced when there is a mismatch between the self and ideal self.

independent variable a variable in an experiment which is systematically varied by the researcher, in order to see what effect it has on behaviour.

individuation Jung's conception of the goal of development, which he described as the expansion of conscious awareness by the ego making contact with the unconscious portions of the self.

induction a process of reasoning based on forming general principles from specific observations.

inference the process of drawing a conclusion based on logical analysis of what is already known.

inferential statistics the branch of statistics which deals with the interpretation of data, particularly in terms of generalizing from the observed sample to the larger population.

inferiority for Adler, the notion that all children experience a sense of helplessness because of their size and dependence on others; this feeling can also be intensified by real or imagined physical defects, social rejection and other factors.

inferiority complex in Adler's theory, an intense feeling of insecurity based on a failure to resolve the feelings evoked by childhood experiences of helplessness.

information processing a term borrowed from computer science by cognitive psychologists to describe the mental functions which occur between stimulus and response.

initial state in problem solving, the situation at the outset of a problem, including any existing constraints (such as time limits or restrictions on permitted actions).

inner child in the recovery movement, a term referring both to the phenomenological re-experiencing of the feelings and desires of childhood, and also the symbolic representation of the full potential of the individual to grow and be creative.

insight a sudden change in the way one organizes a problem situation (typically this is characterized by a change in behaviour from random responding to rule-based responding); in psychotherapy, awareness of the underlying conflicts which are regarded as the causes of behaviour.

instrumental aggression aggressive behaviour which is maintained because it is positively reinforced.

interference according to associationism, competition between items which can hamper learning and produce forgetting.

internal validity the assessment of the degree to which the design and execution of an experiment are free from bias, confounds and other sources of error.

intersubjective verification a process for validating observations based on agreement by two observers; proposed by Rogers as a means of making subjective impressions useful as scientific data.

interview a method of gathering data in which a researcher asks an individual questions; the format may be pre-planned and highly structured, or relatively free-flowing and unstructured.

introjection of values for Rogers, the incorporation of values into the ideal self due to accepting conditions of worth imposed by others; the term was first used by Freud to refer to a defence mechanism.

introspectionism a method of gathering data in which the individual attempts to analyse the content of their conscious mind; associated with the structuralist approach.

language a system of communication based on symbols or gestures which can vary across individuals and allow for new forms and meanings.

latency stage in Freud's developmental theory, the stage which begins at about age five and extends until puberty, during which the drives appear to be relatively inactive.

latent content in Freud's theory of dreams, the true meaning of a dream, which is transformed by the dream censor into symbolic form as the manifest content.

latent learning a term used by Tolman to describe situations in which learning is distinct from the performance of a behaviour.

law of effect a principle of learning proposed by Thorndike, which stated that any response which leads to an outcome satisfying to the organism is likely to be repeated, and any response which leads to an unpleasant outcome is not likely to be repeated.

learning in behaviourism, a change in behaviour which occurs as the result of experience; in cognitive psychology, the process of gathering information and organizing it into mental schemata.

learning set a learned strategy or set which enables the individual to deal efficiently with problems of the same type; similar in meaning to the Gestalt concept of mental set, except it emphasizes that the set develops as the result of experience.

limbic system a series of subcortical structures which connect the cortex with other parts of the brain and which are important in many basic functions; among the main parts of the limbic system are the thalamus, hypothalamus, amygdala and hippocampus.

localization of function the assumption that specific functions are associated with specific areas of the brain.

logical empiricism in philosophy of science, the assumption that it is possible to compare and evaluate theories in terms of how well they account for the evidence.

logotherapy Viktor Frankl's theory of development and therapy, which is based on the argument that finding a meaning for life is central to individual growth and happiness.

longitudinal study a research design in which a given group of individuals are studied over a period of time.

long-term memory (LTM) the component of memory which is involved with retention over relatively long periods (hours, days, weeks or longer).

maintenance rehearsal the retention of material in STM by means of rote repetition.

manifest content the symbolic content of a dream (disguised by the dream censor) which the conscious mind is aware of, both during sleep and on waking.

materialism the assumption that all behaviour has a physiological basis.

maturation processes in development which seem to be relatively independent of environmental influences; depth perception and walking are examples of behaviours which seem to depend on maturation; implied in the term is the assumption that the characteristics are governed by heredity.

mean (also called 'arithmetic mean') a statistic measuring central tendency, calculated as the sum of all the scores, divided by the number of scores.

measure of central tendency a type of descriptive statistic used to determine what is a representative value for a set of scores.

median a statistic measuring central tendency, calculated as the middle score in a frequency distribution.

mediator a process or event within the individual which comes between a stimulus and a response.

medical model a theory of abnormal behaviour which assumes that all such disorders have physiological causes.

meditation a technique or practice that seeks to achieve mental and physical relaxation, a more passive, receptive awareness, and harmony of mind and nature.

medulla a small swelling at the top of the spinal cord composed of the cell bodies of neurons whose axons extend to the heart and other internal organs; its role is to regulate basic bodily processes.

memory the retention and use of prior learning.

mental set in Gestalt theory, a cognitive schema for a particular situation, such as a problem.

metaneeds in Maslow's theory, need states which are based on a desire to grow rather than an underlying deficiency; expressed as the need for *self-actualization.*

mind the inner subjective experience of conscious awareness; the term has no direct reference to physical form.

mnemonics the study and use of techniques for improving memory (from the Greek for 'memory').

mode a statistic measuring central tendency, calculated as the most frequently occurring value (or interval) in a set of scores.

monism the belief that mind and body are a single entity.

motor nerves those neurons which are responsible for initiating muscle activity.

multiple-personality disorder a severe form of dissociative reaction which can result in several independent personalities being manifested.

mutation a change in the genetic material of a cell; while rare, mutations can result in new characteristics which may be transmitted to descendants of the original cell.

myelin in a neuron, an insulating sheath around the axon, composed of the spirally wound membrane of Schwann cells, which serves to improve the efficiency of neural conduction.

nativism the philosophical view, held by Plato and others, that knowledge and behaviour are innate in origin.

negative correlation a relationship observed between two variables in which increases in one variable occur as the value of the other variable decreases.

negative reinforcement in operant conditioning, a process for increasing the probability of a response in which a response is immediately followed by the removal of an aversive stimulus (negative reinforcer); note that since the response increases in frequency, it is *not* equivalent to punishment.

negative reinforcer an aversive stimulus which when it follows a response serves to decrease the probability of the response in the future.

negative symptoms in abnormal psychology, particularly with reference to schizophrenia, the absence of expected behaviours; negative symptoms include bodily immobility, limited speech, flattened affect (absence of emotional expression) and social withdrawal.

nerve impulse the electrical signal generated when a neuron is active, which normally passes from the dendrites, along the axon, to the terminals.

neuron a cell of the nervous system (also called a nerve cell).

neuropeptide a chemical, comprised of a short chain of amino acids, which can function both as a neurotransmitter and as a hormone; also called a neurohormone.

neurotransmitter a chemical released by the terminals of a neuron which plays a role in communication between neurons, across the synapse.

neutral stimulus in classical conditioning, a stimulus which initially produces no specific response other than provoking attention; as conditioning proceeds, the neutral stimulus becomes a conditioned stimulus.

non-contingent reinforcement in operant conditioning, the occurrence of a reinforcer which is not related to whether the response occurs or not.

non-experimental methods research methods which do not involve direct control of any factor, in contrast to experiments; sometimes called descriptive/correlational designs.

noögenic neuroses in Frankl's theory, conflicts within an individual which are based on existential frustrations, rather than the conflicts of id, ego and superego which Freud saw as the source of anxiety.

normal distribution a type of frequency distribution which resembles a bell-shaped curve; among its special properties, first identified by Gauss, is that its measures of central tendency are all the same.

null hypothesis in research, a hypothesis which asserts that any differences observed between groups are random rather than representing an experimental effect; used for statistical purposes to evaluate results.

occipital lobe the rear-most portion of the cortex, which is devoted solely to vision.

Oedipal conflict in Freud's theory of development, the major conflict associated with the phallic stage which challenges the developing ego; named after the Greek story of Oedipus, who unknowingly killed his father and married his mother.

openness behaviour characterized by a person freely expressing their own sense of self, rather than playing a role or hiding behind a façade; seen by Rogers as a condition for growth.

operant conditioning in the behaviourist approach, the form of learning concerned with changes in emitted responses as a function of their consequences.

operational definition a term whose meaning is derived from the processes or observable events used to measure it.

operator in problem solving, one of the actions permitted in order to solve a problem.

oral stage in Freud's theory of development, the first stage, extending from birth to about 15 months, when the focus of gratification is on the mouth.

organism in Rogers' theory, the biological being which is the source of basic needs (such as food and water), and also the source of a growth motive termed the *actualizing tendency*.

paradigm in Kuhn's analysis of science, a superordinate framework or world-view accepted by a group of researchers, which shapes both theories and evidence; since the paradigm influences the observations one makes, no observations can ever be used to evaluate the paradigm.

parietal lobe the portion of the cortex just behind the central fissure and above the lateral fissure, whose primary function is the sense of touch.

parsimony in the philosophy of science, the principle that states one should always seek the simplest possible explanation for any event.

partial reinforcement in operant conditioning, a contingency of reinforcement in which reinforcement does not follow every response.

participant observation a non-experimental research method in which the researcher becomes part of a group he or she wishes to observe.

peak experience for Maslow, a transient experience of deep intensity which involves enhanced awareness, often accompanied by feelings of being 'fully alive'.

perception the process of selection, organization and interpretation of information about the world conveyed by the senses.

peripheral nervous system (PNS) those nerve pathways which lie outside the central nervous system, involving sensation, motor control and regulation of internal organs.

persistence of set a phenomenon in problem solving, identified by Gestalt psychologists, in which a mental set developed in a previous problem is maintained even though it is no longer appropriate, and tends to interfere with solving a current problem.

persona in Jung's theory, the conscious character or role we assume in presenting ourselves to the world.

personality patterns of behaviour which are characteristic of an individual and which tend to be consistent across situations and over time.

person-centred therapy (also called 'client-centred therapy') a form of therapy developed by Carl Rogers, which emphasizes the responsibility of the individual to determine the direction of change within therapy.

phallic stage in Freud's theory, the third stage of development, extending from about three to five years of age, during which gratification is focused on the genitals, although not in the form of adult sexuality.

phantom limb a mysterious phenomenon in which individuals who have lost a limb will often continue to experience sensations which seem to come from the missing limb.

phenomenal field for Rogers, an individual's unique perception of the world.

phenomenological pertaining to the way things appear or are experienced; in the humanistic approach, a reference to the emphasis on an individual's perceptions and feelings as defining the meaning of their behaviour.

phenotype the observed characteristics of the individual, based on the combination of genetic expression and environmental influences.

phrenology a now-discredited eighteenth-century theory which asserted that one could assess ability by examining the shape of the skull.

pituitary gland a small gland adjacent to the hypothalamus which regulates many endocrine functions, including growth, and also interacts with the nervous system via hypothalamic connections; in stress, it releases a hormone called ACTH, which triggers the release of steroids by the cortex of the adrenal glands; sometimes called 'the master gland' because of its many functions.

placebo effect a phenomenon whereby inert substances labelled as drugs (such as a painkiller) produce effects similar to the real drug.

plateau experience for Maslow, an experience which produces an intensified awareness of the world, and a heightened appreciation for life; a more enduring but less intense state of enhanced awareness than a peak experience.

pleasure principle an early description by Freud of the basis of human motivation, which stated we are driven to maximize pleasure (*Lust* in German) and to avoid that which is unpleasant (*Unlust*).

pons (Latin for 'bridge') a region in the brainstem below the medulla which provides connections between the cortex and cerebellum.

population in statistics, the group whose characteristics one wishes to determine, and from which a sample is chosen.

positive correlation a relationship observed between two variables in which increases in the value of one variable are associated with increases in the value of the other variable.

positive regard love and caring which satisfy a need, which Rogers regarded as universal.

positive reinforcement in operant conditioning, a process of increasing the probability of a response by immediately following the response with a desirable stimulus (a positive reinforcer).

positive reinforcer in operant conditioning, a stimulus which when it follows a response serves to increase the probability of the response in the future.

pragmatism a philosophical doctrine developed by C.S. Peirce, which argues that the significance of thoughts and behaviour can be found by examining their consequences.

preconscious in Freud's theory, that part of the subconscious mind which can be accessed by conscious choice.

preparedness a concept developed by Martin Seligman to describe the degree to which physiological structure influences the occurrence of behaviour.

primary process thinking in Freud's theory, a form of thinking characteristic of the id in which no distinction is made between a wish and its fulfilment.

primary reinforcer a stimulus whose capacity to act as a reinforcer is based on an innate biological significance, such as food or water.

priming a phenomenon whereby a thought or memory increases the activation of associated thoughts or memories (the term is analogous to 'priming a pump' by using a small quantity of water to enhance the flow of water).

proactive interference in memory, a form of interference in which prior experiences make learning and recall of subsequent experiences more difficult.

problem solving the process of determining appropriate actions in order to overcome obstacles that interfere with reaching a desired goal.

procedural memory that component of LTM which stores 'how-to' information, such as how to play a piano or cook a turkey.

projective test a type of personality test used by psychodynamic theorists in which an individual is asked to interpret an ambiguous stimulus; since the stimulus itself is ambiguous, the assumption is that whatever the person says reveals the workings of their own unconscious mind.

prosocial behaviour behaviour which is socially desirable; that is, behaviour which is beneficial to another person or to society as a whole.

psychiatrists medical doctors who specialize in treating mental disorders; by comparison, clinical psychologists typically have a PhD rather than a MD degree.

psychic determinism the assumption made by Freud which states that all behaviour has a cause, and that the cause is to be found in the mind.

psychoactive drug a chemical agent which has a discernible effect on mental state or behaviour.

psychoimmunology the study of mental states and their effect on health, as expressed through the functions of the immune system; sometimes referred to as psychoneuroimmunology.

psychology the scientific study of behaviour and experience.

punishment in operant conditioning, a process whereby a response is followed by a negative reinforcer, which results in a decrease in the probability of the response.

radical behaviourism a position adopted by Watson and Skinner, which argues that mental states are both inaccessible to scientific study and irrelevant to understanding.

random error non-systematic error produced by the variability in sampling or other natural processes.

random sample a sample obtained through a selection procedure in which everyone in the population has an equal chance of being selected.

range a statistical measure of variability which is calculated as the difference between the highest score and the lowest score in a frequency distribution.

rational-emotive therapy a form of therapy developed by Albert Ellis, which focuses on the relationship between thoughts and emotions, particularly negative emotions which arise from an individual's faulty interpretations of experiences.

rationalization a defence mechanism in which one explains behaviour by offering a reason acceptable to the ego in place of the true reason.

ratio variable a characteristic whose measurement is based on a continuous scale, with an obvious zero point.

reaction range in genetics, the limits on the variability of a phenotype (observed characteristic) determined by the genotype; in essence, the limits set by the genes on how environmental influences (whether deprivation or enrichment) can affect the trait.

reaction time the time required to make a response to a stimulus, as measured by the interval between the stimulus and the response.

reactivity the tendency for people to alter their behaviour when they are being observed.

reality principle in Freud's theory, the constraints imposed on the ego by the recognition of the demands of the environment.

recall in memory, the active retrieval of information.

recentring in Gestalt theory, developing an alternative mental set for a situation, such as when trying to solve a problem.

recognition in memory, the process of identifying presented information as familiar.

reconstruction in memory, the process of remembering by actively creating a whole out of partial information.

recovery movement a term used to refer to a variety of humanisitically oriented theories and therapies which share certain similarities in concepts and assumptions; its origins are often traced to the Twelve Step programme of Alcoholics Anonymous.

reflex an unlearned response that can be triggered by specific environmental stimuli, such as a baby's sucking on an object placed in the mouth.

regression in Freud's theory, a defence mechanism in which the individual reverts to an earlier mode of gratification.

rehearsal in STM, the process of repeating information over and over, usually silently.

reinforcement the process by which a reinforcer increases the probability of a response.

reinforcer in operant conditioning, a stimulus which, when it follows a response, results in an increase in the probability of the response recurring.

relearning in memory, an improvement in performance which occurs by reviewing, despite the inability to recall or recognize the information.

reliability a criterion for evaluating a measurement process, which assesses the consistency of measurements; often measured by comparing the correlation between repeated observations.

representative sample in statistics, a sample whose composition matches the population from which it is drawn.

repression in Freud's theory, a defence mechanism in which impulses, memories or ideas are forcibly blocked from the conscious mind.

research method a procedure for examining a problem and gathering observations; in broad terms, research methods are either experimental or non-experimental.

research setting the context in which research is conducted, either a *laboratory setting* (which involves having participants come to a special location) or a *field setting* (which requires the researcher to go to where the people are that he or she wishes to study).

resistance in psychoanalysis, the rejection by an individual of the analyst's interpretations of the meaning of behaviour; regarded as a defence mechanism.

response in general, any reaction to a stimulus, whether overt or mental; in research, the behaviour which is measured.

reticular formation a diffuse network of nerve fibres which runs through the brainstem and limbic system, with connections both up to the cortex and down to the spinal cord; the reticular formation acts as a relay network controlling sensory inputs, and thereby plays a key role in regulating arousal level, alertness and sleep.

retroactive interference in memory, a form of interference in which recent experiences make it difficult to recall something learned earlier.

sample in statistics, a subgroup drawn from a population; in research, the group which one actually studies.

sampling the process by which one selects observations for research (the sample).

sampling error an error caused by having a non-representative sample, due either to using a biased sampling procedure, or the inherent variability associated with the sampling process.

sampling variability variability due to chance variations among samples randomly drawn from the same population.

schedule of reinforcement in operant conditioning, a description of the conditions which determine when a response will be followed by a reinforcer.

schema (pl. 'schemata') a mental framework which organizes knowledge, beliefs and expectations, and is used to guide behaviour.

schizophrenia a severe form of mental disorder in which there can be distortions of perception, thought, language and emotions.

secondary process thinking in Freud's theory, a form of thinking used by the ego to direct the gratification of drives; unlike primary process thinking, secondary process thinking is accessible to conscious awareness, and recognizes constraints imposed by the external world.

selective attention the perceptual process of selectively focusing on particular stimulus elements.

self in Jung's theory, the self comprises the totality of the person, both conscious and unconscious, and is distinct from both the ego and the persona (conscious aspects of personality); for Rogers, the self is an organized cognitive structure based on our experience of our own being.

self-actualization for Maslow, self-actualization is the most advanced human need, and is based on the desire to grow and use one's capacities to their fullest; as such, it is process-oriented, not based on an underlying deficiency.

self-fulfilling prophecy a phenomenon whereby our expectations about other people leads to acting in ways which elicit the expected response from them; the everyday equivalent to experimenter bias.

self-report a method of gathering data which involves asking an individual to describe their behaviour or mental state in some way, such as an interview, survey or psychological inventory.

self-selected sample a sampling procedure which allows members of the population to decide whether to be included or not, as when a survey has a low rate of response.

self theory a general term for theories of behaviour which focus on an individual's self-concept and subjective experience of the world; pioneered by G.H. Mead, and adapted by many humanistic theorists.

semantic memory the component of LTM which involves general knowledge of the world.

sensory memory a modality-specific transient form of memory which serves as a buffer between the senses and STM.

sensory nerves neural pathways in the PNS which carry information from the sense receptors to the CNS.

sequential design a research design which combines features of both longitudinal and cross-sectional studies by selecting groups of different ages (like a cross-sectional design), and then following them over a period of time (like a longitudinal study) sufficient to create overlap in the ages represented by different groups; comparing the behaviour of individuals from different groups at the same age then allows an evaluation for possible confounds or other problems which sometimes arise in simple cross-sectional studies.

sex roles patterns of behaviour which a culture defines as being appropriate for each gender.

shadow in Jung's theory, that part of the contents of the unconscious which is personal, related to the experiences of the individual.

shame a negative feeling evoked by a perceived loss of self-esteem associated with a particular behaviour.

shaping in operant conditioning, the process of guiding the acquisition of a new response by reinforcing successive approximations to the desired response.

short-term memory (STM) the component of memory which handles retention over relatively brief intervals of up to approximately fifteen seconds.

significance level in inferential statistics, a statement of the probability that an observed outcome is due only to chance.

significance tests in statistics, the general name given to inferential statistical procedures which are used to determine whether observed results reflect real differences rather than chance variations.

sign stimuli in ethology, environmental cues which regulate the expression of behaviours related to innate drives.

single-blind design an experiment set up in such a way that subjects are kept uninformed of any details which might lead to bias.

skewed distribution an asymmetrical frequency distribution with a single mode; with a skewed distribution, the median is usually more representative than the mean as a measure of central tendency.

social cognition the mental processes involved in the way people perceive and react to social situations.

social influence a general term for the various ways in which an individual's behaviour is affected by others, such as conformity pressures and social expectations and norms.

species-specific behaviour behaviours which are characteristic of all members of a particular species; these response patterns (sometimes popularly called 'instincts') apply to behaviours such as mating, finding food, defence and raising offspring.

spontaneous recovery in classical conditioning, the reoccurrence of the CR when the CS is presented after some time has elapsed since extinction training.

spontaneous remission in medicine or therapy, improvement in an individual's condition in the absence of treatment.

stages in developmental theory, the belief that development is based on distinct periods with clear boundaries, with behaviour at each stage governed by different underlying processes; Freud's theory of psychosexual stages is one such theory.

standard deviation a commonly used measure of variability, calculated as the square root of the mean of the squared deviations from the mean of a set of scores.

state-dependent forgetting forgetting related to changes in context associated with internal cues of physical and mental state, as opposed to the context defined by the the external environment.

statistics the branch of mathematics that is concerned with the description and interpretation of sets of scores, such as scientific data.

stereotype an oversimplified and often inaccurate perception of an individual based on generalizing from schemata related to the individual's group membership.

steroids hormones produced by the cortex of the adrenal glands which are involved in the regulation of water and sugar metabolism, immune system function, and other basic bodily processes; sometimes called 'corticosteroids'.

stigma a mark or label which identifies an individual as deviant, resulting in social rejection.

stimulant a drug which increases activation of the CNS and the autonomic nervous system; these drugs tend to decrease fatigue, increase physical activity and alertness, diminish hunger and produce a temporary elevation of mood.

stimulus (often abbreviated as S) in general, any event, situation, object or factor that may affect behaviour; for the behaviourists, a stimulus must be a measurable change in the environment.

stimulus discrimination in classical conditioning, selective responding to the CS, but not to stimuli which are similar in some way, as a result of training.

stimulus generalization in classical conditioning, the tendency to produce a CR to both the original CS and to stimuli which are similar to it in some way.

stress a term coined by Hans Selye to describe the non-specific response of the body to any demand on it.

stressor any factor which triggers a stress response in an individual.

structuralism an approach to psychology pioneered by Wundt which attempted to analyse the contents of the mind, using the introspectionist method.

style of life a term used by Adler to describe an individual's unique way of adapting to and interacting with the world, which is an expression of the person's life history and goals.

subconscious in Freud's theory, the portions of the mind which are below the level of conscious awareness.

subject in research, an individual who is the object of study or the participant in an experiment.

subject bias in an experiment, systematic error created because the subjects in different groups have different information (for example, knowing whether they are in the control group or experimental group).

sublimation in Freud's theory, a defence mechanism in which drive energy is redirected towards a socially desirable creative activity.

superego in Freud's theory, that portion of the psyche which represents the moral demands of family and society, and is therefore governed by moral constraints.

superiority complex in Adler's theory, a response to feelings of inferiority in which the individual attempts to mask their weakness by adopting an attitude of exaggerated self-importance.

survey a technique for determining attitudes of many individuals by providing a pre-planned series of questions to which individuals respond.

symbiotic attachment an intense interdependency between a mother and child which prevents the child from developing a healthy, distinct ego; seen by psychodynamic theorist Margaret Mahler as the basis of schizophrenia.

symptom substitution in psychodynamic theory, the assumption that changing overt behaviour without addressing the underlying dynamics will lead to the expression of the problem in a new way.

synapse the junction between two neurons, represented by a small physical gap which is bridged by the flow of neurotransmitter chemicals from the terminals of the 'sending' neuron.

systematic desensitization a technique based on classical conditioning which is designed to treat phobias (unrealistic fears) and related anxiety disorders by gradually diminishing the undesired response.

*t***-test** in inferential statistics, a procedure for determining the significance of observed differences; a common use is to decide whether the difference between the means of two groups is due only to sampling variability.

temperament behavioural tendencies which are believed to be determined by heredity; examples include emotionality, sociability and fearfulness.

temporal lobe the region of the cortex below the lateral fissure; its primary functions are hearing and memory.

theory a structured set of principles intended to explain a set of phenomena.

think-aloud protocol a transcript of the comments made when an individual is asked to describe their thoughts and behaviour while working on a task such as problem solving.

thought disturbances in abnormal psychology, distortions of thinking processes such as violations of logic, incoherent speech and inappropriate shifts in word usage.

token economy a form of behaviour modification based on operant conditioning; most commonly used in institutional settings, it involves giving conditioned reinforcers ('tokens') for doing specific behaviours.

toxic shame in the recovery movement, feelings of shame which are applied to one's whole being rather than specific actions, resulting in severe loss of self-worth.

trait a behaviour pattern which occurs consistently across a range of situations; a specific personality characteristic.

transference in psychoanalysis, the displacement of drive energy from past relationships, often between the individual and a parent, to the relationship between the individual and the therapist.

unconditional positive regard acceptance and caring given to a person as a human being, without imposing conditions on how the person behaves.

unconditioned response in classical conditioning, a reflexive response produced by a specific stimulus, such as pupil contraction to bright light.

unconditioned stimulus in classical conditioning, a stimulus which elicits a reflexive (unconditioned) response.

unconscious in Freud's theory, that portion of the subconscious which cannot be accessed directly by the conscious mind; nonetheless, impulses and thoughts from the unconscious can 'leak out' in fragmentary intrusions into conscious awareness, either directly or in symbolic form.

unigenic inheritance genetic transmission which is dependent on the action of a single pair of genes; also called Mendelian inheritance, in recognition of Gregor Mendel's pioneering work.

unlearning an alternative interpretation of the interference theory of memory, which holds that the build-up of interference can lead to the breaking of associations, and therefore the destruction of memories.

unobtrusive measure an indirect measure of behaviour intended to avoid the reactivity which can occur with direct observation; such measures typically require making complex assumptions about the relationship of the measure to actual behaviour.

vacuum activities in ethology, behaviours which arise in the absence of appropriate environmental stimuli when drive levels are very high.

validity a criterion for evaluating a measurement process, which assesses whether the variable measures the intended characteristic, as opposed to some other characteristic.

variability in statistics, the dispersion of scores within a set of data.

variable any measured characteristic which shows variation across cases or conditions.

variable interval (VI) schedule in operant conditioning, a reinforcement contingency defined by the average time interval which must elapse since the last reinforcer before a response will be reinforced; thus, on a VI 15 sec schedule, over a long period the average duration would be fifteen seconds.

variable ratio (VR) schedule in operant conditioning, a reinforcement contingency defined in terms of the average number of responses required to receive a reinforcer; thus, VR 10 means that on average every tenth response is reinforced.

visual agnosia a general term for disorders which result in disruption of visual recognition.

voluntary response a response which is controlled by the individual (i.e. emitted) rather than being triggered by specific stimuli as reflexes are.

wish fulfilment in Freud's theory, the symbolic expression of drives in fantasy form, as in dreams.

would–should dilemma the conflict between one's own needs, expressed through the actualizing tendency, and the demands of others, expressed through the ideal self.

References

Abrams, J. (Ed.) (1990) *Reclaiming the Inner Child*. Los Angeles, CA: Jeremy P. Tarcher.

Ader, R. and Cohen, N. (1975) Behaviorally conditioned immunosuppression. *Psychosomatic Medicine*, **37**, 333–40.

Ader, R. and Cohen, N. (1985) CNS-immune system interactions: Conditioning phenomena. *Behavioral and Brain Sciences*, **8**, 379–94.

Allport, G. (1955) *Becoming*. New Haven, CT: Yale University Press.

Amábile-Cuevas, C.F. and Chicurel, M.E. (1993) Horizontal gene transfer. *American Scientist*, **81**, 332–41.

American Psychiatric Association (1978) *Diagnostic and Statistical Manual of Mental Disorders*. 3rd edn. revised. Washington DC: American Psychiatric Association.

Amsel, E., Langer, R. and Lontzenhiser, L. (1991) Do lawyers reason differently from psychologists? A comparative design for studying expertise. In R.J. Sternberg and P.A. Frensch (Eds), *Complex Problem Solving: Principles and Mechanisms*, pp. 223–50. Hillsdale, NJ: Lawrence Erlbaum Associates.

Anderson, E. (1994) The code of the streets. *The Atlantic Monthly*, May, 81–94.

Angell, M. (1985) Editorial, *New England Journal of Medicine*, June, 6–7.

Ansbacher, H.L. and Ansbacher, R. (Eds) (1956) *The Individual Psychology of Alfred Adler: A Systematic Presentation in Selections from his Writings*. New York: Basic Books.

Arieti, S. (1974) An overview of schizophrenia from a predominantly psychological approach. *American Journal of Psychiatry*, **131**(3), 241–9.

Aronson, E. (1976) *The Social Animal*, 2nd edn. San Francisco, CA: W.H. Freeman.

Atkinson, R.C. and Shiffrin, R.M. (1968) Human memory: A proposed system and its control processes. In K.W. Spence and J.T. Spence (Eds), *The Psychology of Learning and Memory*, Vol. 2. New York: Academic Press.

Atthowe, J. and Krasner, L. (1968) Preliminary report on the application of contingent reinforcement procedures (token economy) on a 'chronic' psychiatric ward. *Journal of Abnormal Psychology*, **73**(1), 37–43.

Ayllon, T. and Azrin, N.H. (1968) *The Token Economy: A Motivational System For Therapy and Rehabilitation*. Englewood Cliffs, N.J.: Prentice-Hall.

Azrin, N.H. and Holz, W.C. (1966) Punishment. In N.K. Honig (Ed.), *Operant Behavior*, pp. 380–447. New York: Appleton-Century-Crofts.

Baars, B.J. (1986) *The Cognitive Revolution in Psychology*. New York: Guilford Press.

Baker, B.L. (1969) Symptom treatment and symptom substitution in enuresis. *Journal of Abnormal Psychology*, **74**, 42–9.

Bandura, A. (1970) Modelling therapy. In W.S. Sahakian (Ed.), *Psychopathology Today: Experimentation, Theory, and Research*. Itasca, IL: Peacock Press.

Bandura, A. (1973) *Aggression: A Social Learning Analysis*. Englewood Cliffs, NJ: Prentice-Hall.

Bandura, A. (1977) *Social Learning Theory*. Englewood Cliffs, NJ: Prentice-Hall.

Bandura, A. (1986) *Social Foundations of Thought and Action: A Social Cognitive Theory*. Englewood Cliffs, NJ: Prentice-Hall.

Bandura, A., Ross, D. and Ross, S.A. (1961) Transmission of aggression through imitation of aggressive models. *Journal of Abnormal and Social Psychology*, **63**, 575–82.

Baronides, S. (1993) *Molecules and Mental Illness*. New York: Scientific American Library.

Bartlett, F.C. (1932) *Remembering: A Study in Experimental and Social Psychology*. Cambridge: Cambridge University Press.

Bassuk, E.L. and Gerson, S. (1978) Deinstitutionalization and mental health services. *Scientific American*, **238**, 46–53.

Bateson, G., Jackson, D.D., Haley, J. and Weakland, J.H. (1956) Toward a theory of schizophrenia. *Behavioral Science*, **1**, 251–64.

Baumrind, D. (1964) Some thoughts on ethics of research: After reading Milgram's 'Behavioral study of obedience'. *American Psychologist*, **19**, 421–3.

Beadle, G. and Beadle, M. (1966) *The Language of Life*. New York: Doubleday.

Bell, A.P., Weinberg, M.S. and Hammersmith, S.K. (1981) *Sexual Preference: Its Development in Men and Women*. Bloomington, IN: Indiana University Press.

Belson, W.A. (1978) *Television Violence and the Adolescent Boy*. Hampshire, England: Saxon House.

Benson, H. (1976) *The Relaxation Response*. New York: Morrow.

Berkowitz, L. (1975) *A Survey of Social Psychology*. Hillsdale, IL: Dryden Press.

Berkowitz, L. (1978) Whatever happened to the frustration–aggression hypothesis? *American Behavioral Scientist*, **21**, 691–708.

Berkowitz, L. (1983) Aversively stimulated aggression. *American Psychologist*, **38**, 1135–44.

Berkowitz, L. (1984) Some effects of thoughts on anti- and prosocial influences of media events: A cognitive-neoassociation analysis. *Psychological Bulletin*, **95**, 410–27.

Berlyne, D.E. (1975) Behaviourism? Cognitive theory? Humanistic psychology? – To Hull with them all! *Canadian Psychological Review*, **16**, 69–80.

Berne, E. (1961) *Transactional Analysis in Psychotherapy*. New York: Grove Press.

Berne, E. (1973) *Games People Play*. New York: Grove Press.

Bick, P.A. and Kinsbourne, M. (1987) Auditory hallucinations and subvocal speech in schizophrenic patients. *American Journal of Psychiatry*, **144**, 222–5.

Blackburn, T. (1971) Sensuous–intellectual complementarity in science. *Science*, **172**, 1003–7.

Blakemore, C. (1977) *Mechanisms of the Mind*. Cambridge: Cambridge University Press.

Block, N. (1990) The computer model of the mind. In D.N. Osherson and E.E. Smith (Eds), *An Invitation to Cognitive Science, Vol. 3: Thinking*. Cambridge, MA: MIT Press.

Bloom, H.E. (1981) *The Linguistic Shaping of Thought: A Study of the Impact of Language on Thinking in China and the West*. Hillsdale, NJ: Lawrence Erlbaum Associates.

Borysenko, J. (1990) *Guilt is the Teacher, Love is the Lesson*. New York: Warner.

Bouchard, T.J., Jr, Lykken, D.T., McGue, M., Segal, N.L. and Tellegen, A. (1990) Sources of human psychological differences: The Minnesota study of twins reared apart. *Science*, **250**, 223–8.

Bower, T.G.R. (1979) *Human Development*. San Francisco, CA: W.H. Freeman.

Bowlby, J. (1969) *Attachment and Loss, Vol. 1: Attachment*. London: Hogarth Press.

Bradshaw, J. (1988) *Healing the Shame that Binds You*. Deerfield Beach, FL.: Health Communications.

Brandt, L.W. (1982) *Psychologists Caught: A Psycho-Logic of Psychology*. Toronto: University of Toronto Press.

Bregman, E. (1934) An attempt to modify emotional attitude of infants by the conditioned response technique. *Journal of Genetic Psychology*, **45**, 169–98.

Brenner, C. (1955) *An Elementary Textbook of Psychoanalysis*. Garden City, NY: Doubleday Anchor.

Brenner, C. (1957) Appendix. In J. Rickman (Ed.), *A General Selection From The Works of Sigmund Freud*. Garden City, NY: Doubleday.

Brown, G.W. and Harris, T.O. (Eds) (1989) *Life Events and Illness*. New York: Guilford Press.

Brown, R. (1972) Schizophrenia, language, and reality. Eastern Psychological Association Presidential Address, Boston.

Brown, R. (1973) Development of the first language in the human species. *American Psychologist*, **28**, 97–106.

Brown, R. and Herrnstein, R.J. (1975) *Psychology*. Boston, MA: Little, Brown.

Bruner, J.S., Goodnow, J.J. and Austin, G.A. (1956) *A Study of Thinking*. New York: John Wiley.

Buford, B. (1991) *Among the Thugs*. London: Mandarin.

Buss, A. (1963) Physical aggression in relation to different frustrations. *Journal of Abnormal and Social Psychology*, **67**, 1–7.

Byne, W. (1994) The biological evidence challenged. *Scientific American*, **270**, 50–5.

Campbell, J. (1982) *Grammatical Man: Information, Entropy, Language and Life*. New York: Simon and Schuster.

Caporeal, L.R. (1976) Ergotism: The Satan loosed in Salem? *Science*, **192**, 21–6.

Carlson, N. (1990) *Psychology: The Science of Behavior*. Boston, MA: Allyn and Bacon.

Carlsson, A. (1978) Antipsychotic drugs, neurotransmitters, and schizophrenia. *American Journal of Psychiatry*, **135**, 164–73.

Carmichael, L., Hogan, H.P. and Walter, A.A. (1932) An experimental study of the effect of language on the reproduction of visually perceived items. *Journal of Experimental Psychology*, **15**, 73–86.

Cermak, T.L. (1985) *A Primer on Adult Children of Alcoholics*. Pompano Beach, FL: Health Communications.

Chance, P. (1988) *Learning and Behavior*, 2nd edn. Belmont, CA: Wadsworth.

Chapman, J. (1966) The early symptoms of schizophrenia. *British Journal of Psychiatry*, **112**, 225–51.

Chomsky, N. (1988) *Language and Problems of Knowledge*. Cambridge, MA: MIT Press.

Chorover, S.L. (1985) Psychology in cultural context: The division of labor and the fragmentation of experience. In S. Koch and D.E. Leary (Eds), *A Century of Psychology as Science*, pp. 870–9. New York: McGraw-Hill.

Clausen, J.A. (1981) Stigma and mental disorder: Phenomena and mental terminology. *Psychiatry*, **44**, 287–96.

Cooper, J.R., Bloom, F.E. and Roth, R.H. (1991) *The Biochemical Basis of Neuropharmacology*, 6th edn. New York: Oxford University Press.

Cousins, N. (1989) *Head First: The Biology of Hope*. New York: E.P. Dutton.

Craik, F.I.M. and Lockhart, R.S. (1972) Levels of processing: A framework for memory research. *Journal of Verbal Learning and Verbal Behavior*, **11**, 671–84.

Cramer, D. (1992) *Personality and Psychotherapy: Theory, Practice and Research*. Milton Keynes: Open University Press.

Crick, F. and Koch, C. (1992) The problem of consciousness. *Scientific American*, September, 153–9.

Crowder, R. and Morton, J. (1969) Pre-categorical acoustic storage (PAS). *Perception and Psychophysics*, **8**, 815–20.

Cytowic, R.E. (1993) *The Man Who Tasted Shapes*. New York: Tarcher/Putnam.

Darwin, C. (1859) *The Origin of Species*. New York: Washington Square Press (reprinted 1963).

Darwin, C. (1872) *The Expression of the Emotions in Man and Animals*. Chicago, IL: University of Chicago Press (reprinted 1965).

Davis, P.J. and Schwartz, G.E. (1987) Repression and the inaccessibility of affective memories. *Journal of Personality and Social Psychology*, **52**, 155–62.

Deaux, K. (1985) Sex and gender. *Annual Review of Psychology*, **36**, 49–81.

deBono, E. (1976) *Practical Thinking*. Harmondsworth: Penguin.

Delgado, J.M.R. (1969) *Physical Control of the Mind: Toward a Psycho-civilized Society*. New York: Harper and Row.

Delgado, J.M.R., Roberts, W.W. and Miller, N.E. (1954) Learning motivated by electrical stimulation of the brain. *American Journal of Physiology*, **179**, 587–93.

Dollard, J. and Miller, N.E. (1950) *Personality and Psychotherapy*. New York: McGraw-Hill.

Dollard, J., Doob, L., Miller, N., Mowrer, O. and Sears, R. (1939) *Frustration and Aggression*. New Haven, CT: Yale University Press.

Dourley, J.P. (1992) *A Strategy for a Loss of Faith: Jung's Proposal*. Toronto: Inner City Books.

D'Zurilla, T. (1965) Recall efficiency and mediating cognitive events in 'experimental repression'. *Journal of Personality and Social Psychology*, **1**, 253–7.

Eaton, W.O. and Enns, L.R. (1986) Sex differences in human motor activity. *Psychological Bulletin*, **100**, 19–28.

Edelman, G.M. (1992) *Bright Air, Brilliant Fire*. New York: Basic Books.

Editors (1993) High anxiety. *Consumer Reports*, January, 19–24.

Elkin, I., Shea, M.T., Watkins, J.T., Imber, S.D., Sotsky, S.M., Collins, J.F., Glass, D.R., Pilkonis, P.A., Leber, W.R., Kocherty, J.P., Fiester, S.J. and Parloff, M.B. (1989) National Institutes of Mental Health treatment of depression collaborative research program: General effectiveness of treatments. *Archives of General Psychiatry*, **46**, 971–82.

Ellis, A. (1993) Fundamentals of rational-emotive therapy for the 1990s. In W. Dryden, and L.K. Hill (Eds), *Innovations in Rational-emotive Therapy*. Newbury Park, CA: Sage.

Ellis, L., Ames, M.A., Peckham, W. and Burke, D. (1988) Sexual orientation of human offspring may be altered by severe maternal stress during pregnancy. *Journal of Sex Research*, **25**, 152–7.

Emmelkamp, P.M.G., Kuipers, A.C.M. and Eggeraat, J.B. (1978) Cognitive modification versus prolonged exposure *in vivo*: A comparison with agoraphobics as subjects. *Behavior Research and Therapy*, **16**, 33–42.

Endler, N.S. (1982) *Holiday of Darkness: A Psychologist's Personal Journey out of His Depression*. New York: John Wiley.

Ericsson, K.A. and Chase, W.A. (1982) Exceptional memory. *American Scientist*, **70**, 607–15.

Erikson, E.H. (1962) *Young Man Luther*. New York: W.W. Norton.

Erikson, E.H. (1963) *Childhood and Society*, 2nd edn. New York: W.W. Norton.

Eron, L.D. (1963) Relationship of TV viewing habits and aggressive behavior in children. *Journal of Abnormal and Social Psychology*, **67**, 193–6.

Eron, L.D. (1982) Parent–child interaction, television violence, and aggression of children. *American Psychologist*, **37**, 197–211.

Eron, L.D., Walder, L.O. and Lefkowitz, M.M. (1971) *The Learning of Aggression in Children*. Boston, MA: Little, Brown.

Eysenck, M.W. (1993) *Principles of Cognitive Psychology*. Hillsdale, NJ: Lawrence Erlbaum Associates.

Fadiman, J. and Frager, R. (1976) *Personality and Personal Growth*. New York: Harper and Row.

Faller, K.C. (1988) *Child Sexual Abuse: An Interdisciplinary Manual for Diagnosis, Case Management, and Treatment*. New York: Columbia University Press.

Fancher, R.E. (1979) *Pioneers of Psychology*. New York: W.W. Norton.

Ferguson, G.A. (1981) *Statistical Analysis in Psychology and Education*, 5th edn. New York: McGraw-Hill.

Ferster, C.B. and Skinner, B.F. (1957) *Schedules of Reinforcement*. New York: Appleton-Century-Crofts.

Feshbach, S. (1955) The drive-reducing function of fantasy behavior. *Journal of Abnormal and Social Psychology*, **50**, 3–11.

Festinger, L. (1957) *A Theory of Cognitive Dissonance*. Stanford, CA: Stanford University Press.

Festinger, L. and Carlsmith, J.M. (1959) Cognitive consequences of forced compliance. *Journal of Abnormal and Social Psychology*, **58**, 203–10.

Feynman, R. (1988) *What Do You Care What People Think? Further Adventures of a Curious Character*. New York: W.W. Norton.

Ford, C.S. and Beach, F.A. (1951) *Patterns of Sexual Behavior*. New York: Harper and Row.

Forest, D.V. (1976) Nonsense and sense in schizophrenic language. *Schizophrenia Bulletin*, **2**, 286–381.

Forrest, G.G. (1985) Antabuse treatment. In T.E. Bratter, and G.G. Forrest (Eds), *Alcoholism and Substance Abuse: Strategies for Clinical Intervention*. New York: Free Press.

Fouts, R.S., Hirsch, A. and Fouts, D. (1983) Cultural transmission of a human language in a chimpanzee mother/infant relationship. In H.E. Fitzgerald, J.A. Mullins and P. Page (Eds), *Psychological Perspectives: Child Nurturance Series*, Vol. III. New York: Plenum Press.

Frank, J.D. (1963) *Persuasion and Healing*. New York: Schocken Books.

Frankl, V.E. (1992) *Man's Search for Meaning*, 4th edn. Boston, MA: Beacon Press.

Fraser, C. (1987) Social psychology. In R.L. Gregory (Ed.), *The Oxford Companion to the Mind*, pp. 721–3. New York: Oxford University Press.

Freedman, J.L. (1984) Effect of television violence on aggressiveness. *Psychological Bulletin*, **96**, 227–46.

Freedman, J.L. (1986) Television violence and aggression: A rejoinder. *Psychological Bulletin*, **100**, 372–8.

Freidrich-Cofer, L. and Huston, A.C. (1986) Television violence and aggression: The debate continues. *Psychological Bulletin*, **98**, 1–20.

Freud, A. (1936) *The Ego and the Mechanisms of Defense* (C.M. Baines, Trans.). New York: International Universities Press (reprinted 1946).

Freud, S. (1900) *The Interpretation of Dreams*. (This reference refers to the original German date of publication for a volume later printed in translation as part of J. Strachey (Ed.), *The Standard Edition of the Complete Psychological Works of Sigmund Freud*, Vols 1–24. London: Hogarth Press, 1953–66.)

Freud, S. (1904) *Psychopathology in Everyday Life*. Reprinted in S. Freud, *A General Introduction to Psychoanalysis* (J. Riviere, Trans.). New York: Washington Square Press (reprinted 1952).

Freud, S. (1905) *Three Essays on Sexuality* (This reference refers to the original German date of publication for a volume later printed in translation as part of J. Strachey (Ed.), *The Standard Edition of the Complete Psychological Works of Sigmund Freud*, Vols 1–24. London: Hogarth Press, 1953–66.)

Freud, S. (1913) *Totem and Taboo* op cit.

Freud, S. (1920) *Beyond the Pleasure Principle* op cit.

Freud, S. (1923) *The Ego and the Id* op cit.

Freud, S. (1924) *A General Introduction to Psychoanalysis* (J. Riviere, Trans.). New York: Washington Square Press (reprinted 1952).

Freud, S. (1926) *The Problem of Anxiety* (H.A. Bunker, Trans.) New York: W.W. Norton (reprinted 1936).

Freud, S. (1930) *Civilization and its Discontents*. (This reference refers to the original German date of publication for a volume later printed in translation as part of J. Strachey (Ed.), *The Standard Edition of the Complete Psychological Works of Sigmund Freud*, Vols 1–24. London: Hogarth Press, 1953–66.)

Frey, D. (1986) Recent research on selective exposure to information. *Advances in Experimental Social Psychology*, **19**, 41–80.

Fromkin, V.A. (1973) *Speech Errors as Linguistic Evidence*. The Hague: Mouton.

Gantt, W.H. (1966) Reflexology, schizokinesis, and autokinesis. *Conditioned Reflex*, **1**, 57–68.

Garcia, J., Hankins, W.G. and Rusniak, K. (1974) Behavioral regulation of the milieu interne in man and rat. *Science*, **185**, 824–31.

Gardner, A. and Gardner, B. (1969) Teaching sign language to a chimpanzee. *Science*, **165**, 664–77.

Gardner, H. (1985) *The Mind's New Science: A History of the Cognitive Revolution*. New York: Basic Books.

Geen, R. (1976) Observing violence in the mass media: Implications of basic research. In R. Geen and E. O'Neal (Eds), *Perspectives on Aggression*. New York: Academic Press.

Geen, R.G., Stonner, D. and Shope, G.I. (1975) The facilitation of aggression by aggression: A study in response inhibition and disinhibition. *Journal of Personality and Social Psychology*, **31**, 721–6.

Gershon, E.S. and Rieder, R.O. (1992) Major disorders of mind and brain. *Scientific American*, September, 127–33.

Glass, D.C. and Singer, J.E. (1972) *Urban Stress*. New York: Academic Press.

Glassman, W.E. (1972) Subvocal activity and acoustic confusions in short-term memory. *Journal of Experimental Psychology*, **96**, 164–9.

Godden, D. and Baddeley, A.D. (1975) Context-dependent memory in two natural environments. *British Journal of Psychology*, **66**, 325–31.

Goffman, E. (1963) *Stigma*. Englewood Cliffs, NJ: Prentice-Hall.

Goldiamond, I. (1973) A diary of self-modification. *Psychology Today*, November, 53–7.

Goldstein, K. (1939) *The Organism*. New York: American Book Co.

Goldstein, K. (1950) Prefrontal lobotomy: Analysis and warning. *Scientific American*, February, 36–41.

Goleman, D. (1993) Studying the pivotal role of bystanders, *The New York Times*, June 22, C1, C6.

Goodall, J. (1990) *Through a Window: My Thirty Years with the Chimpanzees of Gombe*. Boston, MA: Houghton Mifflin.

Gorcynski, R.M., Macrae, S. and Kennedy, M. (1982) Conditioned immune response associated with allogenic skin grafts in mice. *Journal of Immunology*, **29**, 704–9.

Gould, S.J. (1981) *The Mismeasure of Man*. New York: W.W. Norton.

Green, M.E. (1993) Cognitive remediation in schizophrenia: Is it time yet? *American Journal of Psychiatry*, **150**, 178–87.

Grice, G.R. and Hunter, J.J. (1964) Stimulus intensity effects depend on the type of experimental design. *Psychological Review*, **71**, 247–56.

Guilford, J.P. (1967) *The Nature of Human Intelligence.* New York: McGraw-Hill.

Hall, G.S. (1924) Preface to the American edition. In S. Freud, *A General Introduction to Psychoanalysis* (J. Riviere, Trans.). New York: Washington Square Press (reprinted 1952).

Hall, M.H. (1968) A conversation with Abraham Maslow. *Psychology Today*, 2(2), 34–7, 54–7.

Halpern, D. (1989) *Thought and Knowledge: An Introduction to Critical Thinking*, 2nd edn. Hillsdale, NJ: Lawrence Erlbaum Associates.

Harlow, H.F. (1949) The formation of learning sets. *Psychological Review*, **56**, 51–65.

Heath, R.G. (1972) Pleasure and brain activity in man. *Journal of Nervous and Mental Disease*, **154**, 3–18.

Hebb, D.O. (1953) Heredity and environment in mammalian behaviour. *British Journal of Animal Behaviour*, **1**, 43–7.

Heider, F. (1958) *The Psychology of Interpersonal Relations.* New York: John Wiley.

Heinrichs, R.W. (1993) Schizophrenia and the brain: Conditions for a neuropsychology of madness. *American Psychologist*, **48**, 221–33.

Hetherington, E.M. and Frankie, G. (1967) Effect of parental dominance, warmth, and conflict on imitation in children. *Journal of Personality and Social Psychology*, **6**, 119–25.

Hilborn, R.C. (1994) *Chaos and Nonlinear Dynamics: An Introduction for Scientists and Engineers.* New York: Oxford University Press.

Hirai, T. (1978) *Zen and the Mind.* Tokyo: Japan Publications.

Hirsch, J. (1963) Behavior genetics and individuality understood. *Science*, **142**, 1436–42.

Hite, S. (1987) *The Hite Report. Women and Love: A Cultural Revolution in Progress.* New York: Knopf.

Hofling, C.K., Brotzman, E., Dalrymple, S., Graves, N. and Pierce, C.M. (1966) An experimental study in nurse–physician relationships. *Journal of Nervous and Mental Disease*, **143**, 171–80.

Hofstadter, D.R. (1979) *Gödel, Escher, Bach: An Eternal Golden Braid.* New York: Basic Books.

Hohmann, G.W. (1966) Some effects of spinal cord lesions on experienced emotional feelings, *Psychophysiology*, **3**, 143–56.

Horney, K. (1950) *Neurosis and Human Growth: The Struggle Toward Self-Realization.* New York: W.W. Norton.

Huber, P.W. (1991) *Galileo's Revenge: Junk Science in the Courtroom.* New York: Basic Books.

Hunt, E. (1991) Some comments on the study of complexity. In R.J. Sternberg and P.A. Frensch (Eds), *Complex Problem Solving: Principles and Mechanisms.* Hillsdale, NJ: Lawrence Erlbaum Associates.

Hunt, M. (1993) *The Story of Psychology.* New York: Doubleday.

Huston, A.C., Carpenter, C.J. and Atwater, J.B. (1986) Gender, adult structuring of activities, and social behavior in middle childhood. *Child Development*, **57**, 1200–9.

Isaacs, W., Thomas, J. and Goldiamond, I. (1960) Application of operant conditioning to reinstate verbal behavior in psychotics. *Journal of Speech and Hearing Disorders*, **25**, 8–12.

Jablensky, A., Sartorius, N., Ernberg, G., Anker, M., Korten, A., Cooper, J.E., Day, R. and Bertelsen, A. (1992) Schizophrenia: Manifestations, incidence and course in different cultures. A World Health Organization ten-country study. *Psychological Medicine, Monograph Supplements*, **20** (Whole issue).

James, W. (1884) Some omissions of introspective psychology. *Mind*, **9**, 1–26.

James, W. (1890) *The Principles of Psychology*. New York: Dover (reprinted 1950).

James, W. (1902) *The Varieties of Religious Experience*. New York: Collier (reprinted 1961).

Jenkins, J.G. and Dallenbach, K.M. (1924) Oblivescence during sleep and waking. *American Journal of Psychology*, **35**, 605–12.

Jones, E.E. and Pulos, S.M. (1993) Comparing the process in psychodynamic and cognitive-behavioral therapies. *Journal of Consulting and Clinical Psychology*, **61**, 306–16.

Joy, L.A., Kimball, M.M. and Zabrack, M.I. (1986) Television and children's aggressive behavior. In T.W. Williams (Ed.), *The Impact of Television: A Natural Experiment in Three Communities*, pp. 303–60. New York: Academic Press.

Jung, C.G. (1958) The psychology of the child archetype. In V.S. deLaszlo (Ed.), *Psyche and Symbol*. Garden City, NY: Doubleday.

Jung, C.G. (1963) *Memories, Dreams, Reflections*. New York: Pantheon Books.

Jung, C.G. and von Franz, M.-L. (Eds) (1964) *Man and His Symbols*. London: Aldus.

Kabat-Zinn, J., Lipworth, L. and Burney, R. (1985) The clinical use of mindfulness meditation for the self-regulation of chronic pain. *Journal of Behavioral Medicine*, **8**, 163–90.

Kagan, J. (1989) Temperamental contributions to social behavior. *American Psychologist*, **44**, 668–74.

Kaminer, W. (1993) *I'm Dysfunctional, You're Dysfunctional*. New York: Vintage Books.

Karen, R. (1992) Shame. *The Atlantic Monthly*, February, 40–70.

Kazdin, A.E. and Wilson, G.T. (1980) *Evaluation of Behavior Therapy: Issues, Evidence, and Research Strategies*. Lincoln, NB: University of Nebraska Press.

Kellogg, R. (1967) *The Psychology of Children's Art*. San Diego, CA: CRM.

Kelly, G.A. (1955) *A Theory of Personality: The Psychology of Personal Constructs*. New York: W.W. Norton.

Kelman, H.C. (1967) Human use of human subjects: The problem of deception in social psychological experiments. *Psychological Bulletin*, **67**, 1–11.

Kelsoe, J.R., Ginns, E.I., Egeland, J.A., Gerhard, D.S., Goldstein, A.M., Bale, S.J., Pauls, D.L., Long, R.T., Kidd, K.K., Conte, G., Housman, D.E. and Paul, S.M. (1989) Re-evaluation of the linkage relationship between chromosome 11p loci and the gene for bipolar disorder in the Old Order Amish. *Nature*, **342**, 238–43.

Kendell, R.E. (1987) Schizophrenia. In R.L. Gregory (Ed.), *The Oxford Companion to the Mind*, pp. 697–9. New York: Oxford University Press.

Keneally, T. (1982) *Schindler's List*. New York: Simon and Schuster.

Kimura, D. (1992) Sex differences in the brain. *Scientific American*, **267**, 118–25.

King, A. (1971) *A Married Couple*. Toronto: NFB Films.

Klama, J. (1988) *Aggression: Conflict in Animals and Humans Reconsidered*. London: Longman.

Kluver, H. (1966) *Mescal and Mechanisms of Hallucinations*. Chicago, IL: University of Chicago Press.

Koch, S. (1985) The nature and limits of psychological knowledge: Lessons of a century *qua* 'science'. In S. Koch and D.E. Leary (Eds), *A Century of Psychology as a Science*, pp. 75–97. New York: McGraw-Hill.

Koch, S. and Leary, D.E. (Eds) (1985) *A Century of Psychology as a Science*. New York: McGraw-Hill.

Kohlberg, L. (1966) A cognitive-developmental analysis of children's sex-role concepts and attitudes. In E.E. Maccoby (Ed.), *The Development of Sex Differences*. Stanford, CA: Stanford University Press.

Kohler, W. (1925) *The Mentality of Apes*. New York: Harcourt, Brace and World.

Konner, M. (1982) *The Tangled Web: Biological Constraints on the Human Spirit*. New York: Holt, Rinehart and Winston.

Krasner, L. (1976) On the death of behavior modification: Some comments from a mourner. *American Psychologist*, **31**, 387–8.

Krippner, S. (1972) The plateau experience: A.H. Maslow and others. *Journal of Transpersonal Psychology*, **4**, 107–20.

Kuhn, T. (1970) *The Structure of Scientific Revolutions*, 2nd edn. London: Cambridge University Press.

Labouvie-Vief, G. (1985) Intelligence and cognition. In J.E. Birren and K.W. Schaie (Eds), *Handbook of the Psychology of Aging*, 2nd edn. New York: Van Nostrand.

LaFond, J.Q. and Durham, M.L. (1992) *Back to the Asylum*. New York: Oxford University Press.

Laing, R.D. (1965) *The Divided Self: An Existential Study in Sanity and Madness*. Baltimore, MD: Penguin.

Laing, R.D. (1967) *The Politics of Experience*. New York: Pantheon.

Langer, E.J. and Rodin, J. (1976) The effects of choice and enhanced personal responsibility for the aged: A field experiment in an institutional setting. *Journal of Personality and Social Psychology*, **34**, 191–8.

LaPiere, R.T. (1934) Attitudes and actions. *Social Forces*, **13**, 230–37.

Latané, B. and Darley, J. (1969) Bystander 'Apathy'. *American Scientist*, **57**, 222–68.

Lee, T.F. (1991) *The Human Genome Project: Cracking the Genetic Code of Life*. New York: Plenum Press.

Lenneberg, E.H. (1967) *Biological Foundations of Language*. New York: John Wiley.

Leo, J. (1985) A therapist in every corner. *Time*, 23 December, 39.

LeVay, S. (1993) *The Sexual Brain*. Cambridge, MA: MIT Press.

LeVay, S. and Hamer, D.H. (1994) Evidence for a biological influence in male homosexuality. *Scientific American*, **270**, 44–9.

Levine, M. (1976) Hunting for hypotheses. In M.H. Siegel and H.P. Ziegler (Eds), *Psychological Research: The Inside Story*. New York: Harper and Row.

Liebert, R.M. and Sprafkin, J. (1988) *The Early Window: Effects of Television on Children and Youth*, 3rd edn. Oxford: Pergamon Press.

Lin, K. and Kleinman, A.M. (1988) Psychopathology and clinical course of schizophrenia: A cross-cultural perspective. *Schizophrenia Bulletin*, **14**, 555–67.

Locke, J. (1690) *An Essay Concerning Human Understanding*. Oxford: P.H. Nidditch (reprinted 1975).

Loftus, E. (1980) *Memory*. Reading, MA: Addison-Wesley.

Loftus, E. and Hoffman, H. (1989) Misinformation and memory: The creation of new memories. *Journal of Experimental Psychology: General*, **118**, 100–4.

Logue, A.W. (1988) A comparison of taste aversion learning in humans and other vertebrates: Evolutionary pressures in common. In R.C. Bolles, and M.D. Beecher (Eds), *Evolution and Learning*. Hillsdale, NJ: Lawrence Erlbaum Associates.

London, P. (1974) From the long couch for the sick to the push button for the bored. *Psychology Today*, June, 63–8.

Lorenz, K. (1967) *On Aggression*. New York: Bantam.

Luborsky, L. and Spence, D.P. (1978) Quantitative research on psychoanalytic therapy. In A.E. Bergin and S.L. Garfield (Eds), *Handbook of Psychotherapy and Behavior Change: An Empirical Analysis*, 2nd edn. New York: John Wiley.

Luchins, A.S. (1942) Mechanization in problem-solving: The effect of *einstellung*. *Psychological Monographs*, **54**, No. 248 (Whole issue).

Luria, A.R. (1968) *The Mind of a Mnemonist*. New York: Basic Books.

Maccoby, E.E. (1992) The role of parents in the socialization of children: An historical overview. *Developmental Psychology*, **28**, 1006–17.

Maccoby, E.E. and Jacklin, C.N. (1974) *The Psychology of Sex Differences*. Stanford, CA: Stanford University Press.

MacLean, P.D. (1990) *The Triune Brain in Evolution: Role in Paleocerebral Functions*. New York: Plenum Press.

Maddi, S. (1974) Freud's most famous patient: The victimization of Dora. *Psychology Today*, September, 32–5.

Maher, B. (1972) The language of schizophrenia: A review and interpretation. *British Journal of Psychiatry*, **120**, 3–17.

Mahler, M.S., Pine, F. and Bergman, A. (1975) *The Psychological Birth of the Human Infant*. New York: Basic Books.

Maier, S.F. and Laudenslager, M. (1985) Stress and health: Exploring the links. *Psychology Today*, August, 44–9.

Marcus, D.E. and Overton, W.F. (1978) The development of cognitive gender constancy and sex-role preferences. *Child Development*, **49**, 434–44.

Mark, V.H. and Ervin, F.R. (1970) *Violence and the Brain*. New York: Harper and Row.

Marler, P. (1970) A comparative approach to vocal learning: Song development in white-crowned sparrows. *Journal of Comparative and Physiological Psychology*, **7**, 1–25.

Martin, C.L. and Halverson, C.E., Jr (1983) The effects of sex-typing schemas on young children's memory. *Child Development*, **54**, 563–74.

Martin, C.L. and Halverson, C.E., Jr (1987) The roles of cognition in sex-roles and sex-typing. In D.B. Carter (Ed.), *Current Conceptions of Sex Roles and Sex-typing: Theory and Research*. New York: Praeger.

Maslow, A. (1964) *Religions, Values and Peak Experiences*. Columbus, OH: State University Press.

Maslow, A. (1968) *Toward a Psychology of Being*, 2nd edn. New York: Van Nostrand.

Maslow, A. (1970) *Motivation and Personality*. New York: Harper and Row.

Masson, J. (1984) *The Assault on Truth: Freud's Suppression of the Seduction Theory*. New York: Farrar, Strauss and Giroux.

Masters, J.C., Ford, M.E., Arend, R., Grotevant, H.D. and Clark, L.V. (1979) Modeling and labeling as integrated determinants of children's sex-typed imitative behavior. *Child Development*, **50**, 364–71.

Mattern, K.K. and Lindholm, B.W. (1985) Maternal condemnation of TV violence during mother and child viewing, perceptions of violence and aggressive behavior in 61–73 month olds: Extension of research by B.F. Fontes. *Journal of Genetic Psychology*, **146**, 133–4.

May, R. (1961) The emergence of existential psychology. In R. May (Ed.), *Existential Psychology*. New York: Random House.

McCloskey, M., and Zaragoza, M. (1985) Misleading postevent information and memory for events: Arguments and evidence against memory impairment hypotheses. *Journal of Experimental Psychology: General*, **114**, 1–16.

McConnell, J.V. (1974) Behavior mod. Letter-to-the-editor. *APA Monitor*, **5**, 2–3.

McCord, W., McCord, J. and Howard, A. (1961) Familial correlates of aggression in nondelinquent male children. *Journal of Abnormal and Social Psychology*, **62**, 79–93.

McGhie, A. (1970) Attention and perception in schizophrenia. In B.A. Maher (Ed.), *Progress in Experimental Personality Research*, Vol. 5, pp. 1–35. New York: Academic Press.

McGuire, W.J. (1985) Toward social psychology's second century. In S. Koch and D.E. Leary (Eds), *A Century of Psychology as a Science*, pp. 558–90. New York: McGraw-Hill.

Mead, G.H. (1934) *Mind, Self, and Society*. Chicago, IL: University of Chicago Press.

Mead, M. (1935) *Sex and Temperament in Three Primitive Societies*. New York: William Morrow.

Meador, B.D. and Rogers, C.R. (1979) Person-centered therapy. In R.J. Corsini (Ed.), *Current Psychotherapies*, 2nd edn, pp. 131–84. Itasca, IL: Peacock Press.

Meehl, P. (1971) Law and the fireside inductions: Some reflections of a clinical psychologist. *Journal of Social Issues*, **27**, 65–100.

Meichenbaum, D. (1977) *Cognitive-behavior Modification: An Integrative Approach*. New York: Plenum Press.

Melzack, R. (1973) *The Puzzle of Pain*. New York: Basic Books.

Melzack, R. (1992) Phantom limbs. *Scientific American*, April, 120–6.

Melzack, R. and Wall, P.D. (1982) *The Challenge of Pain*. New York: Basic Books.

Mercer, D. (1986) *Biofeedback and Related Therapies in Clinical Practice*. Rockville, MD: Aspen Systems.

Milgram, S. (1963) A behavioral study of obedience. *Journal of Abnormal and Social Psychology*, **67**, 371–8.

Milgram, S. (1964) Issues in the study of obedience: A reply to Baumrind. *American Psychologist*, **19**, 848–52.

Miller, G.A. (1956) The magical number seven plus or minus two: Some limits on our capacity for processing information. *Psychological Review*, **63**, 81–97.

Miller, G.A. (1985) The constitutive problem of psychology. In S. Koch and D.E. Leary (Eds), *A Century of Psychology as a Science*, pp. 40–5. New York: McGraw-Hill.

Miller, N. (1941) The frustration–aggression hypothesis. *Psychological Review*, **48**, 337–42.

Miller, N. (1969) Learning of visceral and glandular responses. *Science*, **163**, 434–45.

Miller, N. (1985) The value of behavioral research on animals. *American Psychologist*, **40**, 423–40.

Milner, B. (1965) Memory disturbance after bilateral hippocampal lesions. In P. Milner and S. Glickman (Eds), *Cognitive Processes and the Brain*. Princeton, NJ: Van Nostrand.

Mischel, W. (1968) *Personality and Assessment*. New York: John Wiley.

Money, J. and Tucker, P. (1975) *Sexual Signatures: On Being a Man or a Woman*. Boston, MA: Little, Brown.

Moskowitz, B.A. (1978) The acquisition of language. *Scientific American*, **239**, 92–108.

Motley, M.T. (1985) Slips of the tongue. *Scientific American*, September, 116–27.

Mowrer, O.H. (1956) Two-factor learning theory reconsidered, with special reference to secondary reinforcement and the concept of habit. *Psychological Review*, **63**, 114–28.

Moyer, K. (1976) *The Psychobiology of Aggression*. New York: Harper and Row.

Moyer, K. (1983) Violence. In S.H. Kadish (Ed.), *Encyclopedia of Crime and Justice*, Vol. 4, pp. 1618–25. New York: Free Press.

Moyers, B. (1993) *Healing and the Mind*. New York: Doubleday.

Newell, A. and Simon, H.A. (1972) *Human Problem Solving*. Englewood Cliffs, NJ: Prentice-Hall.

Newell, A., Shaw, J.C. and Simon, H.A. (1958) Elements of a theory of human problem solving. *Psychological Review*, **65**, 151–66.

Nicol, S.E. and Gottesman, I.I. (1983) Clues to the genetics and neurobiology of schizophrenia. *American Scientist*, **71**, 398–404.

Öhman, A. (1986) Face the beast and fear the face: Animal and social fears as prototypes for evolutionary analysis of emotion. *Psychophysiology*, **23**, 123–45.

Olds, J. and Milner, P. (1954) Positive reinforcement produced by electrical stimulation of septal area and other regions of the rat brain. *Journal of Comparative and Physiological Psychology*, **47**, 419–27.

Orne, M.T. (1962) On the social psychology of the psychological experiment: With particular reference to demand characteristics and their implications. *American Psychologist*, **17**, 776–83.

Ornstein, R. (1972) *The Psychology of Consciousness*. San Francisco, CA: W.H. Freeman.

Ornstein, R. and Swencionis, C. (Eds) (1990) *The Healing Brain: A Scientific Reader*. New York: Guilford Press.

Osherson, D.N. and Smith, E.S. (Eds) (1990) *An Invitation to Cognitive Science*, 3 Vols. Cambridge, MA: MIT Press.

Padel, J.H. (1987) Freudianism: Later developments. In R.L. Gregory (Ed.), *The Oxford Companion to the Mind*, pp. 270–4. New York: Oxford University Press.

Paivio, A. (1971) *Imagery and Verbal Processes*. New York: Holt, Rinehart and Winston.

Patterson, F.G. and Linden, E. (1981) *The Education of Koko*. New York: Holt, Rinehart and Winston.

Pavlov, I.P. (1927) *Conditioned Reflexes* (Ed. and Trans. by G.V. Anrep). New York: Dover (reprinted 1960).

Penfield, W. (1975) *The Mystery of the Mind*. Princeton, NJ: Princeton University Press.

Penfield, W. and Rasmussen, T. (1957) *The Cerebral Cortex of Man*. New York: Macmillan.

Persons, J. (1991) Psychotherapy outcome studies do not accurately represent current models of psychotherapy. *American Psychologist*, **46**, 99–106.

Pert, C.B. (1990) The wisdom of the receptors: Neuropeptides, the emotions, and body–mind. In R. Ornstein and C. Swencionis (Eds), *The Healing Brain: A Scientific Reader*, pp. 147–58. New York: Guilford Press.

Pervin, L.A. (1989) *Personality: Theory and Research*, 5th edn. New York: John Wiley.

Peterson, D. (Ed.) (1982) *A Mad People's History of Madness*. Pittsburgh, PA: University of Pittsburgh Press.

Peterson, N. (1962) Effect of monochromatic rearing on the control of responding by wavelength. *Science*, **136**, 774–5.

Pfungst, O. (1911) *Clever Hans: The Horse of Mr. von Osten* (C.L. Rahn, Trans.) New York: Holt, Rinehart and Winston (reprinted 1965).

Piaget, J. (1954) *The Construction of Reality in the Child*. New York: Basic Books.

Plomin, R., DeFries, J.C. and Fulker, D.W. (1988) *Nature and Nurture during Infancy and Early Childhood*. New York: Cambridge University Press.

Potter, M.C. (1990) Remembering. In D.N. Osherson and E.S. Smith (Eds), *An Invitation to Cognitive Science, Vol. 3: Thinking*. Cambridge, MA: MIT Press.

Prather, E.M., Hedrick, D.L. and Kern, C.A. (1975) Articulation development in children aged two to four years. *Journal of Speech and Hearing Disorders*, **40**, 179–91.

Premack, D. (1983) The codes of man and beasts. *Behavioral and Brain Sciences*, **6**, 125–67.

Rahe, R.H. (1972) Subjects' recent life changes and their near-future illness susceptibility. *Advances in Psychosomatic Medicine*, **8**, 2–19.

Regier, D.A., Boyd, J.H., Burke, J.D., Rae, D.S., Myers, J.K., Kramer, M., Robins, L.N., George, L.K., Karno, M. and Locke, B.Z. (1988) One-month prevalence of mental disorders in the United States. *Archives of General Psychiatry*, **45**, 977–86.

Rescorla, R.A. and Solomon, R.I. (1967) Two-process learning theory: Relationships between Pavlovian conditioning and instrumental learning. *Psychological Review*, **74**, 212–21.

Richards, J.E. and Rader, N. (1983) Affective, behavioral, and avoidance responses on the visual cliff: Effect of crawling onset age, crawling experience, and testing age. *Psychophysiology*, **20**, 633–42.

Roazen, P. (1975) *Freud and His Followers*. New York: Knopf.

Robinson, D.N. (1979) *Systems of Modern Psychology*. New York: Columbia University Press.

Robinson, D.N. (1985) Science, psychology, and explanation: Synonyms or antonyms? In S. Koch and D.E. Leary (Eds), *A Century of Psychology as a Science*, pp. 60–74. New York: McGraw-Hill.

Rochester, S.R. (1977) A hard look at studies of language in schizophrenia. Paper presented at Canadian Psychological Association Annual Meeting, June, Vancouver.

Rogers, C.R. (1939) *The Clinical Treatment of the Problem Child*. Boston, MA: Houghton-Mifflin.

Rogers, C.R. (1951) *Client-centered Therapy*. Boston, MA: Houghton-Mifflin.

Rogers, C.R. (1959) A theory of therapy, theory, and interpersonal relationships, as developed in the client-centred framework. In S. Koch (Ed.), *Psychology: The Study of a Science*, Vol. 3, pp. 184–256. New York: McGraw-Hill.

Rogers, C.R. (1964) Towards a science of the person. In T.W. Wann (Ed.), *Behaviorism and Phenomenology: Contrasting Bases for Modern Psychology*, pp. 109–33. Chicago, IL: University of Chicago Press.

Rogers, C.R. (Ed.) (1967) *The Therapeutic Relationship and its Impact: A Study of Psychotherapy with Schizophrenics*. Madison, WI: University of Wisconsin Press.

Rogers, C.R. (1969) *Freedom to Learn*. Columbus, OH: Charles E. Merrill.

Rogers, C.R. (1973) My philosophy of interpersonal relationships and how it grew. *Journal of Humanistic Psychology*, **13**, 3–16.

Rogers, C.R. and Dymond, R.E. (1954) *Psychotherapy and Personality Change*. Chicago, IL: University of Chicago Press.

Rogers, C.R. and Skinner, B.F. (1956) Some issues concerning the control of human behavior. *Science*, **124**, 1057–66.

Rokeach, M. (1981) *The Three Christs of Ypsilanti*. New York: Columbia University Press.

Rosenhan, D.L. (1973) On being sane in insane places. *Science*, **179**, 250–8.

Rosenthal, R. and Jacobson, L. (1968) *Pygmalion in the Classroom*. New York: Holt, Rinehart and Winston.

Ross, L. (1977) The intuitive psychologist and his shortcomings: Distortions in the attribution process. In L. Berkowitz (Ed.), *Advances in Experimental Social Psychology*. New York: Academic Press.

Rosser, R. (1994) *Cognitive Development: Psychological and Biological Perspectives*. Toronto: Allyn and Bacon.

Rothbart, M.K. (1981) Measurement of temperament in infancy. *Child Development*, **52**, 569–78.

Rubenstein, E.A., Liebert, R.M., Neale, J.M. and Poulos, R.W. (1974) *Assessing Television's Influence on Children's Prosocial Behavior*. New York: Brookdale International Institute.

Ruble, T.L. (1983) Sexual stereotypes: Issues of change in the 70s. *Sex Roles*, **9**, 397–402.

Sacks, O. (1985) *The Man Who Mistook His Wife for a Hat*. New York: Summit.

Sartre, J.P. (1948) *Existentialism and Humanism* (P. Mariet, Trans.). London: Methuen.

Savage, C.W. (Ed.) (1990) *Scientific Theories*. Minnesota Studies in the Philosophy of Science, Vol. 14. Minneapolis, MN: University of Minnesota Press.

Scarr, S. and McCartney, K. (1983) How people make their own environments: A theory of genotype environment effects. *Child Development*, **54**, 424–35.

Schachter, S. and Singer, J.E. (1962) Cognitive, social, and physiological determinants of emotional state. *Psychological Review*, **69**, 379–99.

Schaefer, H.H. and Martin, P.L. (1966) Behavioral therapy for 'apathy' of hospitalized schizophrenics. *Psychological Reports*, **19**, 1147–58.

Schank, R.C. (1984) *The Cognitive Computer: On Language, Learning, and Artificial Intelligence*. Reading, MA: Addison-Wesley.

Seligman, M.E.P. (1970) On the generality of the laws of learning. *Psychological Review*, **77**, 406–18.

Selye, H. (1976) *The Stress of Life*. New York: McGraw-Hill.

Selye, H. (1978) They all looked sick to me. *Human Nature*, February, 58–63.

Shepard, R.N. and Metzler, J. (1971) Mental rotation of three-dimensional objects. *Science*, **171**, 701–3.

Shettleworth, S. (1972) Constraints on learning. In D.S. Lehrman, R.A. Hinde and H. Shaw (Eds), *Advances in the Study of Behavior*, Vol. 4. New York: Academic Press.

Shields, J. (1962) *Monozygotic Twins Brought Up Apart and Brought Up Together*. London: Oxford University Press.

Siegel, S. (1976) Morphine analgesia tolerance: Its situation specificity supports a Pavlovian conditioning model. *Science*, **193**, 323–5.

Siegel, S., Krank, M.D. and Hinson, R.E. (1988) Anticipation of pharmacological and nonpharmacological events: Classical conditioning and addictive behavior. In S. Peele (Ed.), *Visions of Addiction*. Lexington, MA: Lexington Books.

Singer, J.L. and Singer, D.G. (1981) *Television, Imagination, and Aggression: A Study of Preschoolers*. Hillsdale, NJ: Lawrence Erlbaum Associates.

Skinner, B.F. (1948a) Superstition in the pigeon. *Journal of Experimental Psychology*, **38**, 168–72.

Skinner, B.F. (1948b) *Walden Two*. New York: Macmillan.

Skinner, B.F. (1950) Are theories of learning necessary? *Psychological Review*, **57**, 193–216.

Skinner, B.F. (1957) *Verbal Behavior*. New York: Appleton-Century-Crofts.

Skinner, B.F. (1967) B.F. Skinner. In E.G. Boring and G. Lindzey (Eds), *A History of Psychology in Autobiography*, Vol. 5. New York: Appleton-Century-Crofts.

Skinner, B.F. (1971) *Beyond Freedom and Dignity*. New York: Vintage.

Skinner, B.F. (1974) *About Behaviorism*. New York: Knopf.

Skinner, B.F. (1987) Behaviourism, Skinner on. In R.L. Gregory (Ed.), *The Oxford Companion to the Mind*, pp. 74–5. New York: Oxford University Press.

Sloane, R.B., Staples, F.R., Cristo, A.H., Yorkston, N.J. and Whipple, K. (1975) *Psychotherapy Versus Behavior Therapy*. Cambridge, MA: Harvard University Press.

Smith, D. (1982) Trends in counselling and psychotherapy. *American Psychologist*, **37**, 802–9.

Smith, M.L., Glass, G.V. and Miller, T.I. (1980) *The Benefits of Psychotherapy*. Baltimore, MD: Johns Hopkins University Press.

Snyder, S. (1980) *Biological Aspects of Mental Disorder*. New York: Oxford University Press.

Solomon, G.F. (1990) Emotions, stress, and immunity. In R. Ornstein and C. Swencionis (Eds), *The Healing Brain: A Scientific Reader*, pp. 174–81. New York: Guilford Press.

Sperling, G. (1960) The information available in brief visual presentations. *Psychological Monographs*, **74** (11, Whole No. 498).

Sperry, R. (1968) Hemispheric deconnection and unity in conscious awareness. *American Psychologist*, **23**, 723–33.

Sperry, R. (1969) A modified concept of consciousness. *Psychological Review*, **76**, 532–6.

Sprafkin, J.N., Liebert, R.M. and Poulos, R.W. (1975) Effects of a prosocial televised example on children's helping. *Journal of Experimental Child Psychology*, **20**, 119–26.

Steiner, C. (1974) *Scripts People Live – Transactional Analysis of Life Scripts*. New York: Grove Press.

Sterman, M.B. (1978) Biofeedback and epilepsy. *Human Nature*, May, 50–7.

Sternberg, R. (1985) *Beyond IQ: A Triarchic Theory of Human Intelligence*. Cambridge: Cambridge University Press.

Stevenson, M.R. and Black, K.N. (1988) Paternal absence and sex-role development: A meta-analysis. *Child Development*, **59**, 793–814.

Stiles, W.B., Shapiro, D.A. and Elliott, R. (1986) Are all psychotherapies equivalent? *American Psychologist*, **41**, 165–80.

Stone, J. (1988) Sex and the single gorilla. *Discover*, August, 78–80.

Strupp, H.H. (1989) Psychotherapy: Can the practitioner learn from the researcher? *American Psychologist*, **44**, 717–24.

Sulloway, F. (1979) *Freud: Biologist of the Mind*. New York: Basic Books.

Szasz, T.S. (1961) *The Myth of Mental Illness*. New York: Harper and Row.

Tandon, R. and Kane, J.M. (1993) Neuropharmacologic basis for clozapine's unique profile. *Archives of General Psychiatry*, **50**, 158–9.

Terrace, H.S., Petitto, L.A., Sanders, R.J. and Bever, T.G. (1979) Can an ape create a sentence? *Science*, **206**, 891–902.

Thomas, A. and Chess, A. (1977) *Temperament and Development*. New York: Brunner/Mazel.

Thomas, L. (1981) On the need for asylums. *Discover*, December, 68–71.

Thompson, S.K. (1975) Gender labels and early sex-role development. *Child Development*, **46**, 339–47.

Thorndike, E.L. (1898) Animal intelligence. *Psychological Review Monograph Supplement*, **2** (4, Whole No. 8).

Tolman, E.C. (1932) *Purposive Behavior in Animals and Man*. New York: Appleton-Century-Crofts.

Toulin, A. (1993) Liberals head to majority, new poll says. *The Financial Post*, 2 October, 1.

Trevarthen, C. (1987) Split-brain and the mind. In R.L. Gregory (Ed.), *The Oxford Companion to the Mind*, pp. 740–47. New York: Oxford University Press.

Truax, C.B. (1966) Reinforcement and non-reinforcement in Rogerian psychotherapy. *Journal of Abnormal Psychology*, **71**, 1–9.

Tulving, E. (1974) Recall and recognition of semantically encoded words. *Journal of Experimental Psychology*, **102**, 778–87.

Tulving, E. (1985) How many memory systems are there? *American Psychologist*, **40**, 385–98.

Tulving, E. (1986) What kind of hypothesis is the distinction between episodic and semantic memory? *Journal of Experimental Psychology: Learning, Memory, and Cognition*, **12**, 307–11.

Tulving, E. and Madigan, S. (1970) Memory and verbal learning. *Annual Review of Psychology*, **21**, 457–84.

Tulving, E. and Thompson, D.M. (1971) Retrieval processes in recognition memory. *Journal of Experimental Psychology*, **87**, 116–24.

Turing, A. (1950) Computing machinery and intelligence. *Mind*, **59**, 433–60.

Valins, S. (1966) Cognitive effects of false heart-rate feedback. *Journal of Personality and Social Psychology*, **4**, 400–8.

Villet, B. (1978) Opiates of the mind. *The Atlantic Monthly*, June, 82–9.

Vonnegut, M. (1975) *The Eden Express*. New York: Bantam.

Wachtel, P.L. (1977) *Psychoanalysis and Behavior Therapy*. New York: Basic Books.

Wallace, R.K. and Benson, H. (1972) The physiology of meditation. *Scientific American*, February, 84–90.

Wallerstein, R.S. (1989) The psychotherapy research project of the Meninger Foundation: An overview. *Journal of Consulting and Clinical Psychology*, **57**, 195–205.

Warner, R.E. (1991) A survey of theoretical orientations of Canadian clinical psychologists. *Canadian Psychology*, **32**, 525–8.

Warwick, D.P. (1975) Deceptive research: Social scientists ought to stop lying. *Psychology Today*, February, 63–5.

Watson, J.B. (1930) *Behaviourism*. New York: W.W. Norton (reprinted 1970).

Watson, J.B. and Rayner, L. (1920) Conditioned emotional reactions. *Journal of Experimental Psychology*, **3**, 1–14.

Waugh, N.C. and Norman, D.A. (1965) Primary memory. *Psychological Review*, **72**, 89–104.

Webb, E.J., Campbell, D.T., Schwartz, R.D. and Sechrest, L. (1972) *Unobtrusive Measures: Non-reactive Research in the Social Sciences*. Chicago, IL: Rand McNally.

Weimer, W.B. (1973) Psycholinguistics and Plato's paradoxes of the Meno. *American Psychologist*, January, 15–33.

Weinberger, D.A., Schwartz, G.E. and Davidson, R.J. (1979) Low-anxious, high-anxious, and repressive coping styles: Psychometric patterns and behavioral and physiological responses to stress. *Journal of Abnormal Psychology*, **88**, 369–80.

Weizenbaum, J. (1966) ELIZA – a computer program for the study of natural language communication between man and machine. *Communications of the Association for Computing Machinery*, **9**, 36–45.

Wender, P.H. and Klein, D.F. (1981) The promise of biological psychiatry. *Psychology Today*, February, 25–41.

Wenrich, W.W. (1970) *A Primer of Behavior Modification*. Belmont, CA: Brooks/Cole.

White, R.W. (1975) *Lives in Progress: A Study of the Natural Growth of Personality*, 3rd edn. New York: Holt, Rinehart and Winston.

Whorf, B.L. (1956) *Language, Thought, and Reality*. Cambridge, MA: MIT Press.

Wicker, A. (1971) Attitudes *vs* action: The relationship between verbal and overt behavior responses to attitude objects. *Journal of Social Issues*, **25**, 41–78.

Wolpe, J. (1973) *The Practice of Behavior Therapy*, 2nd edn. New York: Pergamon Press.

Yates, F.A. (1966) *The Art of Memory*. Chicago, IL: University of Chicago Press.

Zaner, R.M. (1985) The *Logos* of *Psyche*: Phenomenological variations on a theme. In S. Koch and D. E. Leary (Eds), *A Century of Psychology as a Science*, pp. 618–37. New York: McGraw-Hill.

Zangwill, O. (1987) Sigmund Freud. In R.L. Gregory (Ed.), *The Oxford Companion to the Mind*, pp. 268–70. New York: Oxford University Press.

Zeig, J. (Ed.) (1987) *The Evolution of Psychotherapy*. New York: Brunner/Mazell.

Zimbardo, P.G. (1992) *Psychology and Life*, 13th edn. New York: HarperCollins.

Index